The Good Tourist

Katie Wood is a name many travellers are familiar
with. As a well established travel writer and journalist,
she has tackled everything from backpacking in her
bestseller *Europe by Train*, to the deluxe world of
country house hotels and continent-hopping in the
Round the World Air Guide. With eighteen successful
guidebooks to her name, and a string of freelance
commissions, from the *Guardian*, *Independent* and
Scotsman to the *Observer* and *Traveller* magazine, she is
well qualified to comment on all aspects of the travel
industry. She also regularly broadcasts for the BBC and
undertakes TV travel shows.

Following on from *The Good Tourist* this series is
the next logical step, to show tourists how to have a
positive, not negative, impact on their host country.

The perfect marriage of minds, from this series'
point of view, has resulted from her marriage to Syd
House. Syd is a graduate of ecological sciences and
has considerable experience of practical management
in conservation. Working as a Forest District Manager
for the Forestry Commission, he is responsible for
the management and conservation of a large part of
Scotland. He has travelled the world in his own right,
before combining his skills with those of his wife and
looking at the impact of tourism on the environment.

Together they bring you the definitive work on
'green travel', examined from both the tourist and the
environmental points of view. Syd and Katie are both
graduates of Edinburgh University and share a Scottish
background. Katie was born in Edinburgh. Following
graduation she worked in journalism, and following
an eighteen month spell backpacking in Europe, her
first travel guide was published in 1983. A Fellowship
from the Royal Geographical Society, several travel
consultancies and fifty-seven countries later she is
still writing and travelling full-time. Syd, originally

from Gourock, travelled the world before returning to Scotland, where he became immersed in conservation matters and resumed managerial work within the Forestry Commission. He too is a Fellow of the Royal Geographic Society.

The couple married in 1984. They have two young sons, Andrew and Euan, live in Perth, Scotland, and lead a lifestyle punctuated with foreign travel, midnight writing, and an active involvement in conservation matters. They have recently completed consultancy work for, among others, the English Tourist Board, working on a policy document on green tourism.

By the same author

Europe by Train
The Round the World Air Guide
European City Breaks
The Best of British Country House Hotels
Holiday Ireland
Holiday Scotland
The Cheap Sleep Guide to Europe
The 100 Greatest Holidays in the World★
The 1992 Business Travel Guide★
The Good Tourist in the UK★
The Good Tourist★

★Also available from Mandarin Paperbacks

The Good Tourist in France

KATIE WOOD & SYD HOUSE

Mandarin

A Mandarin Paperback
THE GOOD TOURIST IN FRANCE

First published in Great Britain 1992
by Mandarin Paperbacks
Michelin House, 81 Fulham Road, London SW3 6RB

Mandarin is an imprint of the Octopus Publishing Group,
a division of Reed International Books Limited

Copyright © Katie Wood & Syd House 1992

A CIP catalogue record for this title
is available from the British Library
ISBN 0 7493 0808 7

Typeset by Falcon Typographic Art Ltd,
Edinburgh
Printed and bound in Great Britain
by Cox & Wyman Ltd, Reading, Berks

The Good Tourist Series

This book is aimed at the educated, probably well travelled, but most importantly environmentally-aware person. The person who loves travel but doesn't want to spoil what he or she sets out to see. It is quite different from any other guide you are likely to have seen. It is not written for the extremist Green fringe. We don't advocate everyone cycles everywhere, eats vegan and sleeps in communes. It's a soft but effective green message you'll get from this guide, and indeed any book in the Good Tourist series. But it works and is practical.

This series aims to show you how to visit a country in a way that gives you the most pleasure and also does the least harm (and often does actual good) for the region you are holidaying in. So, for example, we recommend you to try alternative routes rather than the crowded, well-documented ones; suggest you stay in a family-run B&B, rather than check in to the sanitised chain-hotel down the road; and we encourage you to meet the locals, giving practical suggestions on where to do this, and to learn about the impact that tourism has (and therefore the impact YOU will have) in that region. It's amazing to think that no other guidebook in the bookshop will actually tell you, the tourist, things like how many other tourists go to that area; how much money you and other visitors bring to the region in the form of tourism, and where tourism is having a detrimental impact on the environment or society, and what you can do to help.

The new breed of tourists are interested in this. They are keen to learn as much as possible about where they're travelling, not just have run-of-the-mill info regurgitated in a bland style. We give you the sort of info only the locals will tell you. **Because we've**

asked the locals: we've asked them to tell us where the best places to go, stay and eat are; we've asked them how tourists can be more sensitive in their area; we've asked for their opinions. Everyone from the local Ecological Group to the regional tourist councils have been canvassed and have had their say where tourists should go, and what they should know about their region. Not exactly earth shattering stuff, you might think. But, believe it or not, it's not been done before, and you'll soon see the different it makes. Now you really can experience a genuine slice of local culture, not one put on for the tourist hordes.

Our contributors and researchers all know and have travelled extensively in (and in 99% of cases, actually lived in) the regions on which they comment. Syd House and I have laid our thoughts on tourism out in the guide which launched this series – *The Good Tourist* – a worldwide guide for the green traveller (Mandarin Paperbacks £5.99). We believe that whilst immense problems are created by mass tourism and its associated developments, there **are** ways in which tourism can be developed which bring benefits not only to tourists, but also to the host countries and the natural environment. We hope through this series to encourage the tourist to be aware of the issues, and by following the practical guidelines found in the books, to enjoy being what until recently has been called a contradiction in terms – a 'good tourist'.

We welcome comments. Please write to us care of the publishers:

Katie Wood & Syd House
Mandarin Paperbacks
Michelin House
81 Fulham Road
London SW3 6RB

Contents

Acknowledgements

Our thanks are owed to the following people, who worked long and hard on this project:

Editorial Assistant: Vicky Lewis

A graduate in French and German from Oxford University, Vicky has lived in France and knows the country well. She undertook an extensive research trip for this guide and has covered much new ground, bringing together the French green movement's thoughts and applying them for the first time to the travel industry's infrastructure. She now works full time as Katie Wood's assistant in the world of travel writing, and is actively involved in sustainable tourism issues.

Researchers:

Vicky Lewis: Brittany; Picardy; Paris and the Ile-de-France; Champagne-Ardenne; Lorraine; Alsace; Franche-Comté; Burgundy; The Rhône Valley; Dauphiny and Savoy – the Alps; Provence–Alpes; Cote d'Azur; Midi-Pyrénées; The Loire. **Jane Chappell** also contributed to the research of Brittany and Midi-Pyrénées.

David & Dorothy Burrows: Normandy; Nord & Pas-de-Calais; Poitou-Charentes; Auvergne. Teachers Dorothy & David Burrows have travelled on an annual basis in the parts of France on which they write. They are actively involved with the sustainable tourism movement and are members of Tourism Concern.

Marcus Dalrymple: The Loire; Limousin; Aquitaine. Journalist for a London-based Japanese newspaper, Marcus Dalrymple has travelled extensively and is involved in green tourism issues.

Rob Davidson: Languedoc-Roussillon; general research. Lecturer in tourism in France; living in France and author of *Tourism*, Rob Davidson is a leading expert on French green tourism, as well as being a highly respected lecturer on the subject in the UK and France.

1. The Départments of France

2. **North-East France**

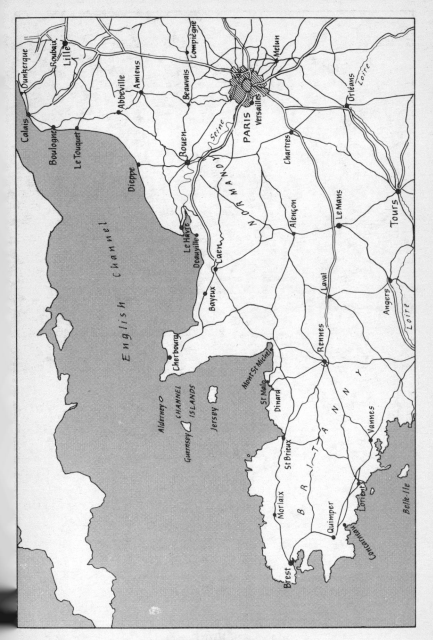

3. North-West France

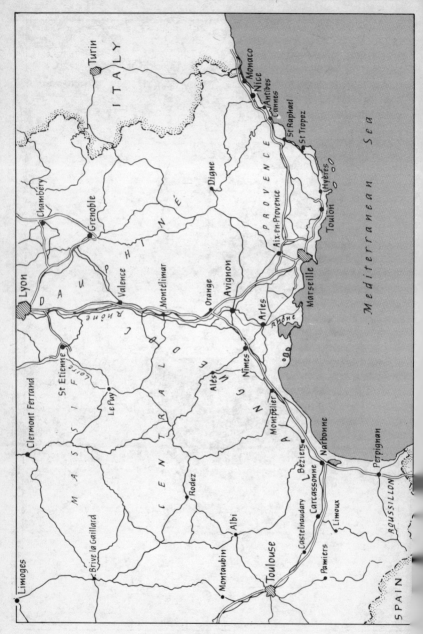

4. South-East France

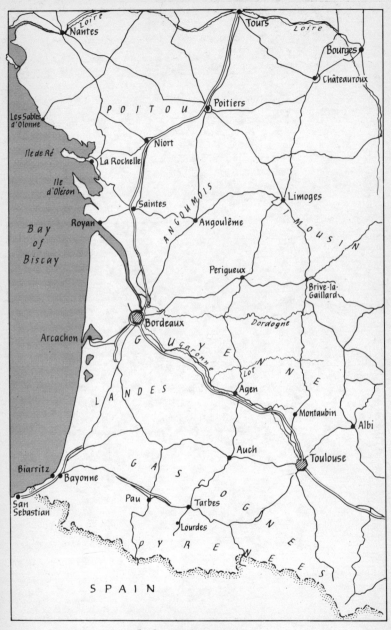

5. South-West France

Introduction

Highlights of France

A common first impression formed by visitors to France is of that country's great beauty and charm. 'La belle France' is the phrase most often used by the French themselves when talking about their own country, and it is no meaningless exaggeration. The physical beauty of France's vast and largely unspoilt natural landscape is fully matched by its immense variety. From the rugged granite coast of Brittany, through the sweeping northern plains and the volcano-studded landscape of the Massif Central to the vineyard-planted foothills sloping down to the Mediterranean, France offers an abundance of visual delights. But much of its attractiveness is also due to man's interaction with this environment. The evidence of human endeavours throughout the centuries can be seen in the great wealth of handsome constructions which constitute France's architectural heritage: Roman roads and aqueducts, Gothic churches, Norman fortresses and Renaissance châteaux, Paris's wide majestic boulevards – they all contribute to the beauty and splendour of this fascinating country. And it is not only the imposing grandeur of France which is so pleasing to the eye. Much of what is everyday and commonplace also has great visual appeal. Sleepy hamlets which appear to grow out of the hillsides; half-timbered Normandy farmhouses; shuttered and balconied apartment buildings in the old quarters of large cities; shaded, plane-tree-lined village squares – France abounds in the picturesque and charming as well as the awe-inspiring.

But, striking though this is, it would be wrong to think that visual gratification is all that France has to offer the visitor. France provides a feast for all the senses – and not least through the rich delights it offers to please the palate. The importance of food and drink to the French has exalted the production and preparation of these vital elements into an art form; and the visitor to France profits from the extremely high standards of care, attention and imagination which give French cooking its high reputation. In fact, the only disappointment with French food and wine is that there is such an abundant variety that you would find it impossible to sample everything in even twenty visits! The local produce changes as much as the landscape, with every region making its own contribution to the French table: wild mushrooms from the Cévennes, seafood from Brittany, snails from Poitou-Charentes, dark prunes from Agen, and, of course, cheeses from *everywhere*. And once again, the humble and everyday shows the same concern for quality as the refined and elevated. A simple salade niçoise with chunks of freshly-baked bread, washed down with a few glasses of the local red wine, can provide as authentic and delicious a taste of French cooking as some of the more fanciful offerings of haute cuisine. French food and wine should be sampled to the full – from a do-it-yourself lunch composed of take-away charcuterie products to at least one blow-out meal in a recommended restaurant.

The great variety of regional cooking is one aspect of the huge regional diversity of this country. It is impossible to travel around France without noticing the striking contrasts between one region and the next. The proud Celtic culture of the people of Brittany, with their bagpipes and their own Breton language, seems far away indeed from the bullfights and pavement-café life of the Latinate peoples of the French Mediterranean. Yet they, together with those living in the Flemish north, the fiercely independent inhabitants of the Basque region, the people of Alsace and Lorraine with their own German heritage, and all the other separate civilisations which make up France, make this country a colourful and ever-changing patchwork of different cultures. Discovering these differences and appreciating the nuances between regions is part of the pleasure of a visit to France, and a reason for returning and exploring completely contrasting areas.

This nation of contrasts, however, is united by the consciousness of its own historical and cultural identity. France is one of the oldest, and historically and culturally most important nations of Europe. Its history, so central to that of Europe as a whole, is there to be seen in monuments, festivals, and the many marks left by the ancient civilisations who have passed over this land. In terms of its contributions to the cultural domain, France has always held a high place, from the Gothic architecture which originated in its dukedoms and provinces in the Middle Ages, to the broad humanism which so shaped modern ideas and which came from French thinking during the Renaissance and the Enlightenment. The sciences, too, have been expanded by various French discoveries while in the arts, France has contributed richly, producing figures of world stature in literature, painting and music. The French are proud of their national heroes, to the point of chauvinism, and take as a great compliment the interest of visitors seeking out the house where Alain-Fournier, author of *Le Grand Meaulnes*, spent his childhood, or the village which inspired Proust's *A la recherche du temps perdu*, for example.

With its roots in such a rich historic and cultural heritage, it is not surprising that France abounds in excellent museums on a wide range of subjects. The most prestigious are the Fine Arts museums of Paris, such as the Louvre and the Musée d'Orsay. But every region of France makes an impressive effort, not only to display works of art, but also to show off its own history and culture, and to celebrate local heroes. Albi has its Toulouse-Lautrec museum exhibiting the works of the locally-born artist; the Breton culture is celebrated in Rennes' Musée de Bretagne; Joan of Arc's house in Orléans has been turned into a museum, and so on, through most towns and cities of France.

With so many reasons for going there, where do you start in deciding which part of France to visit? Any attempt to 'do' all of France in one go would result in a frenetic blur of unsatisfying and shallow impressions, and nothing else. Instead, choose a theme for your trip: an activity holiday in a mountainous area or along a stretch of canal, for example; a thematic tour, such as one based on the châteaux of the Dukes of Savoy or the abbeys of Yvelines; or base your trip in one city, exploring it and the surrounding region. It's easy to see why **Paris**, with its monuments, shops and entertainment is so popular. But there are many other French cities which, rewarding and fascinating in themselves, also make useful bases for exploring some of the most interesting areas of the country. **Bordeaux**, with its High Gothic churches and 18th century centre, is well-situated for exploring the vineyards, châteaux and prehistoric sites of Aquitaine; the pedestrian lanes of **Strasbourg**, the elegant capital of Alsace, make it a joy to linger and stroll around, while the nearby Rhine valley and Vosges mountains provide opportunities for more rigorous exercise; **Lyon**, all too often passed over quickly on the mad dash to the south, is of particular cultural as well as gastronomic interest, being home to the schools which produce France's most reputed chefs; vastly under-rated too is **Lille**, which has one of the most beautiful historic centres in France; three excellent bases from which to explore the Alps are **Grenoble,** **Chambéry** and **Annecy**, all in magnificent settings and each one interesting enough in itself to provide a few days' sightseeing; **Montpellier** and **Nîmes** are distinctly Mediterranean cities rich in traces of past civilisations which have settled on this coast, and each well-placed for trips to the Camargue or the Cévennes Hills. Other important regional centres well worth considering as holiday bases are **Aix-en-Provence** for the Provence countryside, **Nice**, especially at festival time, **Toulouse**, for the Pyrenees, and **Rennes**, for the Celtic culture and medieval towns and villages of Brittany.

Finally, with all the opportunities for touring and sightseeing, it is easy to overlook the fact that the key to understanding France and appreciating it fully is also to make some effort to get to know the French people themselves. Discovering the sometimes subtle and sometimes not-so-subtle differences between them and the British is fascinating in itself, and an enjoyable and rewarding element of a holiday in France. Their own *joie de vivre* is part of what makes their country such a pleasure to visit, but this is only one aspect of a national character, which is as complex and contradictory, at times, as that of their British neighbours. However, they are a loquacious people, and the open-spirited among them are as curious to get to know their visitors, too. The kind of visitor who will get the most out of a trip to France is someone who extends their interest in the country's culture and history to the French people themselves. In taking the plunge and making an effort to communicate as equals with their hosts, visitors should learn something about themselves, too!

Natural History

The fauna and flora of France are as varied as the range of topography and climate. From the limestone cliffs around Marseille to the dense woods of Normandy, there are a multitude of different habitats for wildlife and a rich variety of plant life.

France has 6000 plant species, 200 of which are endemic to the country. Forests cover a quarter of the land area. The deciduous temperate forests of the north and centre are mainly of oak and beech, while in the mountainous zones, silver fir and Norway spruce dominate. The forests of the south contain pine and scrubby oak trees, though the eucalyptus, originally imported from Australia, is commonly planted in Provence. France's forests abound in many forms of wildlife, including polecats, pine-marten, voles, wild boar, roe deer and the rarer red deer. Wildcats, contrary to legend, are harmless, and in fact serve to keep down rodents. Among the birdlife, insectivores predominate, with many species, including coal tits, nuthatches and woodpeckers. Many forest birds are magnificently colourful, such as the golden oriole and the woodpecker. Reptile life appears particularly in humid forests, with the slow-worm and the much-persecuted viper, which is by nature timid, biting in self-defence only.

On the whole, the French, with the oldest Forest Service in Europe, have conserved their forests well. The main threats to forests today are from fire, pesticides, urbanisation, and the ever-growing network of France's motorways. There is little incentive for the planners to avoid putting a motorway through a forest, as this is much cheaper than buying up agricultural land. Thousands of acres of forest are lost every year in France through the building of roads.

The extensive marshlands and lagoons of France have their own particular, but no less rich, flora and fauna. The Camargue is one of the most important wildlife refuges remaining in Europe. Carp, tench and perch swim among the reeds and bullrushes, serving as food for herons, while storks feed on frogs and toads. The duckweed and water irises of these regions attract a wide range of insect life, which in turn brings sedge warblers and marsh warblers to marshlands. Look out, too, for the bright orange and blue kingfisher which makes its home in tiny holes on the banks of these areas. France's rivers contain, according to the region, roach, bream, tench, chub, trout and salmon. The more brackish waters, found in the Gironde, for example, contain mullet, sturgeon and eels. River banks are home to otters and beavers, both protected species now in France. The latter has been reintroduced into the Rhône valley, and a few live in the gorges of the Gardon.

Lowland areas are principally devoted to intensive agriculture over much of France, but mountain areas offer a great variety of wildlife and plantlife. In regions such as the Massif Central, between 800 metres and 1500 metres above sea-level, fir, spruce and beech trees provide homes for capercaillies and hazel grouse, with fox, hare, squirrel, pine-marten and deer common. At higher elevations the lynx and the wolf are found, albeit in ever-decreasing numbers.

while the brown bear survives in the Pyrenees only, under constant threat from human inroads into its habitat. The flora changes also, with larch typical at this altitude, along with alpine flowers such as the anemone and gentian. Above the treelines in the Alps and the Pyrenees, there are extensive areas where the vegetation is little modified by man, except for summer grazing. These lofty regions are home to the chamois, alpine hare, ibex and the marmot, the ptarmigan and pipit. Plantlife over 2100 metres is limited to generally montane species such as edelweiss, bilberry and saxifrage.

Geography

Covering an area of 545,000 square kilometres, France is the second largest country in Europe, after the USSR. It occupies a privileged position between the ocean and the continental mass of Europe, with 3000 kilometres of coastline facing the English Channel, the Mediterranean sea and the Atlantic ocean. Except in the north-east, where it merges gradually into Belgium, the country is bound on all other sides by natural frontiers – the Alps, the Pyrenees and the River Rhine. Within these boundaries, France has all the variety of natural characteristics to be found elsewhere in the continent of Europe: flat, fertile lands in the north, snow-capped mountain ranges in the east, the rolling green landscape of the Loire valley, the sharp, towering Pyrenees in the south, and the semi-tropical Mediterranean coastline.

The country is divided almost equally into either areas of plains and lowlands, or areas characterised by hills or mountains. The highest and most extensive range is the Alps in the south-east, bordering on Italy and Switzerland, and including the highest mountain in Europe, Mont Blanc, at 4807 metres. Despite their imposing stature, the Alps are easily crossed by a number of valleys leading to passes. North of this range lie the Vosges and the Jura. The rugged Vosges border on the north-east plateaux, a wooded region, where most of France's iron-ore deposits lie. This region's other mountains are the Ardennes, which continue on into Belgium and Luxembourg. Finally, the Pyrenees span the neck of land between the Mediterranean and the Atlantic.

The core of France is the Paris Basin, a large circular area drained by the Seine and other rivers. This forms part of the fertile northern French plains, which merge into the low, rounded hills of Brittany and Normandy to the north-west. The northern plains are connected, in the south-west, with the Aquitaine lowlands. This region's lowlands are characterised by wide, sandy beaches along the coast, and rolling plains and pine forests inland. Access to the Mediterranean coast from the north is through the valley of the Rhône, which, with the valley of its tributary, the Saône, forms broad passageways through the otherwise impenetrable Massif Central. This ancient, worn-down upland, topped with extinct volcanoes, is the largest geographical region in France, covering about one sixth of the country's surface area. The land is thinly populated, with poor soils, except in the valleys, and forests predominate on the higher slopes. The Massif Central provides the sources of many of France's rivers: the Seine flows from there into the English Channel, while the Garonne and the Loire flow into the Atlantic.

The Rhône valley itself, like the Mediterranean lowlands through which it flows before reaching the Mediterranean, is a highly-productive farming area. Irrigation is commonly used, to help produce the extensive range of crops, the most widespread of which is the vine.

France has about half the density of population of Britain, and fewer large cities. After Paris and its suburbs, with a population of ten million, and Lyon, Marseille and Lille, with about a million inhabitants each, most of France's other well-known cities have much smaller populations. The next rank of cities, such as Strasbourg, Nancy, Grenoble, Nice, Rouen and Saint-Etienne all have populations of between 300,000 and 400,000, including their suburbs.

For administrative purposes, France is divided into twenty-two Regions, most of which coincide with the pre-Revolution 'provinces', and ninety-five *Départements*. These *départements* are named after a geographical feature (usually a river or mountain range) and are numbered according to an alphabetical system. All postcodes in a *département* will start with that *département's* number, which will also appear on car number plates. Since 1983, these *départements* have been given more and more powers and resources, devolved from Paris to their assemblies, through the French government's policy of decentralisation. They all now operate with much more political and administrative autonomy than their British counterparts.

Climate

The French climate tends to be varied but reliable. With the exception of the Mediterranean coast, with its long, hot, dry summers and mild, wetter winters, France's climate falls wholly within the more moderate section of the temperate zone. Within that zone, however, France's ocean-facing position and variety of relief produce three variations on the climate. It is oceanic in the west, strongly affected by the winds from the Atlantic which bring mild temperatures, moderate rainfall, less frequent in summer, and cool, not cold, winters; north-western areas tend to be wetter than south-western ones. Eastern and central France have a continental climate, with warmer summers and colder winters; to the east, towards the mountains, the westerly air streams rise, cool, and give further precipitation, creating dreary conditions often, in Alsace and Lorraine. Finally, there is a mountain climate in the upland regions, with cool summers and cold, sunny winters.

The biggest variations in temperature between different regions are found in the winter. The average December daily maximum temperature for Paris is 7.8°C, for Alsace, 4.7°C, while those on the Riviera are enjoying a mild 14.1°C. Summer temperatures peak in August, with 25.6°C in Paris, and over 28°C in the south. Average sea temperatures in August range from 17°C in the English Channel, through 18 or 19°C along the Atlantic coast, to a comfortable 21°C in the Mediterranean. From November until April, there is snow cover anywhere over 1000 metres.

Industry

After fast economic growth in the 1960s and 1970s, France is now among the top six industrial countries in the world, well ahead of Britain. Practically self-sufficient in agricultural produce, France is the largest agricultural producer in Europe. The main cereal crops are wheat, barley and maize, with wine production concentrated in the south. However, in most areas, livestock breeding takes precedence over crop production, with cattle accounting for about half of this. Their great surplus in dairy produce makes France the world's second most important exporter of cheese. On the other hand, it has a deficit of fruit and vegetables, which must be imported. Forestry and fishing are other important natural sources of national income.

Apart from deposits of iron-ore and coal in the north-east corner, France is not rich in mineral resources, and has to rely on imports for most of its needs. It has to import almost all of its oil, domestic production accounting for only 2% of its requirements.

The principal manufacturing industries are steel, and steel-related products such as armaments and motor cars, with Renault and Peugeot-Citroën dominating the latter in terms of exports. France's aircraft industry is a dynamic one, too, and very active on the export front, due mainly to the efforts of Aérospatiale and Dassault. Textiles and perfumes are also important exports. The latter, together with champagne, wines and spirits, *pâté de foie gras* and truffles, contributes to the common perception of France as an exporter of luxury goods. Tourism itself is one of France's most successful service industries, now bringing in almost $20 billion each year in foreign currency. Since the French themselves spend just over half this amount on travel outside their own country, tourism on the whole makes a major contribution to their balance of payments as a net 'export', comparable to the motor car industry or the agriculture and food sector.

History

France has a long and colourful history, inextricably linked with that of Britain. Throughout the centuries, the two countries have invaded each other, fought against common enemies, and developed, each in their own way, into modern states, with much in common. As in Britain, the history of France is written in its monuments, traditions, language and racial mix. Some familiarity with the main events which shaped France will enormously enhance your understanding of that country.

Until the climatic improvements of the 10th century BC, pre-historic human communities in France were largely concentrated in the warmer south-west. It is in this area that the early cave-dwelling hunters have left their marks, in the form of remarkable cave-paintings, such as those of Lascaux and Niaux. By the time the Romans, under Julius Caesar, finally conquered the country which is now France, it was occupied by the **Gauls**, a loose confederation of tribes living to the west of the Loire and more often than not at war with each other. The Gauls were a Celtic people, whose culture lives on today among the inhabitants of Brittany, distinguishing them from the rest of the French. The Gauls united under **Vercingétorix** to fight the legions of Rome, but were defeated at Alesia, in what is now Burgundy, in 52 BC. During the following four centuries, Gaul was part of the vast Roman empire. The frontiers of this empire were constantly under threat from barbarian raiding parties, and in the fifth century, the entire empire finally fell to Germanic invaders. Visigoths, Vandals and Franks crossed into Gaul, and divided it into a number of small chiefdoms. It was the Franks, a rough alliance of peoples under a series of petty kings, who were to lay the foundations of France, the most powerful kingdom of medieval Europe. By 500 AD, under their king **Clovis**, they had become the dominant power, driving the Visigoths out into Spain, and making Paris their capital. By the time of Clovis' death, his power extended to the Atlantic in the west and only a narrow band separated Frankish territory from the Mediterranean. By the middle of the sixth century, the natural boundaries of France – the seas, mountains and rivers which enclose it today – had been reached. In 751, the next dynasty, that of the **Carolingians**, was ushered in peacefully under **Charlemagne** (said to be seven feet tall, with a bushy moustache and a high-pitched voice). He instigated a great many military, economic and political successes, and was crowned emperor of the Holy Roman Empire in 800. Following his death, his grandsons squabbled over who was to inherit which lands. At the Treaty of Verdun in 843, they divided up the territory, with **Charles the Bald** inheriting those lands west of the Rhône, which were to become modern France. Increasing attacks from Vikings, Normans and Norsemen made necessary more and more delegation of powers to those appointed to govern the provinces of the Carolingian empire. Before long, the power of the king was limited to the Ile-de-France region, with the rest of the country a series of practically independent feudal states.

Reunification under the crown came during the **Capetian** dynasty, named after its first king, Hugh Capet, who came to power in 987. For 350 years, an unbroken Capetian line added to its domain and consolidated royal authority. During that period, the history of France and Britain became intertwined, beginning with the invasion of England in 1066 by **William I, the Conqueror**, Duke of Normandy, who became king of England. In 1152 another Norman king of England, **Henry II**, through marriage, inherited Aquitaine, the western half of France, stretching from the English Channel to the Pyrenees. For the following 300 years, the English were a thorn in the side of all French kings. In 1328, the English king Edward III challenged the succession of **Philip VI**, of the House of Valois, to the

Capetian line. This led to the **100 Years War**. Although France was the most powerful nation in Europe, with a population of 15 million, several of its provinces were still held by the English. The 100 Years War settled the contest. The English inflicted crushing defeats on the French at **Crécy** in 1346 and at **Agincourt** in 1415. But the French, inspired by **Joan of Arc**, defeated the English at **Orléans** in 1429, and expelled them from most of France. Final victory went to the French at **Castillon** in 1453, and all the provinces passed into the control of the crown – except for Calais which remained in English hands until the middle of the 16th century.

The **Bourbon** dynasty began with the reign of **Henry IV of Navarre**, whose first task was to reconstruct and reconcile the nation, after bitter religious controversy between Roman Catholics and the Protestant Huguenot followers of the reformer John Calvin had led to a civil **war of religions** in 1562. The **Edict of Nantes** which he signed in 1598 accorded limited freedom of worship to the Huguenots. French influence increased during the 17th century, partly under **Cardinal de Richelieu**, chief minister to **Louis XIII**, and partly under **Cardinal Jules Mazerin**, minister to **Louis XIV, the Sun King**. Absolute monarchy reached its culmination in the reign of the latter, who sought supremacy over Europe, symbolised by his glittering palace at Versailles. While the king's extravagance reached dizzy heights, the country was increasingly impoverished by his futile wars with the Dutch and the Spanish. His great-grandson, King Louis XV's dying words, '*Après moi, le déluge*' proved prophetic when in 1789, **Louis XVI**'s bungling attempts to solve the country's deepening economic crisis triggered off the French **Revolution**. In order to introduce a new tax to finance the national debt, he recalled the **Estates-General**, which represented the nobility, the clergy and the bourgeoisie – the **Third Estate**. Exasperated and in revolutionary mood, the Third Estate, fearing that it would be outvoted by the other two, dramatically declared itself the National Assembly, usurping the more privileged sections. Although at first appearing to accept the situation, the king finally called in the troops to expel the National Assembly, sparking off the storming of the Bastille by the Paris mob. Amid similar uprisings all over the country, the National Assembly proceeded to vote away all peasant obligations and rents, abolish the feudal rights and privileges of the nobility, and adopt the Declaration of the **Rights of Man**. A bloodbath ensued when, four years later, the radical **Jacobins** ushered in a **Reign of Terror**, beginning with their execution of the king, and continuing with the guillotining of anyone else perceived to be an enemy of the Revolution.

A new authoritarianism followed, under **Napoleon Bonaparte**, who had successfully defended the fledgling republic from foreign attack. As First Consul, he established the political and administrative framework which still operates in modern France. Naming himself Emperor in 1804, he led the French into a series of daring but ruinous military campaigns, whose early successes were followed by defeats, first by the Russian winter as his army marched on Moscow, then by Wellington at **Waterloo** in 1815. The **Congress of Vienna** of that year sought to restore the monarchy, in the person of **Louis XVIII**, but increasing industrialisation and the French middle classes, both fostered under Napoleon, had built irresistable pressure for change, and the following thirty years were characterised by mounting tension between royalists and those inspired by Napoleonic and Revolutionary reforms. Finally, in 1848, this tension culminated in the overthrowing of the reigning monarch, **Louis-Philippe**, by the **February Revolution**, which forced him into exile. A **Second Republic** elected as its president **Prince Louis Napoleon**, nephew of Napoleon I, who declared the **Second Empire** in 1852, and took the throne as Napoleon III. Napoleon's opposition to the rising power of **Prussia** ignited the **Franco-Prussian War**, 1870–71, which ended in his defeat and abdication, and the loss of Alsace and Lorraine to the victor. The post-war **Third Republic** was plagued by political instability and chaos, with no satisfactory form of representative government in place. The citizens of Paris set up the **Paris Commune** as an attempt at self-government, but it was ruthlessly crushed by government forces directed by **Thiers**.

During the 1890s, Britain and France were the two great colonial powers, and fierce competition existed between them. This was ended by the Entente Cordiale of 1904, which heralded a new era of cooperation between them both, but also led to the increasing isolation of Germany, and a host of ill-fated alliances which in 1914 brought France and Germany into armed conflict. During **World War I**, France and Britain united against the common enemy. France emerged victorious but exhausted from the war in 1918, some of the bloodiest battles having been fought on her soil. Her foreign policy was then aimed at keeping Germany at bay, through a system of alliances and the construction of the **Maginot Line** of defences in north-east France. Neither was successful in stopping the rise of Hitler or his troops, who marched into Paris in 1940.

to begin the **Occupation. Marshal Henri Philippe Pétain** signed an armistice, and the country was divided into an occupied north and an unoccupied south, the latter being governed by Pétain. The **French Committee of National Liberation**, formed in Algiers in 1943, constituted a provisional government under the Resistance leader **Charles de Gaulle** in Paris when the Allies liberated France, the following year. Then began the remarkable post-war renewal which turned France into one of the world's most dynamic and successful economies. The humiliation of the 1940 defeat and Occupation seemed to provide France with a much-needed shock to awaken it from its traditional backwards-looking sloth and economic stagnation, to become a thoroughly progressive and energetic industrial nation. This was a time of reform and growth, and the beginning of the population's great move off the land and into the towns and cities.

Dissatisfaction with the past, and in particular France's constitution, was one of the reasons why de Gaulle's presidency was so short-lived. His resignation in 1946 left the coalition **Fourth Republic** governments to cope with a war against Communist insurgents in **Indochina** in 1954 and a rebellion by the army and French settlers in **Algeria** in 1958. During that year, the National Assembly invited de Gaulle to return as premier, with extraordinary powers, to sort out the crisis. He drafted a new constitution for the **Fifth Republic**, strengthening the powers of the president, to which position he was promptly elected. The 1958 constitution and the Fifth Republic are still operational today, with executive power being held by the president, and legislative power belonging to a Parliament composed of the Senate and the National Assembly. De Gaulle resolved the Algerian crisis by granting that country its independence in 1962. On the economic front, he presided over the country during the first years of its membership of the **EEC**, in the formation of which France had played a leading role. If the French motives behind its formation were mainly political – springing from the post-war desire for reform and closer European cooperation – industrialists' fears over the removal of protectionism proved to be unfounded and, overall, the French economy benefited from membership.

The internal unrest which culminated in the student and worker riots of **May 1968** led de Gaulle to call a general election the following year. Despite an overwhelming victory for his party, the president was to resign, for the second time in his political life, in 1969, when a referendum on certain constitutional amendments went against him. His successor, **Georges Pompidou** continued de Gaulle's policies of modernising France, but in 1971 endorsed Britain's entry into the Common Market, thereby reversing the previous president's decision. For their turn in power, the Left had to wait for **François Mitterand**'s 1981 victory over **Valéry Giscard d'Estaing**, Pompidou's successor and the candidate of the Gaullist alliance. A vast programme of nationalisation and decentralisation followed, the latter giving extensive powers to France's regional and departmental assemblies. The first two years of Mitterand's social reforms resulted in a 12% inflation rate, a huge trade deficit and devaluations of the franc. To counteract these, he embarked on an austerity programme in 1983, moving to the political centre the following year, with the appointment of **Laurent Fabius** as Prime Minister. The Socialist-Communist coalition was ended, and more conservative economic policies replaced the extravagance of previous years.

In 1986, a period of **cohabitation** began, between President Mitterand and **Jacques Chirac**, the leader of the centre-right coalition which won a slim majority in that year's legislative elections. This uneasy cooperation was marked by a spate of denationalisation, and a harder line on security issues. However, with Mitterand's decisive re-election as president in 1987, Chirac was replaced by the socialist **Michel Rocard**. The president called a general election, hoping for a Socialist Party majority, but failed to achieve this. Today, the socialists still lack an absolute parliamentary majority; ad hoc support tends to come from the left or right as necessary. Their term in government is made easier by continuing divisions in the mainstream right, which helps by offsetting the re-emerging factionalism within the socialist party itself. Even so, their programme is a conservative one, with fiscal policy remaining tight. Spring 1991 saw the appointment of France's first woman Prime Minister, **Edith Cresson**.

The Real France

How does the real France differ from the version put over by the tourist industry in their zeal to persuade us to go there? And what surprises are in store for those whose image of France is formed solely by the media?

Discovering the French themselves comes as a pleasant surprise.

It is they, after all, who enliven and animate the cities and countryside of France. On the whole, they are an energetic, stylish and hedonistic people, with a great love of argument and discussion. For the French, appearance is important, and life for them is theatre to a much greater extent than it is for the generally more reserved British: street life, café life, life in any public place – they are all infused with the colour and sparkle of the French themselves. However, the characteristic energy of the French has led them to pursue certain enthusiasms which go unrecorded in the tourist brochures.

Firstly, France is a much more modern and technologically-advanced country than the tourist industry would lead you to believe. The most obvious manifestation of this is the architecture. Still standing in almost every town and city are the results of the craze for modernisation and architectural experimentation which swept across France in the 1960s. At that time, skyscrapers shot up in Paris, and much of the country's poor housing was replaced by (much-needed) blocks of flats – mercifully on the outskirts of towns, leaving most of the centres intact. French interest in the avant-garde expands into architecture, as much as the other arts, and the results are on permanent public display – sometimes imaginative, such as the glass pyramid of the Louvre, sometimes plain garish, but always just as much a part of French life as the well-photographed 'historic centres' of cities. The French themselves are proud of much of this heritage and their technological prowess. The ultra-modernistic Pompidou Centre and the skyscrapers of La Défense are, for them, as much part of Paris's attractions as the picturesque cobbled streets of Montmartre. And they would certainly want you to visit the gigantic arts-leisure-and-science complex of La Villette in the north-east suburbs, if only to see the vast collection of French high-tech achievements in the world's largest science museum!

Alongside the rush towards things modern, the French have plunged headlong into the consumer society. Visitors, especially the more discreet British, are often startled by French people's evident urge to make money, and the obvious pleasure they get from spending it. This shouldn't come as a surprise; the French love of pleasure extends effortlessly to the weekly shopping expedition. To see the French consumer in action requires an expedition to another place you won't find in the brochures – the out-of-town hypermarket. The French have the largest hypermarkets in Europe – but also the good taste to place them far away from their town centres. These 'commercial zones', with their loud neon signs, enormous car-parks and what the French expressively call the 'grandes surfaces' – shops the size of small towns – seem distinctly American in scale and appearance. Yet they are an essential part of the French way-of-life, and well worth a visit, if only to compare them with the British equivalent.

Some of the food products on the hypermarket and supermarket shelves come as something of a surprise to tourists used to believing that France is the Mecca for 'la gastronomie', fresh foods and traditional home cooking. Convenience foods abound, from tinned 'cassoulet' to boil-in-the-bag 'canard à l'orange', while frozen-food counters stretch for hundreds of metres. The fast-selling packs of twenty frozen beefburgers remind the visitor, uneasily, of the ubiquitous McDonalds to be found in every French town centre, with the hot-dog snack bars and other examples of what the French term 'le fast-food'. Over the past thirty years, French eating habits and the range of products available have undergone massive changes. Gone are the days when the average French housewife would spend the greater part of every day shopping in the market and preparing two major meals of three or four courses each for her family. The changing role of women, more working mothers and shorter lunch-breaks have all paved the way for the increase in popularity of time-saving convenience foods and fast-food outlets. (Many run-of-the-mill restaurants, too, have turned to the use of processed foods and mass-production techniques, to keep their costs down; a practice unheard of in France until recently.) The result is that, in their day-to-day eating at home, the French have moved much closer to the habits of other Europeans, having shorter and simpler meals, often a combination of some convenience food plus fresh vegetables, and, of course, wine. The French gastronomic zeal is still there, and as strong as ever. The only difference is that now, it tends to be channelled into two or three culinary events a week – meals taken in quality restaurants, the long Sunday lunch, or a dinner party with friends, for example. But the tourist should not imagine that the average French family at home enjoys every evening the same elaborately-prepared dishes which he is served in restaurants. Chances are they are tucking in to microwaved pizzas while watching TV.

The huge hypermarket car-parks are a clue to another aspect of French culture, which clashes with the tourist's received image of this country as a peaceful haven of village squares whose tranquillity is broken only by the appearance of the occasional bicycle. The French obsession with the motor-car and speed will become immediately and shockingly evident if you drive there. The French have one of the highest levels of car ownership in Europe, and this is still increasing at 3% a year, despite successive oil crises. Behind the wheel, the average Frenchman becomes a near-omnipotent being, whose impatience to get from A to B in an unreasonably short time is one of the reasons why the fatal car accident rate in France – about 10,000 a year – is roughly double that of Britain. The combination of this impatience and a permitted alcohol level higher than that of many European countries is deadly: nearly half of all fatal road accidents are the result of drunk driving. The French obsession with fast driving is often put down to the Latin element in their nature. Yet, compared to the French, the Italians are more polite, and, while just as impatient, are usually more in control of their vehicles. French car parking habits also tend to raise the eyebrows of foreign visitors. Illegal, if sometimes quite ingenious, parking is widespread, especially in cities in the evenings, when it is quite common to see cars parked perpendicular to the kerb, in order to squeeze between two other vehicles. On holiday or on outings to the beach or countryside, the French like to park as near as possible to the spot where they plan to sunbathe or picnic. The more audacious will on occasion actually drive along the beach, contravening every regulation in the book!

However, the French love-affair with speed, progress and materialism has to be seen in the context of recent moves towards the rediscovery by French people of their own traditions and heritage. Despite, or maybe because of, the rise of convenience foods, interest in cuisine is running high among the French. In spite of the flirt with 'la nouvelle cuisine', sound regional cooking is enjoying a revival of interest among those who make the time to cook well at home once or twice a week. In a country where regional attachments have always remained strong (in Paris, office workers from the provinces often put up photographs of their beloved 'pays' around their desks), people are increasingly searching out their rural roots, for example, by spending holidays in the countryside which they or their parents left behind. This accounts for much of the upsurge in rural tourism in France. Tourism has also played a part in the recent resurgence of interest in France's regional languages, folk culture and history, although this is perhaps more due to the novelty of post-war urbanisation and modernisation wearing off, and French people acting to save aspects of their own culture at risk of disappearing. These trends showing the French turning back to their own traditions are less obvious to the tourist, but they are real and they put the more surprising trends, above, in perspective.

Another surprise in store is the discovery that the population of France is much more of a racial mix than you would guess from a perusal of a brochure. Those old men sitting picturesquely around a café table may, in actual fact, turn out to be Arabs. During the years of the industrial expansion of the 1960s, France relied heavily on her former colonies for labour – mainly Muslims from North Africa. Consequently, France now has about two million immigrant Moroccans, Algerians and Tunisians living there. These are the most obvious ethnic group, but there are another two and a half million immigrants, composed mainly of Portuguese, Italians and Spaniards. As in Britain, unemployment among immigrants is higher than that in the general population, and this, combined with the tendency for immigrants to be housed together in out-of-town housing estates, has led to mounting tension and the recent outbreak of riots in these areas. Yet France's immigrant population, much higher than Britain's, is more evenly spread throughout the country, including rural areas, and now very much part of the French demographic landscape. The high profile given to France's ethnic unrest and the rantings of the National Front leader Jean-Marie Le Pen tend to eclipse the fact that, through mixed marriages, for example, much of the immigrant population is gradually assimilating. As in Britain, they have also enriched the range of culinary offerings, through the many North African restaurants – particularly Moroccan, the best cooks.

Finally, one aspect of the real France which conforms exactly to the version put over by the tourist boards and the media is rural life. The idealised image of the life of the French countryside received by foreigners is rarely disappointed when experiencing the real thing. France is still largely a rural nation, and much of its identity comes from the awareness of its agricultural heritage. There is a much stronger town/countryside divide in France than in Britain, and you don't have to go far into the rural landscape to find yourself in what townpeople somewhat disparagingly call 'La France profonde' – deepest, darkest France. Apart from the big arable and cattle farms of the Paris basin, in other regions it is quite common to come across peasants farming the land as their ancestors did, eking a living out of a few dozen acres with a market garden and some animals – a nightmare for the Common Agricultural Policy perhaps, but an essential part of French rural life, and one which exists side-by-side with the modernisation which has come to much of French farming since the Second World War. Drive along some 'D' roads to discover the charm of French village life. Their physical beauty, and the intricate rituals of their markets, cafés and shops are of a quality that no brochure could exaggerate.

The Tourist Industry

After many years of losing out to other, newer destinations, France is once again in the ascendancy, as changing tourism trends move in its favour. Before the Second World War, France was the most visited country in the world, the destination for one in every four international tourists. This was the era of travel for the élite only – the wealthy and leisured who were prepared to pay well for the very best in accommodation, haute cuisine and access to art and culture. France was able to supply all of these, in abundance. With the rise of mass tourism during the 1960s, however, France faced new competition from Spanish, Italian and other Mediterranean destinations, which were able to provide what the new mass consumers of international travel were seeking: sun, sea and sand holidays at the lowest price possible. Mercifully, France was little affected by this new wave of tourism, which was to transform the coasts of other Mediterranean countries. To this day, it remains a favoured destination for foreign visitors, in particular the British. 12% of all British people's holidays of four days or more, and 43% of their short breaks (up to four days) are spent in France, making it their number one overseas destination. France is also popular among the French themselves: about 75% of all holidays taken by French people are taken in their own country.

So, why this revival in popularity? Two trends currently favour France as a tourist destination. The first is the widespread move in favour of quality. As members of the holiday-buying public become more confident and more sophisticated in their selection of destinations, they are increasingly rejecting cheap package tours in favour of a better quality product. Tired of sun, sea and sand, they are looking for something extra: culture, cuisine, activities – all of which France is excellently placed to offer. At the same time, the higher quality of amenities, services and facilities now being sought by tourists are also to be found there. The other trend in France's favour is a growing environmental awareness on the part of tourists. It is exactly this awareness which has led tourists to turn their backs on destinations where the human or natural environment has been allowed to deteriorate – through uncontrolled development, or pollution, for example. Clean water for bathing, unpolluted air, the absence of litter, large expanses of unspoilt land and a greater authenticity of holiday experience: these are all features increasingly in demand from holidaymakers. As a result, France, widely perceived to be better placed to offer these than many other European countries, is now climbing back up the list of the world's top international destinations. It recently overtook Italy to move into third place, behind Spain and the USA.

Tourism is now one of France's biggest industries, and a key sector of the economy. The annual turnover of the tourism industry in France is currently about 450 billion FF – more than that of French agriculture, and double that of the textile industry. The spectacular annual rises in spending on tourism in France have dropped slightly from the heady days of the late 1970s, when it stood at about 15% a year, to today's level of around 8%. Nevertheless, tourism still represents some 9% of the GDP (Gross Domestic Product) of France as a whole. Generally speaking, the economic impact of tourism, region by region, becomes more important the further south you go. For the Nord/Pas-de-Calais, tourism accounts for less than 2% of the regional GDP; in Auvergne, between 5 and 10%; but in Languedoc-Roussillon and Corsica, for example, it is responsible for well over 10% of the regions' GDP – an uneasily high proportion, perhaps, with the tourist season so short and given the seasonal nature of the employment it creates.

Tourism is an important source of foreign income for France. It brings in more foreign cash than the car industry, and almost as much as their highly lucrative armaments industry. More than forty-one million foreign tourists spent a total of 105 billion FF in France in 1989, a record year. The eight million British visitors currently making trips to France each year are the second most important market for that country, coming just after the Germans. Spain, the USA, Switzerland, Belgium, the Netherlands and Italy are the other principal markets for inbound tourism in France. With all of these countries spending more and more on tourism in France every year, while the French themselves are currently spending only about 65 billion FF on tourism outside their own country, France shows a healthy positive travel balance of payments, at around

$7 billion. This compares favourably with, for example Britain's travel balance, which currently shows an annual net **loss** of about $7 billion.

The other major advantage of tourism, for France, is the amount of employment it creates. While employment in the French economy, in general, is stagnating, the number of tourism jobs is rising at the rate of 3% a year. Taking jobs created directly and indirectly by tourism, a total of about 1.6 million French people owe their living to this industry – about 8% of the total employed population.

The economic importance of tourism for France is the reason why so much effort is made in marketing the country as a destination. Central government involvement comes through the Ministry of Tourism, responsible for overseeing the expansion and development of tourism in France. Part of the Ministry's resources goes to funding the work of the French Government Tourist Office, known as 'La Maison de la France', which works overseas to promote France as an international tourist destination. The FGTO has thirty-six offices in twenty-six foreign countries, the 'shop windows' for tourism in France. Each FGTO represents the French tourism industry, mounting marketing campaigns, producing brochures, and attending travel fairs, to persuade people to visit France.

In France itself, tourism marketing is undertaken by a range of regional, departmental and communal organisations. On the regional level, each 'Comité Régional de Tourisme' (Regional Tourist Board) is responsible not only for marketing the region for tourism, but also for coordinating tourism development and training in that region. The regions of France are also marketed through a number of 'Maisons Régionales' in Paris. Some twenty-two regional tourist boards have opened these attractive tourism 'shops' in Paris, to promote their region to Parisians as well as to foreign visitors to the capital. They organise promotion campaigns, distribute tourist information, and make hotel bookings.

On a smaller scale, each *département* in France has its own 'Comité Départemental de Tourisme', basically to promote the *département* and to carry out research into its tourist facilities, but also to advise the local planning authorities on matters of tourism development.

The most public face of tourism promotion and marketing in France is seen in the 'Offices de Tourisme' and 'Syndicats d'Initiative', the tourist information centres (often marked on maps as O.T.S.I). Operating at the level of the individual 'commune', the smallest unit of democracy in France, these offices, open to the public, provide tourist information, not only on their own commune, but on the whole *département*. They produce lists of hotels, camping sites, local walks, and any other kind of tourist information. Some also arrange car hire, hotel bookings and concert tickets, for example. Rent, materials and salaries are paid for by the communes. However, in smaller towns and villages, or places with a very short tourist season, these offices are often staffed by volunteers; while the larger offices, open all year round in cities, have staff who, as well as being paid, are more likely to speak foreign languages. Information on a specific town can be obtained simply by addressing a letter to the **Office de Tourisme**, followed by the postcode of the *département* (see map of France p. ix) and the name of the town. Alternatively, contact the **Fédération Nationale des Offices de Tourisme et Syndicats d'Initiative**, 2 rue Linois, 75015 Paris (Tel. (1) 40 59 43 83).

Despite making a massive contribution to the French economy, the vast majority of businesses in the tourism industry are small-scale, family affairs. This is particularly true in the hotel and restaurant sector; 70% of France's hotels have fewer than five employees. The whole industry is characterised by small, independent hotels and restaurants, coach operators and tourist attractions. 'Big names' are rare in the French tourism industry. Even France's biggest tour operator, Club Méditerranée, has only just over a million clients annually, compared to over five million for Britain's Thomson group. (The one exception is the French Accor group, now Europe's largest hotel group, with Ibis/Urbis and the budget hotels Formule 1, its most famous brand names, now being 'exported' to other countries including Britain.)

One significant change is that recently, in the face of growing competition, many hotels have joined forces as consortia, in order to market themselves more effectively. These 'voluntary' hotel chains are associations of independent hotels who combine their resources to produce attractive booklets containing details of all the hotels belonging to the consortium. In this way, they keep all the personal touch and independence of the family hotel, while having the advantages of scale which come from being part of a chain. (See **Accommodation**, page 60).

Unlike Spain and Italy, France is not a major package-tour destination. On average, about 40% of France's tourism is in the hands of tour operators (although this figure more than doubles for winter sports holidays in France). One reason for this may be the fact that France has very few home-grown tour operators of its own working overseas to sell package-tours to France. In Britain, for example, the vast majority of tour operators featuring France in their brochures are British-owned.

And it is not necessarily a question of size; because it is not the largest tour operators who send the greatest numbers of package tourists to France. In Britain, small, specialised companies such as Neilson or Keycamp are each responsible for almost twice the number of tourists sent to France by the mighty Intasun. Tour operators selling French package tours are often specialist companies, dealing with a particular type of accommodation (Gîtes de France, Eurocamp, French Villa Centre), a particular activity (Cycling for Softies, Ski Falcon), or a single region of France (Paris Travel Service, Brittany Direct, NSS Riviera). Many are very small-scale, selling as few as 2000 to 3000 packages a year in some cases.

The other 60% of visits to France are made by independent travellers, arranging their own transport and accommodation. Most use their own car, by far the most common way of travelling to, and around France. Camping and caravanning are widely used forms of accommodation (more than half of the total accommodation stock of France falls into these two categories). There is no doubt that it is this kind of tourist that the French themselves best understand and appreciate. By and large, the French tend to shun travel agents and tour operators (except for long-haul trips to exotic destinations). They will sooner drive to a camping site on the Mediterranean coast, to a second home in Brittany, or to Tante Marie's villa in the Cévennes, than choose a package tour from a brochure. For this reason, they well understand the independent traveller, and recognise him or her as 'one of their own' whenever they meet on the beach or between the aisles of some rural supermarket.

The attitude of the French towards tourists is generally very positive. Demonstrations of hostility towards visitors are extremely rare, and even then are more likely than not to consist of a few choice insults called out to you from the car behind as you dither around the streets of some strange French town in your GB registered car. However, the particular situation of Corsica makes it a special case. There, tourism is a very sensitive issue, due to the locals' fears of foreign speculators and developers dominating the tourism industry and draining away the profits from the island. Bars and tourist developments owned by outsiders have been attacked by the Corsican Nationalist Movement, the FLNC, which, although not opposed to foreign tourists, is determined that tourism on the island should be run by Corsicans. On mainland France, in certain busy resorts, there have been occasional sightings of graffiti daubed on walls, as expressions of the inhabitants' frustration, but this is very rare. Inevitably, the best reception for tourists is found in those regions where they are sufficiently few to remain a focus of novelty and interest for their hosts.

Rural tourism is where the best expression of this attitude is found – farmers offering 'camping à la ferme', couples running bed and breakfasts, families living next door to a gîte: these people tend to be genuinely welcoming, often proud to tell of visitors who have become firm friends and who return to see them year after year. It is not difficult to understand why. The vast French countryside can be a lonely place, with little in the way of added interest or stimulation for the inhabitants. Most of them look forward with great pleasure to the tourist season, not only for the opportunities it brings to supplement their income, but also for the contact with new people which it provides. For many, their main motivation for taking in visitors is for the human contact aspect of this activity.

One of France's biggest tourism assets for the years ahead is its rural tourism or 'le tourisme vert'. Changing tastes are beginning to favour the personal service and authentic, small-scale enterprises which characterise the 'cottage' tourism industry now operating successfully in the French countryside and mountain regions. The tourism tide is moving inland, away from the beaches, with their associations of pollution and idleness, to a countryside rightly perceived to be rich in opportunities for activity, exploration and discovery. The French themselves, as well as foreign tourists, are more and more drawn towards the rural regions, of which France has an abundance. The proliferation of small businesses which constitute the rural tourism industry are increasingly grouping themselves together in order to market themselves more effectively to this growing clientèle. And they are doing everything in their power to make it easy for the tourist to buy the 'product', whether it's a week's bird-watching holiday, a weekend gastronomic tour, or a fortnight's stay in a gîte. (See **The Positive Holidays**, page 39.) The French also regard tourism in their countryside as one of the solutions to the problem of continuing rural depopulation, and what they call 'désertification'. This is the name given to the process by which the rural exodus leads to remoter areas becoming social and cultural deserts. The population in some parts has already fallen below the minimum required to maintain services and make a social life possible – in regions such as Aveyron, and the lonelier parts of the Massif Central, Savoy and the Jura. Recently, vast amounts of public money have been spent to breathe life back into rural communities, through the promotion of tourism, traditional handicrafts using local materials, the development of forestry and the improvement of road and rail communications. For example, as the vogue for rural tourism in France has steadily grown, the government has encouraged the conversion of old farm buildings into gîtes, by awarding generous grants for this purpose. For many farmers in particular, extra income from tourism has become increasingly important as the EC has urged cutbacks in the agricultural production of all member countries. Given the great variety and beauty of the thinly-populated French countryside, there is clearly scope for much more tourism of this type, before it reaches anything like saturation point. And, in contrast with the more fragile mountain environments, and parts of its coastline, the vast countryside of France appears to be robust enough to be spared most of the negative impacts of tourism – erosion of footpaths, for example – seen in Britain.

How Green is France?

If the French need any reminder of the importance of controlling the negative impacts of tourism on the environment, they have only to look across the frontier at their Spanish neighbour. Degraded coastal regions and soulless high-rise hotels blocking the views of the sea have contributed a lot to that country's declining tourism fortunes, as well as damaging one of the most beautiful landscapes in Europe.

Back in the 1960s and 1970s, it looked as though France was set to follow the same downward path as its neighbour, when its philosophy appeared to be one of 'development at any price'. That was the era of the construction of the massive, modernistic new resorts along many French coasts, as concrete walls of holiday flats and obtrusive marinas restricted access to the coast for all but the most affluent in some parts. The Alps, too, were the scene of the rapid expansion of gigantic ski-stations with out-of-place apartment blocks, as a result of the government's 1970 'plan neige' to vastly increase the country's skiing capacity. The grandiose scale of these schemes, and their apparent lack of concern for environmental consequences are now widely criticised. Along with a new awareness of environmental issues (the environment is now second on the French worry list, after unemployment), there are several other factors at play in France which mean that it is unlikely to make the same mistakes as Spain.

For one, despite rising affluence among the French population, about three quarters of all holidays taken by them are taken in their own country. This is not, in most cases, because they can't afford to go abroad, but because they are (rightly) proud of France, and have therefore an interest in seeing its attractions and charms maintained in tourist regions as well as elsewhere. Secondly, the French have a very special interest and affection for their own countryside. Until the end of World War II, France was still a very rural nation, with about 35% of the population at that time still employed in farming. Now that only 8% of the French work in farming, the 'urbanised' population and their offspring still retain a lot of nostalgic affection for the countryside. Its conservation is far more a matter of national concern than it is among the general population in Britain.

The result of this concern has been a series of conservation policies for tourism in France, designed to protect the coast, the mountains and the countryside.

In the 1970s, when Giscard came to power, with his famous slogan, 'A more human kind of growth', he set out to protect the coast from the twin evils of beach pollution and over-building. Already at that time, 51% of the French coast was built up with towns and resorts, about twice the proportion of the British coast. Giscard put a brake on the activities of France's property developers who were building ugly high-rise apartment blocks, in response to the growing desire of the French for private holiday flats by the sea. A 1976 law made it compulsory for **any** major construction project (not only in tourism) to be the subject of an environmental impact study. Now, new holiday property in France is restricted to three storeys and low-density, and it has to be placed either at least 100 metres inland, or perpendicular to the coast, not parallel. The architectural quality of these constructions is also subject to strict controls. The same regulations cover construction around large inland lakes, estuaries and river deltas, forbidding the construction of roads on the edge of shores, and guaranteeing the total protection of all shores to a distance of 100 metres back from the water's edge.

Further protection is provided by the 'Conservatoire de l'espace littoral', the Coastal Conservatory. Inspired by the British National Trust, but with much more power to intervene, and with generous annual grants from the government, the Conservatory buys up parts of the coast under threat. Land coming into its ownership in this way is given to the local communities to manage and maintain. Such parts of the coast must be kept open to general public access, and must be kept free from further construction schemes. In the first ten years of its existence, the Coastal Conservatory bought up 186 different properties in this way, representing about 67,000 acres, a figure doubled by 1990.

France's beaches have, thankfully, come a long way from the days when the Côte d'Azur, for example, was one of the slimiest stretches of coast from Gibraltar to Suez. Even as recently as 1980, one in three samples of seawater taken from the French coast were failing to come up to the (modest) European Community standards for bathing beaches. Now, massive investment in sewerage facilities, and the spending of some 1500 million FF on the south coast alone has put almost 90% of France's beaches into the top two EC standards for the quality of their seawater. Most visitors now have no problem finding French beaches displaying the 'Pavillon Bleu' (blue flag), indicating that they meet the EC's quality standards for beach and bathing water quality. There are 102 of these in France, third from the top in the list of European countries, as opposed to only 29 in Britain, fifth from the bottom.

In mountain areas, ski developments have been responsible for damage to wildlife, through the interruption of nesting and breeding patterns, and for damage to forests, as extensive tree clearances have threatened the environment by increasing the risk of avalanches. Many of the large 'high-tech' resorts of the early 1970s severely detracted from the landscape. In 1977, the government took action, saying that the zone situated above the forest limit was to be developed to a minimum only, and defining certain high valleys which were to remain free from any development. It stressed the vital role of agriculture and forestry in mountain life, and the necessity of maintaining these, and developing them in tandem with tourism; and it affirmed the desirability of local communities benefiting financially from tourist developments, and of those developments being in scale and in keeping with existing settlements. Although the building of new ski resorts has continued, the excesses of earlier times, with their heavy toll on the environment, have been avoided.

The building of some new resorts – Superbagnères and Soussouéou in the Pyrenees, for example – has been challenged on the basis of their environmental impact. More and more, local communities are involved in the management of ski facilities, even when these are owned by foreign companies. A Dutch developer was allowed to build a new resort at Valmorel in the Tarentaise only on condition that the local authority retained responsibility for land management, that all jobs created went to local people, and that contributions were made to the maintenance of local farming activities. The gigantism of certain early ski resorts has not been repeated. Only low-rise, village-type constructions are permitted; architecture must be in harmony with what already exists, if the resort is joined to an existing village; and priority is given to year-round resorts, which offer other mountain activities during the summer, as well as winter skiing. On the whole, these regulations have been well observed, not least because they happen to coincide with a general desire among the French themselves to return to traditional mountain accommodation, and food, when they go skiing. Accommodation on farms, in chalets, family pensions and villages which have kept their charm of yesteryear is now in vogue, and even new ski resorts, such as Valmorel, are being built using the traditional architecture of the region. (See **Activity Holidays**, page 44). There are, however, moves to extend the lift system and ski runs in the Tarentaise region, so as to link all its resorts, which will almost certainly have negative environmental consequences.

In rural France, six National Parks have been created since 1960, each with the aim of protecting a natural area of special interest, and at the same time, opening that area up for tourism and discreet scientific investigation. Each of the parks, five of which are in the mountains, has an uninhabited Inner Zone, where wildlife is protected through a ban on hunting, building and camping. This is surrounded by a Peripheral Zone containing towns and tourist facilities, with the aim of preserving the rural lifestyle in the face of continuing depopulation and erosion of traditional crafts and customs, while at the same time providing facilities for tourism. The National Parks are those of the Cévennes, the Ecrins, Mercantour, Port-Cros, the Pyrénées Occidentales and the Vanoise, whose combined surface area accounts for about 1% of the entire area of France. Twenty-four Regional Parks, representing roughly 7% of the area of France, have the same aims as the Peripheral Zones of the national parks. Most of these are located in medium to high mountain regions, but are also found in more delicate forest regions and marshlands. Wildlife protection in them is minimal, as there is no restriction on hunting, except where a nature reserve has been created within a park. Information on the National and Regional Parks is available from the **Fédération des Parcs Naturels de France**, 4 rue Stockholm, 75008 Paris (Tel. (1) 42 94 90 84). The Parks Federation has now joined forces with the Ministry of the Environment and the Ministry of Tourism, who signed an agreement in 1989 to develop new forms of tourism designed to make the public more sensitive towards the environment; together they have created a dozen 'Voyages au Naturel', which allow visitors to discover various French parks in an environmentally responsible manner. For details, see **Adventure/Activity Holidays** section, page 44.

Finally, eighty-five state Natural Reserves exist to protect the most sensitive sites of France's natural heritage. This number – low for a country the size of France – is partly explained by the fact that the government prefers to seek agreement with private landowners, rather than to purchase the land. For this reason, many additional nature reserves and refuges have been created by private conservation societies, such as the 'Ligue Française pour la Protection des Oiseaux' and the 'Société Nationale de Protection de la Nature'. One conservation association, which manages some state and some private reserves is worth a particular mention. The 'Fédération de Conservatoires Régionaux d'Espaces Naturels' now has fourteen regional divisions throughout France, which model themselves on the British National Trust but have to operate on a shoestring budget. They aim to purchase or rent (often by means of public subscription) the areas of ecological interest in their region, which they feel are most under threat. Wherever possible, they create discovery paths in these areas so that the public may appreciate them.

Green politics started in France at the end of the 1960s, with the rise of ecology groups disenchanted with the older political parties and their ideologies, and prepared to fight on a range of fronts, from nuclear power stations, through uranium mining, to building schemes which threaten the landscape. The rate of success of their lobbying has been mixed: least effective in connection with France's massive nuclear power programme. Even after Chernobyl, the general population remains largely in favour of nuclear power – partly due to Electricité de France's successful public relations exercise to persuade the public that French nuclear stations are much safer than Russian ones, and that without this energy, French living standards would fall.

Out of three separate green political parties in France, 'Les Verts' emerged in 1984. Since then, they have met with a mixed rate of success in elections. In the 1986 legislative elections, green candidates received 3.38% of the total votes in all the *départements* where candidates stood. In the national elections, they had a total of only 305,500 votes, or 2.44% of the total in the *départements* where they were active. Nevertheless, 'Les Verts' performance in the 1989 European elections was excellent, taking over 10% of the total vote in France, earning them nine seats in the European Parliament. In the same year, 1300 green candidates were elected on to French municipal councils. By and large, French ecologists have been disappointed with the environmental policies of the socialists, seeing little difference between them and the policies of more right-wing governments in recent years. Mitterrand's overall policy for the environment has not in the end proved to be very different from that of Giscard and Chirac. True, the nuclear programme has been scaled down slightly, and local opinion is now consulted over any new construction schemes. But the overall policy has not been widened, and many issues of concern to 'Les Verts' – nuclear testing, land-drainage and its effects on wetlands, the endangering of many bird and animal species, for example – go on unchecked.

France has about 100 non-governmental national associations concerned with environmental issues, and many more operating on a regional or more local basis. While each one is effective to a degree in their activities, they are all partly hampered by the absence in France of any independent foundations to which they can turn for funding. Consequently, their continuing survival depends on a mixture of local and regional government grants, and donations.

'Amis de la Terre' (15 rue Gambey, 75001 Paris, Tel.(1) 47 00 05 05) is the French Friends of the Earth, concerning itself with general environment protection issues. They are joined in this mission by several other national associations including 'Espaces pour Demain' (20 avenue Mac-Mahon, 75017 Paris, Tel.(1) 47 64 13 38) and 'Greenpeace France' (28 rue Petites Ecuries, 75010 Paris, Tel.(1) 47 70 46 89). The latter continues to take action against French nuclear tests in the South Pacific, despite the scandalous Rainbow Warrior affair of 1985, when their ship was blown up and sunk by French secret agents in Auckland Harbour.

The protection of wildlife is the aim of a number of associations.

prominent among which are the French World Wide Fund for Nature, 'Fonds Mondial pour la Nature' (151 boulevard Reine, 78000 Versailles, Tel.(1) 39 50 75 14), and the 'Ligue Française pour la Protection des Oiseaux' (La Corderie Royale, BP 263, 17305 Rochefort Cedex, Tel.46 99 59 97), the French League for the Protection of Birds – both of whom are largely to be given the credit for the number of preservation orders on most of France's endangered species. Up against France's mighty hunting lobby is the 'Rassemblement des Opposants à la Chasse', (23 rue Gosselot, 59000 Lille, Tel.20 52 12 02), the union of those opposed to hunting

Leading the way in the conservation of France's cultural heritage are 'Vieilles Maisons Françaises', Old French Houses (93 rue de l'Université, 75007 Paris, Tel.(1) 45 51 07 02), and the 'Club du Vieux Manoir', Country House Club (10, rue de la Cossonnerie, 75001 Paris, Tel.(1) 45 08 80 40), associations whose projects range from the restoration of a Renaissance village in the Vosges to the maintenance of gardens around historic houses. A considerable role in cultural conservation is also played by France's numerous *ecomusées*. An *ecomusée* is best described as a 'living' museum. They are often small-scale and rural, though some are to be found in towns or industrial areas, and they all aim to keep the public in touch with local skills, crafts and industries which might otherwise die out. Sometimes you can actually see people at work in the *ecomusée*; sometimes it is more like a conventional museum, merely offering displays on the local history and way of life. But in most cases they provide great insight into the interests of the community.

Unlike its huge British namesake, the French Ministry of the Environment (14–16 boulevard du Général Leclerc, 92524 Neuilly sur Seine Cedex, Tel.(1) 47 58 12 12) sticks to the tasks of nature protection, quality of life, hazards, pollution, research and international issues such as global warming. The Ministry is headed by ecologist and former leader of French Friends of the Earth, Brice Lalonde, who is not a politician, but someone directly appointed by the Prime Minister. In response to the problems created by France's too-rapid post-war urbanisation, most of the environmental issues tackled by this Ministry during the past twenty years have focused on France's cities, home now to 80% of the population. Vast amounts have been spent to make them more habitable and easier to travel around, and the results have been generally impressive. The French national environment plan outlines the Ministry's targets: CFCs outlawed within ten years, CO_2 emissions stabilised in ten to fifteen years, atmospheric pollution cut by 30%, an increase to 50% (from 30%) in recycling of primary materials, and a trebling within five years of the Ministry's budget to 1.9% of GNP (the same as Germany's).

Sightseeing

As France's popularity increases, it becomes more and more difficult to avoid the hordes of other visitors travelling around the country and visiting its attractions. Yet, with some planning, a little imagination and originality, you can still enjoy France at its best, without the crowds.

Summer and winter, the **Parisian region**, Ile-de-France, is where you will find most British visitors to France, as well as tourists from practically any country in the developed world (in August, of course, the only scarce nationality in Paris is the French themselves!). It is vital that you choose the timing of any trip to Paris very carefully. Arrive during the wrong week, and you could end up with the impression that every hotel bed in the city is booked already – except, naturally, for the most expensive. Unless you want to risk feeling like an extra on *Grange Hill*, avoid, at all costs, any British school mid-term holiday week. That's when you will find Paris packed with stressed teachers leading groups of pupils around, and trying not to lose too many of them on the Metro. The French Government Tourist Office, in their free guide 'The Traveller in France' produces a very useful little table, telling you the best weeks to visit Paris in any year, if you want to avoid the crowds.

The next most popular summer destinations for the British, after Paris, are Provence/Côte d'Azur, followed by Burgundy, Brittany and Rhône-Alpes. If you are keen to avoid your fellow countrymen, think about the regions least visited by the British; according to the French Government Tourist Office, these are **Franche-Comté**, **Picardy and Champagne-Ardenne**. These regions are the ones which feature least in tour operators' brochures for France, for the time being . . .

But expect to meet substantial numbers of **French tourists** if you choose to take a holiday in France during July or August. That's when **80%** of French holidays are taken, and most of these are spent in France itself. Where do the French go on holiday in France? More than one in four choose to spend their summer holidays in two regions – Languedoc-Roussillon and Provence-Alpes-Côte d'Azur, in other words, along France's Mediterranean coast. These regions of France reach close to saturation point during July and August, with an influx of about ten million tourists, a quarter of them from Paris. Roads become congested, parking impossible, tempers frayed, and beaches dirty and overcrowded. And with the high-season so short, those running tourism businesses try their hardest to make the maximum amount of money during those two months. So unless you are prepared to pay well over the odds for accommodation and everything else you will need on holiday, you should certainly avoid the congestion of the Mediterranean coast during July and August. Either go somewhere else during those months – try an inland destination – or go earlier or later in the year, if your heart is set on the Med. The next most popular summer destinations for the French themselves are the Brittany and Atlantic coastal resorts, which, during July and August, present some of the problems to be found on the south coast, but not to the same nightmarish extent.

If you want to visit regions which are relatively free of any other tourists at most times of the year, there are four of these, each of which is well worth considering: **Nord/Pas-de-Calais**, **Haute Normandie**, **Lorraine** and **Champagne-Ardenne**. According to the French Ministry of Tourism, these northern regions are the least visited parts of France. Yet, this can't be explained by any great lack of places of interest or things to do there. For they are, every one of them, attractive and rewarding destinations for those prepared to try somewhere off the beaten tourist track. Think about beating your own track there before they get the recognition they really deserve.

At the level of individual towns and tourist attractions, France's most problematic honeypots tend to be in Paris itself, or within a day's return trip from the capital. So be prepared to jostle with countless other tourists if you visit practically any of Paris's better-known attractions in the high-season, or any of the following: **Versailles, Fontainebleau, Chartres, Mont-Saint-Michel, Senlis, Chantilly, Barbizon** or **Vaux-le-Vicomte**. Best of all, avoid the day-trippers from Paris by staying locally and getting an early start for your sightseeing. Then, having satisfied your appetite for culture and history, you can relax over a long lunch, avoiding the afternoon 'rush hours'.

Communications

France's transport system offers various ways of getting around the country, for sightseeing.

The French are justly proud of the SNCF network and its **trains**, which are modern, comfortable, clean and punctual. The network is one of the densest in Europe, connecting all major cities as well as smaller towns. The government's heavy subsidies to the SNCF have resulted in a system of fares which are on average 20–30% cheaper than those charged by British Rail for equivalent journeys. Inevitably, the best services are on those lines radiating from Paris, but with 35,000 km of lines connecting over 5500 destinations throughout France, smaller towns are well-served too. **Motorail** services carry cars, motorbikes and passengers overnight on trains from Boulogne, Calais, Dieppe and Paris to all main holiday areas. Part of the SNCF network is served by the slick orange and white **TGV** trains ('trains à grande vitesse'), which, travelling at over 300 km per hour, have become symbols of France's technological prowess. Since the launch of the first service in 1981 (which brought Lyon within two hours of Paris), many regions of France have battled to win the TGV for their cities, while in others (see **The Art of being a Good Tourist**, page 63) it is not so welcome. Recently, new TGV services have begun between Paris and Le Mans and Paris and Bordeaux, while work continues on the TGV Nord line, which will connect Paris with the Channel Tunnel. Remember that there is a compulsory 'reservation supplement' on all TGV services, and that train tickets bought in France must be punched ('composté'), using the orange machines at the entrance to all platforms before starting your journey.

The SNCF, through their associate company SNCF Tourisme, also run excellent excursions from more than 250 French towns, using either a combination of train + **coach**, or coach only. The excursions range from half-day to several days in length, and use high-comfort operating coaches, usually with multilingual staff on board. Without transport of your own, these excursions are a good way of getting to some of the more out-of-the-way attractions of France, such as the Verdon gorges, the rosary chapel at Vence, or even Mont Blanc. Railway stations can point you in the direction of the nearest SNCF Tourisme office.

French **roads** take a real hammering every year, an effect exacerbated by tourist traffic. The British are partly to blame. By far the majority of British visitors to France use their own cars to get around the country, struggling to cope with driving on the 'wrong' side of the road in cars with the steering wheel on the 'wrong' side too. To add to the problem, three quarters of the French themselves also use their private cars to go on holiday in their own country. For the sake of your own sanity and safety, you should really try to avoid joining **them** in the annual race for the sun. Above all, keep off the roads during 'le grand départ' of the last weekend in July or the first weekend in August, when some two million French cars are heading south.

France got off to a late start in constructing its **motorways**, 'les autoroutes'. By 1967, it only had 780 km of motorway, fewer, even, than the Netherlands. One reason for this was its excellent network of **main and secondary roads**, which are still there today, and which offer useful alternatives to motorway travel. These roads form part of what is the best network in Europe, logically arranged and well engineered, to connect all of France's cities and towns. Unless you are in a desperate hurry, avoid the motorways where there is now a **minimum** speed of 80 kph during good visibility, and use the less stressful and much more interesting main and secondary roads. There is always a good main road, a 'route nationale', prefixed with an 'N', along roughly the same route as any motorway – often parallel – and as well as saving wear and tear on your nerves and vehicle, you'll save the money you would have spent on tolls. But if you are not in a hurry, then the secondary, 'routes départementales', with a 'D' prefix, are ideal. They are quieter, safer, and will take you into some beautiful countryside.

One of the busiest summer routes in France is the road to the south. If you are driving all the way down, you can either use the motorways, like most people (and pay about £35 in tolls at the 'péages', the additional price for getting there in the shortest time possible); or, if you are in less of a hurry, you can use a bit of imagination, and make the trip an enjoyable and memorable part of the holiday. If the Riviera is your destination, drive down via Champagne country, through the Aube to Burgundy then Grenoble, coming into Cannes via the back roads of Sisteron and Grasse. If heading towards the Spanish border, you could keep well west, visiting inland Brittany before dropping down to Bordeaux. Or take a route through the Touraine and Limousin.

If you do find that you have to use a motorway (and the French now have 6,500 km of these – double the amount in Britain), you will notice that they have managed to avoid some of the environmental damage wreaked by other countries' motorways. In France, they are elegantly landscaped, with extensive use of greenery, where Britain, for example, has concrete. There are none of the unsightly advertising hoardings which deface Italy's motorways; instead, brown pictorial signs every few kilometres add interest to the journey by telling you that you are passing some famous vineyard, or castle, or historic town.

However you decide to go, if you are driving, look out for the advice of the 'Bison Futé' (the wily bison). This helpful character makes his appearance every year at peak motoring times. You will see roadside signs telling you that the 'wily bison' advises you to avoid using the roads at particular times, i.e. when they are at their most congested. You would do well to follow this advice, if you want to avoid long delays, for even the traffic on France's motorways can be brought to a frustrating standstill at these peak periods. France has the most elaborate domestic **air network** in Europe, operated by the state-owned domestic airline, Air Inter and about ten smaller, private airlines. Air Inter underwent rapid expansion during the 1960s, and, like the railways, benefits from generous subsidies from a government desperate to keep road transport to a minimum. As a result, its fares are among the least expensive in Europe. With over 300 flights per day, the network is much more highly-developed than Britain's. It links thirty provincial towns to each other, as well as to Paris, and with impressive daily frequencies, makes it possible to cross France in an average flight-time of one hour.

Red Tape

For all its obsession with red tape and bureaucratic procedures, France presents very few problems of this kind for visitors. To get into France, a full British Passport, valid ten years, or a British Visitor's Passport, valid one year is needed. Alternatively, a British Excursion Document for travel to France (from the Post Office) is valid for one month, for trips of up to sixty hours. No visa is necessary for visitors from EC countries, though Australians still need a visa. (Contact the Visa Section, 6A Cromwell Place, London SW7; Tel. 071 823 9555, 9am–11.30am).

You can take unlimited amounts of currency into France, but must declare it if you are likely to re-export notes to the value of 50,000FF or more. The basic unit of currency is the French franc (FF), with coins to the value of 1, 2, 5, and 10FF, and notes to the value of 20, 50, 100, 500FF. The franc is divided into 100 centimes, with 5, 10, 20 and 50 centimes coins. For the best exchange rates, use banks rather than the money-exchange counters in airports, railway stations and city-centres. As in most places, it is not advisable to carry around vast sums of cash. Credit cards such as American Express, Visa/Barclaycard, Mastercard/Access or Diners Club are widely accepted. Other alternatives to cash are travellers' cheques and Eurocheques. The former are available from banks and some building societies, and the Eurocheque system comprises a chequebook and card – available from banks – used just like a normal chequebook and card.

Should fate decree it, visitors from EC countries are entitled to use the French health services. The form E111 is required. Application forms for these are available from Post Offices and DSS offices in Britain. This entitles the visitor to the same health benefits as the French themselves: 80–85% refund of medical expenses incurred. For 100% refund, take out a travel insurance policy which offers comprehensive health insurance. If in need of medicine, look for the nearest chemist's shop, or 'pharmacie', easily identified by the neon green cross outside. At night and on Sundays, if you have problems finding one, ask at the Commissariat de Police. To call an ambulance, the number to dial is 15. No special immunisations are necessary for travel to France.

The main public holidays in France are: January 1, Easter, Easter Monday, Ascension Thursday, May 1, May 8, Whit Monday, July 14, August 15, November 1, November 11 and Christmas. On these days, banks, shops and almost everything else will be closed.

For the telephone system, there are now only two regions, Paris and the provinces (Province). To call Paris from Paris, simply dial the eight-figure number. For Paris to Province, dial 16 and then the eight-figure number. For Province to Paris, dial 16 then 1 then the eight-figure number. Finally, for Province to Province, dial the eight-figure number alone.

To call Britain from France, dial 19, wait until the dialling tone recurs, then dial 44 followed by the STD code minus the initial 0, and the number. Especially when calling overseas, phonecards (Télécartes – sold in newsagents, tobacconists and Post Offices, and available in two sizes – Petite (around £5) and Grande (around £10) are useful, as most telephone booths now take only these.

Emergency numbers: Fire 18, Police 17, Ambulance 15, Operator 13, Directory Enquiries 12.

Budgeting

For British visitors, France is no more and no less expensive than holidaying at home. An average comfortable 2-star hotel will cost from 150–250FF for a room for two, plus between 25FF and 30FF for breakfast. In Paris, the cost of a 2-star room for two rises to anywhere between 250 and 350FF per night. It is possible to dine out well in France without breaking the bank. Even in Paris, there are many good restaurants offering three or four-course set-menu meals for 50–90FF (add another 30–40FF per person for wine and coffee with the meal). What **does** run away with the francs is that cup of coffee and a cake, taken at a café table overlooking a village square or some lively street scene, and two people partaking of this little indulgence would be lucky to get change back out of a 50FF note.

Taxis charge about 10FF just for picking you up, and about 3FF per km. Rail fares are calculated on a rough scale of 1FF for every 2 km to be travelled. Travel by coach is slightly less expensive than by rail, but services tend to cover routes outside the SNCF network. Petrol costs hover around about 5–6FF a litre; and, for using the motorways, expect to pay about 100FF in tolls for every 300 km covered. Car hire costs around 400–550FF a day, plus 6–7FF per km.

Entry charges for museums and monuments vary between on average 10–20FF, although many museums have one day a week when entry is free or reduced.

All in all, a budget of about 350FF per person per day will guarantee a reasonably comfortable existence, staying in clean, safe accommodation, doing a bit of sightseeing, and eating out twice a day in not-too-basic restaurants. But add another 100FF or so for days spent in Paris, or if you are travelling alone, with no-one to share the cost of the bedroom.

When to Go

The temptation to visit France in the off-peak season is enormous. Paris after a fall of snow is a breathtaking sight, and an excellent backdrop for Christmas shopping with a difference.

From mid-November until the end of February, many Parisian hotels offer two nights for the price of one (details in the 'Bon Weekend à Paris' guide, from the French Government Tourist Office). Or join those drinking hot chocolate during January and February in the outdoor cafés of the Mediterranean cities, blissfully calm, for a change, outside the high-season. French destinations in general outside the Easter and summer school holidays are relatively free from crowds and the inflationary effect they have on prices, but be prepared for the down side of this, which is that some hotels and tourist attractions close down for the winter, and Tourist Information Centres, monuments and museums often have reduced opening hours during the off-peak season.

For a change of climate during a trip to France, it is necessary to travel a long way south, as there is no great difference between Britain's weather and that of the northern half of France. From May until the end of October, average temperatures south of the Loire are in the 20s (°C). Winters are short and mild in the south, but during the 'shoulder' months of October, March and April, there can be days on end of rain and overcast skies.

Another attractive possibility is to plan a trip to France around a special event in that country. As a result of France's Minister of Culture, Jack Lang's policy of creating a 'non-stop atmosphere of carnival', most towns have an annual festival, often on quite esoteric themes – a festival of cartoons, of street music, of jam, of negro spirituals, or even of Scrabble! A list of all of these, together with the more widely-known such as the Nice Carnival, the Cannes Film Festival, the Strasbourg Music Festival and the Avignon Festival, for example, is available from the French Government Tourist Office.

Where are the Positive Holidays?

How is it possible to recognise a good, or in green travel terms, a 'positive' holiday package, when choosing from the hundreds on offer in France? First of all, you can tell a lot about a travel company from their brochure. Things to look for are: information about the cultural and ecological background of the holiday region; guidelines on appropriate, tactful behaviour at the destinations; mention of any contributions which the company makes to conservation bodies; and text and photographs which avoid clichés and stereotypes. Does the brochure give a respectful description of those living at the destination? Is the brochure itself over-glossy and flashy, or does it show an honest attempt to keep costs down and use resources responsibly? (Increasingly you may find it printed on recycled paper). Secondly, there are certain characteristics to look out for in the nature of the package itself. Is it small in scale, and therefore more likely to be low-impact? Does it draw on the character of the countryside: its beauty, culture, history and wildlife? And does the travel company show signs of being socially and environmentally considerate in what it proposes? For example, does it support the local economy by employing local people, serving local produce? Does it offer the kinds of accommodation used by members of the local society? Does it favour, or at least consider the use of public transport? If it is a touring holiday, does the overall pace provide enough time for you to create or accept opportunities to meet local people?

General Holidays

France takes second place after Spain as a destination programmed by British tour operators. Organised packages account for 39% of holidays in France lasting more than four days, and 82% of winter sports holidays. About 370 British tour operators include France in their programme – 290 for summer holidays and 80 for winter breaks. There are quite a few advantages in opting for an all-inclusive tour to France. One is the price. Because the tour operators get concessions from the ferry companies and the airlines, this keeps down the overall cost of the holiday (especially if you travel during the week). And there is little in the way of travel agents' commission to be passed on to customers. Only 25% of packages to France are purchased through travel agents. This is because France has long been the domain of direct-sell tour operators, selling directly to the public instead of through travel agents. The majority of the tour operators listed below fall into this category, and you will have to contact them directly for their brochures. Tour operators are also a good source of useful information for those with little experience of travelling in France. For example, if you opt for a self-drive holiday, the tour operator will usually provide maps, advice on the best route, advice on insurance and how to prepare your car, what to do if there are problems, etc. The other most obvious advantage of inclusive tours is the security which they bring – the knowledge that at the end of the journey lies someone who is expecting you, with a hotel room, rented accommodation or place in a campsite. It is also easier to budget, because you know what has been paid for in the package, and what has not.

One of the most low-impact kinds of destination-orientated holiday is the self-catering package, renting a real French house, owned by someone local, and usually in a rural setting. Of course, the Sunday papers are full of small ads for holiday properties in France. But more often than not, their owners are absentee British people, who would not be there to welcome you in person. And, more seriously, what come-back do you have if you arrive and find that the property has been wrongly described, or that it is overrun with rats? Rather than risk this, choose from one of the better companies offering packages for this type of holiday.

VFB Holidays (Normandy House, High Street, Cheltenham GL50 3HW, Tel. 0242 526338), the UK pioneers of gîte holidays in France, set high standards with their 'Cottage Holidays' programme. Their policy of insisting on gîtes owned by the French guarantees customers a good welcome and means that they are helping put money back into the local economy, instead of the pocket of some distant British owner. They also use only those properties which are built in the traditional style of the region concerned. From about £100 per person in a party of four for two weeks' self-catering accommodation and car ferry, to £160 per person in the high season.

La France des Villages (Model Farm, Rattlesden, Nr Bury St Edmunds, Suffolk, IP30 0SY, Tel. 0449 737664) specialise in ferry plus self-catering or *chambres d'hôte* holidays in parts of France normally missed by tourists, such as the Mâconnais – most often seen as a blur on the mad dash south past Lyon. The company has made an effort to find hosts and hostesses with a genuine interest in taking guests because of the contact this provides or in order to keep their homes living. There are quite a few châteaux, but also farmhouses and country cottages. From £175 per person for two weeks' self-catering accommodation and ferry crossing.

Vacances en Campagne (Bignor, Pulborough, West Sussex RH20 1QD, Tel. 07987 433) also offer ferry plus self-catering accommodation in areas of France untouched by the trappings of mass tourism. Their brochure gives excellent details on all aspects of the destinations. From £190 per person, for two weeks' accommodation and ferry crossing.

Also worth considering: **Allez France** (27 West Street, Storrington, Pulborough, West Sussex RH20 4DZ, Tel. 0903 745793) for cottages and châteaux. From £300 per person in the low season, including car ferry.

Bowhills (Mayhill Farm, Swanmore, Southampton SO3 2QW, Tel. 0489 877627) for cottages, farmhouses, châteaux and watermills. From £60 per person per week including ferry crossing.

Sally Holidays (81 Piccadilly, London W1V 9HF, Tel. 071 355 2266) offers family apartments on the Atlantic and Mediterranean coasts and gîtes in Burgundy and the Massif Central. From £90 to £200 per person for two weeks, ferry included.

For Corsica, **France Voyages** (145 Oxford Street, London W1R 1TB, Tel. 071 494 3155) fly-drive self-catering packages based on scheduled flights. Two weeks from £30 to £360 per person, for four people sharing a studio apartment.

Camping and caravanning holidays are the single most popular kind of inclusive tours to France for the British, who are attracted by the flexibility and inexpensive nature of this kind of holiday. 420,000 packages were sold last year, mainly by specialist British tour operators. Even so, the Dutch are France's biggest customers for camping and caravanning, accounting for 66% of foreign visitors to French sites. The classic formula from Britain is the self-drive package including the ferry crossing and a fully-equipped family tent or caravan. In general, the products on offer are of a fairly high standard, with organised activities for children included, as well as 'extras' such as cheese-and-wine receptions.

The British market is dominated by the mighty **Caravan Club, Canvas Holidays** and **Eurocamp**. Eurocamp alone has 6600 places permanently rented on sites throughout France, for 100 days of the year, and sells over 150,000 packages each year. However, there are many smaller companies specialising in this field:

Carefree Camping (126 Hempstead Road, Kings Langley, WD4 8AL, Tel. 0923 261311) features the Loire, the Dordogne, the French Alps, Burgundy, Brittany, Normandy, the Mediterranean and Atlantic coasts, and even Paris. Stays in fully-equipped tents or luxury mobile homes are on offer in beach, countryside or mountain sites, with free holidays for children under fourteen and children's couriers on most sites.

Sunsites (22–24 Princess Street, Knutsford WA16 6BW, Tel. 0565 55644) have sites throughout France, with the average price of £400, for a family of four going on a two-week camping holiday with a short sea ferry crossing.

Carisma Holidays (Bethel House, Heronsgate Road, Chorley-wood WD3 5BB, Tel. 09278 261311) have mobile homes, tents and caravans on sites in Brittany, the Western Loire and Aquitaine.

Keycamp Holidays (92–96 Lind Road, Sutton, Surrey SM1 4PL, Tel. 081 661 7334) offer self-drive holidays to attractive sites in most parts of France, including Paris.

With food and wine such attractive aspects of a holiday in France, it is easy to see why the 'traditional' package of transport plus transfer and hotel is so popular among the British. Short breaks, longer holidays and touring holidays in hotel accommodation are widely available, and again prices are kept down, as tour operators are usually able to negotiate concessions from hotels, which individual guests cannot. The following companies show particular care in the hotels they use:

Inn-Travel (The Old Station, Helmsley, York YO6 5BZ, Tel. 0439 71111) offer self-drive holidays in Flanders, Picardy and Normandy, and fly-drive to the Pyrenees, Provence and Languedoc-Roussillon, based on their handpicked hotels of character. Out-of-season short breaks are available, such as three nights' fly-drive to a village hotel near Toulouse, half-board, from £250 per person.

Sally Holidays (address above) use Logis de France hotels and auberges, as well as châteaux for their 'Go As You Please' programme of tailor-made holidays. A six-night Mini-tour using Logis costs £176 per adult, including a midweek ferry crossing, outside July and August.

Time Off (2a Chester Close, London SW1X 7BQ, Tel. 071 235 8070) offers short breaks or longer holidays in Paris, in hotels ranging from 1-star to luxury, using air, rail or coach travel, with helpful maps and guides included. Prices from £65 per person.

Travelscene (11–15 St Ann's Road, Harrow HA1 1AS, Tel. 081 427 4445) has short breaks in Paris with a range of accommodation from budget to luxury, with the possibility of having a two-centre holiday with Lyon, using the TGV to get there.

VFB Holidays (address above) use charming hotels in the Latin Quarter for their Paris holidays, and family-run hotels all over France, including lesser-known regions such as the Auvergne and the Jura, for their Auberge Holidays. The company has a policy of booking no more than a third of a hotel's capacity, in order to maintain its French ambience. Prices from £150 per person in a party of two for three nights' half-board accommodation, inclusive of ferry-crossing.

Château holidays including accommodation and ferry crossing are available from **Just France** (1 Belmont, Lansdown Road, Bath BA1 5DZ, Tel. 0225 446328) for Normandy, Brittany, the Loire Valley, Bordeaux and the Dordogne, from £250 per person for seven nights; and from **Unicorn Holidays** (Intech House, 34–35 Cam Centre, Wilbury Way, Hitchin SG4 ORL, Tel. 0462 422223) for the Western Loire, Provence and other regions, for packaged three-night breaks from £145 per person.

Well worth considering, too, are **Roue Libre Voyages** (Le Poteau, 69210 Fleurieux, Tel. 74 01 07 40). This small-scale tour operator promotes alternative travel for small groups, providing opportunities for real contact with local people and their everyday life. One% of the price of their trips goes to finance small-scale development projects at the destination. Although specialising in holidays outside France, they can also arrange tailor-made holidays in France for groups.

Adventure/Activity Holidays

France has long been a favourite destination for British visitors in search of activities to pursue while on holiday. According to the FGTO, about 17% of British visitors to France come for the purposes of walking, horseriding or cycling, for example.

Walking

When it comes to hiking, the French have a saying, 'Walking is the gastronomy of the eye', and if this is true of anywhere in the world it is France. The entire country is criss-crossed by the magnificent marked long-distance footpaths, the 'sentiers de grande randonnée' (GR), often based on ancient routes, such as those taken by pilgrims, or crossing mountain ranges, or taking in the National Parks. Tackling some of the GRs is a mammoth undertaking, and a whole holiday can be taken up on just one, following the red and white stripes which mark the route. Some of the footpaths and the vegetation around them take such a pounding from walkers that measures have been taken to limit their use. For example, in the Mercantour National Park, the Vallée des Merveilles is open to accompanied hiking groups only.

Many travel companies organise walking holidays based on the GRs. A good example is **SVP France** (The Garden House, Main

Road, Nutbourne, Chichester, West Sussex PD18 8RL, Tel. 0243 377862), who offer inclusive GR holidays, with *gîte d'étape* accommodation, and fully-qualified guides. Their groups are of up to twelve people, and include French hikers, so some knowledge of French is useful, to benefit fully from the experience. For those who prefer a luxury hike, walking tours with hotel accommodation are also available. Itineraries range from the lakes and volcanoes of the Auvergne, and prehistoric Dordogne, to the gorges of the Tarn. Travel options with the tours include air, air/rail, ferry/rail and self-drive. A six-night accompanied walking tour of the Cantal, moving from hotel to hotel every other night, with full-board, costs between £340 per person for self-drive and £410 per person for rail or air/rail.

Inn-Travel (address above) offer accompanied and unaccompanied mountain walking holidays, with luggage being transferred ahead to the next hotel, in the Vosges, Pyrenees and the French Alps. A six-night walking holiday in the Dordogne costs from £250 for the accommodation and activity alone, to £375 for rail travel included in high-season.

Headwater Holidays (146 London Road, Northwich CW9 5HH, Tel. 0606 48699) offer walking holidays in the Loire Valley, the Vercors, the Lot, the Jura and the Auvergne. On Headwater holidays, there are never more than six or eight people in each group, and you can be as sociable or as independent as you like, because you plan your own daily itinerary on the basis of the comprehensive notes, maps and recommended routes supplied by the company. Accommodation is in family-run hotels, *fermes-auberges* and *chambres d'hôtes*, and hoteliers are encouraged to offer typically regional dishes. You can either opt for a 'moving on' holiday, touring from one hotel to another, with your luggage being transported ahead, or 'stay put' in one place. Travel arrangements are very flexible: BR/hovercraft/SNCF, self-drive with ferry, by air, or you can even make your own travel arrangements. You can add nights to the beginning or end of the holiday, either in a hotel in your destination area, or in a good stopover area such as Paris, Champagne or Toulouse – the company will make the hotel bookings. Prices start at £170 for a six-night rambling holiday in Trièves.

A good map is vital, especially if travelling without a guide: a 'topoguide' is published for each GR by the National Committee for Long-Distance Footpaths, the FFRP, 8 avenue Marceau, 75008

Paris, who can also supply a map showing all GRs. Information on France's other, less taxing, paths and trails, of which there are thousands, is available from local Syndicats d'Initiative, or from the Centre d'Information Sentiers et Randonnée, 64, rue de Gergovie, 75014 Paris (Tel. (1) 45 45 31 02).

Holidays Afloat

One of the most interesting innovations in French tourism during the past ten years has been the use of France's navigable canals and rivers for pleasure cruising. There are more than 8500 km of navigable waterways in France, and a total of 250 companies offer tourist products based on this form of transport. Choose from two different types of holiday: a houseboat or a cruise.

The houseboats which are available for hire have been designed for easy, safe sailing, and even complete novices will easily master the skills needed to steer, moor and navigate.

Cruises began a few years ago, using barges as 'floating hotels', with accommodation facilities, but river cruises using what amount to small liners are now also available – particularly on the Rhône and the Seine. This relaxing activity provides access to areas of France, often inaccessible otherwise, giving a privileged insight into the life of the river or canal itself, as well as those French people who live their quiet lives along the banks. If hiring your own craft, take bicycles on board and explore the countryside along the rivers and canals, taking some exercise at the same time. The excellent leaflet, 'Afloat in France', from the French Government Tourist Office gives details of this kind of holiday.

Clearwater Holidays (17 Heath Terrace, Leamington Spa, Warwickshire CV32 5NA, Tel. 0926 450002) have pledged a £2 donation to the Whale and Dolphin Society for every holiday booked. They offer yacht charters around the coast and on the rivers of Brittany, the Côte d'Azur and Corsica, and canal boats on the rivers and canals of Brittany and the Loire Valley. Packages including accommodation in local Breton-style cottages plus the hire of a small dinghy boat are also available. Prices start at £500 in low-season for the hire of a two-four berth 'albatros' canal boat, plus the ferry crossing for one car.

VFB Holidays (address above) offer canal cruising holidays on the canals of Alsace, Burgundy and the Midi. There are five different craft, sleeping from two to ten persons, available for seven, ten, or fourteen-night holidays, and you can hire a boat at one base and leave it at another, where your car will have been brought for you.

A range of interesting canoe and kayak holidays, for all levels of competence, are on offer from **SVP France** (address above). Discover the Auvergne by kayak on a six-day holiday under canvas; or canoe along the Vendée's *Route du Sel*, for a close-up view of the region's fauna and flora, on an accompanied seven-day tour, with accommodation in hotels, tents and private homes. Prices start at £200 for a seven-night unaccompanied canoeing holiday on the Dordogne, self-drive, with tent accommodation.

Headwater Holidays (address above) offer canoeing holidays in the Loire Valley, Lot and Célé, and the Jura. Luggage is carried for you.

In The Saddle

If the only thing that puts you off cycling holidays is the thought of being stuck with all that luggage, fear not. Several regions have put together cycling holiday 'packages' which enable visitors to roam around unburdened all day, while their luggage is transferred ahead to that evening's pre-booked hotel accommodation.

One of the best examples of this is the **Vélo Bleu Vélo Vert** scheme in the Western Loire region. Started up in 1982 on the initiative of the Comité Regional du Tourisme, the scheme has been a great success, opening up cycling holidays to a whole new clientèle. Special touring bicycles are provided, as well as detailed maps and itineraries. And luggage is transferred on ahead – leaving cyclists free to ride through the shady pine forests, meadows and beaches of the region. For details, write to the French Government Tourist Office for the Western Loire Information Pack. Or contact one of the tour operators offering packages using the scheme.

SVP France (address above) offer Vélo Bleu Vélo Vert cycling holidays in the Western Loire, with different travel options including self-drive, air and air/rail. Their cycling holidays are based on themes ranging from the Loire Valley to the Vendée, and the Atlantic coast on the north side of the Loire estuary. From about £220 for four nights, with half-board and self-drive.

Other good cycling holidays in France are available from **Alistair Sawday's Tours** (44 Ambra Vale East, Bristol BS8 4RE, Tel. 0272 299921), **Madron's Cycling for Softies** (22 Lloyds Street, Manchester M2 5WA, Tel. 061 834 6800), **Inn-Travel** (address above) and **Headwater Holidays** (address above). Information on touring in general is available from the **Fédération Française de Cyclotourisme**, 8 rue Jean Marie Jégo, 75013 Paris (Tel. (1) 45 80 30 21).

The other way of holidaying in the saddle is to go **horseriding**, on an inclusive riding holiday. Inexperience is no bar to enjoying this kind of activity holiday. Most packages based on horseriding are designed for groups of a maximum of eight people, guaranteeing complete beginners all the tuition and attention they will need from the guide who accompanies the group. Inclusive riding holidays are usually based on a weeks' tour of a particular region, using accommodation ranging from the dormitories of *gîtes d'étapes* and *ferme auberges* through 2-star *logis* to, for those with a taste for luxury, *grand châteaux*. Luggage is transferred ahead to the accommodation, leaving riders completely unencumbered.

Stick to centres listed by the **Association Nationale de Tourisme Equestre**, whose annual handbook is available from the French Government Tourist Office (send £1 in stamps). Independent and accompanied horseriding holidays are offered by **Inn-Travel** (address above), with prices starting at just over £300 for a seven-night accompanied horseback tour of Cerdagne, for the activity and accommodation only.

Horseback holidays in France are also offered by **Cavalry Tours** (14 Cromwell Crescent, London SW5 9QW, Tel. 071 602 8433); holidays on horseback including château tours are available from **Jean-Paul et Françoise Bonnetat** (La Martinière, 37510 Savonnières, Tel. 47 50 04 46).

Skiing

Each year, about 300,000 British visitors go to France to ski, making that country the number one destination for British skiers, with more than one in three heading there each year. The several million skiers who take to the French mountains annually are for the most part unaware of the impact which this activity has on this fragile environment. The construction of resorts for Alpine (downhill) skiing replaces the easily-drained soil of mountain areas with the hard, impermeable surfaces of car parks, roads, and so on, and the result has been extensive and damaging flooding in some areas.

At high altitudes, alpine grass is essential to bind the soil, but skiing on shallow snow, or, even worse, bulldozing a ski-run can cause damage to the grass and other Alpine plants, which may never be repaired. The building of Alpine ski-runs also damages forest areas. Trees are the first line of defence against avalanches, but local pollution, traffic, and forest clearances for the skiing industry put this form of natural protection at risk.

Cross-country (Nordic) skiing has many advantages over Alpine skiing. It is far less environmentally damaging, for the most part following paths used by walkers in summer, or even roads which are impassable due to snow. No great swathes of woodland are cut down to provide pistes, and there are no ugly scars left on the countryside when the snow melts. Cross-country skiing really lets you get away from it all and enjoy the French countryside at its best. You can choose between forest paths and more open routes, but in either case, it is possible to go for miles without seeing another soul. There is no queuing for ski-lifts, and most cross-country ski resorts are small-scale and rural. Try to time your ski trip to avoid the French early spring school holidays, if you can. These one-week breaks are staggered from region to region during the months of February and March, in order to let French schoolchildren loose on the slopes. The dates change every year, but it's worth finding out when they fall, if you want to avoid heavily-congested pistes.

Headwater Holidays (address above) offer excellent cross-country skiing holidays in the Auvergne and in the Vercors mountains of the Dauphiny region. Accommodation is in family-run hotels though there is also a self-catering option for holidays in the village of Autrans in the Vercors Regional Park. Headwater also offer Alpine skiing options.

SVP France (address above) offer cross-country skiing holidays among the snow-capped volcanoes and medieval villages of the highlands of central France – the Massif Central and Vercors. Accommodation is either in *gîtes d'étapes*, or in hotels which are part of the very fabric of the villages they are in, and whose owners are local people – 'enfants du pays'. (Should the snow fail to materialise, the summer programme of walks, picnics, and flora and fauna study comes into play). Prices start at about £250 for seven days' cross-country skiing, with self-drive and full-board.

Inn-Travel (The Old Station, Helmsley, York YO6 5BZ, Tel. 0439 71111) also run cross-country skiing holidays, using village hotels of character, as well as self-catering accommodation.

Some tour operators also help support mountain resorts during the summer. The summer programme of **VFB Holidays** (address above) helps maintain two traditional Alpine villages which are ski resorts in winter. Their 'Alp Actif' activity holidays between July and September are set in the Haute-Savoie villages of La Clusaz and Valloire, and come complete with the VFB Activity Passport, giving a choice of sports including tennis, mountain bikes, archery, pony trekking, grass tobogganing and guided mountain walks. Seven, ten, eleven and fourteen-night options are available.

Lakes and Mountains (The Red House, Garstons Close, Titchfield, Fareham PO14 4EW), are a small, family-owned company offering summer activity holiday packages in two French alpine villages. Accommodation in Le Grand Bornand is in modern apartments 1km from the village; and in St Jorioz, on the western shore of Lake Annecy, the apartments are generally part of the owner's house or chalet. Swimming, cycling, tennis, watersports and excursions are among the activities included. Prices start at around £160 per person, based on four people sharing, for a self-catering apartment, including ferry travel.

An excellent combination for an activity/interest holiday is to make your own transport arrangements, but to book the accommodation and activity element through a **Loisirs-Accueil** reservation service. These operate in about sixty out of France's ninety-five *départements*, on behalf of hundreds of independent rural tourism businesses. All of these small-scale businesses offer a combination of accommodation and activity holiday, but lack the means to market themselves nationally or internationally. Through their local, non-profit-making, Loisirs-Accueil service, they have all their marketing and reservations taken care of for them. The advantage of booking through a Loisirs-Accueil service is that you know that the 'product' has passed their regular quality control checks. (Maybe that is why their motto is 'Visit France in full confidence'.)

The type of activities include learning local crafts, gastronomic short breaks, hillwalking, cycling and potholing; and accommodation is in 'logis' hotels, 'gîtes', B&Bs or camping. Prices are very reasonable. For example, a long weekend cycling/canoeing break in the Valençay, with half-board in a 1-star 'logis' works out at 450FF per person; a one-week painting holiday in the Périgord, with tuition and half-board in a 2-star 'logis', 2950FF; one week aboard a hotel-boat on the rivers and canals of the Loiret department, with half-board, 2250FF.

These holidays are open to foreign visitors as well as to the

French themselves. Groups, families and single travellers are equally welcome, although by the very nature of the holidays, numbers are limited, often to around ten or twelve participants. The **Fédération Nationale des Services de Réservation Loisirs-Accueil** 2 rue Linois, 75015 Paris (Tel. (1) 40 59 44 12) publishes an annual guide (in French) to all their activity holidays. It costs 80FF but is well worth it. Alternatively, a selection of their rambling and cycling holidays is featured in the Loisirs-Accueil brochure available from **Gîtes de France Ltd.**, Loisirs-Accueil Department, 178 Piccadilly, London W1V 9DB (Tel. 071 493 3480 or 071 408 1343). If there are any departmental Loisirs-Accueil services in your chosen holiday region, *The Good Tourist in France* details them in that region's Good Alternatives section.

Another excellent scheme has recently been started up by the **Fédération des Parcs Naturels de France**, the Ministry of the Environment and the Ministry of Tourism. A brochure, entitled 'Voyages au Naturel', contains a dozen holidays, on most of which individuals travel together in small groups, exploring one of France's beautiful national or regional parks in an environmentally responsible manner. Holidays on offer range from six days walking across the largest and wildest nature reserve in France, with luggage carried by mules and accommodation in comfortable gîtes (around 2200FF per person), to seven days' discovery of the Armorique Regional Park in Brittany, by foot, bicycle, boat and plane, staying full-board in 2-star hotels (around 5500FF per person).

The brochure is available from **Clés de France** (13–15 rue St-Louis, 78100 St-Germain-en-Laye, Tel. (1) 30 61 23 23), who are in charge of bookings. It is also possible to book these holidays directly with the regional parks or their representatives. Details of their addresses and the trips they offer can be found in the Good Alternatives sections of the following chapters: Brittany; Alsace; The Loire; Dauphiny and Savoy; Provence-Alpes; Côte d'Azur; Aquitaine.

Wildlife/Ecological Holidays

Until recently, escorted wildlife and cultural tours were available only to 'exotic' destinations – fine for gorilla-watching in Rwanda or cruising in the Galapagos. But British tour operators have woken up to the fact that there is a great interest in French wildlife and cultural holidays.

Conservation of environmental resources, wildlife and habitats is of vital importance to **EcoSafaris** (146 Gloucester Road, London SW7 4SZ, Tel. 071 370 5032) who support the work of the World Wide Fund for Nature and the Royal Society for Nature Conservation. Their tours, for small groups, range from one-week cultural and activity holidays set in the heart of Brittany's Armorique Regional Park, nature walking, pony trekking, studying local music, art and history, cuisine, and trying boating and photography, to two-week wildlife and cultural tours of the Camargue, a haven for birdwatchers and naturalists.

Cox and Kings' (PO Box 2, Ellesmere Port, South Wirral, L64 3EA, Tel. 051 355 7175) Environmental Journeys programme includes botany tours in the French Pyrenees for those in search of the distinctive and beautiful alpine flora of this region. The walking tour includes Saillagouse in the eastern Pyrenees, the centre for French solar energy research. Their other French product is a flora and fauna photography tour of Southern France, including trips into the Maritime Alps region, the Massif des Maures in Provence, and the Camargue. The company contributes to conservation by buying an acre of rainforest in Belize or sponsoring a week's research to the Whale and Dolphin Conservation Society for every traveller on their wildlife programme.

Voyages Jules Verne (21 Dorset Square, London NW1 6QG, Tel. 071 724 6624) include several French destinations in their Natural World programme, with accompanied botanical study trips to the French Pyrenees, Corsica, the Hautes-Alpes, and the Causses and Cévennes Hills of southern France. Scheduled flights and half-board accommodation are included in the packages.

Other companies offering interesting guided tours to study French flora and fauna are **Branta Travel** (11 Uxbridge Street, London W8 7TQ, Tel. 071 229 7231), **Canvas Holidays** (9/13 Bull Plain, Hertford SG14 1DY, Tel. 0992 553535), and **LSG** (Leicester Study Groups (201 Main Street, Thornton LE6 1AH, Tel. 0509 231713).

Shorter outings for the purposes of nature study are offered by the French environmental organisations, **La Ligue Française pour la Protection des Oiseaux** (French League for the Protection of Birds) La Corderie Royale, BP263, 17305 Rochefort Cedex (Tel. 46 99 59 97); and **La Société Nationale de Protection de la Nature,** (National Society for the Protection of Nature), 57 rue Cuvier 75005 Paris (Tel. (1) 47 07 31 95).

The French farming system is quite different to that of Britain, being still largely based on the small, family-farm unit. The average size of a French farm is only sixty acres, and half the agricultural land is owned and cultivated by smallholders. As such, it is of particular interest to British people, and there are several organisations which specialise in holidays on working farms. The association **Agriculture et Tourisme** (9 avenue Georges V, 75008 Paris, Tel.(1) 47 23 55 40) produces an annual directory, 'Bienvenue à la Ferme', listing visits and holidays available on about 2500 French farms.

Agricultural study tours to all parts of France are available from the **Agricultural Travel Bureau**, 14 Chain Lane, Newark NG24 1AU (Tel. 0636 705612). Individuals between sixteen and twenty-six years old can experience life on farms in Picardy and Lot through **Euro-Academy**, 77a George Street, Croydon CR0 1LD (Tel. 081 686 2363).

Volunteer/Conservation Holidays

Those on holiday can help preserve part of France by volunteering to work with an organisation responsible for the maintenance of the country's natural or built environment. A good example is the **Club du Vieux Manoir**, 10 rue de la Cossonnerie, 75001 Paris (Tel.(1) 45 08 80 40). This not-for-profit association welcomes those over fifteen for periods of fifteen days minimum, all year round. Volunteers live and work on one of France's historic sites or monuments, helping to restore it – and improving their command of French at the same time. Accommodation (under canvas in summer) is provided free, but volunteers pay about £6 a day for food.

A similar organisation is the **Union Rempart**, 1 rue des Guillemites, 75004 Paris (Tel.(1) 42 71 96 55) which welcomes volunteers (over fourteen years old) wishing to take part in restoration or conservation workshops (or archaeological digs). A contribution towards food of around £4 a day is required.

Travelling Independently

France is a favourite destination for the independent traveller: only about one in three British tourists going to France do so on an inclusive tour. Much to travel agents' chagrin, the wide range of travel and accommodation options has long made it easy for the

British to arrange their own trips to France. Of course, independent travellers have to use a bit more initiative than those opting for an inclusive tour, especially if on the kind of freewheeling touring holiday which requires accommodation and travel to be arranged as you go along. But with a bit of forward planning, there is not much that can go wrong. Where it is most possible to come unstuck is in arriving late at a destination, with no accommodation booked. The great concentration of French holidays in July and August make this a particularly risky business during those months. In cities, it is usually possible to find something, but at a price. Even large resorts on the Riviera will have spare hotel capacity at the height of summer – but in their top grade hotels only. Avoid having to fall back on this kind of enforced luxury by booking ahead – see **Accommodation Options**, page 57.

The book-ahead principle also applies to any sustainable tourism programmes which interest you, especially where these are restricted to small groups only. Use the **Loisirs-Accueil** services (see **Positive Holidays**, page 50.) to book programmes of semi-independent activity or interest holidays (you make your own travel arrangements). Another source of information on good sustainable tourism activities and accommodation are France's 190 **Pays d'Accueil**. A Pays d'Accueil is an association of all the small tourism businesses in a given area, usually based on a natural feature – a mountain range, piece of coastline, river, etc. – rather than an administrative area. Each one produces an annual programme, with prices, of the accommodation, activity/interest short breaks and catering services provided by its members, bookable directly with the small businesses concerned. Most include details of local sites and monuments, sporting and cultural activities, and opportunities for ecology and nature study. As with the Loisirs-Accueil, capacity for each programme of activities is limited, and a knowledge of French is necessary, not only to make the booking, but to communicate with the others on the programme. Contact the **Fédération Nationale des Pays d'Accueil Touristiques**, 19 avenue du Maine, 75015 Paris (Tel. (1) 49 55 53 08) saying which regions you intend visiting.

Syndicats d'Initiative and **Offices de Tourisme** can also help those arriving in their areas in search of sustainable tourism on spec. They can supply useful contacts, such as details of local hiking associations (randonnées), as well as the usual information on accommodation and transport. Otherwise, ask them for the address of the local **Conservatoire Régionale** or **Maison de**

l'Environnement. These are offices which have details of local ecology tours and visits to protected sites, for example.

Transport Options

Travel to France by **coach** is offered by **Eurolines** (52 Grosvenor Gardens, London SW1W 0AU, Tel. 071 730 8235), with scheduled departures from London to the Channel Ports, Rouen, Paris, Montpellier, Perpignan, Lyon, Bordeaux, Marseille, Cannes, Nice and Reims, and most other main destinations. Fares range from around £50 return, London to Paris, to just over £100 return, London to the south of France. **Hoverspeed** (Maybrook House, Queens Gardens, Dover CT17 9UQ, Tel. 0304 241241) offer a service between London and Paris, using a coach plus hovercraft combination, at around £50 return.

By **rail**: the **France Vacances Pass** is the SNCF's rover ticket which allows unlimited travel around France. A fifteen-day second-class pass usable on any four days within that period costs £75 for adults and £37.50 for children, while a one-month pass usable on any nine days costs £127 for adults and £63.50 for children. Combining this pass with accommodation is the SNCF's one-week rail-and-stay programme **Liberté**, which offers any four days of unlimited travel on the French rail network and seven nights' half-board accommodation at a choice of more than 140 hotels throughout France.

Combination **air/rail** tickets from Air France and the SNCF are good value. It is possible to fly from regional airports (as well as London) to Paris, and from there either travel to one destination, or combine the air ticket with a France Vacances Pass and travel to several. For example, a return flight from Edinburgh to Paris plus a France Vacances Pass costs £212 for four days' rail travel and £264 for nine days.

Another combination is **Flexiplan**, which offers return Air France flights from Heathrow to any one of eleven airports in France, plus a France Vacances Pass. One advantage of this is that you can return from a different airport to the one you flew in to. £176 and £228 are the prices for a return flight from Heathrow to any French Provincial airport served by Air France, plus four and nine days' rail travel respectively, with a £20 supplement in each case for the high season.

The SNCF's **Motorail** services carry cars, motorbikes and passengers overnight on the same train from Boulogne, Calais, Dieppe and Paris to all main areas. Contact the SNCF's London office at French Railways House, 179 Piccadilly, London W1V 0BA.

British Rail's **InterRail** pass, £175, offers unlimited travel for a month on Europe's railways, and half-price travel in Britain and on the Channel ferries.

By **air: scheduled flights** serve mainly Paris, but it is increasingly possible to fly direct to the French regions. **Air France** has flights from London to ten regional cities – Biarritz, Bordeaux, Lille, Lyon, Marseille, Montpellier, Nantes, Nice, Strasbourg and Toulouse. Air France also offers regular flights to Paris from Aberdeen, Birmingham, Bristol, Cardiff, Dublin, Edinburgh, Glasgow, Jersey and Southampton.

British Airways serves Bordeaux, Lyon, Nice, Toulouse and Marseille out of Heathrow, and Nice out of Manchester and Birmingham.

Dan Air flies to Paris, Montpellier, Perpignan, Toulouse, Lourdes/Tarbes and Nice, from Gatwick. The best deals from these three companies are their **Superapex** tickets. These must be reserved at least two weeks in advance; the trip must include a Saturday night, and the return date must be fixed at the time of booking, with no subsequent changes.

British Midland operates eight fights a day between Heathrow and Paris.

British Independent Airways serves the French port of Le Touquet out of Lydd airport in Kent; and **Brit Air** flies daily from Gatwick to Le Havre, Caen, Brest, Quimper and Rennes. Recent expansion of Manchester airport means that it now has services to Paris, Lyon, Bordeaux, Nice, Toulouse and Strasbourg, with plans for an even wider network.

Charter flights between Britain and France are limited, and almost exclusively fly out of London, but they provide good value if you can get on one.

Nouvelles Frontières (Tel. 071 629 7772) sell London-Paris flights at around £75 return, and their own daily charters to Paris, Montpellier, Nice and Toulouse.

Euro Express (Gatwick office, Tel. 0293 511125) has flights to Paris six times daily, to Nice twelve times weekly, to Corsica and Lourdes three times weekly, and weekly to Bordeaux.

For students under thirty-two and anyone under twenty-six **STA Travel** (6 Wright's Lane, London W8, Tel. 071 937 9921) offers good value flights to Paris, starting at £65 return, and other cities. Winter ski charters to Lyon and Chambéry/Aix-les-Bains are increasingly available, from London City, Gatwick and Plymouth.

By sea: the main cross-Channel ferry companies are **Sealink, Sally Lines, Hoverspeed, Brittany Ferries** and **P&O European Ferries**. For Normandy, Sealink's Portsmouth-Cherbourg/Le Havre, Newhaven-Dieppe and Weymouth-Cherbourg routes, Brittany Ferries' Portsmouth-Caen and Poole-Cherbourg routes, or P&O's Portsmouth-Le Havre/Cherbourg routes could save driving and money; as could Brittany Ferries' Portsmouth-St Malo and Plymouth/Cork-Roscoff routes for destinations in Brittany. Otherwise, the cross-Channel ferry routes are Dover-Calais/Boulogne by Hoverspeed (at 35 minutes' crossing, the fastest way to go), P&O and Sealink, Folkestone-Boulogne by Sealink, and Ramsgate-Dunkerque by Sally Line.

From Scotland, the north of England or the Midlands, **North Sea Ferries'** (King George Dock, Hedon Road, Hull HU9 5QA) route from Hull-Zeebrugge (50 km from the French border) could cut driving time, depending on your final destination.

Accommodation Options

For those going it alone, the accommodation options increase according to how out-of-season one goes. In most regions, there is no point going to the Syndicat d'Initiative (SI) in July or August, in search of available local accommodation to let, because the chances are it will all be already booked, probably by the French themselves. However, outside the busy holiday periods, the SIs – or the 'mairies' if the SI is closed – are usually able to fix up on-spec enquirers with a choice of interesting accommodation. Most rural SIs keep lists of local people with a gîte or flat to let, for those staying a few days or more. It is possible to book a gîte on its own, through the Gîtes de France booking service, but it is usually cheaper to book it with the Channel crossing included (see **Accommodation**, page 60).

For overnight stays on touring holidays, a range of options is available. Those travelling alone, with no-one to share the cost of a room, could find accommodation in a youth hostel – **auberge de jeunesse** – a good bet. France's 900 youth hostels offer dormitory accommodation, sharing with between seven and fifteen others, for about 50FF a night, with another 10F for breakfast. Equipment needed is: a sheet sleeping bag and membership of the Youth Hostel Association (details from YHA, Trevelyan House, St Stephens Hill, St Albans, Herts AL1 2DY, Tel. 0727 55215, or the Scottish YHA,

7 Glebe Crescent, Stirling, FK8 2JA, Tel. 0786 51181). A list of French youth hostels is available from these organisations.

Basic rural accommodation for cyclists, horseriders and hikers comes in the form of the **gîte d'étape**. There are about 400 of these municipal hostels in France, mainly in hillwalking regions. For a place in the fairly spartan bedrooms shared with half-a-dozen others, guests pay about the same price as in youth hostels. Addresses available from Syndicats d'Initiative.

One French equivalent of the 'Bed and Breakfast' is the *chambres d'hôtes*. There are over 5000 of these in France, almost all of them in rural areas. Ideal for overnight stops, *chambres d'hôte* cost from about 100FF per night, including breakfast. This has to be one of the most convivial ways of meeting French people in their own homes and getting an authentic insight into their everyday lives. Look out for those B&Bs also offering *table d'hôte* – reasonably-priced evening meals, usually including generous and delicious helpings of local specialities. Lists of local *chambres* and *tables d'hôte* are available from Syndicats d'Initiative, or through Gîtes de France Ltd.

An alternative form of B&B accommodation is available through the **Café-Couette** organisation, which provides over a thousand addresses of French people offering B&B in their own homes: country villas, well-located flats and houses of character. A room for two people costs between about 250–450FF, depending on the degree of luxury. To receive a copy of the Guide, join the Café-Couette Club, which costs £10 per person. Reservation and payment is done centrally, through Café-Couette. Details from: Café-Couette, 8 rue de l'Isly, 75008 Paris (Tel. (1) 42 94 92 00).

Camping and caravanning sites are another possibility. For a family of four with tent and car, expect to pay around 60FF for a 1-star site, and 150FF for a 4-star site per day. Charges must, by law, be posted at the site entrance, so study these before going in. Popular sites, especially on the coast, tend to fill up quickly in the high season, so book ahead. This can be done in the UK through specialist companies such as **Select Site Reservations** (Travel House, Pandy, nr Abergavenny, Gwent NP7 8DH, Tel. 0873 89058) or **The French Connection** (111 Stoke Common Road, Bishopstoke, Hants SO5 6DW, Tel. 0703 617192) who can provide information on some of the best sites in France, and make reservations. A good investment is the official guide of the **Fédération Française de Camping et Caravanning**, available in French only, but with an English supplement for easy understanding, from the FFCC, Springdene, Shepherd's Way, Fairlight, Sussex TN35 4BB, £7.45.

The useful French Government Tourist Office publication, 'The Camping Traveller in France' (available in return for 80p in stamps) carries a wealth of advice for the independent camper, and includes a sample letter in French which can be used to book a pitch at a particular site. Don't be tempted to camp without permission on a farm, beach or forest. This can bring heavy penalties with it: at best a fine, and at worst a full-scale attack from the farmer's dogs!

There are five grades of French hotels, from 1 star to 4-star luxury. An average comfortable 2-star hotel costs somewhere in the region of 180–260FF (250–380FF in Paris) for a room for two. Allow another 22–28FF per person for breakfast. It's worth sharing, because a double room is usually only marginally more expensive than a room for one person. And you normally pay only around 30% extra for a third bed. Most hotels with their own restaurants will have a good go at persuading you to take dinner there, but make sure you know what this is likely to cost, before agreeing.

Many individual hotels have formed themselves into consortia. While maintaining their independent status, they have joined together for the purposes of marketing, and have agreed on standards of quality. Once in France, members of these consortia can make reservations for you, booking ahead with other members in other parts of the country. To book French hotels from Britain, either correspond directly with the hotel itself, or use a centralised booking service in Britain, such as **Voyages Vacances Ltd** (197 Knightsbridge, London SW7 1RB, Tel. 071 589 6769) who can book any of Climat de France's 138 2-star hotels in France; or **France Accueil Hotels (UK) Ltd** (10 Salisbury Hollow, Edington, Westbury BA13 4PF, Tel. 0380 830125) who have 140 family-run hotels throughout France, including Paris. A full selection of British central booking services and French hotel groups appears in the free FGTO publication, 'The Traveller in France'. This also gives details of centralised booking services in France, useful for those touring around and needing to book ahead as they go.

Alternatively, a clever new system in the French Government Tourist Office in Piccadilly is available to those in the London region. A computer displays pictures and data on touch screens, allowing the public to locate and select any of 2100 hotels in France.

The **Loisirs-Accueil** reservation services (see **Positive Holidays**, page 50) can also help by reserving hotels, gîtes and camp sites, usually charging no fee.

Accommodation

The French take great pride in the quality of their **campsites**, and rightly so. The quantity is just as impressive – about 11,000 officially-graded sites at the last count, more than any other country in Europe. Graded sites must be laid out so as to respect the natural setting, and must have at least 10% of the ground devoted to shrubs or trees, and they must have permanent covered washing and sanitary equipment, and a daily refuse collection. The maximum number of people per hectare (about 2^1/2 acres) is 300, although this rule is often relaxed at peak periods, when all sites are under considerable strain. Sites range from small, basic 'campings à la ferme' – farm sites – to 4-star sites, resembling complete holiday centres, with supermarkets, swimming pools, tennis courts, restaurants and luxury toilet blocks. Sites graded 2-star and above must have communal buildings lit, a central meeting place, points for electric razors, a surrounding fence with guard, hot showers, safety deposits, telephones and shops on or close by the site. The greatest concentration of sites is found in the recognised holiday areas, on the coast, but there are also plenty of notable areas inland, too.

A **gîte** is one form of simple, reasonably-priced, self-catering holiday accommodation, which can be rented by the week. Gîtes are either part of a house or an entire house, almost invariably in the deep countryside, although some are within reach of the coast. Some are completely detached and remote, while others are in a group of farm buildings, in a house containing more than one gîte, or are self-contained flats in the owner's house. While a gîte should not be compared to a luxurious villa or hotel (prices clearly reflect that – average rent is from 900–1500FF a week for a gîte for four–six people), guests do have the security of knowing that the national association, the **Fédération Nationale des Gîtes**, has inspected and graded the standard of comfort and quality of each one of its 45,000 properties. Gîtes are classified by ears of corn, from one to three, according to criteria such as the geographical location, the recreational activities available nearby, and/or the degree of comfort.

A week or two in a gîte transports guests into the very heart of rural France, with all its quirks and customs, as well as its tranquillity. Whether on some unpretentious farm, hamlet or village, daily working life goes on, and guests might have to get used to the 'dawn chorus' of rural life, as the cockerel crows or the tractor sets out for the fields in the early morning. But the plus side of gîte holidays is that the owners and neighbours are often interested in more than simply the commercial side of renting property. They are usually genuinely friendly, welcoming people who enjoy real contact with visitors, and are happy to provide information and advice about the locality.

The official *Gîtes de France Handbook* listing all the properties is available on payment of the £3 membership fee. This annual membership is necessary to receive all the details of the gîtes and make a booking. Inevitably, the golden rule is **book early** for June, July and August. For details, send s.a.e. to Gîtes de France Ltd, 178 Piccadilly, London W1V 9DB, Tel. 071 493 3480). It is possible to book the gîte only, but it usually works out cheaper to book an all-inclusive gîte holiday with travel arrangements. Gîtes de France have worked out favourable terms with ferry companies and Motorail, the network of special overnight trains carrying passengers with their cars or motorbikes over long distances.

If looking for a hotel with the personal touch, then consider a **logis**, a country inn. Logis are small or medium-sized family-run, mostly 1 or 2-star hotel-restaurants, many of which are situated outside urban areas, often in beautiful French villages. There are over 5000 of these in France, classified using a 'fireplace' rating, according to the quality of the rooms, reception areas and restaurants. Those running logis sign a Quality Charter which guarantees guests a warm personal welcome as a 'paying guest', cooking that makes a feature of regional dishes and the chef's own specialities, and prices listed inclusive of service. Booking is carried out directly with the hotel. A free guide listing them all is available from the French Government Tourist Office (send 80p in stamps for postage). If the thought of corresponding in French with the logis owner is all too much, it is possible to book in Britain with either of two companies, each of which offers a selection of logis: **Logis en vacances'**, through Gîtes de France (address above), or **Logis en liberté'**, through The Voyage Organisation, 134a Uxbridge Road, London W12 8AA (Tel. 081 743 5233).

Finally, for those in search of a taste of luxury, there are various organisations specialising in château accommodation. One example is **Château Acceuil**, an association of private château owners offering a warm personal welcome in their own homes. A great advantage of this 'meet the locals' scheme with a difference is that the hosts are usually a great source of information on the history, architecture, cultural events and gastronomy of their regions – ideal for those touring or beginning a longer holiday in a particular region. Average prices for a double room are 600–700FF per night. Contact Château Accueil through their president, M. le Marquis de Chénerilles, Château du Gerfaut, 37190 Azay-le-Rideau (Tel. 47 45 40 16).

Other organisations providing château accommodation are: **Châteaux**, Destination Marketing Limited, 2 Cinnamon Row, Plantation Wharf, York Place, London SW11 3TW (Tel. 071 978 5212); **Châteaux d'en France**, 8 rue de l'Isly, 75008 Paris (Tel. (1) 42 94 92 00); **Relais et Châteaux**, 9 avenue Marceau, 75116 Paris (Tel. (1) 47 23 41 42); and **Châteaux, Demeures et Tables des Vignobles**, BP40, 13360 Roquevaire (Tel. 42 04 41 97), which lists restaurants specialising in regional dishes, as well as châteaux and other quality accommodation.

House-swapping offers many advantages. It is rent-free. It cuts down on the need to eat out so much. It can offer the opportunity of swapping cars as well, eliminating the need to drive to the destination. And your own home is occupied during your absence. **Green Theme Home Exchange Holiday Service** (Little Rylands Farm, Redmoor, Bodmin, Cornwall PL30 5AR, Tel. 0208 873123) have a very good listing of French families interested in swapping their homes with British people for holidays. It costs £10 to register, after which they will send you a carefully-chosen shortlist of properties, with colour photographs.

Interlink (BP 1124, 69203 Lyon Cedex 01, Tel. 78 27 96 00), for a payment of 600FF, can match up individual clients with French people wishing to swap their houses or flats. Alternatively, for 480FF, clients can arrange to appear in one of their catalogues and deal directly with interested French families.

Home Base Holidays (7 Park Avenue, London N13 5PG, Tel. 081 886 8752) can also arrange house-swaps with French families, and charge £24 for inclusion in their listings booklet.

For stays with French people, **En Famille Overseas** is a good example of a company offering visits to French host families, as well as language holidays. They can be contacted at The Old Stables, 60b Maltravers Street, Arundel, West Sussex BN18 9BG (Tel. 0903 883266). Other organisations which can provide details of French host families are **Accueil France Famille**, 5 rue François Coppée, 75015 Paris (Tel. (1) 45 54 22 39), and **Amicale Culturelle Internationale**, 27 rue Godot de Mauroy, 75009 Paris (Tel. (1) 47 42 94 21). The **Experiment in International Living** (EIL) is an independent educational organisation founded to promote an international homestay exchange programme which would foster mutual friendships and understanding. Its French offices are at 8 rue Mercoeur, 44000 Nantes (Tel. 40 35 74 75).

Syndicats d'Initiative and Offices de Tourisme will gladly provide information on all of the forms of accommodation listed above. An alternative way of booking in advance is to contact the **Loisirs-Accueil** in the *département* you intend visiting. These are officially-backed booking services, usually charging no fee, and with someone there who speaks English. They can reserve hotels, *gîtes* and campsites, as well as special activity or sports holidays, Send a s.a.e. off to the French Government Tourist Office for a list of the Loisirs-Accueil organisations in France. In the rest of this guide, low-impact, traditional, family-run establishments have been recommended, with price brackets for accommodation and eating out breaking down as follows: *First Class*: over 500FF per double room or meal for two (starter, main course, dessert); *Middle Range*: 250–500FF; and *Economy*: under 250FF.

The Art of Being a Good Tourist

The art of being a Good Tourist in France can be split into two stages: the first starts at the planning stage of the trip, with the choice of destination, accommodation and means of transport. Should lovers of France avoid certain areas which are already spoiled by tourism, or go off-season to avoid already overcrowded places? What kind of transport inflicts least damage on the environment? And what kind of accommodation is most in keeping with the destination? The second stage concerns tourists' behaviour during their time in France. How should they conduct themselves in order to fit in harmoniously with the French themselves, and best preserve the country they have come to see?

For getting to, and around, France, **rail travel** is hard to beat, from the environmental point of view. The reduced load on France's roads partly explains the French government's motivation for the heavy subsidies which it pays to the SNCF. **Motorail** services also help keep down road traffic. **TGV** trains have been the focus of some controversy in recent years. But, despite the ongoing protestations over the proposed TGV route through Provence, said to threaten the last of that region's unspoilt farmland, the TGV generally has a good environmental record, with the SNCF constructing sound-smothering embankments and hiding the train in tunnels as much as possible.

Another way to keep more cars off France's roads is to **car-share** with someone already planning to make the journey by car, instead of taking your own. Sharing with a French driver offers the added attraction of getting to know one of the 'locals' while travelling; **Allostop Provoya** (84 passage Brady, 75010 Paris, Tel.(1) 47 70 02 01) puts drivers and passengers in touch with each other, quoting fares such as 125FF for Paris to Marseille and 100FF from Nancy to Avignon.

If driving your own car, remember that **lead-free petrol** ('sans plomb') is widely available throughout France, and is cheaper too; so, if planning to cover large distances, this could be the moment to convert to lead-free if you haven't done so already.

House-letting, particularly in the countryside, is one of the best ways of merging in with the background. And if the house belongs to someone local, the rent paid could be a valuable part of their supplementary income as well as a contribution to the fragile rural economy. The same applies to the form of accommodation based on people opening up their own homes to paying guests. These range from the simple **chambres d'hôte**, the French version of B&B, to the grandeur of staying with the owner in his **château**. The bonus of using this kind of accommodation is the opportunity it brings for getting to know local people.

Family-run **hotels** of the **logis de France** and **auberges de France** type are most often small to medium-sized establishments, built, more often than not, in the vernacular style, and on a scale in keeping with the locality. (Details of all of these under Accommodation, page 61). **Camping** in coastal regions, where 75% of all camping in France takes place, poses its own environmental problems, and the Good Tourist should think twice before adding to these. In areas such as the Côte d'Azur where there is a great concentration of camping in summer, the ecological impact ranges from the disappearance of vegetation to the total sterilisation of the soil in places; and sites in Aquitaine, the Vendée and the Côte d'Opale have been known to harm the fragile dunes of these regions. Coastal camping sites also create problems for the local authorities, who receive very little income from them, yet who have to build expensive drainage and sewerage facilities for these sites, which are used only in the high-season. Try inland sites instead – of the 200 new campsites created each year in France, a growing number are being built inland, with facilities such as swimming pools and games areas to compensate for the lack of a nearby beach. If you are prepared to do without sophisticated facilities, another option is 'camping à la ferme': at these sites, the farmer offers his field to a very small number of campers, who are often made to feel more like guests.

The French coast is also where the greatest concentration of tourists are to be found during summer, and part of the art of practising 'good tourism' is to avoid adding to the problems of those areas which suffer from this annual invasion. The Mediterranean beaches during July and August are the closest to saturation point, followed by those on the Atlantic and Brittany coasts. Visit these areas outside these months, or try the Normandy and Channel coast resorts, for summer seaside. In winter, the Alps, in particular the northern peaks, suffer from an over-concentration of winter-sports visitors; while resorts in the Pyrenees, the Jura, the Vosges and Auvergne all have spare capacity. Use either low-altitude village resorts, which have a life outside the skiing season, or 'Fourth Generation' resorts when possible. The latter is a term used to describe some recently constructed resorts, which have been built with more sensitivity to their location and to a reasonable scale.

It is understandably in the overcrowded destinations that some resentment towards tourists can be found. Residents of the 'mega-resorts' on the Mediterranean coast have been known, in their exasperation, to spray the slogan 'Touriste = Con' ('bloody idiot') on walls, as a message to the tourist hordes. But those living in rural regions, too, struggling with the hardships of farming life and the continuing depopulation of their regions, often resent the annual influx of wealthier tourists. 'Les touristes passent, le paysan trépasse' (tourists walk by, while the countryside is dying) and 'Nous ne sommes pas des Indiens!' are examples of the graffiti expressing their sentiments. In these regions in particular, the tourist needs to be sensitive to the difficulties of the local people, and make every effort not to exacerbate them. Which raises the question: what constitutes Good Tourist behaviour?

Having arrived in France, British visitors usually find that daily life and customs are familiar enough, and if they demonstrate a reasonable degree of sensitivity and consideration for other people and for the place they are visiting, few problems will arise. Some pointers, however, may help visitors avoid the principal pitfalls.

On a very simple level, it is important to remember that the French use **greetings** much more than the British do. 'Bonjour monsieur, bonjour madame' (at around 5 or 6p.m. it becomes 'bonsoir') are used a lot: when meeting neighbours, when about to ask for some information, or when entering a shop, for example. Not to open with this simple formula makes foreigners appear slightly brusque to the French. It is also usual to shake hands virtually every time you see someone you know, and **always** if you are meeting someone for the first time.

Although anyone in France under the age of thirty is likely to have at least a smattering of English (and more often a great deal) at their disposal, this is no reason for tourists automatically launching into English, without at least a preliminary 'Parlez-vous anglais?' Older French people in particular can be sensitive to what they see as the linguistic imperialism of English. So master at least the basic tourist vocabulary needed for a trip to France, particularly if heading for a rural destination, where fluent speakers of English may be rare.

When it comes to **photographing people**, remember that although some French people, the young and fashionable in particular, may dress in order to turn heads in the street, they are inviting **discreet** attention, not offering themselves as models for holiday photographs. The rule is always to ask permission – using sign-language if necessary – before photographing that group of 'boules' players, pavement mime-artist, or organ-grinder. (Street entertainers appreciate – and deserve – a few francs dropped into the hat, in return for the favour.)

There are two places where the use of cameras is particularly sensitive: in churches and on naturist beaches. France is not the strongly Catholic country it was a century ago; only 14% of the population regularly attend mass now (although this figure can be as high as 50–60% in rural areas). But, it is important to appreciate that places of worship are still more than tourist attractions to some of those present in them. As well as being mindful of what you wear in churches (no beachwear, gaudy sportswear or bare shoulders), remember that flash photography destroys the tranquillity which people are often seeking in churches, and, out of consideration for worshippers, should be avoided. In the unwritten etiquette of French naturist beaches, the most rigorous rule of all is No Photography of people you do not know. Snapping nude sunbathers unawares is the quickest way to stir up trouble on the sand, so even if photographing your own group, take care not to inadvertently include any others in the frame.

Women are now able to travel around France with the same degree of freedom from harassment that they would expect in Britain. French women are now fiercely intolerant of 'machismo' behaviour in the streets (which perhaps explains why it is most often expressed now behind the safety of the steering wheel!) and female visitors to France should encounter no more and no less in the way of pestering than in their own country. Nevertheless, a Good Tourist rule is always to be aware of women travelling alone, and to offer help, if it is thought that this would be appreciated.

Rural tourism, bringing visitors into contact with country people as it often does, necessitates a particular code of conduct on the part of the tourists, especially those renting property on or near to farms. As well as being liberal with the customary greetings, they should remember that, while they are on holiday, perhaps staying up late and sleeping in, the neighbours' often very hard-working life goes on. The French 'paysan' will usually rise in the morning with the sun to start work, and therefore does not take too kindly to noisy late-night parties or car doors slamming at 1a.m.

Another common source of grievance is the phenomenon of visitors arriving at their gîte or campsite with enough provisions in the back of the car to last the entire holiday. Country people fully realise that this kind of tourist brings little benefit to the rural economy. So Shop Local is a good rule here, not only to stimulate the local economy, but to sample the local produce, too. Particularly if staying on a farm, ask if any of their produce is for sale. The other, vitally important, Good Tourism rule in rural areas is to treat the countryside itself with the greatest respect. For all its size, the French countryside is no less fragile than that of Britain, and it needs to be treated with care. In the south, avoid, above all, lighting fires out of doors. In this increasingly arid part of France, thousands of acres of forest are burned and lives are lost every year, often due to the thoughtlessness of tourists. As well as observing the other guidelines of the Countryside Code involving litter, noise and keeping to paths, refrain from collecting fruits, mushrooms, flowers and other plants growing wild. Even where such things are growing on common land, they are often a supplementary source of revenue for country people in rural areas of France.

Checklist for the Good Tourist

1. Have I learned enough about my destination to be able to properly appreciate it and understand the issues facing this area when I arrive?

2. Can I go out of season to avoid further tourist congestion?

3. Can I use local tour operators, local transport and stay with local people?

4. If going with a tour operator, check that the company:

* works with the local community and ensures their operations are as environmentally friendly and socially acceptable as possible;

* contributes to local initiatives to keep the destination in good condition;

* creates local employment;

* uses local guides and locally owned accommodation and transport;

* integrates tourists with locals and teaches you, prior to departure, about the destination.

5. When there, consume local produce; use public transport.

6. Remove all excess packaging before packing your case, and take biodegradable sunscreens and toiletries

7. Buy souvenirs that are locally made and reflect the indigenous culture. Avoid all produce made from endangered species. Help conserve the native fauna and flora.

8. Be sensitive to the local customs regarding photography and tipping.

All these and many more positive ideas on how to be a good tourist and get more fun out of your holiday are found in *The Good Tourist – a worldwide guide for the green traveller* (Mandarin Paperbacks. £5.99)

Further Information

General Environmental Issues

Amis de la Terre, 15 rue Gambey, 75001 Paris (Tel. (1) 47 00 05 05)

Espaces pour Demain, 20 avenue MacMahon, 75017 Paris (Tel. (1) 47 64 13 38)

Greenpeace France, 28 rue Petites Ecuries, 75010 Paris (Tel. (1) 47 70 46 89)

France, Nature, Environnement, Maison de Chevreul, 57 rue Cuvier, 75231 Paris Cedex 05 (Tel. (1) 43 36 79 95)

Union Nationale des Centres Permanents d'Initiation à l'Environnment, 2 rue Washington, 75008 Paris (Tel. (1) 45 63 99 48)

Fédération des Parcs Naturels de France, 4 rue Stockholm, 75008 Paris (Tel. (1) 42 94 90 84)

Fédération des Conservatoires Régionaux d'Espaces Naturels, Ecomusée de Haute Alsace, 68190 Ungersheim (Tel. 89 48 02 42)

Wildlife Protection

Fonds Mondial pour la Nature, 151 boulevard Reine, 78000 Versailles (Tel. (1) 39 50 75 14)

Ligue Française pour la Protection des Oiseaux, La Corderie Royale, BP 263, 17305 Rochefort Cedex (Tel. 46 99 59 97)

Association pour la Protection des Animaux Sauvages et du Patrimoine Naturel, BP 34, 26270 Loriol (Tel. 75 62 64 86)

Rassemblement des Opposants à la Chasse, 23 rue Gosselot, 59000 Lille (Tel. 20 52 12 02), the union of those opposed to hunting.

Heritage Conservation

Caisse Nationale des Monuments Historiques et des Sites, Hôtel de Sully, 62 rue Saint-Antoine, 75004 Paris (Tel. (1) 42 74 22 22)

Vieilles Maisons Françaises, 93 rue de l'Université, 75007 Paris (Tel. (1) 45 51 07 02)

Club du Vieux Manoir, 10 rue de la Cossonnerie, 75001 Paris (Tel. (1) 45 08 80 40)

Union Rempart, 1 rue des Guillemites, 75004 Paris (Tel. (1) 42 71 96 55).

Government

French Ministry of the Environment, 14–16 boulevard du Général Leclerc, 92524 Neuilly sur Seine Cedex (Tel. (1) 47 58 12 12)

French Ministry of Tourism, 2 rue Linois, 75740 Paris Cédex (Tel. (1) 45 75 62 16)

Conservatoire de l'Espace Littoral et des Rivages Lacustres (the conservation of sea shores and lake shores), 72 rue Regnault, 75013 Paris (Tel. (1) 45 70 74 75)

Office National des Forêts, 2 avenue de Saint-Mandé, 75012 Paris (Tel. (1) 40 19 58 00)

Tourism Network (Britain-Based)

La Maison de la France (French Government Tourist Office), 178 Piccadilly, London W1V 0AL (Tel. 071 491 7622).
(Publications: Logis de France handbook; handbook of horse-riding associations; list of Loisirs-Accueil organisations; information packs on specific regions; Festivals guide; *The Traveller in France*; *The Camping Traveller in France*; *Afloat in France*; *The Active Traveller in France*; *The Touring Traveller in France*; *The Ski Traveller in France*).

Gîtes de France Ltd, 178 Piccadilly, London W1V 9DB (Tel. 071 493 3480 or 071 408 1343). (Information concerning all types of gite, plus chambres d'hôte, camping à la ferme, and the Loisirs-Accueil cycling/rambling brochure.)

Tourism Network (France-Based)

La Maison de la France, 8 avenue de l'Opéra, 75001 Paris (Tel. (1) 42 96 10 23) (Information useful for the planning of a holiday in any part of France – for Paris-based 'Maisons' with information on specific regions, see Appendix.)

Fédération Nationale des Gîtes de France, Maison du Tourisme Vert, 35 rue Godot de Mauroy, 75009 Paris (Tel. (1) 47 42 20 20) (Information on all types of gîte, plus chambres d'hôte and camping à la ferme – brochures for every French département.)

Fédération Nationale des Services de Réservation Loisirs-Accueil, Direction de l'Industrie Touristique, 2 rue Linois, 75015 Paris (Tel. (1) 40 59 44 12) (Not-for-profit organisation offering accommodation and low-impact, locally arranged thematic and activity holidays in around sixty French *départements* – see **Adventure/Activity Holidays** for details. For the addresses of departmental Loisirs-Accueil services in your chosen holiday region, look in that region's **Good Alternatives** section.)

Fédération Nationale des Pays d'Accueil Touristiques, 19 avenue du Maine, 75015 Paris (Tel. (1) 49 55 53 08) (Similar to Loisirs-Accueil organisation, but based in natural, rather than administrative, areas.)

Fédération Nationale des Offices de Tourisme et Syndicats d'Initiative, 2 rue Linois, 75015 Paris (Tel. (1) 40 59 43 83) (Information on specific towns and cities.)

Service d'Utilité Agricole 'Agriculture et Tourisme' (SUAAT), Assemblée Permanente des Chambres d'Agriculture, 9 avenue Georges V, 75008 Paris (Tel. (1) 47 23 55 40) (Supplies list of departmental Chambers of Agriculture organising stays with local farmers under the 'Bienvenue à la Ferme' initiative.)

Special Interests
Walking/Rambling
Comité National des Sentiers de Grande Randonnée, 8 avenue Marceau, 75008 Paris (Tel. (1) 47 23 62 32)

Cycling
Fédération Française de Cyclotourisme, 8 rue Jean-Jego, 75013 Paris (Tel. (1) 45 80 30 21)

Horse-riding
Association Nationale du Tourisme Equestre, 15 rue de Bruxelles, 75009 Paris (Tel. (1) 42 81 42 82)

Winter Sports
Associations des Maires des Stations Françaises de Sports

d'Hiver, Ski-France, 61 boulevard Haussmann, 75008 Paris (Tel. (1) 47 42 23 32)

River Tourism
Fédération des Industries Nautiques, Syndicat National des Loueurs de Bateaux de Plaisance, Port de la Bourdonnais, 75007 Paris (Tel. (1) 45 55 10 49)

Naturism
Fédération Française de Naturisme, 53 rue de la Chaussée d'Antin, 75009 Paris (Tel. (1) 42 80 05 21)

Thermalism
La Fédération Thermale et Climatique Française, 16 rue de l'Estrapade, 75005 Paris (Tel. (1) 43 25 11 85)

Thalassotherapy
La Maison de la Thalassotherapie, 128 avenue de Malakoff, 75116 Paris (Tel. (1) 45 00 58 00)

These national associations are supplemented by numerous regionally based groups, many of which specialise in issues of local interest. Contacting them, preferably in advance of your trip, is a good way of discovering more about the local community and its priorities; their addresses are listed in the **Useful Local Contacts** section of each chapter.

You will find a list of regional and departmental tourist boards with Paris offices in the **Appendix**.

1 Brittany

Right from the start, Brittany will strike the visitor as a thoroughly independent region, different from anywhere else in France. The best way to approach the Brittany peninsula is, without a doubt, by sea, for the sea plays a special role here and is vital to both culture and livelihood. Indeed, Brittany has over 1200 kilometres of coastline – more than any other French region. Fishing is the traditional occupation and the Breton people call the coastal fringe of their country Armor, meaning 'the Sea'. The more sparsely populated inland parts are known as Argoat or 'the Woods', though sadly little of the original forest remains.

The Celtic culture is still fundamental to the Breton way of life. Many similarities exist between the languages and traditions of Brittany, Ireland, Wales, Cornwall and parts of northern Spain, whose inhabitants gather together at Lorient each August for the 'Festival Interceltique', where their Celtic roots are celebrated. Regional costume is worn, including the delicate white lace *coiffe* head-dress for women; bagpipes (*cornemuses*) are played; Celtic dancing and Breton wrestling take place. Smaller festivals occur thoughout Brittany during the summer, and in some villages traditional dress is still worn by older people outside festival time – on market days, for example – though this is not nearly as frequent as tourist board posters would imply.

Another classic image of Brittany is one of granite calvary crosses, eery and stark against a dramatic sunset. These, too, are less common than one might imagine, but this makes it all the more startling to come across one (preferably out of season when its atmosphere is not destroyed by throngs of visitors). Prehistoric stone circles and lines can be seen in Morbihan, adding to the mythical aura which seems to pervade the whole of Brittany.

Perhaps the best way to gain a glimpse into this unusual culture is to stay with the exceptionally welcoming Breton people, whether in a simple *chambres d'hôte* or an imposing château. Tales of King Arthur and the various other local legends are certainly appreciated best over an earthenware bowl full of cider and an authentic Breton crêpe. A lesser known feature of Brittany is its abundance of castles; the region is home to no less than 4000 of France's 10,000 châteaux, many of which are in the true story-book mould, with medieval ramparts, moats, turrets and draw-bridges. Brittany also boasts a whole string of sandy beaches; a range of good (and cheap) golf courses; various small islands which can be visited on day-trips; and some of the most spectacular coastline in France.

History

It was as long ago as 4670 BC that megalithic civilisation began in Brittany, remnants of which can still be seen in the stone circles of Carnac. In the sixth century BC the Celts arrived, calling the area Armor, but they were conquered, first by the Romans, then the Barbarians. It was not until AD 460 that the region was given its current name, Bretagne (meaning 'Little Britain'), by Celts fleeing from Great Britain after invasions by the Angles and Saxons. Having emigrated to the ancient land of Armor, the Celts proceeded to convert it to Christianity, making many of their religious leaders into saints, and faith has remained strong here ever since, particularly in the interior. People lived and were governed in parish communities and a bond was formed between Brittany and the other Celtic strongholds of Wales, Cornwall and Ireland.

Medieval Brittany suffered from being the battleground between nobles laying claim to its rule. In the fourteenth century, Bertrand du Guesclin, a heroic inhabitant of Dinan, won battles for the province during the Anglo-French wars. In 1488, the Duchess Anne became the last ruler of independent Brittany. As a result of her marriages, first to Charles VIII and then to Louis XII, Brittany was annexed to France in 1532. Anne did, however, succeed in negotiating concessions for her people, which meant that Bretons enjoyed a unique status in France: they were neither obliged to pay taxes, stand trial, nor defend the nation. In 1666, Colbert established the East India Company at Port-Louis, forming a new town, at first known as L'Orient (the East), but becoming Lorient in 1830. Spices and porcelain were imported from the Indies and this was the beginning of the rivalry between the French and the British concerning superiority at sea.

The French Revolution was generally welcomed in Brittany,

but Breton Royalist revolts led to a certain amount of bloodshed. Further heavy loss of life was incurred in the First World War, and considerable destruction (of towns like Lorient and Brest) came with the closing stages of the Second. More recent damage has been in the shape of oil spillages – the *Torrey Canyon* disaster in 1967, and the *Amoco Cadiz* in 1978.

The sea around Brittany has long been used as a source of food and income. Traditionally, Breton fishermen used small trawlers and risked unpredictable local catches. Things changed in the 1960s, when cooperatives were formed, auctions (called 'criées') were held, and new, larger and more powerful boats began to venture to Cornish and Irish waters for mass catches of brill, whiting, sole, skate and cod. Nowadays, some traditional fishing areas have been fished out and EC regulations control catches, but fish and seafood are as popular as ever.

Brittany still has a strong regional identity, not only in matters of cuisine, but also in customs, festivals and language. The ferocity of Breton nationalism has hardly abated since the days of the Duchess Anne. In 1951, a committee was created to safeguard Breton interests and stimulate the local economy and in 1978, a charter was signed to protect Brittany's cultural heritage. The Breton language has managed to survive and is spoken fairly widely; it also appears, along with French, on road signs. As England is to the Welsh, France is to the Bretons – another country. The historical links with its big sister, *Grande Bretagne*, have not made Brittany any more 'British' but, rather, less mainstream French.

Geography

As the most westerly part of France, Brittany is a peninsula jutting out from the grazing lands of Normandy and the sheltered Loire valley into the Atlantic ocean. The region is made up of four *départements*: the most westerly (and least French) is Finistère, whose capital is Quimper (60,000 inhabitants); along the southern Atlantic coast runs Morbihan, whose capital is Vannes (46,000); in the east is the predominantly inland *département* of Ille-et-Vilaine, whose capital, Rennes, is also the regional capital and has a population of 200,000; finally, the *département* stretching along the northern Channel coast, known until 1990 as Côtes-du-Nord, has just been rechristened as the more romantic-sounding Côtes d'Armor – its capital is St-Brieuc, with 52,000 inhabitants. You will find in Brittany a wealth of surnames and place names beginning with Ker – as the word means 'village' or 'house' in Breton.

The entire coastline (of which there is 1200 km) is extended by inlets, bays, gulfs, spits, estuaries and islands. Some of these islands, known as the Iles du Ponant, are uninhabited; others are home to fishing communities, whose livelihood is dependent on the whims of the temperamental sea, with its abundance of fish and crustaceans. As well as being divided into Armor (the coast) and Argoat (the interior), Brittany falls into Low Brittany (Basse-Bretagne), which, confusingly, is the partly mountainous western area, and High Brittany (Haute-Bretagne) in the low-lying east. The landscape inland is unspectacular, agricultural and wooded (though it has lost almost all of the original forest which gave it the name Argoat); it is intersected by pretty rivers along which there is no shortage of charming towns with considerable medieval character. The many villages are concerned with farming maize, wheat, vegetables, apples and livestock rearing. The 600 km of navigable waterway, notably the Nantes à Brest canal which bisects the region, are busy with children in kayaks during summer. Meanwhile, on the coast, the constant cycle of high and low tides makes for a varied seascape.

Though Brittany has only one regional park, the Armorique, it is fairly rich in *réserves naturelles*, where there is strict protection of the natural heritage. Perhaps the most important of these, the Sept-Iles, is an archipelago of rocky islands off the Côtes d'Armor. The islands are a favourite haunt of grey seals and nesting sea birds, of which there are twelve species including the gannet, kittiwake, storm petrel, auk and puffin. The last two were disastrously affected by oil pollution from the *Torrey Canyon* and *Amoco Cadiz*, which reduced the puffin population from 2000 to 240. There is an ornithological station on the Ile Grande and visitors can take boat trips from Perros-Guirec to the largest island, Ile aux Moines. West of Douarnenez is the lesser known Cap Sizun reserve, whose bird-life is similar to that of the Sept Iles. On the Ile de Groix, offshore from Lorient in the Morbihan *département*, is another reserve, this time geological, where a diversity of minerals can be seen, left by the collision of two tectonic plates 400 million years ago. Offshore from Fouesnant and Concarneau, in Finistère, is the St-Nicolas-des-Glénan reserve, which contains a fixed dune on a rocky island, with interesting flora including narcissus.

The Armorique regional park itself includes a maritime and insular sector and an inland one, which covers the hilly Monts d'Arrée region. The islands are situated in the Iroise sea, one of the most important maritime reserves in the world, which has recently been declared an International Biosphere Reserve by UNESCO. Colonies of seals and dolphins live here, as well as almost 300 species of sea bird. The Armorique park's coastline is a spectacular combination of granite indentations, sandstone cliffs and dunes, while inland the Breton moor is punctuated by small woods. Sadly, the hurricanes of October 1987 caused extensive damage in some areas, as can be seen from the forest walks around Huelgoat. Clearance and replanting are ongoing. Along the Ellez, Roudouhir and Roudoudour rivers are signs of the only visible beaver colony in Brittany; salmon and otters also live within the park area, and fallow deer and wild boar inhabit its forests.

Climate

The summer in Brittany tends to be only moderately warm (average 17°C), as a result of bracing breezes coming from the Atlantic gulf stream. During recent hot dry summers, the tempering maritime influences have been welcome in the region's interior. There are occasional summer showers which are usually heavier on the coast. Spring and autumn can be windy and rainy, but this is easily compensated for by the colours of flowers and foliage, the whipped-up-seas and the dramatic, shifting skies. Winters are mild and Brittany enjoys a similar temperature to that on the Mediterranean coast, though winds can blow up unexpectedly. There are rarely frosts and some Mediterranean plants grow on the coast and islands. The traditional 'Breton knit' striped sweaters are, however, a wise addition to the holiday wardrobe at most times of year.

Attractions

Like England's West Country, Brittany's appeal lies in its endless coastline, varied countryside, charming towns and villages, and strong regional identity. A holiday in Brittany means a trip into foreign territory, for British and French visitors alike. Besides stunning scenery, the seaside offers the usual facilities for bathing, sailing, a host of watersports and fishing, as well as strolling the picturesque promenades and tasting the 'fruits de la mer' in the abundant quayside restaurants. In addition to the smaller fishing villages, it is worth exploring towns like St-Malo with its granite ramparts, Quimper with its cobbled streets and colourful pottery, and the walled city of Vannes. Brittany's islands with their flourishing bird-life add yet another string to its bow.

Inland there is space to stay away from the coastal bustle, to enjoy medieval market towns, the historic city of Rennes, and other important reminders of the region's past inhabitants. Try not to miss the ancient mystical megaliths forming circles and lines in the area of Carnac; the grey slate turrets of the many Breton castles; the intricate Parish-Close village constructions, consisting of complex stone monuments engraved with figures telling the story of the Crucifixion, which were built in the seventeenth century to repel a plague epidemic; and the imposing granite crosses known as calvaries. These last are the focal point of *pardons*, pilgrimages made for absolution, which are a feature of traditional Breton culture. The procession, taking place in local costume and accompanied by bagpipe music, is followed by wrestling, dancing, fireworks and other festivities, which sometimes last through the night. *Pardons* take place throughout the summer in different villages. They, along with Brittany's many other traditional festivals, form a major attraction of the region. Another perspective on the regional way of life is offered by the wealth of *ecomusées*, which illuminate areas as diverse as fishing, iron-making and the unsual Ouessantine culture.

Cuisine

It is on the tables of Brittany that local seafood specialities blend with the cream, cider and calvados of Normandy and the wines of the Loire. From the sea, crustaceans such as lobster, crab and crayfish are popular, as are shellfish, particularly mussels and oysters. Many types of fish, in every conceivable form, feature on menus. Fish soup and *assiette de mer* (seafood platter) are usually on the fixed price menu, and fish is often the basis of the *Plat du Jour*. *Farz Breton* is a local dish from an ancient recipe, which has a Yorkshire pudding-like consistency; a sweetened version with prunes is most commonly served these days. *Pré-salé* lamb from the salt-marsh grazing lands is a delicacy. Rennes is known for its tasty chickens, Morlaix for its flavoursome ham, and Quimperlé for its chitterlings. Local vegetables include artichokes, peas, cauliflowers and potatoes, while strawberries, melons and cherries also grow in the region. Crêpes (made with wheat or buckwheat, depending on whether the filling is to be savoury or sweet) and *galettes* (a kind of flat scone) are regional specialities and there is virtually no food which cannot be folded into them.

Crêpes, and indeed most Breton dishes, are best washed down with the local *cidre* (which conoisseurs consider inferior to that of Normandy). This is usually served in earthenware bowls. *Eau-de-Vie de Cidre* is also made, as well as a delicious *Plougastel Fraise* (strawberry) liqueur. Although wine is not produced in Brittany, the crisp white wines from neighbouring Loire are an excellent accompaniment to Breton cooking, especially Muscadet, which comes from the area around Nantes, formerly a part of Brittany.

Level of Tourism

Brittany comes sixth in the league of French tourist-receiving regions, hosting about 5.2% of the nation's hotel visits. Although only around 16% of visitors come from outside France, tourism is Brittany's second largest source of income. Of the foreign visitors, the British and Irish make up around 40%, followed closely by the Germans, with a handful of Italians and Dutch. At present, virtually all holidays to Brittany take place between June and September (most of them in the school summer holidays). However, with its mild winters and so much natural beauty, there is scope to extend the season to welcome visitors in spring and autumn, for short breaks, including nature discovery and activity holidays such as walking and sailing. If you have the opportunity to see the region outside the relatively short tourist season, you will enjoy spectacularly colourful, unspoilt landscapes, shining seas, empty bays, deserted roads and uncrowded restaurants.

During summer, camping is popular with both French and British families, who either use their own tents and caravans, or else sited ones on the south coast. From Bénodet downwards the bathing is sheltered and sites along this stretch of coast are therefore popular among families with young children. If staying here, you are also more than likely to have fellow Brits as neighbours. There are a large number of rural *gîtes* scattered about the region, many of which are old buildings which would have fallen into ruin were it not for the restoration grants offered by the authorities to those willing to convert their property into small-scale, authentic holiday accommodation.

During summer Brittany has its fair share of 'honeypot' sites, including picturesque towns like Dinan and St-Malo and the well-advertised 'typical jewel of the 16th century', Poul-Fetan, though you will find these places transformed if you visit them out of season. The coastal parts are obviously the most crowded in summer, and it is easy to forget that much of the coastline belongs to a protected zone due to its ecological fragility. It is particularly important to dispose sensibly of your rubbish here, and to use biodegradable sunscreens etc. Bear in mind that the fish you eat for dinner probably came from nearby.

Finistère is the *département* which receives most tourists in Brittany, and it is not far from the top of the league of all the French *départements*. Wishing to maintain this position, the departmental tourist board has decided it is important to place the emphasis on quality. Projects are under way to get local communities and organisations to work together in the promotion of tourism; to adapt the type of accommodation on offer in different areas to the demand; and to structure and make more interesting the practice of different activities (e.g. to signpost walking trails and explore the possibilities of both sea and river fishing holidays). Other areas in expansion are business tourism, cultural tourism, health tourism, river tourism and sports such as sailing and golf. In Finistère an emphasis is being laid on good publicity and the tourist board has produced numerous thematic brochures. Their main concern, however, is to persuade people to come outside the peak holiday season: a suggestion which would benefit local people and visitors alike.

Good Alternatives

Meeting People

All the festivals held in Brittany make it relatively easy to meet local people, especially if you choose to attend a small, village celebration rather than one of the well-known ones. A list of the festivals taking place within the Armorique regional park is contained in the 'Animation' leaflet for the appropriate year, available from the **Maison du Parc**, Menez-Meur, Hanvec, BP 35, 29460 Daoulas (Tel. 98 21 90 69). The **Comité Régional du Tourisme** will be able to supply you with lists of festivals thoughout Brittany (though these are less likely to include the small, lesser known ones than is the park's brochure); contact the CRT at 3 rue d'Espagne, BP 4175, 35041 Rennes (Tel. 99 50 11 15).

Another good way of meeting people is to stay in locally-owned accommodation. There are a large number of family-run 'Logis de France' hotels in the region, as well as attractive rural *gîtes* and welcoming *chambres d'hôte*. At the other end of the scale, it is possible to check in to a genuine Breton château, where you will be usually be treated like a guest of the family, enjoying good regional cuisine, long chats about the local way of life, and numerous tips on walks and places to visit which only a local person would know about. You can book through **Château Accueil** (see p. **62**); alternatively, information on Bed and Breakfast château accommodation in Brittany is available from **Châteaux et Manoirs de Bretagne**, Sophie Goodfellow, Brittany Chamber of Commerce – Service Tourisme, 69 Cannon St, London EC4N 5AB. Some simple château accommodation is also listed in the Gîtes de France handbook for each *département*. At one particular residence, the family offers guided discovery tours of the region's châteaux to its guests: contact M. Pourdieu le Coz, **Château de Pontgamp**, 22150 Plougenast (Tel. 96 28 72 32). Children between the ages of 6 and 12, whose parents feel they would enjoy the experience of traditional Breton farm life, are offered a warm welcome in farms throughout Finistère, through the **Association Accueil d'Enfants à la Ferme**, Mme Fily, Ménec, Le Folgoët, 29260 Lesneven (Tel. 98 83 06 48). Students wishing to improve their French through work experience in a Breton town could consider staying in the residential centre run by Alan and Hélène Line, converted, with students in mind, from a typical Breton mill. Their address is **Moulin de Kergoual**, 56 Pluméliau. Those requiring information on joining archaeological digs should apply to the **Direction des Antiquités**, Hôtel de Blossac, 6 rue du Chapître, 35000 Rennes (Tel. 99 79 21 32).

Finally, a different kind of holiday is offered by the Thalasso-therapy centres of Brittany. The therapeutic nature of the sea is taken much more seriously by the French and there are several centres for rehabilitation (as at Sables Blancs, near Douarnenez), run by the French health service to help the healing of limbs. Sophisticated and healthy holidays are possible at **Carnac Thalassothérapie**, Avenue de l'Atlantique, BP 83, 56341 Carnac (Tel. 97 52 52 00). Alternatively, inclusive holidays to this resort can be arranged from the UK through **Erna Low Consultants Ltd**, 9 Reece Mews, London SW7 3HE (Tel. 071 584 2841).

Discovering Places

Three of Britanny's *départements* have **Loisirs-Accueil** services, offering reservation of accommodation, as well as locally run, small-scale holiday packages, collected together in brochure form. Brochures and information are available from **Loisirs-Accueil Côtes d'Armor**, 5 rue Baratoux, 22000 St-Brieuc (Tel. 96 62 12 40); **Loisirs-Accueil Ille-et-Vilaine**, 1 rue Martenot, 35000 Rennes (Tel. 99 02 97 41); and **Loisirs-Accueil Morbihan**, Hôtel du Département, BP 400, 56009 Vannes (Tel. 97 42 61 60).

In summer, outings are organised by various associations belonging to the Armorique regional park. A full list is contained in the park's 'Animation' leaflet, but examples are as follows: you can learn how to bake old-fashioned bread, or make traditional wooden spoons, or explore the St-Rivoal 'bocage', through the **Ecomusée des Monts d'Arrée**, Moulins de Kerouat, Commana, 29237 Sizun (Tel. 98 68 87 76); you can go for a nocturnal walk across a marsh rich in legends, or watch the departure of migrating birds, through the **Centre d'Etudes et de Découverte de l'Environnement des Monts d'Arrée** (Tel. 98 81 41 21); you can discover the characteristics of Breton rivers with the **Maison de la Rivière, de l'Eau et de la Pêche**, Moulin de Vergraon, 29237 Sizun (Tel. 98 68 86 33); or you can go walking or mountain biking around the cliffs of Crozon or Camaret with the **Maison des Minéraux**, route du Cap de la Chèvre, St-Hernot, 29160 Crozon (Tel. 98 27 19 73). The park is also the venue for a seven-day discovery trip, organised by **Havas Voyages Brest**, 33 rue Jean Macé, 29200 Brest (Tel. 98 80 05 43), and also marketed by **Clés de France** (see p. 51), with the seal of approval of the Natural Parks Federation. The trip is called 'Lands at the End of the Earth', costs around 5500 FF, and includes full board, bike hire, transport, entrance fees to museums, a flight over a nature reserve and the services of qualified local guides.

Walkers should look out for the new hotel label 'Baladhôtel'. This classification has been granted to fifteen or so Brittany hotels, which reserve a special welcome for walkers, offering transfer of bags, regional dishes and local information. Details are available from **Abri**, 9 rue des Portes Mordelaises, 35000 Rennes (Tel. 99 31 59 44). The Abri association also runs various week-long or weekend holidays (with or without a guide), mainly walking, but also including a sea kayak excursion at Paimpol. Abri joins forces with Logis de France to offer the 'Bike Brittany' programme, whose cycling tours start and finish at railway stations, allow for luggage to be transferred for you to your next hotel, and offer accommodation in pleasant family-run hotels. What makes this programme particularly flexible is that the minimum number for participating is only two people. Numerous possibilities exist in Brittany for horseriding holidays and details are contained in the brochure 'La Bretagne à Cheval', available from the **Comité Régional du Tourisme** (address above). The range of boating holidays is, if anything, greater, with numerous local companies offering good-value boat-hire opportunities; details are in the 'Tourisme Fluvial en Bretagne' brochure, prepared by the **Comité de Promotion Touristique des Canaux Bretons et des Voies Navigables de l'Ouest**, Office de Tourisme, Place du Parlement, 35600 Redon. From Douarnenez it is possible (June to Sept.) not only to take a boat trip across the bay to see its unusual caves, but also to join an early morning or evening fishing party; contact **Vedettes Rosmeur**, BP 91, 29176 Douarnenez (Tel. 98 92 83 83 or – off season – 98 27 10 71). Other possible activities in Brittany include diving at Camaret-sur-Mer or taking an off-the-beaten-track mini-bus trip with **Atlantour**, rue Leur-ar-veil, 29132 Penmarc'h (Tel. 98 58 52 30).

UK specialists in holiday accommodation in Brittany are **Brittany Direct Holidays** (362 Sutton Common Road, Sutton, Surrey SM3 9PL, Tel. 081 641 6060). **Brittany Ferries** also offer an extensive programme of holidays, mainly for the motorist: contact The Brittany Centre, Wharf Road, Portsmouth PO2 3RU (Tel. 0705 751833).

Communications

How to Get There

There are **airports** at Brest, Rennes and Quimper, though the fact that you will usually have to change in Paris makes this an impractical option for most travellers. Brit Air offer some direct flights from London to Brittany: contact them at the Aerodrome de Ploujean-Morlaix (Tel. 98 62 10 22).

Brittany Ferries run year-round **ferry** services from Plymouth to Roscoff (Tel. 0752 221321) and from Portsmouth to St-Malo (Tel. 0705 827701). Using Brittany Ferries, Eurolines offer a **coach** service from London, through Exeter and Plymouth, to Roscoff (for around £50 return). There is also a daily Eurolines service to St-Malo. Bicycles travel free on ferries and trains except at peak times. **Trains** from Paris to Rennes take around three hours, those to Brest or Quimper around five and a half.

When You're There

Anyone planning a holiday by public transport in Brittany should get hold of the invaluable 'Guide Régional des Transports', which gives detailed timetables and routes for regional trains, buses and boats, and even includes some town maps. It is available from **SNCF Direction Régionale Bretagne**, 22 boulevard de Beaumont, BP 2022, 35040 Rennes (Tel. 99 29 11 20).

Rail – the main train stations are at Rennes, Quimper, Brest, Vannes and St-Brieuc and there is a good train service around the coast, though the only routes into the middle of the peninsula are those to Carhaix and Loudéac.

Bus – buses and coaches supplement the train network, especially in the interior and on the Finistère peninsulas where trains cannot go. Buses linking smaller towns are, regrettably, infrequent, but they are nonetheless reliable and most problems should be able to be overcome through sensible advance planning. For the address of a company offering off-the-beaten-track mini-bus excursions, see **Good Alternatives**.

Car – most visitors to Brittany bring their car, though, particularly in summer, this can be a barrier to communication with local people; consider instead bringing your bicycle over on the ferry. The routes from the ports are pleasantly free from heavy commercial vehicles, as most of these travel via the more northerly ports. There are almost no toll autoroutes, and the main roads do not often get congested. Most traffic jams occur along single access roads to popular resorts, like the road to Quiberon in high summer. In recent years, signposting has improved greatly. Whether by bike or car, exploration of Brittany's minor roads in the deserted off-season is a rare pleasure.

Boat – many of Brittany's outlying islands can be reached on organised boat trips (details are in the Regional Transport guide mentioned above). The ports to head for if you wish to take an island trip are Paimpol, Roscoff, Perros Guirec, Le Conquet, Brest, Le Fret, Audierne, Loctudy, Bénodet, Quimper, Concarneau, Lorient and Quiberon. Brittany also has 600 km of navigable waterway and those interested in hiring a boat should contact the **Comité de Promotion Touristique des Canaux Bretons et des Voies Navigables de l'Ouest**, Office de Tourisme, Place du Parlement, 35600 Redon. Canoeists can obtain information from **LBCK**, M. Hunaut, Ponthoen Servel, 22300 Lannion; and rowers should address the **Ligue de Bretagne d'Aviron**, M. Guengant, 1 bis rue de la Mairie, 29000 Quimper.

Cycling – Brittany is an ideal area for cycling holidays and bikes can be hired from main SNCF stations or cycle shops if necessary. Organised cycle tours, which can be adapted to your needs are run by **Abri** under their 'Bike Brittany' programme – see **Good Alternatives**.

Walking – walking and rambling are well catered for. The beautiful GR 34 runs along the northern Brittany coast (the Pink Granite coast), and other paths cross the region's interior. The Tour des Monts d'Arrée, which includes parish closes, is a magnificent one. The towpath of the Nantes-Brest canal also crosses the region from east to west. Maps, publications, information about hotels specially suitable for walkers, and organised holidays with or without guide are available from **Abri** (see **Good Alternatives**).

Riding – horseriding possibilities are contained in the 'Bretagne à Cheval' brochure, produced by the **Comité Régional de Tourisme** and mentioned under **Good Alternatives**.

Useful Local Contacts

A long-established regional nature protection organisation is the **Société d'Etude et de Protection de la Nature en Bretagne (SEPNB)**, 182 rue Anatole France, BP 32, 29276 Brest (Tel. 98 49 07 18), which has ten local groups, presides over a network of nature reserves and publishes a quarterly magazine. Information on the reserves is available from the SEPNB at Faculté des Sciences, Avenue le Gorgeu, 29200 Brest. Bird-watchers may wish to contact the **Station Ornithologique**, Réserve Naturelle les Sept-Iles, 22560 Pleumeur-Bodou. The headquarters of the **Parc Naturel Régional de l'Armorique** are at Menez Meur, Hanvec, BP 35, 29460 Daoulas (Tel. 98 21 90 69). For the addresses of some of its installations which offer outings providing particular insight into the local culture, see **Good Alternatives**. Information on the unusual culture of the Ile d'Ouessant is available from the **CEMO** (Ouessant Regional Study Centre), 29242 Ouessant (Tel. 98 48 82 65).

Geographical Breakdown of Region

Côtes d'Armor & Finistère

The recently rechristened Côtes d'Armor, whose new name harks back to Brittany's Celtic roots, and the popular *département* of Finis-tère, meaning 'world's end', contain between them the vast majority of Brittany's coastline, including the famous Pink Granite Coast and the jagged points which give Finistère its name. Inland are woods and hills, along with the unusual parish closes, unique to this part.

Dinan, in the north-eastern corner of the Côtes d'Armor, is a short and pleasant boat or train journey from the coast (St-Malo) up the river Rance. Its location made it historically important as an inland port and trading place, and its strategic castle and ramparts perch on a high plateau above the river. Dinan is a delightful town to wander round, its medieval streets full of charming half-timbered, top-heavy houses, many of which are now shops or cafés. Above the stone alleyways are artisans' hanging signs, window-boxes, steeples, turrets and lanterns. Below are souvenir stalls mostly selling handicrafts in brass or stained glass. Look out for the Place des Merciers, rue du Jerzual, Clock Tower and Governor's House in the old town, and the rue du Petit-Fort, a former craftsmen's street leading down to the river. In mid-July Dinan hosts the International Festival of Celtic Harp, and throughout October there is a Festival of the Ramparts. If planning a visit to Dinan, bear in mind that it is more rewarding to come out of season so as to avoid the crowds.

Back on the coast, the 70-metre vertical cliffs of **Cap Fréhel** are an unusual red-grey colour and offer spectacular views, particularly if you are energetic enough to climb the 145 steps to the platform of the lighthouse. **St-Brieuc** is the capital of Côtes d'Armor; the Cathédrale St-Etienne and the medieval quarter to its north are worth visiting, and there is a good view of the Aubet valley from the Tertre Aubé hill. A little way inland, **Lamballe** has a Golden Gorse Festival in mid-July, while **Mur-de-Bretagne**, right in the interior of the peninsula is a good base for walking or, indeed, for any off-the-beaten-track exploration of the countryside. **Guingamp** holds a Festival of Breton Dancing in mid-August. On the most northerly section of Brittany's coast is **Perros-Guirec**, from where you can take boats out to the Ile aux Moines, the largest of the islands belonging to the Sept-Iles nature reserve. The stretch of coast from Perros-Guirec to **Trébeurden** is part of the Pink Granite Coast (Côte de Granit Rose), and the cliffs are hugged by a spectacular road known as the 'Corniche Bretonne', which gives splendid panoramas. You can also explore the coast by taking the 'Sentier des Douaniers' (Cliff Path of the Customs Officers) between Perros-Guirec and **Ploumanac'h**. On the Corniche Bretonne is **Trégastel**, a popular resort which describes itself as the 'Jewel of the Pink Granite Coast': the unusual rocks which you will find here, on Ile Renote, Plage de Coz-Porz and the Grève Blanche, certainly make it worth a visit. It also has an interesting thirteenth century church and a sea-water aquarium housed in caves.

Over the border in Finistère is the town of **Morlaix**. Attractively huddled beneath a double-tier pink granite railway viaduct, Morlaix sits in the gorge carved by the confluence of the Jarlot and Queffleuth with the Morlaix river. The central streets (Grand Rue and Place des Halles) are filled with half-timbered houses, notably the Maison de la Reine Anne, while the more bohemian St-Mathieu quarter has several inexpensive restaurants. A landmark in Morlaix's history was 1522 when English sailors came up the river to ransack the town. Its citizens, who had been away at neighbouring fairs, returned to find the English getting drunk in their cellars, and battle broke out. Nowadays English tastes can be indulged in 'coreff', the town's locally brewed English-style real ale. Morlaix is an ideal base for touring some of northern Brittany's attractions, situated as it is with the Pink Granite Coast to the north-east; the Arrée Mountains to the south; and the parish close villages of **St-Thégonnec, Guimiliau** and **Lampaul-Guimiliau** to the west.

To the north-west of Morlaix is an intensive market gardening area, where fields of cabbages and artichokes seem to stretch to the horizon. At one point they are dominated by the twin spires of the twelfth- to sixteenth-century cathedral of **St-Pol-de-Léon**. Next to St-Pol is the port of **Roscoff**. This is where Brittany Ferries' service from Plymouth docks and, surprisingly, the town makes a good choice for a family summer holiday. Tourist facilities are well developed but have not detracted from the charm and character of the port and town. You can take a short boat trip to the **Ile de Batz** from here, and Roscoff also has an exotic garden, marine aquarium and algae centre. To the south-west, the town of **Lesneven** claims to be the 'most scholarly in France': out of a population of 7000, 5000 are currently attending educational establishments! The highlights of the town are its Place le Flô and Musée de Léon; the latter is housed in a chapel and presents the history and life of the Léon area from earliest times to this century. **Plouguerneau** is a popular seaside resort, well-situated for exploring some of the historical stone monuments and buildings inland.

From **Le Conquet**, further down the rocky coastline, it is possible to take boats to the islands of Molène and Ouessant (also called Ushant), situated in what is known as the Iroise Sea, and part of the Armorique regional park. The Ouessantine culture is unique, reflecting the dictates of life on an island, and is presented and promoted in the Maison Ouessantine in the hamlet of Niou-Hella. Ouessant also has a Lighthouse and Beacon museum, centring around the Creach lighthouse. For discovery of a truly foreign culture, a visit to the island is highly recommended. A complete contrast is provided by the city of **Brest**, almost wholly rebuilt after the war. The remains of its maritime past can be seen in its château and the Tour Tanguy. It also has a botanical conservatory (at 52 allée du Bot) and some pleasant flower gardens. **Plougastel-Daoulas** is the site of a typical calvary, built of granite and ochre in 1602–4 to celebrate the end of the 1598 plague. Neighbouring **Daoulas** has a parish close and fifteenth- to sixteenth-century abbey with medicinal plant garden. The headquarters of the Armorique regional park are just inland at the Domaine de **Ménez-Meur – Hanvec**, an estate developed by a gold prospector in the middle of beautiful woods. There is also an animal park, with areas for wild animals, farm animals and for the genetically recreated aurochs (wild ox). Interesting forest walks start from here, and there is also a Breton Horse Museum which shows the importance of the horse in rural Breton society.

Scattered thoughout the park are a number of museums, craft centres and *écomusées*: the Ecomusée des Monts d'Arrée is split between the Moulins de Kerouat at **Commana**, where there are two traditional water-mills and a tannery, and the Maison Cornec at **St-Rivoal**, a 1702-house typical of the region. The Moulin de Vergraon, near **Sizun** houses the Water, River and Fishing museum, with a fish-farming museum in an annex, while the Pilhaouerien museum at the former presbytery in **Loqueffret** recalls the history of the semi-nomadic rag-and-bone men of the Monts d'Arrée. The Ferme St-Michel at **Brasparts** houses the Maison des Artisans craft museum, where 250 highly regarded craftworkers and artists display their creations.

At the eastern edge of the park, **Huelgoat** (meaning 'high wood') is a popular centre for exploring the Monts d'Arrée area. The mountains rise to 400 metres and their sharp granite peaks (**Roc'h Trévézal**, for example) are wild and barren. The lower slopes resemble open moorland and are clothed in gorse and heather in autumn, while the valleys and lake areas are thickly forested (mainly with deciduous trees, though there was considerable damage during the October 1987 hurricanes) and well-covered with ferns, mosses and bog-plants. The whole mountain area is marvellous walking country and information about routes and wildlife species is available either from Tourist Information in Huelgoat or from the park headquarters at Menez-Meur. Huelgoat is famous for its unique rock formations resulting from erosion and deposits of massive granite rocks: the rounded shapes have been given evocative names like 'Chaos du Moulin', 'Grotte du Diable', 'Ménage de la Vierge' (The Virgin's Kitchen Pots), and 'Roche Tremblante'.

Further south, at **Châteauneuf-du-Faou**, mid-August brings an International Festival of Traditional and Popular Dancing and, just across the river Aulne, the park of the Château de **Trévarez** has a unique collection of ornamental shrubs. If you follow the river Aulne almost to the sea, you will come to **Trégarvan**, where the school has been turned into a museum presenting the history of schooling in rural Brittany. On a promontory nearby stand the ruins of the fifth-century abbey of **Landévennec**, with its museum retracing the settlement of monks in Brittany in the early middle ages. Palm trees grow here and the Celtic connections are very strong, right down to the 'St Patrick Bar' which serves Irish beer. You are now on the **Crozon peninsula**. The French consider the outline of the Brittany peninsula as a whole to resemble a wolf's head with open jaws, snapping at the Atlantic: according to this image, the Crozon peninsula forms the wolf's tongue. Here you will find the kind of rugged, moss-covered, grey-stone fishermen's cottages typical of the Lizard or County Kerry, and it is certainly worth staying over in this mellow backwater, rather than simply making it a day trip as do most people. **Camaret-sur-Mer** and **Morgat** are small resorts, good for family holidays as they offer plenty of seafaring activities. 'Club Leo' at Camaret has a sailing school, as well as scuba diving, surfing, sailboarding and fishing. The town is an old lobster port with authentic quayside seafood restaurants. Morgat offers boat trips to nearby caves, and the Maison des Minéraux at **St-Hernot** displays fossils and minerals tracing the 700 million years of Armorican geology; it is also the starting point for guided geological tours, either by foot or mountain bike (see **Good Alternatives**).

Back at the entrance to the peninsula is the 330-metre **Menez Hom** (meaning 'giant hill'), isolated to the west of the main mountain range. **Châteaulin** is a pleasant town with shady quaysides, which is far enough up-river to be non-tidal and, therefore, a centre for salmon-fishing. At the beginning of the year it draws crowds of enthusiasts, all eager to see the fish swim and leap upstream to spawn. **Locronan** is a cameo medieval granite village, situated below the Locronan mountain in a gap between forests. It is a popular tourist attraction whose focal point is the fifteenth-century Le Pénity church. The cobble-stoned village has gained fame from use in film sets, notably in Polanski's *Tess* to portray a Wessex village. Today the well preserved stone buildings mostly sell pricey arts and crafts. Nearby **Douarnenez** is a commercial port where fresh catches of lobster, sardine and deep sea fish are sold on the quayside at Port de Rosmeur. It can also be reached by ferry, across the Bay of Douarnenez, from Morgat. The Musée du Bateau here has good exhibits which help explain the maritime background of the people of the bay. From Douarnenez, boat excursions will take you to the bay's beauty spots. There is a delightful stretch of coast between **Tréboul**, a sailing port, and the **Sables Blanc** beach, linked by a winding coastal path lined with charming village houses, and the area in general is good for coastal walks. Watching the sun setting over Crozon opposite, while sail-boats bob below, is a special treat.

Audierne is an attractive fishing port on the way out to the westerly *pointes* – outposts lashed by the Atlantic – and boat trips to the Ile de Sein start from here. In summer, it is not worth joining the crawl of tourist traffic to see the **Pointe de Raz**, which is, in any case, mutilated by tourism paraphernalia. The **Pointe du Van** and **Baie des Trépassés** offer more natural panoramas. On Brittany's south coast, **Pont-l'Abbé** has a turreted castle which houses the Bigouden museum, offering an introduction to the way of life in the Pays de Bigouden, a remote corner to the west of Bénodet, where traditions have been slow to change. **Bénodet** itself is charmingly situated at the mouth of the picturesque Odet river. The view from the Odet bridge of the port flanked by wooded valley slopes is particularly scenic, and there is a good beach with plenty of watersports and other holiday activities. Boat trips to the **Iles de Glénan**, where

there is a nature reserve, can be taken from Bénodet, **Fouesnant**
and **Concarneau**. The latter is a popular resort, whose beach (to
the west of town) is rather unsightly, but whose old town is on a
narrow island surrounded by granite ramparts. This 'Ville Close'
was built between the fourteenth and seventeenth centuries and is
linked to the port by two bridges. The Museum of Fishing is housed
in the old Armoury. Further along the sheltered and popular stretch
of coast known as **Cornouaille** is **Pont-Aven**, which is famous for
being where Paul Gauguin lived and established a school of painters
before working in Tahiti. The Musée de la Ville exhibits some of
their works, and you can walk to the adjoining Bois d'Armour to
see the scenes which inspired them. The most attractive approach
to the town of **Quimperlé** follows the Laita river from the coast,
through the Forêt de Carnoët; the town itself is picturesque, with a
medieval quarter containing the Ste-Croix Abbey and Notre-Dame
de l'Assumption church.

Accommodation

First Class

Château de Kerminaouët, 29128 Tregunc (Tel. 98 97 62 20): 18
rooms in imposing, turn-of-the-century family manor house with
park. **Manoir de Kergrec'h**, 22820 Plougrescant (Tel. 96 92 56 06
and 96 92 51 29): 4 rooms in charming 17th century manor house on
Pink Granite coast; *tables d'hôte* on request. **Hostellerie de Keraven**,
50 rue de Côteau de Keranperc'heg, 29123 Pont-Aven (Tel. 98 06 16
11 and 98 06 16 50): 8 rooms in tree-shaded château-hotel in heart
of Gauguin country.

Middle Range

Repaire de Kerroch, 29 quai Morand, Port de Plaisance, 22500
Paimpol (Tel. 96 20 50 13): 7 rooms in 18th century house on fishing
port quay; restaurant serving classic dishes. **Ti Al-Lannec**, Allée de
Mezo-Guen, BP 3, 22560 Trébeurden (Tel. 96 23 57 26): 22 rooms
in airy family house offering friendly welcome; good restaurant with
sea view.

Economy

Hôtel Julia, 43 rue de Treflez, 29160 Crozon-Morgat (Tel. 98 27
05 89): 22 rooms in family-run hotel on Crozon peninsula; restaurant. **Hôtel les Voyageurs**, quai St-Laurent, 29120 Pont-l'Abbé

(Tel. 98 87 00 37): 19 rooms in pleasant, family-run hotel next to castle.

Eating Out

First Class

D'Avaugour, 1 Place du Champ-Clos, 22100 Dinan (Tel. 96 39 07 49): classic cuisine, based on seafood and varying according to the day's catch; also has 27 rooms.

Middle Range

Le Relais du Roy, 42 Place du Centre, 22200 Guingamp (Tel. 96 43 76 62): gastronomic regional cuisine in elegant surroundings; also has some rooms.

Middle Range/Economy

Hôtel des Sables Blancs, Plage des Sables Blancs, 29110 Concarneau (Tel. 98 97 01 39 or 98 97 86 93): finalist in 1989/90 Logis de France regional cuisine competition; also has 48 rooms.

Economy

Hôtel de l'Ecu, Place du Martray, 22270 Jugon-les-Lacs (Tel. 96 31 61 41): good value *prix fixe* menus.

Quimper

Formerly the capital of the Cornouaille province, some people here still wear local costumes on market days and at church.

The old town offers a good collection of half-timbered houses and town mansions, centred around the impressive **St-Corentin Cathedral**. The cathedral was built between the thirteenth and nineteenth centuries in a harmonious Gothic style. Inside, it is worth looking out for the fifteenth century flamboyant stained glass windows, high up in the nave and transept, and the frescoed side chapel. The **St-Mathieu church** and the riverside Romanesque **Notre-Dame de Locmaria** are also of interest. In the **Musée des Beaux Arts**, housed in the town hall, a variety of art-work is displayed, including a wide range of seventeenth century Flemish and Dutch paintings, nineteenth and twentieth century Breton paintings and some pictures of the Pont-Aven school, as well as work by Quimper-born Max Jacob and Pierre de Belay. The **Musée Départemental Breton** is also worth visiting, as it is housed in the former Bishops' Palace and contains exhibits on regional archaeology, ethnology, economy and way of life. Quimper is known for its colourful pottery, which has been practised in the Locmaria quarter since ancient times. The **Faïencerie de Quimper** contains an interesting pottery museum, and the **Henriot** pottery workshop (route de Bénodet, rue Haute, Tel. 98 90 09 36) and **Keraluc** workshop (14 rue de la Troménie, Tel. 98 90 25 29) can be visited by the public.

Accommodation

First Class/Middle Range

Hôtel Griffon, route Bénodet (Tel. 98 90 33 33): 49 luxurious rooms in hotel 3 kilometres from town; good restaurant.

Middle Range

Hôtel Gradlon, 30 rue de Brest (Tel. 98 95 04 39): 24 rooms in family-run hotel. **La Tour d'Auvergne,** 13 rue des Réguaires (Tel. 98 95 08 70): 43 rooms in family-run hotel; restaurant.

Economy

Hôtel le Transvaal, 57 rue J-Jaurès (Tel. 98 90 09 91): 44 rooms in family-run hotel with restaurant. **Hôtel de l'Ouest,** 63 rue le Déan (Tel. 98 90 28 35): comfortable rooms in friendly hotel convenient for station.

Eating Out

First Class/Middle Range

Le Capucin Gourmand, 29 rue des Réguaires (Tel. 98 95 43 12): good regional cooking with house specialities. **La Roseraie de Bel-Air,** route de Pont-l'Abbé, 29700 Pluguffan (Tel. 98 53 50 80): high quality restaurant, 4½ km out of town.

Middle Range

L'Ambroisie, 49 rue Elie-Fréron (Tel. 98 95 00 02): good cooking in reasonably central restaurant.

Economy

Le Steinway, 20 rue des Gentilshommes: good value *plats du jour* with seafood specialities in elegant setting. **Crêperie Victoria**, rue Ste-Catherine: serves typical Breton crêpes.

Entertainments

Experiencing a market day in Quimper or a traditional Breton language church service will bring you close to the Celtic heart of this town. The Festival de Cornouaille, which takes place here during the week before the fourth Sunday in July is another unique experience. In March, the town hosts an Art and Cinema Festival, in May various photography exhibitions, and, in August, numerous concerts. There are a dozen art galleries in the town centre, a good town theatre, and concerts are often performed at the Auditorium de Musique, in a former Jesuit chapel.

Useful Addresses

The extremely helpful **Tourist Office** is on Place de la Résistance (Tel. 98 95 04 69). The **Post Office** is at bd Amiral de Kerguélen and rue de Juniville. The **Hospital** is Centre Hospitalier Laennec, 14 bis ave Yves-Thépot (Tel. 98 52 60 60).

Transport Options

The tourist office offers good advice on any transport queries you may have. They run a twice daily guided tour of the town between mid-June and mid-September, and at other times on request. Bicycles can be hired from the train station or from **M. Hénaff**, 107 ave de Ty Bos. Town buses start from Place de la Résistance and tickets are valid for 40 minutes. Quimper is also a good base for making bus trips further afield (ask tourist office). It is a pleasant boat trip down the Odet to Bénodet or Loctudy, or as far as the Iles de Glénan.

Morbihan & Ille-Et-Vilaine

These two *départements* tend to be less visited, despite the fact that Morbihan's southern coastline enjoys an almost sub-tropical climate, and both *départements* have plenty of cultural attractions to offer.

From the modern town of **Lorient**, famous for its enormous

Interceltic Festival in the first fortnight in August, you can take a boat to the **Ile de Groix**. Here you will find the 'François le Bail' geological reserve and, at **Port-Tudy**, the Ile de Groix *ecomusée*, which contains a permanent exhibition on the natural, historical and ethnographical heritage of the island, and is the starting point for paths which allow you to discover elements of the maritime environment, including an inshore fishing boat. If you follow the river Blavet from Lorient inland, its valley becomes very attractive around the typical sixteenth-century Breton village of **Poul-Fetan**. Though the demonstration of rural crafts and traditions is quite obviously being put on for visitors, it still provides an insight into local life and helps to keep the crafts alive. **Pontivy**, situated further up the Blavet valley, where the river meets the Canal de Nantes à Brest, has a moated castle and good local cider, and makes an excellent base for exploring the surrounding area, including the beautiful **Forêt de Quénécan** to its north.

The castle of **Josselin** is the largest in Brittany and dates back to the 14th century. Rising majestically above the River Oust and completely dominating the picturesque little town, the château also houses a doll museum. At nearby **Guéhenno**, you can see one of the finest calvary crosses in Brittany. At **Brec'h**, on 2 rue du Penhoët, is the St-Dégan *ecomusée*, which presents the natural history and traditions of the Pays d'Auray. Brec'h is a terraced village on the banks of the river Loc'h and the museum, which preserves a group of Morbihannais buildings, suggests a walking trail across the village for visitors who wish to gain an insight into how local people live and work. **St-Anne d'Auray** is an important place of pilgrimage and the scene of the largest annual 'Pardon' in mid-July. There is also a good wax museum here. The Loc'h promenade gives a splendid view over the river to the medieval quarter of St-Goustin, which is well worth a visit.

No trip to Morbihan is complete without seeing **Carnac**'s staggering assembly of prehistoric stones, or megaliths. Breton names for the various types of stone, such as *menhir* and *dolmen*, have become universal. The most famous and interesting of the many formations of stone in the Carnac area are the *Alignements du Ménec*, which are massive upright stones stretching in straight lines for a full kilometre and probably erected between the second and fourth centuries BC. There are over 1000 menhirs, of which the tallest is over 4 metres. Why and how the stones came to be there remains a mystery, though there are no shortage of theories, some of which will be expounded to you if you choose to join one of the guided tours. The Musée de Préhistoire in Carnac presents plentiful artefacts found during excavations, many of which come from the St-Michel Tumulus, a 120-metre mound of burial chambers, covered with earth and stones to a height of twelve metres. There is a calvary on top of the tumulus and a fine viewing point of this site, which is the most ancient evidence of human activity in Europe.

From **Quiberon**, on the end of its own peninsula, you can take a boat to the **Belle-Ile**, a popular day-trip destination. Some ferries go to the pretty, Cornish-style village of **Sauzon**, though most head for **Le Palais**, the main town. The ferries take cars, and bicycles can be hired at the port; cycling is, perhaps, the best way to explore this island's varied and beautiful scenery, with its menhirs and castles. It is not surprising that the island boasts such historic residents as Claude Monet and Sarah Bernhardt. Belle-Ile offers you Brittany in miniature: tranquillity, picturesque coastal landscapes, historical curiosities and, most importantly, the sea. It is certainly worth staying here longer than the customary day-trip if you possibly can.

Locmariaquer, at the entrance to the Golfe du Morbihan, is famous for its oysters, which can be enjoyed in one of the various harbour-side restaurants; this is an infinitely more pleasurable experience than fighting your way to the town's congested beach! On Locmariaquer's outskirts are some further examples of megalithic structures, including the 'Table des Marchands', a set of table-like formations. This used to be the site of the largest menhir, the Witches' Stone, which was 20 metres high and weighed nearly 350 tons. Around 1800, it is said to have been struck by lightening and broken into four pieces, now known as the 'Grand Menhir'.

Vannes is the capital of Morbihan and the main port of the Morbihan Gulf. Its extensive medieval city, built in a series of squares composed of overhanging houses, backed by ramparts, comes to life on market day (Wednesday), when fine arrays of locally produced fruit, vegetables, cheese, honey, cider and flowers fill the streets, and the fish hall displays the Atlantic's best. The main attractions are the Cathédrale St-Pierre, the ramparts and the old wash-houses beside them, Place Henri-IV, the Maisons de Vannes and St-Vincent-Ferrier, and the Archaeological museum. The tourist office (1 rue Thiers) will give you a leaflet to inform you as you explore the old town. A visit to the wooded **Ile aux Moines** on one of the Vedettes Vertes which ply the gulf is a restful way to spend the afternoon. On summer Saturday evenings, the trip up to **Largoët Castle** (known as the Elven Towers) is rewarded by a superb *Son et Lumière* production, during which you can watch the figures of Tristan and Yseulte gliding across the lake, while dragons, horses, jousting, battles and flames help to tell their tragic story. The quiet backwater town of **Questembert** has an impressive covered market hall, built in 1552, and nearby **Malestroit** is home to the Breton Resistance Museum.

Over the border in Ille-et-Vilaine there are fewer places of interest and the *departement* is noticeably less Breton in atmosphere. However, the towns of **Vitré** and **Fougères**, almost on the frontier with Mayenne and mainstream France, are worth a visit. Vitré has some superb half-timbered houses and a castle which is one of the best remaining specimens of medieval Breton military architecture. The castle contains a museum of sculpture and decorative arts which help relate the history of the town. Vitré's Augustine monastery can also be visited. Fougères is another place with a medieval château and impressive old town, where evening street entertainment takes place in July and August. Greenery can be found in its public garden and the Fougères forest to the north-east, which is an excellent source of walks. Off to the north-west, **Bazouges-la-Pérouse** is the site of the Jardin de la Ballue, a succession of thematic gardens, including mazes, open only from 1 March to 15 April, and from 5 August to 15 September. Near **Bécherel**, the Caradeuc château has a large classical park, with statues, which offers a panoramic view of the upper Rance Valley.

Back on the coast, **St-Malo,** though crowded in summer, should not be missed. You can walk its massive granite 12th century ramparts for spectacular views of the city and sea, shop for Breton lace in its bustling streets, or visit the Gothic-style Cathédrale St-Vincent or the Quic-en-Groigne tower museum. What is most impressive about St-Malo is that the town was severely damaged during the Second World War, yet was painstakingly restored in its original style. Boat trips from here will take you to most places of interest along the Emerald Coast, and it is only a short hop across the Rance estuary to **Dinard,** a town attractively situated among headlands, bays and sandy beaches. It became a popular holiday resort in the nineteenth century, a fact to which its grand hotels, villas, casino and rows of striped canvas beach huts bear witness. **Saint-Briac-sur-Mer** hosts a Seagull Festival in mid-August and, a little way inland, the terraces of Le Montmarin at **Pleurtuit** dominate the Rance with their informal and formal gardens.

Accommodation

First Class

Château de Léauville, Landujan, 35360 Montauban-de-Bretagne (Tel. 99 61 10 10): 6 rooms in charming, tree-shaded château with friendly atmosphere; bicycles available and dinner on reservation. **Château de la Motte-Beaumanoir**, 35720 Pleugueneuc (Tel. 99 69 46 01): 8 rooms in château with lake and park; *tables d'hôte* on reservation. **Château des Blosses**, 35460 St-Ouen-la-Rouerie (Tel. 99 98 36 16): 6 rooms in historic 19th century château; *tables d'hôte* on advance reservation.

Middle Range

La Korrigane, 39 rue le Pomellec, 35403 St-Malo (Tel. 99 81 65 85): 10 rooms in elegant mansion, furnished with antiques, just south of harbour. **Auberge des Deux Magots**, 1 Place du Bouffay, 56130 La Roche-Bernard (Tel. 99 90 60 75): 14 rooms in 17th century house with welcoming owners; restaurant serves traditional regional dishes.

Middle Range/Economy

Le Roof, Presqu'île de Conleau, 56000 Vannes (Tel. 97 63 47 47): 13 rooms in smart, welcoming hotel on Gulf of Morbihan; restaurant with seafood specialities.

Economy

Hôtel de la Mairie, 26 Place de la Mairie, 56400 Aurey (Tel. 97 24 04 65): 21 rooms in family hotel with restaurant. **Hôtel le Villeneuve**, Route de Vannes, 56300 Pontivy (Tel. 97 39 83 10): 10 rooms in family hotel with restaurant.

Eating Out

First Class

Château de Locguénolé, route de Port-Louis, 56700 Hennebont (Tel. 97 76 29 04): rich Brittany cuisine in exceptionally attractive setting; also has 35 luxury rooms. **Restaurant le Bricourt**, 1 rue Duguesclin, 35260 Cancale (Tel. 99 89 64 76): gastronomic restaurant with charming welcome and seafood specialities, in eighteenth-century family house.

Middle Range

Auberge Bretonne, 2 Place du Guesclin, 56130 La Roche-Bernard (Tel. 99 90 60 28): light cuisine in fixed price menu form, using freshest local ingredients; also has 5 rooms. **La Taverne de l'Ecu**, 12 rue de la Baudrairie, 35500 Vitré (Tel. 99 75 11 09): gastronomic and traditional cuisine in 16th century half-timbered house.

Economy

Crêperie Chez Chantal, 2 Place aux Herbes, 35400 St-Malo (Tel. 99 40 93 97): one of the best-value and most authentic crêperies in Brittany. **Auberge au Gai Bec**, 4 rue des Lauriers, 35400 St-Malo (Tel. 99 40 82 16): excellent seafood and friendly atmosphere.

Rennes

The capital of Brittany, Rennes, is a flourishing city with medieval, classical and modern quarters. The seventeenth-century **Palais de Justice**, formerly the Brittany Houses of Parliament, is impressive both outside and in; the richly decorated interior may be visited. The **Mordelaise Gate** marks the entrance to the medieval quarter, whose half-timbered houses have inner courtyards and wooden staircases. The nineteenth-century **Cathédrale St-Pierre** and the **Eglise St-Sauveur** are both worth a visit, as is the 18th century **Town Hall** on Place de la Mairie. The **Musée de Bretagne** recalls the regional history of Brittany, from prehistoric times to the present day, and the **Musée des Beaux Arts** contains works of art ranging from fourteenth- to twentieth-century, including a fine collection of eighteenth-century pottery. On the route de Châtillon-sur-Seiche in the south of the city is the **Ecomusée de la Bintinais**, which traces the daily life of the inhabitants of a Bintinais farm over five centuries, so giving a clear insight into the social, cultural, architectural and environmental evolution of the Pays de Rennes. Peace and quiet can be enjoyed in the nineteenth-century **Thabor Garden** on Place Ste-Mélanie, a former abbey garden, landscaped in different fashions and dotted with various structures including sculptures.

Accommodation

Rennes' first-class hotels are all of the large-scale chain variety. Try instead:

Middle Range

Hôtel le Président, 27 ave Janvier (Tel. 99 65 42 22): 34 rooms in hotel in south of town. **Hôtel Germinal**, 9 cours de la Vilaine, au bourg, 35510 Cesson Sévigné (Tel. 99 83 11 01): 20 rooms in old mill-house with garden, on Vilaine river 6 km from town; restaurant. **Les Forges**, 22 ave du Général-de-Gaulle, 35530 Noyal-sur-Vilaine (Tel. 99 00 51 08): 11 pretty rooms in peaceful hotel near autoroute, 12 km from town; excellent restaurant.

Economy

Garden Hotel, 3 rue Duhamel (Tel. 99 65 45 06): 24 quiet rooms in hotel with courtyard, close to river. **Hôtel de Léon**, 15 rue de Léon (Tel. 99 30 55 28): comfortable rooms in friendly hotel near river.

Eating Out

First Class

Ti-Koz, 3 rue St-Guillaume (Tel. 99 79 33 89): imaginative cuisine with regional nuances served in early 16th century historic house with carved wooden façade, antique furniture and exhibition of Breton costumes; booking advisable. **Le Palais**, 7 Place du Parlement (Tel. 99 79 45 01): light cuisine using freshest ingredients (fish dishes recommended) in well-situated restuarant.

Middle Range

Le Corsaire, 52 rue d'Antrain (Tel. 99 36 33 69): classical cuisine which varies with the season. **L'Auberge St-Sauveur**, 6 rue St-Sauveur (Tel. 99 79 32 56): traditional cuisine in 15th century half-timbered house.

Economy

Le Boulaingrain, 25 rue St-Melaine (Tel. 99 38 75 11): cosy restarant with wide range of crêpes, housed in former prison. **Au Jardin des Plantes**, 32 rue St-Melaine (Tel. 99 38 74 46): good value fixed price menus in attractive half-timbered house, popular with local clientèle.

Entertainments

Ask the tourist office for its 'Spectacles, Informations' leaflet. The Maison de la Culture on Avenue Janvier, designed by the architect of the Palais de Chaillot in Paris, contains a theatre, cinema, exhibition gallery and discotheque. At the end of June or beginning of July comes the 'Tombées de la Nuit' festival, involving dancing and special events with a regional emphasis. There is an antiques fair in October, and the 'Transmusicales' rock festival in December.

Useful Addresses

The **Tourist Office** is at Pont de Nemours (Tel. 99 79 01 98). The **Post Office** can be found on Place de la République, and the **Hospital** is Hôpital de Pontchaillon, Rue Henri-le-Guilaux (Tel. 99 59 16 04). For emergency **medical assistance** phone SAMU on 99 28 43 15.

Transport Options

The tourist office runs daily or twice daily guided tours from 15 June to 15 September, though these can be arranged throughout the rest of the year on request. Bicycles can be hired at the railway station, and buses from Bd Magenta serve many neighbouring towns and villages. If planning to explore the area by bicycle, horseback, canoe or on foot, drop in to the ABRI association at 9 rue des Portes Mordelaises (Tel. 99 31 59 44) for friendly advice.

2 Normandy

For the British, Normandy is an easily accessible and popular destination. With a landscape and climate similar to those of southern England, it has cultural and gastronomic attractions that are undeniably French. Often compared unfavourably to neighbouring Brittany, it does have its own distinct charm and character which has long made it popular with Parisians and artists alike.

There are two distinct aspects to the landscape of Normandy. Along the coastline, jagged abrupt chalk cliffs that defy the attack of the channel tides alternate with deserted beaches and sand-dunes made famous by the D-Day landings of June 1944. Each part of the coast has been given a tourist tag; the Alabaster Coast of Upper Normandy, the Côte Fleurie and Pearl Coast of Lower Normandy. Arriving by ferry in Le Havre or Dieppe is a more pleasant introduction to France than that afforded by the more northerly ports of entry. Dieppe in particular is a bustling place with good restaurants and colourful markets. Along the coast are other towns of interest: Fécamp and Honfleur, fishing ports and holiday resorts with a certain provincial charm, and Deauville with its upmarket but faded elegance, a collection of holiday villas, a casino and racecourse. At the most westerly point, where Normandy meets Brittany, lies the impressive, though touristy, Mont-St-Michel with its medieval abbey and endless souvenir shops.

Inland, it is a country of apple orchards, grazing dairy cows, rolling green hills punctuated with woodland and forest. The prettiest parts are perhaps the Pays d'Auge, with its imposing manor houses and half-timbered farm buildings, and some parts of the meandering Seine Valley leading to Giverny, the one-time residence of Claude Monet. The major city is Rouen, whose cathedral is immortalised in a series of paintings by Monet. Caen was heavily bombed during the war and offers less for the tourist than nearby Bayeux, whose famous tapestry is far more interesting than school-book reproductions may suggest.

In France itself, Normandy is best known for its gastronomy. The rich grazing land produces butter and cheeses of which Camembert is the most famous. The cuisine is characterised by rich sauces. The apples are made into cider and calvados, while Benedictine liqueur is distilled in Fécamp.

The people of Normandy have a strong feeling of regional identity. Colonisation by the Norsemen, long periods of independence, then years of English rule – all have served to set them apart from the rest of France and give Normandy its unique character.

History

Normandy owes its name to the Vikings or Norsemen who first pillaged and then occupied the region during the ninth and tenth centuries. These Viking settlers were not, however, the first to invade Normandy; they were following in the footsteps of the Romans in 58 BC and then the Franks. It was the Franks who established the first abbeys, such as the one at Jumièges, and built up the wealth that subsequently attracted the attention of the Vikings. Their raids were devastating, particularly in the valley of the Seine, where they forced the monks to flee and the peasants to desert their fields. Finally a treaty was signed – perhaps because there was no booty left to loot – and the Viking Earl Rollo became Robert, the first Duke of Normandy.

There then followed a period of three hundred years in which Normandy was an independent dukedom. It was a period of prosperity: the monasteries destroyed by the Vikings were restored, the Benedictine abbey at Mont-St-Michel was built, as were beautiful cathedrals at Bayeux and Coutances. It was during this period that William the Bastard invaded England and became William the Conqueror, King of England and Duke of Normandy.

In 1205 Normandy became part of the Kingdom of France until, in 1415, the region was conquered by England's Henry V. This was the time of Joan of Arc, the French heroine who stood up against the English and was burnt at the stake for her troubles.

In 1450 the English left and Normandy became part of France once and for all. The subsequent centuries saw the development of Dieppe and Le Havre as flourishing ports, whilst agriculture was expanding to meet the demands of Parisians. The coming of the railways in the nineteenth century brought tourism to Normandy for the first time and Dieppe and Deauville became fashionable resorts.

The First World War left the region relatively unscathed, but the Battle of Normandy, which raged after the allied landings, destroyed villages and towns, leaving many civilians, as well as soldiers, dead or injured. Since 1945, much has been restored or reconstructed. New industries have been established and Normandy has been the site for the construction of two of France's nuclear power stations.

Geography

The varied landscapes of Normandy, its dramatic cliffs, its gentle pastures, are a legacy of the geological history of the region which naturally splits Normandy into two parts. The east was formed from layers of chalk and limestone later covered by fine soil which has become the lush green farmland of Upper Normandy. Where the chalk has been exposed by the waves of the English Channel, spectacular cliffs have been sculpted. The west is shale, sandstone and granite which has been folded, split and eroded to form the 'Alps' of Maine and the hills and valleys of Suisse Normande and, on the coast, the granite outcrops of the Cotentin peninsula. Upper Normandy (Haute-Normandie) comprises the Seine-Maritime and Eure *départements*, and its capital is Rouen; while Lower Normandy (Basse-Normandie) is made up of Orne, Calvados and Manche and has Caen as its capital.

In Normandy, each *pays* or landscape region has its own name, which does not correspond to the five administrative *départements*. In the east of Upper Normandy, the **Pays de Bray** is a pretty landscape of pastureland, orchards and woodland. Further west lies the **Pays de Caux** a chalk plain given over to arable farming, and the **Pays d'Auge**, an undulating region where cattle graze and cider apples grow. Winding through Upper Normandy is the **Seine Valley**, whose industries form, according to some ecologists, a potentially dangerous 'chemical corridor', which is counterbalanced by one of Normandy's two natural parks, the **Parc Naturel Régional de Brotonne**, an area of rich and varied forest and woodland which also includes the **Réserve Naturelle des Mannevilles**, a specially protected area of marshland. The park was first conceived (in 1974) as a green barrier between the industrial regions of Rouen and Le Havre. It has managed to combine the maintenance of agriculture, the development of artisanal activities, the rise in 'discovery' tourism and the protection of a cultural and architectural heritage threatened by anarchic urbanisation. In Lower Normandy, extending from the

Pays d'Auge to the Cotentin peninsula is the **Bocage** of Normandy, a landscape of small fields divided by hedgerows and earth banks which in springtime are covered in wild flowers. Further south are the hills of **Suisse Normande** and the **Parc Naturel Régional Normandie-Maine**. This park, created in 1975, extends into the Loire region. It is rich in beech copses and oak forests, and efforts have been made to develop forestry so as to encourage old traditions of carpentry and wood-carving. Cider-making also flourishes.

Such diversity of landscape results in a rich variety of flora and fauna. The beaches, dunes and cliffs of the coastline attract many different kinds of birdlife including gulls and terns, sandpipers, oystercatchers, teal, wigeon and shoveler duck. Inland, the forests of oak, beech and pine provide shelter for hundreds of species of wild plants including many types of edible mushroom. The forests are inhabited by foxes, hare, deer and even wild boar. Normandy boasts a large number of Nature Reserves, notably in the Manche and Calvados *départements*, many of which contain interesting plant and insect life. At the Cap Romain Geological Reserve there are remarkable reefs formed by fossilised sponges 165 million years old.

Climate

Considering their proximity, it's not surprising that Normandy's temperate climate is rather like that of England's south coast. Mild winters (January average maximum temperature: 8°C) and pleasant summers (August average maximum 20°C) are the norm – along with a fairly high annual rainfall. Although it rains more frequently in spring and late autumn, you might hit the odd downpour in summer so be prepared and pack a mac! (In August the average rainfall is 71mm.) If it does rain, don't despair. The chances are the weather will soon change, thanks to the influence of the sea.

Generally speaking, the coast enjoys a slightly milder climate than inland Normandy. However, if you are planning a beach resort holiday and hoping for a dip in the sea, your best bet is from June to September. As in southern England, the water can be decidedly chilly outside the high season!

Attractions

From the early nineteenth century, painters and holiday-makers were coming to Normandy to sample the delights of its coastline, and this is still a major attraction of the region. Honfleur is perhaps the pick of the coastal resorts with a busy port and quaysides bustling with tourists. Fécamp is more of a family resort although the beach is shingle. A visit to the Benedictine distillery is worthwhile. Deauville, one of the *original* seaside resorts of Normandy, aims for an upmarket clientèle with its casino and horse-racing. The most spectacular natural coastal scenery is at Etretat where a cliff top walk to see the chalk arches and needles is essential. The D-Day landing beaches which lie between Le Havre and Cherbourg are well signposted for visitors. There are few remaining clues to the battles which raged there: at Arromanches the artificial *Mulberry* harbour still lies in the sea; elsewhere, there are the cemeteries, memorials and museums which keep alive the memory of June 1944. The final attraction of the Normandy coastline must be Mont-St-Michel, completely swamped by tourists, yet undeniably an impressive sight, and designated a World Heritage Site by UNESCO.

Inland, the chief attraction of Normandy is its rural landscape. The woods, meadows and orchards of the Pays d'Auge, the meandering Seine Valley with its ruined abbeys and the regional park of Brotonne, the hills and valleys of Suisse Normande. Of the inland towns, Rouen holds the most interest for the visitor, particularly the cathedral of Notre-Dame and the half-timbered houses of Old Rouen. Bayeux is the other town the tourist will want to visit, not just for the tapestry, but also to see the wonderful Gothic cathedral.

Cuisine

Slimmers beware! If you're counting calories, Normandy's rich cuisine is not for you! One of France's truly great gastronomic regions, the chefs here specialise in cooking with cream. The culinary term *à la normande* means that a dish is served with a cream sauce usually laced with cider or calvados.

It's not surprising that cream is so widely used when you consider that Normandy's cattle provide more than half of France's total dairy output. Norman butter and *crème fraîche* (clotted cream) are renowned throughout the country as are several of its excellent soft cheeses. *Pont l'Eveque, livarot* and *camembert* are the best known of the thirty or so locally produced cheeses.

Thanks to its coastline, seafood features prominently in the cuisine. You can sample shrimps, lobsters, cockles, clams, mussels and scallops. Oysters are farmed around several coastal towns including St Vaast-la-Hougue and Courseulles-sur-Mer. Turbot, brill, mackerel and sole will often appear on the menu. Dieppe is famous for *sole à la dieppoise* (sole poached in cider or wine with cream, butter and mussels) and *marmite dieppoise* (fish and shellfish stew cooked with cider and cream).

Meat delicacies include *andouille de Vire* (a smoked chitterling sausage usually served cold), *rillettes* (soft potted pork) and lamb from the salt marshes of the Cotentin peninsula – ask for *agneau de pré salé*.

Caen is famous for *tripes à la mode de Caen* (featuring cows' stomachs, leeks, onions, carrots, calves' feet, herbs and cider or calvados). Rouen specialises in *caneton rouennais* (duck roasted in blood sauce after the bird has been strangled!), and Mont-St-Michel in *Omelette mère poulard* (a souffléd omelette invented in the hotel of the same name).

Normandy's orchards provide the apples or pears which are the basic ingredient in many local desserts. The sweet trolley may well tempt you with some delicious variation on *tarte aux pommes*, typically served with a generous dollop of cream! Look out for *bourdelos* (apple turnovers covered and baked in suet pastry), *douillons* (pear turnovers) and *beignets de pomme* (apple fritters). For an iced dessert try *coup normandie* (apple sorbet laced with calvados and a helping of cream).

Normandy may not boast any vineyards but it is famous for its ciders. The best are from the Vallée d'Auge. If you want to try 'pear cider' ask for *poiré*. Calvados is an apple brandy drunk traditionally in the middle of a meal to make space in your appetite, a *trou normand*, leaving room for yet more food. Pommeau, a mixture of calvados and apple juice, is also popular. The local liqueur is Benedictine, distilled in Fécamp.

Level of Tourism

Normandy is one of the oldest tourist regions in France. In the nineteenth century, Trouville and Deauville became established as fashionable resorts, while a cross-channel ferry service from Newhaven brought British tourists to Dieppe. The opening of the railway from Paris also made Dieppe a popular day-trip for Parisians. The growth of popular tourism in the south of France in the 1960s was a threat to Normandy's tourist trade but nowadays, despite being seen as something of a second best to the rival Brittany, it reports steady growth in the number of visitors each year. Lower Normandy is still more than half way down the hit parade of French tourist regions though, while Upper Normandy is near the bottom.

Normandy is positioned close to a large potential tourist market. It has the nearest seaside resorts to Paris; it is easily accessible by ferry from Britain (over two million tourists a year pass through Dieppe and Le Havre, for example); and it is only a day's journey from Belgium and parts of Germany and Holland. The French make up the largest proportion of the tourists who visit Normandy, followed by the Dutch, then the British, then the Germans. Around 24% of the region's visitors come from abroad. Tourism in Normandy comprises, in roughly equal proportions, long-stay high-season tourism; tourists who are passing through; weekend and short-stay tourists and, finally, second-home owners. The average length of a stay in a hotel in Upper Normandy is 1.5 nights and the average campsite stay is 3 nights.

In general terms, tourism is concentrated on the coast of Normandy, while the inland area remains quiet. Especially if you are *not* following a recommended tourist board trail, it is fairly easy to find quiet routes through attractive countryside and picturesque villages. The main exceptions to this rule are Giverny and the Seine Valley. The home of Claude Monet is the biggest attraction in the Eure *département* and, despite being open only from April to October, it receives more than a quarter of a million visitors each year. The Seine Valley is on all the guidebook itineraries and you are unlikely to be able to get away from other tourists as you visit the abbeys of Jumièges and St Martin-de-Boscherville. Rouen and Bayeux are the two cities which attract the most tourists.

Tourism on the coast is a seasonal affair. Beginning in July, it reaches a peak in the first two weeks of August and then begins to fall back. During this time accommodation is at a premium and the traveller without a reservation will have problems finding a room. The number of tourists has meant an increase in the services available, whether that means hiring a windsurfer or choosing a restaurant. The main resorts on the coast are Le Tréport, Fécamp, Honfleur, Trouville and Deauville. They do in fact look their best in high season when the crowds give the beaches, quaysides, promenades and restaurants a lively atmosphere. In the low season, when hotels and bars are often shut up, they can become lifeless places.

Mont-St-Michel, the sweetest honeypot in the whole of provincial France, with around 700,000 visitors a year, deserves special consideration. From a distance it retains a fairytale quality, a cluster of buildings on a rock fortress, topped by a graceful abbey spire, and all rising magically from the sea – or mudflats, depending on your timing. However, entering the gates you soon find yourself fighting through crowds of tourists, and climbing the winding road to the top, you are assailed from all sides by the worst in souvenirs and trashy trinkets. It goes without saying that any feeling of mystery you may have retained will be wiped out by the queue for the tour of the Abbey. The site is also under threat due to silting up and a rescue project is under way.

Good Alternatives

Meeting People

Gîtes de France offer an 'Almanach' of activities in Normandy covering a wide range of interests from flower arranging to a tour of angora goat farming. In addition, they have lists of farm holidays. The regional tourist boards will have details; otherwise contact the **Maison du Tourisme Vert**, Gîtes de France, 35 rue Godot-de-Mauroy, 75009 Paris. The **Chambre d'Agriculture de l'Orne** gives a list of farms where tourists can taste local products, whilst the Calvados tourist board offers a weekend course in cider-making – only available in November of course. Contact **Calvados Tourism**, Place du Canada, 14000 Caen. The Manche tourist board has a list of food producers who welcome visitors, including vegetable growers, mussel and oyster-bed farmers, and even two artificial insemination centres! They also organise a four-day 'package' tour of folk traditions of the area including cider-making and crafts. Contact the **Office Départemental du Tourisme de la Manche**, rte de Villedieu, 50008 Saint-Lô.

Perhaps one of the best places to meet people in Normandy is in the markets of the towns and villages. In a region where food is one of the priorities of life, the visit to the market is taken seriously. Each local tourist office will give details of market days in its area. Normandy also has its fair share of festivals. One of the most traditional is said to be the Fair of the Holy Cross at **Lessay**, south of Cherbourg. It takes place on the moor outside the town in September. There is also the Fête de Jeanne d'Arc at **Rouen** in May, a medieval festival at **Orbec**, a carnival in Dieppe and a sea festival at **Granville** all in August. The **Mont-St-Michel** has a July and a September pilgrimage, although both can be crowded.

Information about joining archaeological digs in Lower Normandy is available from the **Direction des Antiquités**, 22 rue Jean-Eudes, 14000 Caen (Tel. 31 86 37 10). For details of those in Upper Normandy, contact **Direction des Antiquités**, 12 rue Ursin Scheid', 76140 Le Petit Quevilly (Tel. 35 73 75 59).

Discovering Places

Normandy is admirably suited for walking or cycling and nearly a dozen GR footpaths cross the region. Two of the best are the GR 22/223 which follows the coast of the **Cotentin** Peninsula and the GR 221 through the hills of **Suisse Normande**. Either buy a map and guidebook and work out your own route, or follow a suggested *circuit*. Alternatively, join one of the organised tours, of which the departmental tourist offices often have their own; the Manche tourist board for example, in a brochure entitled 'Accueil et Loisirs', offers a range of walking and cycling tours on the Cotentin peninsula, while their horseback tour to the **Mont-St-Michel**, giving superb views of the abbey, is a good alternative to jostling with the other tourists on the *mont* itself. The Calvados tourist board publishes a leaflet called 'Circuits Vélo', a package which includes lodging, cycle hire, luggage transfer and all necessary maps. **Gîtes de France** in Calvados, and an association in Eure called **Rando-Risle**, 75 rue de la République, 27500 Pont-Audemer also have packages on offer. Details of horseriding tours can be obtained from the same sources.

The two regional parks of Normandy have their own programme of activities. Information on the **Parc Naturel Régional de Brotonne** can be obtained from the Maison du Parc, 2 Rond-Point Marbec, 76580 Le Trait (Tel. 35 37 23 16). The park has marked trails for walkers, pony-trekkers and cyclists and guided tours are also available, including bird-watching. The **Centre de Découverte de la Nature** takes parties into the Mannevilles reserve; contact CE.DE.NA., Place de l'Eglise, 27680 Sainte-Opportune-la-Mer. In and around the park are a collection of craft *Ecomusées* including a **Maison des Métiers** with Sunday afternoon demonstrations. The **Parc Naturel Régional Normandie-Maine** has 2900 km of signposted routes for walkers, cyclists and pony-trekkers.

Information and maps are available from the Maison du Parc, 'Le Chapître', BP 05, 61320 Carrouges (Tel. 33 27 21 15). The Cotentin marshland near **Carentan** is rich in flora and fauna and trips can be made in a small barge called a *gabare*. The local tourist office can arrange guided tours. They also offer trips around the coves and dunes of the Cotentin coastline and visits to the **Tourbière de Mathon** nature reserve.

Each tourist board in Normandy has a selection of tourist routes in its region. Each of these is on a theme such as cider or cheese. For something different, there is a dovecote (*colombier*) route in Seine-Maritime and a watermill route and granite route in Calvados. For the bookworm there is a *Route des Maisons d'Ecrivains* which includes museums related to the life and work of Flaubert and Victor Hugo. These routes are usually designed for the motorist, although parts can often be adapted for the cyclist. Details from the tourist boards of the region. The addresses for the Manche and Calvados tourist boards can be found under **Meeting People**. The **Office Départemental du Tourisme de Seine-Maritime** is at 2 bis rue du Petit-Salut, 76000 Rouen, and information on the whole of Normandy can be obtained from the **Comité Régional de Tourisme de Normandie**, 46 ave Foch, 27000 Evreux (Tel. 32 31 05 89).

Communications

How to Get There

Flights are available from London to Caen and Le Havre (Brit Air), Deauville (Aigle Azur) and Rouen (Air Vendée). There may soon be a flight from Manchester to Rouen.

Most people will, however, prefer the **ferry** option. Brittany Ferries run a service from Portsmouth to Caen (6 hrs) and a Truckline service from Poole to Cherbourg (4 hrs 15 mins); P&O leave Portsmouth for Le Havre (5 hrs 45 mins) and Cherbourg (4 hrs 45 mins); Sealink go from Newhaven to Dieppe (4 hrs) or from Southampton to Cherbourg (6 hrs). Bicycles are carried free of charge on all ferries, and combined train plus ferry tickets linking towns either side of the channel can be purchased.

A **coach** service is operated by Eurolines UK as far as Le Havre. For those travelling from South Wales, Bristol, Bath, and Salisbury, there is a service, via Portsmouth, to Rouen; and for those travelling from Birmingham, Oxford, Reading and London, there is a route, also via Portsmouth, to Caen.

When You're There

Rail – there is an extensive rail network in Normandy, with frequent trains and particularly good connections between the main coastal resorts and Paris. Major stations can be found at Rouen, Lisieux, Cherbourg, Granville, Caen, Alençon and Evreux, with plenty of minor ones in between. Three special tourist trains in the Manche *département* are the Marshland train from Carentan to Baupte; the Island Coast train from Carteret to Portbail, and the Mont-St-Michel Bay train, a steam train from Pontaubault to St-Hilaire. Timetable details are available from local tourist offices.

Bus – there is a reasonably comprehensive bus service linking the large towns, run by companies such as **Bus Vert** and **SNCF**, but their timetables are not really designed for sightseers.

Car – though Normandy has few motorways (the notable exception being the A13 'autoroute de Normandie', which links Paris to Rouen, Le Havre and Caen), its main roads are fast and straight. It is, however, a region whose best parts can be reached only by minor roads; this is particularly true on the Cotentin peninsula.

Boat – the coast has many places where boats or windsurfers may be hired. It is also possible to take cruises along the coastline or to Jersey, Guernsey or the Chausey Islands off the Cotentin coast. Trips can be made on inland waterways such as the Carentan canal and the rivers Douve and Seine.

Cycling – cycling is a good way of seeing Normandy. Bikes can be hired from many railway stations and the Normandie-Maine regional park offers information on cycling circuits.

Walking – many GR footpaths cross Normandy from east to west and north to south, the most important one being the GR 36 which links Normandy to the Mediterranean; it starts at Ouistreham. There are also many signposted short walks. Depending on your chosen area, information on the walking possibilities can be obtained from the headquarters of the regional parks, or from the **Comité Départemental de la Randonnée Pedestre**, BP 666, 76008 Rouen.

Riding – horseriding is popular in the region and there are many centres for it. Information is available from tourist offices, which will also have details on horse-drawn caravan hire.

Useful Local Contacts

The **Conservatoire des Sites Naturels de Normandie** shares its headquarters with the Nature Discovery Centre CE.DE.NA at

Place de l'Eglise, 27680 Sainte-Opportune-la-Mer) Tel. 32 42 02 37). The Conservatoire is a new association, created in 1989, which aims to safeguard the region's natural heritage. Information on the architectural and environmental heritage of Basse-Normandie can be obtained from the **DRAE de Basse-Normandie**, 1 bis rue Leroy, 14037 Caen (Tel. 31 44 45 00). The headquarters of Normandy's two regional parks are: **Parc Naturel Régional de Brotonne**, 2 Rond-Point Marbec, 76580 Le Trait (Tel. 35 37 23 16); and **Parc Naturel Régional Normandie-Maine**, 'Le Chapître', BP 05, 61320 Carrouges (Tel. 33 27 21 15).

Geographical Breakdown of Region

Haute-Normandie

This less-frequented, eastern part of Normandy comprises the Seine-Maritime and Eure *départements*. It has Rouen for its capital.

Rouen

Cut in half by the meandering River Seine, Rouen is a city of two personalities. On the one hand it is a leading tourist attraction, the site of many old and beautiful medieval and Renaissance buildings. On the other it is France's fourth largest port, the place where freight bound for Paris is transferred from barge to juggernaut. Its importance as a port was one of the reasons why the city suffered so badly during the Second World War. Since then, an ambitious and costly programme of restoration and reconstruction has brought the city centre back to something of its former glory.

All that the tourist will want to see in Rouen is confined to a small area on the *Rive Droite*, the right bank of the Seine. A good place to begin a tour is in the **Place du Vieux Marché**, the site on which Joan of Arc was burnt in 1431. There is a large **Croix de Réhabilitation** to mark the spot, a modern **Eglise de Jeanne d'Arc** which skilfully incorporates a sixteenth-century stained glass window from the Eglise de St-Vincent which was destroyed in the war. Less tasteful is the **Musée de Jeanne d'Arc** waxworks museum – an inappropriate medium to choose for one who was burnt to death. East from the square down the pedestrianised **rue du Gros Horloge**, there are many fine fourteenth-century half-timbered houses. The **Gros Horloge** itself is a large gilded clock mounted on a Renaissance arch which spans the street. The street opens out into the **Place de la Cathédrale** at the foot of the magnificent west facade of the **Cathédrale de Notre Dame**. This was the viewpoint that so fascinated Monet and led him to undertake his series of paintings which recorded the change of light on the Gothic carvings (albeit carvings untouched by twentieth-century air pollution). One of the Monet paintings can be seen at the **Musée des Beaux Arts** in Rouen. The cathedral was built between the twelfth and sixteen centuries although the tall cast-iron steeple was added in the nineteenth century. Inside, the two storeys of the Gothic nave are lit by light filtering through the beautiful stained glass windows. Look out for the tomb of Richard the Lionheart. It apparently contains just the heart. Behind the cathedral is the restored **Eglise St-Maclou** and, of perhaps more interest, the **Aître St-Maclou**, cloisters which were used as a charnel house for the victims of the plague. Carvings on the beams depict gruesome graveyard scenes. The nearby **rue Damiette** and **rue Eau-de-Robec** are lined with attractive old houses. The rue Damiette leads to the **Eglise St-Ouen**, a fine example of pure Gothic architecture as large and almost as imposing as the cathedral.

The most important collection of antique wrought-ironwork in the world can be seen in the **Musée Le Secq des Tournelles**. For a relaxing stroll, visit the **Jardin des Plantes** on avenue des Martyrs-de-la-Résistance, where there are many rare plants including a giant water-lily from the Amazon.

Accommodation

First Class

Hôtel de Dieppe, Place Bernard-Tissot (Tel. 35 71 96 00): 42 rooms in very pleasant hotel run by the same family since 1880: restaurant (see below). **Colin's**, 15 rue Pie (Tel. 35 71 00 88): the only other first class hotel in Rouen with under 50 rooms.

Middle Range

Versan, 3 rue Thiers (Tel. 35 70 22 00): 34 rooms in comfortable hotel.

Middle Range / Economy

Hôtel de la Cathédrale, 12 rue St-Romain (Tel. 35 71 57 95): 24 rooms in traditional hotel with half-timbered facade.

Economy

Hostellerie du Vieux Logis, 5 rue de Joyeuse (Tel. 35 71 46 44): pleasant rooms in old house: good restaurant. **Hôtel Normandya**, 32 rue du Cordier (Tel. 35 71 46 15): attractively decorated hotel.

Eating Out

First Class

Gill, 60 rue St-Nicolas (Tel. 35 71 16 14): restaurant run by a top chef not afraid to offer simple, homey regional cuisine. **Le Quatre Saisons**, Place Bernard-Tissot (Tel. 35 71 96 00): reputed restaurant belonging to the Hôtel de Dieppe; many regional specialities including duck.

Middle Range

Le Réverbère, 5 Place de la République (Tel. 35 07 03 14): restaurant with wide range of dishes including a delicious 'menu du marché'. **Le Saint Nicaise**, 17 rue de la Roche (Tel. 35 07 41 79): cosy restaurant in heart of old town; imaginative cuisine.

Economy

Les Flandres, 5 rue des Bons-Enfants (Tel. 35 98 45 16): friendly service of traditional dishes. **Pascaline**, 5 rue de la Poterne (Tel. 35 89 67 44): good value regional dishes.

Entertainments

Guided tours of the historic area of Rouen are available. It is also possible to have a tour of the ports. Details are available from the Tourist Office. There are two main festivals during the year: the Fête de Jeanne d'Arc at the end of May (processions and street theatre) and the Fête d'Eté de Seine-Maritime, a music and drama festival during July and August.

St-Maclou has a programme of organ recitals in August.

Useful Addresses

Local **Tourist Information** is at 25 Place de la Cathédrale (Tel. 35 71 41 77). The **Tourist Board** for Seine-Maritime is at 2 bis rue du Petit-Salut. The **Post Office** is 45 rue Jeanne d'Arc and the **Hospital** (Hôpital Charles-Nicolle) is 1 rue de Germont (Tel. 35 08 81 81).

Transport Options

Much of the old centre of Rouen is pedestrianised, so walking is the only way to get around. There is a comprehensive town bus service (information: TCAR, 79 rue Thiers), and another local service if you want to explore across the river. The station for buses to Le Havre and Dieppe is south-west of the Vieux-Marché in the rue des Charettes. The railway station is in the Place Tissot, north of the old town. **Clamageran Voyages**, 29 rue du Buffon run tours of the area. Bicycles can be hired from **Rouen Cycles**, 45 rue St-Eloi (Tel. 35 71 34 30).

Rest of Haute-Normandie

If you follow the Seine downstream from Rouen, you will find yourself on the popular tourist route known as the *Route des Abbayes du Val de Seine*. The first one you will come across is the ruined, though still imposing, **Jumièges Abbey**, situated among orchards just inside the Brotonne Regional Park. The park's headquarters are at **Le Trait**, where you will also find the **Ecomusée de Basse-Seine**, which presents the Seine economy, with its sailor-fisherman, traditional agricultural practices and ways of life, and its natural and cultural heritage. Across the river (by ferry) from here, and a little way south, is the **Moulin de Pierre** at **Hauville**, a thirteenth-century windmill, which is the only one in Normandy still to produce flour. At nearby **La Haye-de-Routot** is the **Four à Pain**, a faithful reconstruction of a nineteenth-century bakery, which functions one Sunday a month and organises bread-baking courses for both children and adults; you will also find a comprehensive clog museum, the Maison du Sabotier. Also worth a visit is the **Maison des Métiers** at **Bourneville**, which presents the traditional crafts of the region and includes studios, exhibitions, a museum and a shop.

The other side of the Forêt de Brotonne and across the Seine is the **Abbaye de St-Wandrille**, originally founded in the seventh century but still in use. The **Musée de la Marine de Seine** at **Caudebec-en-Caux** is devoted to the Seine river and those who make their living from it. The last Sunday in September sees a Cider Festival here. The **Musée du Pays de Caux** at **Yvetot** offers the most complete collection of objects associated with regional life. This is complemented by the **Musée de la Nature** at **Allouville-Bellefosse,** which presents Normandy's plants and animals as well as offering field trips (information from park headquarters). Also near Allouville is a 1000 year old oak tree, whose trunk is big enough to house two chapels, but which is sadly suffering from old age. Back near the Seine are the **Musée Victor-Hugo** at **Villequier** and the beautiful Renaissance **Château d'Etelan** at **St-Maurice.** Over the river, **Quillebeuf-sur-Seine** is an active port with a 'historical path'. **Sainte-Opportune-la-Mer** offers a fascinating **Maison de la Pomme,** which presents the apple in all its forms, from seedling to cider and calvados; its products are for sale. There is also a traditional blacksmith's forge here. **St-Samson de la Roque** boasts an impressive lighthouse and discovery paths. Further south, **Pont-Audemer** is an attractive old town.

The concrete city of **Le Havre,** now the second largest commercial port in France, is the work of the architect Auguste Perret, who was entrusted with the reconstruction of the city after its almost total destruction in the Second World War. Amongst Perret's constructions, the **Eglise St-Joseph** is worth singling out as the most successful. Le Havre's chief attraction is, however, the **Musée des Beaux-Arts André Malraux** on Boulevard J-F-Kennedy. The purpose-built galleries house a fine collection of nineteenth and twentieth century paintings by the Impressionists and the Fauvists, notably locally born artists Raoul Dufy and Eugène Boudin. Some boat trips start from Le Havre, taking you around the docks, up the Seine, or along the coast. A sea festival takes place here in July and a flower festival in August. North of Le Havre is the coastal resort of **Etretat,** where the chalk cliffs of the **Côte d'Albâtre** form arches and needles. Beyond here is the largest resort along this coastline, **Fécamp,** which used to have a substantial fishing fleet whose catches came from the waters of Newfoundland. Nowadays it is still a fishing port, but that economy is supplemented by the tourist trade. Its biggest attraction is its Benedictine distillery, open daily from Easter to November for tasting.

Up near **Varengeville-sur-Mer,** just south of Dieppe, is the **Parc Floral des Moutiers,** a stunning landscaped garden perched on a cliff-top, which seems at times almost Mediterranean in tone; it is open from mid-March to mid-November. The channel port of **Dieppe** deserves more than a cursory glance *en route* for the ferry. It is an active fishing port, the fifth largest in France, and has been an important seaside resort for the French since the nineteeth century. In 1942 it was the place chosen by the Allied Command for the 'Jubilee' raid, a costly rehearsal for D-Day; nearly a hundred Canadian soldiers lost their lives. The quayside is an ideal place on which to get a feel for the real Dieppe. While fishing boats offload on the east side of the Bassin Duquesne, fishermen sell their catch from the quay. The pedestrianised Grand'Rue is the site of a Saturday morning market. Nearby is the Eglise St-Jacques. The municipal museum, which is housed in a fifteenth-century château, has an interesting collection including maritime exhibits, ivory carvings (ivory was imported to Dieppe from Africa) and prints by the cubist Georges Braque. Two kilometres west of the town is the **Musée de la Guerre et du Raid du 19 Août 1942**, which tells the story of the Jubilee Raid. Dieppe has a carnival in mid-August and a November herring festival.

Right down in the Eure *département*, the Château Gaillard at **Les Andelys** offers a good introduction to the history of Normandy. The fortress, which is situated on a promontory overlooking a loop in the Seine, offers a magnificent view and bears witness to the area's bloody past. Further upstream is **Giverny**, where the Impressionist painter Claude Monet spent the last forty years of his life. This is a 'Site Naturel Classé' and both studio and gardens have been perfectly restored. The gardens, designed by Monet himself, became the artist's favourite subject for paintings, notably the famous water-lilies. The museum and gardens are open every day except Mondays, from 1 April to 31 October. Another impressive garden near **Vernon** is the park of the Château de Bizy, with its fountains, waterfalls and yew trees. In the market town of **Evreux**, you will find the beautiful Notre-Dame cathedral and a museum of popular arts and crafts. **Le Neubourg** and the 600-year-old château of **Harcourt** are both worth visiting. Harcourt also has an arboretum with a collection of rare trees.

Accommodation & Eating Out

First Class

Château de Brécourt, 27120 Pacy-sur-Eure Douains (Tel. 32 52 40 50 or 32 52 41 39): 24 rooms in elegant Louis XIII château, surrounded by moat and situated in a wooded park.

First Class/Middle Range

Manoir de Rétival, 76490 Caudebec-en-Caux (Tel. 35 96 11 22): 10 rooms in idyllically situated manor house in park; antique furniture: restaurant offering regional and seasonal specialities.

Middle Range

Auberge du Clos Normand, 22 rue Henri IV, Martin-Eglise, 76370 Neuville-les-Dieppe (Tel. 35 82 71 01): 9 rooms in simple village inn in heart of countryside; wooden beams: restaurant serving typically rich Norman cuisine. **Auberge du Vieux Puits**, 6 rue Notre-Dame du Pre, 27500 Pont-Audemer (Tel. 32 41 01 48): 14 rooms in family-run, half-timbered inn: cosy, highly-praised restaurant.

Economy

Les Airelles, 2 Passage Michu, 76270 Neufchâtel-en-Bray (Tel. 35 93 14 60): 14 rooms in family-run hotel: restaurant was finalist in the 1989/90 Logis de France regional cuisine competition. **M. et Mme Chatel**, rue de Quesny, Jumièges, 76480 Duclair (Tel. 35 37 24 98): 3 *chambres d'hôte* in restored Norman farmhouse owned by welcoming family.

Basse-Normandie

This more popular part of Normandy is composed of the Pays d'Auge and Suisse Normande, inland rural areas to the east and south of Caen; the southern Orne *département* with its regional park; and the long coastal area known as the Cotentin peninsula.

Caen

Caen was the Ducal seat of William the Conqueror in the eleventh century. It is now the capital of Lower Normandy. Like many of the towns in this area, Caen suffered badly during the Second World War. Three-quarters of the buildings were destroyed by Allied bombing as part of the D-Day offensive. Unlike Le Havre, some of the old monuments did remain intact although Caen cannot be said to be a beautiful city.

The **Abbaye aux Hommes** and the **Abbaye aux Dames** were built by Duke William and his wife Matilda as an act of penance; distant cousins, their kinship was objected to by the Pope and they were excommunicated. The building of the abbeys followed the lifting of the excommunication. The Abbaye des Hommes is a fine example of lofty Norman Romanesque architecture. William was buried here, but his grave was desecrated in the sixteenth century. Other old buildings dating from the thirteenth century are in the area around the Place St-Saveur and the rue aux Fromages. Look out also for the fourteenth-century **Eglise St-Pierre**, and, within the walls of William's ruined **château**, the exceptionally good **Musée des Beaux-Arts**. Also within the château walls is the **Musée de Normandie**, which focuses on the history of rural Norman life. The **Caen Memorial Museum**, north of town, is designed to be a museum of peace rather than war. For a pleasant stroll, try the spacious **Jardin des Plantes** on Place Blot.

Accommodation

First Class

Le Relais des Gourmets, 15 rue de Geôle (Tel. 31 86 06 01): 32 luxurious rooms in imposing, well-situated hotel: two good restaurants.

Middle Range

Le Dauphin, 29 rue Gémare (Tel. 31 86 22 26): 21 cosy rooms in former monastery: restaurant (see below).

Economy

Hôtel de la Paix, 14 rue Neuve-St-Jean (Tel. 31 86 18 99): comfortable rooms in friendly hotel. **Hôtel Demolombe**, 36 rue Demolombe (Tel. 31 85 48 70): centrally located.

Eating Out

First Class

Le Dauphin (for address, see above): excellent regional dishes, home-made with imagination. **La Bourride**, 15 rue du Vaugueux (Tel. 31 93 50 76): a wide variety of regional dishes using all-local produce.

Middle Range

Auberge de l'Ile Enchantée, 1 rue St-André, 14000 Fleury-sur-Orne (Tel. 31 52 15 52): riverside inn, 3 km from Caen, with traditional yet imaginative cuisine.

Middle Range/Economy

La Petite Marmite, 43 rue des Jacobins: elegant restaurant with Norman specialities.

Economy

Le Boeuf Ferré, 10 rue des Croisiers: generous portions of traditional cooking.

Entertainments

CROUS, a university-run office on 23 ave de Bruxelles, will supply you with a copy of 'Le Mois à Caen', which lists the month's theatre, concerts and exhibitions. Local people tend to frequent the jazz concerts given at the **Retro Piano Bar**, 9 rue Fresnel.

Useful Addresses

The **Tourist Office** at Place St-Pierre (Tel. 31 86 27 65) offers information not only on Caen itself, but also on the whole of Lower Normandy. The **Post Office** is on Place Gambetta, and the **Hospital** is Hôpital Clemenceau, ave Côte de Nacre (Tel. 31 44 81 12).

Transport Options

Bicycles can be rented from the train station (Place de la Gare, south-east of town centre). Buses ('Bus Verts') leave from next to the station to nearby towns, and **Viking Voyages**, 16 rue Général-Giraud, offer tours of the surrounding area.

Rest of Basse-Normandie

The coast stretching away to the north-east of Caen, between Cabourg and Trouville, is known as the **Côte Fleurie**. On it are a number of small seaside resorts, all crowded in the high season. **Cabourg** is the model for 'Balbec', the resort described in such detail in Proust's *A la Recherche du Temps Perdu*. The fashionable **Deauville**, whose successful casino was, incidentally, pinched from its twin resort, Trouville, has a short 'season' of horse-racing, when the international jet set congregate on the wooden boardwalk promenade along the seafront, known as 'Les Planches'. If Deauville lays claim to being the height of sophistication, then the older Trouville, on the other side of the River Touques, has retained a certain amount of its original fishing-village atmosphere.

Further along the coast, **Honfleur** is a picturesque port which has lost its beach to the slow silting up of the Seine estuary – the Boulevard Charles V was once the seafront. Boats can still tie up at the quayside however, although the Vieux Bassin is now filled with pleasure craft; the fishing boats use the Quai de la Quarantine. The Vieux Bassin is surrounded by attractive old buildings, many now turned into restaurants or private art galleries. This is painters' territory and modern pretenders are often seen trying to draw inspiration from the home of Eugène Boudin. Boudin used to meet with fellow impressionists in the Ferme St-Siméon, now a luxury hotel. The Eglise Saint-Catherine is worth a visit; it was built at the end of the Hundred Years' War by local shipwrights, using materials and techniques that they were familiar with, which is why the structure of the roof is reminiscent of an upturned boat. The Tourist Office is at 33 cours Fossés, next to the bus station.

The area around **Lisieux** is known as the Pays d'Auge and offers a glimpse of quintessential Normandy; a landscape of green rolling pastureland dotted with cows, apple orchards and half-timbered manor houses. Lisieux itself is a destination for pilgrims who come to the domed Basilique de Ste-Thérèse. Thérèse Martin, a Carmelite nun who entered the convent in Lisieux in 1888, was canonised in 1925 and is now the second patron saint of France. This area contains many picturesque small towns such as **Orbec**, whose streets are lined with houses constructed from timbers infilled with patterned brick. Nearby are the towns of **Livarot** and **Camembert**, which have given their names to the cheeses first produced there; Camembert even has a statue to Marie Harel who invented the famous cheese.

West of the Pays d'Auge, where the River Orne cuts through the **Gorge de St-Aubert**, is the area of wooded hills and valleys called **Suisse Normande**. It is a part much loved by walkers, pony-trekkers and canoeists. **Thury-Harcourt** and **Clécy** are two centres from which the area can be explored, and the tourist offices of both towns have details of activities in the area. A recommended walk from Clécy is to the **Pain de Sucre**, an outcrop above the Orne which gives magnificent views. In the town, the Manoir de Placy has been converted into a Norman craft and folk museum.

The area in the south-eastern corner of the Orne *département*, beyond **Mortagny-au-Perche**, is very sparsely populated and completely off the tourist track; exploring round here offers true immersion in rural French life. To its west is the **Parc Naturel Régional Normandie-Maine**, part of which extends down into the Loire region. The park offers good facilities for walking, cycling and horseriding (it has 1000 km of footpath and bridleway), and there is a short botanical discovery path through the Forêt d'Ecouves, starting from **Vingt-Hanaps**. The park's headquarters are at **Carrouges**, housed in a fifteenth century building belonging to the château. Apple and pear trees, of varieties in danger of extinction, form an orchard round the Maison du Parc. Information on the park and its activities can be obtained here. The town also hosts craft exhibitions, concerts and other displays designed to make the public aware of the local environment, architecture and traditions. **La Ferrière-aux-Etangs** is the starting point for another discovery path, and there is a **Maison de la Pomme et de la Poire** at **Barenton**, over in the Manche *département*. This contains a museum of traditions, displays of 'cidre' and 'poiré'-making, and a promotion centre for the final products.

The west coast of Normandy starts with the Mont-St-Michel in the south, gradually turning into the Cotentin peninsula in the north. Both belong to the Manche *département*, which offers a landscape of granite cliffs and, inland, areas of scrubland, bocage and marsh, woods and gentle hills. **Mont-St-Michel**, provincial France's top attraction and a UNESCO World Heritage site, goes back a long way. A monastic community was first established on the granite mound as early as the eighth century. Ramparts were built from the earliest times to defend the monastery from attackers, including the English. The medieval abbey comprises a Romanesque church and Gothic choir, crypt and cloisters which, together with the refectory, form the **Merveille**. A view of the ensemble from across the bay can be had from the Jardin des Plantes at **Avranches**. Further up the coast, **Granville** is a lovely fishing port with an eighteenth-century fortified **Haute Ville**. Boats leave for the Channel Islands from here. **Coutances** is the most attractive inland town, perched on a hill and crowned with the towers of the cathedral and the churches of St-Nicolas and St-Pierre. With mountainous dunes as a backdrop, vast areas of flat sandy beaches are revealed at low tide around **Carteret**. The dramatic cliffs at the **Nez de Jobourg** and at the **Cap de la Hague**, at the western tip of the peninsula, are some of the tallest in Europe. It is probably not worth lingering in the area's main town, **Cherbourg**, which is in the middle of the rocky north coast.

In contrast to the north and west, the east coast of the peninsula is sheltered. The two chief resorts are **Barfleur** and **St-Vaast-la-Hougue**, famous for its oysters. The dunes and sandy beaches of the Calvados coastline are where the Allies landed on D-Day, 6 June 1944. Except for the 'Mulberry Harbour' at **Arromanches**, there are few physical clues to the battles that raged from the Cotentin peninsula in the east to **Ouistreham** in the west. There are however many memorials, musuems (at **Pegasus Bridge, Arromanches** and

Caen), and cemeteries (**Hermanville, St-Laurent-sur-Mer** and **La Cambe** for example), which serve as a reminder.

A reminder of still earlier battles comes in the form of the tapestry to be found at **Bayeux**, just inland. In France the embroidered linen cloth tapestry is known as 'La Telle du Conquest', but it is also a great attraction for British visitors, as 1066 is the one date in history about which most people feel knowledgeable. The tapestry is well displayed at the Centre Culturel Guillaume le Conquérant. It is also worth visiting the nearby Cathédrale de Notre-Dame, a fine example of thirteenth-century Gothic architecture with Romanesque elements.

Accommodation & Eating Out

First Class

M. et Mme Chahine, Le Prieuré St-Michel, 61120 Crouttes (Tel. 33 39 15 15): 5 beautiful rooms in a Benedictine priory founded in the tenth century (open Easter to November). **Le Castel**, 7 rue de la Cambette, 14400 Bayeux (Tel. 31 92 05 86): 4 *chambres d'hôte* in eighteenth century town mansion in park on outskirts of Bayeux.

Middle Range

Château de la Salle, Montpichon, 50210 Cerisy-la-Salle (Tel. 33 46 95 19): 10 spacious rooms in comfortable château-hotel: restaurant. **Hôtel de la Marine**, quai du Canada, 14117 Arromanches (Tel. 31 22 34 19): 30 rooms in family-run hotel: restaurant was finalist in 1989/90 Logis de France regional cuisine competition.

Middle Range / Economy

Hôtel de la Coupe d'Or, 49 rue Pont Mortain, 14100 Lisieux (Tel. 31 31 16 84): 18 rooms in quiet, family-run hotel: restaurant.

Economy

Mme Courtois, Le Bas Chêne, St-Victor-de-Réno, 61290 Longny-au-Perche (Tel. 33 73 65 22): *chambres d'hôte* accommodation – attractive rooms and authentic farm welcome: *tables d'hôte*. **Mme Vermes**, Ferme d'Ailly, 14170 Bernières d'Ailly (Tel. 31 90 73 58): 4 *chambres d'hôte* in old farmhouse owned by friendly family: *tables d'hôte*. **Mme Lemarie**, Ferme de l'Hermerel, Gefosse Fontenay, 14230 Isigny-sur-Mer (Tel. 31 22 64 12): 3 *chambres d'hôte* in seventeenth century manor house near sea: *tables d'hôte*.

3 Nord & Pas-de-Calais

Ask any British tourist who has been to France for an opinion about Nord/Pas-de-Calais and you are likely to get predictable replies. They will either recall flat agricultural plains divided into monotonous green, yellow and brown fields or a heavily industrialised landscape of ugly factories and belching chimneys. These will have been the tourists who simply used the region as a preface to their 'real' French holiday. On the other hand, for those who are just day trippers keen to get their money's worth from a trip to the Continent, the North may appear simply to be one vast hypermarket crowded with fellow Brits cramming their trolleys with beer and Boursin.

Of course there is more to the region than this, but it would be pointless to try to argue that Nord/Pas-de-Calais offers hidden jewels to rival the delights of Paris or more southerly regions of France. However, for the tourist on a short-stay travel hop, or for the traveller who has mistimed the return to the Channel port, there are attractions in the region which would reward time spent there.

Whether it is cliff-top walks, lazing amongst the dunes, wind-surfing or bird-watching, it is the coastline of the region called the Côte d'Opale which holds the most attractions for those who love the outdoors. The extreme tip of the coastline, high chalk cliffs called the Deux Caps, is a designated national beauty spot. Boulogne is the most pleasant of the Channel ports and inland there are towns worth visiting, notably Lille with its fine citadel, Douai, St-Omer and Arras, the latter being very much the pick of the bunch. There are cultural attractions; the *Musée des Beaux Arts de Lille* is said to be second only to the Louvre, whilst a different type of museum is the *Centre Minier Historique* at Lewarde. Finally, the visitor could not miss the neat monuments and cemeteries, testament to the ferocity of the fighting of the two World Wars which took place throughout the whole of the north.

The position of Nord/Pas-de-Calais made it inevitable that the ground would become well trodden by conquering armies – Celts,

Franks, Germanic tribes, Romans and even the English have laid claim to the soil at one time or another. With one eye on the white cliffs of Dover and one on the Flemish speaking Belgians, it is not surprising that the northern French seem a different race from their southern cousins and that the British visitor who takes time to stop and sample this region can feel so much at home.

History

In order to see the history of Nord/Pas-de-Calais in its true perspective, the key date to be remembered is 1713 when the whole region became part of France for the very first time. Its history up until then is one of changing masters and shifting borders.

The region was inhabited by Celtic tribes until the first century, when the Romans made it part of their Belgian province. Their hold was broken after the second century by the invasion of Germanic armies. The region suffered Viking raids in the ninth century, but this did not prevent the establishment and subsequent growth of the principalities of Flanders in the West, Artois in the South and Hainaut in the East.

The thirteenth century saw these principalities allied with the English crown. Although this alliance was not to last long, Shakespeare ensures we will not forget the battle and English victory at Agincourt on St Crispin's Day 1415; Calais continued to belong to the English until 1558.

Gradually, piece by piece, the region became part of the Kingdom of France and the Treaty of Utrecht in 1713 established the borders that exist today. It is perhaps not surprising, however, that despite those political borders, Flemish patois can still be heard in Lille – a legacy of that previous deep-rooted allegiance.

The eighteenth and nineteenth centuries saw growing prosperity come to the region. The development of modern agricultural methods was followed by the discovery of coal which brought with it the growth of heavy industry, as chronicled by Zola in *Germinal*.

The fields of Flanders will of course be remembered as the battleground for some of the fiercest confrontations of the First World War. Some of the heaviest Allied losses were suffered where the Hindenburg (or Siegfried to the Germans) line passed through Vimy and Cambrai. There was scarcely less devastation in the

Second World War when the region fell under the control of the German Reich.

Nowadays, Nord/Pas-de-Calais sees itself as a forward-looking region with the old coal-based industry replaced by high-tech manufacturing. It boasts the youngest average population in France and it has a key geographical position in the context of a united Europe, a position which can only be emphasised by the opening of the Channel Tunnel.

Geography

Nord/Pas-de-Calais is the most northerly region of France. It has a 350 km border with Belgium and 140 km of coastline. The old principalities of Flanders and Artois have been replaced by two *départements*; Nord in the north-east and Pas-de-Calais in the south-west, which function together as one administrative region whose capital is Lille. There are nearly four million inhabitants in the region and it boasts the highest population density of all the provincial regions of France.

The landscape is not dramatic but neither is it monotonous. In the north the maritime plain is barely above sea-level: indeed an area called Les Moeres is below sea-level. The 'high' land (rarely over 200metres) is to be found in the beginnings of the Ardennes at the eastern end of the region, a pleasant landscape of wooded plateaux and winding valleys, and in what used to be Artois in the south-west. Nearly three-quarters of the land is farmed and, in the north especially, there are wide open fields with isolated farmhouses in the Flemish style while in the south, farms are grouped within villages. The area from Béthune to Valenciennes is industrial rather than agricultural and this was where coal was found under the chalk in the nineteenth century. Meanwhile the coastline alternates between wide dunes, peaceful beaches and high chalk cliffs such as the Cap Blanc-Nez. The northern coastline is threatened by erosion while, along the south-west, the dunes are being extended as the Channel tides deposit more sand.

Nord/Pas-de-Calais has a Regional Park divided into three sectors: the marshland of **Audomarois** near St-Omer, the habitat of heron, harrier and woodpecker, the gentle hills of **Le Boulonnais** inland from Boulogne, and **La Plaine de la Scarpe et de l'Escaut**, an alluvial plain with rivers, lakes and forests containing wild boar and deer. In addition, the coastline is rich in birdlife and there are nature reserves at Le Platier d'Oye, at Canche Bay and at Bray-Dunes

Climate

Nord/Pas-de-Calais enjoys a temperate climate, with winds which can come from any point of the compass. In this region the wind even has its own feast day!

Wet and windy winters can be followed by blustery spring rains. However, despite some cloudy weather, the summers are often mild and sunny with the average July temperature for the Lille area reaching 18.5°C. The autumn months are also mild but the weather is less predictable.

Attractions

Like every region of France, Nord/Pas-de-Calais has much to offer, although here the attractions may take longer to dig out.

For the tourist interested in walking and nature there is the long coastline, the Côte d'Opale, and the three areas of the Regional Park which offer a variety of scenery and wildlife. You can take a punt in the Audomarois or go horseriding in the Boulonnais. There are opportunities for watersports off the coast.

The cultural attractions of the region are to be found in the towns. Arras is not to be missed. Despite being damaged during the First World War, it retains attractive architectural features. It is also famous for its Flemish lace. Vieux Lille, the old centre of the capital of the region, retains fine seventeenth- and eighteenth-century houses and is well worth a visit. Lille also has an acclaimed art museum. Other museums in the region include the mining museum at Lewarde and the Channel Tunnel museum at Sangatte.

Tourists are often diverted from their intended route by one of the immaculately kept war cemeteries which dot the landscape. Even the smallest give a powerful reminder of the tragedy of war. Vimy Ridge with its vast Canadian cemetery is perhaps the most dramatic in the region.

Finally, for the tourist interested in folklore, the *Fêtes de Gayant* featuring wickerwork giants must rate as the most spectacular festivals of the region. They take place in many towns and villages at different times of the year.

Cuisine

The region prides itself on its traditional *cuisine flamande*. Beer, used in many Flemish recipes, features in the famous *la carbonade flamande* (beef and onions cooked in beer sauce and spices). You might also like to try *le lapin aux pruneaux, coq à la bière, le pigeon aux cerises* and *andouillettes* which are small sausages made of offal and are a speciality of several towns including Arras. Pâtés are made from fowl such as duck and partridge and also from freshwater fish. *Anguilles au vert* is a pâté made from eels, wine sauce and herbs. Coastal restaurants offer a wide selection of seafood. You can taste fresh mackerel, turbot, sole and oysters, while salted and pickled fish are also plentiful. Dunkirk specialises in small smoked herrings called *craquelots*. Shellfish in general and *moules* (mussels) in particular appear in many dishes.

Local cheeses are typically strong flavoured. *Maroilles*, a soft brownish cheese washed in beer, is the most prestigious. Vegetarians should note that chicory, artichokes and leeks are grown here. If you don't eat meat or fish, you could be in for a bit of a lean time. However, for those determined not to head for the nearest pizzeria or crêperie, *soupe a l'oignon du nord* may be meatless. The sweet-toothed will want to sample the local *pâtisseries*. Macaroons are popular, along with *gaufres* (waffles) and *crêpes*.

An important beer-producing region, here it is beer rather than wine which is the traditional accompaniment to a meal. If you want a light bitter, ask for *bière blonde* or, for a sweeter taste, try *bière brune*. For a *digestif*, genièvre is a local brandy made from juniper berries. Genièvre can also be added to black coffee; ask for a *bistoulle*.

Level of Tourism

Nine million travellers per year pass through the port of Calais, making it the busiest in the whole of France (the second most popular is Boulogne). However, Nord/Pas-de-Calais can only boast a figure of 1.5 million visitors who annually spend the night in the region. All in all, it comes about halfway down the list of French tourist regions, hosting 2.7% of all national visits. Though 23% of its visitors come from abroad, the majority are just passing through.

Tourism here is of a transitory nature and the only real examples of mass tourism are the bottlenecks at the Channel ports during the high season. However, even these quickly disperse down the rarely crowded autoroutes and will be further eased by the opening of the new coastal autoroute in 1993. For train passengers, the new TGV link will further speed their transit through the region. The opening of the Channel Tunnel in 1993 at Sangatte, just outside Calais, will take even more traffic away from the ports.

The **Conseil Régional** is proud of the fast road and rail links in Nord/Pas-de-Calais. It does not see that it is necessarily damaging to the rural environment, neither does it see that it will simply speed travellers **out** of the region. Instead, with Nord/Pas-de-Calais easy to get to and easy to leave, two types of tourism are being promoted. The first is business tourism: three convention centres have been developed at Lille, Le Touquet and Dunkirk. Secondly, the council is promoting short-stay tourism – the British day tripper is an important part of this market.

Over one million British tourists annually make the day-trip across the Channel. During July and August Calais becomes an extension of the British seaside circuit – a veritable *Calais-on-Sea*. You are as likely to be sitting next to a Brit as a Frenchman when you order your morning *crème*, and certainly the number of Anglophones can make a visit to one of the hypermarkets seem like a trip to Tesco. The locals do their best to accommodate the tourists; menus in English, 'Pubs' with English beers, and at times it can seem that Calais has been reconquered. However, this type of transitory tourism does not encourage good cuisine and meals in a Channel port are often very disappointing.

The opening of the 'Chunnel' will inevitably increase the popularity of the region for short-stay tourism and the Regional Council has launched a mutually beneficial joint tourism programme with Kent. The council acknowledges the potential threat to the environment that the project could bring and it has ensured that development of the road and rail system is 'integrated into the countryside', preserving rural and farming life. Much is made of the work of the **Espace Naturel Régional**, the body which has worked to preserve sites of interest including the three regional parks and nature reserves such as the Platier d'Oye.

The **Espace Naturel Régional** has teamed up with the British **Countryside Commission** and designated the coastlines around the tunnel entrances on both sides of the Channel 'Eurosites'. The aim of the project is to protect wildlife, encourage people to explore the areas, explain the countryside to people of all ages and maintain an attractive landscape. Time will be the judge of their success.

Good Alternatives

Meeting People

The traditional culture of the Nord/Pas-de-Calais is strongly promoted by the regional tourist board, yet few British tourists fully appreciate this aspect of the region. The Dunkirk Carnival is one of the best examples. A type of French *mardi gras*, it takes place at a weekend in mid-February with a carnival ball on the Saturday night and procession on Sunday. A local tradition are the wickerwork giants called *Gayants*, which appear at Dunkirk and other festivals in the region, including Douai.

The **Association Accueil à la Ferme**, BP 1177, 59013 Lille (Tel. 20 52 22 22) offers visits to farms in the Nord to taste local produce. They also organise *chambres d'hôte, gite*, horseriding and camping on farms.

The **Centre Permanent d'Initiation a l'Environnement** at **Auxi-le-Château** provides opportunities to join conservation work-parties. Information from **C.P.I.E.**, BP 23, Auxi-le-Château.

Each part of the *département* has its own walking club which organises weekend rambles. These are often open to the public. A calender of events is available from **La Maison de la Nature et de l'Environnement**, 23 rue Gosselet, 59000 Lille. Information on joining archaeological digs in the region can be obtained from the **Direction des Antiquités**, Ferme St-Sauveur, avenue du Bois, BP 51, 59651 Villeneuve d'Ascq (Tel. 20 91 38 69).

Discovering Places

Walking tours and bird-watching are available in the three Regional Park sectors. Contact: Maison du Parc, 'Le Luron', 357 rue Notre-Dame-d'Amour, 59230 Saint-Amand-Les-Eaux (Tel. 27 27 88 27) for the **Plaine de la Scarpe et de l'Escaut**. 'Le Grand Vannage-Les Quatre-Faces', 62510 Arques (Tel. 21 98 62 98) for the **Audomarois**. Manoir du Huisbois, Le Wast, 62142 Colembert

(Tel. 21 83 38 79) for the **Boulonnais**. Organised bird-watching is also available at Armentières near Lille; contact **Base des Près du Hem**, avenue Marc Sangnier, 59 Armentières.

The heron and the iris of the **Audomarois** are ideally seen from one of the traditional flat-bottomed punts called *bacôves*. They can be hired from **Clairmarais, Salperwick, St-Omer** or **Tilques**.

The coastline of the region is said to be the best protected in France and is designated an *Espace naturel régional*. Details about nature walks along the northern coast, the **Littoral Nord**, can be obtained from 'Casteel Houck', rue du Lac, 59380 Armbouts-Cappe (Tel. 28 60 06 94). Information on the nature reserve at the **Platier d'Oye**, famous for its birdlife, and the rest of the **Littoral Pas-de-Calais** with its signposted trails and information point can be obtained from 30 avenue Foch, 62930 Wimereux (Tel. 21 32 13 74). More specifically, guided tours of the sand-dunes in the north-western corner can be arranged by the **Office Intercommunal de Bray-Dunes/Zuydecoote**, Marie de Bray-Dunes, 59123 Bray-Dunes.

Tours of the battlefields in the region are organised by a number of British firms. **Major and Mrs Holt's Battlefield Tours** (Tel. 0304 612248) run coach tours which include Dunkirk. **Galina International** (Tel. 0482 894409) and **Martin Middlebrook** (Tel. 0205 364555) visit Arras on their tours.

The pressure on the Al trunk road leading south from the Channel ports has largely been relieved by the A26 autoroute and heavy traffic will be further siphoned off when the new autoroute via Amiens is opened. With the vast majority of tourists concentrated onto these through-routes, the remaining N roads and D roads are left to light local traffic and any tourist who has taken the time to linger in the region. In addition to the regional park and the coastline, the easterly Avesnois region, 'la petite Suisse du Nord' is to be recommended, whilst Flanders has its own distinct charm.

A wide variety of tours and holiday packages run by small local operators throughout the region are organised by the **Loisirs-Accueil Services**. The address for Nord is 15/17 rue du Nouveau Siècle. BP 135, 59027 Lille (Tel. 20 57 00 61), and for Pas-de-Calais it is Antenne Départementale, rue Désille, 62200 Boulogne-sur-Mer (Tel. 21 83 32 59). The **Comité Régional de Tourisme** will also give details of tours available, including those of local bus companies. Its address is 26 Place Rihour, 59800 Lille (Tel. 20 60 60 60)

Communications

How to Get There

Until the Channel Tunnel is open (June 1993), **ferry** or **hovercraft** is the obvious way to get to Nord/Pas-de-Calais. Sally Line runs a service from Ramsgate to Dunkirk, which takes $2^1/2$ hours; Sealink Stena Line's Dover to Calais service takes $1^1/2$ hours, while its Folkestone-Boulogne service takes 1 hour 50 minutes; P & O takes 1 hour 40 minutes from Dover to Boulogne and only 1 hour 15 minutes from Dover to Calais. On Hoverspeed, you can get from Dover to Boulogne in 40 minutes and to Calais in 35 minutes. Ferries carry **bicycles** free.

Rail travellers can purchase combined rail/ferry tickets linking main towns on either side of the Channel. Once the Channel Tunnel is open, Lille will serve as a connection for onward TGV services to the south of France. Hoverspeed's 'City Sprint' **coach** service goes to Calais and Lille, as does National Express with its 'Eurolines' service. Eurolines offers a daily service to Calais and Boulogne on special 'Channel Hopper' fares, as well as day trips to Calais. The Paris autoroute has just been extended into the centre of Calais.

For those in a hurry, Air France run a service from London City or Heathrow **airport** to Lille, and British Independent Airways fly to Le Touquet. A Manchester to Lille service is on the cards.

When You're There

Rail – the region is served by the T.E.R., a regular local rail network which links 250 stations. The express service links the main towns in the region (e.g. Calais-Lille in 1 hour) and beyond (e.g. Calais-Paris in 2 hours 50 minutes).

The main lines are those running along the coast (Dunkirk, Calais, Boulogne, Etaples Le Touquet) and radiating from Lille to Hazebrouck, Calais, Dunkirk, Tourcoing, Valenciennes, Douai, Arras, Lens and Béthune. The extension of the TGV, coinciding with the opening of the Channel Tunnel, will cut some journey times in the region.

Bus – bus services link the main towns in the region, but

there is not a comprehensive rural service on which the tourist can rely.

Car – the region is well served by motorway: the A26 Calais-Reims-Paris; the A25 Dunkirk-Lille-Belgium, and soon the A16 along the coast. This leaves other roads uncongested outside the towns, with many quiet D roads.

Boat – Nord/Pas-de-Calais is criss-crossed by some 680 km of canal and navigable river. There are many opportunities, therefore, for 'tourisme fluvial', either taking boat trips or hiring a vessel. Contact the **Association Régionale pour le Développement du Tourisme Fluvial**, 5/7 avenue Marc Sangnier, BP 46, 59426 Armentières. Boating holidays are particularly popular in the Audomarois; details from Le Grand Vannage (see **Good Alternatives**).

Cycling – the region's uncrowded D roads are ideal for cyclists. Bicycles can be hired at many railway stations, including those at Le Quesnoy, Fourmies, Saint-Amand, Arras, Calais-Ville, St-Omer and Boulogne. Some campsites, youth hostels and even Tourist Information centres also have bicycles for hire.

Walking – the Grand Randonnée trails GR 120, 121, 122 and 128 cross the region. Information on these and other walks is available from the **Maison de la Nature** in Lille (for address, see **Good Alternatives**).

Riding – horseriding is particularly popular in the Regional Park areas and forests, where there are often marked trails. The organisation which which will provide information on different areas is the **Association Régionale pour le Tourisme Equestre**, 'Le Paddock', 62223 St-Laurent-Blagny.

Useful Local Contacts

The different areas of the regional park can usually provide detailed information about their sector. The park is divided into three and comes under the auspices of the **Espace Naturel Régional**, 17 rue Jean-Roisin, 59800 Lille (Tel. 20 60 60 60). The **Audomarois** sector is dealt with by 'Le Grand Vannage – Les Quatre-Faces', 62510 Arques (Tel. 21 98 62 98); the **Boulonnais** sector by Manoir du Huisbois, Le Wast, 62142 Colembert (Tel. 21 83 38 79); and the **Plaine de la Scarpe et de l'Escaut** sector by 'Le Luron', 357 rue Notre-Dame-d'Amour, 59230 St-Amand-les-Eaux (Tel. 27 27 88 27). Information on the coast of the Nord *département* is provided by the **Littoral Nord**,

'Casteel Houck', rue du Lac, 59380 Armbouts-Cappel (Tel. 28 60 06 94); and the Pas-de-Calais coastline is covered by the **Littoral Pas-de-Calais**, 30 avenue Foch, 62930 Wimereux (Tel. 21 32 13 74).

The **Groupe Ornothologique Nord** and the **Fédération Nord-Nature** are both concerned with nature conservation and environmental issues in the region. They can be contacted at the **Maison de la Nature et de l'Environnement de Lille**, 23 rue Gosselet, 59000 Lille.

Geographical Breakdown of Region

Pas-de-Calais

The Pas-de-Calais *département* covers the south-west of the region, including the majority of the coastline. Its gentle countryside is punctuated both by pockets of industry and charming old towns like its capital, Arras.

Arras

Arras used to be a cloth town, famed for its tapestries. Like many French towns, it is promoted by the tourist board as one of the most beautiful in Europe. Its claim to fame lies in the two squares which, after careful restoration following heavy bombardment in the two World Wars, offer fine examples of seventeenth century architectural style.

The tourist will of course begin with the **Grand Place** and the **Place des Héros** or Petit Place. The former is the pride of Arras, a huge cobbled square bordered by 155 Flemish Renaissance mansions with elegant arcades. The latter is dominated by the imposing **Hôtel de Ville**, a wonderful example of careful restoration as it was severely damaged in 1918, and it is topped by a graceful belfry. Underneath the Hôtel de Ville lies a hidden surprise; extensive underground vaults that can be visited by tourists. These vaults were used by the British during World War I as barracks and hospital.

Accommodation

There are no small-scale first class hotels in Arras. Instead, try the following:

Middle Range

L'Univers, 3 Place Croix-Rouge (Tel. 21 71 34 01): 33 rooms in very comfortable hotel with restaurant. Ostel les Trois Luppars, 49 Grande Place (Tel. 21 07 41 41): 42 rooms in pleasant hotel on Arras' most beautiful square.

Economy

Le Chanzy, 8 rue Chanzy (Tel. 21 71 02 02): 23 individually decorated rooms belonging to well-known restaurant (see below). **Hôtel les Grandes Arcades**, 12 Grande Place (Tel. 21 23 30 89): beautifully situated hotel with popular local restaurant. **Hôtel le Rallye**, 9 rue Gambetta (Tel. 21 51 44 96): hotel near station with popular bar.

Eating Out

First Class

La Faisanderie, 45 Grande Place (Tel. 21 48 20 76): gourmet restaurant, with light cuisine and regional menu, in cosy room on main square.

First Class / Middle Range

L'Ambassadeur, Place Foch (Tel. 21 23 29 80): high-quality cuisine in Louis XVI style dining room.

Middle Range

Le Chanzy (address above): classic cuisine in restaurant with incredible wine cellar.

Economy

La Rapière, 44 Grande Place (Tel. 21 55 09 92): ideally situated restaurant with excellent value menu.

Entertainments

Colourful markets fill the Place des Héros and nearby squares on Wednesday and Saturday mornings. A lively night-spot is **Café de la Plage** at 6 bd Faidherbe.

Useful Addresses

The **Tourist Office** is on Place des Héros in the Town Hall (Tel. 21 51 26 95). The **Post Office** is on rue Gambetta and the **Hospital** at 57 ave Winston Churchill (Tel. 21 21 48 01).

Transport Options

Bicycle hire is available from the train station, and all the town buses, run by STCRA, stop there too.

Rest of Pas-de-Calais

Near Arras, **Vimy Ridge** is the site of a memorial to the Canadian troops who died there. Restored trenches attempt to recreate the field of battle, but the grass is too green. Over on the coast, the town of **Calais** holds little interest for the visitor. There are, however, three sites which serve as a reminder to the English influence in this, the last part of France to be held by the English. There is an imposing town hall with a statue by Rodin to commemorate the surrender of the six Burghers of the town to Edward III, the lace museum (**Musée des Beaux-Arts et de la Dentelle** – lace-making was introduced by the British in the nineteenth century) and the church of **Notre-Dame** built in the English Perpendicular style. There is also a popular beach. Tourist information is at 12 boulevard Clemenceau.

East of Calais is the **Plage d'Oye**, a coastal nature reserve where cows and Scottish ponies graze and a wide variety of birdlife may be observed. To the west is **Sangatte** and the Channel Tunnel museum. Further along the coast, **Wissant** has an excellent beach whilst the two capes, **Cap Blanc Nez** and **Cap Gris Nez**, are worth a detour for a windy walk. Inland is **St-Omer**, a pleasant country town with a majestic basilica and an excellent museum of eighteenth century France, housed in the 1776 Hôtel Sandelin. St-Omer is surrounded by marshland known as the Audomarois, which has been drained to form a network of canals. Boats can be hired, including the traditional flat-bottomed punts (contact Mme Lalart, Pont de la Guillotine, Le Rivage, Tilques, or the Maison de Tourisme, bd Pierre Guillain, St-Omer.)

The Audomarois also offers good and varied walking country. A sensible starting point is the 'Grange-Nature' at **Clairmarais** which hosts exhibitions on the area, as well as giving information on walks and cycle rides. One walking circuit in the **Romelaere** reserve explains the flora and fauna of the marsh. Back on the coast, around Boulogne, is the area known as the Boulonnais, a green land which turns into coastal dunes and is punctuated by châteaux, manors and white-washed houses. The **Marquise** area is one of marble quarrying and even has a 'quarry circuit'. **Rinxent** is home to a 'Maison du Marbre et de la Géologie', and there are plenty of good walking paths in the estuary of the River Slack. Just to the north of Boulogne, is **Wimereux**, a seaside resort popular in the early nineteenth century.

Boulogne itself is the most attractive of the Channel ports. Although, like its neighbours, it was heavily bombed during World War II, much of the **Haute-Ville** survived. Fine eighteenth-century houses are contained within its rectangular ramparts, narrow streets are lined with restaurants, bars and souvenir shops. There is the **Basilica of Nôtre Dame** which has an eleventh-century crypt and the **Musée du Château**. The lower town is less attractive, but the shopping is good and the restaurants can be better value. Tourist information is on the quai de la Poste.

Just to the south is **Le Touquet**, a fashionable resort with casinos, golf, horse-riding, sand-yachting and watersports. Southeast is the town of **Montreuil**, once a seaside town but now some distance from the sea. Here you will find another Vauban citadel.

Inland once again is the town of **Béthune**, which has a pleasant Art Deco garden, dating from 1927 and known as the Jardin de l'Union Gauthier-Germond.

Accommodation

First Class

Château de Montreuil, 4 Chaussée des Capucins, 62170 Montreuil-sur-Mer (Tel. 21 81 53 04): 16 rooms in luxurious country house with restaurant.

Middle Range

Moulin de Mombreux, route de Bayenghem, 62380 Lumbres (Tel. 21 39 62 44): 30 rooms in converted mill with restaurant. **Hostellerie des Trois Mousquetaires**, Château du Fort de la Redoute, 62120 Aire-sur-la-Lys (Tel. 21 39 01 11): 27 rooms in family-run nineteenth-century château hotel with good restaurant – book well ahead.

Economy

Hôtel la Sapinière, D 208, 62500 St-Omer (Wisques), (Tel. 21 95 14 59): 9 rooms in family-run hotel with restaurant.

Eating Out

First Class

Flavio, avenue du Verger, 62520 Le Touquet (Tel. 21 05 10 22): top-class, imaginative cuisine.

Middle Range / Economy

La Vie Claire, 15 rue Coquelin, 62200 Boulogne: vegetarian meals prepared from whatever ingredients happen to be in the house. **Hôtel de l'Escale**, rue de la Mer, 62179 Escalles (Tel. 21 85 25 09): finalist in the 1989/90 Logis de France regional cuisine competition; also has 26 rooms.

Nord

The town names, cuisine and architecture of the Nord *département* give it a distinctly Flemish feel.

Lille

Lille was the old capital of Flanders and is now the regional capital of Nord/Pas-de-Calais. It is an industrial town but nevertheless has an attractive centre. The city has the fifth largest population in France, with a considerable student community.

Most tourists aim for **Vieux-Lille**, an area between the Place Rihour and the Citadel. Here stands the **Ancienne Bourse**, the old stock exchange built in Flemish Renaissance style. It is surrounded by an attractive area of arcades now given over to second hand shops and gift shops. Nearby is the seventeenth-century **Hospice Comtesse**, initially founded in 1236 but much restored since then. Originally a hospital, it then became an old people's home and is now a museum.

The **Citadel** is a pentagonal construction by Vauban and is said to have used sixty million bricks. It is one of the best surviving examples of his work. The Citadel is still used by the army, but guided tours are run on Sundays. Its garden is very beautiful. Outside Vieux-Lille, by the fountains of the **Place de la République**, stands the **Musée des Beaux Arts**. The museum has a much acclaimed collection of paintings including works by Goya, Rubens, Delacroix and various Flemish painters.

Accommodation

There are no small-scale first-class hotels in Lille. Instead try the following:

Middle Range

Hôtel Treille, 7 Place L. de Bettignies (Tel. 20 55 45 46): 40 rooms in comfortable hotel. **Hôtel Paix**, 46 bis rue Paris (Tel. 20 54 63 93): 35 rooms.

Economy

Hôtel Constantin, 5 rue des Fossés (Tel. 20 54 32 26): generous rooms in hotel in pedestrian zone. **Hôtel Chopin**, 4 rue de Tournai (Tel. 20 06 35 80): friendly small hotel.

Eating Out

First Class

A l'Huîtrière, 3 rue des Chats-Bossus (Tel. 20 55 43 41): traditional cuisine with fish specialities. **Le Compostelle**, 4 rue St-Etienne (Tel. 20 54 02 49): classical cuisine in vaulted 16th century pilgrims' hostel.

Middle Range

Le Champlain, 13 rue Nicolas-Leblanc (Tel. 20 54 01 38): varying but consistently good dishes in former family house. **Charlot II**, 26 bd Jean-Baptiste Lebois (Tel. 20 52 53 38): fresh seafood specialities with excellent wines.

Economy

Aux Moules, 34 rue de Béthune: various dishes involving mussels; popular local haunt. **Bistro Romain**, 20–22 Place Rihour (Tel. 20 54 53 69): good *nouvelle cuisine* in attractive setting.

Entertainments

A monthly guide to entertainments in Lille, called *Chtimi*, is available from the tourist office. The most famous of Lille's festivals is the 'Braderie de Lille', a weekend at the end of August when the town turns into one huge street jumble sale. For forty-eight hours, non-stop, people tour the streets looking for bargains, stopping only to drink beer and eat vast quantities of mussels and chips (ask for 'moules-frites')

Useful Addresses

The **Tourist Office** is in the Palais Rihour (on Place Rihour – Tel. 20 30 81 00). There is another, smaller branch at the railway station, and the **Comité Régional de Tourisme**, which will supply information on the whole Nord/Pas-de-Calais region, is at 26 place Rihour (Tel. 20 57 40 04). The **Post Office** is 7 Place de la République and the **Hospital** complex at Place de Verdun (Tel. 20 44 59 61).

Transport Options

Lille is best seen on foot, especially as Vieux-Lille is pedestrianised. To travel longer distances in the town, try the automated Métro, the VAL, claimed to be the most modern in the world. There are information centres for both the Métro and town buses next to the train station, and a telephone information service on 20 98 50 50.

Rest of Nord

The Flemish town of **Douai**, attractively situated on the River Scarpe, is an important industrial centre despite the closure of the coal mines in the surrounding area. It was severely damaged during the two World Wars but much has been restored or rebuilt. It is worth visiting the Place d'Armes, an attractive square dominated by a belfry which appears in a painting by Corot. Douai is famous in the region for its Fête de Gayants, a July festival in which wickerwork giants are paraded around the streets. Tourist information is from Hôtel du Dauphin, 70 Place d'Armes.

In the Centre Historique Minier at **Lewarde**, you can 'follow in the footsteps of the coalminers' – but only through reconstructed tunnels. The guides, however, are retired miners (tours are available in English).

Cambrai is one of France's oldest cities, famous for its textile industry (*cambric* is made in Cambrai). It was almost completely destroyed in 1918 and much has had to be rebuilt. The area between the cathedral and the church of Saint Gery is the most interesting for the tourist. Tourist information from Maison Espagnol, 48 rue de Noyon. Musée Matisse at **Le Cateau-Cambresis** was created by Matisse himself and contains a fine collection of his work.

At **Fourmies**, you will find the **Ecomusée de Fourmies-Trélon** (on rue François-Delaplace), which incorporates a museum of textiles and local lifestyles, a glass-maker's workshop, an exhibition on the 'bocage' country, and a museum of religious heritage. Different sections of the *ecomusée* are scattered in the surrounding villages, along with protected natural sites, which can be explored by means of observation paths. **Le Quesnoy**, a town contained within the brick-built fortifications of Vauban, has been called 'the pearl of the Avesnois district'. It withstood a number of sieges, the most recent being in 1918 when New Zealand troops scaled the walls by ladder to defeat a German garrison. **Condé-sur-l'Escaut** is another town fortified by Vauban. Nearby, the abbey tower of **St-Amand-les-Eaux** contains a good ceramics museum, and **Marchiennes** is another historic town with an impressive abbey. They all fall within the sector of the regional park known as La Plaine de la Scarpe et de l'Escaut, which is noted for its vast forests, inhabited by deer and wild boar, its lakes and its military architecture. On the outskirts of Lille is **Villeneuve-d'Ascq**, whose excellent modern art museum is built on the edge of the city park.

Over on the coast, just west of Dunkirk, is **Gravelines** with a Vauban-constructed arsenal and large nuclear power station. As a contrast to this form of power production, there is also a small windmill which can be visited: contact the *mairie*. **Dunkirk** (*Dunkerque*) itself is a most unprepossessing town, despite being the third largest port in France. You can still see the long sandy beaches from which British soldiers were evacuated in 1940. There are two art museums: the Musée d'Art Contemporain, a collection of paintings from the last four decades, attractively situated in a sculpture garden, and the Musée des Beaux-Arts. There are opportunities for a variety of sporting activities including canoeing and windsurfing. It is certainly worth coming here for the pre-Lent carnival if you are in the area. Tourist information can be found at St-Eloi church, rue de l'Amiral-Ronarc'h. To the east of Dunkirk are the dunes of **Zuydecoote**, **Bray** and **Dewulf**. The Bray dunes have been made into a nature reserve where glacial flora can be seen. There are marked trails on all the dunes and guided tours can be arranged: contact the **Office Intercommunal de Bray-Dunes/Zuydecoote**, Mairie de Bray-Dunes, 59123 Bray-Dunes.

Accommodation

First Class / Middle Range

Auberge du Bon Fermier, 66 rue de Famars, 59300 Valenciennes (Tel. 27 46 68 25): 16 rooms in former post-house with old-fashioned atmosphere; restaurant with local specialities. **La Terrace**, 36 terrace St-Pierre, 59500 Douai (Tel. 27 88 70 04): 24 rooms in pleasant family-run hotel with restaurant.

Middle Range / Economy

Hôtel du XIXᵉ Siècle, 1 Place de la Gare, 59140 Dunkerque (Tel. 28 66 79 28 or 28 66 27 72): 14 rooms in family-run hotel with restaurant.

Economy

La Chope, 17 rue des Docks, 59400 Cambrai (Tel. 27 81 36 78): 18 rooms in family-run hotel with restaurant.

Eating Out

The following *First Class* restaurants deserve special mention:

La Crémaillère, 26 place Général-Leclerc, 59440 Avesnes-sur-Helpe (Tel. 20 61 02 30): family-run restaurant with lighter alternatives as well as traditional dishes. **L'Alberoi**, Place de la Gare, 59300 Valenciennes (Tel. 27 46 86 30): former Buffet de la Gare, gone upmarket; many good house specialities.

4 Picardy

Picardy is a region that suffers from a decidedly blurred and often undeservedly negative image. In a recent poll at Paris-Gare du Nord (gateway to Picardy and the North), only 15% of participants came up with an accurate description of Picardy. Indeed, many tourists who make day-trips from Paris to places like Chantilly and Compiègne have no idea that they are even *in* Picardy. The most common misconception is that the region is environmentally monotonous and industrially overdeveloped. This is far from the truth. Instead, you will find in Picardy a region of immense cultural and ecological variety that has scarcely been touched by the blinkered tourist industry. And it lies right on Britain's doorstep.

In Picardy you are never far from water: the sand-dunes and chalk cliffs of the *Baie de Somme* constitute some of the least developed coastline in France, and the 1200 kilometres of river flowing through the region have spawned countless ponds and lakes. The land around them is fertile and its expanse of gently undulating fields produces a quarter of all French agricultural exports. Picardy's watery landscape attracts an enormous number of migrating birds, making it an ornithologist's – and often a hunter's – heaven.

Other local pastimes include a whole collection of traditional games, many of which are variations on handball, tennis or archery. There is also a strong interest in music and theatre, and sharp social comment can be found in the traditional marionette shows. On the architectural front, Picardy is by no means barren either. It boasts the highest concentration of Gothic monuments anywhere in the world; numerous châteaux, often situated in mid-forest; and an area containing over sixty fortified churches. The latter bear witness to its war-scarred past.

Though the birthplace and one-time capital of France, Picardy's role dwindled to that of Paris's protective shield. Over and again, it served as a battleground on which to fight invaders, culminating in the horrendous Battle of the Somme in 1916. Memories of this century's wars are kept alive with memorials and museums, and there is still a distinct sense of fellowship with the British. Picardy's history has also made its inhabitants unusually resilient: they tend to be quiet but industrious perfectionists. Though tourism is only just beginning to be considered important for the region, and has hitherto been handled, at best, naïvely, Picardy is simply bursting with potential for 'soft' tourism and full of ideas on harmonising conservation and economic growth.

History

Around 300 BC some Celtic tribes, known as the Belgae, took over the north of Gaul, but were subjected to Roman rule from 57 BC. In AD 406 the Franks invaded and in 486 Clovis defeated the Roman army at Soissons, making it the first capital of the kingdom of Francia. The sixth and seventh centuries saw the creation of bishoprics and the founding of abbeys at St-Riquier, Soissons and Corbie. In the ninth century, during the Norman invasions, the first underground hide-outs were dug at Naours – later to be used by smugglers and even by the Germans in the Second World War. After two hundred years of invasions the powerful duke, Hugues Capet, was elected king of France at Senlis in 987 and so began the Capetian dynasty that was to rule the country for eight centuries.

It was from St-Valéry-sur-Somme that William the Conqueror set off for England in 1066. With the Middle Ages began a period of prosperity linked to the development of the textile industry. Picardy became the birthplace of Gothic architecture, eventually producing its six famous cathedrals. After the Hundred Years' War, including the famous Battle of Crécy in 1346, the arts were able to flourish, and many other impressive buildings and fortified castles were built.

Mention the Somme and most people think of the First World War. This *département* did indeed suffer greatly: one third of it was razed to the ground. The Battle of the Somme in July 1916 left a million victims, of thirty different nationalities. The Battle of Picardy (1918) was also of major importance, leading to the signing of the Armistice at Rethondes in the Compiègne forest on 11 November.

This century has seen the growth of both agriculture and manufacturing industries such as mechanical construction, glass and rubber. Between 1950 and 1970, in the years of post-war economic expansion, the people of Picardy threw themselves into the modernisation necessary to succeed in the EC. In those twenty years, 20% of all jobs created in France were located in Picardy. The current youthful population and high level of training puts the region in a position to do well in the single European market.

Famous inhabitants of Picardy include men of faith like Calvin, one of the disseminators of Protestantism; men of action like Camille Desmoulins, St-Just and Maréchal Leclerc; numerous writers including La Fontaine, Racine, Rousseau, Dumas and Jules Verne; and painters such as the Le Nain brothers and the eighteenth-century pastellist, Quentin de La Tour.

Geography

Picardy is the roughly rectangular region just above the Ile-de-France and is divided into three *départements*: the Somme, whose north-western boundary is the English Channel; the Oise, which is nearest to the Paris region in the south; and the Aisne, in the east, which borders on Champagne-Ardenne. Each *département* is named after the main river flowing through it. The regional capital is Amiens (150,000 inhabitants) in the Somme, and the next largest towns (well under half the size) are Beauvais (Oise) and St-Quentin (Aisne), though the administrative capital of Aisne is not St-Quentin but the fortified little hill-top town of Laon.

East of the reclaimed land and fragile dunes of the Somme estuary, the region becomes hilly north of Amiens, changing into hedge-trimmed pastures or 'bocages' in the north-eastern Thiérache area, with wooded hills and wide valleys around Laon, and 5000 acres of champagne vineyard in the south-east near Château-Thierry. Forests cover a good deal of southern Picardy: particularly noteworthy is the massive Forêt Domaniale de Compiègne. The dominant trees are oak and beech, though there are also many poplars. The vast chalky plateaux of central and western Picardy are particularly suitable for cultivation.

The crops which help make Picardy such an agriculturally rich region are cereals (especially wheat), sugar beet and potatoes. Cattle and sheep are also reared. Fishing is naturally the prime industry on the coast, but river and pond-fishing are also practised inland. It is the damp areas around coast and waterways that attract wildfowl and, consequently, hunters. Unfortunately shooting has so diminished the number of wildfowl, and so discouraged migrating birds from making a stop, that ecologists describe the situation in some areas as critical. They are, however, confident that despite the strong tradition of hunting in Picardy, sufficient anti-bloodsport feeling exists to force a tightening of the laws. Another threat to wildlife has been posed by a past lack of concern for these valuable damp habitats: a project is now under way though, to clean up the ponds of the Haute-Somme in order to re-encourage their original flora and fauna.

Plants found in Picardy include sea lavender on the coast, numerous types of orchid, and, round peatbogs, protected sundews and rare ferns. Seals live in the Baie de Somme and the racoon has recently appeared in forests around Laon. Another surprising inhabitant of Picardy is the black woodpecker. The Marquenterre ornithological reserve on the coast offers peace, quiet and protection to countless species, including avocets, white storks, and various geese and ducks. It is also particularly hospitable to migrating birds.

There are several other protected areas in Picardy. The fragile nature of the sandy Hâble d'Ault site, in the south of the Somme estuary, has recently been appreciated and steps have been taken to look after it. Also protected are the unique *hortillonnages* in and around Amiens: these are miniature market gardens planted on marshy parcels of land which float at the edges of the Somme river and are accessible, in the main, only by rowing boat. The town of St-Quentin boasts the world's only nature reserve to be situated in a wholly urban environment: the 30-acre Parc de l'Isle is open to the public and includes a marsh reservation and botanical gardens. Also open to the public, though on a more limited basis, are 'discovery' paths criss-crossing the fragile Cessières marshes.

Climate

Picardy has a temperate climate, with average maximum temperatures ranging from around 5.6°C in February to 24°C in August. The region enjoys fairly mild winters, but, even in July and August, temperatures are rarely higher than those in the south of England. Rain is quite frequent in autumn and winter and not unusual in summer.

Attractions

The seven most visited attractions in Picardy are all situated in the Oise *département*. One of the main reasons for their popularity is their proximity to Paris: the majority of visitors are simply on day-trips. Among these sites are the château at Compiègne, the medieval town of Senlis, the little cathedral town of Noyon, and the Château de Pierrefonds. These places are the only ones in Picardy ever likely to be truly crowded – and then only in high-season when coaches from Paris are more frequent. The next most popular sites are all in the Somme and include two leisure parks, the Marquenterre ornithological reserve, Amiens zoo and cathedral, and an underground city at Naours. This leaves Aisne as the least visited and most natural *département* – though none of them could possibly be described as overdeveloped.

It is a little known fact that Picardy is the French region with the highest number of classified historical monuments. Its first claim to cultural fame must surely be its Gothic architecture. As well as the famous cathedral at Amiens (deemed by UNESCO to be one of the twelve most beautiful monuments in the world), there are others at Beauvais, Senlis, Noyon, Soissons and Laon, and a basilica at St-Quentin. It is in Picardy, too, that the oldest European skull was excavated, for Picardy is also the region of France richest in archaeological finds. Other attractions include its abbeys and fortified churches, its war memorials and museums, its festivals, its sandy beaches and its suitability for both nature and activity tourism.

Cuisine

The cooking in Picardy is heavily based on local produce. On the coast, this is naturally seafood – ranging from little shrimps nick-named *sauterelles* (grasshoppers), to cockles and mussels or the fish of the day. Inland, fish is also popular – particularly eels, pike, perch and trout. Hunting, as well as fishing, has made its contribution to regional cuisine, notably in various game pâtés and the Amiens *pâté de canard*, a pie made from a whole duck conserved in spices, to which no less a man than Rabelais is said to have been partial. There are also many dishes which originated in peasant culture: leek or onion tarts called *flamiches*, hot cheese tarts called *goyères*, or *caudière* – a kind of fish soup. A more recent introduction is the famous *ficelle picarde*, a pancake stuffed with ham, mushroom and cream. Macaroons and *gâteau battu*, a jam sponge cake, are also popular. The regional cheese, *maroilles* (which actually comes from over the border in Nord/Pas-de-Calais) is rich and salty, and best washed down with beer or cider. Cider is the traditional drink of the region, though of course champagne is widespread in the vine-growing country around Château-Thierry.

Level of Tourism

Picardy is the second least visited region in France, hosting only 1.5% of all national visits. This is mainly due to misconceived notions and a lack of reliable information to set them right. Picardy has suffered severely from haphazard attempts to appeal to every type of clientèle, but, since 1990, a marketing strategy has been in place to try to change this. Up till now, most tourists have been elderly French people from the Ile-de-France, the North and Picardy itself, who want to spend time in the country or by the sea but cannot afford to travel far. Of its meagre number of visitors, 28% come from abroad: nearly half of those are from Britain, followed by the Germans, the Dutch and the Belgians. 80% of them come in summer.

The new marketing policy aims to exploit Picardy's potential for short-stay, off-season visitors and concentrates on the British and Parisian markets. It also concentrates, for the moment at least, on individuals rather than groups, for the simple reason that there are scarcely any hotels large enough to accommodate the latter. One facility Picardy is well provided with is rural *gîtes* – particularly in the north-eastern Thiérache area – and the potential for nature tourism is enormous.

The only tourist-related problem admitted to by regional authorities is that there are not enough of them! This means that certain improvements are often not yet economically viable: for example, extending museum visiting hours, or offering organised trips to out-of-the-way places. Such developments will happen, given time, but we are talking not simply of developments in the tourist industry but, virtually, of *the* development of *a* tourist industry. Fundamental policy decisions are more likely to be in line with the 'soft' tourism philosophy, which is recognised as having much to recommend it. One example is the realisation that 65 kilometres of undeveloped coastline is a rare but fragile asset. Certainly some controversial building has occurred but, on the whole, the image that the tourist authority wishes to promote is that of a well-preserved coast. To this end there is a policy banning motorised sports. Many ingenious alternatives, such as sand-yachting and sea-canoeing, are practised, but those who wish to water-ski will just have to go elsewhere.

Secondary residences on the coast, the creation of the leisure park Aquaclub Côte Picarde, and the necessary road-building involved, have all contributed to some erosion of the dunes. Even less environment-friendly developments still to come are the inevitable consequences of the Channel Tunnel: not only will the TGV link between London and Paris run through Picardy, but there are also four new autoroutes planned, including one which will be the final link in a motorway system running all the way from Britain to Spain.

Perhaps the most encouraging attitude to be found in Picardy is the very positive and practical one of environmentalists vis-à-vis tourism. The majority are of the opinion that, in order for our natural heritage to be valued, it must first be known and understood. For this reason, sites of environmental importance are perceived not as something to hide away, but as a vital opportunity to interest first the local public, then visitors, in the natural assets of the region. The same attitude exists towards cultural heritage, and Picardy is awash with associations running archaeological digs and restoration workshops.

The tourist authority's plans for the immediate future concentrate on using existing resources to the full, with the accent on the animations provided by the various regional festivals. The only reminder of their naïve efforts to please everybody is their continuing insistence on trying simultaneously to promote both nature tourism and hunting, a policy whose inherent contradiction ecologists are determined to make them understand.

Good Alternatives

Meeting People

For a calendar of the numerous regional festivals, ask a major tourist office for the brochure 'L'Art de la Fête en Picardie'. Smaller tourist offices or syndicats d'initiative often produce lists of fêtes occurring in the immediate vicinity. Young people may be interested in taking part in a *chantier de bénévoles*: these are working holidays, involving either archaeological digs, renovation of old buildings or environmental conservation activities. The digs tend to take place in July and August and volunteers bringing their own camping equipment are always welcome. For information, contact the **Direction des Antiquités Historiques et Préhistoriques de Picardie**, 5 rue Henri Daussy, 80044 Amiens (Tel. 22 97 33 45). An international *chantier* to conserve the *hortillonnage* gardens is organised in summer by the **Maison pour Tous**, rue Jean Moulin, 80450 Camon (Tel. 22 46 13 56). Other working holidays of all kinds are run by **Concordia Picardie CEAVR**, rue Chamiteau, 02830 St-Michel (Tel. 23 98 65 65). If you are in the Somme and interested in learning one of the traditional French sports of the seventeenth century which have died out elswhere but are still practised in Picardy (*Jeu de Paume* tennis, the *Jeu de l'Assiette*, or *Javelot*), write to MM, Mondouet et Moreau, **Direction Départementale de la Jeunesse et des Sports**, 56 rue Jules-Barni, 80040 Amiens (Tel. 22 91 53 41), to find out where this is possible. An alternative to the hunting so popular among local people is clay pigeon shooting at Neuilly-l'Hôpital, or the traditional sport of archery (if in Aisne, contact M. Ponthieux, **Comité Départementale de la Fédération Française de Tir à l'Arc**, 02470 Dammard, Tel. 23 71 03 16).

Discovering Places

A selection of short breaks, from one day to five, is set out in the 'Weekends Away' brochure, available from the **Comité Régional du Tourisme**, 3 rue Vincent Auriol, BP 2616, 80026 Amiens (Tel. 22 91 10 15). These breaks range from learning how to make a marionette, ride a horse or race a sand-cart, to a day at sea with local fishermen, a gastronomic weekend in a château or a week's holiday for five to twelve-year-olds on a family farm. It is hoped that holidays designed specifically for bird-watchers will soon be on the agenda. As it is, free guided ornithological excursions take place, for which a calendar is supplied by **GEPOP**, 103 rue Octave Tierce, 80000 Amiens (Tel. 22 43 26 88). Details about guided botanical and geological walks are available from the **Société Linnéenne Nord-Picardie**, 15 rue P. de Commynes, 80000 Amiens. Information on where you will find exhibitions of rural life can be obtained from the **Maison du Tourisme Vert**, 49 bis rue du Général Leclerc, 60690 Marseille-en-Beauvaisis (Tel. 44 46 32 20). If you are interested in the ecological aspects of the region, it is worth enquiring whether the **Conservatoire des Sites Naturels de Picardie** (Conseil Régional, 11 Mail Albert 1er, 80000 Amiens, Tel. 22 97 37 37) is offering any guided visits to its sites. In Aisne, there are monthly 'environmental discovery' jeep trips from Easter to November: contact M. Samin, **Relais Franco-Belge**, Place Victor Hugo, 02000 Laon (Tel. 23 23 25 73 or 23 20 45 54).

Communications

How to Get There

Paris's Roissy-Charles de Gaulle **airport** is only ten minutes from Senlis and Chantilly, and half an hour from Compiègne. Direct flights from Britain are also available to the airport at Beauvais.

There are direct **trains** to Amiens from London, via either Dover-Calais or Folkestone-Boulogne, which take around 7 hours at present, but will of course be much quicker when the planned TGV line is built. The train journey from Boulogne to Amiens is 1 hour 20 mins, and from Calais it takes 2 hours.

When You're There

Rail – regional rail links are not particularly good: to get from Amiens to Compiègne, you may find it's quickest to go via Paris! The fastest lines are the ones fanning out from Paris: Paris-Beauvais, Paris-Creil-Longueau-Amiens-Abbéville, Paris-Creil-Compiègne-Tergnier-St-Quentin, Paris-Soissons-Laon, and Paris-Château Thierry (only 50 minutes, as it's on the main line to the north-east). Some cross-country routes exist. There are scenic steam trains from Le Crotoy to Cayeux-sur-Mer round the *Baie de Somme*, from Froissy to Dompierre along the upper Somme near Péronne, round the forest at the Château de Pierrefonds, and along the Oise valley from St-Quentin-Gauchy to Origny-Ste Benoite (see appropriate section in **Geographical Breakdown** for details).

Bus – there is a large bus station next to the train station in Amiens. From here local buses run in many directions including Abbéville-Le Tréport, Doullens, Albert, Péronne-St-Quentin, Roye, Montdidier, and Breteuil-Beauvais. Organised coach or mini-bus trips are only just starting up: a 3-hour evening drive around floodlit sights leaves from Fort-Mahon in summer (reservations from **Fort-Mahon Maison du Tourisme**, Tel. 22 27 70 75); mini-bus trips from Amiens to the battlegrounds of the Somme and various other destinations are planned – enquire at the tourist office.

Car – Amiens is around 2 hours by road from Calais and it takes roughly the same time to drive from Amiens to Paris. The main motorway to cross the region is the A1 from Belgium to Paris, though the A26 also passes St-Quentin and Laon, on its way from Calais to Reims. Various new autoroutes are planned to coincide with the opening of the Channel Tunnel, including one connecting

Abbéville to Rouen. Aside from the autoroutes, however, Picardy possesses a good network of N and D roads.

Boat – recently there has been a boom in river tourism in Picardy, which has 700 kilometres of navigable waterway. For information on renting a barge on the Oise river, contact the **Compiègne Tourist Office**, Place de l'Hôtel de Ville, 60200 Compiègne (Tel. 44 40 01 00); or M. Stassart, **Château Sourivière**, Cramoisy, 60660 Cires les Mello (Tel. 47 27 10 41). More general information on river tourism can be obtained from the **Maison du Tourisme Fluvial**, 31 rue Bélu, 80000 Amiens (Tel. 22 97 88 55). Facilities for canoeing are good: the **Service Loisirs-Accueil Somme**, 21 rue Ernest Cauvin, 80000 Amiens (Tel. 22 92 26 39), offers sea kayak courses amongst other boating holidays; details on canoeing possibilities in Aisne is supplied by M. Dourlet, **Comité Départemental de Canoë Kayak**, 55 rue Blondel, 02240 Ribemont (Tel. 23 63 74 81).

Cycling – maps of circuits using the very comprehensive network of back roads are available free from most tourist offices – as are lists of cycle hire shops. Bicycles can also be hired from the SNCF stations at Beauvais, Compiègne, Laon and Rue. The **Service Loisirs-Accueil Somme** (for address, see **Boat** section) offers cycling holidays. Detailed information on cycling possibilities can be obtained, in the Somme, from the **Comité Départementale de Cyclotourisme**, 5 bd du Poilu, 80200 Péronne (Tel. 22 84 23 30); and, in Aisne, from the **Comité de l'Aisne Cyclotourisme**, 64 rue Paul Houël, 02130 Fère-en-Tardenois.

Walking – six *Grande Randonnée* paths cross Picardy: GR 12A which explores the forests of Compiègne, Laigue and St-Gobain; GR 125 which links Hendaye and the *Baie de Somme*; GR 122 which winds among the fortified churches of the Thiérache; and GR 123, 124 and 225. Eight shorter walks (1–3 hours) are proposed by the **Pays d'Accueil du Ponthieu-Marquenterre**, rue de l'Ecole des Filles, 80135 St-Riquier (Tel. 22 28 90 90). In the Somme there are numerous accompanied Sunday rambles, open to all: for a list, contact the **Comité Départemental de la Randonnée Pédestre**, BP 65, 80092 Amiens. For thematic walks, see under **Good Alternatives**. Information on walking in Aisne is available from the **Comité Départemental de la FFRP**, 58 rue de la Mare Aubry, 02400 Château-Thierry.

Riding – horseriding is extremely popular in Picardy: Chantilly is the horseriding capital of France, and the *Baie de Somme* has its own sturdy breed of horse, the Henson. For organised riding holidays in the Somme, contact the **Service Loisirs-Accueil Somme** (address in **Boat** section). General information is available from the **Association Régionale du Tourisme Equestre de Picardie**, 8 rue Fournier Savolèze, BP 354, 60203 Compiègne (Tel. 44 40 19 54). If you would rather hire a horse-drawn caravan for a day – or a week – contact '**Ateliers du Val de Selle**', 47 route de Loeuilly, 80160 Conty (Tel. 22 41 23 31).

Useful Local Contacts

The **Conservatoire des Sites Naturels de Picardie** Conseil Régional de Picardie, 11 Mail Albert 1er, 80000 Amiens, Tel. 22 97 37 37 or the **Délégation Régionale à l'Architecture et à l'Environnement de Picardie (DRAE)** 56 rue Jules-Barni, 80040 Amiens, will be able to give you information on sites of special ecological interest. Ornithologists should contact the **Groupe Environnement, Protection, Ornithologie de Picardie (GEPOP)**, 103 rue Octave Tierce, 80000 Amiens (Tel. 22 43 26 88), or the **Parc Ornithologique du Marquenterre**, St-Quentin-en-Tourmont, 80120 Rue (Tel. 22 25 03 06).

Geographical Breakdown of Region

Somme

The Somme offers an enormous range of things to do and see. The coast provides all the usual seaside pleasures, plus several less usual ones, and inland there are numerous sites whose interest is broadly classifiable under the umbrella term 'culture'. A wealth of information is contained in the tourist office brochure 'Bienvenue Pays de Somme'.

Amiens

At first sight Amiens is a slightly grey city, but it has several unusual attractions which more than make up for this. The stunning Gothic **Cathédrale de Notre-Dame**, begun in 1220, is one of UNESCO's World Heritage Sites: particularly impressive are the carved wooden choir-stalls and the treasury. A joint ticket can be obtained for the **Musée de Picardie**, with its comprehensive local archaeology and painting collections, and the **Musée d'Art Local et d'Histoire**

Régionale at the Hôtel de Berny, a more homely museum of old wooden furniture, hand-painted plates and much else. There is also a costume museum and a stained-glass window museum, as well as the house of Jules Verne. The medieval quarter of Amiens is called **St-Leu** and is criss-crossed by canals. It is the place to come for antiques, bric-a-brac and crafts. Nearby are the protected **Hortillonnages**, floating market gardens, which it is possible to visit on foot, by bike or by boat (see **Transport Options**). There is a lively centre explaining the site's ecology on the **Ile aux Fagots** (Tel. 22 91 44 96).

Accommodation

You will be hard pushed to find an expensive hotel in Amiens. The following are recommended:

Middle Range

Hôtel le Prieuré, 17 rue Porion (Tel. 22 92 22 67): 25 rooms in family hotel with restaurant. **Grand Hôtel de l'Univers**, 2 rue Noyon (Tel. 22 91 52 51): 41 rooms in comfortable, well-situated hotel.

Middle Range / Economy

Hôtel Alsace-Lorraine, 18 rue de la Morlière (Tel. 22 91 35 71): 14 rooms in hotel near station. **Hôtel de Normandie**, 1 bis rue Lamartine (Tel. 22 91 74 99): 26 rooms in well-situated hotel.

Economy

Hôtel de la Renaissance, 8 bis rue André (Tel. 22 91 70 23): views of cathedral. **Bar-Hôtel des Touristes**, 22 Place Notre-Dame (Tel. 22 91 33 45): 11 rooms with views of cathedral. **Hostellerie de Belloy**, 29 route Nationale, Belloy-sur-Somme, 80310 Picquigny (Tel. 22 51 41 05): 9 rooms in pleasant hotel outside town, near Samara.

Eating Out

First Class

Les Marissons, 68 rue des Marissons, Pont de la Dodanne (Tel. 22 92 96 66): gastronomic restaurant in fifteenth-century boat-builder's workshop near waterside market. **Le Mermoz**, 7 rue Jean-Mermoz (Tel. 22 91 50 63): excellent regional dishes.

Middle Range

Le Vivier, 593 route de Rouen, (Tel. 22 89 12 21): good fish specialities. **Aux As du Don**, 1 Place du Don (Tel. 22 92 41 65): traditional cuisine in the town's oldest bistro, with its eighteenth century wood panelling. **La Capitainerie**, 31 rue Bélu (Tel. 22 91 88 55): Picardy specialities (also does boat-hire).

Economy

La Couronne, 64 rue St-Leu (Tel. 22 91 88 57): local specialities. **La Soupe à Cailloux**, 16 rue des Bondes (Tel. 22 91 92 70): relaxed restaurant with traditional dishes and vegetarian/organic options.

Entertainments

There is a 'market on water' on Saturday mornings at Place Parmentier and all day Thursday and Saturday at Place des Halles, where fruit, vegetables and flowers from the Hortillonnages are sold. Le Passage Bélu is filled with antique shops and craftsmen's workshops. Try to find time for a visit to the workshop of J-Pierre Facquier, marionette-maker, at Place du Don (Tel. 22 92 49 52). There is a Maison de la Marionnette at 24 rue St-Leu where you can find out about traditional puppet shows in the area. Amiens also has a lively Maison de la Culture, which organises concerts, plays, films and exhibitions (Tel. 22 91 83 36). The *Son et Lumière* put on at the cathedral in the evenings from mid-April to mid-October is excellent. The local carnival and Fête des Hortillonnages take place in May. If you are in Amiens in late September, your visit may coincide with the Traditional Picardy Sports and Games Day.

Useful Addresses

The main **Tourist Office** is at rue Jean Catelas (Tel. 22 91 79 28), with branches at the train station and outside the cathedral – summer only. The **Office Départementale du Tourisme**, which tells you about the whole Somme area, is at 21 rue Ernest Cauvin (Tel. 22 92 26 39), and the address of the **Comité Régional du Tourisme**, which provides information on the whole of Picardy, is 3 rue Vincent Auriol, BP 2616, 80026 Amiens (Tel. 22 91 10 15). The **Post Office** is 7 rue des Vergeaux and the **Hospital** at Place Victor Pauchet (Tel. 22 44 25 25).

Transport Options

Amiens is small enough to explore on foot, though there are regular town buses, all of which stop in front of the train station. The ideal way to see the Hortillonnages is in a traditional 'barque a corne' boat, with commentary by a member of the **Association pour la Protection et la Sauvegarde du Site des Hortillonnages**. Boats leave throughout the day from 56 boulevard Beauvillé (Tel: 22 92 12 18) with groups of about ten: there is a guaranteed departure at 3 p.m. even if you are the only one there. A cruise on the Boat-Restaurant *Picardie* is another possibility; you can also hire small boats yourself – information at 31 rue Bélu (Tel. 22 91 88 55 or 22 92 16 40). Rowing boats to explore the Hortillonnages can also be hired from the Auberge du Vert Galant, 57 chemin de Halage (Tel. 22 91 31 66).

Rest of Somme

From **Fort-Mahon** it is possible to take evening coach trips as described in the **Communications** section under **Bus**. One of the places visited is the Cistercian **Abbaye de Valloires**, which has magnificent gardens. It is a true botanical park with several rare varieties of roses and other plants, some of which may be purchased. Nature walks abound both in the Fort-Mahon area and in the **Forest of Crécy**. The **Parc Ornithologique du Marquenterre** is a private reserve, created in 1973 as a zone to protect birds from the excesses of hunters. It does, however, adjoin a 5000 acre hunting reserve. Since 1986 the park has been under the management of the **Conservatoire du Littoral** and now welcomes 100,000 visitors a year. It is situated on reclaimed dune-land, created by means of dykes and canals, and recently planted with trees. The park is open to the public from late March to mid-November and it is possible to hire anything from binoculars to umbrellas and baby-slings at its **Pavillon d'Accueil**. There are two possible circuits to follow: the initiation circuit, which is shorter and has explanatory signs concerning the semi-wild birds you will see; and a longer observation circuit through the dunes, from hide to hide. Dedicated ornithologists, with a knowledge of French, should consider writing to the DRAE or GEPOP (addresses under **Useful Local Contacts**) to ask for a copy of the 'Guide des Oiseaux de la Baie de Somme', which suggests ten ornithological walking routes, describing the birds you will see, and includes a section on the impact of tourism. The park also has a riding centre and offers guided rides (even for complete beginners) on the steady Henson horses native to the Bay. Among the seaside resorts of the *Baie de Somme* is the fishing village of **St-Crotoy**, whose south-facing beach is particularly pleasant. It is from here that the Somme Bay Steam Train, which has been running for over a century, departs for Noyelles, St-Valéry-sur-Somme and Cayeux-sur-Mer (info: Tel. 22 26 96 96). At **Cayeux** it is possible to visit the lighthouse in June, July and August. It is also the starting point for five mountain bike circuits, from 1^{1}/2 to 4 hours: contact **Centre de Loisirs Permanent**, Résidence Club Côte Picarde, rue du Général Leclerc, 80410 Cayeux-sur-Mer (Tel. 22 26 62 56). Not far from here, at the Carrefour du Hourdel (Lanchères), is the **Maison de l'Oiseau**, an exhibition which calls itself an 'anti-museum' and displays over 400 stuffed birds in natural environments recreated using various methods including audio-visual ones. This is open during the same period as the Marquenterre Park, but has been criticised as somewhat glorifying hunting.

If you follow the valley of the River **Bresle** inland, you will come across numerous old glassworks. Information as to which ones are open to the public is available from local tourist offices. The mills of the **Vimeu** region can be seen if you follow the '*circuit des moulins*', drawn up by **Les Amis des Moulins Picards**, Le Moulin 'le Marottin', Plachy-Buyon, 80160 Conty (Tel. 22 42 75 12). An exhibition is set up in the **Moulin de St-Maxent** at Oisemont. If in this area, do not miss the **Forteresse Féodale de Rambures**. Up at **Abbéville** is the lovely Château and Jardin de Bagatelle (open in July and August in the afternoon only), the Boucher de Perthes Museum of regional history and the flamboyant Gothic church of St-Vulfran. Other magnificent examples of this style are the Chapelle du Saint Esprit at **Rue** and the abbey at **St-Riquier**. The latter is part of a cultural complex including permanent exhibitions on the evolution of Gothic art and rural life in Picardy, as well as other thematic displays and a pleasant park. If at St-Riquier in the second fortnight of July, be sure to attend some of the events of the Summer Classical Music Festival. On Sunday afternoons you can enjoy an excellent guided visit of the **Muches de Domqueur**, which are late medieval underground refuges. The more famous **Grottes de Naours** are open every day and have 300 underground rooms, crossroads, stables, wells and an unusual chapel. Outside there is an exhibition of old trades. **Doullens, Albert** and **Péronne** are the places to go for memorials and museums of the First World War.

Particularly worth seeing is the 'Historical de la Grande Guerre' at Péronne. Nearby, you can explore the ponds of the Somme by steam train between Froissy and Dompierre on certain afternoons (enquire at a tourist office).

In the vicinity of Amiens is the village of **Ailly-sur-Noye** where 1200 local people put on a *Son et Lumière* History of Picardy on Friday and Saturday evenings in late August and September. At **Saleux** is the Ferme d'Antan, an accurately recreated working farm of the beginning of the century, which will particularly appeal to children and is a starting point for walks in the Creuse forest. The archaeological park **Samara**, north-west of Amiens, is also fascinating: it contains a botanical garden and arboretum; a peat-bog with peat-cutter's equipment; prehistoric dwellings reconstructed after archaeological digs at 'Oppidum – Camp César', the most important fortified site in northern France, situated on the hill behind; demonstrations of prehistoric techniques such as flint-cutting; and exhibitions both of life in the past and of projected future ecosystems.

Accommodation & Eating Out

In the Somme, it is possible to have a room and breakfast in a park-surrounded château for less than 150FF. To be recommended are:

First Class

Château de Remaisnil, 80600 Doullens (Tel. 22 77 07 47): 20 rooms in eighteenth century château. **Château – Vauchelles les Domart**, 80620 Domart en Ponthieu (Tel. 22 51 62 51): 5 rooms in seventeenth- and eighteenth-century château.

Middle Range / Economy

Mme Raymond, 25 quai Perrée, 80230 St-Valéry-sur-Somme (Tel. 22 60 82 41): 1 *chambres d'hôte* in pleasant house near harbour.

Economy

Grand Hôtel de la Paix, 39–47 rue Victor-Hugo, 80300 Albert (Tel. 22 75 01 64): 15 rooms in family-run hotel whose restaurant was finalist in the 1989/90 Logis de France regional cuisine competition. **M. Goisque**, Château de Digeon, 80590 Morvillers-St-Saturnin

(Tel. 22 38 07 12): 3 *chambres d'hôte* in château with park. **Les Amis du Moulin**, 80140 St-Maxent (Tel. 22 28 52 28): 4 rooms in former mill-house. **Abbaye du Gard**, Crouy, 80310 Picquigny (Tel. 22 51 40 50): 5 rooms in eighteenth-century house with park.

If you wish to rent an apartment on the coast (minimum two nights), contact **Loisirs-Accueil**, 21 rue E. Cauvin, 80000 Amiens (Tel. 22 92 26 39). For a simple, truly regional restaurant, try **La Clé des Champs** at Favières.

Aisne

Aisne is considered the best *département* in France for environmental education. Though its natural attractions are the most obvious, there are many others besides, most of which are described in the tourist office brochure 'L'Aisne au Culturel'.

Laon

This pocket-sized administrative capital of Aisne is a town which should not be missed. Once capital of France under the Carolingian kings, it is located on top of a hill (you must climb 280 steps to reach the *Ville Haute*) and surrounded by 8 kilometres of medieval ramparts. It also contains some eighty classified buildings of architectural interest. Laon's early Gothic **Cathédrale de Notre-Dame**, begun in the twelfth century, still has traces of the Romanesque. Its most striking features are its beautiful façade and its five ornamented towers (originally there were seven) – look out for the carved oxen peeping between the columns. The former **Bishop's Palace** next door (now the law courts) bears witness to the transition from the Romanesque to the Gothic. An example of a later, more simple Gothic church is the **Eglise St-Martin** at the other end of the *Ville Haute*. The **Chapelle des Templiers** is an interesting octagonal building from the twelfth century, set in its own garden; nearby rue Vinchon boasts many attractive old buildings. The **Musée Municipal** on Rue Georges Hermant has a collection of local archaeological finds and paintings by the Le Nain brothers among others. Make sure you walk round the ramparts; you will be impressed not only by the view, but also by the medieval gates, the Porte d'Ardon, Porte de Chenizelles and Porte de Soissons.

Accommodation

There are no top-of-the-range hotels, but the following are recommended:

Middle Range

Hôtel de la Bannière de France, 11 rue Franklin-Roosevelt (Tel. 23 23 21 44): 19 rooms in seventeenth century coaching inn with restaurant (see below).

Middle Range / Economy

Les Chevaliers, 3 rue Sérurier (Tel. 23 23 43 78): 15 rooms in hotel with restaurant serving regional specialities.

Economy

Hôtel du Commerce, 13 Place de la Gare (Tel. 23 79 10 38): 25 rooms in hotel near station. **Hôtel Welcome**, 2 ave Carnot (Tel. 23 23 06 11): 12 rooms. **Les Roses de Picardie**, 11 rue Clémenceau, 02410 St-Gobain (Tel. 23 52 88 74): 13 rooms in hotel some way out of town.

Eating Out

First Class

Hôtel de la Bannière de France (address as above): traditional French cuisine.

Middle Range

La Petite Auberge, 45 bd Brossolette (Tel. 23 23 02 38): nouvelle cuisine; good selection of wines. **Les Chenizelles**, 1 rue du Bourg (Tel. 23 23 02 34): brasserie style restaurant.

Economy

La Porte d'Ardon, 2/4 rue Vinchon (Tel. 23 20 64 62): traditional cuisine with fish specialities. **L'Assiette Laonnaise**, 31 rue Fernand Thuillard (Tel. 23 79 26 93): traditional cooking.

Entertainments

The **Maison des Arts et des Loisirs** (Place Aubry) regularly puts on concerts, plays and exhibitions. At the tourist office you will find various leaflets distributed by local societies who welcome visitors to their meetings or excursions: it is also well worth getting hold of the Laon newspaper supplement, *Elan*. If you are there in early September, you will experience the lively **Heures Médiévales** festival. Laon is a town with many artists, whose studios are often open to the public. The indoor swimming pool at the end of the rampart-edged Promenade St-Martin is worth trying out.

Useful Addresses

The **Tourist Office** is in Place du Parvis (Tel. 23 20 28 62); it will give you information about guided tours of the town amongst other things. The **Comité Départemental du Tourisme**, which will provide information on the whole Aisne region and often hires out bikes (cyclists should ask for the brochure *Cyclotourisme: guide pratique*), is at Maison de Refuge St-Vincent, 1 rue St-Martin (Tel. 23 20 45 54). The **Post Office** is at Place des Frères Le Nain (at the end of rue Pourier). The **Hospital** is Centre Hospitalier de Laon, rue Dévisme (next to Eglise St-Martin – Tel. 23 24 33 33 or 23 20 20 20).

Transport Options

If you don't fancy the 280 steps up from the train station to the *Ville Haute*, there is a cable-car system called POMA 2000 which makes the journey at frequent intervals. The only way to appreciate fully the view from the top is a walk all round the ramparts, with regular stops. This and other town walking circuits are facilitated by a system of signposts designed specifically for pedestrians. There are also town buses, and bicycles can be rented from the train station.

Rest of Aisne

St-Quentin boasts not only the Marais d'Isle nature reserve but also a Maison de la Nature which explains the ecosystem of the Somme river, its ponds and marshes. The Gothic basilica is worth seeing, as is the Antoine Lecuyer museum of regional history (including eighty of Quentin de la Tour's pastel drawings), the insect museum, the historical theatre and the numerous antique and craft shops (visit the wood-carver's workshop at 153 rue de la Chaussée-Romaine). From the Gauchy station at St-Quentin, a little tourist train runs to Origny-Ste-Benoite on summer Sundays. The hedge-crossed **Thiérache** area is good for walking, cycling and riding and has many rural *gîtes*. It also has a unique concentration of over sixty fortified churches: try to visit the one at **Jeantes** and the beautiful village of **Parfondeval**. Further south at **Corbeny** is the Museum of the Living Bee, and at the nearby **Abbaye de Vauclair** are fascinating gardens of medicinal plants. From the little village of **Bourguignon**, near Laon, regular group walks set off: information about these and local festivals is available from the Syndicat d'Initiative (Mairie). The **Cessières** marsh has been declared a site of international value for its rich flora and insect life and the unusual juxtaposition of acidic and alkaline peat. 'Discovery' paths exist, and nearby is the **Château de Coucy**. At **Tergnier** is a regional museum of resistance and deportation, and, in the grounds of the Abbey of St-Jean-des-Vignes in **Soissons**, is a reconstruction of a sixth century Frankish house and garden. Soissons also has a remarkable Gothic cathedral, several local jewellery-makers (try 4 rue St-Martin) and, in June, hosts the *Lumiscenies*, a spectacular *Son et Lumière* presentation at the abbey. **Château-Thierry**, in the heart of the Champagne vineyards of the Marne valley, was the birth-place of the fable-writer Jean de la Fontaine, who naturally has a museum devoted to him and a festival in June.

Accommodation & Eating Out

First Class

Grand Hotel, 6 rue Dachery, 02100 St-Quentin (Tel. 23 62 69 77): 24 rooms in luxurious, attractively decorated hotel.

Middle Range

La Tour du Roy, 45 rue du Général-Leclerc, 02140 Vervins (Tel. 23 98 00 11): 15 rooms in turreted sixteenth century mansion with excellent restaurant. **Hôtel de l'Abbaye**, Rue des Tourelles, 02600 Longpont (Tel. 23 96 02 44): 12 rooms in ivy-covered hotel. **Mme Royol**, Les Patrus, 02540 L'Epine au Bois (Tel. 23 82 67 87): 5 *chambres d'hôte* in seventeenth century farmhouse.

Economy

Mme Sendron, Ferme 'Le Château', 02540 Montfaucon (Tel. 23 82 82 34): 2 *chambres d'hôte* in farmhouse doubling as *ferme-auberge*.

Oise

Oise is the most densely wooded *département* of Picardy, and walking, riding or cycling between its fairy-tale castles and their very varied parks is the ideal way to see them. Ask for the tourist office brochure 'Du Roman au Gothique par les Forêts Royales de l'Oise', which contains maps and practical information.

Compiègne

This town grew up around a palace established here in 873 by Charles the Bald, and became a favourite place of retreat for French monarchs. The present **château** is predominantly late eighteenth century and somewhat severely classical. The interior decorations are, however, magnificent, and the château also houses a **Museum of the Second Empire** and a **Car Museum**. The formal park is pleasant to stroll in. The **Vivenel Museum**, whose garden is a public park, includes archaeological and art collections of the nineteenth-century architect Vivenel. There is also a **Museum of Historical Figurines** in which tin soldiers recreate the Battle of Waterloo, helped along by audiovisual effects. The **Town Hall** is a remarkable building with a statue-covered facade, which combines Gothic and Renaissance styles. The thirteenth-century **Eglise St-Jacques** is where Joan of Arc took communion on the day she was captured by the English, an event to which the **Beauregard Tower** also bears witness.

Accommodation

First Class / Middle Range

Hostellerie du Royal Lieu, 9 rue de Senlis (Tel. 44 20 10 24): 20 comfortable rooms in quiet old hotel on edge of forest; with restaurant (see below).

Middle Range

Hôtel du Nord, 1 Place de la Gare (Tel. 44 83 22 30): 20 rooms in family-run hotel with restaurant. **Hôtel de Harlay**, 3 rue de Harlay (Tel. 44 23 01 50): 20 rooms.

Middle Range / Economy

Hôtel de France et Rôtisserie du Chat qui Tourne, 17 rue Eugène-Floquet (Tel. 44 40 02 74): 22 rooms in family-run hotel with restaurant (see below).

Economy

Le Solférino, 4 rue Solférino (Tel. 44 23 33 18): 15 rooms. **Hôtel du Lion d'Or**, 4 rue Général Leclerc (Tel, 44 23 32 17): 21 rooms in pleasant hotel.

Eating Out

First Class

Hostellerie du Royal Lieu (address above): classical cuisine using fresh ingredients which vary according to the season, **Auberge du Pont**, 21 rue du Maréchal-Foch, 60153 Rethondes (Tel. 44 85 60 24): light, imaginative cuisine in historic building, 9 km out of town.

Middle Range

Le Relais Impérial, ZAC de Mercières, BP 636 (Tel. 44 20 11 11): good regional and house specialities. **Rôtisserie du Chat qui Tourne** (address above): house specialities.

Economy

Restaurant de la Poste, 4 rue Napoléon (Tel. 44 40 10 64). **Le Solférino** (address above): good value.

Entertainments

From late May to early June is the Fête des Séries, which involves dynamic street theatre and dancing. If you are fortunate enough to be here over the fourth weekend in September, do not miss the *Son et Lumière* in the park of the château. Remember Compiègne is a good place to start river tours on the Oise – ask at the tourist office.

Useful Addresses

The **Tourist Office** is in the Hôtel de Ville, Place Hôtel de Ville, BP 106 (Tel. 44 40 01 00). The **Post Office** is at rue des Domeliers and the **Hospital** at 42 rue de Paris (Tel. 44 20 16 36).

Transport Options

Most attractions can be reached on foot, though a free bus service runs from the station, with most buses stopping at the Hôtel de Ville. The tourist office provides a full bus timetable for both town buses and those going further afield. The bus station is at 10 rue d'Amiens. Bicycles can be rented from the train station.

Rest of Oise

The **Noyon** area has long been one of fruit cultivation and there is a 'Red Fruit Festival' in the town each July. Noyon is also famous for its twelfth-century **Cathédrale de Notre-Dame**, the Jean Calvin Museum (in the house where he was born on Place Aristide Briand), and the sixteenth-century library with its huge collection of precious volumes, including a ninth-century manuscript. Cycleways and footpaths follow streams and gorges in the forests of **Laigue** and **Compiègne**, where bicycles can be hired. It was in a railway carriage in a clearing of the Compiègne Forest that the Armistice was signed on 11 November 1918: a replica of the carriage remains there on display, along with a giant statue of Maréchal Foch. Nearby **Pierrefonds** castle, a restored medieval fortress of great splendour, overlooks the pleasant little town and lake of Pierrefonds. A steam train can be taken through the woods. From **Crépy-en-Valois**, you can explore the **Vallée d'Automne** with its thirty-five village churches. Crépy itself has a ruined castle, an abbey and the Geresmes park. At the **Parc Jean-Jacques Rousseau** at **Ermenonville** you can make a pilgrimage to the memorial of the writer and philosopher on the **Ile des Peupliers**. The informal landscape of the park is an early and accurate evocation of Rousseau's philosophy. In the woods a geological freak has laid bare a vast expanse of sand, known as the **Mer de Sable**, which makes an interesting destination for a walk. North-west is the town of **Senlis** with its flamboyant Gothic cathedral, numerous museums, modest château, and the remains of a Gallo-Roman amphitheatre, which combine to create a strong sense of history. In September there is a festival during which the town is closed to traffic. **Chantilly**'s château is anything but modest; it is built on two islands in the middle of a lake and surrounded by an immaculate park. Mid-June brings to it an impressive firework festival. The château houses the magnificent Condé Museum, which includes rare manuscripts and miniatures, along with paintings by

Raphaël and Botticelli. Chantilly is also a horseriding centre – the Newmarket of France – and the stables opposite the château are part of the 'Living Horse Museum', which gives dressage displays. Beyond **Creil**, where you can visit the Gallé-Juillet museum of nineteenth-century furniture and accessories or hire a barge, and **Clermont**, with its fourteenth-century town hall, is the departmental capital, **Beauvais**. Here, the **Comité Départemental du Tourisme** (1 rue Villiers de l'Isle Adam, BP 822, 60008 Beauvais, Tel. 44 45 82 12) will give you information about the whole of Oise. Beauvais is worth visiting despite occasional unpleasant whiffs from a nearby tyre factory, for the town boasts a Gothic cathedral (inside which you could fit the Arc de Triomphe) as well as the National Tapestry Museum and an *ecomusée* at 2 rue du Franc-Marché. The *ecomusée* has exhibitions on Picardy's industrial and agricultural heritage, the rural way of life and regional ethnology, as well as organising guided visits to different monuments. Try to find time to see the Benedictine abbey at **St-Germer-de-Fly** and the beautiful medieval village of **Gerberoy**.

Accommodation & Eating Out

First Class / Middle Range

Auberge 'A la Bonne Idée', 3 rue des Meuniers, 60350 St-Jean-aux-Bois (Tel. 44 42 84 09): 24 spacious rooms in eighteenth century building on edge of forest; excellent restaurant.

Middle Range

Hôtel des Etrangers, 10 rue du Baudron, 60350 Pierrefonds (Tel. 44 42 80 18 or 87 11): 18 rooms in family-run hotel. **Auberge de Fontaine**, 22 Grand-Rue, 60300 Fontaine-Chaalis (Tel. 44 54 20 22): 8 rooms in family-run hotel. **L'Oustal**, 36 rue Nationale, Sérifontaine, 60590 Trie-Château (Tel. 44 49 73 38): 4 rooms in family guest house.

Economy

Le Relais St-Denis, 7 rue de l'Eglise, 60340 Villers-sous-St-Leu (Tel. 44 56 31 87): 9 rooms in family-run hotel. **La Taverne**, Lieu-dit la Folie, D 916, Beauvoir, 60120 Breteuil-sur-Noye (Tel. 44 07 03 57): 11 rooms in family-run hotel.

5 Paris and the Ile-de-France

The dazzling reputation of Paris is frequently allowed to eclipse the splendours of the surrounding area. All too often, even the highlights of the rest of the Ile-de-France are given cursory attention (with several crammed together in day-trip form), and its many other sources of interest are virtually ignored. This is unfortunate when one considers that, even without Paris at its centre, the Ile-de-France would be one of the most culturally varied and exciting parts of the country. It must be remembered that Paris is only one of eight *départements* in its region, and that the capital's vibrancy and the astounding density of its attractions are pleasantly balanced by the calmer pace and wider spaces of the rest.

One reason for the magnetic pull exerted by Paris is its sheer compactness. Unlike London, you can walk across Paris quite comfortably in a single afternoon, and only just over two million people live in the city itself. Yet it contains an extraordinary number of world-famous monuments, museums, galleries, streets and buildings. Inevitably, such places are the destinations of hordes of holiday-makers, especially in summer, and their appeal is, on occasion, heightened by the sense of competition. But this is coupled with a reluctant descent to the 'been-there-done-that' mentality. The crowds and bustle can be exciting, and certainly add to Paris's cosmopolitan atmosphere, but they can also be frustrating and a barrier to personal contact. One solution is to visit Paris off-season, perhaps in April or October, when things are slightly less frenetic. Another solution is to make your base outside the capital, perhaps in a *chambres d'hôte* somewhere in the 270,000 acre greenbelt area surrounding the city, and, using the extremely efficient train system, visit Paris on a daily basis from there. This reverses the usual way of doing things, and is obviously not appropriate if you wish to make the most of Parisian nightlife, but it is considerably cheaper than staying in Paris and allows a breathing space between visits, especially welcome for families with children.

The essence of Paris is 'culture' in a highly concentrated form, diluted only by the city's parks and other green areas; the rest of the Ile-de-France is more like the 'real world', albeit a particularly rich slice of it. The extensive wheatfields, poplar-lined roads, the winding river Seine, dense forests and squat village steeples form the region's backdrop. The foreground consists of prehistoric remains, medieval towns, royal châteaux and stately homes from every architectural period, a comprehensive network of footpaths and a wealth of outdoor pursuits. Even quite close to Paris, you can find a regional park and much unspoilt countryside. The people who live here, the *Franciliens*, are naturally less hassled than the Parisians and have more time for tourists, especially if you make the effort to address them in French.

Complementing the Eiffel Tower, the Arc de Triomphe, the Champs-Elysées and Paris high-life with leisurely walks through landscaped parks, charming villages or deer-filled forests, is a sensible idea. You're far less likely to need a second holiday to recover from the first.

History

From the sixth century BC, Celtic tribes settled in the valleys of the Paris Basin, the Parisii making their home on what is now the Ile de la Cité (an island on the Seine in the heart of Paris). Caesar conquered the area in 52 BC and, a century on, the Gallo-Romans built the city of Lutetia, whose first bishop, St Denis, was martyred in Montmartre around AD 250. The name Lutetia was changed to Paris in 380. It was in 508 that Clovis, king of Francia, made this little town his capital, though it was abandoned by Charlemagne in the eighth century and left to decline. Capital once more in the thirteenth century, King Philippe Auguste built a wall around it and, in 1215, the University was founded. The Hundred Years' War caused considerable damage all over the Ile-de-France, which was in English hands until the liberation of Pontoise in 1441; Henry VI of England was even King of France for seven years.

Much ambitious building work was carried out during the seventeenth century, including Paris's Luxembourg Palace and the extravagant Palace of Versailles, commissioned by Louis XIV as the new home of the monarchy. The end of the eighteenth century saw the construction of a further wall (the fifth one) around the expanding capital. It was called the Farmers General Wall and included fifty-seven controversial toll-houses, designed by the architect Claude-Nicolas Ledoux. The Revolution brought us the most famous date in French history: the storming of the Bastille on 14 July 1789. It was not, however, until 1792 that the Tuileries were taken, the monarchy fell and a Republic was proclaimed. The period known as the Terror gripped Paris in 1793 and 1794. Ten years later, Napoleon was crowned in Notre-Dame, then took up residence in Malmaison. The Arc de Triomphe, among other monuments, was built during his rule, which ended with the invasion of France by the Allies in 1814 and his abdication at Fontainebleau. The Bourbons were restored to power, canals dug, the first French railway line opened, and yet another wall, the Thiers fortifications, was built, becoming the official limits of the capital in 1859. Baron Haussmann was commissioned to change the layout of Paris, creating the great boulevards and dividing it into its twenty *arrondissements*.

In 1870, the Third Republic was proclaimed, but soon afterwards the Prussians invaded Paris, defeating the revolutionaries of the Paris Commune and forcing the French government to move to Versailles until 1878. The Eiffel Tower was built for the World Exhibition in 1889 and the first Metro line opened in 1900. The Battle of the Marne saved Paris from attack in the First World War, which ended with the 1919 Treaty of Versailles. 1940 brought the occupation of Paris, followed by its liberation in August 1944.

In 1964 the region around Paris was reorganised into its present *départements* and a regional Town and Development Plan brought into being various new towns. May 1968 saw many strikes and demonstrations and, in 1970, the University was decentralised to form thirteen autonomous ones. It was not until 1976 that the Ile-de-France region was officially created. Since 1977, Paris has had an elected mayor, who works alongside the town halls of the different *arrondissements*; present projects include the revitalisation of depressed areas.

Of course, vast numbers of famous people have associations with this part of France, which has always been an automatic destination for intellectuals, politicians, aristocrats, artists and exiles of many nationalities. Among the names which crop up the most frequently are Le Vau and Mansart, major seventeenth-century architects, together with Le Brun, the main decorator, and Le Nôtre, the famous landscape gardener. In the art world there were Camille Corot, Théodore Rousseau, Henri de Toulouse-Lautrec, Camille Pissarro, and many of the Impressionist School. Paris also figures strongly in works by numerous authors including Voltaire, Victor Hugo, Balzac and Zola.

Geography

The Ile-de-France is made up of eight *départements* (including Paris), which radiate from the capital. Immediately round Paris are the little suburban *départements* of (clockwise) Seine-St-Denis, Val-de-Marne and Hauts-de-Seine. Their administrative capitals are, respectively, Bobigny, Créteil and Nanterre. Surrounding these is another ring of *départements*: Val-d'Oise (capital Pontoise), Seine-et-Marne (capital Melun), Essonne (capital Evry), and Yvelines (capital Versailles). Both Paris and the Ile-de-France as a whole are shaped roughly like a rugby ball. The region covers an area of 12,000 square kilometres, has 10.2 million inhabitants (18.5% of the French population), and produces 27% of the Gross National Product. Paris itself is only 100 square kilometres (40 square miles) and has a population of 2.2 million.

The Ile-de-France is a low limestone plateau which boasts ten major rivers, with 600 km of navigable waterway through orchard-lined valleys, and eight major forests, criss-crossed by 4000 km of marked footpaths. The wheat-fields and meadows in between are a sign of the area's agricultural richness: it is famed not only for its cereals and beef cattle, but also for cheeses, honey, fruits and vegetables (watercress, lettuce, radish and beetroot), flowers, pot-plants and trees. Much of the local industry is associated with energy production and concentrated around Paris, Creil, Mantes and Melun.

The lowest point of the Paris Basin is the Seine valley; on either side of this, the country undulates considerably. The other main rivers include the Oise, the Marne and the Essonne. The forests are either private, local authority or state; the latter are known as 'forêts domaniales' and are run by the Office National des Forêts. They sometimes contain what are known as 'biological reserves', which, though open to the public, are protected areas. The forests of the Ile-de-France are made up mainly of oak, beech, hornbeam, chestnut, birch and Scots pine, and are carefully managed. The most famous are probably Rambouillet and Fontainebleau, which has fourteen biological reserves. There is an information and documentation service on French forests, called Allo-Forêt, at 1 ter ave de Lowendal, 75007 Paris, (Tel. 45 51 61 71).

The Ile-de-France sprouts colourful broom in spring and summer, and the forests favour a cycle of flowers, ferns, mushrooms, nuts and berries, which extends round the year. Deer are quite a common sight. Various animal reserves have been set up, notably the **Parc Animalier des Yvelines** at Sonchamp (closed during the breeding season), and the Parc de St-Vrain in Essonne. There is an ornithological reserve at the Château de Sauvage at Emance (Yvelines). The only officially established nature reserve is an urban pond at St-Quentin-en-Yvelines, which is often used for educational purposes.

Yvelines is also home to the only regional park in the Paris area. It is called the Parc Naturel Régional de la Haute Vallée de Chevreuse, covers 63,250 acres of river valley, woodland and agricultural land, and contains nearly one thousand buildings of interest. Its aim is the protection of the natural and architectural heritage and the prevention of urbanisation. It has some excellent projects underway, but its footpaths, museums, châteaux and gardens (a welcome escape from the metropolis), attract rather too many weekend visitors and it is wiser to come mid-week.

Climate

The Parisian climate is variable, with a fair amount of rain in autumn and summer. The temperature ranges from an average of about 2.5 °C in January to one of about 18.5°C in July and August, though top temperatures can be considerably higher. On average, around six days a year are above 30°C. Sunshine hours range from about two a day in November, December and January, to around eight a day in June. Climate-wise, good times to visit the area are late April through to June, and September/October, though winter in Paris can be a magical experience if your visit coincides with a fall of snow.

Attractions

The Ile-de-France contains an astounding 2000 classified historical monuments and 200 museums (with eighty museums and 200 art galleries in Paris alone). Twelve out of the fourteen most visited attractions in France are situated in the Ile-de-France (eleven of them in Paris). Those which receive more than 1 million visitors a year are the Pompidou Centre, the Eiffel Tower, the Cité des

Sciences et de l'Industrie, the Louvre Museum, the Château de Versailles, and the Orsay Museum.

Obviously, most people's reasons for visiting this area are, broadly speaking, 'cultural'. Because Paris is so culturally rich, many visitors do not venture outside the centre, or, if they do, make a bee-line for Versailles or Fontainebleau. The lesser known châteaux of the Ile-de-France, of which there are dozens, including Breteuil (with its wax historical figures); Maisons-Laffitte, Dampierre, and St-Jean-de-Beauregard, are less crowded and often give an equally good idea of how life was (and, in some cases, still is) for the French aristocracy. As opening times vary from Sunday afternoons only to every day of the year, it is worth enquiring in advance. Many towns associated with famous people have good museums: the J-J Rousseau Museum at Montmorency, the Rodin Museum at Meudon, and the House of Chateaubriand at Châtenay-Malabry, for example.

With all its forests and waterways, the Ile-de-France is also ideal for nature and activity tourism. Not only rambling but all types of sport, are well catered for, whether you wish to take advantage of one of the comprehensive leisure parks or to take off independently, on bike, boat or horseback. The Ile-de-France even has its own spa town: Enghien-les-Bains in the Val-d'Oise.

Cuisine

This part of the country does not really have its own cuisine, though Paris is the place to come if you wish to sample traditional dishes from regions throughout France and its colonies. North African dishes such as couscous are popular and have been absorbed into everyday French cooking, often as a less expensive alternative. It is worth getting hold of the the weekly 'L'Officiel des Spectacles' which lists restaurants serving both French and foreign specialities.

The nearest the Ile-de-France gets to a regional cuisine are the various game dishes served during the hunting season. It is also famous for its delicious pastries, gâtinais honey, mimolette and brie cheeses, and meaux mustard.

Level of Tourism

The level of tourism here is the highest in France, but is rather unevenly spread. The Ile-de-France hosts over 14 million hotel visits a year (about 50% more than the next most popular region – Rhône-Alpes). The average hotel stay lasts a little over two nights, and just over half the visitors come from abroad. It is interesting that trends show a recent decrease in hotel-based visits to provincial France, while those to the Ile-de-France have increased. The influx of tourists means that Paris experiences a doubling of its population in the summer season. Visitors include back-packers and business people, coach-trippers and honeymooners. Paris is known both as the ultimate romantic destination and the world's top congress city. Its tourists are of all nationalities, including many Americans and Japanese, and projects to promote the city in Eastern Europe are now under way.

It is just as well that the region has the densest and most modern transport network in the world. Even this is under considerable pressure, with 3 million vehicles entering and leaving Paris daily, adding to those of the Parisians themselves. You would have to be mad to choose to drive in Paris, or on its ring-roads: traffic jams are often worse than in London, penalties for traffic offences are steep, parking is non-existent . . . and the public transport system is efficient, clean and cheap. Nor is it advisable to go to Paris in July or August. Most Parisians are on their own summer holidays in the south of France at this time, so tourists by far outnumber local people, and there is a distinct lack of facilities. In addition, the weather is often hot and oppressive.

Tourism-related problems all seem to stem from the fact that too many people choose to visit the same things at the same time. Summer weekends are the worst. The fact that admission to the Louvre is half-price on Sundays means that you can barely see the paintings. It is worth paying more to go during the week, or, better still, buy the *Carte Inter-Musées*, which is very good value, allowing entrance to sixty museums and monuments in and around Paris, without queuing, and is valid for one, three or five days, depending on how much you pay. Queuing up in sweltering heat to climb the stairs of the Arc de Triomphe or to purchase tickets for the Château de Versailles is not fun. It is therefore wise to arrive at the most popular tourist attractions early in the morning. One consolation for the fact that most of Montmartre is a 'tourist trap' is that it always has been; at least, ever since the 1890s, when Toulouse-Lautrec and friends decided it would be a money-spinner to spread the myth that it was a den of loose living and artistic talent. There is, of course, a positive side to the 'famous monument tourist crush': namely, that all the less well known destinations are virtually empty. Even in popular forests like Fontainebleau, it is possible to find deserted paths, as most people stay near the château – though the task is made infinitely easier if you go mid-week.

So many local people make their living through the tourist industry that there is generally little resentment, unless, perhaps, you get in the way of a flustered commuter during rush-hour on the Metro. The regional park's efforts to prevent further urbanisation south-west of Paris have been successful so far. The French government usually thinks quite hard before putting up new buildings, and, however controversial the results, they are somehow representative of twentieth-century French culture and taste. One new addition does, however, seem unlikely to make many concessions to local culture. The enormous Euro-Disneyland, at Marne-la-Vallée just east of Paris, which cost some 23 billion FF to build, offers 5200 new hotel rooms and is due to attract 11 million visitors a year. But, apart from the inclusion of some characters from European fairy-tales, this controversial development is 100% American.

Good Alternatives

Meeting People

Like most capital cities, Paris is not particularly conducive to meeting local people, unless you are prepared to make an effort. Often the best places to meet people or just to soak up the atmosphere of the city are the markets, including the famous flea markets (see **Paris – Entertainments**). If you are interested in contemporary art, why not visit some artists' studios: the ones on quai de la Gare (13e), rather than Montmartre. Alternatively, contact C. Katz, **Cercle des Artistes Plasticiens**, 44 rue du Faubourg du Temple, 75011 Paris (Tel. 43 38 31 85), who will arrange for you to make a tour of artists' studios in the Bastille area. The **Maison de la Vigne et du Vin de France**, 21 rue François 1er, 75008 Paris (Tel. 47 20 20 76), offers audio-visual presentations of French wines, rounded off with tastings. Keen archaeologists should contact **Union Rempart**, 1 rue de Guillemites, 75004 Paris (Tel. 42 71 96 55), an association which organises restoration workshops and archaeological digs. A similar organisation is the **Club du Vieux Manoir**, 10 rue de la Cossonnerie, 75001 Paris (Tel. 45 08 80 40). Further information on digs in the Ile-de-France is available from the **Direction des**

Antiquités, Château de Vincennes, Donjon du Vieux Fort, Avenue de Paris, 94300 Vincennes (Tel. 48 08 60 66).

A good way of getting to know local people is simply to choose bed and breakfast accommodation. Three organisations offer accommodation in Parisian homes: **Café-Couette** (literally 'Coffee-Quilt'), arranges B&B accommodation nationwide and has some Paris addresses. Contact Café-Couette, 8 rue de l'Isly, 75008 Paris (Tel. 42 94 92 00) for information on membership. **Bed and Breakfast**, 73 rue Notre-Dame-des-Champs, 75006 Paris (Tel. 43 25 43 97) has many hosts in Paris. Alternatively, try **Accueil VVF**, at Comité Régional VVF Ile-de-France, 40 bd Edgar Quinet, 75014 Paris (Tel. 43 22 24 14). Bear in mind, however, that the B&B concept is relatively new to France, especially to city-dwellers, and that Parisians are often very busy people. You will almost certainly experience a warmer welcome if you are able to stay outside Paris itself, booking your accommodation either through one of the above associations or through the national *chambres d'hôte* network. The **Maison du Tourisme Vert**, 35 rue Godot-de-Mauroy, 75009 Paris (Tel. 47 42 25 43), can give you a list of *chambres d'hôte* in any region, including the Ile-de-France. If you want to meet a lot of friendly Parisians all at once, go to the Champs-Elysées or Boulevard St-Michel on New Year's Eve!

Discovering Places

The tourist office leaflet 'Saisons de Paris' lists all exhibitions, fairs, performances and events: you may well find that your special interest features in some form. If that happens to be history, and if you are staying in Paris for a while, it may be worth enquiring about membership of **CLIO – Les Amis de l'Histoire**, an association which organises lectures, cultural outings with specialist guides, and even holidays for its members. The address is **CLIO**, 34 rue du Hameau, 75015 Paris (Tel. 48 42 15 15). Guided tours of the older parts of Paris, in particular the Marais area, are arranged by the **Association pour la Sauvegarde et la Mise en Valeur du Paris Historique**, 44–6 rue François Miron, 75004 Paris. If you require any further information on matters cultural in the Ile-de-France, write to the **Direction Régionale des Affaires Culturelles de l'Ile-de-France**, Grand-Palais Porte C, avenue Franklin-Roosevelt, 75008 Paris.

The **Société Nationale de Protection de la Nature**, 57 rue Cuvier, BP 405, 75231 Paris Cedex 05 (Tel. 47 07 31 95), is the oldest conservation society in France and offers nature study day-trips, weekends and longer holidays to its members. Many day-long hikes are arranged by the **Randonneurs d'Ile-de-France**, 66 rue de Gergovie, 75014 Paris (Tel. 45 42 24 72). These usually start from a Paris station and visitors may join two excursions before becoming a member. The **Mouvement de Défense de la Bicyclette**, 32 rue Raymond Losserand, 75014 Paris, operates a similar scheme for cycling trips, some of which last a full weekend.

The non-profit-making organisation 'Grand R', La Maison de la Randonnée, 140 rue de Picpus, 75012 Paris (Tel. 43 47 31 10), cooperates with the regional tourist board to offer walking, cycling, horseriding, canoeing, boating and sporting holidays at very reasonable rates. You can join one of their group holidays or design your own itinerary. Two of the Ile-de-France *départements* have their own tour operators: **Service Loisirs-Accueil de Seine-et-Marne**, Château Soubiran, 170 ave Henri-Barbusse, 77190 Dammarie-lès-Lys (Tel. 64 37 19 36); and **Sevice Loisirs-Accueil du Val-d'Oise**, Hôtel du Département, 2 le Campus, 95032 Cergy-Pontoise (Tel. 34 25 32 52). Both organise small-scale local trips. Information on how to recognise and where to buy food and crafts which are local and produced using traditional techniques is available from the **Chambre Régionale d'Agriculture**, 42 rue du Louvre, 75001 Paris (Tel. 42 36 73 51).

Communications

How to Get There

The two Paris **airports** are Roissy-Charles de Gaulle (north-east of the capital) and Orly (to the south). British Airways (Tel. 081 897 4000) and Air France (Tel. 081 499 9511) both offer ten flights a day between London and Paris, while British Midland (Tel. 081 589 5599) flies the Heathrow-Paris route eight times a day. Air France provides regular flights to Paris from Aberdeen, Birmingham, Bristol, Cardiff, Edinburgh, Glasgow, Manchester and Southampton. The Manchester-Paris route is also served by British Airways and Aer Lingus. The cheapest return prices for London-Paris start at around £65 for students. Both Paris airports have bus and train connections to central Paris.

There are direct **trains** from London to Paris. Those which go via Newhaven – Dieppe arrive at Gare St-Lazare; those going via Dover – Calais, or Folkestone – Boulogne arrive at Gare du Nord. At present, the journey takes between 6 and 10 hours.

Eurolines run a daily **coach** service to Paris from London, South Wales, Bristol, Bath, Salisbury and Bournemouth. Hoverspeed also run a Citysprint coach service between the two capitals. Prices start from around £45 return. Most coaches from abroad, including Britain, arrive at the Gare Routière Internationale, 3 ave de la Porte de la Villette, 75019 Paris.

Those **driving** to Paris from one of the northern Channel ports will enter the capital on the A1; those arriving from one of the Normandy ports will need the A13.

When You're There

Rail – each of the six Paris stations specialises in certain destinations, as follows: Gare St-Lazare – Normandy; Gare du Nord – northern France; Gare de l'Est – eastern France; Gare de Lyon – southern and south-eastern France; Gare d'Austerlitz – south-western France; Gare de Montparnasse – Brittany. Each station also has a separate section for trains to the suburbs (*banlieue*). In addition, the high-speed RER network extends to many places quite a long way out of Paris, including St-Rémy-lès-Chevreuse, St-Quentin-en-Yvelines, Versailles and St-Germain-en-Laye, and selected stations connect with the SNCF network.

Bus – in the Ile-de-France, local trains are generally used more frequently than buses. Numerous Paris coach tour operators do trips to sights in the Ile-de-France; ask for a list at the tourist office.

Car – using a car for a visit to Paris makes no sense at all. You will save money, the environment and your own sanity by using public transport. Even if you plan to spend your whole holiday outside Paris, touring the Ile-de-France, think twice before bringing the car; or consider going to **ACAR Réseau**, 77 rue de Lagny, 75020 Paris (Tel. 43 79 76 48), which is a non-advertising small business, renting second-hand cars.

Boat – several Paris-based companies offer boat trips on the Seine, Marne or local canals, lasting from 1 hour to a full day. Among them are **Paris Canal**, Bassin de la Villette, 11 quai de la Loire, 75019 Paris (Tel. 42 40 96 97); and **Canauxrama**, Bassin de la Villette, 13 quai de la Loire, 75019 Paris (Tel. 42 39 15 00). It is also possible to join cruises in the Seine-et-Marne, Yvelines and Val-d'Oise *départements*: ask local tourist offices for details. Various companies hire out family-sized boats, including **Ourcq Loisirs**, Bassin de la Villette, 12 quai de la Seine, 75019 Paris (Tel. 40 38 95 35) and **Marne Loisirs**, BP 43, Chemin de Halage, 77360

Vaires-sur-Marne (Tel. 64 72 97 87). Canoeists should contact **La Maison du Canoë-kayak**, 2 rue Noël Ballay, 75020 Paris (Tel. 43 72 16 97).

Cycling – bicycles can be hired from the following SNCF stations: Coulommiers, Dourdan, Etampes, La Ferté-sous-Jouarre, Fontainebleau-Avon, Mantes-la-Jolie, Meaux, Montfort-L'Amaury-Méré, Nemours-St-Pierre, Pontoise and Rambouillet. **Le Bicyclub de France**, 8 place de la Porte-de-Champerret, 75017 Paris (Tel. 47 66 55 92), operates a bicycle-hire service (*Roue Libre*) in conjunction with the RATP regional transport network. The Ile-de-France has many cycle paths; particularly good areas are along the Canal de l'Ourcq, round Milly-la-Forêt and Dourdan, in the Rambouillet Forest, and, for the more energetic, the Parc de St-Cloud circuit. See also **Good Alternatives** section.

Walking – the Ile-de-France has 4200 km of marked paths, including twelve *Grande Randonnée* paths. The best information and maps can be obtained from **CORANDIF**, 64 rue de Gergovie, 75014 Paris (Tel. 45 45 31 02). For organised rambles, see under **Good Alternatives**.

Riding – there are numerous riding clubs in the Ile-de-France. For information, contact the **Association Régionale du Tourisme Equestre en Ile-de-France**, 15 rue de Bruxelles, 75009 Paris (Tel. 48 94 53 15).

Useful Local Contacts

The **Bureau de Liaison des Associations de Sauvegarde de l'Environnement de l'Ile-de-France**, 1 ave de Père Lachaise, 75020 Paris (Tel. 43 66 12 79), publishes a list of environmental organisations in the Ile-de-France, together with a map which locates them. **Pro-Natura Ile-de-France** is the recently established Ile-de-France division of the Conservatory of Natural Sites, which operates from 21 rue des Provenceaux, 77300 Fontainebleau. The **Société Nationale de Protection de la Nature**, 57 rue Cuvier, BP 405, 75231 Paris Cedex 05 (Tel. 47 07 31 95), also has useful information. The French Friends of the Earth network, called **Amis de la Terre**, is based at 15 rue Gambey, 75011 Paris (Tel. 47 00 05 05). Responsible projects are undertaken by **Robin des Bois**, 15 rue Ferdinand-Duval, 75004 Paris (Tel. 48 04 09 36); it also sells ecological products. Many of these organisations have limited resources and, therefore, restricted working hours – so keep trying. Ecological topics are a speciality of the bookshop

Parallèles, 47 rue St-Honoré, 75001 Paris (Tel. 42 33 62 70). Another interesting concern is **Vieilles Maisons Françaises**, 93 rue de l'Université, 75007 Paris (Tel. 45 51 07 02); this organisation renovates historic houses, which might otherwise be neglected. The association **Dev-Tour** (Développement Tourisme) is based at 42 rue de Cambronne, 75015 Paris (Tel. 45 62 25 54). It has various important objectives, including the promotion of a tourism of dialogue and development, whose structures are based on the participation of local people.

Geographical Breakdown of Region

Paris

Despite a rather daunting reputation, Paris must be one of the easiest capital cities to explore. This is due partly to its compact nature, and partly to its logical, almost symmetrical, layout. It still has approximately the same structure as it did in the thirteenth century: with Politics, Law and Religion concentrated on the Ile de la Cité, Learning on the Left Bank, and Commerce on the Right Bank. The latter is north of the Seine, slightly larger, and crescent-shaped; the former is shaped more like a melon, and the two are linked by numerous bridges. The Seine itself links the two 'lungs' of the city, the Bois de Boulogne on the west side, and the Bois de Vincennes to the east. The twenty *arrondissements* into which Paris is divided form a clockwise spiral, working outwards from the 1er (*premier*) to the 20e (*vingtième*). Each *arrondissement* has its own character and the ones which boast the best-known sights are the 1er (Louvre & Tuileries), 4e (Notre Dame), 5e (the Sorbonne), 6e (Luxembourg Palace), 7e (Eiffel Tower), 8e (Champs-Elysées & Arc de Triomphe) and 18e (Montmartre). With the exception of Montmartre, the top attractions are in the centre. Before setting off, ask the tourist office for a copy of 'Musées et Monuments', an invaluable guide which classes every museum and monument alphabetically, thematically and by location, and tells you what's open when.

Some practical tips for the visitor. To form a Paris postal code, take 750 and add the number of the *arrondissement*: an address in the 9e will be 75009, and one in the 19e will be 75019. To make a telephone call to the French provinces from Paris, dial 16 before the eight-figure number. If you are calling Paris from the provinces, dial 161 before the eight-figure number. Calls within Paris require the standard eight-figure number alone.

The **1er** *arrondissement* includes the western tip of the Ile de la Cité, where you will find the Gothic ensemble of the **Palais de Justice** (law courts since the thirteenth century), **Ste-Chapelle**, and **Conciergerie**, the prison where many people, including Marie-Antoinette, were held before execution. The sixteenth century **Pont Neuf** is the oldest bridge in Paris, but if you cross to the Right Bank at the **Pont au Change**, you come to **Rue St-Denis** which leads to the modern **Forum des Halles** complex. This contains various museums including a branch of the **Grévin Waxworks**, with its *Son et Lumière* scenes of turn-of-the-century Paris, and the highly original **Cousteau Oceanic Centre**. Look out for **St-Eustache** church (modelled on Notre Dame) and the peaceful **Palais Royal** on your way to the **Louvre**, with its controversial pyramid entrance. Beyond the world-famous art museum, the **Tuileries Gardens** stretch along the riverbank, landscaped by Le Nôtre and one of the largest green spaces in central Paris. To the north is the chic **Place Vendôme**.

The **2e** contains the **National Library** and the Stock Exchange (**La Bourse**), both of which can be visited, alongside the trafficky and seedy **Sentier** quarter. The **3e** is certainly the place to come for museums. The **Conservatoire des Arts et Métiers** houses a museum of technical progress down the ages. Off Rue des Archives are the **French History Museum** and the **Musée de la Chasse et de la Nature**, which links nature and hunting in typical French manner. The **Musée Picasso** and **Musée Carnavalet** (a history museum) are nearby.

Just across in the Marais quarter of the **4e** is the beautifully symmetrical **Place des Vosges**, where Victor Hugo's house is also a museum. While still on the Right Bank, do not miss the **Pompidou Centre**, otherwise known as the Beaubourg. The 'inside-out' architecture of this contemporary art centre is well worth seeing, as is some of the eccentric street entertainment that goes on outside. The Third Republic style **Hôtel de Ville** dominates the riverbank, opposite the Gothic masterpiece of **Notre Dame** on Ile de la Cité. The cathedral's 70-metre-high platform offers a wonderful view. It is worth crossing the **Pont St-Louis** to see the narrow streets and picturesque quays of **Ile St-Louis**.

Over on the Left Bank, the **5e** is known as the Latin Quarter, as Latin was the official language of the University until the 18th century. You can visit not only the **Sorbonne**, but also many museums and churches. The **Hôtel de Cluny** houses Roman thermal baths, of the same era as the nearby **Arènes de Lutèce**; **St-Etienne du Mont** is a fifteenth-century church in a mixture of styles, and the **Panthéon** is an impressive building which contains the ashes of many famous people. In the east of the *arrondissement*, opposite a green-and-white mosque, is the **Jardin des Plantes**. As well as being a pleasant place for a stroll, it has an alpine garden, greenhouses with tropical plants, a **Natural History Museum**, and changing exhibitions.

In the **6e** are the Italiante **Luxembourg Palace**, with its lovely gardens, and the churches of **St-Sulpice** and **St-Germain-des-Près**. If you are at the Sèvres-Babylone Metro, look out for its miniature museum on the environment. In the **7e**, follow the famous **Boulevard St-Germain** with its art galleries, antique shops and cafés, to the **Assemblée Nationale**, making sure you take the detour to the waterfront **Musée d'Orsay**, a former railway station that is now a museum of nineteenth- and early twentieth-century art. Beyond the National Assembly is the symmetrical **Esplanade des Invalides**, leading down to the spacious **Hôtel des Invalides**, a magnificent building which once housed 5000 retired soldiers, and now contains various museums and churches. Nearby are the **Rodin Museum** and the **Ecole Militaire**, from whose gateway you can view the **Eiffel Tower**, with the full length of the **Champ de Mars** park in the foreground, and the river Seine behind.

If you cross the river again, at **Place de la Résistance**, you will find yourself in the **8e**. Following the Seine downstream will take you past the **Palais de la Découverte**, a dynamic science museum, and the ornate **Pont Alexandre III**, which affords excellent views of both the Invalides and the **Grand** and **Petit Palais**. A little further on is the exceedingly busy **Place de la Concorde**, from where you can head up the **Champs-Elysées**, which remains an impressive avenue, despite its bizarre combination of exclusive shops and fastfoods outlets. Off to the right are **La Madeleine** church and, further along, the **Elysées Palace**, home of the French president. To the left, **avenue Montaigne** is where all the big names of fashion (Chanel, Dior, et al.) have their shops. At the end of the Champs-Elysées is the **Arc de Triomphe**, at the top of which is a museum and a stunning view. Try **Boulevard Haussmann** for shopping and, if you need a rest, the **Parc de Monceau** is pleasant.

The main attraction of the **9e** is the **Opera**, though there are a few museums, including the **Fragonard** Perfume Museum on rue Scribe, and the main **Grévin Waxworks**, whose 500 wax figures bring alive French history, on boulevard Montmartre. Neither the **10e** nor the **11e** has much to offer the visitor. In the north-west corner of the **12e** is the **Place de la Bastille**, with its July column commemorating those killed in the 1830 riots; opposite is the controversial modern **Bastille Opera**. The south-east of the *arrondissement* opens up into the **Bois de Vincennes**. This is laid out like an English park, has several lakes, a zoo, a seventy acre flower garden, a race-course and a twelfth-century château. On Route du Pesage, there is also a farm which serves as a Maison de la Nature.

Back on the Left Bank, the **Quai de la Gare**, in the **13e**, is a mass of artists' studios where you can browse. The **Manufacture des Gobelins** is also worth a visit; tapestries have been made here since the seventeenth century, and traditional methods are still used. The **14e** contains the Paris **Observatory**, which dates from 1668, and the **Montparnasse** area, with its arty cafés and a cemetery where Baudelaire, Sartre and other famous figures are buried. In the south of the large **15e** *arrondissement* is the quiet **Parc Georges Brassens**, where there is a miniature vineyard and a scent garden, created for the blind.

Much of the **16e**, which is over the river again, is upmarket and residential, though there are some interesting museums here. At the end of rue des Eaux (near Pont Bir Hakeim) is the **Wine Museum**, where the admission fee includes wine-tasting. The **Palais de Chaillot**, built opposite the Eiffel Tower in 1937, houses various museums including the **Musée du Cinéma**, the **Musée des Monuments Français**, and the anthropological **Musée de l'Homme**. Further along the bank, the **Palais de Tokyo** houses the **Modern Art Museum**. The west of the 16e is taken up by the **Bois de Boulogne**. Here you can find lakes, racecourses, cycle paths, riding schools, a tree nursery, a yacht club and an area for playing *boules*. The **Château de Bagatelle** is an eighteenth-century folly, built for Marie-Antoinette, whose garden is artistically laid out. Plays and concerts are performed there in summer. In the **Jardin d'Acclimatation**, to the north of the wood, is the **Musée National des Arts et Traditions Populaires**. This is the nearest Paris gets to an *ecomusée*, and concentrates on French ethnography. Nearby is the **Musée en Herbe** (literally 'the budding museum'), which has changing exhibitions especially chosen to interest children.

There is little of interest in the **17e**, except, perhaps, a centre which contains exhibition space dedicated to the role of birds in the biosphere. This is at 51 rue Laugier. It is the streets off the Boulevard de Clichy, at the south of the **18e**, which form the heart of the Parisian red light district, and it is unwise to use the Metro stations round here if you're on your own at night. Not far away is **Montmartre**. Unless you are really foot-sore, it is not worth using the tourist train or the *Montmartrobus*, as they will only take you to the most obvious sights; wandering aimlessly is much more satisfactory. **Place du Tertre** is the centre of it all, though very commercialised; to its west is the beautiful white-domed **Sacré Cœur Basilica**, which offers a tremendous view over Paris. Do not miss the **Musée de Montmartre**, which tells the area's history and overlooks the Montmartre vineyard. Under the auspices of the museum, the **Société du Vieux Montmartre** arranges open evenings and exhibitions.

It is from the **Bassin de la Villette**, in the **19e**, that many boat trips depart. In the north-east of the *arrondissement* is the **Cité des Sciences et de l'Industrie**, home of the vast steel globe, known as **La Géode**, and various scientific exhibitions, ranging in matter from outer space and the environment to computers and human behaviour. In the south-west is one of Paris's largest parks, the **Parc des Buttes Chaumont**. The only major attraction of the **20e** *arrondissement* is an unusual one: the enormous **Père Lachaise Cemetery**, which is among the most visited in the world and contains the graves of Balzac, Delacroix, Chopin, Oscar Wilde and other ex-celebrities.

Accommodation

There are numerous high-class small-scale hotels in Paris, often with correspondingly high prices. If you cannot resist the temptation of staying in one of the larger Palace Hotels, try to make it **Le Crillon**, 10 place de la Concorde, 8e (Tel. 42 65 24 24), as this is the only one which is still wholly French-owned.

The following smaller hotels are recommended:

First Class

Résidence du Bois, 16 rue Chalgrin, 16e (Tel. 45 00 50 59): 19 rooms in quiet Third Empire mansion, run by friendly lady; restaurant.
Hôtel le Ste-Beuve, 9 rue Ste-Beuve, 6e (Tel. 45 48 20 07): 22 light,

airy rooms in elegant town hotel. **Hôtel d'Angleterre**, 44 rue Jacob, 6e (Tel. 42 60 34 72): 29 classically furnished rooms; calm situation. **Hôtel de la Bretonnerie**, 22 rue Ste-Croix-de-la-Bretonnerie, 4e (Tel. 48 87 77 63): 32 spacious rooms in a characterful 17th century townhouse. **Hôtel Monceau Lenox**, 18 rue Léon Jost, 17e (Tel. 46 22 60 70): 18 rooms in welcoming and well-situated turn-of-the-century house. **Hôtel Gaillon Opéra**, 9 rue Gaillon, 2e (Tel. 47 42 47 74): 26 rooms in quiet, though centrally placed, hotel with rustic interior.

Middle Range

Hôtel St-Louis, 75 rue St-Louis-en-l'Ile, 4e (Tel. 46 34 04 80): 21 rooms in welcoming hotel in converted 17th century townhouse. **Hôtel St-Merry**, 78 rue de la Verrerie, 4e (Tel. 42 78 14 15): 12 gothic-style rooms with heavy wood panelling in former presbytery. **Hôtel des Célestins**, 1 rue Charles V. 4e (Tel. 48 87 87 04): 15 cosy rooms in 17th century building. **Hôtel de la Place des Vosges**, 12 rue de Birague, 4e (Tel. 42 72 60 46): 16 rooms in 17th century house built in typical style for the area. **Hôtel le Pavillon**, 54 rue St-Dominique, 7e (Tel. 45 51 42 87): 18 small but pretty rooms in 18th century former convent.

Economy

Hôtel des Grandes Ecoles, 75 rue de Cardinal Lemoine, 5e (Tel. 43 26 79 23): 46 rooms in country-house type hotel with large garden. **Hôtel Prima Lepic**, 29 rue Lepic, 18e (Tel. 46 06 44 64): 38 rooms in characterful family-run Montmartre hotel. **Hôtel Esméralda**, 4 rue St-Julien-le-Pauvre, 5e (Tel. 43 54 19 20): 20 rooms in romantic, 'arty' hotel with wonderful views. **Hôtel Henri IV**, 25 place Dauphine, 1er (Tel. 43 54 44 53): simple rooms in seventeenth-century townhouse; be sure to book long in advance. **Hôtel du Marais**, 2 bis rue des Commines, 3e (Tel. 48 87 78 27): simple rooms in good location. **Hôtel du Séjour**, 32 rue du Grenier St-Lazare, 3e (Tel. 48 87 40 36): small, bright friendly hotel.

For bed and breakfast options, see **Good Alternatives**. Young people can take advantage of the free booking service offered by the youth tourist office **Accueil des Jeunes en France (AJF)**, whose central office is at 119 rue St-Martin, 4e (Tel. 42 77 87 80). This can also fix accommodation in student hotels or hostels in the 4e, 5e, 11e, 12e, 13e, and 17e *arrondissements*.

Eating Out

First Class

Jacques Cagna, 14 rue des Grands Augustins, 6e (Tel. 43 26 49 39): chef-owned restaurant in pretty 17th century house, serving subtle *haute cuisine*. **Gérard Besson**, 5 rue du Coq-Héron, 1er (Tel. 42 33 14 74): small, chef-owned restaurant serving classic cuisine. **Relais Louis XIII**, 8 rue des Grands Augustins, 6e (Tel. 43 26 75 96): fine restaurant with excellent wine cellar, in historic building. **Timgad**, 21 rue Brunel, 17e (Tel. 45 74 23 70): high class Moroccan restaurant, popular with Parisians.

Middle Range

Les Chants du Piano, 10 rue Lambert, 18e (Tel. 42 62 02 14): small, chef-owned restaurant near Montmartre vineyard; inventive cuisine. **Le Petit Doué**, 66 rue de Douai, 9e (Tel. 45 96 06 81): small and unpretentious. **Brasserie de la Poste**, 54 rue de Longchamp, 16e (Tel. 47 55 01 31): traditional brasserie atmosphere and fare.

Economy

Chartier, 7 rue du Faubourg Montmartre, 9e (Tel. 47 70 86 29): simple, authentic French food served at shared tables. **Polidor**, 41 rue Monsieur-le-Prince, 6e (Tel. 43 26 95 34): simple French cooking in faded setting, popular with Parisians. **Chez Hamadi**, 12 rue Boutebrie, 5e (Tel. 43 54 03 30): good value and popular North African restaurant.

Most of the above will serve vegetarian meals on request. Otherwise try one of Paris's specifically vegetarian restaurants, all of which fall into the *Economy* category: Le Macrobiotheque, 17 rue de Savoie, 6e (Tel. 43 25 04 96): small, friendly rustic-style restaurant with macrobiotic cuisine. **Aquarius**, 54 rue Ste-Croix-de-la-Bretonnerie, 4e (Tel. 48 87 48 71): small restaurant serving organic vegetables; unlicensed and no smoking. **Piccolo**, 6 rue des Ecouffes, 4e (Tel. 42 72 17 79): imaginative food in pleasant setting. **Végétarien**, 3 rue Villedo, 1er (Tel. 42 96 08 33): simple, high-quality cooking and local atmosphere.

Entertainments

Some of the best entertainment in Paris can be enjoyed absolutely (or virtually) free. People-watching is an infinitely varied sport:

you can opt for the high fashion of Place St-Germain-des-Près (6e), the seedy cosmopolitanism of the Goutte d'Or area (18e), or the unconventionality of the Beaubourg (4e). Ardent window-shoppers will be impressed by avenue Montaigne and rue du Faubourg-St-Honoré (don't expect prices to be marked) and bargain-hunters should make for the flea markets. The largest one is on Saturdays, Sundays and Mondays at Porte de Clignancourt in the 18e – beware of pickpockets. You could also try the markets at the Porte de Montreuil (20e; Sat.–Mon.) or the Porte de Vanves (14e; Sat.–Sun.). There is an organic market on Sunday mornings in boulevard Raspail, 6e (above its intersection with rue de Rennes).

Paris monuments are always illuminated until midnight and there is a *Son et Lumière* at the **Invalides** in summer. Underground sources of 'entertainment' are the catacombs and the sewers. The former house the bones of several million Parisians in a labyrinthine series of galleries, and are accessible from 2 Place Denfert-Rochereau, 14e. The sewers (*Egoûts de Paris*) are the site of an intriguing museum, open from Saturday–Wednesday. The entrance is opposite 93 quai d'Orsay, 7e.

Paris theatre comes in many forms. The majestic **Comédie Française** is at 2 rue de Richelieu, 1er (Tel. 40 15 00 15) and puts on the classics. The **Théâtre de la Ville**, 2 Place Châtelet, 4e (Tel. 42 74 22 77) shows a wide range of plays. For summertime outdoor theatre, try the **Jardin Shakespeare – Pré Catelan**, Bois de Boulogne, 16e (Tel. 42 40 05 32), where plays (including Shakespeare in French) are performed. There is also the **Théâtre à Ciel Ouvert**, Place du Marché Ste-Catherine, 4e (Tel. 48 77 01 59), which is fun and free. *Guignol* shows (the French equivalent of Punch & Judy) are often put on outside too, and are great for children. The most traditional is in Square de Choisy, 13e; another is in the Jardin d'Acclimatation in the Bois de Boulogne. Check with the tourist office for performance times. Cafés-Théâtres put on satirical sketches, some with political emphasis: try **Au Bec Fin**, 6 rue Thérèse, 1er (Tel. 42 96 29 35), or **Café d'Edgar**, 58 bd Edgar-Quinet, 14e (Tel. 42 79 97 97) – but only if your French is up to it. At *Chansonniers*, traditional folk songs are performed, often with audience participation: the **Caveau de la République**, 1 bd St-Martin, 3e (Tel. 42 78 44 45) has particular character. Of course, it is cabarets for which Paris is most famous. The best known are the **Moulin Rouge**, the **Folies Bergère** and the **Lido**. Visits to any of these are very expensive: moreover, the audiences are made up almost exclusively of tourists and the girls they watch are fairly likely to be British. Parisians tend to go to the **Crazy Horse Saloon**, 12 ave George V, 8e (Tel. 47 23 32 32), or one of the smaller – and cheaper – venues listed in the *Officiel des Spectacles*. This comes out weekly (on Wednesday) and is available from news-stands and *tabacs*. Like its slightly more expensive counterpart, *Pariscope*, it lists restaurants and bars as well as films, plays, exhibitions, festivals, and other current entertainments.

The dates of various events – of both religious and secular orientation – are worth noting. On the Sunday nearest 21 January, a mass is held at the **Chapelle Expiatoire**, 29 rue Pasquier, 8e, to commemorate Louis XVI's execution in 1793. This is the best occasion to see French aristocracy and keen royalists. In mid-June, a day is set aside for the Garçons de Café race. 500 waiters and waitresses, carrying trays of drinks, run a five mile circuit, starting from the **Hôtel de Ville** in the 4e. Bastille Day is celebrated all over Paris on 3 and 14 July with fireworks, parades and dancing in the streets. The first Saturday in October is the Fête des Vendanges at Montmartre. There are great festivities, but you'd be lucky to sample the wine, as the only Parisian vineyard produces a mere 500 bottles. Another festival with alcoholic focus is the arrival of the Beaujolais Nouveau, usually on the third Thursday in November. This unmatured Beaujolais causes Paris to flock to its wine-bars and cafés. Finally, from about the third week in December, there is a life-sized Nativity scene in front of the **Hôtel de Ville** in the 4e. Admission fees go to charity.

Useful Addresses

The main **Tourist Office** is at 127 ave des Champs-Elysées, 8e (Tel. 47 23 61 72) – be prepared for a wait in summer. There are also branches at the Eiffel Tower, 7e (Tel. 45 51 22 15 – summer only); the Gare du Nord, 10e (Tel. 45 26 94 82); Gare de l'Est, 10e (Tel. 46 07 17 73); Gare de Lyon, 12e (Tel. 43 43 33 24); and Gare d'Austerlitz, 13e (Tel. 45 84 91 70). For young people's tourist office, see **Accommodation**. The **Comité Régional du Tourisme**, 73–5 rue Cambronne, 15e (Tel. 45 67 89 41), can provide information on the whole of the Ile-de-France; and the **Maison de la France**, 8 ave de l'Opéra, 1er (Tel. 42 96 10 23) does the same for the whole of France. A tape-recorded message, in English, listing the week's events in Paris, can be heard on 47 20 88 98. The main **Post Office** is at

52 rue du Louvre, 1er. There are many other branches throughout the city. For emergency medical assistance, phone SAMU on 45 67 50 50. The **Hôpital Cochin** is at 27 rue du Faubourg-St-Jacques, 14e (Tel. 42 34 12 12). If you need an English-speaking medic, go to the **Hôpital Franco-Britannique de Paris**, 48 rue de Villiers (in Levallois-Perret, just outside the 17e; Tel. 47 58 13 12). The only 24-hour chemist is at 84 ave des Champs-Elysées, 8e (Tel. 45 62 02 41).

Transport Options

Details of organised **walking** tours are available from the tourist office. Although walking is the best way to see the central sights of Paris, you will undoubtedly need to use public transport too. The **Metro** may be unbearably crowded during rush hour, but at least it is efficient, clean and cheap. Tickets for the Metro are interchangeable with those for RATP buses and many RER trains, and can also be used on the cable car up to Montmartre. One ticket will take you anywhere within Paris, though several are needed if travelling to the suburbs. Instead of buying individual tickets, it is well worth getting a *carnet* of ten. If you plan to use public transport a lot on any one day, buy a *Formule 1* pass. Three or five day passes, called *Paris Visite*, are also available. Passport photos are required for the *Coupon Jaune* and *Carte Orange* (weekly and monthly passes). Information on all these services is available from RATP (Paris Transport), 53 ter quai des Grands Augustins, 6e (Tel. 40 46 41 41), and from many Metro stations. It is also worth asking for the RATP leaflet 'Paris Bus Métro RER!'

There are thirteen Metro lines, which are numbered, but referred to by their ultimate destination. These are supplemented by four RER **train** lines (A to D), which can take you to various destinations within Paris, as well as to the surrounding countryside. Before using the **bus**, which is a good way of seeing Paris, ask the tourist office for the free 'Autobus Paris – Plan du Réseau', which will enable you to plan your journeys more effectively. Bus routes worth taking for their scenic value alone are 20, 24, 52, 82 and 95.

Coach trips round the major sights are run by **Cityrama**, bus stop – 4 Place des Pyramides, 1er (Tel. 42 60 30 14); and **Paris Vision**, bus stop – 214 rue de Rivoli, 1er (Tel. 42 60 31 25). Both have pre-recorded commentaries – Cityrama's are available as individual cassettes in different languages.

Another pleasant way to see the city is by **boat**. The nearest to a river-bus service is the summer-only **Batobus**; details of its various pick-up points are available at the tourist office or from RATP. Regular hour-long cruises with commentary are organised by several companies, including the famous **Bateaux Mouches**, which leave from the Pont de l'Alma. Others leave from the Pont d'Iéna.

Cycling in Paris itself is dangerous, though it is a good way to see the Bois de Boulogne and Bois de Vincennes. For bicycle hire, try **Bicyclub 'Roue Libre'**, 8 Place de la Porte de Champerret, 17e (Tel. 47 66 55 92), which has the cooperation of the RATP transport network; or **Paris by Cycle**, 99 rue de la Jonquière, 17e (Tel. 42 63 36 63), which organises tourist circuits.

If you wish to take a **taxi**, it is better to go to one of the numerous taxi ranks than to try to hail one in the street. It would be crazy to hire a car, except for touring outside Paris (see **Communications**).

West – Hauts-de-Seine and Yvelines

This is the direction most people head if they want to spend some time outside Paris. It contains not only Versailles, but also a regional park and some wonderful walking country. Walkers should ask a tourist office for the leaflet 'Circuits Pédestres en Yvelines' which suggests two- to six-hour circuits, all starting from stations, and provides maps, useful addresses and details of local attractions.

On the outskirts of Paris, in Hauts-de-Seine, is the business district of **La Défense**. Its latest landmark is a vast open cube, La Grande Arche, whose roof offers incredible views, and whose halls display exhibitions connected with the Human Rights Foundation which it houses. Nature in an urban environment is the theme of the Maison de la Nature des Hauts-de-Seine, at 9 quai du 4 septembre, **Boulogne-Billancourt**, next to the lovely Jardins Kahn. At **St-Cloud**, there are special walking paths in the parks; try to visit the **Rueil-Malmaison** château. **Sèvres** has a ceramic museum, and **Meudon** was the home of the famous sculptor, Rodin. Its Musée de Rodin complements the Paris museum of the same name. The Comité Départemental du Tourisme des Hauts-de-Seine is at 22 rue Pierre et Marie Curie, 92140 Clamart (Tel. 46 42 17 95)

– information on the *département* is available here. **Sceaux** has a park designed by Le Nôtre, and, in the Vallée aux Loups at **Châtenay-Malabry**, the writer Chateaubriand planted many rare trees.

Out in the Yvelines, you will come to **Versailles**. The magnificent château was commissioned by Louis XIV, designed by Mansart, and constructed by 22,000 workmen between 1661 and 1710. Its park, nearly 15,000 acres, was drawn up by Le Nôtre. It is best to visit the château as soon as it opens in the morning, and the park and outlying buildings in the afternoon. There is a fountain display at 3.30 p.m. on summer Sundays. A guided tour of the town is also possible, and it is here that you will find the Comité Départemental du Tourisme des Yvelines – at 2 Place André Mignot, 78012 Versailles. (Tel. 39 02 78 78). Near to the new town of **St-Quentin-en-Yvelines** are an urban pond nature reserve, and an *ecomusée* devoted to industry and agriculture past and present, whose address is Commanderie des Templiers de la Villedieu, 78990 Elancourt (Tel. 30 50 82 21).

To the south is the regional park of the **Haute-Vallée de Chevreuse**. The Maison du Parc is at Château de la Madeleine, BP 73, 78460 Chevreuse (Tel. 30 52 09 09), where much information is available. The area is covered in oak and beech forest, ponds and rivers, and agricultural land where farmers are encouraged to use non-intensive methods. There are various *gîtes*, footpaths and sites of interest. 'Discovery' paths can be found at **Maincourt** and **Mérantais**, and there are four botanical paths. Suggestions of thematic circuits are supplied by the Maison du Parc or the Syndicat d'Initiative at **St-Rémy-lès-Chevreuse**, where the Coubertin garden is full of bronze sculptures. Other places to visit in the park are the Musée National des Granges and Musée des Ruines de l'Abbaye de Port-Royal at **Magny-les-Hameaux**; the Château de Dampierre, also designed by Mansart, at **Dampierre-en-Yvelines**; the animal park at **Sonchamp**, where deer and wild boar wander at liberty; the Forester's House at **Haut-Besnières**, which has been turned into a Nature Initiation Centre; and the Château de Breteuil at **Choisel**, brought to life by figures from the Grévin waxworks.

At the Château de Sauvage, to the west, is an ornithological reserve. The **Rambouillet** château and forest are worth exploring, as is the lovely medieval town of **Montfort-l'Amaury**, with its sixteenth-century stained-glass windows. There is another château at **Thoiry**, owned by the same family for thirty-four generations, with Le Nôtre gardens and an African animal reserve. Further châteaux can be found at **Maisons-Laffitte** (Mansart-designed), and **St-Germain-en-Laye**, where there is a national antiquities museum and beautiful woods. **Marly-le-Roi** also has a park and forest, and nearby **Rocquencourt** is the site of the Arboretum de Chèvreloup, a museum of tree-types, open on weekends and Mondays.

Accommodation

First Class

Château de Villepreux, 78450 Villepreux (Tel. 30 56 20 06): 11 rooms in elegant eighteenth-century château in Versailles plain; *table d'hôtes* on request. **Château de Villiers-le-Mahieu**, 78770 Villiers-le-Mahieu (Tel. 34 87 44 25); 30 luxurious rooms in moated thirteenth-century château-fort.

Middle Range

Le Gros Marronnier, 3 Place de l'Eglise, Senlisse, 78720 Dampierre-en-Yvelines (Tel. 30 52 51 69): 12 rooms in simple inn surrounded by peaceful garden. **Mme Reams**, 32 bd de la Reine, 78000 Versailles (Tel. 39 50 48 85): 2 spacious *chambres d'hôte* in comfortable town house; 2 nights minimum.

Economy

Hôtel des Voyageurs, 49–51 rue de Paris, 78490 Montfort-l'Amaury (Tel. 34 86 00 14): 7 rooms in family-run hotel. **Auberge Villa Marinette**, 20 ave du Général de Gaulle, Gazeran, 78120 Rambouillet (Tel. 34 83 19 01): 6 rooms in family-run hotel. **Mme Magny**, La Butte de Bréval, 78980 Bréval (Tel. 34 78 32 85): 2 comfortable *chambres d'hôte* in wing of a former farm. **Mme Rossi**, 7 rue de la Grande-Vallée, 78120 La Boissière-Ecole (Tel. 34 85 06 18): 3 *chambres d'hôte* in quiet, green setting.

Eating Out

First Class

Cazaudehore, 1 ave du Président-Kennedy, 78100 St-Germain-en-Laye (Tel. 39 73 36 60): traditional cuisine in rustic context; also has 24 luxurious rooms and 6 suites. **La Feuilleraie**, 78200

Follainville-Dennemont (Tel. 34 77 17 66): inventive cuisine in elegant country restaurant.

Middle Range

Le Potager du Roy, 1 rue du Maréchal-Joffre, 78000 Versailles (Tel. 39 50 35 34): upmarket bistro-style food; popular due to its excellent value, so you'll need a reservation.

Economy

Le Boeuf à la Mode, 4 rue du Pain, 78000 Versailles (Tel. 39 50 31 99): traditional homey cooking in brasserie-style restaurant.

North – Seine-St-Denis and Val-d'Oise

This area is often ignored, or else driven straight through on the way to Chantilly, Senlis and Compiègne, in Picardy. It does, however, have its own attractions to offer.

St-Denis is a Paris suburb famous for its basilica, whose mausoleum is fascinating. You can find out more about the Seine-St-Denis *département* from the Comité Départemental du Tourisme, 2 rue de la Légion d'Honneur, 93200 St-Denis (Tel. 42 43 33 55). Another part worth visiting is the forest park of **Sevran** on the Canal de l'Ourcq.

Just over the border from St-Denis, in Val-d'Oise, is the spa town of **Enghien-les-Bains**. To the north-east, the Château d'**Ecouen** (access through the woods, on foot) houses an impressive Renaissance Museum. The other side of the **Forêt de Montmorency** is **Auvers-sur-Oise**, a charming hamlet, popular with nineteenth-century artists. The Auberge Ravoux is where Van Gogh ended his life in 1890. The major town of **Pontoise** still has its medieval ramparts, and a restored manor which houses the Pissarro Museum. The Comité Départemental du Tourisme du Val-d'Oise is at 2 le Campus, 95032 Cergy-Pontoise (Tel. 34 25 32 53). At the weekend, it is worth going to the far west of the *département* to see the Italian-influenced Jardin d'Ambleville near **Bray-et-Lu**.

Accommodation & Eating Out

Accommodation here is pretty thin on the ground, except for some charming B&Bs. For other options, ask at local tourist offices.

Economy

Mme Patry, Genainville (Tel. 34 67 05 33): 4 *chambres d'hôtes* in house with big garden. **Mme Thedrel**, Cléry-en-Vexin (Tel. 34 67 44 90): 4 *chambres d'hôtes* in elegant house with park. **Mme Debeaudrap**, Ambleville-Vexin (Tel. 34 67 71 08): 1 *chambre d'hôtes* on farm.

For a meal out, try the *Middle Range* **Hostellerie de Maupértu**, 25 rte d'Anvers, 95300 Pontoise (Tel. 30 38 08 22): country restaurant with modernised classical cuisine.

East – Seine-et-Marne

Seine-et-Marne is by far the largest and most varied *département* of the Ile-de-France, bordering on Champagne in the east, and including the rolling fields of the Meaux area, the attractive Brie valleys and the forests around Fontainebleau.

Due east of Paris are the château and park of **Champs-sur-Marne**, and those of **Ferrières**, where the park is particularly superb. The agricultural town of **Meaux** has a fine Gothic cathedral and other buildings dating from the twelfth century; guided tours are possible, both here and in Provins. **Provins** was a medieval trade centre, now famous for rose-growing, and for the churches, tithe barn and tower of its well-preserved old town. In the southern tip of the *département*, at **Nemours**, you should visit the twelfth- to fifteenth-century castle and the Ile-de-France Prehistory Museum. **Fontainebleau** is obviously a must: the château is essentially Renaissance, though it bears the marks of many monarchs and is consequently rather irregular (which is almost a relief after the perfect symmetry of Versailles). Its museum is excellent, and the forest, which is a mixture of deciduous and coniferous trees, is perfect for walking, with many marked trails. On the forest edge is the pretty village of **Barbizon**, made famous by the school of mid-nineteenth century painting to which it gave its name; Millet's and Rousseau's houses are now museums there. At **Melun**, you can join cruises on the Seine, and nearby is **Vaux-le-Vicomte**, whose château and park, designed by Le Vau and Le Nôtre, caused Louis XIV to become so envious that he threw their owner in prison and copied the design, on a much grander scale, for his own Versailles. Also near Melun is **Vert-St-Denis**, where there is a Nature Initiation Centre called *La Futaie* (Tel. 60 63 69 80), which concentrates on organic gardening, bee-keeping and medicinal plants. **Savigny-le-Temple** has an interesting *ecomusée* – at Ferme du Couleuvrain (Tel. 64 41 75 15) – devoted to the natural and human history of the Brie plateau.

Accommodation & Eating Out

First Class

Le Manoir, 77610 Fontenay-Tresigny (Tel. 64 25 91 17): 11 rooms and 3 suites in quiet half-timbered mansion; excellent restaurant.

Middle Range

Auberge du Cheval Blanc, 55 rue Victor Clairet, 77910 Varreddes-par-Meaux (Tel. 64 33 18 03): 10 rooms in charming inn; good cooking with fresh produce. **Hostellerie du Moulin**, 2 rue du Moulin, Flagy, 77940 Voulx (Tel. 60 96 67 89): 10 rooms in converted 12th century mill; restaurant.

Economy

Mme Taisne, La Fougeraie, Noisy-sur-Ecole (Tel. 64 24 75 97), 1 *chambre d'hôte* in characterful house with landscaped garden; bike hire. **Mme Taillieu**, Ferme les Vaux, Rampillon (Tel. 64 08 06 01): 2 *chambres d'hôte* in isolated farm with friendly family welcome.

When eating out, look out for restaurants belonging to the Association 'Produits du Terroir Seine-et-Marne', who have pledged to use only local products and to promote local dishes. The *First Class* **Le Bas Bréau**, 22 rue Grande, 77630 Barbizon (Tel. 60 66 40 05) offers excellent cuisine using produce from the kitchen garden; it is also a luxury hotel with 12 rooms and 8 suites.

South – Val-de-Marne and Essonne

Just on the border between Val-de-Marne, Essonne and Hauts-de-Seine is the village of **Fresnes**, where an *ecomusée* in a farm at 41 rue Maurice-Tenine presents the rural community. Further south, well into Essonne, is a famous tower at **Montlhéry**. **Evry**, near the Sénart Forest, is where you will find the Comité Départemental du Tourisme de l'Essonne, at 2 cours Monseigneur Roméro (Tel. 64 97 35 13). If you follow the River Essonne, fringed with ponds, you will come to **St-Vrain**, where there is an animal reserve and safari park, with a reconstruction of a prehistoric village. Le Moulin des Noues in **Soisy-sur-Ecole** is a glass-worker's studio and shop, which makes an interesting visit. At **Courances** there is a seventeenth-century château and formal Le Nôtre park, only open at weekends, and nearby **Milly-la-Forêt**, known for its herb-growing, has a fifteenth-century wooden covered market. The Parc de Jeurre, just north of **Etampes**, contains a collection of eighteenth-century buildings. Keen geologists will be interested in the spectacular fossils of the Etampes region and should contact the Hôtel du Département, Boulevard de France, 91012 Evry, for further information. **Dourdan** has a château-museum, open every day except Mon. and Tues. Unfortunately, the remaining châteaux in Essonne are open only on Sunday afternoons: they are the formal-gardened Château du Marais at **St-Chéron**; the seventeenth-century Château de Courson, with its romantic park, at **Bruyères-le-Châtel**; and the impressive Château de St-Jean-du-Beauregard, with its seventeenth-century kitchen garden, just south of **Les Ulis**.

Accommodation & Eating Out

Pleasant accommodation can be found in this area, for very reasonable prices.

First Class / Middle Range

Le Château des Iles, 85 quai Winston Churchill, 94 La Varenne (Tel. 48 89 65 65): 15 rooms in park-surrounded house; restaurant with traditional cuisine.

Middle Range

Hôtel le Tartarin, 94370 Sucy-en-Brie (Tel. 45 90 42 61): 11 comfortable rooms in calm setting; traditional restaurant.

Economy

Auberge du Moulin de Jarcy, rue Boieldieu, Varennes-Jarcy, 91480 Quincy-sous-Sénart (Tel. 69 00 89 20): 5 rooms in converted mill on island. **Aux Armes de France**, 1 bd Jean-Jaurès, 91100 Corbeil-Essonnes (Tel. 64 96 24 04): 11 rooms in family-run hotel; restaurant. **Mme Evian**, 4 hameau le Rouillon, 91410 Dourdan (Tel. 64 59 84 27): 2 *chambres d'hôte* in quiet farmhouse with garden; farm produce for sale and bike hire available.

When eating out, look out for the restaurants of the 'Toques Blanches' association, which use high-quality local products in traditional ways.

6 Champagne-Ardenne

It is easy to make the mistake of assuming that Champagne is a region where life is one long party, which only the wealthy and distinguished are eligible to attend. There is, of course, much more to the region than champagne vineyards, champagne cellars and champagne dinners, though even these attractions can be enjoyed on a limited budget if desired. In sparsely populated Champagne-Ardenne, people and places are surprisingly unostentatious, yet every aspect of your visit will be of the highest quality. This is a place to come for quiet pampering.

There are also plenty of opportunities to be active once your batteries are sufficiently recharged: watersports, cycling, riding, climbing, nature rambles, barge trips – the variety of activities reflects the variety of the region's environment. As well as vineyards, Champagne-Ardenne has dense forests, limestone caves, gouged-out river valleys, peaceful canals, wheat-fields, marshes and the largest artificial lake in Europe. Traditional occupations include basket-work, scissor-making and bee-keeping.

A visit to a champagne cellar, most of which are in the Marne *département*, is essential. Ever since the late seventeenth century, when the blind monk Dom Pérignon perfected the champagne technique and uttered the oft-cited words 'brothers, come quickly – I am drinking stars!' this sparkling wine has played a central role in the life of the region. Cellar visits range from a walk round with the owner to a hi-tech audio-visual experience, but almost all are free and some offer a glass of champagne at the end. Regional cooking, which sometimes involves local fish or game in a delicate champagne sauce is a mouth-watering pleasure, whether sampled at a rustic *ferme-auberge* or at a restaurant fit for – and frequented by – royalty.

Cultural stimulation is provided too, in the form of Gallo-Roman remains, Romanesque and Gothic churches, the vast castle-fortress at Sedan, *Son et Lumière* performances at cathedrals and châteaux, the half-timbered city centre of Troyes, along with its numerous museums, and much else besides.

As a region of passage, Champagne-Ardenne has, in turn, enjoyed the benefits of commerce and suffered the devastation of invasion. The consciousness that, however wealthy one is, life is fragile – which may explain the unpretentiousness of local people – has recently been translated into an increased interest in the environment. Various schemes have been put in place to protect the many areas of special ecological value and to educate the public, and the regional government has pledged support for investment in environmentally appropriate development. It is easy to see why many tourists, who stumble upon the pleasures of Champagne-Ardenne on their way to the south, return the following year to stay a bit longer.

History

Occupation of the region goes back to prehistoric times, though Reims and Langres first became important trade centres after the Roman conquest. Reims has been a prestigious city ever since, sporting a triumphal arch and hosting an assembly on the death of Nero. It was the bishop of Reims who baptised Clovis, first king of the Franks, in AD 498. The tradition of holding royal coronations at Reims began in 816 with Louis the Pious. After the Norman invasions came the high-point of Romanesque architecture, succeeded by the Gothic style whose masterpiece is Reims cathedral, where Joan of Arc escorted Charles VII to be crowned in 1429.

Trade had deteriorated during the Hundred Years War, but the Renaissance brought a few years of peace and economic renewal. The religious wars of the late sixteenth century laid waste over eighty villages in the south of the region, which made a remarkable recovery with the growth of the cutlery industry around Langres and Bassigny in the seventeenth century. It was also about this time that the champagne-making process was discovered.

The fortresses of the Ardennes bear the marks of every war and seige, including the defeats in 1870 at Sedan and Bazeilles, where a handful of men resisted the Prussians to the very end. The First World War brought the two Battles of the Marne, one in 1914 and one in 1918. A new fort was built at Villy-la-Ferté in 1939, but even the valiant efforts of the soldiers, here on the Maginot line, were unable to keep the Germans out. Champagne's liberation came in 1944 and the Armistice was signed at Reims on 8 May 1945.

The Seine reservoir, known now as the Lac de la Forêt d'Orient, was created in 1965, and the area around this was declared a regional park in 1970, the same year as the nuclear power station at Chooz in the Ardennes started up. It was also in 1970 that General de Gaulle died at his retirement home in Colombey-les-Deux-Eglises. Four years later, the Marne reservoir – or Lac du Der-Chantecoq – was formed; plans for two further lakes are under way, The second regional park, the Montagne de Reims, came into being in 1976.

Many famous people are associated with the region, including Viscount Turenne, Marshal of France in the seventeenth century; Colbert, statesman of the same era; Diderot and Danton in the eighteenth century; the philospher Hippolyte Taine and the radical young poet Arthur Rimbaud in the nineteenth.

Geography

Champagne-Ardenne (there is no 's' on Ardenne in the compound designating the region) is roughly crescent-shaped and borders on Belgium in the north. The four *départements* that make up the region are, from north to south, the Ardennes (spelt with an 's'), the Marne, the Aube and the Haute-Marne. The administrative capital of the region (and the Marne) is Châlons-sur-Marne (55,000 inhabitants) and the other departmental capitals are Charleville-Mézières (62,000 – Ardennes), Troyes (65,000 – Aube) and Chaumont (29,000 – Hte-Marne). By far the largest town in the region is, however, Reims (pronounced 'rance'), with a population of 185,000. The region as a whole is very sparsely populated, with only 50 people per square kilometre (the average in France being 100), and the emphasis is firmly agricultural.

Land-use naturally depends on the type of soil and terrain, both of which vary considerably throughout Champagne-Ardenne. The French Ardennes are part of a slate massif which extends into Belgium, and they reach 502 metres at La Croix de Scaille on the Franco-Belgian border. The rivers Meuse and Semoy meander through the Ardennes slopes, which are covered in deciduous forests. Between the Ardennes and Champagne itself is a fertile depression where cereals are grown and cattle reared. Champagne is part of the Parisian Basin and is made up of concentric plateaux of differing natures. The most westerly is the Côte de l'Ile-de-France, a cliff-like projection broken by river valleys, including that of the Marne, the heart of the champagne-growing area. The vineyards are planted in little parcels and cover only 68,000 acres altogether. Reims is situated just at the edge of this area, where it turns into the plateau known as 'Dry Champagne', a chalky swathe of land 80 kilometres wide. This used to be very poor, but now contains Champagne's three most important towns and, as a result of modern fertilisers, produces rich crops of sugar-beet, wheat and barley, as well as expanses of yellow mustard fields. The narrow band called 'Wet Champagne' comes next. This has an easily eroded soil of clay and sand, and was chosen as the site for immense reservoirs. The area is chequered with woods and forests, but the land is also used to graze dairy cows. In the very south of the Champagne-Ardenne crescent is the Plateau de Langres, a high limestone plain covered in forest, where many rivers, including the Seine, have their sources.

Interesting environmental features include petrified waterfalls in the Haute-Marne, caves with stalactites in the Ardennes, and, of course, the region's 25,000 acres of man-made lake. Though originally created to supply the Paris area in times of water shortage, both the Lac du Der-Chantecoq and the Lac de la Forêt d'Orient have become not only tourist attractions, but also important resting places for migrating birds. They are the only known wintering quarters of the sea eagle in France, and the common crane and bean goose are regular visitors to the Forêt d'Orient, which has a totally protected ornithological reserve. Unfortunately bird protection seems to be less of a priority in the Châlons-sur-Marne area, where electric cables caused the death of over seventy birds of prey in six months. Very effective grills have been set up at the mouth of caves near the *Lac Der*, in order to prevent human disturbance of the bats living there. Wild boar, red deer and roe deer are fairly common in the region's forests: you can observe them in semi-liberty at the Parc de Vision de Gibier on a peninsula in the Lac de la Forêt d'Orient. Observatories and hides mean that you do not disturb them. Other places to view local fauna, past and present, are the wildlife reserves of Bannie in the Haute-Marne and Belval in the Ardennes, where not only boar and deer, but bison and even bear can be seen. Species of tree growing in the area include holm oak, silver birch, beech, ash and spruce, which often shelter foxgloves, bilberries and wild mushrooms. Carnivorous plants and orchids can be found around the peat-bogs of the Ardennes, though some trouble has been caused by 'orchidophiles' who pop over the Belgian border to pick orchids.

Champagne-Ardenne is at the forefront of the national programme of ZNIEFFs (natural zones of interest for their animal and plant life), and also has a large number of Nature Initiation Centres. It is concerned to keep its considerable quantity of water unpolluted, and its first official nature reserve has just been created, with more to follow. The region's most interesting phenomenon is, perhaps, its most fragile: near Verzy in the Parc Naturel Régional de la Montagne de Reims are the *Faux de Verzy*. These are a group of over 800 beech trees, stunted and weirdly twisted, and unique in the world. They are the result of some unidentifiable genetic freak, but are suffering severely as a result of visitors trampling the soil beneath them, so it is essential to stay on the marked path.

Though the region's two parks have been criticised (the Montagne de Reims particularly for allowing the use of chemical fertiliser in its champagne vineyards), both have admirable aims and are well-organised. They have a management plan for their architectural as well as ecological heritage, insisting that any new buildings (even bus shelters!) blend in with traditional ones.

Climate

This is similar to that in the south of England. Winter is fairly chilly, though there is less rain, and summer is generally mild, though temperatures tend to be higher than British ones in mid-summer. The annual temperature range is from an average maximum of 5.6°C in February to 24.9°C in August. The countryside is at its most beautiful in spring and autumn, and the weather in October is generally still fine.

Attractions

A top priority when people come to Champagne-Ardenne is usually a visit to some of the great champagne houses. These are found mainly in Reims and Epernay, and many visitors stick to the Reims-Epernay-Châlons-sur-Marne triangle, advertised by the tourist board as 'the sacred triangle of Champagne', perhaps with detours along the Route du Champagne as far as Dormans or Sézanne. Here you will be told how the right to be called 'Champagne' belongs only to wines made in the viticultural zone covered by the Montagne de Reims, the Vallée de la Marne, the Côte des Blancs, and a few designated vineyards in the Aisne and the Aube; how only grapes from the Pinot Noir, Pinot Meunier and Chardonnay vines may be used; and how the wine must go through two fermentations before it receives its final cork and is ready to label. It is this complex and exclusive process which results in the most prestigious and lucrative wine in the world. One acre of vines can be worth well over £40,000, and Epernay, whose avenue de Champagne is lined with mansions bearing the names of the most famous brands, is the richest town in France, paying more tax per capita than any other.

If getting to know your bubbly better strikes you as an over-hedonistic way to spend a holiday, you can always head for other top attractions such as the Gothic cathedrals of Reims and Châlons, and the basilica of L'Epine. Away from 'the sacred triangle', the most popular part is 'the great lakes'. With their watersports facilities, these are particularly suitable for families and young people in summer, but are a paradise for naturalists the rest of the year. Here you will also find many typical half-timbered buildings, including churches.

The other two areas highlighted by the tourist board are less frequented, though no less interesting. The Meuse Valley in the Ardennes is a source of sturdy slate-roofed houses, stunning panoramas and eerie legends; and the 'land of springs' around Langres is unspoilt and committed to its traditions, despite being home to Bourbonne-les-Bains, the top thermal spa in the east of France, with the most modern equipment in Europe. However much of a cliché it is, Champagne-Ardenne really does have something for everyone!

Cuisine

Champagne itself is used in some regional cuisine, including *rognons au champagne* (kidneys), *poulet au champagne* (chicken), and various fish and game dishes. The Ardennes area is the place to go for the latter, where venison and boar ham are specialities, but where even thrushes are used for pâté-making. Several versions of white pudding (a kind of sausage) exist, the most famous of which is that of Rethel. The most popular fish are trout from the Semoy river, and pike or salmon from the Vanne. Specialities from the south of the region include Haute-Marne trout in cream, *matelotte de perches au vin de Coiffy* (perch stew), and Bassigny *pot-au-feu*. Vegetarians should look out for the delicious wild mushrooms, sometimes served in a vol-au-vent as an *entrée*, and for potato dishes such as *cacasse à cul nu*.

Local cheeses include the creamy chaource, produced in the Aube since the 12th century, 'caprice des dieux' from Bourmont, Trappist cheese from Igny, and the hard langres. Reims is well-known for its pink biscuits, *massepains* and *croquignoles*, which accompany champagne. The Ardennes produces a famous sugar cake, as well as various fruit tarts, and the Haute-Marne has a custard dish called *quemeu* tart.

In addition to champagne itself, drunk both as an apéritif and during the meal, the region has a small number of still wines, including the delicious reds of Bouzy, Ay and Cumières. The Rosé des Riceys also enjoys a good reputation. Sloe wine and hazelnut wine are specialities too, along with cider from the Othe region, fruit-flavoured *eaux-de-vie* from the Argonne, and the grape-derived spirits Ratafia and Marc de Champagne.

Level of Tourism

Champagne-Ardenne is near the bottom of the league table of French touristic regions, and the emphasis is on weekend and short-stay visitors. Foreign tourists, who make up 31% of the total number of visitors, tend to come from Belgium, Holland, Germany and Britain, though the type of tourist and level of tourism vary considerably throughout the region. There is no mass tourism, as such: the coach groups who do come tend to follow a historico-cultural theme and stick to the main towns. The region is at its busiest during the grape harvest (September/October) and, believe it or not, far less busy during July and August. The visitors it does receive in high summer are often simply stopping off on their way to the coast. There is, however, considerable loyalty among tourists, with a high rate of return to the region.

Champagne-Ardenne caters well for certain specific types of traveller. Reims is naturally a favourite destination for the business traveller: it has been known for London executives, wishing to impress their clients, to fly them over to Reims for a champagne business lunch. At the other end of the scale, the region is excellent for children's educational visits. It boasts seven Nature Initiation Centres, all of which host 'discovery' trips for schools. Specialist visitors to the region include geologists, drawn by the fascinating quarry at Mailly-Champagne, and ornithologists, drawn by the sea eagle which winters at the lakes. Finally, there are the thermalists of Bourbonne-les-Bains.

Some of the relatively few problems connected with tourism have already been mentioned: the picking of orchids in the Ardennes;

the compression of the earth around the *Faux de Verzy* beeches; and the disturbance of bats in caves near the Lac du Der-Chantecoq. The artificial lake itself was a cause for controversy when it was created in 1974, as it meant the destruction of three villages, but this cannot be blamed on the tourist industry as the lake was developed as a reservoir. Other controversies in the area surround the nuclear power stations at Chooz and Nogent-sur-Seine, and the dumping of nuclear waste at the pretty little village of Soulaines d'Huys, though, even taking these into account, the risk of industrial pollution in the region remains low. Differences of opinion exist concerning the large number of army camps in the area: some claim that their manœuvres are dangerous; others that their ownership of woodland is of great ecological benefit, providing a mini-nature reserve and preventing the land being taken over by agriculture.

There are no great traffic problems, except in Reims and, occasionally, around the port of Mesnil-St-Père on the Forêt d'Orient lake, though measures have been taken to alter the course of the road so that tourists will have to reach the lakeside on foot. There is already a strict speed limit on the lakeside roads, and visitors are encouraged to take a given route when they leave their cars, rather than to disperse into sometimes fragile areas. A new autoroute due to pass close to the regional park will almost certainly cause an influx of tourists, though the park authorities are determined to retain the authenticity of the area.

This determination is reflected in other domains too. Many valuable buildings are falling into disrepair, so the park authorities offer free advice and interest-free loans to individuals or communities prepared to restore them. Similarly, farmers are offered compensation if they sign a contract agreeing not to drain damp prairie-land. There is a general move to improve the quality of life in both regional parks, which includes a scheme to encourage the installation of proper heating, insulation and plumbing in old houses, which might eventually be used by their owners as bed and breakfasts. Building work is done by local people, using traditional techniques, and the money generated is therefore kept within the local economy. It is agreed that the region needs more accommodation, and the authorities seem to have opted for the B&B approach. They are determined to create small-scale accommodation, which offers a welcome of the highest quality; already, even the *gîtes* used by hikers verge on the luxurious. One gets the impression that the aim is to create a product, like champagne itself, which will enjoy such a good reputation that the crude business of promotion is virtually unnecessary!

This pure form of tourism must, of course, take place in a pure environment, and the local government has various programmes to see that it does. Among these are the reduction of all types of pollution, with special attention to rivers, lakes and the fish that live in them, and the planting of trees alongside many roads. Protecting the environment is regarded as an investment and, to see that it is appreciated, plans for 'living' museums and 'pôles de la nature' (nature discovery areas) are underway.

Good Alternatives

Meeting People

Various different leaflets, obtainable from tourist offices in the appropriate area, tell you what is going on. The accommodation lists for the Meuse valley and the 'land of springs' both include local festivals and events. In the Marne, detailed information can be found in the brochure 'La Marne en Fête'. The Parc Régional de la Montagne de Reims also produces both a monthly newsletter and a leaflet of the whole year's events, entitled 'Animations proposées par le parc', which includes excursions.

Those interested in helping out with conservation work should contact the **Conservatoire du Patrimoine Naturel de Champagne-Ardenne**, 08240 Boult-aux-Bois (Tel. 24 30 06 20). This organisation has done some excellent work, including rebuilding a stork's nest, protecting bats, and clearing undergrowth at valuable sites. During winter it runs afternoon *chantiers de bénévoles* at weekends. Anyone can take part and it is a good way to meet people. In addition, there is a two-week international *chantier de jeunes* ('jeune' being under about 30), which usually takes place in August, and where bed and board are provided. The 1990 one won a national award and they are very popular, so enquire well ahead.

Those interested in joining an archaeological dig should contact the **Direction des Antiquités**, 20 rue de Chastillon, 51000 Châlons-sur-Marne (Tel. 26 64 13 75 and 26 68 28 94). If you're self-catering, or on the look out for locally produced food in the Ardennes, it's worth writing to the **Chambre d'Agriculture des Ardennes,** 1 ave du Petit Bois, BP 331, 08105 Charleville-Mézières Théâtre, who will provide you with information on where to buy farm products. A list of every single champagne house is available from the **Union des Maisons de Champagne**, 1 rue Marie-Stuart, 51100 Reims. It is a good idea to visit one from the top of the range (Mercier or Moët et Chandon in Epernay, or Mumm in Reims, for example) just to experience the flawless reception and to appreciate the sheer size of the cellars, and one small-scale grower-producer, who will probably give you a personal tour. The following are recommended: **Champagne Blondel**, Ludes (Tel. 26 03 43 92); **Champagne Cattier**, Chigny-les-Roses (Tel. 26 03 42 11 – not weekends, English spoken); **Champagne Blin & Cie**, Vincelles (Tel. 26 58 20 04 – English spoken). Visits are free, but, as the proprietor himself will probably take time off to show you round, it is polite both to contact him in advance and to buy from him afterwards, if you possibly can.

Discovering Places

Many tourist offices, even quite minor ones, offer organised trips, sometimes just for the day, and sometimes as a short-break package, so, if you're interested, it is always worth asking. A few examples are listed below. The tourist office at Montier-en-Der (Haute-Marne) offers a guided tour of half-timbered churches and sixteenth-century stained-glass windows. The Rocroi tourist office (Ardennes – Tel. 24 54 11 75) does a weekend photo safari in the Riezes marshlands. The Pays de Langres tourist office (Langres, Haute-Marne – Tel. 25 87 67 67) proposes riding, cycling, gastronomic and other trips. In Epernay, Reims and Châlons-sur-Marne, the tourist offices will arrange a whole variety of tours. Local tour operators include **Champagne Découverte**, 18 rue Porte Lucas, 51200 Epernay (Tel. 26 54 19 49), who give guided mini-bus tours of champagne vineyards, and the wide-ranging **Loisirs-Accueil en Ardennes**, 18 ave Georges Corneau, 08000 Charleville-Mézières (Tel. 24 56 00 63).

At the Maison du Parc of both regional parks, you can obtain information on their thematic trails and accompanied excursions, which range from general nature rambles or early-morning bird-watching, to visits to potteries, bee-keepers or local factories. The Montagne de Reims park also provides a list of addresses of local enterprises you can visit, including vine-growers, horticulturalists, sculptors, silk-painters, and even somewhere you can learn weaving. General information on the region and possibilities for holidays in it is available from the **Comité Régional du Tourisme de Champagne-Ardenne**, 5 rue de Jéricho, 51037 Châlons-sur-Marne

(Tel. 26 70 31 31). Specialist nature study, botany and bird-watching holidays to Champagne-Ardenne are arranged in the UK by **Branta Travel** (11 Uxbridge St, London W8 7TQ, Tel. 071 229 7231).

Communications

How to Get There

Flights from Britain to Reims-Champagne airport (51450 Bétheny, Tel. 26 07 18 85) involve a change in Paris.

There is a good **train** service from Paris, with one main line to Epernay (connections to Reims) and Châlons-sur-Marne, and another going further south to Troyes and Langres. Reims and Châlons are both around 1$1/2$ hours from Paris (Gare de l'Est). There is a Eurolines **coach** service between London and Reims, which costs around £60 adult return. The car journey from Paris to Reims on the A4 takes just under 2 hours.

When You're There

Rail – of the two main lines, one passes through Dormans, Epernay, Châlons-sur-Marne, Vitry-le-François and St-Dizier, and the other through Nogent-sur-Seine, Troyes, Bar-sur-Aube, Chaumont, Langres and Chalindrey. From Epernay the line goes north to Reims and Charleville-Mézières, where there are connections to Sedan. There are numerous minor lines, supplemented by an efficient coach service, and details of the whole network are in the 'Guide Régional des Transports – SNCF/TER', available from the Conseil Régional in Châlons. For breathtaking views, take the train along the Meuse valley.

Bus – for the best information, get hold of the guide mentioned above. Bus routes include Chaumont – Bourbonne-les-Bains; Troyes – Brienne-le-Château – Montier-en-Der – St-Dizier; and Troyes – Châlons-sur-Marne – Reims – Rethel – Charleville-Mézières – Rocroi. Tourist offices will be able to tell you about local coach or mini-bus trips.

Car – Reims, Châlons, Troyes and Langres are all connected by swift motorways, though the alternative N and D roads are much more pleasant to drive on, as well as giving better views of the champagne vineyards and the opportunity for spur-of-the-moment stops.

Boat – Champagne-Ardenne has 650 km of navigable waterway and many large lakes. Boat-hire firms of all types are common. In the Ardennes, try **Bouchery Plaisance**, 21 Sous les Roches,

08000 Charleville-Mézières (Tel. 24 59 35 23). In July and August, canal trips leave from Attigny – contact the Syndicat d'Initiative at Vouziers (Tel. 24 71 76 63). For further information, write to **Loisirs-Accueil en Ardennes**, 18 ave Georges Corneau, 08000 Charleville-Mézières (Tel. 24 56 00 63). In the Marne, house-boats can be rented from **Champagne Eaux Coeur**, 25 rue des Rocherets, 51200 Epernay, and from M. Grandhomme, **Le Coche d'Eau**, Chemin du Petit Parc, 51300 Vitry-le-François (Tel. 26 74 05 85), who also organise cruises. Other addresses can be obtained from the **Comité Régional de Tourisme Champagne-Ardenne**, 5 rue de Jéricho, 51037 Châlons-sur-Marne (Tel. 26 70 31 31). Boat trips with commentary are available on the Forêt d'Orient and Der-Chantecoq lakes – ask at the ports (Mesnil-St-Père and Giffaumont, respectively). The lakes also have facilities for sailing, rowing and canoeing, as do those around Langres. Good rivers for canoeing are the Marne, the Aube, and, for the more adventurous, the Blaise, the Saulx, the Rognon and the Aire.

Cycling – bicycles can be hired from various railway stations and local cycle clubs. Good areas for cycling are the Marne meadows and the Ardennes forests. The only cycle hire available in the Montagne de Reims park is from M. Gabriel, Chemin des Remparts, 51160 Avenay-Val-d'Or (Tel. 26 52 31 03). The **Pays de Langres** tourist office (52200 Langres, Tel. 25 87 67 67) proposes 2- and 3-day circuits, touring the 'land of the four lakes'. You can hire both normal bikes and mountain bikes (VTT) from the **Service Pêche**, 51290 Giffaumont (Tel. 26 72 61 16).

Walking – hundreds of miles of marked paths cross Champagne-Ardenne, the main ones being the GR 2, in the south of the region; the GR 24, which passes through the Forêt d'Orient regional park; the GR 12, in the Ardennes; and the GR 14, which crosses the Montagne de Reims park. Other thematic trails are set up by the parks themselves, where walkers' maps are available (addresses of park headquarters below).

Riding – horseriding is popular, and information on riding centres and routes is available from the **Association Champagne-Ardenne pour le Tourisme Equestre**, St-Etienne-à-Arnes, 08310 Juniville (Tel. 24 30 34 52). The **Pays de Langres** tourist office (address under Cycling) organises riding holidays. For riding near the *Lac du Der-Chantecoq*, contact M. Pillard, **Amicale des Cavaliers du Grand Der**, 52220 Planrupt (Tel. 25 04 20 74). In the Montagne de Reims park, riding is not encouraged as the horses' hooves churn up the clay-based ground. Horse-drawn caravans are available. In the Ardennes, try M. Laloua, 08240 Boult-aux-Bois (Tel. 24 30 02 37).

Useful Local Contacts

The **Conservatoire du Patrimoine Naturel de Champagne-Ardenne** (08240 Boult-aux-Bois, Tel. 24 30 06 20) is keen to inform people of its projects. As well as organising *chantiers de bénévoles* and undertaking other conservation work, it has plans for a Maison de la Nature in Boult-aux-Bois, which will bring to life the region's natural heritage for the general public. The headquarters of the two regional parks will be able to inform you about current ecological issues. Their addresses are: **Parc Naturel Régional de la Montagne de Reims**, Maison du Parc, 51480 Pourcy (Tel. 26 59 44 44); and **Parc Naturel Régional de la Forêt d'Orient**, Maison du Parc, 10220 Piney (Tel. 25 41 35 57). Other addresses which might be useful are: **Délégation Régionale à l'Architecture et à l'Environnement**, 15 ave du Maréchal Leclerc, 51037 Châlons-sur-Marne; **Union Régionale Champagne-Ardenne pour la Nature et l'Environnement (URCANE)**, 2 rue Louis Armand, 51000 Châlons-sur-Marne; and **Centre Ornithologique Champagne-Ardenne**, Drosnay, 51290 St-Rémy-en-Bouzemont.

Geographical Breakdown of Region

Ardennes

The word Ardenne is Celtic for 'deep forest' and the name is still appropriate, particularly in the north and east of the *département*. Here, dramatic valleys have been carved by the rivers Meuse and Semoy and, in the south, it is the Aisne which slices through the countryside. Several routes are set out in tourist office leaflets, including the 'legends of Meuse and Semoy' route and the 'forests, lakes and abbeys' route. Perhaps the best way to explore the area is simply to follow the rivers.

The river Meuse crosses from Belgium to France at **Givet**. From here you can visit the imposing **Charlemont** castle and the **Grottes de Nichet**, ancient caves open to the public from April to October. A diversion through the forest to **Hargnies** is worthwhile, before rejoining the river at **Fumay** to see the Slate Museum. West of the Meuse is **Rocroi**, a star-shaped town with sixteenth-century fortifications. From here, there are guided tours to the Rocroi and Hautes-Rivières plateaux to see the acid peat-bogs of the 'Riezes' and the 'Fagnes', with their arctic flora, orchids and carnivorous plants. Back on the Meuse, the most spectacular scenery is between the river bend at **Revin** and its confluence with the Semoy at Monthermé. The **Dames de la Meuse** is a high cliff on which erosion has formed a series of vertical rocks, which overlook the river like protective goddesses. **Monthermé** is an ideal starting place for rambles through the woods, which can lead to the stunning panoramas at the **Longue Roche**, the **Roche à 7 Heures**, the **Roc de la Tour** (ideal for climbers), and to the Phades waterfall in the Semoy valley. Following the Meuse southwards, you will come to the **Rocher des 4 Fils Aymon**, a crest resembling four horsemen of local legend.

There is plenty to see in the main city, **Charleville-Mézières**, originally two towns, but joined together in 1966. You can still see fortifications and a large section of the ramparts of Mézières. The church of Notre-Dame de l'Espérance is late Gothic, with impressive stained-glass windows. Charleville was founded in 1606 and is a lovely example of urban architecture of the period – see the Place Ducale and the Vieux Moulin townhouse, which holds the Rimbaud Museum. From April to September, cruises start from Charleville. You could also visit the **Abbaye des 7 Fontaines**, the **Musée de la Forêt** at Renwez, and the **Lac des Vieilles Forges** with its sailing facilities. Further down the Meuse, just before Sedan, you can cut down to Rethel, along the **Canal des Ardennes**, if time is short.

Sedan has the largest fortified castle in Europe, built between the eleventh and sixteenth centuries. The town itself has many attractive seventeenth- and eighteenth-century slate-roofed houses of yellow stone. Below Sedan, it is worth following the River Chiers, tributary of the Meuse, to the Maginot Line fort of **Villy-la-Ferté**, before returning to the main river at **Mouzon**. This town, where Spanish influence is in evidence, has a magnificent thirteenth-century abbey and a Felt Museum. Leaving the Meuse, which crosses into Lorraine, it is worth visiting the 865-acre animal reserve at **Belval**, with its bison, elk, bear and boar. Visits can be made by car, coach, tourist train or on foot. To the west, in the tiny village of **Boult-aux-Bois**, many environmental organisations have their headquarters, and an old barn is being renovated to become a Maison de la Nature. The surrounding Forêt de la Crois-aux-Bois is a source of pleasant walks and has a marked 'discovery' path. The other side of the wood is **Vouziers**, home of the philosopher Hippolyte Taine. Look out for the triple door of the Renaissance church of St-Maurille, and visit some of the many wickerwork shops and studios. Vouziers is on the Aisne river, which you can follow right across, through **Rethel**, to Picardy.

Accommodation & Eating Out

If you wish to rent furnished rooms during your stay, contact **Loisirs-Accueil en Ardennes**, 18 ave Georges Corneau, 08000 Charleville-Mézières (Tel. 24 56 00 63). The following hotels and B&B are recommended:

First Class

Le Château Bleu, 3 bd L. Pierquin, Warcq, 08000 Charleville-Mézières (Tel. 24 56 18 19): 13 rooms in nineteenth-century mansion with restaurant.

Middle Range

Ferme-Auberge du Pied des Monts, 'Grivy', Grivy-Loisy, 08400 Vouziers (Tel. 24 71 92 38): 5 *chambres d'hôte* in quiet, country farmhouse. **Le Pelican**, 42 ave Leclerc, 08000 Charleville-Mézières (Tel. 24 56 42 73): 20 rooms in family-run hotel with restaurant.

Middle Range / Economy

Le St-Michel, 3 rue St-Michel, 08200 Sedan (Tel. 24 29 04 61): 19 rooms in family-run hotel; restaurant.

Economy

Auberge en Ardenne, 15 rue de l'Hôtel de Ville, Les Hautes-Rivières, 08800 Monthermé (Tel. 24 53 41 93): 14 rooms in family hotel. **'La Brasserie'**, Chémery-sur-Bar, 08450 Raucourt (Tel. 24 35 40 31): 3 *chambres d'hôte* in eighteenth-century house.

The brand name 'Ardennes de France' is an indication of good regional food. Look out also for restaurants displaying a yellow, red and black sign, which indicates the chef proposes typical Ardennes cuisine.

Reims

This town, which hosted the coronation of French royalty for a thousand years, but was considerably damaged in the First World War, is now, along with Epernay, the centre of champagne production. The **Cathédrale de Notre Dame**, which escaped major war damage, is a thirteenth century Gothic masterpiece of golden limestone, which looks its best in the evening sunshine. Look out for the Smiling Angel sculpture (on the left of the facade), the amazingly blue Rose window on the west wall, and the Chagall windows beyond the altar. Next door, the **Palais de Tau**, former episcopal palace, houses the cathedral's treasure, including statuary and tapestries. The **St-Remi Basilica** is said to contain the tombs of some of France's earliest kings, and nearby **Abbaye St-Remi** is a comprehensive archaeological museum. The **Musée des Beaux-Arts**, in the **Abbaye St-Denis**, contains some interesting Cranach sketches and a collection of Corots. **Hôtel le Vergeur** is a restored thirteenth-century house, whose museum traces the expansion of Reims and includes fascinating engravings by Dürer. More recent developments are reflected in the **Car Museum** and the **Salle de Reddition**, the schoolroom where the Germans surrendered to the Allies on 8 May 1945. There is an extensive museum of the First World War at the **Fort de la Pompelle**, 8 kilometres outside Reims. Reminders of Roman times are the **Porte Mars**, a third-century Corinthian style triumphal arch which dominates Place de la République, and the **Cryptoporticos**, second- and third-century galleries, partly underground, which belonged to the Roman Forum. It is also worth wandering through **Place Royale**, restored to look as it did in the time of Louis XV.

Of course, no trip to Reims is complete without a visit to the cellars of a champagne firm. A tourist office leaflet explains where they all are, which ones speak English, which require advance warning, and so on. **Taittinger** and **Pommery** have magnificent cellars; **Mumm** and **Veuve Clicquot-Ponsardin** offer free tasting; and **Piper-Heidsieck** is ideal for the foot-weary as it conducts the whole visit in a miniature electric train. There is a colourful horticultural garden on boulevard Roederer.

Accommodation

First Class

Boyer les Crayères, 64 bd H. Vasnier (Tel. 26 82 80 80): 19 luxurious rooms in 18th century château with private grounds (see **Eating Out**). **Hôtel les Templiers**, 22 rue des Templiers (Tel. 26 88 55 08): 15 very comfortable rooms. **Hôtel Crystal**, 86 Place Drouet d'Erlon (Tel. 26 88 44 44): 31 rooms in attractive building.

Middle Range

Hôtel au Tambour, 60 rue de Magneux (Tel. 26 40 59 22): 14 rooms in family-run hotel with restaurant. **Hôtel les Relais Bleus**, rue Gabriel Voisin (Tel. 26 82 59 79): 40 rooms in charming, airy hotel with restaurant. **Hôtel Dom Pérignon**, 14 rue des Capucins (Tel. 26 47 33 64): 10 rooms.

Economy

Hôtel d'Alsace, 6 rue du Général Sarrail (Tel. 26 47 44 08): 24 spacious rooms in friendly establishment. **Hôtel Linguet**, 14 rue Linguet (Tel. 26 47 31 89): 12 rooms in quiet hotel with courtyard. **Hôtel du Cours Langlet**, 53 cours Langlet (Tel. 26 47 13 89): 12 rooms.

Eating Out

Reims is the French city with the highest total of 'stars' for gastronomic excellence. This is only a small selection of its good restaurants.

First Class

Boyers les Crayères, 64 bd H. Vasnier (Tel. 26 82 80 80): spectacular, light, innovative cuisine in elegant setting. **Le Verzenay**, Cours de la Gare, 2 bd Roederer (Tel. 26 47 54 56): classic cuisine in spacious restaurant.

Middle Range

Restaurant Colbert, 64 Place Drouet d'Erlon (Tel. 26 47 55 79): traditional and modern cuisine harmoniously blended. **Le Vigneron**, Place Paul Jamot (Tel. 26 47 00 71): regional cuisine in what seems like a museum of champagne, with many old posters.

Economy

Le Paysan, 16 rue de Fismes (Tel. 26 40 25 51): classical cuisine in attractive dining room. **L'Ambroisie**, 66 rue Gambetta (Tel. 26 85 46 51): traditional cuisine in rustic-style restaurant with wood panelling.

Entertainments

The tourist office organises regular guided tours of the town. Visits to the workshops of jewellers, furniture-restorers, potters, stringed instrument-makers and other craftsmen are possible – all details are in the 'Guide Officiel de l'Office de Tourisme de Reims'. In June,

July, August and September, there are *Son et Lumière* performances at both the cathedral and the basilica (the former offers programmes on three different themes). There are open-air concerts at various locations during July and August. If you are fortunate enough to be in the town on the second weekend in June, you will experience the lively Joan of Arc Festival.

Useful Addresses

The **Tourist Office** is at 2 rue G. de Machault (Tel. 26 47 25 69), to the left of the cathedral. The **Post Offices** are on Place de Boulingrin (near the Porte Mars) and 1 rue Cérès (Place Royale). Medical assistance can be provided by SAMU, 45 rue Cognacq Jay (Tel. 26 06 07 08).

Transport Options

Information on the comprehensive bus network is available at the TUR office (6 rue Chanzy) or at the tourist office, which also offers its own suggestions on how to get around. It organises thematic walking circuits with a guide; mini-bus trips, both around Reims and into the surrounding vineyards; half-hour circuits by mini-train; and, in July and August, tours of the town in a horse-drawn carriage.

Marne

The part of the Marne with the greatest concentration of things to see and do is the regional park area. This is where most champagne vines are grown, though the summit of the Montagne de Reims is a plateau of thick deciduous forest, and many sections are devoted to agriculture. The park headquarters is a good place to start.

The Maison du Parc at **Pourcy**, which won an architectural prize, has an exhibition room, useful leaflets and advice on all its facilities. Nearby **Marfaux** has a church with an exhibition on Romanesque architecture and is the starting point for a circuit of eighteen Romanesque buildings along the Ardre valley. The Domaine de Commétreuil at **Bouilly** is a 350-acre forest with its own château, which is ideal for walks and has educational trails. From the Chapelle St-Lie, above the village of **Ville-Dommange**, there is an excellent view over what is called 'la petite Montagne'. Working eastwards, through Villers-Allerand, you come to an area with many small-scale champagne producers, and to the geological 'discovery' path at **Mailly-Champagne**. Beyond **Verzenay**, with its unexpected windmill, is **Verzy**, whose 'Mont Sinaï' military observatory is another good view point. Also at Verzy is the sensitive site of the uniquely twisted *Faux de Verzy* beech trees. Unless you like crowds, avoid coming here at the weekend, and remember that the trees' future depends on people staying on the path. In **Ambonnay** you can visit the workshops of a painter-sculptor (3 rue de la Musique), and a bee-keeper (10 rue du Château), both of whom belong to the Association Accueil, set up by the park to help present a rounded picture of rural life. Try the red wine made at nearby **Bouzy** before joining the gentle Marne valley and following it westwards. The vineyards are mainly on the right bank, and many houses in the wine villages look unassuming but have an impressive interior courtyard: one way in which the wealth of the area is played down. **Avenay-Val-d'Or** has an 'interpretation path', starting and finishing at the village station, designed to enable people to discover different facets of the rural community. At **Germaine**, another path takes the walker through the different environments of the area. Both paths are best appreciated if followed in conjunction with the appropriate park brochure. Germaine is also home to the Maison du Bûcheron, which presents the activities of the lumberjack, past and present, along with other forest occupations (open weekends, afternoons only).

Epernay is the true capital of champagne, and this is quite apparent when you pass between the impeccable mansions of the great champagne firms which line the avenue de Champagne. If Moët et Chandon is the most extensive, with over 27 kilometres of cellar, then Mercier is the most flamboyant, with its beautifully carved, century-old Tun, which has a fascinating history and a capacity of 215,000 bottles! De Castellane owns a tower housing an interesting museum. The Musée du Champagne et du Préhistoire is also worth a visit, as is the Jardin des Papillons, where butterflies live in tropical conditions. The tourist office at Epernay arranges excursions and short-break holidays.

Champillon and **Hautvillers** offer splendid views across the Marne valley. The latter is the village where Dom Pérignon, inventor of champagne, was a monk, and you can see his tomb in the abbey. Look out for the traditional coats of arms for different trades, which swing above the doors of most houses. At **Ville-en-Tardenois** is the Centre Artisanal (same opening times as Maison du Bûcheron), which has an exhibition room and offers studios to two local artists or craftspeople to help get their businesses off the ground.

Outside the regional park, the Chapelle de la Marne at **Dormans** is worth a visit, and, further south, the St-Gond marshes, site of many monuments recalling General Foch's victory over the Germans during the first Battle of the Marne.

Boat trips along the Canal de la Marne au Rhin start from **Vitry-le-François**, and may pass through **Sermaize-les-Bains**, where you will find the pleasant park of the Abbaye de 3 Fontaines. Finally, **Ste-Menehould**, birthplace of Dom Pérignon, has a remarkable pink brick Hôtel de Ville and is a good starting place for walks in the Argonne forest.

Accommodation & Eating Out

First Class

Le Royal Champagne, Champillon-Bellevue, 51160 Ay-Champagne (Tel. 26 52 87 11): 26 luxurious rooms in Relais et Châteaux hotel with magnificent panoramic views over vineyards.

Middle Range

'Manoir de Montflambert', 51160 Mutigny (Tel. 26 52 33 21): 5 *chambres d'hôtes* with period furnishings, in seventeenth-century manor surrounded by vineyards; *tables d'hôte*.

Middle Range / Economy

Le Relais Champenois, 157 rue Notre-Dame, 51120 Sézanne (Tel. 26 80 58 03): 14 rooms in old house in regional style; family-run; restaurant with regional specialities. **Le Champenois**, rte Nationale 4, Thiéblemont-Farémont, 51300 Vitry-le-François (Tel. 26 73 81 03): 6 rooms in family-run half-timbered hotel with rustic interior; restaurant with local specialities. **La Touraine Champenoise**, 2 rue du Pont, 51150 Tours-sur-Marne (Tel. 26 58 91 93): 10 rooms in old inn, in same family for three generations; restaurant with regional cuisine.

Economy

Lieudit 'Les Nonettes', Basse Vaucelle, 51210 Boissy-le-Repos (Tel. 26 81 12 63): 2 rooms in seventeenth-century former convent.

Arguably the best restaurant in the area is **Le Royal Champagne** (address above). Those with more limited budgets might try the *ferme-auberges* at Germaine and Vauciennes.

Châlons-sur-Marne

Châlons is a small bourgeois city, lent serenity by its canals, parks and elegant town mansions. The thirteenth-century **Cathédrale St-Etienne** is famed for its stained-glass windows (notice the deep green colour that characterises church windows in Châlons). It also has an interesting treasury. The cathedral is rivalled by the **Eglise Notre-Dame-en-Vaux**, with its Rose windows and peal of 56 bells. Its **Musée du Cloître** boasts 55 early Gothic caryatids (statues forming columns), which were discovered only recently. The **Municipal Museum** and the **Musée Garinet et Musée Goethe-Schiller** both contain interesting, if rather eclectic, selections of objects. The latter is worth visiting, if only to see the nineteenth century bourgeois interior. There is also a **Museum of Regional Military History**.

The old parts of Châlons have some beautifully restored half-timbered houses (on Place de la République, for example), and many seventeenth- and eighteenth-century town mansions. The Mau and Nau canals, formed by tributaries of the Marne, are spanned by attractive old bridges. The **Jardin du Jard** runs alongside the Nau canal, contains the turreted **Château du Marché**, various rare trees and an English garden, and offers good views of the cathedral. Eight kilometres from Châlons is the cathedral-sized **Basilique Notre-Dame de l'Epine**. This has fifteenth-century flamboyant Gothic tracery, many life-like gargoyles, and rises unexpectedly from the wheatfields around it.

Accommodation

First Class

Hôtel d'Angleterre, 19 Place Monseigneur Tissier (Tel. 26 68 21 51): 19 rooms in beautiful, central hotel.

First Class / Middle Range

Hôtel du Pot d'Etain, 18 Place de la République (Tel. 26 68 09 09): 30 spacious rooms in well-situated and friendly hotel.

Middle Range

Hôtel Pasteur, 46 rue Pasteur (Tel. 26 68 10 00): 29 attractive rooms in seventeenth-century building. **Hôtel Bristol**, 77 ave Pierre Semard (Tel. 26 68 24 63): 24 rooms.

Economy

Hôtel au Bon Accueil, 81 rue Léon Bourgeois (Tel. 26 68 09 48):
19 rooms. **Hôtel Jolly**, 12 rue de la Charrière (Tel. 26 68 09 47):
11 rooms in friendly hotel.

Eating Out

First Class

Hôtel d'Angleterre – Restaurant Jacky Michel, 19 Place Monseigneur Tissier (Tel. 26 68 21 51): imaginative cuisine in elegant
hotel restaurant.

Middle Range

Les Ardennes, 34 Place de la République (Tel. 26 68 21 42): local
specialities and classic cuisine in rustic-style restaurant with wooden
beams and central location. **Hôtel Pasteur**, 46 rue Pasteur (Tel. 26
68 10 00): high-quality hotel restaurant.

Economy

L'Avenue, 86 ave de Ste-Menehould. **Les Années Folles**, 75 rue
Léon Bourgeois: good value food in lively restaurant.

Entertainments

The tourist office's guided tours last 2 to 3 hours and are excellent,
covering virtually everything. In summer, they leave from the tourist
office from Tuesday to Saturday at 2.30 p.m. (the rest of the year,
ask in advance). One champagne cellar is open to the public:
Joseph Perrier, 69 ave de Paris. Châlons has many antique and
bric-à-brac shops: try looking down rue Gobet Boisselle and rue
Léon Bourgeois. In summer, a fabulous *Son et Lumière* takes place
at Notre-Dame de l'Epine.

Useful Addresses

The **Tourist Office** is at 3 quai des Arts (Tel: 26 65 17 89); the
Comité Départemental du Tourisme de la Marne is at 2 bis
bd Vaubécourt (Tel. 26 68 37 52); and the **Comité Régional du
Tourisme de Champagne-Ardenne** is at 5 rue de Jéricho (Tel. 26
70 31 31). The **Post Office** is 36 rue Jaurès and **medical assistance**
can be obtained by phoning 26 64 91 91.

Transport Options

Town buses leave from the station and Place Tissier. On Sunday afternoons from June to mid-August, a mini-train leaves Place Godart at regular intervals on a town circuit. Boat trips on the Mau leave Quai Barbat on Sunday afternoons from July to September.

Aube and Haute-Marne

The three main areas to visit are the Der-Chantecoq lake (half of which lies, strictly speaking, in the Marne *département*), the Forêt d'Orient lakes, and the Langres plateau where the rivers Seine, Aube and Marne rise.

There are boat trips, with commentary, on the **Lac du Der-Chantecoq** from April to September. In winter, it is mainly naturalists who come here. **Ste-Marie-du-Lac** is a village made up of reassembled half-timbered buildings, which is a kind of living museum. At **Arrigny**, on rte du Port de Nuisement, you will find the Poterie du Der, where M. Osik gives pottery demonstrations. **Giffaumont** is the port and it is here, at the Maison du Lac, that you will find detailed information about the sports and other activities you can practise on and around the lake. Nearby is the Grange aux Abeilles, with its bee-keeping exhibition, and on the way to **Montier-en-Der** is the Musée Agricole. Montier-en-Der itself is home to the Haras National stud farm, open to the public in the afternoon. The little village of **Lentilles** has a remarkable sixteenth-century half-timbered church with chestnut-wood tiles, and parts of the nearby forest are so untouched as to be impenetrable.

Over in the north-western corner of the Aube *département*, below the champagne village of **Villenauxe-la-Grande**, the valley of the River Noxe is very beautiful, with its mills and old bridges. Near **Nogent-sur-Seine**, you will find the eighteenth-century Château de la Motte-Tilly, with its lovely gardens. South-east of Troyes is the wooded country of the Pays d'Othe, and south-west, around **Les Riceys, Essoyes, Bar-sur-Seine** and **Bar-sur-Aube**, is the Aube's primary champagne-growing area. There is a good wine museum at Essoyes.

Heading towards the Forêt d'Orient regional park, you will pass through **Vendeuvre-sur-Barse**, whose sixteenth- and seventeenth-century château hosts a *Son et Lumière* spectacle in summer. The Mairie at **La Loge-aux-Chèvres** is the starting point for a 6¹/2 kilometre botanical path through copses and woods of 'Wet Champagne': a detailed guide is available from the park headquarters. **Mesnil St-Père** is the port of the Forêt d'Orient lake, which is divided into an ornithological reserve (with observation point), and a part for non-motorised watersports. At **Piney**, whose interesting seventeenth-century hall is being restored and may become a show-place for local products, is the Maison du Parc. This information and exhibition centre also organises guided outings (ask for a programme). At **Brienne-la-Vieille** is an *ecomusée*, with an old forge and wheel-maker's workshop, explanations of agricultural techniques, and a half-timbered mill which runs exhibitions on the theme of water.

The town of **Chaumont** in the Haute-Marne has some very picturesque turreted houses and is famed for its viaduct. Nearby **Nogent-en-Bassigny** is known as a scissor and cutlery-making centre, has a museum on the subject and organises visits to workshops. The Langres plateau is an inexhaustible source of running water, with numerous springs, including the petrified Etufs waterfall, and four lakes. Forests surround the fortified city of **Langres**, whose ramparts, with their six gates and seven towers are very impressive. From its narrow streets rises St-Mammès cathedral, built between the twelfth and eighteenth centuries. The Du Breuil museum is also worth a visit and, in July and August, folklore celebrations take place in Langres. Various trips, including cheese-tasting, Coiffy wine discovery and canal cruises, are organised by the tourist office. **Fayl-Billot** is also on the list, as this is the capital of the local basketwork trade. There is an important Gallo-Roman site at **Andilly-en-Bassigny**, and the thermal spa at **Bourbonne-les-Bains** dates from the same period. Do not miss Bourbonne's arboretum or the Bannie wildlife reserve.

Accommodation & Eating Out

First Class

Hôtel du Château d'Arc, Place Moreau, 52210 Arc-en-Barrois (Tel. 25 02 57 57): 28 rooms in nineteenth-century riverside château with restaurant.

First Class / Middle Range

Le Moulin du Landion, Dolancourt, 10200 Bar-sur-Aube (Tel. 25

26 12 17): 16 rooms in building in regional style, with rustic interior and views of river and mill; restaurant.

Middle Range

Auberge du Lac, Mesnil-St-Père, 10140 Vendeuvre-sur-Barse (Tel. 25 41 27 16): 15 rooms in family-run inn.

Middle Range / Economy

M. Gradelet, St-Vallier, 10110 Bourguignons (Tel. 25 29 84 43): 4 *chambres d'hôte* in charming house in quiet location.

Economy

Le Vieux Logis, Brevonnes, 10220 Piney (Tel. 25 46 30 17): 7 rooms in family-run hotel with restaurant. **'Hameau de Boulancourt'**, Longeville-sur-la-Laines, 52220 Montier-en-Der (Tel. 25 04 60 18): 3 *chambres d'hôte* in private château near farm.

Troyes

The hosiery capital of France, Troyes is a charming city, whose half-timbered old town is shaped like a champagne cork. **The Cathédrale St-Pierre et St-Paul** has 112 stained-glass windows and one of the longest naves in France. You should visit the town's oldest church, the mid-twelfth-century **Eglise Ste-Madeleine**, with its beautiful carved stone rood-screen, and the **Basilica St-Urbain**, with its thirteenth-century stained-glass windows. The Louis XIII-style **Town Hall** is also impressive. There are at least half a dozen museums worth visiting. The most famous, though the newest, is the **Musée d'Art Moderne**, housed in the former episcopal palace, which contains works by Braque, Courbet, Degas and Seurat, among others. The sixteenth-century Hôtel de Vauluisant holds both the **Musée Historique de Troyes et de Champagne** and the **Musée de la Bonneterie**, recalling Troyes' contributions to the hosiery industry (which still employs 20,000 people locally). Other good museums are the **Musée des Beaux Arts et d'Archéologie**, the **Pharmacie-Musée de l'Hôtel-Dieu** (a sixteenth-century apothecary's shop), and the **Maison de l'Outil et de la Pensée Ouvrière**, a museum devoted to crafts using wood, iron, leather and stone, and the tools involved.

However short your visit to Troyes, find time to wander through the streets around the craft museum and the pedestrian precinct, with their wonderfully restored sixteenth-century houses, such as the half-timbered **Maison du Boulanger** and **Tourelle de l'Orfèvre**. Just south of Troyes, at St-Léger-près-Troyes, you can visit a traditional farm (by arrangement only: phone M. Bres on 25 82 42 00).

Accommodation

First Class

Le Grand Hôtel de la Poste, 35 rue Emile Zola (Tel. 25 73 05 05): 34 rooms in grand hotel near old town; elegant restaurant with fine cuisine. **Le Relais St-Jean**, 51 rue Paillot de Montabert (Tel. 25 73 89 90): 22 rooms in smart hotel.

Middle Range

Splendid Hôtel, 44 bd Carnot (Tel. 25 73 08 52): 16 rooms.

Middle Range / Economy

Hôtel de Paris, 54–6 rue Roger Salengro (Tel. 25 73 11 70): 26 rooms in restored 12th century building.

Economy

Hôtel Marigny, 3 rue Charbonnet (Tel. 25 73 10 67): 14 rooms in old, half-timbered hotel. **La Mascotte**, 8 rue de Prieze (Tel. 25 80 96 49): 8 cosy rooms.

Eating Out

First Class

Le Valentino, cours de la Rencontre (Tel. 25 73 14 14): excellent restaurant with fish specialities and pleasant terrace.

First Class / Middle Range

Le Bourgogne, 40 rue du Général de Gaulle (Tel. 25 73 02 67): classical cuisine in attractive restaurant.

Middle Range

La Marée, 3 rue Raymond-Poincaré (Tel. 25 73 80 78): seafood specialities. **River's Café**, quai La Fontaine (Tel. 25 76 00 33): restaurant on board a barge.

Economy

Le Grand Café, 4 rue Champeaux (Tel. 25 73 25 60): half-timbered brasserie-style restaurant in central location. **Le Café du Musée**, 59 rue de la Cité: good local specialities in rustic-style restaurant.

Entertainments

Les Halles market is a mixture of the traditional and the modern. Ask the tourist office about some of the town visits and local tours they do; you could also enquire about visiting the Marinot Glassworks. In summer, a *Son et Lumière* at the cathedral shows off the stained-glass windows at their best.

Useful Addresses

The **Tourist Office** is 16 bd Carnot (Tel. 25 73 00 36), with a branch at 24 quai Dampierre (Tel. 25 73 36 88). The **Comité Départemental du Tourisme de l'Aube** is at the Hôtel du Départment, BP 394 (Tel. 25 42 50 50). The **Post Office** is on rue Louis Ulbach, and **medical assistance** can be obtained by phoning 25 49 55 33.

Transport Options

Buses run from next to the station. Information on routes is available from 15 rue Gustave Michel (or the tourist office).

7 Lorraine

Many French people have completely the wrong idea of Lorraine. Having been taught about its military and industrial past, they think it must be dirty and drab, and would never consider taking a holiday there. In fact, it is a wholly refreshing region. The little remaining mining industry is in easily avoidable pockets, and has, in any case, been made interesting by museums on its history. Nearly three-quarters of the region is rural, with an extreme diversity of agricultural activities. There are pastures, ploughed fields, acres of yellow rape, forests, vineyards, rivers, lakes and mountains. Middens steam outside red-tiled cottages and fruit-trees line country lanes. Crystal is engraved, earthenware glazed, spirits are distilled, and festivals celebrated, just as they have been for centuries. The place is steeped in history, going back to 2500 BC, when inhabitants of the Moselle *département* were raising cattle, hunting deer and weaving baskets. Archaeological sites and museums of local history and lifestyle abound, along with architectural gems like Metz cathedral and Place Stanislas in Nancy, sobering First World War cemeteries and a unique concentration of church organs, ancient and modern. Facilities for walking, cycling, horseriding and cross-country skiing are excellent, and these are undoubtedly the best ways to appreciate the region's natural riches.

Lorraine's inhabitants are used to being on a European cross-roads, whether that has brought trade, friendship or confrontation. Today, the emphasis is on friendship – after all the border disputes of the past, Lorraine is now on good terms with Germany, and it is easy to see why, when you meet the Lorraine people. They are extremely welcoming and genuinely keen to share their region with visitors. Many are attached to the old ways of doing things. They are proud of their heritage, their cuisine, environment, and treat tourism as a means of reaffirming this. Small-scale tourism is encouraged as a way to revive depressed rural areas – and you feel that it is as much to offer these areas outside contact and to rebuild their self-esteem, as for any economic motives. There is a growing number of charming country bed and breakfasts, which are to be strongly recommended. Though the owners are more likely to know German than English, their welcome will almost certainly break down any language barrier and they will point you on the road to discovering the true Lorraine.

History

Lorraine's climate attracted settlers in prehistoric times, and the town that would later become Metz was already in existence in the eighth century BC. Celtic habitation brought the early industries of metallurgy and salt-mining, and the town of Toul was founded. In the third century AD, the region was seized by Germanic invaders, and by the seventh century there was considerable prosperity and monastic expansion. It was in 843 that the Treaty of Verdun divided Charlemagne's empire among his three grandsons, leaving the lands between France and Germany to Lothair I. His son, Lothair II, called the area Lotharingia, which later became Lorraine.

Metz, Toul and Verdun became first bishoprics and then Free Towns in the Middle Ages, when Lorraine belonged to the Saxon dynasty. The decline of the German Empire in the thirteenth century led to disruptions in Lorraine and attempts by French monarchs to take over the area. None of these worked until 1552, when Henri II remained in control of Metz despite a seige by Charles Quint. Gradually, during the course of the culturally and artistically lively Renaissance, the rest of the region followed suit, and, in 1697, Louis XIV was able to incorporate Lorraine into the French political framework. Meanwhile, half the population had been lost in a plague and the Thirty Years' War had caused considerable damage. The strategic importance of the towns of Lorraine was recognised in the seventeenth century, and Vauban was commissioned to fortify many of them, including Metz, Phalsbourg, Marsal and Montmédy.

The eighteenth century brought a golden age, especially for Nancy. Louis XV made his father-in-law, an ex-king of Poland called Stanislas Leszczynski, Duke of Lorraine, on the condition that the region would return to French hands on his death. Fortunately Stanislas remained in charge for nearly thirty years, putting into practice inspired building projects. The industrial revolution of the nineteenth century also helped Lorraine: oil and iron ore were discovered and mining developed, but the region bore the brunt of the Franco-Prussian fighting of 1870–1 and part of it was annexed to Germany. Fortifications began to be constructed once again, including those of General Séré de Rivières in 1874, and later, between the two World Wars, the Maginot Line. It was only after the violent fighting of the First World War, notably at Verdun, that the whole of Lorraine belonged once more to France. It was again annexed by Germany between 1940 and 1944, when it was finally liberated.

The post-war years have brought a rapprochement of France and Germany in the general opening up of Europe, which was engineered, to some degree, by Lorraine-born Robert Schuman, the Minister for Foreign Affairs who came to be known as the 'father of Europe'. Since the decline of the mining industry, from the 1960s onwards, Lorraine has concentrated on its agriculture and, more recently, started looking forward to industries such as tourism and leisure.

Among well-known people connected with Lorraine are Joan of Arc, born at Domrémy-la-Pucelle, who declared her mission to defend France at Vaucouleurs in 1428; Ligier Richier, a Renaissance sculptor based at St-Mihiel; the seventeenth-century landscape painter, Claude Gellée, better known as Claude Lorrain; Jules Ferry, the nineteenth-century founder of compulsory lay education; the First World War writer, Maurice Barrès; and Albert Lebrun, elected to the French Presidency in 1932.

Geography

Lorraine is bordered by Belgium, Luxembourg and Germany to the north, Alsace to the east, Franche-Comté to the south and Champagne-Ardenne to the west. The region is divided into four *départements*, with Moselle in the north-east, hemmed in by the narrow strip of Meurthe-et-Moselle, leaving the west to the Meuse and the south to the Vosges. The regional capital is Metz (pronounced 'mess'), which is in Moselle and has 120,000 inhabitants; the other major city is Nancy (100,000) in Meurthe-et-Moselle. The remaining departmental capitals are Bar-le-Duc (Meuse) and Epinal (Vosges), both considerably smaller.

Lorraine forms the most easterly segment of the rock formation known as the Paris Basin. The region's western edge is slightly hilly, with the Côtes de Meuse bordering the Meuse river, the Côtes de Moselle bordering the Moselle river, and the Woëvre plateau in between. It is in this area that most of the remaining mining operations and vineyards are found, along with fertile crops, woods and pastures. The middle part of Lorraine is taken up by the Lorraine plateau, where there are some crops and much cattle-rearing, with a certain amount of oil industry in the north, and salt-marshes in the centre. To the east, forming the border with Alsace, are the Vosges mountains. On the Lorraine side, the slopes are gentle, with either *chaumes* (pastureland) or peat-bogs on the rounded summits, giving way to forests of beech and fir, and lakes, the largest of which is at Gérardmer. Economic activity revolves around wood, textiles and, to a lesser extent, winter sports. As the ground flattens out, thermal springs occur, around which the spa towns of Plombières-les-Bains, Bains-les-Bains, Vittel and Contrexéville have grown up.

The upper Vosges and the northern Meuse are the areas least affected by human activity. Rural habits in many other areas are compatible with maintaining a balanced environment. Practices which threaten fragile wetland habitats, such as draining them for agriculture or creating lakes for tourism purposes, are now firmly discouraged. Non-intensive farming is the norm, and there are even courses specifically for farmers wishing to switch to organic methods. Diversification is encouraged and leads to a pleasantly varied countryside: alongside cereal fields are orchards whose fruits are distilled or made into tarts, cattle whose water is raised by miniature windmill, prize strawberry fields, and slowly dwindling areas of vineyard. The Moselle river, which passes through both Metz and Nancy, has played an important economic role for Lorraine since the Middle Ages. Below Nancy it has been made into the Canal de la Marne au Rhin, part of 700 kilometres of canal in the region. River tourism is now becoming popular and is proving a useful way of combatting rural unemployment. Lorraine also boasts many ponds and lakes (over 27,000 acres), which often serve the triple objectives of conservation, fishing and tourism, though the requirements of the three functions occasionally conflict. Hunting is widespread in Lorraine, but a quota system is in operation and environmentalists do not consider it a problem.

Lorraine has a great number of ecologically valuable sites, some of which have been made into nature reserves. These areas include peat-bogs and pastureland in the upper Vosges; marshes and salt-marshes; a geological reserve in Moselle where spectacular ammonites have been found; and limestone areas in the north with magnificent insect life and flora, including rare orchids. Montenach, in northern Moselle, has an important collection of hybrid orchids. It is, of course, essential to keep to the paths at all these sites and to leave flowers alone. Sundew, water-lilies and numerous fungi can be found in Lorraine too. There are also alpine flowers in the *chaumes* of the upper Vosges. It is here that you can see the capercaillie, which is a protected bird. Other wildlife includes deer, chamois, wild boar, wild cats, foxes and otters.

Three regional parks cover areas in Lorraine. The Parc Naturel Régional de Lorraine, founded in 1974, extends over 506,500 acres of forest, meadows, vineyards and cropland in Meuse, Meurthe-et-Moselle and Moselle. It offers various open-air activities and keeps alive popular traditions through museums, workshops and craft outlets. The Parc Naturel Régional des Vosges du Nord has its headquarters in Alsace, but extends into the forests and crystal-cutting area of Moselle. Another shared regional park, this time between Lorraine, Alsace and Franche-Comté, is that of the Ballons des Vosges, in the Vosges *département*.

Climate

The climate is continental, with long winters and prolific snow in the Vosges, and hot sunny summers everywhere. Temperatures range from an average maximum of around 4.7°C in December to 26.3°C in August. Summer rains occur fairly frequently, but are quickly discharged in the form of stormy showers. Spring and autumn are excellent times to visit Lorraine, especially early autumn, which often yields an Indian summer.

Attractions

In the past, interest in Lorraine centred on its military history, with fortresses and fortified towns being the main attractions. Nancy's elegant architecture and Metz's Gothic cathedral were also a draw. Only recently has the region's potential for nature and activity tourism been acknowledged and, at the same time, many other sources of appeal have been uncovered.

Lorraine offers opportunities for walking, cross-country skiing, horse riding, watersports and river tourism, and is excellent for cycling and fishing. Many areas of ecological significance are equipped with informative signs, and local organisations have sign-posted public footpaths. Lorraine also boasts an unusual attraction: the only transversal ship-lift in Europe. This is situated near Lutzelbourg and enables boats to by-pass seventeen locks.

The military thread offers an insight into the French past, and Lorraine's archaeological excavations, the most famous of which is the joint Franco-German one at Bliesbruck, provide a glimpse as far back as Gallo-Roman times. The astounding number of museums devoted to popular arts and traditions compliment the local workshops still flourishing today, to give a rounded picture of rural life, past and present. Museums also represent the industries of the area: there is a salt museum at Marsal, a mining museum at Neufchef, and a crystal museum at Meisenthal. Most towns and villages have some attraction, whether it be an ancient church organ, a château, a famous festival, or a street of craftsmen's studios. Local people are happy to share this hidden side of their region with visitors. An enormous fun park near Metz, called Big Bang Schtroumpf, is proving an unqualified disaster, and the tourist industry seems to have learnt that Lorraine's existing assets are of far greater appeal to today's visitor.

Cuisine

Quiche Lorraine is the most famous of many regional specialities, including the bacon casserole, *Potée Lorraine*. Pork is popular and is often accompanied by potato and cabbage; game dishes are common too, as are freshwater fish recipes such as carp cooked with corn or beer, and *matelote* stew. The area's wild mushrooms are delicious. The sweet-toothed are also in for a treat. Local fruits such as plums and bilberries go into excellent tarts, and Bar-le-Duc specialises in currant jams, whose seeds have been painstakingly removed with – would you believe it? – a goose feather! The Metz valley, especially the Woippy area, is famous for its strawberries, which are at their peak in spring. Other local specialities include honey from the Vosges, *madeleine* sponge cakes from Commercy, macaroons from Nancy and Boulay, almond tarts from the Saulnois area, sugared almonds from Verdun, along with chocolate thistles called *chardons* and rum baba. Soft white cheese is popular, as are the rich Géromé and Munster cheeses from the Vosges mountains.

Summer is the season for *mirabelles*, the small golden plums which are distilled into a clear brandy of which Lorraine is justly proud. Other fruit brandies are also worth trying, though ask an expert which ones go together: they fall into four categories and tasting them is an art! The local beers are good and you should certainly sample the region's wines. Despite the fact that vines are now only a minor crop, the white wines of the Côtes de Moselle are fine and dry, and the unusual 'grey' wines of Toul, products of the 2000-year-old vineyards around Lucey-en-Lorraine, are an excellent accompaniment to quiche and fish.

Level of Tourism

Lorraine is not a particularly touristy region, hosting 1.5 million hotel visits a year (i.e. 2.3% of all national visits). It is predominantly a short-stay destination and less than one in five of its visitors comes from outside France. The ones who do come from abroad are mainly from Germany, Belgium, Luxembourg, Switzerland, Holland and Denmark.

Mass tourism, except for coach trips to Metz and Nancy, is unknown, as are the problems associated with it. The smaller towns of Lorraine are never crowded and tourists are received with pleasure in most parts of the region. One representative of a local revitalisation initiative refers not to the reception of tourists, but to the welcome of guests. This is an attitude widely in evidence.

A few controversies are linked to tourism, but mostly indirectly. People ignore signs to keep to the paths in nature reserves or sensitive areas and so cause damage. Sometimes these people are tourists, but they also include the photographers who invade the upper Vosges during the mating season of the capercaillie; unscrupulous naturalists from neighbouring Germany or Luxembourg who pick Lorraine's rare orchids; and even local people keen to gather bilberries. In the past, the appointment of lakes for recreation and leisure has harmed wetland habitats, though the environmentalists of the Conservatoire Régional des Sites Lorrains have successfully raised public awareness of the value of such areas. Now it is local fishermen rather than developers whom they are up against in their desire to turn some lakes into protected sites. This plan would automatically increase the already high numbers of waterfowl which compete with fishermen for fish. The fishing is so good in Lorraine that it is a popular tourist activity. British people wishing to try their hand should make a special effort to be quiet and responsible, so as to restore confidence after unfortunate incidents involving loutish behaviour in the past.

A decrease in tourism to Lorraine in the late 1980s led to a new approach and various new projects. The first thing was to rid the region of its undeserved image as an industrial area (which, in one brochure, involved the romanticisation of the nuclear plant near Cattenom). The next step was the revelation of its natural and cultural assets. Leaflets produced by the regional parks helped to show the diversity of their appeal. Small-scale international cooperation began, with the Thionville area advertising attractions in Luxembourg, and with the trans-boundary Bliesbruck-Reinheim archaeological park on the German frontier. There is also considerable cooperation on the conservation front, with French and Belgian volunteers joining forces to manage sites on the border.

In the Vosges, the agricultural Renaissance village of Châtillon-sur-Saône is being carefully restored by the organisation Vieilles Maisons Françaises. Emphasis is also being placed on the skiing and spa facilities of the area, but it is the Moselle *département* which really seems to have the right idea. Its policy concentrates on calm, relaxation and unspoilt nature. Value is also placed on its cultural heritage: its archaeological excavations; its crystal industry; and its fine collection of church organs, many of which are now being restored. Restoration work is also being carried out on wayside crosses and traditional bread ovens. The tourist accommodation being developed is small-scale: bed & breakfasts, rural *gîtes*, chalets and 2-star hotels. Most of these are not built new, but involve the renovation or adaptation of existing buildings. Signposting for tourists is also being improved and people are encouraged to visit the area in autumn, when it is often at its best. The keen welcome given to tourists all over Lorraine is a manifestation of pleasure that they have finally discovered and come to appreciate the region.

Good Alternatives

Meeting People

There are many ways of meeting the Lorraine people, quite apart from the obvious and very rewarding one of choosing to stay in *chambres d'hôte*. A list of festivals going on in the Meuse *département*, 'La Meuse en Fête', is available from the **Comité Départemental du Tourisme**, Hôtel du Département, 55012 Bar-le-Duc (Tel. 29 79 48 10). Local tourist offices are also more than ready to let you know what's going on where. People are always keen to promote local products and a visit to an *eau-de-vie* distiller, a pottery or a farm can prove fascinating. The Lorraine regional park, whose headquarters are at Domaine de Charmilly, Chemin des Clos, BP

35, 54702 Pont-à-Mousson (Tel. 83 81 11 91), can provide you with a list of local artisans and producers, including a **Centre d'Aide par le Travail** at Domaine du Vieux Moulin, 55210 Lachaussée (Tel. 29 89 36 02), where free-range poultry is raised by handicapped people. If you ask the park for its calendar and 'Animations Manifestations' leaflet, you will discover many events you might otherwise miss. These range from exhibitions, concerts and village fêtes to accompanied walks (sometimes in conjunction with groups from Germany, Luxembourg or Belgium), bird-watching outings, exploration of salt-marshes or the Meusian forest, and introductions to sheep-rearing or archaeological methods. Another organisation, called the **Club Touristique Lorrain**, arranges Sunday walks, skiing outings and weekend breaks; for information, ask at the main tourist office, Place d'Armes, Metz. Further group walks are organised by the **Club Alpin Français**, 5 rue St-Julien, 54000 Nancy (Tel. 83 32 37 73). In the Vosges area, a list of craftspeople can be obtained from the **Association des Artisans de la Vallée des Lacs**, 3 faubourg de Ramberchamp, 88400 Gérardmer (Tel. 29 63 47 41).

The **Foyer Rural** (Centre Permanent d'Initiation à l'Environnement), Maison de l'Arsène, BP 32, 55160 Bonzée-en-Woëvre (Tel. 29 87 36 65), runs courses and outings, usually based on study of the environment, aimed particularly at young people. Volunteers are welcomed at the conservation workshops or *chantiers* arranged by the **Conservatoire des Sites Lorrains**, 7 Place Albert Schweitzer, 57930 Fénétrange (Tel. 87 07 65 61). Most of these last a day and take place on autumn or winter weekends, but there are also a couple of week-long sessions in August, for which applications should be received by June. There is a vast range of digs at which keen archaeologists might help out: a list of those in Meuse is given in the 'Meuse Heureuse' brochure, supplied by the **Comité Départemental du Tourisme** at Bar-le-Duc (address above). You could also try writing to the **Chantier de Fouilles sur le Site Gallo-Romain de Nasium**, Mme C. Gilquin, 3 rue St-Antoine, 55000 Bar-le-Duc. More general information about the possibilities of joining and archaeological dig is available from the **Direction des Antiquités**, 6 Place de Chambre, 57000 Metz (Tel. 87 36 16 70). Parents of 6–12 year-olds, wishing to give them a holiday with French children on a Vosgian farm, should contact **Accueil Nature**, Sauville, 88140 Contrexéville (Tel. 29 09 13 14) for details.

Discovering Places

In addition to those already mentioned, various other local associations or tour operators can either organise trips for individuals or incorporate you into a group trip. The most comprehensive of these is the **Office Départemental du Tourisme de Moselle**, Service Réservation Loisirs-Accueil, Hôtel du Département, BP 1096, 57036 Metz (Tel. 87 37 57 66). Through this, you can explore Moselle on foot, bicycle or horse, staying in *chambres d'hôte* or family-run-hotels, and your luggage is even transported from one nights' stop to the next. Tours on a military theme, lasting from half a day to two days, are also possible, as are relaxing fishing holidays on a boat called *Aux Arches de St-Pierre*, Port du Houillon, 57810 Languimberg (Tel. 87 25 90 75), which doubles as a hotel and restaurant and where the emphasis is on ecologically responsible fishing. At Verdun, the Syndicat d'Initiative runs mini-bus tours of the battlefields. Other coach trips (lasting one, two or three days), along with fishing, riding, cycling and walking holidays, where accommodation is in inns and farmhouses specialising in regional dishes, are organised by the **Association 'Les Séjours des Pays de Meuse'**, 55200 Frémeréville-sous-les-Côtes (Tel. 29 91 46 06). The **Comité Départemental du Tourisme des Vosges** operates an economical *Bonjour les Vosges* 'passport' system, which gives you a certain number of nights' accommodation and use of various sporting and cultural facilities for a fixed sum. Details about the scheme are available from the C.D.T. des Vosges, 7 rue Gilbert, BP 332, 88008 Epinal (Tel. 29 82 49 93). It is also worth asking them for the comprehensive booklet *Bonjour les Vosges*. For a catalogue of guided walks and other trips in the Vosges, contact the non-profitmaking **Vosges Evasion**, 10 rue du 152e R.I., 88400 Gérardmer (Tel. 29 63 17 50). Another local tour operator is **Transvosges Voyages**, which has branches in Gérardmer, Epinal and St-Dié. A whole range of general information on the Lorraine region is available from the **Comité Régional du Tourisme de Lorraine**, 1 Place Gabriel-Hocquart, 57036 Metz Cedex 1 (Tel. 87 33 60 00).

Communications

How to Get There

The nearest international **airports** are Strasbourg and Mulhouse, both in Alsace, but there are regional ones at Metz, Nancy/Essey and Epinal/Mirecourt, which receive flights from Paris.

The fastest **train** from Paris to Nancy takes around 2^1/2 hours. There is a Eurolines **coach** service from London to Metz which costs around £70 adult return. The drive by car from Paris to Metz takes around 3^1/2 hours on the A 4, but allow an extra half hour if you are continuing to Nancy on the A 31.

When You're There

Rail – the regional railway network is fairly good, with the main line running from Luxembourg, through Thionville, Metz and Nancy, to Epinal. Other lines connect with it, allowing travel to many towns including Longwy, Verdun, Bar-le-Duc, Toul, Sarreguemines, Bitche, Sarrebourg, Lunéville, St-Dié, Vittel and Bussang. There are also two steam trains for tourists. One leaves from Abreschviller, not far from Sarrebourg. The other winds along the Canner valley, between Vigy and Hombourg-Budange, at weekends (reservations can be made at the Thionville tourist office, 16 rue du Vieux Collège, Tel. 82 53 33 18).

Bus – the bus service is used less than the train service, except when it comes to reaching Verdun, and in the southern part of the Vosges mountains, where the range is crossed at only one point by train. Here, bus is the usual form of public transport. Frequent coach trips to see the Vosges leave from Gérardmer. Coach trips in the Meuse are organised by **Association 'Les Séjours des Pays de Meuse'**, 55200 Frémeréville-sous-les-Côtes (Tel. 29 91 46 06). The most comprehensive coach service in Lorraine is provided by **Les Rapides de Lorraine**, Gare routière – Place Monseigneur Ruch, 54000 Nancy (Tel. 83 32 34 20), which covers connections between Nancy, Metz, Pont-à-Mousson, Toul, Lunéville, Contrexéville and Epinal.

Car – the A 31 motorway runs north-south right the way from Luxembourg to Dijon, on its way connecting Thionville, Metz and Nancy, and passing close to Contrexéville and Vittel. The A4 runs from Metz to Strasbourg, passing St-Avold, Sarreguemines and Sarre-Union on the way. Great fun can be had exploring on the minor roads, especially in the relatively sparsely populated Meuse *département*, and around the old-fashioned villages of Moselle.

Boat – it is possible to hire boats on the Moselle and Meuse, as well as the Canal de la Marne au Rhin and the Canal de l'Est (Vosges section): ask at the nearest tourist office or **Navilor Plaisance**, 20 rue de Pont-à-Mousson, 57000 Metz (Tel. 87 63 44 25). Thionville is a starting point for cruises on the Moselle and details are available from the tourist office (address under **Train**). For cruises and boat-hire on the Canal de l'Est, try **S.A. Navigu'est**, Fontenoy-le-Château, 88240 Bains-les-Bains (Tel. 29 36 31 47). Watersports are practised on many lakes: information can be obtained from tourist offices or the **Base de Loisirs de Madine**, Madine Accueil, 55210 Nonsard (Tel. 29 89 32 50). Keen canoeists should contact the **Canoë-Kayak Federation**, 38 rue du Général-Brion, 57050 Metz-Plappeville (Tel. 87 30 01 44).

Cycling – bicycles can be hired from the SNCF stations at Bitche, Contrexéville, St-Dié, Sarrebourg and Verdun. Other bike-hire venues include various lakes, as well as **Sarl Chapleur**, 57 rue de la République, 54300 Lunéville (Tel. 83 74 07 20), and **M. Michenon**, 91 ave des 4 Eglises, 54000 Nancy (Tel. 83 36 44 97), both of which also rent mountain bikes and are closed on Sunday and Monday. Lorraine operates a cycling holiday scheme called **Vélorraine**, whose fourteen or more circuits range from three to fifteen days and from 600-5000 FF.

Accommodation is in B&B and family hotels, with an emphasis on regional cuisine. Information can be obtained from the **Office Départemental du Tourisme de Moselle**, Service Réservations Loisirs-Accueil, Hôtel du Département, BP 1096, 57036 Metz (Tel. 87 37 57 63) or from the **Comité Régional du Tourisme de Lorraine**, 1 Place Gabriel Hocquard, BP 1004, 57036 Metz (Tel. 87 33 60 00). Independent cyclists might contact **Cyclotourisme**, 16 rue de Faulquenel, 57070 Metz-Vallières. The villages of the Mortagne valley, in the south of Meurthe-et-Moselle, are linked by $7^{1}/2$ miles of old railway track. This pleasant stretch of country can best be viewed if you hire a bicycle-powered carriage, called a *draisine*, which runs along the track. The hire point is the former railway station at Magnières.

Walking – Lorraine enjoys a comprehensive footpath network which makes for excellent walking holidays, particularly in the Vosges. GR paths 5 and 7 are supplemented by GR 533 and 714, as well as by numerous smaller footpaths, carefully signposted by local associations like the **Club Vosgien**. For guided and group walks, see **Good Alternatives** section. Maps of walking circuits are available at many tourist offices. More detailed maps of circuits in Moselle, often following a thematic route, can be obtained from the **Office Départemental du Tourisme de Moselle** (address under **Cycling**).

Riding – horse riding is popular and riding holidays are organised by the **Office Départemental du Tourisme de Moselle** (for address, see **Cycling** section). Horse-drawn caravans can be hired from **Relais des Ecuries du Château**, 55260 Thillombois (Tel. 29 75 00 94). The **Association Régionale de Tourisme Equestre** is run by M. Baraban, Dombrot-le-Sec, 88140 Contrexéville (Tel. 29 08 28 58).

Useful Local Contacts

The association most active in ecological matters is the **Conservatoire des Sites Lorrains**, 7 Place Albert Schweitzer, 57930 Fénétrange (Tel. 87 07 65 61), which manages many sites of ecological interest, including some nature reserves, as well as running conservation *chantiers*. Leaflets on areas of environmental and architectural interest in Lorraine are available from the **Délégation Régionale à l'Architecture et à l'Environnement**, 29 rue des Murs, 57000 Metz (Tel. 87 36 14 06). The headquarters of the **Parc Naturel Régional de Lorraine** is at Domaine de Charmilly, Chemin des Clos, BP 35, 54702 Pont-à-Mousson (Tel. 83 81 11 91). The other two regional parks with sectors in Lorraine have their headquarters in Alsace: **Maison du Parc Naturel Régional des Vosges du Nord**, 67290 La Petite-Pierre (Tel. 88 70 46 55); and **Maison du Parc Naturel Régional des Ballons des Vosges**, 1 rue de l'Eglise, BP 11, 68140 Munster (Tel. 89 77 29 04). Interesting leaflets are available from all the parks.

Geographical Breakdown of Region

Meuse and Meurthe-et-Moselle

This part of the region is a mixture of vast stretches of sparsely inhabited agricultural land, where time seems to stand still, and little pockets of industry.

In **Stenay**, a riverside town surrounded by forest in the northern Meuse, there is a museum of the local area and an interesting beer museum. Nearby **Montmédy** was fortified by Vauban and archaeological work is going on at its citadel. There is an unexpectedly beautiful basilica church at **Avioth**, on the Belgian border. **Velosnes**, also on the border, is a limestone area with exceptional flora (including orchids) and insect life, notably butterflies. It is an attractive spot with a short but informative botanical path and some abandoned military forts which are now home to bats. At

Longuyon there is an interesting collegiate church, and **Longwy**, an important industrial centre long famous for its *faïencerie*, has a museum of ceramics and enamels. **Verdun**'s memorial museum of the 1916–18 battles emphasises the Franco-German unity felt today. You can also visit Dragée Braquier, where Verdun's famous sugared almonds are made. The Domaine du Vieux Moulin, at **Lachaussée** in the Lorraine regional park, has a centre where physically handicapped people raise free-range poultry, and a *ferme-auberge* where local dishes can be sampled. There are various places of interest in the area of **Vigneulles-lès-Hattonchatel** and it is worth asking the tourist office for information. Vigneulles itself has a Centre de Promotion des Produits Locaux, where traditionally made products are on sale. To the north, there is a Maison de l'Artisanat at **St-Maurice-sous-les-Côtes** and a fascinating Maison des Arts et Traditions Rurales, showing the way people used to live and work, at **Hannonville-sous-les-Côtes**. Numerous walking trails can be found in the forests north-west of Vigneulles. To the south is the Madine Lake, which has watersports facilities and an ornithological park at **Heudicourt-sous-les-Côtes**. **Pont-à-Mousson**, as well as being the headquarters of the regional park, boasts a spectacular waterfront abbey, called the Abbaye des Prémontrés. It is also the start of the hilly area known as Lorraine's 'little Switzerland'.

If you are in the dairy farming country of the western Meuse, it is worth visiting **Bar-le-Duc**'s sixteenth-century old town and the archaeological Musée du Barrois. In July, the Soirées de Jeand'Heurs provide a magnificent *Son et Lumière* display at the château of **Lisle-en-Rigault**. At **Pagny-sur-Meuse** is the biggest marsh in Lorraine, whose valuable plant life had been threatened by reeds which were smothering it and drying it out, until the Conservatoire des Sites Lorrains had the idea of introducing a specially-suited breed of Polish horse to graze there. The Konig Polsky horses are similar to wild ones found in the Vosges until the eighteenth century and have done a splendid job, winning the hearts of local people. An observatory explains about the horses and the plant life, including why it is important not to feed them or enter the marsh. Around **Lucey-en-Lorraine** are the ancient vineyards which produce the 'grey' Côtes de Toul wines and, if you walk down the Grand'Rue at Lucey, you will find many winegrowers who sell directly to the public. In the same street is the Maison Lorraine de Polyculture, a living museum presenting local agricultural activities from the eighteenth to the twentieth century, but only open on summer weekends. At **Bruley** is the Centre de Promotion des Produits des Côtes de Toul, where there are guided tours, tastings of local produce, a museum and a shop. **Toul** itself is known for its cathedral. **Goussaincourt** has a museum of country life and is in an area well-known for its pottery. There are pleasant châteaux at **Haroué** and **Fléville**, just south of Nancy. Also near Nancy is the flamboyant Gothic **St-Nicolas-de-Port** basilica. **Lunéville** château is known as 'Petit Versailles' and is surrounded by eighteenth-century gardens. In the south-east corner of Meurthe-et-Moselle is **Baccarat**, with its famous crystalworks and museum.

Accommodation & Eating Out

First Class

Hostellerie du Château des Monthairons, 55320 Dieue (Tel. 29 87 78 55): 11 rooms in 1857 château with park and restaurant.

First Class / Middle Range

Hôtel des Vannes et sa Résidence, 6 rue Porte-Haute, 54460 Liverdun (Tel. 83 24 46 01): 7 rooms in hotel with views of Moselle river and restaurant serving excellent fish specialities.

Middle Range

Hôtel Bagatelle, 47–9 rue Gambetta, 54700 Pont-à-Mousson (Tel. 83 81 03 64): 18 rooms in family-run hotel with restaurant and solarium.

Economy

Hôtel la Renaissance, 31 rue des Cristalleries, 54120 Baccarat (Tel. 83 75 10 33): 10 rooms in family-run hotel with restaurant. **M. Eichenauer**, Château de Labessière, Ancemont, 55320 Dieue (Tel. 29 85 70 21): 2 *chambres d'hôte* in château. **Mme Guillemin**, Nettancourt, 55800 Revigny-sur-Ornain (Tel. 29 75 13 20): 3 comfortable *chambres d'hôte* in old house.

For local specialities, try the *Economy ferme-auberges* at Lachaussée (Tel. 29 89 36 02) and Vieville-en-Haye (Tel. 83 81 91 27), but make sure you book in advance.

Nancy

The former capital of the Dukes of Lorraine, Nancy is an elegant city, showing French 18th century town planning at its best. Its pride and joy is **Place Stanislas**, a beautifully proportioned square built in the 1750s, with elaborate wrought iron-work, highlighted in gold, on the gates all round it. On the Place itself, which separates the old town and the commercial district, are the **Fine Art Museum**, which contains European paintings from the fourteenth-century onwards, and the **Hôtel de Ville**, whose windows offer the best view of the square. Next to the tourist office, the short **rue Héré**, named after the architect of Place Stanislas, leads to the **Arc de Triomphe** at the entrance of the elongated **Place de la Carrière**, with its elegant eighteenth-century mansions. To the right of this is a pleasant park called **La Pepinière**. At the end of the Place, to the left, is the **Ducal Palace**, housing the **Lorraine History Museum**, which offers a remarkable insight into regional history. Further up the **Grande Rue** is the **Eglise des Cordeliers**, whose cloisters house the **Museum of Popular Arts and Traditions**, which has a fine collection of paintings under glass, as well as many carefully reconstructed interiors. The **Porte de la Craffe** is the only remaining part of the town's fourteenth-century fortifications. The early eighteenth-century cathedral is to the south of Place Stanislas, not far from one of Nancy's two botanical gardens, the **Ste-Catherine**. In order to reach the **Musée de l'Ecole de Nancy**, you will have to explore the area south-west of the station, near **Parc Ste-Marie**. This museum contains collections of Art Nouveau, a movement mainly involving the decorative arts, inspired by artists of the Nancy school in the late nineteenth and early twentieth centuries.

Accommodation

Nancy has many small hotels in the lower budget range, but the first-class ones are often large and modern. The following are recommended:

First Class

Grand Hôtel de la Reine, 2 Place Stanislas (Tel. 83 35 03 01): 51 rooms in eighteenth-century palace on main square; chic restaurant.

Middle Range

Hôtel la Résidence, 30 bd Jean-Jaurès (Tel. 83 40 33 56): 24 rooms.

Middle Range / Economy

Au Bon Coin, 33 rue de Villers (Tel. 83 40 31 24): 22 rooms in family-run hotel with restaurant. **Hôtel Richelieu**, 5 rue Gilbert (Tel. 83 32 03 03): 12 rooms in conveniently situated hotel.

Economy

Hôtel les Portes d'Or, 21 rue Stanislas (Tel. 83 35 42 34): 20 rooms in central hotel. **Hôtel Globe**, 35 rue St-Michel (Tel. 83 35 48 02): 24 rooms in hotel in old town.

Eating Out

Numerous restaurants, including some inexpensive ones, line **rue des Maréchaux**. The following deserve particular recommendation:

First Class

Le Capucin Gourmand, 31 rue Gambetta (Tel. 83 35 26 98): creative cuisine in what has become a Nancy institution. **La Gentilhommière**, 29 rue des Maréchaux (Tel. 83 32 26 44): classical cuisine in grand setting.

Middle Range

Le Wagon, 57 rue des Chaligny (Tel. 83 32 32 16): home cooking in former railway carriage.

Economy

La Boutonnière, 4 rue Braconnot (Tel. 83 36 51 45): small bistro-style restaurant popular with local people. **Le Vaudemont**, 4 Place Vaudemont (Tel. 83 37 05 70): local dishes at low prices in smart surroundings.

Entertainments

Ask for the tourist office leaflet 'Spectacles à Nancy'. Their afternoon or evening tours of the city are also worthwhile. The theatre company, La Comédie de Lorraine is highly regarded. On summer evenings, there is an impressive *Son et Lumière* at place Stanislas. During the day you could visit the **Cristalleries Daum**, 17 rue des Cristalleries, where glass-workers practise their craft. Jazz fans should come to Nancy in mid-October, when an international Jazz festival takes place in a marquee in the **Pepinière Park** – but make sure you book accommodation first.

Useful Addresses

The **Tourist Office** is at 14 Place Stanislas (Tel. 83 35 22 41). The **Post Office** is on rue Pierre-Fourier, just south of Place Stanislas. For emergency **medical assistance** dial 15.

Transport Options

It is possible to see all the main sites on foot but, as Nancy is quite an extensive town, some are more easily reached by bus. There is a good bus network and most stop at the train station.

Moselle

Moselle covers a varied and predominantly rural area but is, inexplicably, often ignored. Local people are charming and easy-going, and there is a wide variety of things to see and do starting with its capital Metz.

Metz

Metz, once voted the second greenest city in France, is justifiably proud of its 3000-year history. The Gothic **Cathédrale St-Etienne**, situated on the eighteenth century **Place d'Armes**, is of impressive proportions and boasts a wide range of stained-glass windows, including some by Chagall. One of France's oldest churches is **St-Pierre-aux-Nonnains**, parts of which date from the fourth century. Metz has many other churches, of which **St-Maximin** and **St-Eucaire** are particularly worth visiting. The latter is on the edge of town, near the **Porte des Allemands**, a beautiful section of Metz's medieval fortified wall. Other reminders of the middle ages are the **Tour Camoufle**, a 1437 artillery tower, and the **Place St-Louis**, with its magnificent medieval mansions.

Good museums include the **Musée Gallo-Romain**, beneath which are remains of thermal baths, and the **Musée d'Art et d'Histoire**, at 2 rue du Haut-Poirier, which is housed in a former convent and divided into History (with a special section on the Middle Ages).

Architecture, and Art (paintings by Delacroix, Corot and regional artists). It also contains military and natural history collections. Make sure you take a stroll along the banks of the Moselle and the Seille: there is a good view of the Moselle and its islands from the **Moyen Pont**, and many green spaces in this area too.

Accommodation

All the top-of-the-range hotels are large and modern. Try instead:

Middle Range

Le Crinouc, 79 rue du Général-Metman (Tel. 87 74 12 46): 9 rooms in hotel with top-class restaurant (see below). **La Bergerie**, Vigy, Metz (Argancy-Rugy) (Tel. 87 77 82 27): 42 rooms in 16th century house, 10 km north of town.

Middle Range / Economy

La Pergola, 13 rte de Plappeville (Tel. 87 32 52 94): 30 rooms.

Economy

Hôtel Lutèce, 11 rue de Paris (Tel. 87 30 27 25): 20 rooms in family-run hotel with restaurant.

Eating Out

First Class

La Dinanderie, 2 rue de Paris (Tel. 87 30 14 40): fine restaurant on island, offering gastronomic delights – the best in Metz. **Le Crinouc**, 79 rue du Général-Metman (Tel. 87 74 12 46): impressive cuisine.

Middle Range

Restaurant Maire, 1 rue du Pont des Morts (Tel. 87 32 43 12): fine food and view over Moselle river from terrace. **L'Aubergerie**, 18 rue des Augustins (Tel. 87 75 54 76): excellent restaurant with rustic interior and modern, creative cuisine.

Economy

La Ville de Lyon, 7 rue des Piques. **L'Etna**, 9 rue Dupont-des-Loges: low-price local specialities.

Entertainments

Ask the tourist office for its 'Calendrier des Manifestations', and take advantage of its informative city tour. Metz has a marionette theatre and a flea market, about which the tourist office can supply details. In late June and early July, the Festival Etonnante Musique offers performances of music and dance. From mid-July to the end of August there is an evening *Son et Lumière* on the Esplanade. The last weekend in August and the first in September bring the parades and fireworks of the Fête de la Mirabelle.

Useful Addresses

The **Tourist Office** has its main branch on Place d'Armes (Tel. 87 75 65 21), with an additional one at the station. The **Office Départemental du Tourisme de Moselle** is extremely helpful and will assist you with accommodation reservations and many other services throughout Moselle. It is situated in the Hôtel du Département (Tel. 87 37 57 66). The **Comité Régional du Tourisme de Lorraine** is at 1 Place Gabriel Hocquard (Tel. 87 33 60 00). The **Post Office** is at 1 Place Général-de-Gaulle, opposite the station. The **hospital** is Hôpital Notre-Dame-de-Bon-Secours, 1 Place Phillippe-de-Vigneulles (Tel. 87 55 31 31). For emergency **medical assistance**, phone SAMU on 87 75 09 83.

Transport Options

Metz is best explored on foot, but the town buses and mini-buses are frequent and efficient. The tourist office will supply a time-table. Boat-hire is available from **Navilor Plaisance**, 20 rue de Pont-à-Mousson, 57000 Metz (Tel. 87 63 44 25).

Rest of Moselle

South-west of Metz, beyond the spectacular Roman aqueduct at **Jouy-aux-Arches**, are the steep winding roads, wayside crosses, fortified churches and narrow villages of part of the Pays Messin. One of these villages is called **Gorze**. It was of regional importance as early as Roman times, and boasts a collegiate church, an elegant Abbey Palace contemporary with Versailles, and a museum devoted to its historical role. The Musée de la Terre de Gorze is at present only open on Sundays between April and October, and you should telephone in advance (Tel. 87 52 02 17 (daytime) or 87 52 00 19 (evening)). Look out for the carved heads above the doorways in the village, and take time to enjoy one of the many walking circuits around it. Just north, at **Gravelotte**, is a museum of battles fought in 1870. Moselle's only spa town is **Amnéville-les-Thermes**, situated in the industrial belt between Metz and **Thionville**. Thionville is capital of the area known as the 'land of iron' and 'three frontier country'. Though industrial, the town has plenty of historical buildings: seventeenth-century fortifications; St-Maximin church with its decorative eighteenth-century organ; the Tour aux Puces, last remnant of a feudal castle and home to the town museum; and the 1629 Clarisse convent, now the town hall. Nearby there is the 1731 Château de la Grange at **Manom**, and the Château de **Volkrange**, at present under restoration. It is also worth visiting the **Guentrange** fort, built by the Germans at the turn of the century and used as part of the Maginot Line in 1940. At **Neufchef**, in the **Vallée de Ste-Neige**, is the main Lorraine iron-mining museum. It is open every afternoon except Monday and takes you underground.

Another mine site which can be visited by the public is at **Aumetz**, but this is only open in summer. At **Hettange-Grande**, just north of Thionville, there is a geological *réserve naturelle*, which is also botanically rich and varied. Spectacular ammonites were found here and the place gave its name to a geological era, the Hettangian. You can actually see what the fossils looked like and where they were found, thanks to the distribution of models identical to the fossils themselves. There is a 'discovery' path with signs capable of arousing enthusiasm for the area's geology in even the most sceptical, and an accompanying leaflet is available from the Hettange Mairie. **Rodemack**, not far from the Luxembourg border, is an attractive medieval village, and **Contz-les-Bains** is the site of one of the last vineyards in Moselle. The village also has a museum of winegrowing, which is open May to October on Saturday at Sunday afternoons, and an early Gothic chapel. From the church of the neighbouring community, **Haute-Kontz**, there is a good view of the river Moselle and the fortified village of **Sierck-les-Bains**. At **Montenach** is a large limestone area with fascinating plant life, including some hybrid orchids, one of which is specific to the site. There is an elaborate and informatively signposted botanical path, which it is essential to keep to, and an exhibition, housed at present in the Mairie.

The gateway of the north-eastern 'bulge' of Moselle, known as the Pays de Bitche, is an important area for ceramics. One of the best displays of this local speciality is in the museum at **Sarreguemines** (15–17 rue Poincaré – open every afternoon except Tuesday).

At nearby **Sarreinsming**, you can see the ruins of an extensive Gallo Roman villa, and, at **Bliesbruck**, a whole village, which obviously specialised in quality brass-and ironwork. Not only can you watch the excavations going on – you can even join in. Try to sample the local goat's cheese at **Rohrbach-lès-Bitche** before going on to **Bitche** itself. Recently, three 'living' museums have been created at Bitche, to dispel the widespread notion that it is nothing more than a military camp. The museums are based at the town's citadel and form part of the chain of museums belonging to the Parc Naturel Régional des Vosges du Nord. Tourism has brought a new lease of life to the town, and the mayor feels that it has made local people appreciate their own area more. At the **Eschviller** mill, near **Volmunster**, there is a centre for rural techniques. The forested area along the border with Alsace is beautiful, with ruined castles a frequent sight. Look out also for the Hanau Lake (Etang de Hanau), where there is a forest path of botanical interest, with signs explaining the slow evolution of the peat-bog it crosses. The flora is at its best between June and September. The nearby Etang de Baerenthal is an excellent spot for bird-watching, the best months being January, February, April and May. A key for the observation post is available from the Mairie at Baerenthal. There is a showroom-cum-museum of the highly regarded St-Louis crystal at **St-Louis-lès-Bitche**, near **Lemberg**, and glass and crystal museums at **Meisenthal**. **Montbronn** has a craft centre which concentrates on wood, crystal and metalwork.

The country round **Sarrebourg**, in the south-east of the *département*, is one of fruit-trees, red-roofed villages and straw-covered middens. At Sarrebourg itself, in the Chapelle des Cordeliers, you will find an awe-inspiring stained-glass window, created by Marc Chagall and dedicated to Peace. It is worth asking for the explanatory leaflet (available in English), or listening to the tape-recorded commentary (French and German only, at present). Ceramics and crystal are traditional to the area, and there is a famous crystalworks at **Vallérysthal**, where you can watch glass-blowing. It can be visited Monday to Friday all day and on Saturday or Sunday afternoons. The sixteenth-century town of **Phalsbourg**, fortified by Vauban in the seventeenth century, has a museum of military uniforms and local arts. Near **Lutzelbourg** and its castle is the Plan Incliné St-Louis-Arzviller, the unusual transversal ship-lift described in **Attractions**, which is open for tours from March to October. There is also a museum of Inland Water Transport History, housed in a barge. As you head south, the area becomes more mountainous. At the little village of **Schaefferhof**, it is worth stopping off at Bruno Lehrer's crystal-cutting studio. You can watch glasses and vases being engraved by hand, and it makes you realise that each of the items in the shop really is unique. At **Dabo** there is a church perched high on a rock, and nearby **Abreschviller** is the starting point for a pleasant steam train ride through the woods. **Vasperviller** church is an amazing construction in the style of Le Corbusier and contrasts with the onion-domed abbey church of **St-Quirin**, famous for its Silbermann organ.

To the west, in the area known as the Saulnois, **Lagarde** is an example of a village which has been pulled out of depression by the development of river tourism. You can hire a boat on the Canal de la Marne au Rhin from **NavigFrance**. The **Lindre Lake** is a stopping place for migratory birds and has an observatory at **Guermange**. The **Tarquimpol** isthmus also provides exceptional views of the lake. At **Mulcey**, on the road between **Dieuze** and Marsal, there is a nature trail, **Marsal** marks the capital of the Salt Country. The river valley in which the fortified town lies is flanked by rusty-reeded salt-marshes. A museum called the Maison du Sel (open every afternoon and Sunday morning) is devoted to the 4000-year history of salt and salt-mining. Another good museum is the history museum housed in the 1456 Gothic Hôtel de la Monnaie in **Vic-sur-Seille**. It concentrates on the sixteenth and seventeenth centuries and includes paintings by Georges de la Tour (open April to November, all week except Monday morning and Tuesday).

A visit to the *eau-de-vie* distiller Girardin-Defrance at **Burlioncourt** is strongly recommended. Here you will meet a man who distils delicious clear fruit brandies in his own house, using entirely traditional methods including a copper distilling vat from 1802. He is happy to give tours and tastings to individuals, though it is wise to phone in advance (Tel. 87 86 60 84), and a purchase is naturally appreciated. Another local artisan is the sculptor and potter M. Gierlowski, L'Atelier des 3 Bouleaux, 30 rue Principale, **Chenois**. Look out for the seventeenth- and eighteenth-century rural houses and orchards at **Tincry**, and the hiking path on the old Roman road at **Delme**. The rue Principale passing through **Marieulles** and **Vezon**, south of Metz, offers a plentiful supply of local wine and spirits producers.

Accommodation

First Class

Hôtel Horizon, Le Crève-Cœur, 57100 Thionville (Tel. 82 88 50

52): 13 rooms in hotel among vineyards. **Château d'Alteville**, 57260 Tarquimpol (Tel. 87 86 92 40): 4 *chambres d'hôte* in sixteenth- to eighteenth-century château near lake.

Middle Range / Economy

Hôtel de France, 3 ave de France, 57400 Sarrebourg (Tel. 87 03 21 47): 33 comfortable rooms in friendly, family-run hotel with restaurant. **Hostellerie du Lion d'Or**, 105 rue du Commerce, Gorze, 57130 Noveant-sur-Moselle (Tel. 87 52 00 90): 20 rooms in charming village inn, run by same family for 35 years; good restaurant.

Economy

Mme Mathis, rue Principale, Lidrezing, 57340 Morhange (Tel. 87 86 14 05): 3 *chambres d'hôte* in typical Lorraine house with delightful family: *tables d'hôte* meals, made mainly with produce from the garden. **M. Schmitt**, 18 rue Principale, 57340 Rodalbe (Tel. 87 01 56 65): 5 *chambres d'hôte*: *tables d'hôte* meals with home-grown produce.

Eating Out

In the Sarrebourg area, look out for restaurants belonging to the Association des Hôteliers et Restaurateurs du Pays de Sarrebourg. If you are in the north-west of the *département*, the *First Class / Middle Range* **Auberge du Crève-Cœur**, Le Crève Cœur, 57100 Thionville (Tel. 82 88 50 52) is to be recommended (it is only a stone's throw from the *First Class* **Hôtel Horizon** – see above).

Vosges

The gentle Lorraine slope of the Vosges mountains is ideal for cross-country skiing in winter. The rest of the year, numerous fairs and local activities go on in little villages with onion-domed churches.

Grand, in the north-western corner of the *département*, is the site of a Roman amphitheatre with accompanying museum of mosaics and Gallo-Roman remains. Not far away is **Domrémy-la-Pucelle**, birthplace of Joan of Arc, where her house is now a museum. **Contrexéville** and **Vittel** are neighbouring spa towns in a wooded area and make good bases for exploring the countryside. Vittel is a larger resort with more facilities. If you are in the area in mid-August, be sure to attend the Harvest Festival celebrations in **Rozerotte**. **Mirecourt** is famous for its stringed-instrument makers; their studios can often be visited and there is a museum on this subject and on the other local traditions of lace-making and embroidery. In **Rambervillers**, a Musée de la Terre has recently been set up, which concentrates on local agriculture and crafts. The first weekend in October sees a cheese fair in **Etival-Clairefontaine**. Near **St-Dié** which itself has an interesting town museum, there is a 'farm museum' called Lé Moho Dé Soyotte (at Faint de Ste-Marguerite, Route Nationale 415), which focuses on rural Vosgian crafts. In nearby **Fraize**, there is a craft fair in mid-July.

The landscape in this part of the Vosges is often compared with that of Scandinavia. The **Tanet – Gazon du Faing** section of the Route des Crêtes (which marks the border with Alsace) is a nature reserve. Unfortunately, too many cars pass this way in summer and people tend to stray from the paths, damaging the fragile peat-bog habitat with its special flora and upsetting the capercaillie. This has led to closing the northern part of the reserve to the public. Leaflets about the reserve are available from the *ferme-auberge* situated half way along the road through it. On the same road, $2^{1}/_{2}$ km south of **Col de la Schlucht**, is the **Jardin d'Altitude du Haut-Chitelet**. Here, woodland, rock and peat-bog are home to 2900 species of alpine plant from different continents, grouped according to region of origin. The road from here to **Gérardmer** is spectacular, passing beneath rocky outcrops and offering views of the region's glacial lakes. The Gérardmer lake is one of few which is equipped for watersports; the town also has a museum of the forest. The area has many traditional saw-mills and unusual wood-carving is a local speciality. **La Bresse** is one of the main ski resorts of the Vosges, for both cross-country and alpine skiing. Another local industry is presented in the textile museum at **Ventron**. **Bussang** is also good for skiing and, in summer, people come from all around to watch the performances of the local residents who make up the Théâtre du Peuple, founded in the nineteenth century. A summer carnival takes place at **Remiremont** in early July. **Epinal**, capital of the Vosges *département*, is built on the Moselle river and is famous for its prints and etchings, to which a section is devoted in the Musée des Vosges et de l'Imagerie. In **Thaon-les-Vosges** there is a fair of 'Man, Nature and the Environment' in September, where organic wines, breads and cheeses are on sale. **Plombières-les-Bains** and **Bains-les-Bains** are spa towns, dating from Roman times. The villages in this part, known as the Vôge Plain, are generally attractive and **Châtillon-sur-Saône**, in the very south, is a Renaissance village under restoration, which is particularly worth visiting.

Accommodation

There is a good deal of pleasant accommodation in the Vosges, particularly in *chambres d'hôte* and *ferme-auberges*. The following accommodation is recommended:

First Class / Middle Range

L'Aubergade, 265 ave des Tilleuls, 88800 Vittel (Tel. 29 08 04 39): 9 rooms in neo-classical hotel with gastronomic restaurant. **Hostellerie des Bas-Rupts et son Chalet Fleuri**, rte de la Bresse, 88400 Gérardmer (Tel. 29 63 09 25): 12 rooms in family-run hotel.

Middle Range

Hôtel Relais des Ducs de Lorraine, 16 quai Colonel Sérot, 88000 Epinal (Tel. 29 34 35 20): 10 rooms in riverbank hotel.

Economy

Hôtel du Tremplin, rue du 3e R.T.A., 88540 Bussang (Tel. 29 61 50 30): 19 rooms in family-run hotel with restaurant (see below). **M. Parmentier**, Villa Ste-Anne, 42 rue Royale, 88480 Etival-Clairefontaine (Tel. 29 41 53 65): 3 *chambres d'hôte* in pleasant family home with garden. **Mme Hernandez**, La Jonquière, Fiménil, 88600 Bruyères (Tel. 29 50 11 17): 3 *chambres d'hôte* with rustic decor on Vosgian farm; *tables d'hôte*. **M. Vaxelaire**, Ferme-Auberge Balveurche, 88400 Xonrupt-Longemer (Tel. 29 63 26 02): 15 rooms in *ferme-auberge*; restaurant with Lorraine specialities; munster cheese, home-made jams and smoked meat for sale.

Eating Out

The national winner of the 1988/89 *Logis de France* award for the promotion of regional cuisine was the *Middle Range / Economy* restaurant of the **Hôtel du Tremplin** at Bussang (address above). In the 1989/90 competition, the restaurant of the *Middle Range / Economy* **Hôtel de la Frezelle**, 88170 Rouvres-la-Chétive (Tel. 29 94 51 51) was a finalist.

8 Alsace

Despite its immensely picturesque nature, Alsace has managed to avoid becoming a British package destination, and is often omitted even from travel guides, or else lumped together with the very different Lorraine. As a result, visitors from Britain are rare and receive a special welcome in this predominantly quiet, wooded corner of north-eastern France.

Bordered by Germany to the north and east and by Switzerland to the south-east, Alsace forms a kind of corridor between the Vosges mountains and the river Rhine. You will immediately be struck by its Germanic atmosphere. German place names abound, softened by French pronunciation – a symbol of the curiously hybrid nature of the whole region. The older generation speak *Alsacien*, a dialect that bears more relation to German than to French. The half-timbered houses with steep gables, storks' nests and flower-filled balconies come straight from Grimm's Fairy Tales, and the crisp white wines from the sunny Alsatian vineyards have well-known names like *Gewurztraminer* and *Riesling*.

No visit to the region is complete without a tour of a wine cellar – together with a *dégustation*, of course. Alsace also makes its own beer (Kronenbourg) and some powerful *eaux-de-vie*. The German influence extends to the cooking. Staple ingredients for much of the 'homey' Alsatian cuisine are pork, white cabbage and potatoes, treated in a number of imaginative manners in dishes such as *choucroute* and *baeckaeoffe*. These are served in the rough-glazed and simple-patterned pottery typical of the region.

Alsace's location at the crossroads of French, German and Italian trade routes has always meant that it was open to a wide variety of influences. Its location also made it susceptible to annexation and some of the oldest inhabitants were actually born German. Although those who experienced the War tend to be staunchly pro-French, it has been known for younger people to assert: 'I am Alsatian by birth, European through choice, and French out of necessity'! There is an explanation for this strange blend of regional pride and cosmopolitanism. The area's chequered history has made it wary of losing its regional identity, causing it to cling tenaciously to all that is Alsatian. Many of those who live in the north of Alsace still dress in regional costume during village festivals, and every Alsatian relishes such occasions. Even cosmopolitan Strasbourg hosts numerous traditional events in its lovingly preserved old town. Yet Strasbourg's role in Europe has offered not only a raising of the region's profile, but also an opportunity for it to broaden its horizons, giving Alsace a truly European outlook.

History

The Celts settled in Alsace in the eighth century BC, though vine-growing began only in AD 222. The tenth century saw the annexation of Alsace by Germany's Holy Roman Empire. Throughout the Middle Ages European trade flourished in the Rhine plain and, in 1354, ten Alsatian towns freed themselves from the feudal yoke to form a confederation called the Décapole. At the end of the Thirty Years' War, in 1648, Alsace passed to the French crown, but returned to the German Empire in 1871 after the Franco-Prussian War. Though liberated by the French in 1918, it was under German occupation during the Second World War, and has only really enjoyed the stability of belonging unambiguously to France since 1945. The only German invasion nowadays is that of the tourists every October.

In 1949 Strasbourg became the seat of the Council of Europe and, in 1979, the meeting place of the European Parliament. It is also the seat of the European Court of Human Rights; these various appointments have brought with them both prestige and a wealth of facilities for business travellers. Alsace's relative prosperity comes after a period of economic restructuring in the 70s, which went hand-in-hand with the building of hydro-electric power stations on the Rhine and a nuclear one at Fessenheim. The **Parc Naturel Régional des Vosges du Nord** was founded in 1976 and classified a World Biosphere Reserve by UNESCO in 1989. Since then a second regional park, the Ballons des Vosges, has been created.

Famous people associated with Alsace include Gutenberg, who worked in Strasbourg on the invention of printing, and Goethe, Napoleon Bonaparte and Metternich, who all studied at Strasbourg University. Auguste Bartholdi, the sculptor who created the Statue of Liberty in New York, was born in Colmar.

Geography

Alsace is a narrow strip of land, 200 km long and 50 km wide, and has only two *départements*: the Bas-Rhin (Lower Rhine), which, confusingly, is in the north, and the Haut-Rhin (Upper Rhine) in the south. The regional capital is Strasbourg, with a population of 400,000 (including suburbs). Although Mulhouse (200,000 inhabitants) is the second largest town in Alsace, its focus is mainly industrial, and the job of administrative capital of the Haut-Rhin is carried out by the considerably smaller (70,000) – and considerably more attractive – Colmar.

Alsace covers the western half of the near symmetrical formation of land flanking the Rhine, which serves as the French-German border. The Vosges mountains, like those of the Black Forest, are predominantly granite, with some pink sandstone, the material used for the building of Strasbourg's vast Gothic cathedral. The mountains reach a greater height in the lake-studded south of the range (Grand Ballon – 1424m), where forest gives way to pastureland on the rounded summits. This land is known as the *hautes chaumes* and offers skiing terrain in winter, a carpet of alpine flowers in spring, and, in summer, grazing for the cows which produce the famous Munster and Géromé cheeses.

The Vosgean forest is made up of beech and fir, with pockets of Scots pine (particularly in the Regional Park) and spruce just below the *chaumes*. This combination makes for interesting seasonal changes which reach a stunning climax in autumn, despite heavy damage from acid rain. Vine terraces cling to the hill-side up to about 600 metres and, below them in the Rhine plain, the land is also fertile, with orchards and barley-fields. It is easy to see why Louis XIV called Alsace 'the garden of France'.

The Regional Park in the northern Vosges is hilly, and encompasses areas of peat-bog, heath, forest and grassland. Rare plants include the spotted catsear and pasque flower, and among protected birds are the peregrine falcon and tengmalm's owl. Throughout Alsace there is concern about the dwindling number of storks coming to nest. The stork is believed to bring good luck to the region and efforts are being made to encourage it back, particularly at the Hunawihr Re-introduction Centre. Re-introduction measures have also brought chamois and even lynx back to the Donon and Hohneck massifs.

Of special ecological significance is the marshy area along the bank of the Rhine. This is known as the 'Ried' and has its own particular flora and fauna. Drainage of the area, both to change the course of the river and to provide agricultural land, has threatened the 'Ried', much of which has been turned into maize fields. A recent public appeal has, however, enabled the **Conservatoire des Sites Alsaciens** to purchase parts of the 'Ried' for conservation purposes. There are four official nature reserves in Alsace at the moment, with more planned. Two are in Rhineland forests, and one on a Vosgean massif, but the only one with facilities for welcoming visitors is the Petite Camargue, an area of reed-beds in the south-east corner of Alsace near Saint-Louis.

Climate

Average maximum temperatures range from about 4°C in December to 26°C in August. Although there are about 7 hours of sunshine a day from May through to August, the summer months are also the ones with the heaviest rainfall. Spring and early autumn are perhaps the best times to visit Alsace, as summer can be rather oppressive on the plain, though pleasant in the mountains. October is often perfect for the first two to three weeks but heavy fog can be a problem after that. Winter tends to be snowy rather than rainy, with some mountain roads becoming impassable, but snow gives way to alpine flowers with the warmth of spring.

Attractions

According to a regional tourist board survey, most visitors to Alsace come for 'the beauty of its scenery, its gastronomy and cultural heritage, and its peace and quiet'.

The scenery certainly is magnificent, whichever time of year you choose. A visit to the ridge at the top of the Vosges, along the convenient Route des Crêtes, is pretty much essential, as is an exploration of the Route du Vin, which meanders through vineyards. Closer contact with the wines of Alsace is naturally an incentive for many visitors. These routes are, however, well-known tourist trails, and during summer at least, peace and quiet is more likely to be found elsewhere: for example, the sleepy Sundgau region in the south, the villages of the Rhine plain, or the forests of the **Parc Régional des Vosges du Nord**.

The most popular cultural attractions of Alsace are the Château du Haut-Koenigsbourg (near Ribeauvillé on the *Route du Vin*); the cathedral and municipal museums of Strasbourg; the famous Unterlinden museum at Colmar, and the Écomusée d'Alsace at Ungersheim (not far from Mulhouse). Visitors are also attracted by the numerous towns and villages with virtually intact medieval quarters, the best-known being Riquewihr on the *Route du Vin*.

The winter facilities for cross-country skiing (together with **some** downhill skiing) tend to draw local people more than those from futher afield.

Cuisine

Alsace is renowned for its solid, 'homey' cuisine. The trademark is *choucroute* – sauerkraut garnished with every conceivable form of pork. Equally typical is *baeckaeoffe*, a long-simmered stew, though lighter alternatives can be found. *Matelote* is a stew made from freshwater fish, and fried carp is the local dish of the Sundgau. Vegetarians should be aware that *lardons* (cubes of crispy bacon fat) may be lurking in apparently meat-free dishes, so it's worth checking in advance. Local specialities which vegetarians can indulge in are *tarte à l'oignon* and *tarte flambée* (a kind of thin, 'flame-licked' pizza, made with special cheese and generally presented on a wooden board, which any decent restaurant will serve without *lardons* if you ask). *Tarte flambée* also turns up as a sweet, a pizza-type base with fruit in syrup (try pear and chocolate). Other delights for the sweet-toothed are the numerous simple fruit tarts (e.g. bilberry – *myrtille*), cheese tart and *kugelhopf* (a sweet, raisin-studded bread). The local cheeses of Munster and the slightly less pungent Géromé (from the Gérardmer area, just over the Lorraine border) should certainly be sampled. A place particularly famous for its wealth of good restaurants is the Strasbourg suburb of La Wantzenau.

As far as wines go, Sylvaner is the lightest and goes with the hors d'œuvre or fish. Riesling and Pinot (*blanc, gris* or *noir* – the latter a lightweight red) go well with the main course. Gewurztraminer and Muscat d'Alsace both suit Alsatian pâtisserie. The *eaux-de-vie* are clear brandies in flavours like quetsch, mirabelle (types of plum), and poire William (pear), which work wonders after a heavy meal.

Level of Tourism

Despite the lack of British visitors, tourism as a whole has a fairly high profile. Alsace comes around tenth in the hit-parade of French touristic regions with about 2.5 million hotel visits a year (3.9% of all national visits). It is predominantly a short-stay region though. 70% of visitors are French, followed by the Germans, the Dutch, the Belgians, the Swiss and, finally, the British at a mere 1%. Most tourists stay in hotels, though a certain number camp or use rural *gîtes*. The Belgians prefer to visit Alsace in July, the French and Dutch in August, the Germans in October – and 70% of visitors have been to Alsace before. Many are relatively wealthy, middle-aged to elderly town-dwellers. 80% of visitors come by car and only 14% are on organised trips. This means that the few tourism-related problems are of the sort associated more with inconsiderate individuals than with package tourism.

Traffic can be a problem during summer, but only really in the wine villages and Strasbourg, and sensible measures have been taken. The old quarters of both Strasbourg and Colmar, like the entire medieval village of Riquewihr, have been closed to cars. Even the construction of new roads is not entirely negative as, each time one is built, the local authority offers compensation to the environmentalists of the Conservatoire des Sites Alsaciens in the form of plots of damp roadside land which provide ideal habitats for toads and many types of bird. One controversial project is, however, the planned TGV line, which will almost certainly pass through an ancient Rhine forest, perhaps even a nature reserve. The mechanised lifts at Vosgean ski resorts such as Le Hohneck also look ugly and, in summer, rather pointless. Most of the skiing in the Vosges is cross-country though, and it would be unfair to lay all the blame with the tourist industry as much of the winter sports clientèle is local.

The Alsatian tourist industry, which employs 3% of the active population, is, generally speaking, well organised. It has not been allowed to get in the way of the local lifestyle, and is often carefully combined with traditional activities: the *marcaireries* (cheese-making buildings in the upper Vosges), which were gradually dying out, have been able to keep going by offering cheese products, simple meals and sometimes accommodation to walkers, while ski runs revert to mountain pastures in summer.

Several preservation groups exist, which regulate building so as not to spoil regional parks, villages and towns. The state pays architects to consult with developers so that new buildings harmonise with old, and large sections of Strasbourg and Colmar have been restored. Most towns are clearly sign-posted and clean, and possess a well-informed tourist office or Syndicat d'Initiative. Along with many useful (but sometimes quite obscure) brochures and maps, they can often supply you with a list of *chambres d'hôte* and *chambres à louer* (longer term accommodation) in the area. As far as the local people are concerned, one gets the impression that they relish the entertainments put on for visitors at least as much as the visitors themselves.

Plans for the future development of tourism have been influenced in a positive way by the UNESCO 'Man and the Biosphere' programme of the Northern Vosges Regional Park, which seeks to promote low-impact 'discovery' tourism. The programme also concentrates on educating the general public in environmental issues through exhibitions and documentation, on encouraging people to value their cultural heritage, and on the sensible use of natural resources both agriculturally and in traditional crafts. All these plans will benefit the local economy, as will the development of rural tourism in the slightly depressed Sundgau region.

Good Alternatives

Meeting People

The Alsatians are enthusiastic festival-goers and village celebrations are an ideal way of meeting people. As a major tourist office for the brochure 'Alsace Manifestations – Distractions', which contains a calendar of every festival, special event, exhibition and excursion in Alsace for the whole year. Visits to small-scale farms and producers of local crafts and specialities in the Bas-Rhin are arranged by the **Relais Départemental du Tourisme Rural du Bas-Rhin**, 7 Place des Meuniers, 67000 Strasbourg (Tel. 88 75 56 50 or 51).

Those not afraid of an afternoon's hard work might opt for a *chantier de bénévoles*. These usually involve conservation work on an ecologically important site (together with experts who will explain its significance) and take place at different venues every Saturday from late November to late March. Some of the *chantiers* in Northern Alsace last a full day, in which case a hot meal is provided. For information, including dates of summer *chantiers*, contact (in advance) either the **Conservatoire des Sites Alsaciens**, Écomusée d'Alsace, 68190 Ungersheim (Tel. 89 48 02 42 – mornings); or Pascal Maurer on 89 45 71 89. Information on the possibilities of joining archaeological digs is available from the **Direction des Antiquités**, Palais du Rhin, 3 place de la République, 67082 Strasbourg (Tel. 88 32 28 37).

Discovering Places

The **Association Fédérale Régionale de Protection de la Nature** organises guided visits and 'green weekends'. For information contact AFRPN, 17 rue du Général Zimmer, 67000 Strasbourg (Tel. 88 37 07 58). In the Haut-Rhin, there is a 'programme of animation and discovery of the rural environment in a warm, family atmosphere' proposed by the **Relais Départemental des Gîtes Ruraux du Haut-Rhin**, 9 rue Bruat, 68000 Colmar (Tel. 89 41 41 99 or 89 23 21 11). The **Parc Régional des Vosges du Nord** offers various 'alternative' holidays, including numerous walking and cycling circuits (bikes may be hired), which use farmhouse inns, *gîtes* or family hotels for accommodation, and offer free transportation of luggage between them. Circuits are often thematic, range from three to eleven days, and cover areas in both Alsace and Lorraine. Two of the circuits feature in the **Parcs Naturels de France** brochure '12 Voyages au Naturel' and have their special seal of approval; these are both six-day walking circuits, one entitled 'Sandstone, Glass and Forests', the other 'Castles and Gastronomy from the Past'. They are designed for individuals or families, rather than groups, and can be booked either through **Clés de France**, 13 rue St-Louis, 78100 St-Germain-en-Laye (Tel. (1) 30 61 23 23) or directly with **Association de Développement des Vosges du Nord**, Maison du Parc, 67270 La Petite Pierre (Tel. 88 70 46 55). The leaflets 'Vélo sans bagages' (cycling holidays) and 'Randonnée sans bagages' (walking holidays), along with details about horseriding holidays, are available from the Maison du Parc at the above address. This also provides a list of the park's museums and a calendar of fascinating excursions, ranging from the cultural to the ecological. Coach tours are organised by the tourist offices at Strasbourg and Colmar (the latter only in high season). SNCF do a wide variety of coach excursions called **Astra Voyages** from Strasbourg (late March to late October), which you can book at Strasbourg tourist offices and hotels or at any train station. Try also **Voyages Scheurer**, 3 route des Romains, 67000 Strasbourg

(Tel. 88 30 01 58); and **LK Tours/ Kunegel**, 42 rue des Jardins, 68000 Colmar (Tel. 89 24 65 50).

Any further information which you require on the Bas-Rhin can be supplied by the **Office Départemental du Bas-Rhin**, 9 rue du Dôme, BP 53, 67061 Strasbourg (Tel. 88 22 01 02); for the Haut-Rhin, contact the **Association Départementale du Tourisme du Haut-Rhin**, Hôtel du Département, 68006 Colmar (Tel. 89 23 21 11). The above address is also that of the **Service Loisirs-Accueil Haut-Rhin** (Tel. 89 41 41 99), through which you can book both accommodation and low-impact, locally run holidays – write for their brochure.

Communications

How to Get There

There are direct **flights** from Britain to Strasbourg International Airport (Air France) and to Basle-Mulhouse-Freiburg Euroairport. Air Littoral has just started flights between Manchester and Strasbourg and there are also daily flights from Paris (Orly-ouest) to Colmar-Houssen airport.

There is a direct **train** from Calais to main stations in Alsace. An Intercity service links Paris (-Est) to Saverne and Strasbourg (4 hrs), and Strasbourg to Basle (1$^{1}/_{2}$ hrs).

Eurolines run a direct **coach** service from London to Strasbourg. If you're **driving** from Paris to Strasbourg, you will need the A4 and it will take around 5 hours.

When You're There

Rail – the main regional railway line runs from Sarrebourg (Lorraine) to Basle, passing through Saverne, Strasbourg (connections to Haguenau, Wissembourg, Lauterbourg and St-Dié), Sélestat (connections to Ste-Marie-aux-Mines and St-Dié), Colmar (connections to Metzeral and Volgelsheim) and Mulhouse (connections to Kruth, Sewen and Belfort) as well as various minor stations. Local lines are supplemented in the hills and mountains by a bus service. Steam trains for tourists exist: one runs alongside the Rhine (see **Boat**), and another between Cernay and Sentheim.

Bus – you can reach Freiburg (Germany) by bus from Colmar for a pleasant day out. Any tourist office will supply you with a local bus timetable. This is, perhaps, the most rewarding way to travel up to some of the villages in the middle and upper Vosges, as it is the way many local people travel to work and to the shops. Try to get a window seat as there are magnificent views. Addresses of regional coach companies which offer excursions can be found under **Good Alternatives**.

Car – the only stretches of motorway in the region are around Strasbourg and Mulhouse. Elsewhere you will find pleasant N and D roads through vineyards and up the mountainside. The road between Sélestat and St-Dié passes through a famous tunnel in the Vosges. If travelling in the Vosges by car in winter, be sure to bring snow chains and to check in advance whether roads are passable.

Boat – information on cruises on the Rhine or Ill is obtainable from **Alsace Croisières**, 12 rue de la Division Leclerc, 67000 Strasbourg (Tel. 88 32 44 55); or from the Syndicat d'Initiative at Huningue. There is a trip by boat and steam train along the Rhine and the Canal d'Alsace, from Neuf-Brisach to Marckolsheim (weekends: June – September). It is also possible to rent barges on the Canal d'Alsace and the Canal de la Marne au Rhin (which links Saverne and Strasbourg).

Cycling – bicycles can be hired from the SNCF stations at Saverne, Strasbourg, Sélestat, Colmar and Mulhouse, and can be borrowed for anything from half a day to ten days. Some *chambres d'hôte* will also hire out bikes to you during your stay. For excellent maps of marked cycle circuits and invaluable advice including train connections, send s.a.e and reply coupon to **Direction Départementale de l'Equipement** (Parcours Cyclables), 5 rue du Général Frère, 67000 Strasbourg, and ask for their leaflets 'Promenades et Randonnées à Bicyclette'. Bicycle is the ideal way to visit the Rhine villages – and you do not even have to be fit, as there is scarcely a gradient in sight. Cycling between the villages of the lower to mid Vosges offers a slightly greater challenge. The zig-zag ascent of the Ballon d'Alsace should, however, be attempted only by those training for the Tour de France!

Walking – Alsace is a good source of walking opportunities – from the GR 53 trail (which runs from Wissembourg, through the Northern Vosges Regional Park and Saverne, to the Col du Donon) down to numerous minor footpaths through vineyards and in the Vosges. Tourist offices will suggest walks and supply ramblers' maps (information on cross-country skiing is available in winter). Serious walkers should enquire about the publications and services of the **Club Vosgien**, Secrétariat: 4 rue de la Douane, 67000

Strasbourg, (Tel 88 32 57 96), a voluntary organisation dedicated to combining the interests of ramblers with the protection of nature. They organise group rambles for their members every Sunday.

Riding – Alsace takes pains to promote equestrian tourism and information can be obtained from M. Ferdinand Schaeffer, **Association Alsacienne de Tourisme Equestre**, 2 rue du Landwasser, 68000 Colmar (Tel. 89 41 52 82). Horse riding is particularly popular in the north-eastern corner, around the Haguenau forest and Northern Vosges Regional Park.

Useful Local Contacts

The **Conservatoire des Sites Alsaciens** will supply information on *chantiers de bénévoles* (for description and address, see **Good Alternatives**). Details of other environmental activities may be obtained from the **Centre Permanent d'Initiation à l'Environnement**, 36 rue de Sélestat, 68060 Muttersholtz (Tel. 88 85 11 30). It is also worth enquiring at the headquarters of the two Regional Parks: **Maison du Parc Naturel Régional des Vosges du Nord**, 67290 La Petite-Pierre (Tel. 88 70 46 55); and **Maison du Parc Naturel Régional des Ballons des Vosges**, 1 rue de l'Eglise, BP 11, 68140 Munster (Tel. 89 77 29 04).

Geographical Breakdown of Region

Bas-Rhin – Northern Alsace

To the north of Strasbourg, Alsace is, for the most part, densely wooded, with the **Forêt de Haguenau** in the east and the **Parc Naturel Régional des Vosges du Nord**, which is shared with Lorraine, in the west. The eastern area contains charming Alsatian villages, where it is not unusual to see people dressed in regional costume during local festivals or *messti*. All along the northern border and throughout the Regional Park are ruined castles and fortresses and huge churches built of local stone.

Near **Saverne** is a pleasant botanical garden and the twelfth-century **Château du Haut-Barr**. Just north, in **Graufthal**, are troglodytic houses which were still in use only thirty years ago. The château at **La Petite-Pierre**, as well as being the Regional Park headquarters, houses an instructive exhibition on the forest. The town also has its own animal reserve and is the starting point for the Geyerstein Nature Trail. **Wingen-sur-Moder** marks the start of the glass and crystal-making region (museum at **Meisenthal** in Lorraine). Three mountain bike trails begin at Wingen, each with a different theme. Detailed maps are available from the Maison du Parc, and local tourist offices, hotels and shops. Mountain bikes (known in France as VTT) can be hired from Bergmann, 7 rue de Zittersheim, 67290 Wingen-sur-Moder (Tel. 88 89 75 06). **Offwiller,** on the forest edge, is home to a Museum of Popular Arts and Traditions; and at **Bouxwiller** begins the 6 km Bastberg Geological Path, which offers remarkable views while explaining the geological history of Alsace.

In the **Wissembourg** and **Haguenau** area, try to see the potters' village of **Betschdorf,** famous for its decorated cobalt-blue earthenware. **Cleebourg** (south-west of Wissembourg) is the most northerly vineyard in France and its Coopérative Viticole is worth a visit.

Accommodation & Eating Out

Middle Range

Auberge d'Imsthal, route Forestière d'Imsthal, 67290 La Petite-Pierre (Tel. 88 70 45 21): 24 rooms in family-run hotel; restaurant.

Middle Range / Economy

Chez Jean, 3 rue de la Gare, 67700 Saverne (Tel. 88 91 10 19): 27 rooms in traditional family-run hotel; excellent restaurant with regional specialities.

Economy

Wenk, 1 rue Principale, 67290 Wingen-sur-Moder (Tel. 88 89 71 01): 19 rooms in pleasant family-run hotel; restaurant. **A la Rose,** 4 rue Nationale, 67160 Wissembourg (Tel. 88 94 03 52): 7 rooms in family-run hotel (closed in Sept.); restaurant.

Strasbourg

The centre of Strasbourg covers an island formed by the two branches of the River Ill and is described by UNESCO as one of the most beautiful city centres in the world. Numerous bridges connect the island to the rest of the city, though most of the attractions are to be found in the centre.

The most famous building is the pink sandstone **Cathédrale**

Notre-Dame. It was begun in 1170 (the spire was completed in 1439) and is the most elaborate example of Gothic architecture in Alsace. Climb the tower for a magnificent view and be there at midday to hear the astronomical clock strike. Any visit to the cathedral should be accompanied by one to the **Musée de l'Œuvre Notre-Dame** which houses original cathedral sculptures and Alsatian art from the Middle Ages to the Renaissance. The **Château des Rohan**, formerly the Bishop's Palace, is home to the **Musée Archéologique**, the **Musée des Arts Décoratifs** (superb ceramic collection), and the **Musée des Beaux-Arts**. The **Musée Alsacien**, on Quai St-Nicolas, is well worth a visit if you are interested in the folk arts, traditions and trades of rural Alsace through the ages (includes reconstructed rooms). The **Musée Zoologique** is at 29 bd de la Victoire. All museums are closed on Tuesdays and between 12 and 2p.m.

The picturesque **Petite France** area, with its 16th and 17th century house, tanners' district and bridges over the Ill merits a leisurely stroll. In addition to the famous **Maison des Tanneurs** (1572), there are old tanners' houses in rue du Bain-aux-Plantes. If you walk down quai Woerthel or quai de la Petite France, you will reach the **Ponts Couverts**, three bridges and four towers which are remnants of the city's 14th century fortifications. Look out for **Maison Kammerzell** and **Pharmacie du Cerf** (1268), both on Place de la Cathédrale. There are numerous squares and parks, including the famous **Parc de l'Orangerie**, designed by Le Nôtre.

Accommodation

For a major city, hotels are not as expensive as you might expect – though you can get better value for money (and smaller scale hotels) if you stay just out of town.

First Class

Hôtel Cathédrale, 12 Place de la Cathédrale, (Tel. 88 22 12 12): 35 rooms in old building with modernised interior; good views of cathedral and square.

First Class / Middle Range

Hôtel des Rohan, 17–19 rue du Moroquin, (Tel. 88 32 85 11): 36 rooms in quiet (except for the cathedral bells) hotel in pedestrian street in heart of old town. **Relais de la Poste**, 21 rue du Général de Gaulle, 67610 La Wantzenau, (Tel. 88 96 20 64): 19 rooms in welcoming, half-timbered family hotel, 12 km from town; gastronomic restaurant with Alsatian specialities.

Middle Range

Hôtel au Cerf d'Or, 6 Place de l'Hôpital (Tel. 88 36 20 05): 16 rooms in family hotel; restaurant. **Hôtel de l'Orangerie**, 58 allée de la Robertsau (Tel. 88 35 10 69): 25 rooms in comfortable hotel. **Le Moulin de la Wantzenau**, 27 route de Strasbourg, 67610 La Wantzenau (Tel. 88 96 27 83): 20 rooms in family hotel in old water mill with attractive garden, 12 km from town; restaurant (see **Eating Out**).

Middle Range / Economy

Hôtel Gutenberg, 31 rue des Serruriers (Tel. 88 32 17 15): 50 simple rooms in old château with atmosphere of artists' inn.

Economy

Hôtel de l'Ill, 8 rue des Bateliers (Tel. 88 36 20 01): 20 rooms in riverbank hotel. **Auberge du Grand Duc**, 33 route de l'Hôpital (Tel. 88 34 31 76): 8 rooms in friendly inn. **Hôtel au Cygne**, 38 rue de la 1ère D.B., 67114 Eschau (Tel. 88 64 04 79): 20 rooms in family-run hotel in Strasbourg suburb; restaurant.

Eating Out

First Class

Le Crocodile, 10 rue de l'Outre (Tel. 88 32 13 02): one of the best restaurants in Alsace, with lightened classical cuisine and regional specialities. **Maison Kammerzell**, 16 Place de la Cathédrale (Tel. 88 32 42 14): sixteenth-century house where Alsatian chef will serve *choucroute au poisson* as well as the more conventional *choucroute alsacienne*.

Middle Range

Au Moulin, 25 route de Strasbourg, 67610 La Wantzenau (Tel. 88 96 20 01): restaurant of **Le Moulin de la Wantzenau**; traditional cuisine in rural setting. **L'Arsenal**, 11 rue de l'Abreuvoir (Tel. 88 35 03 69): unusual restaurant run by young family who cook traditional recipes in a light, modern way (closed at weekends).

Middle Range / Economy

La Florestine, 28 rue des Juifs (Tel. 88 36 81 19): vegetarian dishes on offer. **Adam**, rue Sedillot (Tel. 88 35 70 84): another vegetarian restaurant.

Economy

Strissel, 5 Place de la Grande-Boucherie (Tel. 88 32 14 73): Alsatian food, wines, decor and atmosphere. **S'Marikstuewele**, 6 rue du Marché (Tel. 88 23 24 10): children welcome in this friendly restaurant where Friday and Saturday evenings bring foot-long *tartes flambées* (enough for two).

Entertainments

Traditional markets occur at Place Ste-Marguerite (Wed. & Fri.), Boulevard de la Marne (Tues. & Sat.), Rue de Zurich (Wed.), and a flea market at Place du Vieil-Hôpital (Wed. & Sat.). Guided tours of the town by foot leave the tourist office on Place Gutenberg at 10a.m. and 9p.m. every day in July and August. There are also boat trips (see **Transport**). Every Sunday at 10.30a.m. during June, July and August, there is a traditional Alsatian spectacle in the courtyard of the Château des Rohan. April to September, a *Son et Lumière* takes place in the cathedral every evening (in French and German only). In July and August, there is nautical jousting on the Ill at 8.30p.m. on Mondays and Fridays. At the same time on Tuesday, there is a free concert of traditional Alsatian music at Place Benjamin-Zix – on Wednesday this takes place at Place du Marché-aux-Cochons-de-Lait. The Orangery is illuminated every evening in July and August. For unusual outings, try the **Planetarium** (1 rue de l'Observatoire) or the **Kronenbourg Brewery** (68 route d'Oberhausbergen).

Useful Addresses

The main **Tourist Office** is at 10 Place Gutenberg (Tel. 88 32 57 07). Other branches are at Place de la Gare (Tel. 88 32 51 49) and Pont de l'Europe (Tel. 88 61 39 23). (The tourist offices can arrange for a lecturer from the National Trust of Historical Monuments and Sites to accompany you round a given museum or place of interest.) Information on the whole of the Bas-Rhin is available from the **Office Départemental du Tourisme**, 9 rue du Dôme (Tel. 88 22 01 02). The main **Post Office** is 5 ave de la Marseillaise. For **medical assistance**, ring SAMU on 88 33 33 33.

Transport Options

It is easy to walk round the main sights – you can cross the island east-west in about 25 minutes, and north-south in 15 minutes – and much of this area is pedestrian zone. Cycling is another possibility: bikes can be hired from the station. From March to December, there are boat trips on the Ill and the Rhine (ask at tourist office or contact Port Autonome de Strasbourg, 15 rue de Nantes, Tel. 88 84 13 13). The bus service is good, though less frequent on Sundays, and will take you right out to the suburbs of Graffenstaden, Ostwald, Lingolsheim, Eckbolsheim, Mittelhausbergen, Bischheim and Robertsau, as well as over the German border to Kehl. A mini-train and orange tourist bus take visitors (and local people) on day and night trips round the old town.

Bas-Rhin & Haut-Rhin – Western Alsace

In **Western Alsace**, many visitors make a bee-line for destinations on the very beautiful Route du Vin (Wine road) and Route des Crêtes (Ridge road). The latter is steep, linking all the Vosgean valleys from **Col du Bonhomme** to **Cernay**. The former winds through vineyards between **Marlenheim** and **Thann**. Most tourist offices will provide a map with these two routes marked, along with information on the places you will pass through. The best way to enjoy them is simply to take your time: try browsing in an artist's studio in **Riquewihr**, or staying to ask questions after a *Dégustation de Vin* at **Eguisheim**, for example. Traditional *Kilbe* or wine festivals are still celebrated in many of the villages each summer and autumn. Some 21 villages between **Marlenheim and Soultzmatt** are linked by public footpaths through vineyards (often with informative signs concerning vine-growing and types of wine). These paths offer the best way of exploring Alsatian wine country: for details, ask any tourist office about the *sentiers viticoles*.

West of Strasbourg, **Marlenheim** is an old market town with a seventeenth-century town hall. From here, you can take a trip into the Middle Vosges, which reach a height of around 1100 metres at the **Champ du Feu**. The places of interest include **Wasselonne**, with its seventeenth- and eighteenth-century houses, decorated with the signs of different trades; **Oberhaslach**, with its 1750 St-Florent chapel and two ruined castles (Niedeck and Ringelstein); the old iron mines of **Framont**; the second-century temple on the summit of the **Donon**, and the memorial to victims of the former Nazi concentration camp at **Struthof**. Back on the *Route du Vin*, **Molsheim** is an interesting fortified town, formerly a bishopric, situated on the River Bruche. The huge convent at **Mont Ste-Odile** is a place of pilgrimage, as it was founded by Saint Odile, patron saint of Alsace. **Obernai** is a tourist centre with some fine medieval buildings and a Renaissance well, and a path through the vineyards starts from here. Many of the wine villages are overlooked by eerie ruined castles: there is the Landsberg castle near **Barr**, and the Andlau castle which towers above **Mittelbergheim** (one of the numerous French villages described as 'the most beautiful village in France'!) **Scherwiller** is a charming village with half-timbered houses on the banks of the River Aubach. In mid-August it opens up its wines cellars for the *Fête du Riesling*. Nearby **Albe** is home to a museum of popular arts and traditions.

Sélestat, which was one of the towns belonging to the *Décapole* federation in the fourteenth century, has some interesting Renaissance buildings, ramparts designed by Vauban, and a Humanist library containing a precious medieval survey. It is at nearby **Chatenois** that you must decide whether to continue along the *Route du Vin* or the *Route des Crêtes*. The latter offers characteristic views of the Vosgean mountain chain, but it is worth making detours into some of the valleys which cross it. Footpaths are frequent here in the upper Vosges. Try following the one just north of Col de la Schlucht, which leads down through the woods to the beautiful **Lac Vert**. Because it requires a slight effort to reach it, you will find the lake far less crowded than its better known counterparts, the **Lac Noir** and the **Lac Blanc**. **Col de la Schlucht**, the **Hohneck** and the **Markstein** (where the Alpine Skiing World Cup was held from 1983 to 1987) are somewhat spoilt in summer by the redundant ski lifts, but the road takes you to the highest peak of the Vosges, the **Grand Ballon** (1424m), which offers a view over one of the most famous First World War battlefields, **Le Vieil Armand**. Near **Thann**, the *Route des Crêtes* meets up once again with the *Route du Vin*.

Thann itself is known for its Gothic St-Thiebault church, and its medieval Witches' Tower and Storks' Tower. Nearby **Cernay** is a centre for excursions, mainly to places on the *Route des Crêtes*. In the following the *Route du Vin* northwards again, you will come to **Guebwiller**, with its Dominican church and Musée Florival. A little way off the *Route du Vin*, at **Ungersheim** (south-east of Guebwiller), is the **Ecomusée de Haute-Alsace**. In 1980, a group of students decided to 'rescue' old Alsatian houses due for demolition and to rebuild them here. As well as old-fashioned building and carpentry skills, other dwindling trades are practised in the 'village', where farm animals are kept and storks come to nest. Soultzmatt's *Zinnkoepfle* vineyard is the highest in Alsace. If you are in the area during Ascension week, look in on the lively fair of organic food and drink at **Rouffach**. At **Husseren-les-Châteaux** is what is known as the Five Castles Road (for obvious reasons) which is clearly marked and makes a good cycling circuit. The picturesque village of **Eguisheim**, overlooked by three ruined castles, has numerous small-scale wine producers eager to sell you their wines. There is also an achaeology museum. **Turckheim** is a medieval village, with an old gateway and watch-tower, cobbled streets and attractive well. On summer nights, the night watchman still goes on his round, carrying a lamp and dressed in medieval costume. **Ammerschwihr** and **Kaysersberg** are both worth visiting. The latter is where Albert Schweitzer was born; it has a local history museum, and a traditional fair of crafts at Christmas time. Nearby, at the lovely **Château de Kientzheim**, a deeper understanding of Alsatian wines and vine-growing can be gained by visiting the Musée du Vignoble et des Vins d'Alsace.

Riquewihr is a perfectly preserved medieval town (completely pedestrianised), whose main street is lined with houses, some of whose courtyards have been made into display areas for local artists. Many of the houses date from the sixteenth century and there is a torture chamber in the Thieves' Tower. The village of **Zellenberg** offers a unique panoramic view over the plain of Alsace. At **Hunawihr**, a flower-bedecked wine village with a fourteenth-century fortified church, is the Centre de Réintroduction des Cigognes, which aims to increase the number of storks in Alsace to former levels. **Ribeauvillé** is another pleasant medieval town, situated beneath the three Châteaux de Ribeaupierre; it is a tourist centre and plays host to various festivals. The **Château de Schoppenwihr**, at Ostheim, has an informal romantic park, open to the public all year round. From **St-Hippolyte**, it is a pleasant, though steep, walk or drive up to the impressive twelfth-century **Château de Haut-Koenigsbourg**, restored in 1902. Finally, back near Sélestat, you will come to the medieval **Château de Kintzheim** (not to be confused with the one at Kientzheim), which is used as an acclimatisation centre for around 80 birds of prey. Not far away is the **Montagne des Singes**, where 300 Barbary Apes live.

This endangered species is native to the Algerian and Moroccan mountains, but similar climatic conditions in the Vosges have enabled the World Wide Fund for Nature to reintroduce to Morocco 240 apes reared in Alsace. Both centres can be visited by the public.

Accommodation

Family hotels and B&B are easy to find in the area around the two *Routes*: the trick is to use the tourist office list of *chambres d'hôte* and try less well-known villages in summer, though bear in mind that some owners are unwilling to take you for less than two nights. The following hotels are recommended:

First Class

Le Clos St-Vincent, route de Bergheim, 68150 Ribeauvillé (Tel. 89 73 67 65): 11 rooms in elegant, chalet-style hotel, among vineyards; restaurant with excellent cuisine and wine selection.

First Class / Middle Range

Hôtel Beau Site, Place de l'Eglise, 67530 Ottrott (Tel. 88 95 80 61): 15 rooms in friendly hotel run by wine-growing family; restaurant with house specialities and opportunities to try local wines. **Auberge de Thierenbach**, Thierenbach – Jungholtz, 68500 Guebwiller (Tel. 89 76 93 01): 16 rooms, decorated with antique furniture, in quiet hotel in country surroundings; highly praised home cooking prepared by owner.

Middle Range

Le Cerf, 30 rue du Général-de-Gaulle, 67520 Marlenheim (Tel. 88 87 73 73): 19 rooms in family-owned hotel, formerly a coaching inn; restaurant with regional accent and innovative rustic cuisine.

Middle Range / Economy

Hôtel Winstub Gilg, 1 route du Vin, Mittelbergheim, 67140 Barr (Tel. 88 08 91 37): 10 rooms in family-run hotel; restaurant recommended by *Logis de France* for its promotion of regional cuisine.

For simple and economical accommodation which will help support traditional cheese-making practices, try one of the *marcaireries* which has become a *ferme-auberge*. Most of these are found at the top of the Munster Valley, between **Le Hohneck** and **Le Grand Ballon**:

Economy

Ferme-Auberge du Freundstein, 68760 Willer-sur-Thur (Tel. 89 82 31 63): 2 rooms and one dormitory in low-roofed farm near magnificent forest: traditional *menus marcaires*; butter and munster cheese for sale. **Ferme-Auberge des Trois-Fours**, 68140 Munster (Tel. 89 77 31 14): 9 rooms in farm where, until recently, local shepherds and labourers came for lunch; it has now opened its doors to tourists: *menu marcaire* and Alsatian specialities; munster cheese for sale.

Eating Out

The following restaurants warrant special mention:

First Class

Auberge de l'Ill, Illhaeusern, 68150 Ribeauvillé (Tel. 89 71 83 23): family inn with interesting regional specialities, extensive wine list and international reputation; reservation essential. **Aux Armes de France**, 1 Grand Rue, 68770 Ammerschwihr (Tel. 89 47 10 12): reliable family restaurant with fine regional wines: also has 10 quiet, elegant rooms.

First Class / Middle Range

Edel, 7 rue des Serruriers, 67600 Kintzheim (Tel. 88 92 86 55): excellent regional gastronomy, with fish specialities, in rustic dining room.

Colmar

Like Strasbourg, the centre of Colmar is pleasantly compact and homely. Restoration of the old town is immaculate, to the point of concealing or disguising the television aerials which so often spoil the character of historic buildings elsewhere.

Ask the tourist office for its leaflet 'Colmar, Ville d'Art', which suggests a sensible itinerary. The **Unterlinden Museum** enjoys a reputation as one of the most important museums in France. Situated in a thirteenth-century convent with vine-covered cloisters, its greatest treasure is the early sixteenth-century **Issenheim altar-piece** by Matthias Grünewald, an astounding combination of the mystical and the realistic, of painting and sculpture. The museum also houses a twenty-four panel series of the Passion by Martin Schongauer, and a comprehensive selection of other items, from carved wine barrels and Alsatian folk art to Picassos and Braques. The impressive **Eglise Collégiale St-Martin** is often mistakenly referred to as a cathedral: this thirteenth- and fourteenth- century Gothic church is even situated in Place de la Cathédrale. The nearby **Eglise des Dominicains** (also begun in the thirteenth century) has some magnificent stained-glass windows and, at present, houses Schongauer's famous painting of the **Virgin of the Rose Bush** (1473). The **Musée Bartholdi** is in the house where Bartholdi, sculptor of the Statue of Liberty, was born (30 rue des Marchands). The **Natural History Museum** fills a seventeenth century-house in rue de Turenne.

Do not miss the **Petite Venise** quarter, which is a mass of half-timbered houses and studios on the banks of the diminutive River Lauch. An excellent view is afforded from Pont St-Pierre. From here it is worth taking the back streets – rue de la Poissonnerie, rue des Tanneurs and the narrow and often overlooked Petite Rue des Tanneurs – to the Place de l'**Ancienne Douane**, with its colourful fourteenth- and fifteenth-century customs house. Other buildings of interest are the green-turreted **Maison Pfister** (1537), **Maison Schongauer** just opposite, and **Maison des Têtes**. The 1804 **Champ de Mars** park and the square outside the eighteenth-century Old Hospital (now an Institute of Technology) are good places to sit and relax.

Accommodation

First Class

Hôtel Le Maréchal, 4–6 Place des Six Montagnes Noires (Tel. 89 41 60 32): 32 rooms in sixteenth-century half-timbered house, overlooking La Petite Venise.

Middle Range

Hôtel St-Martin, 38 Grand-Rue (Tel. 89 24 11 51): 22 rooms in quiet hotel in heart of old town, near cathedral. **Kuehn**, quai de la Fecht, 68040 Ingersheim (Tel. 89 27 38 38): 28 rooms in family hotel in vineyard, just outside town; restaurant.

Middle Range / Economy

Auberge du Père Floranc, 9 rue Herzog, 68920 Wettolsheim (Tel. 89 80 79 14): 32 rooms in rustic, family-run hotel near vineyard, outside town; restaurant. **Beau Séjour**, 25 rue du Ladhof (Tel. 89 41 37 16): 28 rooms in hotel with pleasant inner garden, run by same family for five generations; excellent restaurant with regional specialities.

Economy

Hôtel la Chaumière, 74 ave de la République (Tel. 89 41 08 99): 16 simple rooms in central hotel with bar downstairs.

Eating Out

Wandering round the old town, looking for a restaurant, can be almost as much fun as the meal itself. Restaurants are, on the whole, a little more expensive than in Strasbourg.

First Class

Aux Trois Poissons, 15 quai de la Poissonnerie (Tel. 89 41 25 21): fish specialities served in Alsatian house in old town.

Middle Range

Maison des Têtes, 19 rue des Têtes (Tel. 89 24 43 43): pleasant Alsatian specialities in beautiful 1609 house with rustic decor. **Le Caveau d'Eguisheim**, 3 Place du Château, 68420 Eguisheim (Tel. 89 41 08 89): traditional regional specialities and interesting fish dishes with range of local wines, in beautiful surroundings 6 km south of Colmar. **Auberge de l'Ill**, 8 rue de l'Ill (Tel. 89 71 83 23): pleasant inn with regional dishes, 2 km north-east of main town.

Economy

Sparisser Stewwele, 4 Place Jeanne d'Arc (Tel. 89 41 42 33): friendly wine cellar with simple home cooking. **La Taverne**, 2 impasse de la Maison Rouge (off Place du Marché aux Fruits) (Tel. 89 41 70 33): best *tarte flambée* in town, served in cheerful restaurant with rustic interior.

Entertainments

There is a traditional market in Place de l'Ancienne Douane on Thursday mornings and in Place St-Joseph on Saturday mornings.

The tourist office can arrange guided tours on foot or in mini-train (though these usually come only in French or German). There are free concerts and folk entertainment shows at 8.30 p.m. on Tuesdays from mid-May to mid-September in Place de l'Ancienne Douane. Enquire about the frequent church concerts. If you are fortunate enough to be in the area in mid-August, you will experience the famous Colmar Wine Festival. For something different, visit the chocolate-maker's workshop (guided tour with tasting – book 4 days in advance) at **Pâtisserie Sitter**, 18 rue des Clés (Tel. 89 41 32 54 – this is also a pleasant tea-room); or the **Wolfberger Distillery**, Chemin de la Fecht (Tel. 89 79 11 90).

Useful Addresses

The **Tourist Office** is at 4 rue des Unterlinden (Tel. 89 41 02 29). Information on the whole of the Haut-Rhin is available from the **Association Départementale du Tourisme du Haut-Rhin**, Hôtel du Département, 68006 Colmar (Tel. 89 23 21 11). The main **Post Office** is at 36–38 ave de la République. The **Hospital** is Hôpital Pasteur, 39 ave de la Liberté (Tel. 89 80 40 00).

Transport Options

Once again, walking is the best way to see the old town. Alternatively you could book a seat in the mini-train, which completes a tour of Colmar in 50 minutes. There is a comprehensive bus service, which provides mini-buses to destinations in the town itself and normal ones to the outlying areas of Horbourg-Wihr, Ingersheim and Wintzenheim.

Bas-Rhin & Haut-Rhin

Turning now to eastern and southern Alsace, in the east of the region, alongside the Grand Canal d'Alsace and the River Rhine, is a *'terre bénie'*. This is a fertile strip on which anything will flourish, from tobacco and cereals to vegetables and fruit trees. In the south is another sparsely populated agricultural region, known as the Sundgau.

If you start at fortified **Lauterbourg** in the north, you can work down to **Saint-Louis**, right on the Swiss border. The ideal way to make this trip is a combination of bicycle, train and boat. Below Lauterbourg is **Sessenheim**, where Goethe fell in love with the pastor's daughter, Frédérique Brion, who was the inspiration for much of his early poetry. A collection of their letters can be seen in the local inn, Au Boeuf, and there is also a memorial to Goethe. Down beyond Strasbourg, it is around **Rhinau** and **Diebolsheim** that the most typical 'Reid' scenery can be found. It is worth making a detour to **Sermersheim** if you like the idea of an evening exploration of the 'Ried' in small boats, followed by *tarte flambée* and other local products (contact in advance M. Ackermann, 4 rue du Ried, 67230 Sermersheim). Make sure you return to the Rhine via **Ebermunster**'s impressive Baroque abbey. A steam train runs (weekends only) between **Marckolsheim** and **Neuf-Brisach** (which is on the Freiburg-Colmar bus route). **Bantzenheim** has a bird sanctuary and botanical path and could be used as a base for walks in the **Forêt de la Harth**. Near **Saint-Louis** is the Petite Camargue, an area of reed-beds, formed by old branches of the Rhine, now a nature reserve, complete with centre to familiarise people with the wildlife on the river Au.

Mulhouse is a predominantly industrial city, whose main attractions are its museums: an excellent museum of old cars, a railway museum, and an impressive museum of the town's history, housed in the 16th century town hall. Meanwhile, castles, carp pools, low-roofed farms and flower-filled villages punctuate the peaceful Sundgau region, south of Mulhouse. The only town of any size is **Altkirch** (7000 inhabitants), with its Art and History Museum (Musée Sundgovien) housed in a lovely Renaissance mansion. From here, visit **Hirtzbach**, a flowered village with a stream running alongside the main street, a park and the De Reinach castle. In **Grentzingen** there are typical half-timbered houses, many of which retain their original ochre colour. The town of **Ferrette** lies below two ruined castles, accessible by foot through pleasant woods. In **Oltingue** is a rural museum called Maison du Sundgau, which will help you understand the life of this region, and a 15-minute walk from **Leymen** is the ruined Château du Landskron, which offers a magnificent view over the whole Sundgau.

Accommodation & Eating Out

Middle Range / Economy

Hôtel à la Couronne, 24 route du Rhin, Dalhunden, 67770 Sessenheim (Tel. 88 86 97 16): 26 rooms in family-run hotel; restaurant. **Hôtel de la Poste**, 1 rue de Bâle, Bantzenheim, 68490

Ottmarsheim (Tel. 89 26 04 26): 10 rooms in family hotel; simple restaurant.

When in the Sundgau, make sure you try the local speciality of fried carp: look out for the prestigious *Carpe frite* sign at restaurants. The following hotel-restaurants are recommended:

Economy

Au Cheval Blanc, Bettendorf, 68560 Hirsingue (Tel. 89 40 50 58): 7 rooms in family hotel; restaurant with country dishes. **Collin**, 68480 Ferrette (Tel. 89 40 40 72): 10 rooms in family hotel; restaurant with local specialities.

9 Franche-Comté

Franche-Comté is a region whose attractions are largely unknown abroad; even the French tend to overlook them. This is surprising when you consider what it has to offer, starting with its location. Not only is it at the very centre of Western Europe, it also serves as vestibule to the Alps, preparing for them with its own mountain range, the Jura. The region's landscape is varied, with many unusual geographical features including gorges, waterfalls and underground caverns, as well as lakes, rivers, spas, plains, forests and vineyards. Franche-Comté is ideal for the sports of fishing, potholing, mountain biking and skiing (especially cross-country), and it also has good walking, cycling, horseriding and boating facilities.

During the course of its history, the region has come under a wide range of influences, which manifest themselves in its architecture: there are impressive Gallo-Roman remains; sixteenth-century Spanish courtyards; fortified citadels at Belfort and Besançon; and eighteenth-century salt-works designed as part of a utopian city; and a dramatic Le Corbusier chapel from the 1950s. Besançon capital of Franche-Comté, lies within a horseshoe formed by the Doubs river, cocooned by the seven surrounding hills. It is truly in the middle of the countryside, and its many parks and fountains make it France's greenest city.

Outside the main towns, the population density is relatively low. The villages have simple but distinctive churches, and houses are often built in a chalet style. The numerous farms are made of stone, with low roofs practically reaching the ground, and broad chimneys (called *tuyés*) used for smoking meats. In many areas you will find herds of Montbéliard cows, whose milk is used to prepare the prestigious regional cheese, Comté. Vineyards are not particularly widespread and occur in pockets rather than swathes, making for a varied landscape. Local crafts and industries are flourishing: the engines for all the TGV trains in France are made in Franche-Comté, which also specialises in lasers, as well as more traditional occupations such as cutting gemstones, carving wood and pipes, and making watches and clocks. Tissot watches come from here, and the Comtoise clock, which exists in all sizes (from grandfather down), is generally shaped like an elongated pear and made of oak or cherry wood.

It is said that the accuracy and dedication required in the watch-making business is reflected in the daily life of Franche-Comté's inhabitants. Their keen attention to detail suggests an affinity with the Swiss (the region does, after all, share 240 kilometres of border with Switzerland), yet the 'typical' *Franc-Comtois* is also remarkably easy-going. People are more at home in the country than the city, and even the very wealthy are by no means ostentatious. Independence and freedom are highly valued and the region's heritage and environment are recognised as important assets.

Such a region would seem to have all the ingredients of a prime tourist destination, but the level of tourism here is extremely low. Because Franche-Comté is neither overrun with tourists, nor desperate for the extra income they generate, the welcome it extends to visitors is an honest one. This part of France has enough sense not to pander to mass tourism but to hang on to all its charming regional characteristics.

History

The Franche-Comté region has changed hands countless times since it was first settled in the fourth century BC by a tribe from the upper Seine. The great camp known as Vesontio later grew into Besançon. Under Roman rule, other towns flourished: Lons-le-Saunier, Dole, Pontarlier and Salins. In AD 457, the region allowed itself to fall into Burgundian hands. For 77 years, it was part of the Burgundian empire, until that in turn was conquered by Frankish kings. It was only in the sixth century that monks began to penetrate the dense Jura forests, felling parts of them for farmland. After persistent barbarian invasions in the tenth century, control over the Saône area was given to the Dukes of Burgundy, and power over the Jura region to the Counts (*Comtes*) of Burgundy. For this reason, the region started to be known as the Comté. After a spell belonging to the German Empire in the eleventh century, Comté was bought by the French king Philippe le Bel in 1295. The English laid waste to it during the Hundred Years' War, helped along by a terrible plague in 1349. It was 1366 by the time the name Franche-Comté was first used: *franche* means free and signifies the importance of liberty in the eyes of the inhabitants.

In 1384, the marriage of Philippe le Hardi brought Franche-Comté back under the control of the Dukes of Burgundy, though it had a certain political and cultural independence, which it retained for three hundred years. After a brief occupation by the French monarchy in the 1470s, during which the regional capital of the time, Dole, was deliberately burnt to the ground, the area was given to Emperor Maximilian of Austria. His grandson, Charles, became both King of Spain and Emperor of Germany, but showed special fondness for Comté, which became part of the Spanish Empire after his death, and then passed back to Austria in 1598. In the course of the seventeenth century, the French managed to reclaim Franche-Comté, despite resistance not only from Spain, but from the fiercely independent inhabitants of Comté itself.

After the French Revolution, Franche-Comté was divided into its present *départements*. In the nineteenth century, the town of Belfort provided France with no fewer than twenty generals, and came into its own as a military stronghold. Industrialisation brought the Peugeot car factory at Sochaux, which can now be visited as a museum. Franche-Comté experienced a four-year period of German occupation during the Second World War. Today it has turned its traditional talent for accuracy to modern use, in the manufacture of TGV railway engines and optical equipment. It also supplies the whole of France with wooden cheese-boxes!

Among many famous Franc-Comtois, the following stand out: Captain Rouget de Lisle, born in Lons-le-Saunier, who composed the war song that would come to be known as the Marseillaise; the writer Victor Hugo, born in Besançon and famous for such works as *Les Misérables* and *The Hunchback of Notre-Dame*; the nineteenth century realist painter Gustave Courbet, from Ornans; Louis Pasteur, inventor of many vaccines including those against tuberculosis, cholera, yellow fever and rabies; and the Lumière brothers, who made considerable advances in photography at the turn of the century, coming up with the first effective ciné camera and projector and a means of producing colour photographs.

Geography

Franche-Comté is roughly egg-shaped. It is bordered by Switzerland down its eastern side; Burgundy to the west; the Rhône Valley to the south; and Champagne, Lorraine and Alsace to the north. The region comprises four *départements*: Jura in the south (capital Lons-le-Saunier – 22,000 inhabitants); Doubs in the centre and east (capital Besançon – 120,000); Haute-Saône in the north-west (capital Vesoul – 21,000); and, in the north-eastern corner, the smallest *département* in France, the Territoire de Belfort (capital Belfort – 53,000).

Franche-Comté resembles a flight of steps, rising out of the Haute-Saône plain, gradually becoming steeper, until it forms what are known as the 'folded' Jura in the south and east. The Jura mountains are a crescent-shaped range, shared by France, Switzerland and Germany. The highest part – 1717 metres – is in the Ain *département*. Franche-Comté's highest peak (Crêt Pela) is 1495 metres – just higher than its Vosgian counterpart. Though the Jura are obviously not as steep as the Alps, they are much wilder than the Vosges, with plenty of sharp cliffs and jagged rocks. From the Pic de l'Aigle, just south of Champagnole, there is an excellent view of both the 'folded' Jura and the terraced Jura plateaux. Parts of these plateaux are forest, pasture or cropland and parts infertile and rocky. Because of the porous limestone base, there are many spectacular geological features: rivers run through canyon-like valleys; they disappear underground, then re-emerge, having gouged out caves with stalactites; myriad lakes and waterfalls are created. The lower plateaux form gentle undulations, where crops, orchards and vineyards alternate. There used to be 44,500 acres of vineyard in Franche-Comté, but now there are less than 5000.

The word Jura comes from the low Latin 'juria', meaning forest, and 42% of Franche-Comté is, indeed, afforested. It is well worth visiting the beautiful Forêt de la Joux, where a special reserve protects a number of enormous fir trees, called *Présidents*, the largest of which is 45 metres tall. The region also boasts over eighty large lakes, including the 35-kilometre-long Lake Vouglans (third largest reservoir in France), and hundreds of smaller ones. Many can be found in the area east of Lons-le-Saunier, along with the Cascades du Hérisson, a series of 28 waterfalls. The main rivers of the region are the Loue and the Doubs, which has its own 30-metre waterfall. Of the region's 5500 kilometres of river, 320 kilometres are navigable. Six of Franche-Comté's 4000 caves and caverns may be visited; one, the Gouffre de Poudrey, has a record-breaking volume of 2 million cubic metres. Another geographical feature which should not be missed is the cirque at Baume-les-Messieurs.

Franche-Comté's facilities for most sports are very good, whether you wish to take advantage of its waterways (a special effort is made to keep them clean), its snow, or simply relax in one of its four spa towns: Luxueil-les-Bains, Besançon, Salins-les-Bains and Lons-le-Saunier. The most common trees are Scots pine, fir, beech and oak. Beneath ash trees, you may find wild *morille* mushrooms, considered a real delicacy. Flora typical of the region includes yellow gentian and many alpine flowers: the meadows above Lajoux are a colourful sight in spring. In the Haut-Jura regional park, you can find both Arctic and Mediterranean plants. The rivers and ponds of the Haute-Saône provide a good habitat for many birds, including herons, bitterns, kingfishers and nightjars. Deer and wild boar inhabit the forests, bats live in the caves, and red squirrels can be found in the upper Jura, above St-Claude.

A number of nature reserves have been created. In addition to the Réserve de la Glacière in the Joux forest, there is the Lac de Rémoray near Labergement-Ste-Marie; the Sabot de Frotey at Frotey-les-Vesoul, with its limestone vegetation and insect life; and the Ravin de Valbois near Cléron, where there is Mediterranean flora. The Parc Naturel Régional du Haut-Jura covers 153,000 acres of mountainside, and is an ideal area for walking, cross-country skiing or visiting local craftsmen. Part of the Parc Naturel Régional des Ballons des Vosges, whose headquarters are in Alsace, extends into Franche-Comté. It covers the northern tips of Haute-Saône and the Territoire de Belfort, including the former mining area around Giromagny and the 'plateau of a thousand ponds' in the red Vosgian sandstone north of Lure.

Climate

The climate in the Jura is alpine, with low winter temperatures (average 4.8°C in Feb.) and abundant snow (perfect for cross-country skiing), but high temperatures in summer (average of 26.5°C in August). Mid-summer is usually fine, with clear blue skies, but the rest of the year rain is fairly frequent; it is particularly likely between late August and November. Once the snows have melted in spring, the landscape becomes remarkably green, and the rivers and waterfalls are at their most impressive.

Attractions

The most visited attractions in Franche-Comté are the old towns of Besançon and Dole; the citadels of Besançon and Belfort; the Belfort lion, carved by Auguste Bartholdi, sculptor of the Statue of Liberty; the chapel at Ronchamp designed by Le Corbusier; and the semi-circular salt-works at Arc-et-Senans, part of an eighteenth-century utopian city, the rest of which never got further than the drawing board. There is also an impressive Gallo-Roman theatre at Mandeure, numerous châteaux throughout the region, balanced by simple rural architecture, and some good museums of folklore and local industries. Many traditional crafts are still practised today, especially in the regional park, and visitors to studios are usually welcome.

Outdoors, Franche-Comté offers excellent opportunities, of which many people are ignorant. In addition to its caves and waterfalls, it has some of the best fishing rivers in France (notably the Loue), and many boat-hire and canoeing possibilities on the Canal du Rhône au Rhin, the Saône and the Doubs. There are 5000 kilometres of trails for walking and mountain biking; 1200 kilometres of waymarked bridle paths suitable for riding and horse-drawn caravans; and 2000 kilometres of cross-country skiing tracks, including the 400 kilometres Grande Traversée du Jura circuit. In the Jura, downhill skiing resorts are at Métabief and Les Rousses, and there are two more in the Vosges – Belfahy and La Planche des Belles Filles. Another winter sport which has become popular recently is dog-sleigh racing.

Cuisine

Vegetarians may have problems as the local specialities are *brési* (cured beef), *jésus* (cooked mountain sausage from Morteau), ham from Luxueil, and smoked meats in general. *Coq au Vin Jaune* is another speciality, as are fish from the region's well-stocked rivers, including trout, grayling, pike and perch. In the Haute-Saône, they do a bouillabaisse of freshwater fish, called *La Pachouse*. Mushrooms are the best bet for vegetarians: sometimes seven or more varieties are combined to make a delicious filling for the pie known as *croûte forestière*. Another treat is the *Fondue Comtoise*, a cheese fondue, using Comté cheese and usually served with salad. Fruit tarts and sorbets are popular desserts, and the town of Montbozon makes its own special biscuits.

It is almost worth coming to Franche-Comté just for the cheeses. The most famous is the mild hard cheese, Comté, which has been honoured with an *Appellation d'Origine Contrôlée*, like a good wine. It must be made with fresh milk from pure-bred Montbéliard cows, which have fed only on grass or hay. The real connoisseurs can work out the diet of the cow from the taste of the cheese! The capital of Comté is Poligny, where it is possible to visit the cellars in which it matures. Among other regional cheeses are Morbier from the Morez area; Bleu de Gex from round Septmoncel; and Mont d'Or, a soft cheese which has been produced in the Champagnole region since the thirteenth century. Another speciality is Cancoillotte: this is a spread made of cheese, butter, salt, spices and even wine – but beware, it is **very** salty. When buying food, look out for the Franche-Comté label given to products approved by the Comité de Promotion des Produits Régionaux.

Jura wines have a pleasantly distinctive taste, which can be reminiscent of chestnuts or walnuts. Along the narrow strip of country where the vines grow, most villages have their own wine. The most famous are those from Arbois, Pupillin and Château-Chalon. Jura wines come in all colours and strengths – red, white (good with cheese), rosé and sparkling, but also 'yellow' and 'straw'. Yellow wine, or *vin jaune*, comes mainly from Château-Chalon and Arbois, and ferments for six years. Straw wine, or *vin de paille*, is now very rare, as one bottle requires unrealistic quantities of grapes. It can reach 17% proof and is generally drunk as an *apéritif* or *digestif*. Stronger alcohols include Kirsch from Fougerolles; Gentian brandy from the Pontarlier area; and Marc de Franche-Comté, a clear brandy made from the stalks, pips and skin of grapes – if you don't fancy it neat, ask for some on your sorbet.

Level of Tourism

Franche-Comté comes nearly at the bottom of the league of tourist regions in France. It receives only 955,000 hotel visits a year (that is, 1.5% of all national visits). Most of the tourists are short-stay visitors, and 21% of them come from outside France. The foreign tourists are predominantly Swiss, German, Belgian, Dutch and British. An increase in tourism to Franche-Comté was noticeable in the late 1980s, but the region is as far as ever from becoming a mass tourism destination.

There are distinct on and off seasons in Franche-Comté, and the small number of off-season visitors means that many minor museums and sites are closed, or have restricted opening hours, between October and April. The plus side is that the ones which are open often reduce their entrance fees. Tourism-related problems are few and far between: there are not enough downhill ski runs to have ruined the landscape, and summer road congestion is rare. One self-evident piece of advice is that it is important not to pick any of the beautiful alpine flowers unless you are certain they are a common variety. Even then, it is better to leave them alone, as the Edelweiss **used to be** common . . . until indiscriminate picking made it extremely rare.

Accommodation is mainly small-scale. There are a huge number of family-run *Logis de France* hotels in the region. *Gîtes* are also popular, as is camping. Though there are many campsites, very few are visible from the road. Various *ferme-auberges* offer reasonably priced regional specialities.

In Besançon, a sensible policy has been adopted, which stipulates that no high-rise buildings may be built within the horseshoe bend of the River Doubs, which marks the traditional limits of the city. In addition, a good deal of the old town is pedestrianised. The same is true of Dole, which contains the second most historically important protected area in France. Such protection is a high priority and there is a motto that 'preservation is a kind of creation'. Recently, various initiatives have been undertaken with this in mind. Three local businesses – one forge, one glassworks and one ceramics works – have opened their doors to the public in order to show how they operate. Several 'tourist routes' have been created, which follow themes such as wine, cheese, clock-making and châteaux. A disused railway line, between Vesoul and the Ognon valley, has been turned into a *chemin vert* for the use of walkers and cyclists. In Arc-et-Senans, at the Saline Royale salt-works, a bet led to the creation of the Claude-Nicolas Ledoux Foundation, whose aim is to revive public interest in a historic monument (the *Saline*) by means of contemporary projects. The salt-works now hosts numerous – sometimes bizarre – events and exhibitions. Recently, interest in houseboats and mountain bikes has been growing, both of which offer an excellent way of seeing otherwise inaccessible parts. The golden rule in Franche-Comté seems to be to make the best possible use of what already exists.

Good Alternatives

Meeting People

It is worth asking at tourist offices if there are any local festivals or fairs going on: you will almost certainly be in luck during the grape harvest. Less traditional events, often with a futuristic or architectural theme, occur at the Saline Royale at Arc-et-Senans; these offer a good opportunity to meet people, and impressive surroundings into the bargain. Those interested in taking part in an archaeological dig should contact the **Direction des Antiquités**, 9 bis rue Charles Nodier, 25030 Besançon (Tel. 81 81 29 24).

Another possibility is simply to visit local producers of regional specialities. A list of those who have earned the Franche-Comté Label is available from the **Comité de Promotion des Produits Régionaux**, 2 Place Payot, 25043 Besançon (Tel. 81 80 81 11). If you are particularly interested in Jura wines and cheeses, write for information to the **Chambre d'Agriculture**, 45 rue du Colonel de Casteljan, 39016 Lons-le-Saunier (Tel. 84 24 51 56). The tourist board has recently created the *Route du Comté*, which takes you past various cooperative dairies, where visitors are welcomed and shown how Comté cheese is produced. There is also a *Route des Artisans*, which you can follow to discover the craftsmen of the region. Those on the route belong to the Artisans Créateurs Jurassiens association, and their skills range from diamond cutting and pottery to pipe decoration and babywear design. Details about the *Route des Artisans* are available from the **Chambre des Métiers**, 17 rue Jules-Bury, 39000 Lons-le-Saunier. If you choose to eat the regional cuisine offered by the *fermes-auberges*, you are more likely to strike up conversation with your hosts than at more formal restaurants: a list can be obtained from the **Association Régionale des Fermes-Auberges de Franche-Comté**, Mme Robert, 'La Forge d'Isidore', 70400 Villers-sur-Saulnot; or from the **Comité Régional du Tourisme de Franche-Comté**, 9 rue de Pontarlier, 25000 Besançon (Tel. 81 83 50 47), which will also send you a good deal of general information on the region if requested.

Discovering Places

If you are travelling in your own car, it is a good idea to ask the **Comité Régional du Tourisme** (address above) for its suggested thematic routes. A slightly more structured trip can be provided by the three **Loisirs-Acceuil** services in the region. These act as departmental tour operators and offer holidays varying from weekend breaks to twelve night trips, usually staying in small family hotels. The themes of the holidays are immensely varied and include lace-making in Luxeuil, gourmet weekends, children's riding holidays, cycling tours, rambling with a pack-donkey, canoeing, potholing and general sightseeing. The **Comité Régional du Tourisme** can provide you with the brochure 'Nature at its Best', which contains a large selection of these holidays. Even more detailed suggestions are available from the individual *départements*, as follows: **Loisirs-Acceuil Doubs**, 15 ave Edouard Droz, 25000 Besançon (Tel. 81 80 38 18); **Loisirs-Acceuil Jura**, Hôtel du Département, BP 652, 8 ave du 44e R.I., 39021 Lons-le-Saunier (Tel. 84 24 57 70); **Loisirs-Acceuil Haute-Saône et Territoire de Belfort**, BP 117, 6 rue des Bains, 70002 Vesoul (Tel. 84 75 43 66). If you are interested in fishing holidays, contact **Loisirs-Accueil Doubs**. Day-trips to spectacular sites on rivers and lakes are arranged by the **Maison Nationale de la Pêche et de l'Eau**, 36 rue St-Laurent, 25290 Ornans (Tel. 81 57 14 49). Those wishing for an active discovery of the Doubs *départements*'s natural riches should address **Syratu Tourisme et Loisirs**, route de Montgesoye, 25290 Ornans (Tel. 81 57 10 82). Its specialities are mountain biking, canoeing, climbing and caving. The last two are only for those with previous experience, but mountain bike and canoe excursions (accompanied or independent) can be enjoyed by anyone. It is also possible to combine different activities over a period of days, as **Syratu** has links with hotels, *gîtes* and campsites where you can stay. Other local travel agents include **Monts-Jura Tour**, 9 rue Proudhon, 25000 Besançon (Tel. 81 81 41 94); and **Juragence**, 178 rue Regard, 39000 Lons-le-Saunier (Tel. 84 47 27 27). The British tour operator **Headwater Holidays** (see **Introduction** p. 45) offers walking, cycling and canoeing holidays in the Jura.

Communications

How to Get There

Flights from Paris are received at the small regional airport, Dole-Tavaux. Franche-Comté does not have an international airport, but Basle-Mulhouse-Freiburg Euroairport and Geneva airport are both nearby.

By **rail**, the towns of Dole, Mouchard, Besançon, Frasne,

Pontarlier, Vesoul and Belfort are all on the TGV line, so that they can be reached from Paris in 2 to $3^1/2$ hours, which is about 2 hours less than it would take a normal express train. The nearest Eurolines **coach** destinations from London are Dijon (Burgundy) and Strasbourg (Alsace). By car, the jouney from Paris to Besançon takes around $4^1/2$ hours, either via Beaune on the A 6 and A 36, or via Langres and Vesoul on the A 5, N 19 and N 57.

When You're There

Rail – there is a good rail network, with the towns mentioned under **How to Get There** connected by both TGV and slower trains which stop at more minor stations. Main routes also pass through Montbéliard and Lons-le-Saunier.

Bus – the train network is supplemented by SNCF buses. In addition to numerous minor routes, these connect Lons-le-Saunier to Arbois and Dole. The most comprehensive bus company in Franche-Comté is **Cars Monts-Jura**, whose main branch is at 9 rue Proudhon, 25000 Besançon (Tel. 81 88 11 33). They will take you from Besançon to Ornans, Villers-le-Lac, Pontarlier and Salins-les-Bains as well as lesser-known towns and villages. They also do excursions, including some from Dole into the Jura mountains.

Car – the A 36 motorway runs through the region, connecting Dole, Besançon and Belfort if you are in a hurry. Otherwise use the parallel N road, which makes for more pleasant driving. Numerous D roads allow you to explore off the beaten track, but remember to take snow chains if you are driving in the mountains in winter.

Boat – detailed information on river tourism is available from the **Groupement pour le Tourisme Fluvial**, 18 rue Ampère, 25000 Besançon (Tel. 81 88 71 38). Boat trips are possible on the Saône (below Corre), the Doubs, the Canal de l'Est and the Canal du Rhône au Rhin, as well as at Villers-le-Lac, Lac de Vouglans and Gray. For canoeing infomation, contact **Syratu Tourisme et Loisirs**, route de Montgesoye, 25290 Ornans (Tel. 81 57 10 82). In the Haute-Saône, the canoe clubs of Villersexel and Pesmes organise trips (accommodation and equipment included).

Cycling – in Besançon, bicycles can be hired from the railway station and **Cycles Robert**, 6 rue de la Préfecture (Tel. 81 82 19 12). The Besançon tourist office supplies detailed cycle itineraries. Mountain biking is popular, especially in the hills round Vesoul (Hte-Saône). At Ornans (Doubs), mountain bikes can be hired from **Syratu** (address under **Boat**).

Walking – the GR 5 footpath is a good axis for walking holidays. This follows the Swiss border and is linked to its western counterpart, the GR 59, by the GR 595. Other major paths are the GR 9, GR 559 and GR 590. Local tourist offices will give you information about the numerous minor footpaths in the region, which allow you to explore areas such as the Serre massif (north of Dole), the shore of lake Vouglans, and the châteaux around Vesoul. In winter, cross-country skiing offers an ideal way of seeing the Jura. For details of this and other winter sports possibilities, contact the **Espace Nordique Jurassien**, Hôtel de Ville-Annexe, BP 132, 39300 Champagnole (Tel. 84 52 58 10).

Riding – for information on the many miles of marked bridleway in Franche-Comté, as well as on organised riding holidays, contact the **Comité Régional du Tourisme de Franche-Comté**, 9 rue de Pontarlier, 25000 Besançon (Tel. 81 83 50 47). Horse-drawn caravans are a popular way of seeing the countryside; the main starting point is Fontenois-la-Ville.

Useful Local Contacts

The headquarters of the **Parc Naturel Régional du Haut-Jura** are Maison du Haut-Jura, Lajoux, 39310 Septmontcel (Tel. 84 41 20 37). Here, you will find information about park initiatives. The **Ballons des Vosges** regional park has its headquarters in Alsace: 1 rue de l'Eglise, BP 11, 68140 Munster (Tel. 89 77 29 04). Preservation of old fruit trees is undertaken by **Les Croqueurs de Pommes**, BP 707, Place d'Armes, 90020 Belfort. **Alp Action** is supporting a project involving the Lac de Remoray in the Jura; the organisation's address is (The Bellerive Foundation) PO Box 6, 1211 Geneva 3.

Geographical Breakdown of Region

Haute-Saone and Territoire de Belfort

Most of this area is densely wooded plain, dotted with numerous lakes in the north-east, where the gentle slopes of the Vosges mountains begin.

In the north-west of Haute-Saône is **Passavant-la-Rochère**, home to the oldest glassworks in France. This dates from 1475 and the workshop, together with a film and exhibition, can be viewed by the public every afternoon from May to September (except August). At

Corre, it is possible to hire boats for trips on the Saône; a cheese fair is held here in early September. If you pass **Jonvelle**, it is worth stopping to see the Gallo-Roman remains and the Agricultural Museum. Further south, at **Champlitte**, is an eighteenth-century château and a Museum of Popular Arts and Traditions, which contains 34 beautifully reconstructed interiors. Boat-hire is available at **Gray**, where there is also an art museum, called the Musée Baron Martin, housed in a château, and an attractive Renaissance town hall. A *Son et Lumière* takes place in the fortified town of **Pesmes** in August. Look out for the (still inhabited) Renaissance château at **Malans**, and the fifteenth- and seventeenth-century castle-fort which dominates the Saône plain at **Gy**. At **Sorans** is a fortified residence, which typifies the regional architecture of the sixteenth century. It is possible to visit a dairy and taste cheeses at the Société Coopérative Laitière, route nationale 57, **Rioz** (Tel. 84 91 82 30). **Fondremand** is a typical *comtois* village, containing some beautiful houses and a château; in July, art and craft days are arranged. At **Scey-sur-Saône** there is a museum devoted to the history of costume; here, July brings the Festival of the Forest. Nearby **Grandecourt** has a twelfth-century priory.

Although **Vesoul** is capital of the *département*, it contains little of interest for the visitor, apart from a large lake where a festival is held each August. At **Frotey-lès-Vesoul** is the Réserve Naturelle du Sabot de Frotey, where insects and plants flourish on a limestone plateau. The water of the spa town, **Luxeuil-les-Bains**, has just started to be sold commercially. There are guided tours of this pleasant town of pink sandstone, with its historical mansions, its abbey, its basilica, and its museum of art and archaeology, housed in the fifteenth-century Tour des Echevins. At **St-Valbert** there is a seventh-century hermitage and an animal park. **Le Petit Fahys**, near **Fougerolles**, is the site of an *ecomusée* concentrating on the traditional distillation of clear spirits such as Kirsch, as well as associated crafts like barrel-making and wickerwork. It has its own orchard of cherry and plum trees and is open every afternoon except Tuesday, from mid-May to late September. If you cross the **Esmoulières** 'plateau of a thousand pounds', you will come to **Servance**, where it is worth stopping to see the Saut de l'Ognon, a waterfall on the River Ognon. Le Corbusier's famous chapel, built between 1951 and 1955 to harmonise with the landscape despite its uncompromising modernity, can be seen at **Ronchamp**, where there is also a museum of mining. There is a sizeable lake at nearby **Champagney**.

Plancher-Bas hosts a craft festival in July, and over in the Territoire de Belfort, there is a mining festival at **Giromagny** in mid-June. Down the road at **Etueffont** is a forge, which still operates and forms part of a 'living' museum, representing rural life in the lower Vosges from the nineteenth century onwards. If you are in the area at the end of August, go to **Brebotte** for its Harvest Festival. Back in Haute-Saône, there is another mining museum at **Héricourt**. The **Château de Villersexel** is a beautiful nineteenth-century mansion, still lived in, which contains an antique collection and may be visited every afternoon except Monday. At **Filain** is a fifteenth- and sixteenth-century château with a typically regional facade.

Accommodation & Eating Out

First Class

Relais-Château de Nantilly, 70100 Nantilly (Tel. 84 65 20 12): 20 rooms in 4-star château. **Château de Rigny**, route de la Vallée de la Saône, 70101 Gray (Tel. 84 65 25 01): 24 rooms in comfortable residence with park; restaurant with fish and game specialities.

Middle Range

Hôtel Henri IV, 15 rue du Bourg, 70600 Champlitte (Tel. 84 67 66 81): 14 rooms in family-owned hotel; restaurant.

Middle Range / Economy

Hôtel du Lion Vert, 16 rue Carnot, 70300 Luxeuil-les-Bains (Tel. 84 40 50 66): 18 rooms in family-owned hotel; restaurant. **Hôtel de la Terrasse**, 70110 Villersexel (Tel. 84 20 52 11): 15 rooms in family hotel situated on riverbank; restaurant.

Economy

Hôtel la Sapinière, 56 rue du Tilleul, 90200 Giromagny (Tel. 84 29 32 88): 7 rooms in family hotel; restaurant.

In addition to the restaurants of the hotels mentioned above, the *Middle Range* auberge-restaurant at the **Château de Grammont**, 70110 Villersexel (Tel. 84 20 51 53) is recommended. At weekends, you could try the *Economy* ferme-auberge, **'La Forge d'Isidore'**, 70400 Villers-sur-Saulnot (Tel. 84 27 43 94), where the specialities are Comté chicken and fondue.

Belfort

This town of great military significance proudly dominates what is known as the Belfort Gap, a 30-kilometre breach between the Vosges and the Jura mountains, through which invaders frequently sought to enter France. The town seems to represent a half-way house between Alsace and Franche-Comté proper.

The hallmark of Belfort is its impressive red **Lion**. This measures 20 metres in length and was constructed from sandstone blocks by Auguste Bartholdi, sculptor of the Statue of Liberty, in honour of those who defended Belfort during a siege in the Franco-Prussian war. It is a fitting symbol of Franche-Comté's love of freedom. Above it, built on a rock, is a seventeenth-century fortified **castle**, which contains the **Art and History Museum** and offers splendid views. Among the Vauban fortifications which remain is the **Porte de Brisach**. The **Cathédrale St-Christophe** is an eighteenth-century classical building of red sandstone, which shows some Spanish influence and has a beautiful organ. The **theatre** and the **town hall** are also worth visiting. Look out for Bartholdi's other monument on **Place de la République**; this represents France and the great defenders of Belfort. Across the River Savoureuse, in the newer part of town, is **Square E-Lechten**, with its wealth of greenery and flowers.

Accommodation

First Class

Hostellerie du Château Servin, 9 rue Général-Négrier (Tel. 84 21 41 85): 10 rooms in attractive manor house; closed in August.

Middle Range

Les Capucins, 20 faubourg de Montbéliard (Tel. 84 28 04 60): 35 rooms in family-owned hotel.

Middle Range / Economy

Hôtel St-Christophe, Place d'Armes (Tel. 84 28 02 14): 38 rooms in family hotel with view of cathedral. **Hôtel le Turenne**, 1 rue de Turenne (Tel. 84 21 43 60): 39 rooms.

Economy

Hôtel Thiers, 9 rue Thiers (Tel. 84 28 10 24): 16 rooms. **Hôtel le Vauban**, 4 rue du Magasin (Tel. 84 21 59 37): 17 rooms.

Eating Out

First Class

Hostellerie du Château Servin, 9 rue Général-Négrier (Tel. 84 21 41 85): excellent cuisine in lovely setting. **Le Sabot d'Annie**, 5 rue Aristide-Briand, 90300 Offemont (Tel. 84 26 01 71): small, cosy restaurant, a few kilometres out of town.

Middle Range

Le Pot d'Etain, 4 rue de la République, 90400 Danjoutin (Tel. 84 28 31 95): classical cuisine using regional produce, just outside Belfort. **Le Jardin Gourmand**, 33 faubourg des Ancêtres (Tel. 84 28 09 50): good for regional wines and fixed price menus.

Economy

Dame Charlotte, 2 Place de la Grande Fontaine (Tel. 84 28 18 62): good-value meals in pleasant setting. **Hôtel St-Christophe**, Place d'Armes (Tel. 84 28 02 14): hotel-restaurant near cathedral.

Entertainments

Morning markets are held at rue Docteur-Fréry on Wednesday, Friday and Saturday and at ave Jean-Jaurès on Tuesday, Thursday and Sunday. There are regular performances at the theatre (Tel. 84 28 09 98). You could also visit the Planetarium, Cité des Associations, Ave de la Laurencie (Tel. 84 28 10 32), which has shows at 8.30 p.m. on Friday and 3 p.m. on Saturday. Nearby is a tropical aquarium, open in the afternoon except Sunday and Monday. In June, Belfort hosts a festival of European Music. From mid-June to mid-July there are evening performances at the château's *café-théâtre*, and from mid-July to mid-August, concerts are given at the château on Wednesday evenings. Other events are listed in the tourist office leaflet 'Le mois à Belfort'.

Useful Addresses

The **Tourist Office** is at Place de la Commune (Tel. 84 28 12 23). It offers tours of the old town and visits to the cathedral's organ. The **Hospital** is Centre Hôpitalier, 14 rue de Mulhouse (Tel. 84 21 81 33).

Transport Options

It is easy enough to walk round Belfort. The tourist office produces a leaflet called 'Randonnées Pédestres autour de Belfort', which includes a tour of the castle and fortifications, and walks in the countryside. The bus station is on Place Corbis.

Doubs

This *département*, which climbs from Besançon in the north-west towards the lower Jura in the south-east, covers varied terrain, dominated by the attractive valleys of the Doubs and the Loue.

Montbéliard is in an industrial area but is overlooked by the two fifteenth-century towers of its pleasant castle. The town is worth a visit at Christmas time for its extravagant illuminations. At nearby **Sochaux** is the Musée Peugeot, with its collection of Peugeot vehicles, old and new. At **Audincourt** is the Eglise du Sacré Cœur, whose stained-glass windows by Fernand Léger are a fine example of modern sacred art. **Mandeure** is the site of a Gallo-Roman theatre and archaeological exhibition. Near **Maïche**, you will find the Corniche de Goumois, where there is a spectacular cliff road running alongside the Doubs river. Further west is the twelfth-century **Château de Belvoir**, which has some beautiful furniture and seventeenth-century paintings. The *Grotte de la* Glacière near **Chaux-les-Passavant** is a unique cave with astounding stalactites and other bizarre formations; at its Maison des Minéraux, a large number of crystals are displayed. An open-air museum of regional houses can be seen at **Nancray**.

The other side of Besançon, on the edge of the Forêt de Chaux, is the **Grotte d'Osselle**, another beautiful cave. At **Arc-et-Senans**, the royal salt-works has been designated a world heritage site by UNESCO. In 1775, when Claude-Nicolas Ledoux's architectural masterpiece was built, salt was considered 'white gold'. The semi-circular design of the Saline Royale combines the practical and the aesthetic, and it is fascinating to see the exhibition of other plans by Ledoux, most of which were too radical ever to be put into practice. At **Nans-sous-Ste-Anne** is the Taillanderie Philibert, a nineteenth-century tool-cutter's workshop, which has been turned into a working museum and gives a good idea of local industry in the last century. Here you will also find the source of the River

Lison. The **Cléron** area offers much of interest. At La Fromagerie Comtoise, Sa Perin-Vermot, 25330 Cléron (Tel. 81 62 22 70), you can see how Comté cheese is produced and matured. The Château de Cléron is an impressive fourteenth-century fortified castle, built to defend the Salt Road; unfortunately it can be visited only between mid-July and mid-August. There is a réserve naturelle near Cléron, called the Ravin de Valbois, where Mediterranean flora is found. At **Trépot,** on the Place de la Mairie, is a cheese-making museum on the site of a cheese dairy (the local term is *fruitière*) founded in 1818. It is open to the public from 1 July to 15 September. Near **Etalans** is the vast Gouffre de Poudrey cave.

The little town of **Ornans**, on the River Loue, is thought of as the Venice of Franche-Comté and is both attractive and well-situated for excursions. It was the birth-place of nineteenth century painter Gustave Courbet, and his house has been turned into a museum. It is worth visiting La Galerie Comtoise at 30 rue Pierre Vernier, where traditionally made Comtoise clocks are sold. Local crafts such as wooden toys are on sale in the market. Cheese-cellars may be visited, and Ornans is home to the National House of Fishing and Water (36 rue St-Laurent); there are exhibitions and a museum here, on the theme of fishing, water and the environment. Ornans is also the base for Syratu activity tourism (Rte de Montgesoye), which can arrange for you to explore the area by canoe or mountain bike. If this sounds too energetic, get hold of the tourist office's leaflet 'Ornans Loue-Lison', which suggests places to visit along the Loue and Lison valleys. It is certainly worth following the Loue valley to the river's spectacular source. To the north-east, at the **Hameau de Grandfontaine**, near **Orchamps-Vennes**, is the Ferme du Montagnon. Some years ago this 1736 farm received a prize for the best restored rural house in Franche-Comté; it can now be visited and has a museum section as well as a shop selling local produce. The impressive Doubs waterfall is near **Villers-le-Lac**, where there are boat trips on the lake. In the Renaissance-style Château Pertusier at **Morteau** is an interesting clock- and watch-making museum, open from July to September. At **Les Coteys,** near **Gilley,** you can visit the Tuyé de Papy Gaby, a traditional farm with the typical broad chimney used for smoking meats. In July and August, **Montbenoït** Abbey and its decorative cloisters may be viewed. The Château de Joux at **La-Cluse-et-Mijoux,** near **Pontarlier,** dates from the 11th century and contains a museum of eighteenth- and nineteenth-century arms.

To the south are the impressive **St-Point** and **Remoray** lakes. If you are in the area at the end of August, go to **Les-Hôpitaux-Neufs** to see the sheep descend from the pastures. There is an excellent view from the summit of the **Mont d'Or**, which can be reached by foot (GR 5), car or cable-car. The southernmost tip of the Doubs *département* is sparsely populated but near **Chapelle-des-Bois**, at Maison Michaud, La Combe des Cives, is an agricultural museum, open every afternoon except Monday and Saturday.

Accommodation

Quality accommodation at a reasonable price is easy to find. Those seeking self-catering accommodation for a week or more could ask the Ornans tourist office for its list of furnished apartments. The following hotels are recommended:-

First Class

Château de Roche-sur-Loue, 25610 Arc-et-Senans (Tel. 81 57 41 44): 6 *chambres d'hôte* and 1 apartment in eighteenth-century mansion with park, beside Loue river.

Middle Range

Hôtel Taillard, Goumois, 25470 Trevillers (Tel. 81 44 20 75): 16 rooms in family-owned chalet hotel: excellent restaurant. **Hôtel de France**, 51–3 rue Pierre-Vernier, 25290 Ornans (Tel. 81 62 24 44): 31 rooms in family hotel, situated right on the River Loue; restaurant.

Economy

Hôtel de la Truite d'Or, 25930 Lods (Tel. 81 60 95 48): 13 rooms in family hotel, situated between woods and river; good restaurant. **Hôtel de la Poste**, Nans-sous-Ste-Anne, 25330 Amancey (Tel: 81 86 62 57): 11 rooms in family-owned farm-hotel; restaurant.

Eating Out

In addition to the restaurants mentioned above, try the *Middle Range* **Hôtel-Restaurant La Bellevue**, 25160 Malbuisson (Tel. 81 69 30 89), a member of the Tables Gourmandes de Franche-Comté association. Regional specialities are on offer and the owner will give you the names of the other six restaurants in the association. If you

are in Villers-le-Lac, try Mme Dubois' *Economy tables d'hôte*, La
Pierre à Feu (Tel. 81 43 05 41).

Besançon

This charming regional capital has an old town encircled by a river
and overlooked by an impressive citadel. There is a slightly Spanish
feel to the city, harking back to its days as part of the Spanish empire
in the sixteenth century.

A good place to view the town is the **citadel**, built by Vauban in
the seventeenth century, along whose ramparts you can walk, from
the King's Tower to the Queen's Tower. Peacocks and deer roam
in semi-liberty around the vast area enclosed by the fortifications,
where there are also eight museums. These include the **Musée
Populaire Comtois**, where all kinds of regional crafts are on
display; an area devoted to traditional agricultural equipment;
a traditional dairy, which still operates on occasion; a **Natural
History Museum**; and a **Museum of the Resistance**. At the foot
of the citadel is the **Cathédrale St-Jean**. The building is a mixture of
twelfth- and eighteeth-century styles and contains some interesting
paintings and an astronomical clock (try to visit this at 12 or 3 p.m.
when it is striking). Round the corner, on rue de la Convention is
the **Porte Noire**, a second-century Roman Triumphal Arch. Passing
the antique columns of **Square A-Castan**, you will come to **Grande
Rue**, which has been the main thoroughfare of Besançon for 2000
years and much of which is now pedestrianised. Here and in rue des
Martelots, it is worth having a look into the courtyards of the houses
(don't worry, most contain offices and, even if it is a private house,
the owner is unlikely to mind). You will find that there is a distinctly
Spanish feel, with a good deal of wrought-ironwork, and outside
staircases leading to upper storeys, sometimes with sculpted friezes.
Number 140, Grande Rue is where Victor Hugo was born. Do not
miss the **Palais Granvelle**, a beautiful sixteenth-century building,
with courtyard, which houses the **Musée Granvelle**. This offers an
insight into the history of Besançon and its region. The **theatre**,
in rue Megevand, was designed by Ledoux, the eighteenth-century
architect of the Saline Royale at Arc-et-Senans. It is worth making
a detour to see the seventeenth-century **Hôpital St-Jacques**, with
its impressive wrought-iron grill and old pharmacy. Back in the
centre, look out for the **Palais de Justice** (seventeeth-century) and
the **Hôtel de Ville** (sixteenth-century), which is on the town's main

square, **Place du 8 septembre**. Near here is the excellent **Musée des Beaux-Arts**, located in a hall designed by a student of Le Corbusier, which contains works by famous artists (Courbet, Matisse, Goya, Picasso), and a section devoted to watches and clocks. Finally, you should cross the Doubs on the ancient **Pont Battant** into one of the oldest, and liveliest, quarters of Besançon. The city boasts numerous parks in which to relax; for a pleasant stroll, try the **Promenade Micaud**.

Accommodation

All the **First Class** hotels in Besançon belong to large hotel chains. Of these, the best situated is probably **Hôtel Mercure**, 4 ave Carnot (Tel. 81 80 33 11): 67 rooms in old building with views of park. Otherwise try:-

Middle Range

Siatel, 3–5 chemin des Founottes (Tel. 81 80 41 41): 28 rooms in family hotel. **Hôtel des Trois Iles**, rue du Clos, Rochelez-Beaupré, 25220 Besançon-Chalezeule (Tel. 81 61 00 66): 16 rooms in quiet, comfortable hotel, 5 km from town centre.

Middle Range / Economy

Le Franc-Comtois, 24 rue Proudhon (Tel. 81 83 24 35): 22 rooms in town centre hotel. **Hôtel la Granvelle**, 13 rue Général-Lecourbe (Tel. 81 81 33 92): 26 rooms in centrally-placed hotel.

Economy

Hôtel Régina, 91 Grande Rue (Tel. 81 81 50 22): 19 rooms in elegant, centrally-located but quiet hotel. **Hôtel le Vigny**, Morre, 25660 Besançon-Saône (Tel. 81 82 26 12): 8 rooms in family hotel, 5 km from Besançon. **Hôtel le Levant**, 9 rue des Boucheries (Tel. 81 81 07 88): 15 rooms in hotel on pleasant square near river.

Eating Out

First Class Le Chaland, Pont Brégule, Promenade Micaud (Tel. 81 90 61 61): elegant barge-restaurant on Doubs, specialising in sea-food. **Relais de la Moullière**, Parc du Casino, ave Edouard-Droz (Tel. 81 80 61 01): high-quality, good-value restaurant with pleasant terrace.

Middle Range

Barthod Bar à Vins, 25 rue Bersot (Tel. 81 82 27 14): regional produce and wines: central location. **Charlie 1er**, 20 rue de Belfort (Tel. 81 80 50 43): fresh, traditionally caught fish specialities.

Economy

Crocogrill, 77 rue Battant (Tel. 81 83 42 29): rustic-style restaurant where you can grill your own meat at table. **Au Privilège du Roy**, 1 rue de la République (Tel. 81 81 80 91): tea-room offering traditionally made chocolate specialities.

Entertainments

The courtyard of the Palais Granvelle is the venue for free folk dancing and concerts in summer – the tourist office will give you details. In May there is a folklore fair, in June a jazz festival, and in the first half of September an international music festival. Between November and June, numerous plays and concerts are performed.

Useful Addresses

The **Tourist Office** is at 2 place de la 1ère Armée Française, Parc Micaud (Tel. 81 80 92 55). The **Comité Régional du Tourisme**, which can give you information on the whole of Franche-Comté, is at 9 rue de Pontarlier (Tel. 81 83 50 47). The address of the **Loisirs-Accueil Doubs** service, which can arrange holidays and short trips for you in the Doubs *département*, is 15 ave Edouard-Droz (Tel. 81 80 38 18). The **Post Office** is 19 rue Proudhon, and the **Hospital** is 2 Place St-Jacques (Tel. 81 52 33 22). Emergency **medical assistance** can be obtained on 81 52 15 15.

Transport Options

Since much of Besançon is pedestrianised and there are plenty of parks, it is a pleasant town to walk round. The tourist office organises a guided tour of the Battant quarter. Bicycles can be hired at the train station and at **Cycles Robert**, 6 rue de la Préfecture – the tourist office can supply cycle itineraries. There is also an efficient bus system, and a bus tour of the town is run by the tourist office. A mini-train will take you up to the citadel, leaving from the Rivotte car park. Visits of the town by boat, taking you round the edge of the old town, start at Pont de la République, near the tourist office.

Jura

The Jura is a fertile land, with rich brown soil, vineyards, vast forests, stunning gorges and, in the south-east, rugged mountains.

To the south-west of Besançon, between the rivers Doubs and Loue, is the enormous **Forêt de Chaux**, which is an ideal spot for an afternoon stroll. At nearby **Le Deschaux**, on the River Orain, is the eighteeth-century Château de Fabulys. This is a building of local pink stone, situated in an English garden, and the unusual thing about it is that it is inhabited by one hundred life-size automatons. Some of these offer a historically accurate representation of life in the château; some are pure fantasy. The latter will particularly appeal to children but may seem incongruous to less flexible minds! **Salins-les-Bains**, a spa town, used to mine the salt which was transported underground to the royal salt-works at Arc-et-Senans. At Place des Salines, there is a museum on the site of the old salt-works, which was in operation until 1962. It is also worth visiting the Faïencerie at 20 ave Aristide-Briand, where ceramics have been made since 1857; you can watch people at work and visit an exhibition of their products. At **Arbois** there is a shop where you can buy local ceramics at factory prices. Two museums here are worth a visit: the Maison Louis Pasteur, and the Musée de la Vigne et du Vin, which is beneath the Hôtel de Ville. Arbois is the centre of wine production in the Jura and the main producer, Henri Maire, offers free tasting when you visit his cellars. There is a wine festival here in September.

You can view an impressive cave system at **Les-Planches-près-Arbois**, situated at the foot of a 230-metre-high, horseshoe-shaped cliff. Such cliffs are a feature typical of the area and are known as *reculées*. **Poligny** is the capital of Comté cheese production, and the cellars where it matures can be visited. In April there is a wine festival here. At nearby **Molain** is the Grotte des Moidons, another cave. If you are in a car, the minor roads between Poligny and Lons-le-Saunier are well worth exploring. At **Arlay** is an eighteenth-century château in a pre-Romantic park, with a view of medieval ruins. The village of **Château-Chalon** is justifiably proud of the wine it produces. There are spectacular views over the rolling vineyards from here, and in August a *Son et Lumière* takes place. At **Baume-les-Messieurs**, a tiny stream has eroded a vast gorge, with caves and waterfalls, which is the most remarkable example of a *reculée* in the Jura. The village itself is home to an eleventh- to thirteenth-century abbey, but not much else: the younger generation has left this beautiful area, considering it too remote. The most interesting part of the departmental capital, **Lons-le-Saunier**, is the seventeenth-century rue du Commerce. To the east of Lons is Franche-Comté's attractive lake district. At **Marigny**, on the **Lac de Chalain**, are the remains of an important prehistoric city, where there is an exhibition including reconstructions of neolithic huts, which can be visited in the afternoon during July and August. At **Champagnole** you can see the point where the River Ain disappears underground. Try to visit the **Forêt de la Joux** with its reserve of enormous *Président* fir trees. At **Syam** there is an Italian-style villa-château and an exhibition, called 'The Blacksmiths of Syam', in a still-functioning eighteenth-century forge. There is a spectacular series of 28 waterfalls on the river **Hérisson**, just beneath the **Pic de l'Aigle**, which offers a panoramic view of the area.

Bellefontaine, near **Morbier**, is in the north of the Haut-Jura regional park: if you are interested in the local craft of gem-cutting, visit M. Duraffourg's studio. 'La Taillerie'. At **Morez** is a museum devoted to another local trade, spectacle-making. **Les Rousses**, **Lamoura** and **Lajoux** all have various craft studios, with a particular emphasis on woodwork and pottery. The headquarters of the regional park, at Lajoux, is a good source of information on the area. At **Les Moussières** is a cheese-making cooperative, the Maison des Fromages du Haut-Jura. The largest town in the park is **St-Claude**, the pipe-making capital of France. It is well-situated, with a Gothic cathedral and exhibitions on diamond-cutting and, naturally, pipe-making. Sculpted pipes can be purchased from M. Vincent's *atelier*. At **Villards-d'Héria** is Le Pont aux Arches, an important Gallo-Roman site. **Moirans-en-Montagne** specialises in toy-making, and its Maison du Jouet displays many toys, old and new. Wooden dolls are made and sold by Mme Rougemont, whose *atelier* can be visited in July and August. Boat trips are on offer on the long and winding **Lac Vouglans** and there is a fine Romanesque church, to the west, at **Gigny**.

Accommodation & Eating Out

First Class

Moulin de la Mère Michelle, Les Planches, 39600 Arbois (Tel. 84 66 08 17): 10 rooms in restored mill amidst spectacular scenery; good restaurant with wines from own vineyard. **Hôtel de Paris (Jeunet),** 9 rue de l'Hôtel-de-Ville, 39600 Arbois (Tel. 84 66 05 67): 18 rooms in old-fashioned family hotel; excellent traditional restaurant with regional specialities.

Middle Range

Grand Hôtel des Bains, Place des Alliés, 39110 Salins-les-Bains (Tel. 84 37 90 50): 31 comfortable rooms in well-equipped family hotel; excellent restaurant.

Middle Range / Economy

Chalet Bel Air Hôtel, 39330 Mouchard (Tel. 84 37 80 34): 7 rooms in pleasant family hotel; restaurant. **Hôtel du Cheval Rouge,** 47 rue Lecourbe, 39000 Lons-le-Saunier (Tel. 84 47 20 44): 19 rooms in attractive family hotel; restaurant. **Hôtel du Cerf,** Pont-du-Navoy, 39300 Champagnole (Tel. 84 51 20 87): 27 rooms in family hotel in spectacular surroundings on bank of River Ain; restaurant.

Economy

Auberge du Rostaing, Passenans, 39230 Sellières (Tel. 84 85 23 70): 10 rooms in quiet family-owned inn; good restaurant.

Dole

This former capital of Franche-Comté, situated in the region's western plain, enjoyed its golden age during the sixteenth and seventeenth centuries, as part of the Spanish empire.

The best view of Dole can be obtained from the tower of the **Collégiale Notre-Dame,** which dates from the sixteenth century and is the tallest and largest church in Franche-Comté. Don't miss the eighteenth-century sculptured wooden organ. All over Dole are impressive houses, formerly private mansions or convents. Nineteenth-century decorations have usually been stripped off to reveal the original sixteenth- or seventeenth-century facade. Just some of the ones to look out for are: **Hôtel de Vurry,** 7 rue de Besançon (the tallest and oldest – fifteenth century – house in Dole); **Hôtel Champagney,** 20 rue Pasteur (18th century house with beautiful courtyard); **Hôtel Rigollier de Parcey,** 45 rue des Arènes (attractive wrought-ironwork); **Hôtel de Rye,** 40 rue du Gouvernement (sixteenth-century building with Renaissance staircase); and many more on **Rue Mont-Roland,** including number

7 and the **theatre** at number 26. The birthplace of Louis Pasteur (43 rue Pasteur) has been turned into a **museum**. This backs onto the Tanners' Canal from where you can see the remains of the town's sixteenth-century fortifications. The bridges over the **Canal du Rhône au Rhin** and the **Doubs** offer excellent views of the old town. Other buildings which should not be missed are the sixteenth-century Jesuit **Collège de l'Arc** on rue du Collège; the **Palais de Justice** on rue des Arènes; and, on Grande Rue, the former **Hôtel-Dieu** hospital, which dates from the seventeenth century and has an immensely long balcony, some of whose gargoyle-like carvings are modelled on politicians of the time. There is a **Fine Art and Archaeology** museum at 85 rue des Arènes. **Cours St-Mauris**, off Place Grévy, is a pleasant garden with a monument to Pasteur.

Accommodation

There are no top-of-the-range hotels in Dole, but the following are pleasant:-

First Class / Middle Range

Hôtel la Chaumière, 346 ave du Maréchal-Juin (Tel. 84 79 03 45): 18 rooms in charming family-owned hotel, outside town centre.

Middle Range

Hôtel de la Cloche, Place Grévy (Tel. 84 82 00 18): 21 rooms in centrally-located family hotel.

Middle Range / Economy

Le Pourcheresse, 8 ave J-Duhamel (Tel. 84 82 01 05): 21 rooms in family hotel. **Hôtel au Village**, 16 Grande Rue, Brevans (Tel. 84 72 56 40): 14 rooms in family hotel, 2 km from Dole.

Economy

Auberge du Grand Cerf, 6 rue Arney (Tel. 84 72 11 68): 9 rooms in comfortable, central hotel.

Eating Out

First Class

Le Passe Muraille, 2 rue du Prélot (Tel. 84 82 78 21): waterfront hotel with high quality local specialities.

Middle Range

Les Templiers, 35 Grande Rue (Tel. 84 82 78 78): local specialities.
La Romanée, 13 rue des Vieilles-Boucheries (Tel. 84 79 19 05): local
specialities. **Le Grévy**, 2 ave Eisenhower (Tel. 84 82 44 42).

Economy

Le Pourcheresse, 8 ave J-Duhamel (Tel. 84 82 01 05): hotel-
restaurant with good cooking at reasonable price. **La Demi-Lune**,
39 rue Pasteur (Tel. 84 72 65 17): attractive and cheap waterfront
crêperie.

Entertainments

There is a covered market on Place du Marché, which functions
on Tuesday, Thursday and Saturday mornings and sells much
local produce. The tourist office leaflet 'Jura Eté' lists events in
the surrounding area.

Useful Addresses

The **Tourist Office** is at 6 Place Grévy (Tel. 84 72 11 22). The
Post Office is 3 ave Aristide-Briand, and the **Hospital** is on ave
L-Jouhaux (Tel. 84 72 81 21).

Transport Options

The best way to explore is probably on one of the tourist office's
guided tours, which unfortunately are not very frequent. There
are Monts-Jura bus trips into the Jura mountains from 98 bd du
Président-Wilson.

10 Burgundy

Burgundy advertises itself as the red heart of France. At the risk of over-stretching the metaphor, one might suggest that the lifeblood pumped by this particular heart is wine. Burgundy wines have long been praised as 'the best in Christendom' and the region boasts around 100 *Appellation d'Origine Contrôlée* wines – more than the rest of France put together. Many of the vineyards were planted – and owned – by monks, and there is much Cistercian architecture, including wine cellars. Indeed, the houses designed for storing the wine were, in many cases, considered of greater importance than the wine-grower's own living quarters. Immense care is taken of the precious grapes and, in Chablis, braziers are sometimes lit at night to combat spring frosts.

Burgundy was an independent state for 600 years, and protection of the wines goes back to the fourteenth and fifteenth centuries, when the dukes of the region were as powerful as the French monarchy itself. Town names here will undoubtedly sound familiar, for many of them feature on the labels of world-famous wines. The region's wine capital is Beaune, but even the smallest villages have their own variety. And the small-scale wine-growers are a friendly bunch: you will invariably be offered a glass if you visit their *cave* (even at nine in the morning!) and, if you're lucky, you may experience one of the numerous local festivals celebrated to mark some particular stage in the cycle of wine production.

The region is hardly urbanised at all; the only city with more than 100,000 residents is the capital, Dijon, which has a remarkably preserved and extensive old town, and is certainly worth a visit. The vast majority of Burgundy is rural, and the colours of the landscape vary with the seasons in the spectacular way peculiar to vine-growing regions. Gardens exist everywhere – from the parks of old châteaux to the flower-gardens of lock-keepers' cottages, visible only from the canal. One of the best ways of appreciating Burgundy is, in fact, to hire a boat on one of its many navigable waterways. The Saône and the Loire run through Burgundy, which serves as a reservoir for much of France. Of its countless canals, some date back to the seventeenth century. From them, you will be able to see peaceful fields of white Charollais cattle, solid stone farms, Romanesque churches and dilapidated manor houses. On land, exploring the smallest lanes of all will lead you to unexpected finds: a sixteenth-century wayside cross; a monument to Resistance fighters; an ancient dovecote or pigeon-house; a tiny village museum; or a church filled with frescoes. In many parts of the region, time seems to have stood still.

In Burgundy, the traditional way of doing things is almost always considered the best. Organic meat, vegetables and wines, along with cheeses from ancient recipes, are widely available – and not just because they are fashionable. Burgundians care passionately about their food. Meals are long-drawn-out affairs, where conversation is considered one of the foremost *arts de la table*. The inhabitants of Burgundy liken themselves to snails (one of their own regional specialities): they do not like to rush, and tend to retreat into their shell if others try to hurry them; but, with time, this sensitivity gives way to an exceptionally warm hospitality. It has often been said that the Burgundians are the friendliest people in France, though they themselves would never make such a claim. This openness is reflected in their attitude towards tourism: naturally, it is welcomed for its economic benefit, but its potential for creating dialogue is also stressed. Far too many people speed through Burgundy on their way south, failing to see that it is the perfect place to linger.

History

Flints attest to human presence in Burgundy since around 1,000,000 BC and, at Azé, caves may be visited which were inhabited perhaps as far back as 300,000 BC. Burgundy has long been a meeting place of Mediterranean and northern civilisations, and Caesar established himself here in the course of the first century BC. The town of Augustodunum (later to become Autun) was then founded and made the capital of north-eastern Gaul. A period of peace and prosperity lasted until the late fourth century AD, when invasions began. The Burgundians from the Baltic coast settled in the area and gave it its name in the fifth century, but the Franks seized the land from them in AD 534. The borders changed considerably during the following centuries and a hereditary Dukedom of Burgundy was created in 1031.

Burgundy became a centre of Christianity and many influential Cistercian abbeys and monasteries were built. The Golden Age for the Duchy of Burgundy was under the four Valois dukes, between 1364 and 1477. By the end of this period, the dukes also owned much of Franche-Comté, Alsace, Lorraine, Picardy, Flanders, Luxembourg, Belgium and Holland. On the death of Charles the Bold, however, the region was split between the French crown and the Hapsburg empire, with the French portion increasing in size in the seventeenth century. The Duchy continued to enjoy considerable independence throughout this period. During the Second World War, the Resistance was particularly active here.

Famous Burgundians include the seventeenth-century intellectual Bossuet; Vauban, the defender and fortifier of hundreds of French towns; the eighteenth-century novelist, Réstif de la Bretonne; Lamartine, politician and major Romantic poet, whose recent bicentenary was the cause for elaborate celebrations; Nicéphore Niepce, who invented photography in 1822; the nineteenth-century writers, Romain Rolland and Colette; and Canon Kir, mayor of Dijon after the Second World War, who gave his name to the drink made with white wine and cassis.

Geography

Burgundy is a fairly large region to the east of the area described as Central France. It is bordered by the Ile-de-France and Champagne to the north; Franche-Comté to the east; the Rhône Valley to the south; and the Auvergne and Centre Val de Loire to the west. Four *départements* constitute Burgundy: the Yonne in the north-west, beneath which comes the Nièvre, with the Côte d'Or in the east and the Saône-et-Loire in the south. The regional capital is Dijon, which has 146,000 inhabitants and is situated in the Côte d'Or. The other departmental capitals are Auxerre (41,000 – Yonne), Nevers (45,000 – Nièvre), and Mâcon (39,000 – Saône-et-Loire), though the town of Chalon-sur-Sâone is larger than any of these, with a population of 58,000. Burgundy as a whole is sparsely populated, with an average of 50 inhabitants per square kilometre (the French average is 100).

Burgundy is not an area with distinct geographical boundaries and it has few unifying features. Landscapes range from hills and massifs in the south to high limestone plateaus in the centre and plains linked to the Paris basin in the north. What these areas do have in common is water. The Loire flows along Burgundy's western edge, the Saône along its eastern edge, the Rhône to its south and the Seine to its north. Numerous smaller rivers take their source here, making Burgundy into a kind of water tower for France. In addition, there are 1000 km of navigable canals, which have considerable tourism potential because they run through such varied countryside and vegetation. The most prominent type of farming in Burgundy is cattle, usually of the highly regarded Charollais breed (the equivalent of our Aberdeen Angus), of which there are 200,000 in the region. Much of Burgundy is afforested, especially in the Morvan, with timber playing a considerable role in the economy; crops, such as cereals and sugar-beet, are also grown, particularly in the south.

Although the region's vineyards are so important, they tend to occur only in small patches. Burgundy is fortunate enough to be situated at the northern limit for the production of red wines to lay down, and at the southern limit for fruity white wines. The main factors on which wine production depends are the grape variety, soil type and climate. All the great red Burgundies come from the Pinot Noir grape, and the whites usually come from the Chardonnay, though the Aligoté and Gamay are also grown. The best-known vine-growing areas are Chablis, Auxerre, Pouilly-sur-Loire, the Côte de Nuits, the Côte de Beaune, Mercurey and the Mâconnais.

Burgundy's one regional park is the Parc Naturel Régional du Morvan, which covers areas in all four *départements* (administration is consequently rather difficult), and forms an island of granite in Burgundy's limestone environment, having detached itself from the Massif Central. It rises to a height of 900 metres and is a predominantly wild area, with rivers, lakes and rounded tree-covered hills. It was given regional park status in 1970 and current projects include the protection of medicinal plants, the re-introduction of crayfish, and maintaining the diversity of tree species. Foxgloves, broom and bog-myrtle are found throughout the park. The creation of the *réserve naturelle* of La Truchère, among the dunes of Pont Seille, halted plans for a housing estate, and now offers a good habitat for nesting birds, rabbits, green lizards and various mosses and lichens. Several other ecologically valuable sites are managed by the **Conservatoire des Sites Bourguignons**: a pond at Villers-Rottin; two marshes (at Recey-sur-Ource and Le Conois) in the Châtillonais area, where mountainous flora can be found in low-level peat-bogs; and a lake at Bas-Rebourseaux, which welcomes nesting birds. Mediterranean vegetation grows in the Bois du Parc reserve at Mailly-le-Château. Some areas in the Saône and Doubs valleys are threatened by developments on the rivers, but the **Conservatoire** has plans to protect them.

Climate

Burgundy is situated in the temperate zone, whose weather is typically western European. Average temperatures range from around 5.9°C in February to 26.1°C in August. Winters are cold, sometimes frosty; autumn is a good time to visit, with pleasant, sunny weather and spectacular colours; summer can be extremely hot, though occasionally there are showers. Variations occur in the Saône-et-Loire, which displays southern tendencies, and in the Morvan, where there is a mountain climate above 600 metres.

Attractions

For most visitors to Burgundy, the region's appeal is associated with its unspoilt environment and countryside, the fame of its wines and cuisine, and its excellent cultural heritage. Burgundy is, indeed, one of the top French regions for classified monuments and sites. Two of its finest monuments, the Cistercian Abbey at Fontenay and the Romanesque Basilica at Vézelay, have been declared UNESCO world heritage sites. The Saône-et-Loire *département* has an unparalleled collection of Romanesque architecture, whose four great centres are Cluny, Tournus, Paray-le-Monial and Autun. Burgundy's Cistercian architecture includes wine cellars such as the famous Clos de Vougeot, belonging to the Abbey of Cîteaux. Old wine presses can also be visited. Auxerre boasts the earliest known French frescoes, which are to be found in St-Germain Abbey and date from the ninth century.

Reminders of even earlier periods are in evidence at numerous archaeological sites. Autun used to rival Rome in splendour and has the remains of the largest theatre in Roman Gaul. Prehistoric items are on display in a museum at the foot of Solutré hill, which has now become a place of pilgrimage, not for its importance in ancient times, but because President Mitterand and his wife come to climb it every Easter Sunday.

Natural phenomena which attract visitors are the caves and

grottoes which can be found in various parts of the region, and the spas at Maizières, Santenay, St-Honoré-les-Bains and Bourbon-Lancy. Most visitors take an interest in everything connected with the great Burgundy wines, especially the vineyards themselves. There are also wine museums and cellars to be visited, as well as numerous wines to be sampled. The biggest charity sale in the world takes place on the third weekend in November, when the Hospices de Beaune (the largest vineyard in the region) auctions off its fine wines by candlelight, according to a tradition started in 1859. This is used as an excuse for a major festival – as is almost any event in Burgundy. The Chalon-sur-Saône carnival is said to be the friendliest one in France. Burgundy is also home to the oldest horse-race in France, which takes place at Semuren-Auxois. Traditional crafts such as wood-carving, carpentry and pottery are still widely practised; over two thousand potters are employed in the Saône-et-Loire alone. Many small museums bear witness to former local industries, such as crystal-cutting and coal-mining. Old canal-side villages are now being given a new lease of life through river tourism, which is one of Burgundy's greatest assets.

Different people come to Burgundy for different reasons. A recent survey reveals that the British place the countryside top of the list, while the Germans particularly admire the cultural heritage. The French themselves, however, admit candidly that they come to Burgundy for its wines and its gastronomy, which is, at times, almost synonymous with French *haute cuisine*.

Cuisine

The raw materials for most Burgundian cooking come from within its own borders. Its beef, game, poultry, fish, snails, vegetables and fruits are all staple ingredients; so are its wines. Many traditional dishes involve high-quality wines, which necessarily entail high prices. Specialities using wine sauces include *œufs en meurette* (a poached egg dish); *bœuf bourguignon* (beef casserole); *pauchouse* (freshwater fish stew); and *saupiquet* (ham in wine and cream sauce). Other traditional foods are *gougères* (cheese ramekins), *andouillette* sausages, Burgundy vine snails (now reared commercially), and Bresse chicken – the only poultry in the world to be subject to an *Appellation d'Origine Contrôlée*. In order to qualify, the birds must be raised in liberty (i.e. with at least ten square metres of grass each) and fed on white cornmeal, brown wheat and milk. *Fondue bourguignonne* is an imposter, as it originated, fairly recently, in Switzerland. Dijon produces 80% of all French mustard; it is used in the preparation on many dishes and true Dijon mustard should be made with white wine, not vinegar.

Though not famous for its cheeses, Burgundy has many delicious varieties. The best known are the Bouton de Culotte goat's cheese from Mâcon; Crottin de Chavignon goat's cheese; and the cheeses of Cîteaux, Epoisses, La Pierre-qui-vire, and Soumaintrain. Yonne produces excellent cherries, and blackcurrants and raspberries grow in the Hautes-Côtes. Numerous irresistible sweets, biscuits and desserts exists. Dijon makes very special gingerbread, which should be rockhard and is said to be so nutritious that it was used as military rations for the warriors of Genghis Khan! Chablis is known for its meringues, and Nevers for its chocolate caramel Négus. Look out also for *clafoutis*, a blackcurrant and cherry flan, and for *poire belle dijonnaise*, a pear poached in vanilla syrup with raspberry purée, blackcurrant ice-cream and grilled almonds.

Anyone who enjoys wine will be in their element here. It is worth trying wines you have not heard of as well as those you have, as it is not rare to discover a real gem at quite a modest price. As a general rule, the great red Burgundies go well with game, meats in sauce and cheeses which are not too strong; the great white Burgundies should accompany fish and shellfish in sauce, light charcuterie and foie gras, poultry and white meat. In recent years, the white wines from Buxy and Montagny have been particularly successful. If you are thinking of taking wine back home, ask local people which *viticulteur* they buy their wine from: that is the very best recommendation. The centre for the sparkling wine known as Crémant de Bourgogne is Rully. The increasingly popular *apéritif*, Kir, is named after a mayor of Dijon, and the real stuff (rarely served outside Burgundy) is made with one measure of Crème de Cassis de Dijon and two measures of dry white Burgundy Aligoté wine.

Level of Tourism

Burgundy comes about half way down the league table of French touristic regions, but it tends to host a particular type of tourism. A high proportion (40%) of its tourists come from abroad, but the vast majority dash through Burgundy on their way south and the average length of stay is consequently the shortest in France. Because of Burgundy's proximity to Paris there are a large number of second homes in the region (in the Yonne *département*, second homes account for almost 20% of houses and flats). Although tourist accommodation in Burgundy is relatively sparse (if you exclude second homes), and relatively small-scale (the average hotel size is twenty rooms), there are some anomalies. At the village of Taizé, an important ecumenical centre, 1520 visitors can be received at any one time – outnumbering local people by ten to one. Burgundy at present suffers from an uneven spread of tourism. There is a 'tourist axis' running down the right hand side of the region, along the *autoroute du soleil*, which passes through Dijon, Beaune, Chalon, Tournus and Mâcon, and most people stick to the sights on and around this, causing a certain amount of overcrowding in summer; on the other hand, too few tourists venture away from the axis, making the creation of better facilities uneconomical. The tourist board is keen to encourage people to be more imaginative in their touring of the region, as many lesser known areas could benefit considerably from tourism.

The foreign tourists who visit Burgundy come mainly from Germany and Britain. Indeed, it is one of the favourite French destinations of British tourists. Other keen visitors are from Belgium, Luxembourg, Holland, Italy and North America. Almost half of all foreign visitors head for the Côte d'Or *département*. In general, visitors to Burgundy tend to be relatively well-off and in the 30 to 40 age-range and above. The present clientèle is very loyal and appreciates high-quality accommodation, wine, gastronomy and exclusive activities such as excursions by hot-air balloon. The tourist board is now trying to attract a new, younger clientèle with more accessible activities like river tourism and camping. It is also seeking to persuade people to stay longer than a couple of nights – a sensible idea, as Burgundy can be infinitely better appreciated if you take time over your visit. The majority of *gîte* accommodation is to be found in the Saône-et-Loire (the Germans' favourite *département*), where there are also some charming *chambres d'hôte*. If you'd like to avoid the crowds (which are, in any case, minimal away from the tourist axis), bear in mind that most individuals come in July and August, and most groups in September and October.

Facilities are usually small-scale and cater for the individual tourist rather than the group, though the tourist board is trying, by improving and expanding facilities, to increase tourism's role in the local economy. In the Nièvre, fishing is often proposed as a tourist activity and, in the Yonne, the same is true of hunting. Some villages which might otherwise die out are offered hope through tourism; many canal-side communities have already been rescued. Initial difficulties of coordination between the installations of dying industries and those of small-scale river tourism have, for the most part, been overcome. As a result, you can enjoy an unusual kind of boating holiday, which brings you exceptionally close to local people and the countryside. Various sensitive areas, both along canals and elsewhere, deserve more protection than they are currently receiving. Even the La Truchère Natural Reserve suffers from litter and the use of too many trail bikes.

On the whole, local people have a high environmental awareness. In Saône-et-Loire, there was a campaign to persuade the electricity board to lay its power cables underground, rather than in pylon form. The owner of the Château des Nobles and its surrounding vineyards at La-Chapelle-sous-Brancion is using the profits from the sale of his wines to restore parts of the building; a similar policy is followed by nuns at the thirteenth-century priory of Val-St-Benoît, who sell their home-made blue pottery to help restoration work. There is encouragement of traditional carpentry and building methods, so that restoration can be carried out in an authentic manner by local people, but unfortunately some old buildings are falling into disrepair through lack of funds.

Environmental consciousness on the part of the local government is fairly good. The current mayor of Dijon used to be Minister for the Environment under Pompidou, and he is responsible for the creation of many green spaces and pedestrian zones in Dijon, where there is now far less pollution than there was ten years ago. Auxerre's old town has been declared a 'conservation sector', and those wishing to visit the medieval hill-top village of Brancion have to park their cars at the bottom of the hill and walk up. One rather canny move by local authorities was the deliberate creation of a tourist trap. Apparently the town of Berzé-le-Châtel was in a bad way economically, so a marked tourist route which passed close to it was diverted to include Berzé and generate income for it. The joke is that countless people stop here simply because it is marked as a tourist attraction and rarely even notice that there is very little to see!

Good Alternatives

Meeting People

Tourist offices will give you lists of local festivals and you will find details of village fêtes posted in grocers' shops during summer. If you would like to take part in a conservation *chantier* contact Marc Borrel, who works for the **Conservatoire des Sites Bourguignons**, Maison du Parc Naturel Régional du Morvan, St-Brisson, 58230 Montsauche (Tel. 85 30 67 04). Volunteers are also welcome on many archaeological digs in the region. For digs situated in the regional park, contact the **Maison du Parc Naturel Régional du Morvan** (address as above, but different telephone: 86 78 70 16). Information on workcamps (mostly in summer) on archaeological and other cultural sites throughout Burgundy can be obtained from the **Direction Régionale des Affaires Culturelles**, 39 rue Vannerie, 21000 Dijon (Tel. 80 67 22 33 or 80 67 17 67).

If you are in Dijon, the agency known as **Bourgogne Tour Incoming** (14 rue du Chapeau Rouge, 21000 Dijon, Tel. 80 30 49 49) offers an unusual insight into Burgundian cuisine: you can accompany the well-known chef, Jean-Pierre Billoux, when he goes shopping in the morning market, watch him at work and then sample his specialities. Gastronomic weekends in Sens and Joigny are arranged by **Jovitour**, 10 quai Leclerc, 89300 Joigny (Tel. 86 62 16 31). For more active appreciation of exactly what goes into a Burgundian meal, you could attend one of the cookery courses at **'Chez Camille'**, 21230 Arnay-le-Duc (Tel. 80 90 01 38). If you really want to impress your Burgundian hosts (who already consider the British second only to the French in their knowledge of wines), take one of the wine-tasting courses organised by the **Bureau Interprofessionel des Vins de Bourgogne**, which has bases both at 12 bd Bretonnière, 21200 Beaune (Tel. 80 22 21 35) and at 329 ave de Lattre de Tassigny, 71000 Mâcon (Tel. 85 38 20 15). This association also offers courses on vineyard techniques (English is spoken on both types of course), and will supply brochures on all aspects of wine production and consumption. Visits to local wine producers are an essential element of any trip to Burgundy and you will find various recommendations in the **Geographical Breakdown** sections. In addition, the towns of Dijon, Beaune, Pouilly-sur-Loire, Chalon-sur-Saône, Mâcon and Nuits-St-Georges all have **Maisons du Vin**, which will provide lists of local producers.

Detailed information about wine-drinking brotherhoods (such as the **Confrérie des Chevaliers du Tastevin** at Clos de Vougeot château), who allow visitors to attend their initiation ceremonies, is available from the appropriate **Comité Départemental du Tourisme** (CDT), whose addresses are as follows: **CDT de l'Yonne**, Maison Départementale du Tourisme, 1–2 quai de la République, 89000 Auxerre (Tel. 86 52 26 27); **CDT de la Nièvre**, 3 rue du Sort, 58000 Nevers (Tel. 80 36 39 80); **CDT de Saône-et-Loire**, 389 ave Mal-de-Lattre-de-Tassigny, 71000 Mâcon (Tel. 85 39 47 47); and **CDT de Côte d'Or**. Hôtel du Département, BP 1601, 21035 Dijon (postal address), or 14 rue de la Préfecture, 21000 Dijon (Tel. 80 63 66 00 – headquarters). These departmental tourist boards will supply information on most aspects of their particular *département*.

Discovering Places

Those exploring the south of Burgundy by car could use the *Route des Vins Mâconnais Beaujolais*, which passes about fifty Romanesque churches and various châteaux, museums, inns and cellars – simply follow the Suivez la Grappe signs. More detailed information about the route and its places of interest are available from **Mâconnais–Tourisme**, Syndicat d'Initiative de la Route des Vins, 71960 Solutré-Pouilly (Tel. 85 35 81 00); do not, however, stick rigidly to the marked route as the most authentic Burgundian experiences usually occur when you are irretrievably lost on some country lane! A summarised description of an 11-day walking tour (the 'Tour de Puisaye') in northern Burgundy is available from the CDT Yonne (address above). Organised hikes and nature discovery sessions (with luggage transfer and guide if desired) are arranged by **'La Peurtantaine'**, Accueil Morvan Environnement, Ecole du Bourg, 71550 Anost (Tel. 85 82 77 74). For hiking tours in the Cluny area, contact **'La Billebaude'**, Les Bois-de-Vaux, 71220 Suin (Tel. 85 24 76 59). A five-day bicycle tour (which can also be made on foot, horseback or in a horse and cart) in the 'footsteps of the Gauls', between the two Gallo-Roman settlements of Alésia and Bibracte, is organised each summer by **'Les Quatre Chemins'**, 25 rue aux Raz, 71400 Autun (Tel. 85 52 07 91). This association also runs nature discovery sessions.

Horse-riding and horse-drawn caravans are popular in Burgundy. (For addresses providing information on riding excursions and holidays, see Riding section of **Communications**.) Wine tours by horse-drawn carriage, through Beaune and the surrounding vineyards, are arranged by **Ferme de Cussigny**, Corgoloin, 21700 Nuits-St-Georges (Tel. 80 62 97 23). The Morvan regional park can be discovered in a horse and cart through '**A Hue et à Dia**', Sommant, 71540 Lucenay-l'Evêque (Tel. 85 82 66 48). The **Ferme Equestre d'Allye**, 71540 Cussy-en-Morvan (Tel. 85 82 69 12) offers treks with covered wagons, and the **Roulottes en Morvan**, BP 21, 89450 Vézelay (Tel. 86 33 25 77) rents out horse-drawn caravans and does day tours in the Vézelay area. Fully equipped houseboats can be hired for a weekend or longer from various companies (for addresses, see Boat section of **Communications**). Luxury trips on cruise barges are run by **Aquarelle**, Port de Plaisance, quai St-Martin, 89000 Auxerre (Tel. 86 46 96 77); **Carportas SARL**, Villeneuve-sous-Charigny, 21140 Semur-en-Auxois (Tel. 80 97 21 27); and **Duc de Bourgogne** (Mme Benoit), Chemin de Halage, 21370 Plombières-lès-Dijon (Tel. 80 33 66 49). Such cruises can also be booked through **Abercrombie and Kent Ltd**, Sloane Square, Holbein Place, London SW1 W8NS (Tel. 071 730 9600). For those with exclusive tastes, short breaks which include gourmet meals and a hot-air balloon flight are organised by **Air Escargot**, Remigny, 71150 Chagny (Tel. 85 87 12 30).

Guided visits of ornithological sites on the banks of the Loire and botanical sites in Nièvre are arranged by the **Conservatoire des Sites Bourguignons**, through J-L Clavier, 8 rue de la Croix Morin, 58000 Marzy (Tel. 86 59 51 03). Discovery circuits which take in traditional local industries are suggested by the **Association Communautaire de Développement du Tourisme Industriel**, Château de la Verrerie, BP 148, 71204 Le Creusot (Tel. 85 80 40 90). For information on different discovery circuits, excursions by steam train or boat, and numerous other holidays, contact **L'UNAT Bourgogne**, 1 bd Champollion, 21000 Dijon (Tel. 80 71 32 12) – an association made up of a group of local tour operators. Holidays for young people, including lan- guage courses, day-trips and sporting activities, are organised by the **Centre de Rencontres Internationales** (CRISD), which operates from a Dijon Youth Hostel (same address as L'UNAT Bourgogne). The **Service Réservation Loisirs-Accueil de la Nièvre**, 3 rue du Sort, 58000 Nevers (Tel. 86 59 14 22) offers many activity holidays, and is especially good on watersports, as is **Olympique Auxerrois**, ave Hyver Prolongée, 89000 Auxerre (Tel. 86 52 13 86). A wide range of locally-run holidays is also offered by the **Service Réservation Loisirs-Accueil de** l'Yonne, 1–2 quai de la République, 89000 Auxerre (Tel. 86 51 12 05).

Communications

How to Get There

Flights to Dijon-Bourgogne airport (Tel. 80 67 67 67) are via Paris, where there are three connections daily to Dijon. Direct flights from British airports are available to Lyon, Geneva and Basle-Mulhouse airports, which are all close to Burgundy.

Burgundy boasts two TGV stations (Le Creusot and Mâcon-Loché), where most of the high-speed TGV **trains** travelling between Paris and other major cities (e.g. Lyon) will stop. Le Creusot is only 1 hr 20 mins from Paris by TGV. TGV trains from Paris can also take you to Dijon (1 hr 40 mins), Montbard, Beaune and Chlon-sur-Saône. When not travelling by TGV, the Paris-Dijon journey takes 3 hrs 45 mins. There is also a direct liaison down the western side of Burgundy, between Paris and Nevers.

Eurolines operates a **coach** service between London and Dijon for around £75 adult return. The A 6 motorway means that you can reach Beaune from Paris in under 3¹/2 hours by car.

When You're There

Rail – the rail network within Burgundy is exceedingly comprehensive along the main north-south axis of communication (i.e. Sens, Auxerre, Montbard, Dijon, Beaune, Chagny, Chalon-sur-Saône, Mâcon), but more erratic elsewhere. It takes almost three hours to make the east-west journey between Dijon and Nevers, and it is impossible to manage a trip from Dijon to Vézelay and back in one day, as it involves both train and bus journeys. This is one more reason to allow plenty of time for your visit to Burgundy – unless you are content to stick to the over-frequented sites on the tourist axis, that is. Steam train excursions between Dijon and Bligny-sur-Ouche are organised by the **Association du Rail de la Vallée de l'Ouche**, 3 rue Lamartine, 21000 Dijon (Tel. 80 42 07 38). Other scenic railways exist at Massangis and in the Puisaye area (Yonne); between Cercy-la-Tour and Clamecy (Nièvre); and at Plombières-lès-Dijon and Is-sur-Tille (Côte d'Or).

Bus – buses run somewhat infrequently, but connect main towns like Chalon and Mâcon to Cluny, Taizé, Cormatin and Beaune.

From Auxerre, buses run to Avallon and Vézelay; and from Dijon, you can travel to Semur-en-Auxois, Autun, Saulieu, Avallon and Gevrey-Chambertin. A particularly scenic ride is from Dijon, along the *Route du Vin*, to Beaune and Nuits-St-Georges.

Car – as previously explained, the notorious 'autoroute du soleil' (A 6) runs straight through Burgundy, with major exits at Auxerre, Avallon, Pouilly-en-Auxois, Dijon, Beaune, Chalon-sur-Saône, Tournus and Mâcon. This should be avoided in July and August, though it makes a convenient way of getting to the region fast. Once there, make use of the minor roads which are delightful. There is no motorway at all in Nièvre or western Saône-et-Loire, but N roads and D roads make for easy, relatively traffic-free, and much more pleasant connections.

Boat – there are over 1000 km of navigable waterway (both river and canal) in Burgundy, most of which are clear of commercial craft and perfect for leisurely cruising. Boats can be hired in many waterside towns and villages. Fully-equipped houseboats can be hired for a weekend or longer from **Bourgogne Voies Navigables**, 1–2 quai de la République, 89000 Auxerre (Tel. 86 51 12 05); **Locaboat Plaisance**, quai-du-Port-au-Bois, 89300 Joigny (Tel. 86 91 72 72); and **Blue Line Bourgogne**, La Gare d'Eau, St-Usage, 21170 St-Jean-de-Losne (Tel. 80 29 12 86). If you wish to hire a boat for one day only, try **Locadif**, Gissey-sur-Ouche, 21410 Pont-de-Pany (Tel. 80 49 04 76). Mâcon and Digoin are also boat-hire centres. For the addresses of companies offering luxury trips on cruise barges, see **Good Alternatives** section. For less exclusive boat trips, **Au Fil de l'Eau**, Les Tilleuls, Merry-sur-Yonne, 89660 Châtel-Censoir (Tel. 86 42 52 92).

Cycling – cycling round Burgundy's numerous country lanes is an ideal way of discovering the region, and recommended cycle tours are decribed in leaflets available on request from the **Comité Régional du Tourisme**, Conseil Régional, BP 1602, 21035 Dijon (Tel. 80 50 10 20). Bicycles can be hired from many SNCF stations and other outlets. Information on cycle itineraries in the Côte d'Or is available from the **Comité Départemental de Cyclotourisme**, 45 B rue du Tire-Pesseau, 21000 Dijon. See also **Good Alternatives** section.

Walking – various *Grande Randonnée* footpaths cross the region, notably GR 13, which runs from north to south through the Morvan regional park. There are many local footpaths between villages, through vineyards, fields and forests. In the Côte d'Or alone, there are 700 kilometres of hiking trails, and information on eight recommended tours is available from the **Comité Départemental du Tourisme**, Hôtel du Département, BP 1601, 21035 Dijon (Tel. 80 63 66 00). Further details, including maps and notification of group walks, from the **Club Alpin Français**, 34 rue des Forges, 21000 Dijon. For companies offering organised walks and tours, see **Good Alternatives**.

Riding – information on horse riding in Burgundy is available from the **Association Bourguignonne d'Equitation de Loisirs** (ABEL), M. Fourneau, Corlay, 71240 Sennecey-le-Grand (Tel. 85 92 22 94 or 86 20 18 85); and the **Association Régionale de Tourisme Equestre** (ARTE), M. Ramillon, Château de Lantilly, 58800 Corbigny (Tel. 86 20 18 85). For addresses of companies running horse-drawn caravan excursions, see **Good Alternatives**.

Useful Local Contacts

The **Conservatoire Régional des Sites Bourguignons** manages various sites of ecological interest and organises some working parties and guided tours. Its secretariat is BP 2706, 21058 Dijon (Tel. 80 46 69 39), but its headquarters are at the **Parc Naturel Régional du Morvan**, St-Brisson, 58230 Montsauche. The regional park itself will provide information on local environmental issues and the **Maison du Parc** can be contacted at the above address (Tel. 86 78 70 16). Another useful organisation for information on the regional architecture and environment is the **Délégation Régionale à l'Architecture et à l'Environnement** (DRAE), Cité Administrative Dampierre, 6 rue Chancellier de l'Hôpital, 21037 Dijon. An association involved in work on various green issues is **COPRONAT**, rue des Champs Prévois, INSA, 21000 Dijon.

Geographical Breakdown of Region

Yonne and Nievre

The quiet Yonne is a favourite weekend retreat for Parisians but, in late July and August, the areas around the 'autoroute du soleil' can become crowded. The River Loire marks the western boundary of the Nièvre, through which passes the attractive Canal du Nivernais.

Auxerre, capital of Yonne, is a charming medieval town, which overlooks the Yonne river and is situated in the heart of a wine-producing area whose most distinguished ambassador is Chablis. The crypt of

St-Germain Abbey is a rare example of Carolingian architecture, parts of which (the central sanctuary and two lateral naves) were built in the fifth and sixth centuries. You will also find the oldest (ninth century) frescoes in France, depicting the martyrdom of St Stephen, in this unusual building, which is separated from its own Romanesque bell-tower. The Gothic **St-Etienne Cathedral** has some impressive thirteenth- and sixteenth-century stained-glass windows and an eleventh-century crypt, where you can see a unique fresco of Christ on horseback. It is also worth visiting **St-Eusèbe** church, with its twelfth-century tower and fifteenth-century spire. There are some fine medieval half-timbered houses in the centre of Auxerre, which has been declared a 'conservation sector'. **Place de l'Hôtel de Ville** and **Place Charles-Surugue** are particularly attractive. The oldest house in the town is at **5 place Robillard**; it dates from the fourteenth and fifteenth centuries. Temporary art and history exhibitions are held at **3 place du Coche-d'Eau**. The **Art and History Museum**, which includes a Gallo-Roman section, is housed in the conventual buildings of the abbey. The **Leblanc-Duvernoy Museum**, containing impressive Beauvais tapestries, local pottery and paintings, and the **Natural History Museum**, set in its own botanical garden, are also interesting. There are good views of the town from its bridges.

Accommodation

There are no unambiguously first-class hotels in Auxerre. Instead try:

First Class / Middle Range

Hôtel le Maxime, 2 quai de la Marine (Tel. 86 52 14 19): 25 rooms in riverfront hotel.

Middle Range

Péniche l'Anadonta, Maïté et Lobo Britos, quai de la République (Tel. 86 51 58 79): floating *chambres d'hôte*, in barge.

Middle Range / Economy

Le Parc des Maréchaux, 6 ave Foch (Tel. 86 51 43 77): 24 rooms in comfortable townhouse with friendly owners. **Hôtel de Seignelay**, 2 rue du Pont (Tel. 86 52 03 48): 21 rooms in family-run hotel; restaurant.

Economy

Hôtel de la Porte de Paris, 5 rue St-Germain (Tel. 86 46 90 09): 11 rooms in popular hotel on edge of old town. **Hôtel St-Martin**, 9 rue Germain-Bénard (Tel. 86 52 04 16): 10 rooms.

Eating Out

First Class

La Petite Auberge, 2 Place du Passeur, 89290 Vaux (Tel. 86 53 80 08): charming restaurant on banks of Yonne, 4 km from Auxerre.

First Class / Middle Range

Le Jardin Gourmand, 56 bd Vauban (Tel. 86 51 53 52): simple restaurant with delicious cuisine. **Restaurant le Maxime**, 5 quai de la Marine (Tel. 86 52 04 41): high-quality cuisine in pleasant setting.

Middle Range

Salamandre, 84 rue Paris (Tel. 86 52 87 87): excellent restaurant serving seafood specialities.

Economy

Restaurant l'Ancien Chai, 12 rue de la Fraternité (Tel. 86 52 99 62): good value fixed price menus.

Entertainments

On Tuesday, Friday and Saturday mornings, a market is held in Place de l'Arquelouse; the Sunday market is in Place Degas. Simply walking along the quays, watching the lively harbour, can be fascinating.

Useful Addresses

The **Tourist Office** is at 1–2 quai de la République (Tel. 86 52 06 19). At the same address, you will find the **Comité Départemental du Tourisme de l'Yonne** (Tel. 86 52 26 67 – information on Yonne area), and the **Service Réservation Loisirs-Accueil de l'Yonne** (Tel. 86 51 68 47 – local excursions and holidays). There is another branch of the tourist office at 16 Place des Cordeliers (Tel. 86 51 10 27). The **Bureau d'Information Jeunesse de l'Yonne** (BIJY), 70 rue du Pont (Tel. 86 51 68 75) gives much information on the area, including how to join an archaelogical dig. It also has a list of farmers who sell fresh produce and welcome campers. The **Post Office** is at Place Charles-Surugue, and the **Hospital** is on boulevard de Verdun (Tel. 86 46 07 09). For emergency **medical assistance**, call SMUR on 86 46 45 67.

Transport Options

Auxerre is a pleasant town to explore on foot. Bicycles can be hired from the SNCF station, and the bus station is in Place Migraines. You can hire your own house-boat to explore the area's canals from **Bourgogne Voies Navigables**, 1–2 quai de la République (Tel. 86 51 12 05). Alternatively, luxury cruises on barge-hotels are offered by **Aquarelle**, port de Plaisance, quai St-Martin (Tel. 86 46 96 77).

Rest of Yonne and Nièvre

At Sens, a town with many sixteenth- and seventeenth-century houses, you will find the earliest of France's great Gothic cathedrals, St-Etienne, begun around 1130 and allegedly the model for Canterbury cathedral. If you are in the area at harvest time, it is worth visiting the village of **Etigny**, on the River Yonne, for its festival. **Joigny** is another charming riverbank town, where boats may be hired, and just south, at **Laduz**, there is a good arts and crafts museum. In the very west of the region, the town of **Rogny-les-Sept-Ecluses**, situated on the River Briare, puts on an impressive firework display above its series of locks in August. Summer brings a 1½ hour historical pageant to **St-Fargeau**, performed by 600 of the town's inhabitants at the château; ask any local tourist office for the exact dates. Nearby is the **Boutissaint** deer park.

Over in the Nièvre, at **Clamecy**, the River Yonne and the Canal du Nivernais run parallel and there is a water jousting festival on 14 July. On a different river, the town of **Cosne-sur-Loire** has a fine museum of popular arts (the Musée de la Loire Nivernaise). Another good museum is the municipal one in the outlying village of **Cours**: housed in a historical building on Place de la Résistance, it contains countless objects associated with the Loire river and an art collection that includes works by Chagall and Dufy. At **Pouilly-sur-Loire**, you can go to the Cave Coopérative (Tel. 86 39 10 99) to taste local wines, and a wine fair takes place here in August.

Following the Loire still further south, **La Charité-sur-Loire** has a municipal museum which presents various local trades (closed out of season). The capital of Nièvre is **Nevers**, whose old quarter surrounds St-Cyr cathedral. The late eleventh-century St-Etienne church still draws pilgrims to Nevers, which is where Bernadette de Lourdes died. The town's annual fair is held in March, and a flower and animal fair takes place in October. At **La Machine** there is an unusual museum; after twenty centuries of mining coal in the area, the town's mine finally closed in 1974 and the daily life of local people is now captured in a museum. A replica of the mine allows a glimpse of life underground. The spa town of **St-Honoré-les-Bains**, on the edge of the Morvan regional park, holds a flower festival each August. At **Mont-Beuvray**, you will find the most important archaeological dig in France, where excavations of the fortified Gaulish capital of Bibracte are carried out. If you are here in August, try to attend the Bilberry Festival at **Glux-en-Glenne**. Panoramic views are numerous around here, though there is a particularly good view of the nearby mountains from the wayside cross at **Château-Chinon**. To the north-east, pine and larch trees encircle the pleasant **Lac des Settons**. The regional park headquarters are at **St-Brisson** and include an information centre, herbarium (the area is known for its medicinal plants), and museum of the Resistance.

Back in Yonne, a visit to the basilica and hill at **Vézelay** is a must, though you will not be the only one there! The Romanesque Basilique de la Madeleine was both a stopping place for pilgrims on their way to Santiago de Compostella in northern Spain, and a place of pilgrimage in its own right, as it is alleged that Mary Magdalene was buried here. The sculptures on the early twelfth century tympanum deserve particular attention. The foot-sore may wish to take a horse-drawn caravan trip around town. Nearby, the fortified town of **Avallon** has a well-preserved church (St-Lazare) and impressive ramparts. It is worth making a little detour to see the carved wooden stalls in the church at **Montréal**; look out for the drinking session going on in one detail of the carving. Interesting grottoes can be visited at **Arcy-sur-Cure**, on the way to **Chablis**, where there is a large wine festival on the fourth Sunday in November. The lake at **Bas-Rebourseaux** will appeal to ornithologists. **Tanlay** château and its nineteenth-century gardens, which include a canal, are worth a visit, as is the Italian Renaissance château at nearby **Ancy-le-Franc**.

Accommodation

First Class

Château de Mimont, 58320 Pougues-les-Eaux (Tel. 86 68 81 44): 5 *chambres d'hôte* and 2 apartments in château situated between the Loire Valley and the Morvan hills. **Château de Vault de Lugny**, 89200 Avallon (Tel. 86 34 07 86): 11 rooms in 4-star château.

First Class / Middle Range

M. et Mme Laperyrade, 6 rue Joyeuse, 58150 Pouilly-sur-Loire (Tel. 86 39 07 87): 4 luxurious *chambres d'hôte* in centrally situated town house.

Middle Range

Château de Lantilly, 58800 Corbigny (Tel. 86 20 01 22): 9 rooms in moated mansion, with emphasis on simple authenticity; restaurant. **M. Lusardi**, La Coudre, 89210 Perreux (Tel. 86 91 61 42 or 86 91 62 91): 3 *chambres d'hôte* in restored farmhouse with potter's studio.

Middle Range / Economy

Le Castel, Place de l'Eglise, 89660 Mailly-le-Château (Tel. 86 40 43 06): 12 rooms in quiet house with large garden; excellent restaurant.

Economy

M. et Mme Besson, La Haute Epine, 89500 Villeneuve-sur-Yonne (Tel. 86 87 29 01): 3 *chambres d'hôte* in characterful house; *tables d'hôte*. **M. et Mme Adine**, Domaine de la Conciergerie, rue Restif-de-la-Bretonne, 89800 Courgis (Tel. 86 41 41 28): 2 *chambres d'hôte* in vineyard-surrounded house.

Eating Out

Two *First Class* restaurants deserve a special mention, though they are certainly not for those trying to save their pennies: **Hôtel de la Côte St-Jacques**, 14 faubourg de Paris, 89300 Joigny (Tel. 86 62 09 70): splendid family-run restaurant, combining modern innovations and traditional cuisine; also has 15 rooms and suites. **Hôtel de la Renaissance**, Le Bourg, 58470 Magny-Cours (Tel. 86 58 10 40): modernised regional cuisine in opulent dining room of village inn; also has 10 rooms.

Côte d'Or

The name 'Côte d'Or' refers to the spectacular golden colour of the *département's* vineyards in autumn. Life revolves around the vine in this area, and festivals take place all year round: from the St-Vincent Tournante in late January to the Fêtes de la Vigne in August and early September.

Dijon

It would be a pity to miss this friendly regional capital, with its extensive, remarkably preserved old town and lively atmosphere. The place to start is the **Palais des Ducs**, whose classical façade can be viewed best from **Place de la Libération**, an impressive semi-circular square designed by Mansart, architect of Versailles. Unfortunately the atmosphere is spoiled by the numerous coaches which stop between the square and the palace. If you enter the **Cour de Bar** courtyard, look carefully at the architecture: the styles range from fourteenth century to nineteenth with something from every century in between. The fourteenth-century **tower** and the sevententh century staircase which climbs it are of particular interest. The **Fine Arts Museum** is housed in the ducal palace and is certainly worth a visit. Artworks from almost every period can be seen here, but the highlight is the **Salle des Gardes**, which contains the tombs of two of the dukes, Philippe le Hardi and Jean sans Peur, sculpted by the fourteenth-century master Claus Sluter, whose incredible realism was way ahead of his time. (Dijon is ideal for students as, at present, admission to most museums is free for them.) An impression of how the palace looked at the time of the dukes can be gained from behind it, in the **Place des Ducs-de-Bourgogne**, which is overlooked by the Gothic tower of Philippe le Bon.

In **Rue des Forges**, it is worth going down some of the passages alongside the houses to see their decorated courtyards; number 34 has an unusual spiral staircase. If you continue to **Place François-Rude**, look out for the fountain, which depicts a grape-treader at work. Rue François-Rude will lead you to the covered market and, to your right, **rue Musette**. From here, there is an excellent view of the thirteenth-century Gothic **Notre Dame** church. Its façade is covered in ugly gargoyles, said to represent the sins of mankind, which should be left outside when you enter the church. The clock in the top right-hand corner was brought from Flanders in 1382; the little man (known as Jacquemart) who strikes the hours, was given a wife in 1610 and, after 104 barren years, a son to strike the half hours. Eventually they gained a daughter for the quarter hours. The people of Dijon are extremely fond of this clock and life comes to a virtual standstill if, for any reason, Jacquemart and family stop striking. For an alarming view of the gargoyles, walk to the church entrance and look up! To the left of the church is the charming **rue de la Chouette**, where each house is original: one even has a cat sculpted onto its roof. Inside the courtyard of the **Hôtel de Vogüé**, an early seventeenth-century private mansion with a multicoloured roof of glazed tiles, you will see an Italian Renaissance frieze, hidden from the street. Many of the houses on **rue Verrerie** are noteworthy for their imaginatively carved half-timbering.

Other places of interest in Dijon include the **Eglise St-Michel**, with its Renaissance façade and Gothic interior; the Burgundian Gothic **Cathedral of St-Bénigne**, next to which is the **Archaeology Museum**; the quarter around the **Palais de Justice**; the **Botanical Garden** (Jardin de l'Arquebuse), with its **Natural History Museum**; the **Musée de la Vie Bourguignonne** on rue Ste-Anne, which is devoted to Burgundian life in the nineteenth century and has a good costume collection; the neighbouring **Museum of Sacred Art**; and the **Maison de la Nature et du Paysage de Côte d'Or** at 17 rue Cazotte.

Accommodation

There are no small first-class hotels in Dijon, but the following are recommended:

First Class / Middle Range

Hostellerie du Chapeau Rouge, 5 rue Michelet (Tel. 80 30 28 10): 33 rooms in quiet, traditional hotel near cathedral.

Middle Range

Hôtel des Ducs, 5 rue Lammonoye (Tel. 80 67 31 31): 31 rooms in centrally placed hotel. **Hôtel du Parc de la Colombière**, 49 cours du Parc (Tel. 80 65 18 41): 38 rooms in family-run hotel.

Middle Range / Economy

Hôtel le Jacquemart, 32 rue Verrerie (Tel. 80 73 39 74): 32 rooms in charming old-fashioned hotel in medieval street. **Hôtel Castel Burgond**, 3 rte de Troyes (RN 71), 21121 Daix (Tel. 80 56 59 72): 38 rooms in family-run hotel, 6 km from Dijon.

Economy

Hôtel le Chambellan, 92 rue Vannerie (Tel. 80 67 12 67): 20 rooms. **Hôtel du Sauvage**, 64 rue Monge (Tel. 80 41 31 21): 20 comfortable rooms in quiet and attractive situation.

Eating Out

The following are just a small selection of Dijon's good restaurants:

First Class

Restaurant Jean-Pierre Billoux, 14 Place Darcy (Tel. 80 30 11 00): one of the best restaurants in the Côte d'Or.

First Class / Middle Range

Restaurant des Gourmets, 8 rue de Puits de Têt, 21160 Marsannay-la-Côte (Tel. 80 52 16 32): authentic house specialities in vineyard setting, 6 km from Dijon. **La Toison d'Or**, 18 rue Ste-Anne (Tel. 80 30 73 52): gastronomic cuisine in historic building.

Middle Range

Le Chapeau Rouge, 5 rue Michelet (Tel. 80 30 28 10): high-quality, innovative cuisine.

Middle Range / Economy

L'Etape Burgonde, 3 rue de Montigny (Tel. 80 30 18 17): typical Burgundian lunches and snacks, with *dégustation* of local wines. **L'Harmonie du Vin**, 20 Place de la Libération (Tel. 80 30 35 66): another lunchtime venue with *dégustation*.

Economy

Le Grilladou, 29 rue J-J Rousseau (Tel. 80 74 42 23): home cooking over wood-fire. **Au Bec Fin**, 47 rue Jeannin: excellent value fixed price menus (don't miss the regional cheeses). **La Vie**

Saine, 27–29 rue Musette: pleasant vegetarian restaurant above one of rue Musette's two health food shops.

Dijon is notable for its abundance of *pâtisserie* shops and other sources of lunchtime snacks. Try rue Musette, where there is a wonderful cheese shop. If you want to buy genuine Dijon gingerbread (*pain d'épice*), go to one of the three branches of **Mulot et Petitjean** (main shop in rue de la Liberté). For mustard, go to **Grey-Poupon**, 32 rue de la Liberté: the shop was established in 1777 and doubles as a museum of antique mustard jars.

Entertainments

On Tuesday and Friday mornings, a food market takes place all the way along rue François-Rude: the fruit and vegetables are very fresh, often organically grown. Look out for the organic wine stall and the old-fashioned cheese stand. On Saturdays there is also a market, but the emphasis is more on clothes. Dijon has good theatre and cinema facilities: ask the tourist office for the brochure 'Dijon Nuit et Jour'. Various venues offer wine-tasting: try **La Cave du Clos**, 3 rue Jeannin (Tel. 80 65 83 03); or the **Caves de l'Espace Grévin**, 13 ave Albert 1er (Tel. 80 42 03 03), which offers commentaries in different languages and where there is also a waxwork museum. June brings a music festival, and between mid-July and mid-August there is much street theatre, music and dance. Late August and early September see the Fêtes de la Vigne, and in early November, Dijon hosts an International Gastronomic Fair.

Useful Addresses

The main **Tourist Office** is on Place Darcy (Tel. 80 43 42 12), with a branch office at 34 rue des Forges (Tel. 80 30 35 39). (The **Club Alpin**, which gives information on walks in the area, also has its office here.) The **Post Office** is an imposing building on Place Grangier, and the **Hôpital Général** is at 3 rue Faubourg Raines (Tel. 80 41 81 41).

Transport Options

Ask the tourist office about its guided tours of the old town, as they are extremely good, including various historical anecdotes and pointing out many features which might otherwise be overlooked. Alternatively, ask for their leaflet 'Dijon, Capital of Burgundy', which suggests a walking circuit. Bike hire is available from **Cycles de**

Pouilly at 3 place Wilson and 3 rue de Tivoli. The town bus service, known as STRD, is efficient and there is an information and ticket booth on Place Grangier.

Rest of Côte d'Or

A source of great pride to Burgundy is the Vase of Vix, an enormous vase created in the sixth century BC by Greek bronze-smiths, which can be seen in the museum at **Châtillon-sur-Seine**. The **Châtillonais** area is an unusual one. It is described as a 'mountain' because mountain flora grows here, in peat-bogs and marshes only 300–400 metres above sea level. This part of the Côte d'Or is undeveloped and heavily wooded, so deer and other large mammals are a common sight. There are botanical paths at the Marais des Brosses at **Recey-sur-Ource**. The abbey at **Fontenay** is one of the region's most famous attractions; built in 1118, the abbey complex includes buildings used in all aspects of monastic life. At the Domaine des Forges de Buffon, near **Montbard**, an eighteenth-century foundry has been made into a museum of the northern Burgundian iron and steel-making industry. Finds from the Gallic town of Alésia can be seen in the village museum of **Alise-Ste-Reine**. The château at **Bussy-Rabutin** is worth a visit; it has a splendid seventeenth-century garden, with ornamental lakes, fountains and flowerbeds, enclosed by a nineteenth-century park. **Semur-en-Auxios** is a charming village of half-timbered houses perched above the Armançon river, and hosts the 'Festival de Haute-Bourgogne' (theatre, music and dance) in July and August. **Pont-Royal** is one of the many rural ports along the Canal de Bourgogne, for which light river tourism has proved a blessing; here you will find the Maison du Canal Museum. **Saulieu** is famous for its magnificent markets and restaurants, and also has a museum of local crafts (the Musée François Pompon). In mid-August, the 'Fête du Charolais' takes place here. The first museum in France to celebrate the 'arts of the table' can be found at the Maison Régionale des Arts de la Table at **Arnay-le-Duc**. North-east of here, at **Châteauneuf**, is an impressive château.

The covered markets in the village of **Nolay**, in the south of the *département*, date from the fourteenth century. In order to gain an astonishing overview of the one million years of Burgundian human history, you should visit the Archéodrome. This is an open-air museum, just south of Beaune, and contains reconstructions, including the fort of Alésia and a Gallic farm complete with crops and animals. During summer there are even demonstrations of ancient crafts. **Beaune** itself certainly deserves a visit, if only to see the colourful roof of the Hôtel-Dieu, built along the lines of the hospital at Valenciennes, in mid fifteenth-century Gothic-Flemish style. A *Son et Lumière* takes place here between March and October. Beaune also hosts a music festival in July. As is fitting for the wine capital of Burgundy, it has a Musée du Vin in the former Ducal Mansion. Wine-tasting evenings (with commentary) can be attended at the Ambassade du Vin, 20 rue du faubourg Madeleine (Tel. 80 24 79 88). The festival which accompanies the Hospices de Beaune charity wine auction on the third weekend in November is worth a special trip. In **Seurre**, Maison Bossuet houses the Ecomusée du Val de Saône (open from 1 July to 15 September). The Ferme de Cussigny at **Corgoloin**, between Beaune and Nuits-St-Georges, offers horse-drawn carriage tours through Beaune and its vineyards. The Countess of Loisy opens up her ancestral residence at 28 rue du Général-de-Gaulle, 21700 **Nuits-St-Georges** (Tel. 80 61 02 72), for wine-tastings with explanations. The **Abbaye de Cîteaux** and its cellar at the **Clos de Vougeot** have long been associated with the production of good wines. Houseboats can be rented at **St-Jean-de-Losne** on the River Saône, where there is a fishermen's festival in June. Around a pond of ornithological interest at **Villers-Rottin**, the Conservatoire Régional has created pathways, marked with informative signs. Nearby **Auxonne** has a museum of local folklore, called the Musée Bonaparte and housed in the Château Prost. Caves may be visited at **Bèze** and there is a sort of *ecomusée*, known as the 'Maison du Houblon', at **Ruffey-lès-Echirey**, which focuses on local hop-growing and beer production.

Accommodation

First Class

Château de Longecourt, Longecourt-en-Plaine, 21110 Genlis (Tel. 80 39 88 76): 4 rooms in moated, neo-classical Italian-style manor; *tables d'hôte* on request. **Hôtel de la Poste**, bd Clemenceau, 21200 Beaune (Tel. 80 22 08 11): 25 rooms in 4-star hotel; traditional restaurant. **Domaine C.M. de Loisy**, 28 rue du Général-de-Gaulle, 21700 Nuits-St-Georges (Tel. 80 61 02 72): 4 rooms in eighteenth- to nineteenth-century family home with own vineyards and cellar; *tables d'hôte* on reservation.

First Class / Middle Range

Château de Malaisy, Fain les Montbard, 21500 Montbard (Tel. 80 89 46 54): 23 rooms in renovated seventeenth-century château with park; gastronomic restaurant.

Middle Range

Le Montrachet, Puligny Montrachet, 21190 Meursault (Tel. 80 21 30 06): 32 rooms in grand house; restaurant serving excellent regional cuisine.

Economy

Hôtel le Parc, Levernois, 21200 Beaune (Tel. 80 22 22 51): 20 rooms in converted farmhouse, 6 km from Beaune. **Mme Parfait**, Impasse Fleurie, 21640 Vougeot (Tel. 80 62 86 69): 3 *chambres d'hôte* in pleasant house, 5 km from Nuits-St-Georges. **Mme Rabian**, 3 rte de Solonge, 21230 Arnay-le-Duc (Tel. 80 90 01 03): 2 *chambres d'hôte* in house with garden.

Eating Out

In addition to the restaurants recommended above, the following deserve special mention:

First Class

La Côte d'Or, 2 rue d'Argentine, 21210 Saulieu (Tel. 80 64 07 66): exceptionally good restaurant whose chef cooks the freshest ingredients without fat, cream or alcohol, coming up with delicate concoctions, including the rare phenomenon of a vegetarian fixed-price menu; also has 15 rooms and 9 suites. **La Côte d'Or**, 37 rue Thurot, 21700 Nuits-St-Georges (Tel. 80 61 06 10): fine restaurant known for its regional cuisine; also has 7 attractive rooms.

Middle Range

Chez Camille, 1 Place Edouard-Herriot, 21230 Arnay-le-Duc (Tel. 80 90 01 38): cheerful restaurant with regional specialities, where you can watch chef at work through a window; also has 12 comfortable rooms.

Saône-et-Loire

The Saône-et-Loire *département* has been christened the *Jardin Roman*, because it contains such a wealth of Romanesque architecture, including more than 270 churches. This fertile land, where people are especially friendly, also boasts over 600 châteaux and manor houses and numerous less grand monuments to the past: wayside crosses, low-roofed farms, dovecots, pigeon-houses and *lavoirs*. The *lavoir* was where women used to do their washing – and have a good gossip: hence a local saying that 'the cleaner the washing, the dirtier the scandal'!

There is always something going on in the villages of the north-western corner, around Autun: at **St-Léger-sous-Beuvray**, an unusual Chestnut Fair takes place on October weekends, and various farms in the Morvan area offer tours by horse-drawn cart. **Autun** itself was an important town in Roman times and, each summer, 600 of its inhabitants put on a production called 'Once upon a time in Augustodunum' in its ancient Roman theatre. The tympanum in Autun's St-Lazarus cathedral is impressive, and the Temple of Janus and Rolin Museum are also worth a visit. There is an attractive classical Renaissance château at **Sully**, and a thirteenth-century priory at **Val-St-Benoît**, where sale of the nuns' pottery helps restoration work. Between **Couches** and **Chagny** are the castles of Ste-Marguerite-de-Bourgogne and Rully. There is a good Sunday morning market at Chagny, as well as a summer festival of local wine and cooking. At **Verdun-sur-le-Doubs**, a sixteenth-century Common Hall has been turned into a museum of wheat and bread-making. This is one of a series of local museums which belong to the Ecomusée de la Bresse Bourguignonne, whose headquarters are in the seventeenth-century château at **Pierre-de-Bresse**. The *ecomusée* aims to study, protect and raise awareness of the rich local heritage, both natural and cultural. It is responsible for numerous activities in the Bresse area, including the setting up of 'discovery' trails and various thematic exhibitions. Information on all its activities is available from the **Ecomusée de la Bresse Bourguignonne**, Château, 71270 Pierre-de-Bresse (Tel. 85 76 27 16). At present its exhibitions include one on 'Wood and the Forest' (complete with 1 hour walk) at **St-Martin-en-Bresse**; a display of agricultural machinery on route du Sens, **St-Germain-du-Bois**; the workshop of a local newspaper at 29 rue des Dodânes in **Louhans** (which is famous for its Monday market of Bresse chickens and its medieval pharmacy); an exhibition devoted to vine-growing in the château of the Princes of Orange at **Cuiseaux** (look out also for the attractive choir-stalls in the church); and a tilery which exemplifies pre-industrial sixteenth-century Bresse architecture and is situated on the D 996 near **Varennes-St-Sauveur**. At **Romenay**, near **Montpont-en-Bresse**, a museum of Bresse folklore can be visited on July and August afternoons, and at **Rancy** there is an exhibition of chair and wicker-making. Near **Ratenelle**, among the dunes of Pont Seille, is the Réserve Naturelle de la Truchère where informative signs have been erected and pathways constructed, but which is still wary of encouraging too many visitors.

Tournus is one of the great Romanesque centres, with its magnificent tenth- to twelfth-century St-Philibert Abbey. Its seventeenth-century Hôtel-Dieu is also impressive, and the Musée Greuze (Burgundian folklore) and Musée Perrin de Puycousin (Burgundian arts and crafts) are both worth a visit. There are good views from the church at **St-Martin-de-Laives**. The owners of the 'Moulin Neuf' farm at **St-Etienne-en-Bresse** grow organic fruit (strawberries, raspberries, peaches etc.) which they make into jams, purées and sherbets. The largest town in the *département* is **Chalon-sur-Saône** where you will find charming half-timbered houses (in the St-Vincent quarter); the Denon Museum of archaeology and medieval art; the fascinating Nicéphore-Niepce Museum, which traces the history of photography; and the Maison des Vins de la Côte Chalonnaise (on Promenade Ste-Marie), where you can taste local wines and buy local produce. Chalon hosts a lively carnival in February and a street artists' festival in July. About 4 km to the north-east is the spectacular St-Nicolas Rose Garden. Organic wines are sold by Heilly-Huberdeau at **Cercot-Moroges**. The cave at **Buxy** is worth visiting for its sheer range of local wines. At **Le Creusot**, the Château de la Verrerie (former home of Marie-Antoinette's crystal-makers) houses the Musée de l'Homme et l'Industrie, an *ecomusée* which studies in depth the industrial heritage of the community since the nineteenth century. The old houses in the Quartier de l'Horloge at the spa town of **Bourbon-Lancy** and the basilica of **Paray-le-Monial** are both attractive. **Charolles**, the town which gave its name to the prize Charollais cattle, has a Maison du Charolais, where there are exhibitions and a sale of local produce, both edible and non-edible. The Cave des Vignerons de la Région de Genouilly is a cooperative wine cellar (at **Genouilly**), run by friendly people, which offers real bargains. In **Germagny** church, an unusual eleventh-century fresco of the young Christ was discovered only a few years ago. Sadly, the beautiful château at nearby **Bissy-sur-Fley** is gradually collapsing for want of funds. Local honey and related products are available from M. Balland, rue Blondin, **Saint-Boil**. The medieval hill-top village of **Brancion** is worth visiting, along with the nearby Château des Nobles at **La-Chapelle-sous-Brancion**, whose owner will sell you wine from his vineyards. You could also visit the ancient village of **Chapaize** with its eleventh- and twelfth- century monasteries; or the enormous seventeenth-century château at **Cormatin** whose interior decoration is exceptional and where concerts are sometimes held. At **Sailly**, you will find the only combined *lavoir-pigeonnier* (i.e. washing place cum pigeon-house) in France, and nearby, at **Le Gros Chigy**, is a twelfth-century stable which looks just like a church, where cows are still housed.

Cluny is known for its wealth of medieval monuments, including its Romanesque abbey, which can be seen best from the top of the eleventh-century Tour des Fromages. Cluny is a centre for many cultural events, including classical music concerts in August. It is not unusual to find President Mitterand in the Cluny region, as this is where his wife comes from. Do not miss the caves at **Blanot** (a suite of five grottoes) and **Azé**. There is an archaeological museum at the latter, which are 3000 centuries old and have been inhabited by bears and a whole series of human civilisations. At **Berzé-la-Ville** there are rare eleventh-century murals in the Chapelle aux Moines, though you may wish to press on to the Domaine des Giraudières at **Bussières**, where you can sample and buy the 'Grands Vins du Mâconnais'. The Château of **Pierreclos**, built in 1404, was often visited by the Romantic poet Lamartine; now there are museums of bread and wine and a fine cellar here. In **Mâcon**, the mains sights are the former cathedral (Le Vieux St-Vincent), with its uneven towers; the sculptured wooden façade of the Maison du Bois; the Résidence Soufflot and its chapel; and the eighteenth-century domed Hôtel-Dieu, whose pharmacy you can visit between 10 a.m. and noon. The Lamartine Museum, housed in the Regency-style Hôtel Senecé, and the Musée des Ursulines, which is devoted to Mâcon's history are both worth a visit. For wine-tasting, try the seventeenth-century Cellier des Cordeliers on rue Dufour or the Maison Mâconnaise des Vins, ave Maréchal de-Lattre-de-Tassigny, where meals are also available. In May the National Wine Fair takes place in Mâcon. Good Pouilly-Fuissé and various other wines can be tasted and purchased at Domaine Lapierre, **Solutré-Pouilly**. Solutré hill is an unusual shape and offers a splendid view. It was a prehistoric hunting site and excavations have been going on here since 1866. There is now an excellent Departmental Museum of Prehistory at the bottom of the hill. Near **Tramayes** is the Château de St-Point, which belonged to Lamartine. If you arrive at **St-Christophe-en-Brionnais** early on a Thursday morning, you will experience a market of Charollais cattle which has taken place every week since the fifteenth century. Dating from the same period is the unusually decorated Tour du Moulin at **Marcigny**.

Accommodation

In the Saône-et-Loire, high-quality cottages (including sheets and services) can be rented from **'Les Recollets'**, 71110 Marcigny (Tel. 85 25 19 78). Good hotels and *chambres d'hôte* abound.

First Class

Hostellerie du Château de Bellecroix, RN 6, 71150 Chagny (Tel. 85 87 13 86): 19 rooms in 12th and 13th century château; good restaurant. **M. Villard**, Château de St-Germain-du-Plain, 71370 St-Germain-du-Plain (Tel. 85 47 38 13 or 85 47 40 31): 5 *chambres d'hôte* and 2 suites in nineteenth-century château with beautiful park; *tables d'hôte* on reservation.

First Class / Middle Range

Hôtel de Bourgogne, Place de l'Abbaye, 71250 Cluny (Tel. 85 59 00 58): 13 rooms and 3 apartments in famous nineteenth-century hotel opposite abbey; good restaurant with fine, light cuisine.

Middle Range

Mme Badin, 'Les Recollets', 71110 Marcigny (Tel. 85 25 05 16): 4 *chambres d'hôte* and 3 suites in charming family house (converted convent); *tables d'hôte* on reservation.

Middle Range / Economy

Hôtellerie du Val d'Or, Grande-Rue, 71640 Mercurey (Tel. 85 45 13 70): 10 rooms in wine village coaching inn; excellent, simple cooking.

Economy

Hôtel de la Halle, Place de la Halle, 71640 Givry (Tel. 85 44 32 45): 10 rooms in friendly family hotel; traditional Burgundian cuisine. **Mme Derepas**, 'Dulphey', 71240 Mancey (Tel. 85 51 10 22 or 85 51 20 82): 5 comfortable *chambres d'hôte* in large residence with park, 5 km from Tournus. **Mme Marteau**, 'Verchizeuil', 71960 Verze (Tel. 85 33 36 10): 5 *chambres d'hôte* in hamlet, 8 km from Mâcon.

Eating Out

For special occasions, try the following two **First Class** restaurants: **Lameloise**, Place d'Armes, 71150 Chagny (Tel. 85 87 08 85): welcoming family-run restaurant in rustic setting, with regional cuisine from freshest local produce; also has 25 pleasant rooms. **Restaurant Greuze**, 1 rue Albert-Thibaudet, 71700 Tournus (Tel. 85 51 13 52): simple classic Burgundian cuisine.

11 The Loire

The Loire, some 1000 kilometres in length, is France's longest river. It rises in the Massif Central and empties into the Bay of Biscay below Nazaire.

From its source it flows northwest as far as Orléans, and then turns westward through château-dotted countryside, past the towns of Blois, Amboise and Tours, and beyond to Nantes and the sea.

The name Loire has widely come to be applied to the stretch of river, (and the surrounding countryside) between Orléans and Tours – the Val de Loire. Here are concentrated the largest number of châteaux associated with the Valois kings of France. Some of the châteaux stand not on the Loire, but on its tributaries, the Cher, Indre, and Vienne. The countryside is in no way dramatic and, in fact, has often disappointed visitors who have expected to see not only the splendid architecture for which the area is so renowned, but also delightful scenery. The river itself is not especially attractive, and has neither the physical appeal nor the facilities for watersports offered by the Dordogne. The Loire's appeal, however, lies chiefly in its many architectural splendours, and it is the sort of place that rewards leisurely exploration.

Many of the smaller châteaux have been converted into hotels offering a variety of accommodation, and a reputation for good food and wine. These attract a great number of visitors from both within and outside France, causing considerable motor traffic (particularly along the north bank of the river), congested towns and crowded monuments. The minor roads, however, are a delight, the valleys peaceful and the lesser known châteaux rewarding to visit.

Unfortunately, unlike some of France's more rural regions, many of the Loire's traditional activities have long since disappeared. Herbs and spices such as saffron, liquorice and aniseed are no longer grown on a large scale, and the silk industry introduced to Loire by Louis XI has dwindled. During the Middle Ages, and right up to the eighteenth century, the Loire river was a much-used waterway. With the advent of the railway and the motor car, however, river traffic has severely declined.

Although the Loire is not considered to be an area of great industrial output, recent years have seen a growth in subsidiary industries such as food processing. There are Michelin tyre factories in Orléans, Tours and Cholet and nuclear power stations at Avoine, Chinon, Dampierre-en-Burly and St-Laurent-des-Eaux, which help to stimulate the local economy. Service industries too have experienced an increase. Both Tours and Orléans have become national conference centres, and Le Mans has attracted insurance businesses. Tourism too receives a high profile. Apart from the Loire's considerable Renaissance heritage (as witnessed in the many châteaux), forests, theme parks and 570 kilometres of navigable waterway attract both domestic and foreign tourism.

History

During the Iron Age the Loire was inhabited by the Cenomanni, a fierce race of gold miners who resisted the Romans and other foreign invaders. In 52 BC the Cenomanni and their neighbours the Carnutes organised a rebellion against the armies of Julius Caesar. Although this was brutally suppressed, the Loire enjoyed a time of peace and stability during the reign of the Emperor Augustus.

Christianity was introduced to the region in the fourth century by St Gatien, the first bishop of Tours, and under St Martin (the most distinguished bishop of the Gauls) Christianity became firmly established.

From the ninth to the twelfth century, Loire was ruled by powerful barons who were continually warring amongst themselves. In 1154 Henri Count of Anjou became Henry II, the Plantagenet king of England, and the Loire became incorporated into an English kingdom that stretched from the north of England to the Pyrenees. France regained its lost possessions fifty years later when John of England (known as Lackland) was forced to concede the Loire and much of southwestern France to Philippe Auguste.

The Hundred Years' War (1337–1453) saw the return of the English. In 1429 the armies of Henry V of England were on the point of capturing the whole of the French kingdom when Joan of Arc confronted the the Dauphin of France at his court in Chinon and announced her intention of expelling the English. After that historic encounter, the region became identified with the gradual recovery of France and particularly with the restoration of royal power. The relief of Orléans in the same year marked a reversal in English fortunes.

From the reign of Charles VII (crowned in 1429) to the end of the sixteenth century, the Loire, from Orléans to Angers, continued to be the region most favoured by the crown and to which it retreated in times of crisis, notably during the Wars of Religion (1562–1598).

The Italian campaign of Charles VIII, in the late 15th century brought him and his followers into contact with the Italian Renaissance and this affected the choice of artists and architects brought in to build or extend and embellish the royal and other châteaux. Contemporary developments in the area of war made unnecessary the fortification of the castles and houses, and the châteaux as seen today reflect the shift to a more peaceful and often luxurious mode of living.

During the French Revolution the Loire, like so much of western France, was divided as the peasants rose against the townspeople, and family against family. The new fiscal regimes, brought about in 1791 to alleviate the plight of the poor, did nothing to relieve the peasants. The civil war left considerable bitterness and resentment between the people of the Touraine and the Orléanais, who welcomed the revolution wholeheartedly, and the people of Maine and Anjou who did not. In fact, this resentment has continued to be reflected in the very rigid social and political attitudes held by the people of Anjou and Maine right up to the present day.

During the Second World War, the French government moved its headquarters to Tours (later moving to Bordeaux). During the war, the cadets at the cavalry school at Saumur lived up to their historical reputation when they held up the German army for two days. Montoire, however, was the scene of less heroic deeds when, on 24 October 1940, Marshal Pétain met Hitler and agreed to collaborate with the Nazis. The Gestapo gradually gained full control of the Loire through a brutal reign of terror. However, in 1941, the French Resistance was born, and survived to see the liberation of the region in 1944 when the Allied armies began their counter invasion.

Today, the Loire is subject to a more welcome form of invasion: that of tourism. Visitors from far and wide come to the region every year to see the spectacular châteaux and enjoy the first class hospitality for which the Loire is renowned.

Geography

The area covered in this chapter is a large one, encompassing the two administrative regions of Centre Val-de-Loire and Pays-de-la-Loire. The former is situated inland and it is here that the majority of the famous châteaux are to be found. Bordered by Normandy and the Ile-de-France to the north and Burgundy to the east, this very central area of France has Orléans (Loiret *département*) as its capital, with 106,000 inhabitants, and other major towns at Tours (Indre-et-Loire) ard Bourges (Cher). The remaining *départements* in Centre Val-de-Loire are the Indre, Loir-et-Cher and Eure-et-Loir. The Pays-de-la-Loire region includes a section of the Atlantic coast between Brittany and Poitou-Charentes, as well as three inland *départements*. Its capital is Nantes (248,000 inhabitants), despite the fact that the city, and the whole Loire-Atlantique *département*, belonged until fairly recently to Brittany and are still considered by many to be part of that region. The other main city is Le Mans, in the Sarthe, and the remaining *départements* are Mayenne (bordering Normandy and Brittany), Maine-et-Loire (where the châteaux start), and the coastal Vendée.

Naturally, the main point of continuity in these two Loire regions is the famous river itself. There is a distinction in French between a *fleuve* – a river emptying into the sea – and a *rivière*, which does not. The Loire, although a *fleuve*, has not had a continuous history as a significant waterway, despite attempts to maintain it as such. The flow, heaviest in spring and autumn, is irregular and the alluvial deposit heavy. Dykes built to contain flood waters have been breached frequently, sometimes with catastrophic consequences, but they have provided foundations for roads, which run parallel to the river for many kilometres without affording more than an occasional glimpse of it.

The châteaux were built when the river supported traffic as far as Orléans, and they still look best from the water. Sadly, water-borne traffic no longer exists and even canoes have to be carried across sandbanks which impede the river's flow. The scenery is not dramatic, but life on the riverbank is peaceful in contrast to the noise and pollution of the main roads, which carry heavy commercial as well as tourist traffic. The immediate countryside of the Loire is still referred to as the garden of France. From Gien to Orléans, the valley opens out and meadows give way to horticulture and greenhouses. Further west, the river separates the great Forêt d'Orléans from the Sologne, an area of heather and marsh, both of which are popular with hunters. The Beauce, known as the granary of France, lies to the north-west, and, below Amboise, the sloping valleys support the vineyards of Vouvray and Ronlus. Cultivation continues as you continue westwards, with vineyards, fruit trees, vegetables and flowers, interspersed with willow-fringed meadows. Mushrooms are grown in former quarries here, particularly in the Saumur area, where there are also many caves.

The coastal stretch starts in the north with acres of reeds, punctuated by willows and oak trees, and marshland, often former salt-marsh, divided by canals, ponds and points of higher land known as *buttes*. This part belongs to the Brière regional park and is rich in traditions, often centring around the transportation of peat to Nantes and the Isles of Noirmoutier and Yeu, further south. The southern part of the Pays-de-la-Loire coastline, known as the Vendée, is fairly uncommercialised (and plans are to keep it that way). Much of the land bordering the sea consists of low-lying marshes or damp meadows, either reclaimed from the sea or formerly used as salt-pans. Part of it has been made into the important St-Denis-du-Payré nature reserve, which is really a vast meadow, used by local farmers for grazing and providing an ideal habitat for increasingly rare wetland birds and plants such as the Butterfly Iris. Further protection is afforded to the area at the very south of Vendée, favoured by migrating birds, through the Marais Poitevin regional park.

A section in the north of the Mayenne *département* also belongs to a regional park – the Normandie-Maine one – while the Brenne regional park, in the Indre *département*, covers one of the most important inland wetland areas in Europe. This is a wild and sparsely populated place, with thousands of fish ponds, home to bitterns, purple herons, pond terrapins, European mink and various rare plants such as orchids. This valuable but fragile area has been classed as a Category 1 site by the International Union for the Conservation of Nature. Nature protection in the Loir-et-Cher *département* is helped by the Conservatoire (the only departmentally based one in the country), which was founded in 1987 and hopes to save rare birds and orchids whose habitats are the meadows of the Cher valley. Other nature reserves in the region include the Ile de St-Pryve, an ornithologically valuable island in the bed of the Loire near Orléans, and the Grand-Lieu, in Loire-Atlantique, which is home to the largest European colony of Herons Cendrés.

Climate

The climate in the Loire is maritime and generally temperate though, during the winter, heavy rain and snow fall on the higher ground north of the river basin. On the whole its climate is similar to that of southern England, except during high summer, when the temperatures along the Loire tend to be warmer, rising to an average of 25.7°C in July. Spring comes early, with warm, moist winds from the Atlantic causing a higher rainfall on the coast than inland. The weather can sometimes be frosty until May, though the temperature tends to rise sharply in June. Reasonable temperatures and a fair chance of fine weather from March or April through to November make for a long tourist season; for reasons of comfort and cost, visitors are recommended to come at one end or the other of the season.

Attractions

Holiday-makers in search of relaxation and variety will find the Loire an ideal choice. It has advantages over many other regions in that it is set in the very heart of France, with easy access to Paris and good communications with other major towns.

The Loire's foremost attraction is, without a doubt, its Renaissance heritage. Nowhere else in France are there so many magnificent châteaux concentrated within such a relatively small area. A visit to these offers a new perspective on the history of France, bringing it alive for even the most sceptical. The most famous and undeniably impressive of the châteaux are Chambord, Chenonceau, Chinon and Blois, though there are numerous smaller ones, some of them still owner-occupied or converted to practical use, which are more intimate and less crowded, including Beauregard, La Verrerie, Nohant and Azay-le-Rideau. If there are more châteaux on your list of 'ones to visit' than can be comfortably fitted into your schedule of day-time touring, a good option is to attend one of the numerous spectacular *Son et Lumière* performances put on at various châteaux in the evenings.

Among other attractions are picturesque farms; vineyards that once catered for the palates of Valois kings; museums, and churches from all eras, including the oldest one in France, Germigny-des-Prés, founded in the eighth century. The coast offers sedate, uncommercialised resorts, with trips to islands such as Noirmoutier where time seems to have stopped, or visits to the fascinating traditional museums and craftsmen of the regional parks. Throughout the region there are also many towns of interest. Historic Nantes has a decidedly Breton feel; the more modern Le Mans is famed for its twenty-four hour motor race in mid-June; Chartres is known worldwide for the spectacular stained-glass windows of its magnificent cathedral; Saumur is home of the *Cadre Noir*, a famous cavalry unit, and also has a splendid château-fort. Orléans and Tours are lively, bustling cities with plenty to see and do; Chinon is a fine medieval town, which was the birthplace of Rabelais and has associations with Joan of Arc; and Bourges has an extremely fine cathedral and palace. Apart from the larger towns, other smaller places such as Amboise, Châteaudun, Loches and Mézières-en-Brenne should be included on any tour of the region.

Cuisine

Food in the Loire, like everything else, is very varied, but the fish dishes are particularly recommended. Among the delicacies here are pike, salmon or carp, fried in butter; eels cooked with wine, mushrooms and onions; and stuffed bream. Typical main courses include Sologne game, sometimes made into a casserole; pork cooked with prunes; *rillons* or *rillettes* (kinds of potted pork); and veal in white sauce with brandy. Popular vegetables are cabbage (cooked in butter), mushrooms (stuffed with cream sauce) and asparagus. Fruits in the Loire are also very good, particularly the pears, apricots, peaches, strawberries and apples. The latter often appear in the form of apple and quince jelly or, for dessert, apple tart. Orléans and Tours are known for their pastries. The Loire produces several good cheeses. Particularly delicious are chavignol, valençay and st-benoit, as well as ste-maure and crémets, which are made from goats' milk.

Numerous wines are produced in the Loire and, although none of them equal the great Bordeaux or Burgundies, some certainly deserve attention. Of the white wines, Jasnières, which comes from around Vendôme, is a good bet. Other whites include Muscadet, Vouvray, Sancerre and Pouilly-sur-Loire. For red wine, try St-Nicolas-de-Bourgueil and Montlouis. As for rosés, Anjou and Touraine are popular throughout France.

Level of Tourism

Tourism statistics for the Loire area are divided into those for the Pays-de-la-Loire and those for Centre Val-de-Loire, though the latter are the only ones currently available. They place the Centre (where most of the châteaux are concentrated) eighth in the pecking order of France's touristic regions, hosting 2,963,000 hotel visits a year (i.e. 4.7% of the total hotel visits to France). It is predominantly a short-stay region, though 30% of its visitors are from abroad. The Italians and British tend to dominate the foreign market, and British interest in the Loire châteaux has recently shot up. The region is also sufficiently close to Paris to attract many Parisians at weekends. Of course, it is the châteaux which form the major attraction in the Loire. Even in the Cher *département*, which is relatively lean in major châteaux, two (Apremont and Châteauneuf) manage to drum up visitor rates of over 30,000 each summer, along with Noirlac Abbey, and the Palais Jacques-Coeur and cathedral in Bourges.

Considering the amount of tourism the region receives, it is surprising how little commerce and industry there is. This is partly due to the demise of water-based traffic (since the last century) and to the physical obstacle to both major rail and road networks that the river presents. Another reason has to do with the quality of tourism. Visitors come to see the châteaux and to eat and drink well, not to pass the time shopping, in bars or in nightclubs. One aspect of tourism that does thrive is the hotel business. Local people take great pride in their historical heritage and the Loire's age-old reputation for first-class hospitality. In this sense, tourists are greatly welcomed and have supported the local economy for well over a century. The hordes of 'culture vultures' who arrive in their coachloads for two days of their week in France have had a negative effect on the prices and quality in some hotels; but such establishments can easily be avoided simply by checking in to a small family-run hotel or B&B whose size would not allow it to cater for groups.

Overcrowding is also a by-product of the Loire's considerable popularity; even the most magnificent châteaux lose a high proportion of their charm when congested with human traffic. Visiting out of season, particularly in spring or autumn, is therefore strongly recommended. Even if you are limited to a summer trip, bear in mind that early-morning visits to the most popular châteaux are advisable, to avoid both the crowds and the worst of the day's heat. Peak periods (late morning and mid-afternoon) should be spent visiting lesser-known châteaux (by taking an early lunch, you can often see most of another château before coach visitors have even arrived). You could then attend a *Son et Lumière* performance in the evening, when crowds do not have such a detrimental effect on the atmosphere. Obviously such an agenda should only be undertaken by those whose prime objective is to see as many châteaux as possible, and who know themselves to be immune to cultural indigestion! Most people will be better off diluting château visits with some other activity.

It is important to bear in mind that the majority of the great châteaux are empty, architectural masterpieces, magnificent in their setting, but often unfurnished and lacking the appeal that comes from uninterrupted use, such as the stately homes of Britain usually enjoy. A number of the smaller châteaux are, however, owner-occupied, and taking the time to visit some of these may give you a new perspective on the region and its people. It should also be remembered that the scenery of the Loire in no way matches its architectural splendours. Many people see Tourist Board posters of the châteaux, assume they must be in a spectacular location, and are therefore disappointed by the rather ordinary reality. Disappointment is further fuelled by the sight of ugly power stations (often nuclear), which punctuate the landscape, even impinging on historical châteaux such as Chinon and St-Benoit-sur-Loire.

In this region of France, it is particularly important to ask yourself exactly **what** you want out of your holiday. Those for whom the cultural heritage is paramount will find the majority of châteaux (and of fellow tourists) in the Maine-et-Loire, Indre-et-Loire, Loir-et-Cher and Loiret *départements*. Others, particularly nature lovers, should consider a spell in one of the regional parks: either the Brière or Marias Poitevin, in the west of the region; the Normandie–Maine in the north of Mayenne; or the ponds of Brenne in Indre. The Cher *département* is a good bet for those looking for peace and quiet; it advertises itself as ideal for 'the traveller who is bored with mass tourism holiday destinations' and 'the holiday-maker who appreciates the relaxing calm of a way of life still paced by the cycle of the seasons'. Beach holidays are catered for at the quiet, uncommercialised resorts of the Vendée, which make a pleasant alternative to more sought-after French coastal destinations.

In some places, good solutions to tourism-related problems have been found. The Brière regional park was threatened by the tourist influx of neighbouring city-dwellers, so decided to concentrate its welcome of them in the village of Kerhinet. The village has undergone extensive restoration and authentic local activities which were dying out have been re-encouraged. The park has developed a tourism policy which involves canalising tourists to avoid over-frequentation of certain sites; informing visitors and offering them several centres of interest; and, perhaps most importantly, reassuring local people and offering them the opportunity to benefit from tourism without compromising their way of life. This policy has led to the creation of two *auberges* serving traditional regional food, the training of local people as guides, and the creation of a Brière park 'label of quality'. Rozé, which used to be a big port in the early nineteenth century, but whose trade had been dwindling with the decline of the peat business, is now able to use its traditional peat-carrying boats (*chaloupes*) to give visitors tours of the marshes. The Brière park is a good example of how a clear policy and sensible management can turn potentially threatening tourist activity to local benefit.

Good Alternatives

Meeting People

A good way of meeting people is to attend some of the numerous festivals held in the region throughout the year. These include the Joan of Arc Festival held in Orléans in early May, when there is a religious ceremony in the cathedral and a military parade to commemorate Sainte Jeanne; the Anjou festival of theatre, music, dance and poetry held in July; the Chinon medieval market held in August, which features street entertainers, period costumes and traditional crafts; and the Nautelets Mass held in Anjou on Christmas Eve, when traditional Angevin carols are sung. For a list of events (both festivals and outings) organised by the Brière regional park, contact the **Maison du Parc**, 180 Ile de Fédrun, 4470 St-Joachim.

Another good way to come into close contact with local people is to choose locally owned accommodation. This can range from the simple B&B, of which there are many lovely examples, particularly in the Indre *département*, to the grand château. Do not reject the possibility of the latter out of hand, as the lists of *chambres d'hôte* often contain the addresses of small châteaux which offer basic accommodation at remarkably low prices. In many of these architectural gems, set in peaceful, attractive surroundings, you are treated more as a guest than a client and are given a unique opportunity to interact with local families, who are often extremely knowledgeable about the area. Moving upmarket, you come to the châteaux belonging to associations such as **Relais et Châteaux** or **Château-Accueil** (addresses for both in **Accommodation** section of Introduction). The latter is the marketing body for over sixty French châteaux, almost a quarter of which are in Centre Val-de-Loire. The emphasis is very definitely on 'accueil' (welcome) and most owners speak fluent English, though this option is firmly in the top price bracket.

At the other end of the scale, you could meet people by offering your services on an archaeological dig. Information on those in Centre Val-de-Loire is available from the **Direction des Antiquités**, 6 rue de la Manufacture, 45000 Orléans (Tel. 38 68 16 60 or 38 53 91 38); while details of those in the Pays-de-la-Loire come from Direction des Antiquités, 2 allée du Commandant Charcot, 44035 Nantes (Tel. 40 29 32 55). General information on the two regions which make up the Loire, including lists of festivals and accommodation, is available from the **Comité Régional du Tourisme Val-de-Loire**, 9 rue St-Pierre Lentin, 45041 Orléans (Tel. 38 54 95 42/43); and the **Comité Régional du Tourisme des Pays-de-la-Loire**, Maison du Tourisme, Place du Commerce, 44000 Nantes (Tel. 40 48 15 45).

Discovering Places

In the Brière regional park, thematic walks, cycle rides or canoeing expeditions are organised in July and August. The type of excursion depends on the day of the week, so you could, for example, go walking one day, cycling the next, and then canoeing. This is a very good value way of seeing an interesting area and benefiting from guides with local knowledge. Information on the summer's programme is available from the **Syndicat d'Initiative de Brière**, Maison du Sabotier, 2 rue des Ecluses, 44410 La Chapelle-des-Marais, who can also give you details of local associations dealing with any special interest you may have.

In the Brenne regional park, a four to five day discovery trip 'In the land of a thousand ponds' is run between April and October. Individuals are grouped together up to a maximum of ten, and the cost (around 3750FF) includes full-board in a 2-star château-hotel, bike-hire, a day out in a horse-drawn carriage, a flight over the Brenne ponds in a three-seater plane, the services of guides and local experts, entrance to monuments and châteaux, and visits within the park. The trip has the Federation of Natural Parks seal of approval and is distributed by **Clés de France** (see p. 51).

Information on cave dwellings in the region, as well as itineraries linking them, is available from **Carrefour Anjou-Touraine-Poitou**, Place des Récollets, 49400 Saumur. A catalogue of walking trips organised by the regional branch of the non-profit-making 'Grand R' association, and possible with or without a guide, can be requested from **Abri**, 7 rue de la Clavurerie, 44000 Nantes (Tel. 40 20 20 62).

Those without their own transport could consider basing themselves in Amboise, Blois, Orléans or Tours, as individuals can join mini-bus tours from here to various châteaux and sights of interest. A departure is guaranteed as long as four or more people turn up and there is a different itinerary each day of the week. Off-season, daily visits to either Azay-le-Rideau and Villandry, or Amboise and Chenonceau take place from Tours, even if there are only two people wishing to attend. Information is available from **Touraine Evasion**, 8–10–12 rue du Docteur Herpin, 37000 Tours (Tel. 47 66 51 32 – office hours). Other mini-bus trips starting from Tours are run by **Marques Dos Santos**, 6 rue Jean Messire, 37000 Tours (Tel. 47 37 15 60); and coach excursions are available from **Bureaux des Châteaux de la Loire**, Gare SNCF, 37000 Tours (Tel. 47 05 46 09). Boat trips also depart from Blois, Orléans and Briare. Information on these and other locally arranged excursions, short breaks or holidays is available from the appropriate *département's* **Loisirs-Accueil** service. The addresses of those in Centre Val-de-Loire are as follows: **Cher** – 10 rue de la Chappe, 18000 Bourges (Tel. 48 70 74 75); **Eure-et-Loir** – 19 Place des Epars, BP 67, 28002 Chartres (Tel. 37 21 37 22); **Indre** – Gare Routière, 36 rue Bourdillon, 36000 Châteauroux (Tel. 54 22 91 20); **Indre-et-Loire** – 38 rue Augustin-Fresnel, BP 139, 37171 Chambray-les-Tours (Tel.

47 48 37 27); **Loir-et-Cher** – 11 Place du Château, 41000 Blois (Tel. 54 78 55 50); and **Loiret** – 3 rue de la Bretonnerie, 45000 Orléans (Tel. 38 62 04 88). The Loisirs-Accueil for the *départements* in Pays-de-la-Loire are: **Loire-Atlantique** – Maison du Tourisme, Place du Commerce, 44000 Nantes (Tel. 40 48 15 45); **Mayenne** – 84 ave R-Buron, BP 343, 53018 Laval (Tel. 43 53 18 18); and **Vendée** – 8 Place Napoléon-Bonaparte, 85000 La Roche-sur-Yon (Tel. 51 62 65 27).

Communications

How to Get There

If you wish to travel by **plane**, Air France operate a flight between London and Nantes, though one of the Paris airports would be more convenient for most of the Centre Val-de-Loire region. A Manchester-Nantes service is on the cards. The French airline, TAT, runs a twice-weekly service on 48-seater aircraft between Gatwick and Tours. This takes 95 minutes and reservations are possible through Air France (Tel. 081 499 9511).

Tours and Le Mans are now on the TGV Atlantique **train** route, which cuts journey times considerably. The train journey from Paris to Nantes takes just over 3 hours, while Paris-Tours takes around 2 hours and Paris-Orléans only 1 hour. Services are frequent.

Eurolines operates a **coach** service from the UK to Orléans and Tours.

When You're There

Rail – the main SNCF stations are at Orléans, Chartres, Le Mans, Tours, Châteauroux, Saumur, Nantes, Bourges, Blois and La-Roche-sur-Yon. Connections within the region are very good, except for the few destinations east of Orléans, which require travel via either Paris or Bourges and Nevers. Where a place of interest is not on the rail network, it is almost always served by bus.

Bus – there are regular services on **Les Rapides Touraines** between Tours, Amboise, Chenonceau and many of the Loire châteaux. See also the mini-bus and coach tours mentioned under **Good Alternatives**.

Car – the region's main autoroutes are the A10–A11 from Paris to Le Mans and on to Nantes. This splits off at Le Mans as the A81. The A10 takes you down to Orléans, then Tours, while the A17 from Orléans leads to Bourges and St-Amand-Montrond. The journey time from Paris to Nantes, right in the west of the Loire region is around 4 hours. This comprehensive motorway network is supplemented by good N and D roads.

Boat – the Loire's waterways provide an alternative way of discovering its many hidden charms. The following stretches of river are easily navigable: the Mayenne, from Laval downstream; the Sarthe, from Le Mans onwards; and the Briare canal. Boats can be hired, or boat trips joined, at Angers, Le Mans, Château Gontier, Laval and Noyen-sur-Sarthe, Blois, Briare and Orléans. Further information is available from the regional tourist boards and the **Syndicat Interdépartemental du Bassin Maine**, Place du Président Kennedy, BP 2207, 49022 Angers (Tel. 44 88 99 38).

Cycling – although the countryside around the Loire is rather flat and undramatic, cycling offers visitors a good opportunity of getting off the beaten track and of exploring the forest tracks of the Sologne and the quiet riverbanks of the Loire and its tributaries. For information, contact the regional or departmental tourist board or, in the Indre, the **Comité Départemental de Cyclotourisme de l'Indre** (M. Blenert), route de Luant, 36500 Neuillay-les-Bois (Tel. 54 84 08 92).

Walking – a walking tour of the region is a good way of combining sightseeing and exercise. The following long-distance footpaths have been designed to enable visitors to see both scenic Loire and some of the more famous historical and architectural sights of the region: the GR 3, which follows the Loire valley and passes through the forests of Chinon and Orléans; the GR 46, which follows the Indre valley; the GR 31, which runs from the Boulogne forest to the Sologne woods; and the GR 32, which traverses the Orléans forest from north to south. Those planning walks in the Indre could contact the **Commission Randonnée Pédestre UFOLEP**, 1 bd St-Denis, 36000 Châteauroux (Tel. 54 22 21 47).

Riding – the Loire is noted for its stud farms, particularly those in the region of Saumur, home of the Cadre Noir cavalry unit. There are numerous riding centres in the region, many of which offer accommodation and trekking holidays. Trekking guides and further information are available from local tourist offices and from **ARTE Centre Val-de-Loire**, 66 rue Delvide, 37000 Tours (Tel. 47 54 51 23).

Useful Local Contacts

The **Conservatoire des Sites de Loir-et-Cher**, based at the Centre Administratif, 41020 Blois (Tel. 54 74 62 22 ext. 2322), was founded in 1987 and is the only departmentally based conservatoire in France. Current projects include the purchase of damp prairies in the Cher valley (a nesting site for rare birds), and liaison with local farmers concerning non-damaging methods. Information about the St-Denis-du-Payré nature reserve and other sites of ecological interest in the Vendée *département* is available from the **Association de Défense de l'Environnement en Vendée**, 33 rue Paul-Doumer, 85000 La Roche-sur-Yon. There is an environmental initiation centre (**CPIE**) at Château d'Azay-le-Ferron, 36290 Mézières-en-Brenne (Tel. 54 39 23 43). The headquarters of the **Brière Regional Park** are at Maison du Parc, 180 Ile-de-Fédrun, 44720 St-Joachim; the **Brenne Regional Park** is based at Maison du Parc, Hameau du Bouchet, 36300 Rosnay (Tel. 54 37 75 84). Finally, there are two regional parks, which have areas within the region, though their headquarters are outside it: **Parc Naturel Régional Normandie-Maine**, BP 05, 61320 Carrouges; and **Parc Natural Régional du Marais Poitevin**, La Ronde, 17170 Courcon.

Geographical Breakdown of Region

Pays-de-la-Loire

The administrative region of the Pays-de-la-Loire is extremely varied, with a quiet coastline in the south-west, Normandy-style countryside in the north-east and – between them – in the *département* of Maine-et-Loire, the beginnings of the ribbon of châteaux which stretches along the Loire river. The coast and the châteaux are what lure most people to the region, though it also has a city of great interest in its capital, Nantes.

Nantes

Formerly capital of Brittany, and still regarded as part of that region by many of its inhabitants, Nantes is a historic city of wide boulevards, situated at the point where the Loire becomes tidal.

A major site of interest is the **Château des Ducs de Bretagne**, an imposing fortified building dating from the fifteenth century. Surrounded by wide moats and with six solid towers, it was here that Henry IV signed the Edict of Nantes (which granted the Protestants religious freedom) in 1598. Once inside, look out for the Tour de la Couronne d'Or and the wrought-iron well. The château also contains three museums: the **Musée des Salorges**, which covers the commercial and maritime history of Nantes; the **Musée des Arts Populaires Régionaux**, displaying Breton head-dresses, costumes and furniture; and the **Musée des Arts Décoratifs**, which holds temporary exhibitions of living artists. Bear in mind that all the above are closed on Tuesdays. Just next-door to the château is the **Cathédrale St-Pierre et St-Paul**, started in the fifteenth century but not completed until the end of the nineteenth. The light stone vaulting inside is impressive (higher than that of Notre-Dame in Paris), as is the tomb of François II to the right of the transept. Note the unusual spire of the **Chapelle de l'Immaculée**, behind the cathedral on rue Malherbe.

The **Musée des Beaux Arts** is worth a visit; its exhibition space is extensive, and paintings by artists like Rubens and Courbet are complemented by ever-changing displays of contemporary art. The **Natural History Museum** on rue Voltaire is a source of information on regional fauna. You could visit the **Ancienne Ile Feydeau**, formerly an island and still regarded as such by the *Nantais*, despite the fact that the water either side of it has now been replaced by streets. There are many elegant shipbuilders' houses here, and there is a museum dedicated to Jules Verne, who was born here, at 3 rue de l'Hermitage. The **Passage Pommeraye** on rue Crébillon is an elaborate nineteenth-century shopping gallery. Modern architecture enthusiasts should ask the tourist office about buses out to Le Corbusier's **Cité Radieuse**. An opportunity for peace and quiet is offered by the **Jardin des Plantes** on rue Gambetta.

Accommodation

First Class

L'Abbaye de Villeneuve, Les Sorinières, Route de la Roche-sur-Yon (Tel. 40 04 40 25): 20 luxurious rooms with wooden beams and stone fireplaces in former Cistercian abbey, 10 minutes from town centre; restaurant.

First Class / Middle Range

Domaine d'Orvault, Chemin des Marais du Cens, 44700 Orvault (Tel. 40 76 84 02): 30 rooms in Relais et Châteaux hotel with extensive grounds, 7 km from Nantes; excellent restaurant with dishes based on regional products.

Middle Range

L'Hôtel, rue Henri-IV, 6 Place Duchesse-Anne (Tel. 40 29 30 31): 31 pleasant rooms in quiet but central hotel. **Hôtel Colonies**, 5 rue Chapeau-Rouge (Tel. 40 48 79 76): 39 rooms in comfortable hotel.

Economy

Hôtel Fourcroy, 11 rue Fourcroy (Tel. 40 44 68 00): 19 rooms in friendly hotel. **Hôtel Calypso**, 16 rue de Strasbourg (Tel. 40 47 54 47): neat, comfortable rooms.

Eating Out

First Class

Delphin, Pont de Bellevue, 44470 Ste-Luce (Tel. 40 49 04 13): dishes from local produce served in elegant riverbank restaurant, 9 km from Nantes. **Mon Rêve**, route des Bords de Loire (D 751), 44115 Basse-Goulaine (Tel. 40 03 55 50): fresh ingredients used in country house restaurant, 8 km from Nantes.

First Class/Middle Range

Le Gavroche, 139 rue des Hauts-Pavés (Tel. 40 76 22 49): high quality mixture of traditional and modern cuisine.

Middle Range

Auberge du Château, 5 Place Duchesse-Anne (Tel. 40 74 05 51): pleasant restaurant next to ducal château.

Economy

La Cigale, 4 Place Graslin (Tel. 40 69 76 41): good value turn-of-the-century brasserie-style restaurant. **La Mangeoire**, 16 rue des Petites Ecuries: quiet, elegant, but cheap. **Espace Aquarius**, 3 rue Simeon-Foucault (Tel. 40 89 50 70): vegetarian restaurant attached to bookshop; open for lunch and afternoon tea only.

Entertainments

Between June and August, you could join one of the tourist office tours of the Feydeau or Vignoble areas. Cinemas and the town theatre can be found around Place Graslin, and the area north of rue Crébillon is popular with students at night. The Médiathèque is a modern library with bookshops and video-watching facilities. If you are going to be in Nantes during the first fortnight of July, be sure to book rooms in advance, as Les Fêtes d'Eté brings hundreds of dance, musical and theatrical events to the town.

Useful Addresses

The **Tourist Office** is on Place du Commerce (Tel. 40 47 04 51) and the **Comité Régional du Tourisme,** which will supply information on the whole of the Pays-de-la-Loire region, is in the same building, but the telephone number is 40 48 15 45. The **Post Office** is on Place de Bretagne, and the **Hospital** on Place Alexis-Ricordeau (Tel. 40 48 33 83). For emergency **medical assistance**, dial 40 48 35 35 for SAMU.

Transport Options

Town buses stop at Place du Commerce and a single ticket entitles you to unlimited travel on both buses and trams for one hour. The trams run along the old riverfront, past the train and bus station. TTO buses, Cars Brisseau and Cars Groussin cover destinations outside town, but check for trains first as the fare is often cheaper.

Rest of Pays-de-la-Loire

North-west of Nantes, at the little village of **Le Croisic,** which belongs to the Brière regional park and is attractively situated opposite an expanse of salt marsh on a peninsula above the Loire estuary, you can visit the Les Salicornes pottery at 28 rue du Traict or the hand-made doll shop at 22 rue Pierre-Curie. These are just two of many traditional craft outlets encouraged by the park and allowed to exhibit at its Maison des Artisans at Kerhinet (see below). Nearby **Guérande** is home to others, including a wood-turner on rue de Saillé, a potter on rue du Rocher Saillé, and a pewterer on rue de la Juiverie. The park's 'pilot' village, which it has taken great trouble to restore and equip for discovery tourism is at **Kerhinet-St-Lyphard.** Here, in addition to the Maison des Artisans, you will find a museum of costume and a weaver's studio. Many more craftsmen can be found on rue Clément-Ader in **St-Nazaire** at the mouth of the Loire, where there is also an *ecomusée* focusing on the culture of the port and its industrial and social history.

   Rozé, just beyond St-Malo-de-Guersac, is home to a natural history museum and a nature park. The park recreates all the natural milieux encountered in the 'Grande Brière Mottière', which consist mainly of ponds, prairies, marshland and reedbeds. It sees itself as a window on the living marsh and there is an observation path, which takes you 1 km along the Canal du Rozé and includes hides and information boards; alternatively you can explore by *chaland*, the local boat. The park is open every day from May to September (and during Easter holidays); you can either make your own way, hiring binoculars from the reception building, where exhibitions and audio-visuals can be viewed, or join one of the guided tours which leave between 10 a.m. and 3 p.m. The nearby Maison de l'Eclusier is a recently formed natural history museum which complements the park. The Brière regional park headquarters are at 180 Ile de Fédrun, **St-Joachim**. Number 308 Ile de Fédrun is a reconstruction of a traditional Brière cottage and there are various artists' studios in the vicinity. Visits of the marshes by boat are on offer at **Fédrun** and nearby **Kerfeuille**. Documentation on the Brière region is available from the Syndicat d'Initiative de Brière, which is housed in the Maison du Sabotier, a shoe-making museum, at 2 rue des Ecluses, **La Chapelle-de-Marais** (Tel. 40 66 85 01), but is open daily only in July and August (rest of year Wednesday afternoons only).

Further down the coast, the flat, marshy **Ile de Noirmoutier** can be reached by bridge (or causeway at low tide). Expanses of oyster bed and saltpan are complemented by a fifteenth-century castle, museum and Romanesque church in the island's one town. Still further south, **Les Sables d'Olonne** combines its role as fishing port with that of family resort, with its busy quay, wide promenades and long sandy beaches. On Route de Verdun, the Musée de l'Abbaye Ste-Croix, housed in an old Benedictine convent, displays the modern works of artists Gaston Chaissac and Victor Brauner. If you head inland, you will pass through sectors of the **Marais Poitevin** regional park, whose marshes are criss-crossed with canals.

Up to the north-east, on a level with Nantes, is the town of **Saumur**. Built on both banks of the Loire, it is a busy, somewhat sprawling place, whose main sources of income are its sparkling white wine, the local mushrooms and the 'Cadre Noir', a prestigious cavalry school which attracts both local and international attention. The fourteenth-century château houses a splendid collection of equestrian equipment and saddlery, and is also of architectural interest, with its octagonal corner towers, shaped anachronistically like modern missiles! There are good views from Tour Guet. The

Musée des Arts Décoratifs is also worth seeing, if only for its fascinating fifteenth- and sixteenth-century tapestries. Each July, the Cadre Noir stages its celebrated carousel event, featuring dressage performances, stunts and jumping, which takes place in the Place Hôtel de Ville. If you are interested in wine, you should head for the St-Hilaire suburb, where a number of local wine houses hold tasting sessions: try Ackermann Laurence, 19 rue Palustre, St-Hilaire – St-Florent (Tel. 41 50 25 33).

This area contains many cave dwellings, some of which are still inhabited. Near **Doué-la-Fontaine**, just beyond Forges, several underground sites can be visited, including a seventeenth-century farming hamlet. The country east of Saumur is the **Poitou Plains**, an area of gently rolling hills interrupted by small towns and villages. **Fontrevaud** (10 km south-east) is the site of a magnificent abbey. Several notable Plantagenets are buried here, among them Richard I (the Lion Heart), Henry II and Eleanor of Aquitaine. The monastery was built in the eleventh century and added to in the sixteenth. **Montsoreau**, 2 km up the road, is another medieval village on the southern bank of the Loire. The elegant fifteenth-century château was the setting for Alexandre Dumas' novel *La Dame de Montsoreau* and houses a museum devoted to the Moroccan cavalry.

North-west of Saumur, on the more attractive and less frequented road which runs alongside the southern bank of the Loire, is **Chênehutte-les-Tuffeaux**, a charming village set in soft, shady truffle country. Its thirteenth-century priory has been converted into a very good hotel. Several châteaux in the area are worth visiting, notaby the fifteenth-century **Château Brissac**, which is magnificently decorated and houses a fine collection of family portraits. Wine enthusiasts will be interested in the selection of local wines on show in its eleventh-century cellar, a tour of which includes a wine-tasting session.

Angers, once capital of Anjou, guards the western approach to the Loire Valley. It is a large, sprawling city of some 200,000 inhabitants and its main point of interest is its château. This thirteenth-century building was built by the Dukes of Anjou (ancestors of the Plantagenets) and besieged in the Hundred Years' War by the armies of Henry III. It is an austere fort, built of dark, cold stone and surrounded by a dry moat and high walls. More interesting than its medieval military masonry are the magnificent tapestries it houses, particularly the Tapestry of the Apocalypse, which is considered a masterpiece of medieval art. The collection also includes some fine fifteenth-century works woven of wool and gold thread. Further medieval tapestries can be seen in the St-Maurice cathedral, and a display of contemporary ones is contained in the Lurcat Museum of Contemporary Art on the north bank of the Maine river.

West of Angers is the **Château de Serrant**, an imposing, but nonetheless beautiful, Renaissance castle. Both Vaubrun's tomb and the graceful staircase are fine examples of Baroque style, and the château is another one with a good medieval tapestry collection. To the north-east is the **Château du Plessis Bourré**, whose interest lies in a series of highly comical allegorical paintings on the ceiling of the guards' room.

Up in the Mayenne *département* is the **Château de Craon**, whose beautiful eighteenth-century gardens are open to the public in the afternoon, from April to November. Straddling the Mayenne and Sarthe *départements* are parts of the Normandie-Maine regional park, including the Forêt de Sillé and Forêt de Perseigne, which both offer good walking possibilities. A panoramic view of the park can be had from the Jardin du Donjon de **Ballon**, 20 km north of **Le Mans** (of motor-racing fame), whose Musée de Tessé, at 2 ave de Paderborn, houses interesting collections of paintings, sculptures, decorative arts and archaeology. It was in the old town of Le Mans that *Cyrano de Bergerac* was filmed.

Accommodation

First Class

'**Le Château**', 85450 Moreilles (Tel. 51 56 17 56): 8 rooms and friendly welcome at ivy-covered country house; *tables d'hôte* on request. **Château de Craon**, 53400 Craon (Tel. 43 06 11 02): 5 rooms in elegant eighteenth-century Anjou château. **Château de la Jaillière**, La Chapelle St-Sauveur, 44370 Varades (Tel. 40 98 62 54): 4 rooms in quiet château belonging to same family since 15th century; *tables d'hôte* with family recipes.

Middle Range

Manoir le Goulet, 85520 St-Vincent-sur-Jard (Tel. 51 33 42 31): 5 rooms in pleasant house in pine grove, with private beach. **Château des Briottières**, 49330 Champigné (Tel. 41 42 00 02): 8 rooms in 18th century château with extensive grounds, in the same family for 200 years; *tables d'hôte*. **Château du Plessis**, La Jaille-Yvon, 49220

Le Lion d'Angers (Tel. 41 95 12 75): 6 rooms in sixteenth- and seventeenth-century château with family atmosphere; *tables d'hôte* on reservation.

Economy

Hôtel de France, 72320 La-Chartre-sur-le-Loir (Tel. 43 44 40 16): 28 rooms in family-run hotel; restaurant. **Mme Gendron**, N 12, 53500 Ernée (Tel. 43 05 70 80): delightful *chambres d'hôte* in traditional home offering local produce.

Eating Out

First Class

Le Toussaint, 7 rue Toussaint, 49000 Angers (Tel. 41 87 46 20): traditional local cuisine and wine in beautiful old dining room.

Middle Range

Auberge de l'Hermetière, St-Vincent-du-Loroüer, 72150 Le Grand Lucé (Tel. 43 44 84 45): rustic lakeside restaurant in forest clearing, with local specialities.

Eure-et-Loir, Loir-et-Cher & Indre-et-Loire

In the Eure-et-Loir *département*, **Chartres**, famous for the magnificent stained-glass windows of its cathedral and designated a UNESCO World Heritage site, deserves more than the cursory half-hour allocated on the typical coach tour from Paris. There are winding cobbled streets to explore, which lead past half-timbered houses to the River Eure, and the Stained-Glass Window Centre to visit. It is also a memorable experience to attend one of the organ concerts that take place in the cathedral in July and August. **Maintenon**, on the banks of the Eure, boasts a château whose gardens were designed by Le Nôtre, landscapist of Versailles, while nearby **Gallardon** has a twelfth-century church with an unusual wooden ceiling painted in blue, ochre and terracotta. Further south is **Châteaudun**, with its carefully restored medieval château and lively Thursday market.

Down in Loir-et-Cher, **Vendôme** is worth a visit. Built on several islands in the River Loir (not Loire), it is a town of old streets, bridges, parks and gardens, with a fine eleventh-century abbey and a Gothic church. Downstream, **Montoire-sur-le-Loir** has a beautiful chapel, the St-Gilles, and hosts a festival of world folklore in August. At **Mesland**, you can go wine-tasting at the Caves Brossillon, Domaine de Lusqueneau (Tel. 54 70 28 23), before joining the Loire once again and heading for Blois.

Blois was the capital of the Loire Valley during the Renaissance and, during the fifteenth and sixteenth centuries, its royal court is reputed to have been 15,000 strong. The château (one of the four most famous ones in the region) displays a four-century range of architectural styles, its best known feature being an open octagonal spiral staircase, adorned with sculptured salamanders, which provides a magnificent example of Renaissance flamboyance. Other points of interest are its secret passages, hidden behind wood panelling, its wonderful tapestries and the richly decorated bedroom of Catherine de Medici. Three museums are housed in the château, focusing in turn on Archaeology, Fine Art and Religious Art. The château commands a position on a hill above the northern bank of the river, dominating the bustling little town with its picturesque old quarter, lively shopping area, overflowing street cafés and good museums. It would, however, be wise to time your visit outside the high season. For most of the year, the château puts on a *Son et Lumière* performance (in English). Boat trips on the river also start from here. On the edge of the Forêt de Russy, you will find the more intimate Château de **Beauregard**, which is well-proportioned, has an impressive portrait gallery, a fully equipped sixteenth-century kitchen and parkland sloping away to a lake.

Nearby **Cheverny** is one of the few great châteaux to have been built by a lady. It is a stately home, dating from the early seventeenth century, with a fine classical façade, and readers of *Tintin* (the famous French comic strip whose eponymous hero is an unorthodox journalist) may well recognise it as the model for Tintin's mansion, Moulinsart. Cheverny's interior is lavishly furnished with its original seventeenth-century collection of antiques, furniture, tapestries and paintings, and it is reassuring to know that the château has been inhabited by the same family for over 400 years.

Chambord is arguably the most breathtaking of all the Loire châteaux. Built on a huge scale and surrounded by a vast forest, it is precisely the sort of castle found in fairy-tales. Built from plans inspired by Leonardo da Vinci, it emerges from behind the trees as you approach it through the forest. Its most famous feature is the celebrated double spiral stairway, though the overall impression given by the simple white walls, crowned by a fantastic roofscape of towers, turrets, tiny windows, chimneys and gables, is what makes it so special. With its 440 rooms and eighty-three staircases, it has been designated a UNESCO World Heritage Site. The château plays host to a *Son et Lumière* from May to September, and a regional festival of theatre, music and dance in May and June. All around, the heather, birch trees and lakes of the **Sologne** countryside provide ideal terrain for hunters and fishermen, and offer a harmonious sight in autumn.

To the south-west, at **Montrichard** on the River Cher, you can taste wines at the Caves Monmousseau, 71 rue de Vierzon (Tel. 54 32 07 04), before heading towards another of the great châteaux, **Chenonceau**, just over the border in the Indre-et-Loire *département*. This château was a gift from Henry II to his mistress, Diane de Poitiers, and is many people's favourite Loire château. It is magnificently situated, appearing to be suspended weightlessly above the Cher by a series of graceful arches. The formal gardens are a mass of box hedges and begonias, and the interior of the château contains some fine furniture, tapestries and paintings. However, as with all the most popular sites, it pays to arrive early in the morning to avoid the crowds. **Amboise,** to the north, is also worth visiting. A picturesque town and birthplace of Charles VIII, its château sits perched on a hill, still an imposing presence despite having been partially razed during the Revolution. Look out for its unusual spiral Tour des Minimes. Along the cliff from the castle, on rue Victor-Hugo, you can see numerous cave dwellings, many of which have now been converted into holiday homes, complete with running water and electricity. Also nearby is **Clos Lucé**, where Leonardo da Vinci spent the last years of his life; a museum of his 'fabulous inventions' has been created there. In Amboise, wines can be tasted at Cave Girault-Artois, 7 quai des Violettes (Tel. 47 57 07 71), and July and August bring *Son et Lumière* performances and a summer festival.

There is also wine-tasting at **Chançay, Vouvray** and **Montlouis,** all between Amboise and **Tours,** a medieval city in the very centre of the Loire Valley, which has been capital of its region (the Touraine) since the Roman period. Once past the rather unpleasant industrial suburbs, the recently restored half-timbered gables of the houses in the old town, especially around Place Foire-le-Roi, are a treat. Look out particularly for the Hôtel Gouin, 25 rue du Commerce, with its fine Renaissance façade, and the two towers nearby: the Tour Horloge and Tour de Charlemagne are all that remain of the basilica church of St-Martin, on the pilgrim route to Santiago de Compostella in Spain. The thirteenth century Gatien Cathedral has some lovely clear stained-glass windows and is the site of Charles VIII's tomb. The Compagnonnage museum, housed in a beautiful eleventh-century abbey, has an interesting collection of craftsmen's masterpieces, while the Musée des Beaux-Arts, on rue Jules-Simon, houses collections of Renaissance paintings and has peaceful gardens.

Downstream, not far from the point where the Cher meets the Loire, is the château of **Villandry**. This classical Renaissance palace is notable less for its achitecture than its horticulture; people come for miles to see its wonderful formal gardens. **Langeais**, whose forbidding feudal castle was built in the fourteenth century for Louis XI, boasts the oldest dungeon in France (late tenth century). The castle is architecturally interesting because it has remained largely unaltered for 500 years; inside, it is decorated exactly as it would have been in the fifteenth century, giving a good idea of how the nobility lived at that period. **Azay-le-Rideau**, the most popular château in the Tours area, is set in pastoral surroundings on the banks of the Indre. It offers a fine example of the transition from military architecture to high Renaissance style. The moat and towers are vestiges of a past martial era, while the graceful parklands and luxurious interior hark back to more settled times. A *Son et Lumière* is held there from April to September, and wine-tasting is possible at the Château de l'Aulée. From here, it is possible to drive straight through the forest of Chinon on the River Vienne.

Chinon is another of the most famous Loire châteaux, built by Henry II of England and the place of his death. Its imposing medieval bastions contain fine collections of sculpture and tapestries, as well as a Great Hall where a plaque commemorates Joan of Arc's first meeting with the Dauphin, Down in the town are attractive timber-framed houses, some of them over 700 years old. Rabelais spent his childhood here and it is not difficult to imagine the little alleyways and cobbled streets peopled with Rabelaisian characters. The 'Entonneurs Rabelaisiens' brotherhood give lectures in June and September. The centre of old Chinon is known as the Grand Carroi and every July or August a splendid medieval market is set up in the main square, featuring traditional stalls, local arts and crafts, and street entertainers. Wine-tasting cellars can be found on quai Pasteur and the helpful tourist office is on Place Voltaire (Tel. 97 93 17 85).

To the east of Chinon, on the other side of the River Vienne, the little hamlet of **Tavant** has a remarkable Romanesque chapel with frescoes. At **Champigny-sur-Veude** stand the remains of a palatial château, whose Renaissance chapel has some wonderful stained-glass windows. In summer, a steam train runs between Chinon and **Richelieu**, an unspoilt medieval village complete with town walls and gate. Further east, **Loches**, a fortified town perched on a rocky hill above the Indre, is best approached via the old Renaissance quarter, comprising a series of streets flanked by old houses and leading to the town centre, with its impressive gateway and belfry. A *Son et Lumière* takes place here in July and August. Across the valley, **Montrésor** is a delightful medieval town of half-timbered and old stone buildings. The ancient walls of its tenth-century riverside château (built by Fulk Nerra, one of Anjou's greatest counts) surround a beautifully restored and furnished manor house.

Accommodation

First Class

Château de Colliers, 41500 Muides-sur-Loire (Tel. 54 87 50 75): 5 rooms in sixteenth- and eighteenth-century château on left bank of Loire, near Chambord; *tables d'hôte* on reservation. **Château de Chissay**, Chissay-en-Touraine, 41400 Montrichard (Tel. 54 32 32 01): 30 rooms and apartments in recently renovated royal château with park and wood; restaurant.

Middle Range

Château de Gerfaut, 37190 Azay-le-Rideau (Tel. 47 45 40 16): 5 rooms in imposing château with wooded grounds (2 nights minimum); *tables d'hôte* on reservation. **Château de la Huberdière**, 37530 Nazelles (Tel. 47 57 39 32): 4 rooms in 18th century lakeside hunting lodge with period furnishings; *tables d'hôte*.

Middle Range / Economy

Mme Bouchet, 1 Place de la Gare, Nevoy-le-Roi, 37370 Ste-Paterne-Racan (Tel. 47 29 21 67): small, family-run hotel with large garden and vegetarian restaurant.

Economy

Hôtel du Boeuf Couronné, 15 Place Châtelet, 28000 Chartres (Tel. 37 21 11 26 or 37 21 89 07): 27 rooms in family-run hotel with restaurant. **Auberge de la Madeleine**, 6 Place de la Madeleine, 41100 Vendôme (Tel. 54 77 20 79): 9 rooms in family-run inn with good restaurant.

Eating Out

First Class

Hostellerie de la Lanterne, 48 quai de la Loire, RN 152, Rochecorbon, 37210 Vouvray (Tel. 47 52 50 02): local specialities using seasonal produce, in 18th century building; also has some rooms.

Middle Range

Hostellerie du Château de l'Isle, Château de l'Isle, 37150 Civray-de-Touraine (Tel. 47 23 80 09): hearty cuisine in 18th century house with park; also has 8 rooms.

Indre, Cher & Loiret

These *départements* pride themselves on their location, right in the heart of France, and their attractions range from the wild landscape of the Brenne ponds to a wealth of historic monuments, including the oldest church in the country.

Bourges

Capital of the Cher *département* and the Berry province, Bourges was a cultural centre in the fifteenth century and has strong associations with Charles VII's minister of finance, Jacques Coeur. The highlights of Bourges are undoubtedly **Jacques Coeur's palace** and the cathedral. The elaborate medieval architecture of this palace reflects Coeur's high opinion of himself: even the stonework is decorated with symbols of his name (not only hearts, but also scallop shells – *coquilles St-Jacques*). A guided tour is obligatory, but the detail (including a visit to the original toilets!) makes it worth it. The **Cathédrale St-Etienne** is a magnificent Gothic edifice, whose stained-glass windows, are famous throughout France and span five centuries twelfth to seventeenth). The **Hôtel Lallemant** is a luxurious medieval mansion, containing furnishings from different periods, and the **Hôtel Cujas** (**Musée de Berry**) is certainly worth visiting for its displays of prehistoric and Gallo-Roman remains. You can see the work of locally born artist Maurice Estève in the **Musée**

Estève. Green spaces are provided by the **Jardins de l'Archevêché**, near the cathedral, and the lovely **Jardins des Prés-Fichaux**, beside the River Yèvre.

Accommodation

There is no first class small-scale accommodation in Bourges. Instead try:

Middle Range

Hôtel Angleterre, 1 Place Quatre Piliers (Tel. 48 24 68 51): 31 rooms in comfortable hotel with restaurant. **Hostellerie Grand Argentier**, 9 rue Parerie (Tel. 48 70 84 31): 14 rooms in well-situated hotel.

Economy

Hôtel l'Etape, 4 rue Raphael-Cassanova (Tel. 48 70 59 47): quiet, central, welcoming hotel. **Hôtel de la Nation**, 24 Place de la Nation (Tel. 48 24 11 96): small, well-located hotel. **Hôtel St-Jean**, 23 ave Marx-Dormoy (Tel. 48 24 13 48): 24 rooms in hotel on outskirts of town.

Eating Out

First Class

La Gueulardière, Berry Bouy, 18500 Mehun-sur-Yèvre (Tel. 48 26 81 45): imaginative cuisine at country inn, 7 km from Bourges.

Middle Range

L'Ile d'Or, 39 bd Juranville (Tel. 48 24 29 15): house specialities in pleasant setting. **Le Jardin Gourmand**, 15 bis ave E-Renan (Tel. 48 21 35 91): excellent restaurant just out of town.

Economy

Au Rendez-vous des Amis, 6 ave Marx-Dormoy (Tel. 48 70 81 80): good value and welcoming, family-run hotel-restaurant; also has rooms. **D'Antan Sancerois**, 50 rue Bourbonnoux (Tel. 48 65 96 26): Berry specialities in restaurant frequented by local people.

Entertainments

Spring brings the musical Festival Printemps de Bourges, and more musical events hit town from mid-July to late August, with the Ballades à Bourges. In between, from mid-June to mid-July, various cultural celebrations mark the Fête de Jacques Coeur. Free organ concerts, by well-known organists, are put on in the cathedral during summer. A lively food market takes place at Place de la Nation on Saturday mornings. Night-life outside festival time is on the quiet side, though there is a café-théâtre upstairs at **Le Guillotin**, 15 rue Edouard-Vaillant.

Useful Addresses

The **Tourist Office** is near the cathedral at 21 rue Victor-Hugo (Tel. 48 24 75 33). The **Post Office** is at 29 rue Moyenne, and the **Hospital** at Centre Hospitalier, 34 rue Gambon (Tel. 48 68 40 00). For emergency **medical assistance**, dial SAMU on 48 65 15 15.

Transport Options

The tourist office runs 2-hour walking tours of the town between July and September. Bicycle rental is possible from the train station, the youth hostel (22 rue Henri-Sellier), and Loca Bourges (rue Edouard-Vaillant). A less than comprehensive bus service operates to neighbouring towns, leaving from the Gare Routière, rue du Champ-de-Foire.

Rest of Indre, Cher & Loiret

Valençay, in the north-west of the Indre *département* is a magnificent example of classical Renaissance architecture. Unlike many of the other châteaux in the area, Valençay is a mainly nineteenth-century building and was home to one of France's greatest diplomats, Charles Maurice de Talleyrand. The characteristic features of this château are the enormous round towers and the surrounding parklands, populated with sheep, deer, peacocks, swans and cranes. The interior is also suitably lavish, with all kinds of marvellous *objets d'art* and Louis XVI furniture. A *Son et Lumière* is held here in July and August. The departmental capital is the town of **Châteauroux**, whose Musée Hôtel Bertrand is worth a visit for its collections of paintings, sculptures, decorative arts and archaeology, as well as its section on traditional Berry life.

To the west of here are the ponds of **Brenne**, which are said to be the fourth most important wetland area in Europe and have been made into a regional park. Stories of sorcerers, fairies and giants abound in this wild and sparsely populated region, where the carp-fishing industry has now been supplemented by the manufacture of light aircraft and the encouragement of nature tourism. Tourist offices can supply motorists or cyclists with details of the 'Route de la Brenne'. The region's historical capital is the pleasant town of **Mézières-en-Brenne**, where medieval houses line the village canal and traditional local festivals are commonplace. Nearby **Azay-le-Ferron** is home to a CPIE (Environment Initiation Centre), which is housed in a renovated fifteenth-century château with lovely gardens and a park. A national natural history museum with 1000 animals can also be found here, in the 1200-acre wooded Parc de la Haute Touche. The abbey at **Fontgombault** is worth visiting, and the regional park headquarters are at Hameau du Bouchet, **Rosnay**, whose medieval fortress offers panoramic views over the Brenne.

Just over the border in the Cher *département*, the town of **Châteaumeillant**, with its attractive Romanesque church, nestles among vineyards, while, nearby, the tenth- and fifteenth-century château at **Culan** forms part of the Jacques-Coeur circuit of lesser known châteaux and stately homes (all still inhabited), details of which are available from tourist offices. Another of the Jacques-Coeur residences is the imposing fifteenth-century **Ainay-le-Vieil** château, near **St-Amand-Montrond** (famous for its jewel-workers), whose landscaped park is criss-crossed by canals and contains a rose garden and medicinal plant garden. Along with Bourges cathedral and the Palais Jacques Coeur, **Noirlac** Abbey must be one of the most magnificent buildings in the Cher. Exhibitions and concerts are put on here, from June to September. The châteaux at **Meillant** and **Châteauneuf-sur-Cher** are both popular, and, further north, **Mehun-sur-Yèvre** and **Vierzon** are famous for their porcelain. The Romanesque church and old town of **Aix d'Angillon** are worth a short visit, before going on to **La Chapelle-d'Angillon**'s feudal château and the vineyard-surrounded **Sancerre**, where wine can be tasted at Cave de la Cresle, Domaine Laporte (Tel. 48 54 04 07).

Over in Loiret, **Briare** is a good starting point for boat trips on the Loire. On its outskirts, at **St-Firmin**, is the unusual Pont-Canal, designed by Gustave Eiffel (of Eiffel Tower fame), a relatively unknown attraction which carries the waters of the Briare Canal across the Loire. The fifteenth-century red-brick château of **Gien** (also famed for its porcelain) houses a hunting museum, while **Sully**, further downstream, boasts a magnificent fourteenth-century fortress with intricate dungeons and a moat in which it is reflected.

The Romanesque basilica of **St-Benoit-sur-Loire** has some fine sculptures in the porch and an interesting crypt. Mass is sung there by monks on Sunday morning, and the town has an excellent market. **Germigny-des-Prés** is a rather ordinary little hamlet on the Loire, but contains the oldest church in France. It is Carolingian, built around 795, and has a mosaic-decorated dome, a lovely carved wooden statue of the Pieta and windows made from transparent alabaster. What is more, relatively few people go to see it.

The city of **Orléans** is a pleasant, civilised city, but rather obsessed with Joan of Arc. Although it was half-destroyed during the Second World War, various sights are still worth visiting. Its elaborate grey-stone Ste-Croix cathedral and the nearby Hôtel Groslot, built in 1550 and serving as town hall since 1790, are two of these. The latter contains sumptuous decorations and a collection of Joan of Arc memorabilia. One of the cathedral chapels is dedicated to Joan, with stained-glass windows depicting scenes from her life. The cathedral itself has an unusual mosaic floor. Further tributes are paid to Joan at the Maison de Jeanne d'Arc, 3 Place de Gaulle, where her contribution to both Orléans and France is commemorated through pictures, documents and an audio-visual recreation of her life and times. The Musée des Beaux-Arts, on rue Paul-Belmondo, has wide-ranging collections and is considered one of the best in France. Orléans is transformed in May, when a colourful historical pageant escorts a modern-day 'Joan of Arc' through the streets. The source of the Loiret bubbles up from an underground spring at nearby **Orléans-la-Source**, where an area of parkland contains a magnificent floral garden. The village of **Olivet** is particularly picturesque and wine-tasting can be enjoyed at Covifruit, 613 rue du Pressoir-Tonneau. Back on the Loire, slightly further downstream, the pretty old town of **Meung-sur-Loire** has associations with the literary figures Jean de Meung, author of the medieval classic *Le Roman de la Rose*, and the poet Villon, who was incarcerated in its château.

Accommodation & Eating Out

First Class

Château de la Beuvrière, St-Hilaire-de-Court, 18100 Vierzon (Tel. 48 75 08 14 or 48 75 14 63): 15 rooms in turreted eleventh-century family-run hotel; restaurant. **Château de la Commanderie**, Farges-Allichamps, 18200 St-Amand-Montrond (Tel. 48 61 04 19):

8 rooms in imposing, well-situated and welcoming château; *tables d'hôte* on reservation. **Château de la Verrerie**, Oizon, 18700 Aubigny-sur-Nère (Tel. 48 58 06 91): 11 rooms in fifteenth-century lakeside château in forest; *tables d'hôte* on reservation, or small restaurant in the grounds. **Château de la Tour**, Rivarennes, 36800 St-Gaultier (Tel. 54 47 06 12 or 54 47 06 08): 10 rooms in fourteenth-century riverside castle; meals on reservation.

Middle Range

Mme Lefebure, 'Domaine des Vigneaux', 36260 Mézières-en-Brenne (Tel. 54 38 11 32 and 54 38 10 03): 4 *chambres d'hôte* in unusual house with large grounds with bike hire. **M. Rijpstra**, 'Le Moulin des Chézeaux', 36800 St-Gaultier (Tel. 54 47 01 84): 3 *chambres d'hôte* in fourteenth-century former mill-house.

Economy

M Metz, Le Chalet, Route de Verneuil, St-Chartier, 36400 La Châtre (Tel. 54 31 05 76): 4 *chambres d'hôte* in quiet residence with park and nearby restaurant. **Mme Mitaty**, 63 Le Petit Epôt, 36300 Le Poinçonnet (Tel. 54 35 40 20): 2 *chambres d'hôte* in large, characterful, ivy-covered house.

12 Poitou-Charentes

The Poitou-Charentes is a region once crossed by the well-marked pilgrim trail that took half a million travellers each year to the shrine of Santiago de Compostella in northern Spain. Nowadays, travellers pass through the region on the A 10 autoroute, bound for Bordeaux or Biarritz.

Tourists who have chosen to make this region their holiday destination almost invariably head for the coast, Charentes-Maritime, whose much vaunted sunshine record equals that of the Mediterranean. It is easy to find attractive, gently shelving beaches backed by pine trees, but this coastline does lack the established elegance and class of the Mediterranean resorts. However, in La Rochelle, it has one of France's most attractive coastal towns.

Inland, the flat agricultural plain has none of the prettiness of the neighbouring Loire or Dordogne regions. The chief attraction for the tourist are the countless Romanesque churches, a legacy of the eleventh- and twelfth-century pilgrimages for which they were built.

Where the plain flattens out almost to sea level, north of La Rochelle, lies the Marais-Poitevin, a vast area of reclaimed marshland and one of France's regional parks. It attracts the serious naturalist as well as the tourist who simply likes to mess about on the river.

The people of the Poitou-Charentes have always looked to the sea or the soil for their livelihood. Fishing trawlers leave from the port of La Rochelle to search for their catch in the Atlantic; oyster and mussel farming thrives on the coast. Inland, the traditional *bocage*, small fields divided by hedgerows, sustains small-scale farming and these old-fashioned ways have only in part been replaced by large-scale mechanisation. In the hills around Cognac the grapes are grown which will make brandy, just as they have for over three centuries.

This is a thinly populated region of isolated hamlets reached by narrow, straight D roads. It is not surprising that the inhabitants of the area are conservative people with traditional tastes. It is said that the *Charentais*, the people of the southerly part of Poitou-Charentes, have the relaxed attitude to life more usually associated with inhabitants of the Midi. They are nicknamed after the *cagouille*, a snail that munches its way through the vines of the region.

History

For the tourist, probably the most important period of history for the region of Poitou-Charentes was the tenth and eleventh centuries, for it was then that the many Romanesque churches, those masterpieces of medieval architecture, were built.

The tenth century was the first era of peace and stability for this vulnerable coastal region then called Aquitaine. Until that time, a succession of armies had swept across the land: Celts, Romans, Visigoths, Moslems and Vikings. As the invasions ceased, slowly the Church began to exert its authority; the people responded with an upsurge of faith and the great period of Romanesque architecture began, with hundreds of churches being built here and all over France. At the same time it became safe for pilgrims to travel and many set out on the road to Santiago de Compostella. The most important of these routes ran through Poitiers, Aulnay and Saintes and consequently this was where many of the religious buildings sprang up to cater for the spiritual and material needs of the pilgrims.

Unfortunately, this interlude of peace was not to last. In 1152, Eleanor of Aquitaine, the divorced wife of Louis VII, married Henry Plantagenet. When, two years later, Henry became king of England, the whole of Aquitaine became English territory. For the next three hundred years the English retained their hold on this part of France, the battle being taken up on the English side by Richard the Lionheart and then the Black Prince – it is not surprising that this is a region of castles and walled towns. However, in 1453 at the battle of Castillon, the English were finally driven out.

The coming of the Reformation in the sixteenth century brought more strife to the region. La Rochelle had become a Protestant stronghold and was besieged by the army of Cardinal Richelieu. With the English fleet unable to give relief, the city fell, after resisting for fifteen months.

The seventeenth and eighteenth centuries saw the discovery of the method for the distillation of Cognac. There was also increased prosperity through trade with Canada where many many people from the region had earlier emigrated. The nineteenth century saw the beginnings of the tourist industry with the opening of the casino at Royan. Tourism has continued to develop in this century with the construction of the bridges to the islands and the opening of the A 10 autoroute.

Geography

The region of Poitou-Charentes is divided into four *départements*. The 450 km of Atlantic coastline including the main towns of La Rochelle, Saintes and Royan lie within Charente-Maritime. Inland, the town of Niort is the capital of Deux-Sèvres, Poitiers is the capital of Vienne and Angoulême is the capital of Charente.

The flat coastline is lined with sandy beaches, dunes and pine woods. There are also wide estuaries and vast areas of marshland. The scenery changes dramatically between high and low tide; with the sea retreating as much as two or three kilometres, large areas of mud are exposed at low tide and the estuaries are reduced to a murky trickle. This landscape is an ideal habitat for the many different species of birds which breed in the nature reserves found along this coast. In the Marais de Brouage, there is the Marais de Moëze nature reserve and near Rochefort is the Marais d'Yves where a large lagoon attracts a variety of waders and waterfowl. Curlews, avocets, mallards, teal and plover are all to be seen.

This coast boasts the second largest island in France, the Ile d'Oléron, over 30 km long. It has fine sandy beaches and wooded dunes on its north and west coast but the east coast is entirely given over to oyster farming, the economic backbone of the island. North of the Ile d'Oléron is the Ile de Ré, only a few kilometres shorter than its neighbour but much narrower. Vines are grown on the fertile eastern half of the island. There are sandy beaches on the south coast but the north-east is marshland where oysters are cultivated and salt is dried. There is a nature reserve at Lilleau des Niges where spoonbill. teal, golden plover and many other types of bird can be seen. Between these two islands lies the much smaller Ile d'Aix with beaches and a prison once occupied by Napoleon.

On the northern fringes of the region, west of Niort, lies the Parc Naturel Régional du Marais Poitevin, a large area of reclaimed marshland which has earned the tag *Venise Verte*. Neat fields are divided by narrow canals and waterways, green with duckweed and shaded by overhanging willows and groves of poplars.

Further inland, the flat fertile agricultural plains support intensive arable farming, although the fields of wheat and maize are relieved by areas of *bocage*, small fields where cattle or goats graze. In the south of the region, the River Charente makes its slow tortuous progress towards the Atlantic. On the gentle hillsides above the river between Angoulême and Saintes, grow the vines which produce the *eau-de-vie* of Cognac.

Climate

As the region's tourist board brochures proudly indicate, Poitou-Charentes is one of the country's sunniest areas. On a par with France's Mediterranean resorts, the Charente-Maritime can enjoy over 2250 hours of annual sunshine. With mid-summer air temperatures sometimes reaching 23°C, the summer climate can be particularly pleasant along the coast where the heat is freshened by the sea-breezes. Apart from storms at the time of the spring and summer equinox, the coast has a mild, gentle climate throughout the year. Thanks to the Atlantic gulf stream, spring arrives early, summers are long, winters short. As you travel further inland however, the ocean's moderating influence decreases and the seasonal extremes in temperature increase as does the overall rainfall.

Attractions

Seventy-five% of the tourists who make Poitou-Charentes their holiday destination head for the coast. Either they settle for a mainland resort such as Royan, or they choose the distinctive island quality of the Ile d'Oléron or the Ile de Ré. Not content with simply lazing in the sun, many holiday-makers spend the day grappling with windsurfers or dinghies. The nature reserves along the coastline offer the opportunity for studying birdlife and marine life (including the edible variety – oysters and mussels are a speciality of the Charente-Maritime.)

Most tourists pay at least one visit to La Rochelle, the capital of the region and an attractive and lively town with its port and streets of Renaissance houses with arcades which protect the fashionable shops and restaurants.

There are other attractions inland, worthy of day-trips or longer excursions. The Marais-Poitevin, or *Venise Verte*, west of Niort, is an area of reclaimed marshland intersected by a network of narrow green canals. Buy bread, cheese and wine, hire one of the typical flat-bottomed punts and enjoy a perfect picnic in this unique landscape.

The most important cultural attraction of the region is the Romanesque architecture of the churches of Poitiers and Saintes.

Cuisine

The ocean is the source of many of the dishes of this region. The Atlantic provides a wide range of fish, including turbot, hake and sole. However the region's specialities are its oysters, farmed in the region of Marennes, and mussels grown on wooden posts on the Ile d'Oléron and in the bay of Aiguillon. Oysters are eaten raw or lightly cooked in cream. Mussels are served as *moules mouclades* (a marinière sauce enriched with cream and egg yoke), or *moules éclades* (served on a wooden board then set alight!)

The rivers produce fresh-water fish and eels. The eels are used in a dish called *bouilliture d'anguille* (eels with garlic and wine). Snails are much prized. They are stuffed and served with a red wine *sauce aux lumas*. Meat specialities include lamb and goat. Locally produced smoked ham frequently appears on the menu as does *Tourtière*, a raised pie containing chicken and salsify. Pâté de foie gras is produced around Angoulême and you might also find partridge and lark pâté.

The typical 'peasant' dish of the region is *mojettes*, white beans, often cooked with locally produced butter and sometimes cream. *Far* is a mixture of vegetables such as chard, spinach and cabbage cooked with onions and bacon to which eggs and cream are later added. This region specialises in goats cheese such as chabichou and *fromage de St-Loup*. Soft white goats' cheese is an ingredient of *torteau fromager* a baked cheese-cake, the most famous dessert of the region often served with a raspberry sauce. Another typical sweet is *clafoutis* – fruit flan or thick pancake. From the pâtisserie try the macaroons from Poitiers and the angelica from Niort.

Vineyards of the Haut-Poitou region produce red, white and rosé wines, but the most famous vineyards are those around Cognac whose wine is distilled and matured for 30 months (three star ***), 4½ years (V.S.O.P. or ****), or 10 years (Napoléon). Eighty% of the cognac is exported and the inhabitants of Cognac itself are more likely to be drinking *pineau*, an aperitif made from a mixture of grape juice and cognac and served chilled.

Level of Tourism

Poitou-Charentes is somewhere near the bottom of the league when it comes to French touristic regions, attracting a mere 1.9% of all national visits. Of its visitors, only 11% come from outside France. It would, however, be wrong to think that, with these low figures and with the majority of tourists heading for the beaches of Charente-Maritime, tourism is non-existent inland. The peaceful backwaters of the Sèvres-Niortaise and the Charente have long been favourite retreats for the French holiday-maker. Campsites are often full in the high season with families who have 'dug in' for the summer, husbands and sons spending the day with the fishing rod, wives watering the pots of geraniums. A recent growth in tourism away from the coastal resorts has been in the Marais-Poitevin where the traditional flat-bottomed punts used by farmers to reach their island fields have been taken over by tourists. Villages like Coulon and St-Hilaire-la-Palud in the heart of the *Venise Verte* have become touristy and the waterways echo with the cries of novice boatmen. The Romanesque churches of the region have, of course, always been well-known by travellers and tourist offices, and many guidebooks have published routes which link the most impressive examples.

One very recent move to boost inland tourism is the opening of the Futuroscope park north of Poitiers. Its futuristic architecture houses a collection of high-tech cinemas, a 'journey into the future' and a children's theme park. Restaurants, hotels and conference facilities make this more than just a destination for day-trippers.

The tourism potential of the coast is enthusiastically promoted by the tourist board of Charente-Maritime; 250 km of sandy beaches, 21 marinas and watersports centres, 30 sailing schools and Europe's largest marina. Their brochures are careful to promote more than simply sea, sand and sail; there is equal emphasis given to *Tourisme Nature*, the *vie protégée* of the nature reserves. Considerable investment has been put into infrastructure; a new toll-bridge, for example, has recently been opened to link the Ile de Ré to the mainland. Accommodation has also been developed, and in this region alone they record more than 30 million overnight stays each year, of which 25% are by tourists from outside France. Tourism has become a major employer, creating directly or indirectly an estimated

70,000 jobs. Tourism in Charente-Maritime accounts for a turnover equal to that of agriculture.

This development is not necessarily good news for the tourist seeking peace and quiet. In the past, the Atlantic coast was a good alternative to the overcrowded Mediterranean resorts. Now it faces overcrowding itself. Despite having 539 hotels, 327 campsites and thousands of apartments and *gîtes* to rent, accommodation can be very hard to find during the seasonal onslaught. The Ile de Ré, for example, is invaded by nearly half a million visitors each year and the other two islands are similarly swamped by crowds. On the mainland, Royan is the biggest resort between Brittany and Biarritz, sporting a casino and rows of apartments, tourist shops and restaurants, all seething with tourists. Perhaps of all the resorts, La Rochelle has coped with the tourist invasion most successfully. It is crowded in summer, when windsurfing schools may appear to be as important as the fishing industry, but it does have an important existence outside July and August and therefore retains an authentic feel.

Good Alternatives

Meeting People

The coastal region of Poitou-Charentes is very much a holiday region where the emphasis is on watersports and the locals are as likely to be leading a windsurfing class as mending the nets. To understand one of the remaining traditional occupations of the region, there is an **oyster museum** (*ostréicole*) at Le Château d'Oléron and a **mussel museum** (*mytiliculture*) at Esnandes in the Marais-Poitevin, but to meet the people who do the work, an early morning visit to a fish market such as the one at the **Bassin à flot** in La Rochelle is recommended. Inland, the promotion of *produits régionaux*, whether food or local crafts, gives the opportunity to meet farmers and craftsmen. For example there is a cycle route on the Ile d'Oléron, 'deux roues pour une île', which takes the cyclist to farms offering a variety of products. Details for other areas from the local tourist offices, or from the **Comité Régional du Tourisme**, 2 rue Sainte-Opportune, BP 56, 86002 Poitiers (Tel. 49 88 38 94), which will also supply general information on the whole region.

Poitou-Charentes has its fair share of festivals. For example Nouaillé-Maupertuis has a medieval festival in mid-June when the locals dress in period costume and ride through the streets on horseback; Cognac has a grape harvest festival in October and La Rochelle hosts a festival of French songs called Les Francofolies.

Those interested in joining an archaeological dig in the region could request details from the **Direction des Antiquités**, Hôtel Jean du Moulin de Rochefort, 102 Grande Rue, 86020 Poitiers (Tel. 49 88 12 29).

In June and July, working holidays for young people are run by the **Centre Social et Culturel de Pons**, 4 rue du Président Roosevelt, BP 51, 17800 Pons (Tel. 46 94 08 17). These take place in Charente-Maritime.

Discovering Places

The concentration of tourists into the confined areas of the popular beach resorts of the Charente-Maritime makes it relatively easy to find alternatives and get away from the crowds.

All of the nature reserves in the region offer either signposted trails or guided tours. Details for the **Parc Naturel Régional du Marais-Poitevin** from Maison du Parc, 17170 La Ronde (Tel. 46 27 82 44). Information for the Lilleau des Niges, Moeze and Marais d'Yves nature reserves can be obtained from the **Ligue Française pour la Protection des Oiseaux**, La Corderie Royale, BP 263, 17305 Rochefort. The L.P.O. run a year-round programme of guided visits; ask for their leaflet 'Découvrez les Oiseaux de Charente-Maritime'. The **Société pour l'Etude et la Protection de la Nature en Aunis et Saintonge** (SEPRONAS) offer guided shore walks on the Ile de Ré; information from the tourist information in Saint Martin de Ré.

The forests of Poitou-Charentes such as Braconne near la Rochefoucauld also have well-marked trails. The **Society for the Protection of the Environment** in the Vienne has information on the forests around Poitiers, the most interesting of which is the forest of Moulière, north-east of Poitiers, once the hunting ground of the dukes of Aquitaine. North of Moulière is the *little forest* of Pinail where there are many rare plants growing. Contact M. Baron, 35 résidence de l'Ermitage, 86280 St-Benoit or the tourist office in Poitiers.

For those who love walking, there are four GR footpaths in the region and this is an ideal way of escaping the crowds. The absence of steep hills also makes this good cycling country; local tourist offices have details of bicycle hire. The regional tourist board, BP 56, 86002 Poitiers Cedex publish a booklet of *Circuits Bicyclettes* which includes for example a package bicycle tour of the Cognac country. The same office produce a *Canoë-Kayak* and a *Roulotte* (horse-drawn caravan) brochure. The departmental tourist office of Charente offer beginners courses in pony trekking; contact **Loisirs-Accueil**, Place Boullaud, 16021 Angoulême (Tel. 45 92 24 43). They also arrange various other holidays, often revolving around an activity and always small-scale. This is also true of the region's other Loisirs-Accueil service: **Loisirs-Accueil Vienne**, 11 rue Victor-Hugo, BP 287, 86007 Poitiers (Tel. 49 88 89 79)

Communications

How to Get There

TAT run a direct **flight** service from Stansted to Poitiers. Otherwise it is necessary to fly to Paris and then take a 1½ hour internal flight to La Rochelle (all year) or Royan (weekends in summer).

Eurolines run a direct **coach** service between London and Poitiers which costs around £80 adult return.

There will be a 3-hour high speed TGV **train** service from Paris to La Rochelle beginning in 1993. At present, that journey takes nearly 4 hours, while the Paris – Poitiers trip takes a minimum of 2 hours 20 minutes.

The A10 autoroute means that the region is only 4 hours drive from Paris.

When You're There

Rail – the local train service links all the main towns of the region, including those on the coast. The Ile d'Oléron has its own narrow gauge tourist tramway and there is also a tourist train from Saujon, near Royan, to La Tremblade.

Bus – the coastal regions of Poitou-Charentes are well served by local bus services thanks to the numbers of tourists and it is possible to reach all the towns and islands. Inland, the service is less convenient.

Car – the only motorway in the region is the A10 linking Poitiers and Bordeaux. The coastal roads can become congested in summer, but minor roads inland are generally clear all year round.

Boat – there are numerous possibilities for travel by boat. Cruises around the islands are available from La Rochelle and Rochefort; reservations from Inter-îles, 14 bis cours des Dames, 17000 La Rochelle (Tel. 46 50 55 54). Cruises of the Marais-Poitevin leave from Arçais; reservations from SARL Nouvelles Croisières, Route de Damvix, 17 Arçais (Tel: 49 35 37 80). You can also hire your own boat from many of the towns in the Marais. It is also possible to cruise down the Charente river setting out from Saintes, Cognac or Jarnac; reservations from Charente-Plaisance. Place Solençon, 16100 Cognac. British companies such as Clearwater Holidays offer cruising holidays in the area. There are also trips to the various islands and along the coast, leaving from St-Gilles-Croix-de-Vie, L'Herbaudière, Tranche-sur-Mer, Pornic, Fouras, Royan and La Rochelle. The regions rivers are ideal for canoeists of all standards, and it is possible to practise sea kayak at Fouras.

Cycling – travel by bicycle is a realistic alternative to the car, particularly as inland the roads are quiet and the hills not at all daunting. Bicycles can be hired from the SNCF stations at St-Gilles-Croix-de-Vie, Niort, Rochefort, La Rochelle-Ville and Royan.

Walking – various *Grande Randonnée* footpaths cross the region: the GR 4 crosses Charente as far as Angoulême; the GR 360 forms a circuit allowing you to visit a selection of Romanesque churches; and the GR 36 crosses the Deux-Sèvres. Further information is available from the appropriate Comité Départemental de la Randonnée Pédestre (addresses from the Comité Régional du Tourisme).

Riding – many areas of Poitou-Charentes are ideal for horseriding. Local tourist offices and the regional tourist board will have details. If you are planning to ride in Deux-Sèvres, contact M. Bouillaud, La Charnière, 79200 Gourgé.

Useful Local Contacts

The address of the Marais-Poitevin regional park headquarters is **Maison du Parc**, 17170 La Ronde (Tel. 46 27 82 44). Other associations connected with the park are **SABAUD** (protection of the Poitou mule), Maison de l'Ane du Poitou, La Tillauderie, 17 Dampierre-sur-Boutonne and **Association ACEDEM** (study and protection of marsh environment), Maison du Petit Poitou, Maison commune, 85 Chaillé-le-Marais.

Geographical Breakdown of Region

Charente-Maritime & Charente

La Rochelle

In the seventeenth century, Cardinal Richelieu wanted La Rochelle so badly that he laid siege to it for 15 months. Nowadays, the town is more welcoming to visitors who will find that the combination of a busy harbour, beautiful Renaissance buildings and lively restaurants, bars and casino, makes La Rochelle an ideal holiday destination.

Richelieu destroyed most of the medieval fortifications of the town, but there are three original towers still standing which can all be visited. The entrance to the harbour is guarded by the **Tour St-Nicolas** and the **Tour de la Chaîne**; a chain used to be stretched across the harbour entrance at night time, hence the name (the chain is now in the garden of the Musée d'Orbigny). The third tower is the **Tour de la Lanterne** which used to be a lighthouse. La Rochelle harbour, the **Vieux Port**, is nowadays more likely to be full of pleasure boats than trawlers, but the **Quai Duperre** is nevertheless an enjoyable place for a stroll before heading for the heart of the old town through the **Porte de la Grosse Horloge**, a medieval gateway to the once walled town. To the right and left of the main rue du Palais lie streets of fine sixteenth- and seventeenth-century houses, the ground floor shops and restaurants protected by arcades. The **rue des Gentilshommes** and **Grande rue des Merciers** have some of the best examples, and it is here that you will find the **Hôtel de Ville**, a Gothic and Renaissance building with an intricately decorated facade in the courtyard. Amongst the museums in La Rochelle, are the **Musée des Automates** (mechanical dolls) in the Ville en Bois, the **Musée du Nouveau Monde** in the rue Fleuriau (an exhibition illustrating the strong ties between La Rochelle and North America) and the **Musée des Beaux Arts**. The large, busy **Place de Verdun** at the end of the rue Chaudrier has a wonderfully ornate *fin de siècle* **Café de la Paix**, the perfect place to rest after a tour of the town.

Accommodation

First Class

Hôtel les Brises, Chemin digue Richelieu, ave P-Vincent, (Tel. 46 43 89 37): 48 rooms in charming hotel with island views. **Hôtel France-Angleterre et Champlain**, 20 rue Rambaud (Tel. 46 41 34 66): 33 rooms in attractive hotel with garden, near town ramparts.

Middle Range

Hôtel Trianon et Plage, 6 rue Monnaie (Tel. 46 41 21 35): 25 rooms in hotel on edge of park, with garden and restaurant. **Tour**

de Nesle, 2 quai L-Durand (Tel. 46 41 05 86): 31 rooms in hotel near old port.

Middle Range/Economy

Hôtel François 1er, 15 rue Bazouges (Tel. 46 41 28 46): 38 rooms in elegant hotel, quietly situated in old town.

Economy

Hôtel Printania, 9–11 rue du Brave Rondeau (Tel. 46 41 22 86): good value accommodation; reservation essential for July and August. **Hôtel le Bordeaux**, 45 rue St-Nicolas (Tel. 46 41 31 22): 9 rooms in pleasant hotel near pedestrian zone; book ahead.

Eating Out

The restaurants in this town were definitely conceived with lovers of fresh seafood in mind:

First Class

Richard Coutanceau, Plage de la Concurrence (Tel. 46 41 48 19): regional fish specialities in luxurious dining room with sea views.

First Class/Middle Range

Serge, 46 rue des Dames (Tel. 46 41 18 80): exclusively seafood restaurant with terrace in old port.

Middle Range

La Marée, quai Louis-Prunier (Tel. 46 41 19 92): bistro-style restaurant in middle of fish market.

Middle Range/Economy

Le Claridge, 1 rue Admyrauld (Tel. 46 41 35 75): small welcoming restaurant with home-cooked specialities.

Economy

Le Pilote, 18 rue du Port: small seafood restaurant in lively area. **Le Cordon Bleu**, 20 rue du Cordouan: good value, solid *plat du jour*.

Entertainments

Guided tours are available on a variety of themes, including fishing and history, from the Caisse Nationale des Monuments Historiques.

Information from the tourist office who can also arrange tours out of the town to mussel farms, Cognac distilleries etc.. They also organise talks and slide shows on a variety of subjects. At the end of May, it is International Sail Week in La Rochelle. In June and July there is a film festival, and the popular Francofolies song festival is in July.

Useful Addresses

Tourist Information is at Place de la Petite-Sirène, quai de Gabut (Tel. 46 41 14 68). The **Departmental tourist office** for Charente-Maritime is at 11 rue des Augustins (Tel. 46 41 43 33). Two local coach firms are Océcars, (Tel. 46 41 93 93) and Charentes-Evasions, (Tel. 46 41 10 11). The **Post Office** is on Place de l'Hôtel de Ville, and the **Hospital** is on rue du Docteur-Schweitzer (Tel. 46 27 33 33). For emergency **medical assistance** dial 46 27 15 15 for SAMU.

Transport Options

Much of the old town of La Rochelle is pedestrianised, making walking the only option. The train station is south of the harbour on boulevard Joffre and the bus station is in the Place de Verdun, both for town and country buses. Bicycles can be hired from the train station but there is also a free municipal bike-hire service from the quai Valin. There is a ferry which runs between the old and the new port, whilst boats for the Ile de Ré, Aix and Oléron leave from the old port. There is a car ferry to the Ile de Ré from La Pallice.

Rest of Charente-Maritime & Charente

Rochefort was an arsenal and shipyard built by Colbert in the 17th century. There is now a large naval museum and rope museum. The capital of Charente, **Angoulême**, is situated on a rocky plateau overlooking the River Charente. The old town of Angoulême, the ville haute is enclosed within medieval ramparts. The ramparts themselves give an excellent introduction to the town as it is possible to walk around them. The Romanesque cathedral stands just inside the ramparts. It has a west facade which almost equals that of Notre-Dame in Poitiers for intricately carved stone. Within the ramparts there is a warren of narrow streets with many old houses dating from the Renaissance. The ville basse is the industrial part of Angoulême. Life used to revolve around paper-making, with nearly one hundred mills in operation in the seventeenth century. Nowadays, the only surviving mills are at nearby **Nersac** and **Puymoyen**. 15 km north-east of Angoulême is the town of **La Rochefoucauld**, the site of a huge Renaissance château. There is a *Son et Lumière* at weekends in July. To the west are the towns of **Cognac** and **Saintes**. Cognac is of course best known for the drink, and the warehouses, the *chais*, can be visited. The town itself has many attractive streets of old buildings darkened by the fungi which, encouraged by the brandy fumes, grow on the stone. There are pleasant walks along the banks of the Charente with views of the surrounding vineyards. Saintes, further downstream, was an important stop on the pilgrim trail. The Abbaye aux Dames is one of the most beautiful in the region with a remarkable bell tower and portico, whilst the church of St-Eutrope has a fine crypt. There are also a number of Roman remains in the town as Saintes was once the Roman capital of south-west France.

Accommodation

First Class/Middle Range

Moulin du Maine Brun, La Vigerie, 16290 Hiersac (Tel. 45 90 83 00): 20 antique-furnished rooms in family hotel, housed in sixteenth-century mill with park; mill has own Cognac distillery.

Middle Range

Hostellerie Ste-Catherine, 16220 Montbron (Tel. 45 23 60 03): 18 rooms in friendly seventeenth-century château hotel with park; good restaurant. **Moulin de Cierzac**, St-Fort-sur-le-Né, 16660 Cognac (Tel. 45 83 01 32): 10 rooms in rustic 17th century mill with attractive dining room.

Middle Range/Economy

Le Prieuré, 17380 Tonnay-Boutonne (Tel. 46 33 20 18): 18 rooms in friendly village hotel in typical regional style; good restaurant.

Economy

La Boule d'Or, 9 bd Gambetta, 16300 Barbezieux (Tel. 45 78 22 72): 28 rooms in charming hotel; restaurant with excellent regional cuisine. **Hôtel l'Etape**, 2 ave d'Angoulême, 16100 Cognac (Tel. 45 32 16 15): 22 rooms in family-run hotel with restaurant.

Eating Out

In addition to the restaurants recommended above, try:

First Class/Middle Range

L'Auberge Pontoise, 23 ave Gambetta, 17800 Pons (Tel. 46 94 00 99): high quality traditional dishes; also has 22 spacious rooms.

Middle Range

Le Rustica, St-Léger, 17800 Pons (Tel. 46 96 91 75): excellent food in popular local restaurant; also has 8 cosy rooms.

Middle Range/Economy

La Braisière, 16210 St-Romain (Tel. 45 98 51 35): restaurant was finalist in the 1989/90 Logis de France regional cuisine competition; also has 11 rooms.

Vienne and Deux-Sevres

Poiters

Old Poitiers is attractively situated on a hill above the rivers Boivre and Clain, which skirt the town, then merge on its northern edge. It is unfortunate that such a location has been somewhat marred by ugly suburbs. Poitiers is a town that rests on former glories. Once the stronghold of the Duke of Aquitaine, it was an important religious and political centre, which explains the number of richly decorated monuments in the town. Since the seventeenth century, there has been a period of stagnation, although now Poitiers is a lively university town.

It is the churches of Poitiers that tourists come to see, with Notre-Dame-la-Grande and St-Hilaire-le-Grand attracting most attention. The west facade of the **Eglise de Notre-Dame** gives a perfect example of the Poitiers school of Romanesque architecture characterised by its intricate, almost fussy, carved detail. Above the lower arches are carvings depicting assorted biblical scenes, then come two further sets of carvings in the arches above whilst, high above them all, sits Christ in Majesty. The whole facade is set off by a pair of pine cone towers. The interior of the church is dark and sombre; there are twelfth-century wall paintings surviving in the crypt. The eleventh- and twelfth-century **Eglise de St-Hilaire-le-Grand** has an unusual interior. A fire in the twelfth-century destroyed the original wooden roof and it was necessary to erect extra pillars to support the new stone one, hence the three aisles on either side of the central nave. Other buildings to visit in Poitiers include the cathedral of **St-Pierre**, the baptistry of **St-Jean** and the **Palais de Justice** behind whose nineteenth-century facade hides the medieval palace of the Dukes of Aquitaine and Berry.

Accommodation

There are no small first class hotels in Poitiers itself. Instead try:

First Class/Middle Range

Château Clos de la Ribaudière, Près Mairie, 86360 Chasseneuil-du-Poitou (Tel. 49 52 86 66): 19 rooms in hotel with park, 9 km from town.

Middle Range

Hôtel de France et Royal Poitou, 215 rte de Paris (Tel. 49 01 74 74 or 49 01 72 86): elegant and extensive hotel in picturesque setting; excellent restaurant serving typical regional dishes. **Le Continental**, 2 bd Solférino (Tel. 49 37 93 93): 39 rooms in hotel in park.

Economy

Le Chalet de Venise, 6 rue du Square, 86280 St-Benoit (Tel. 49 88 45 07): 10 attractive rooms in quiet green surroundings, 5 km from town; simple restaurant offering tasty regional dishes. **Hôtel de Paris**, 123 bd du Grand Cerf (Tel. 49 58 39 37): 10 rooms in convenient family-run hotel; simple country cuisine in homely setting.

Eating Out

First Class/Middle Range

Le St-Hilaire, 65 rue T-Renaudot (Tel. 49 41 15 45): good restaurant in fairly central twelfth-century building. **Maxime**, 4 rue St-Nicolas (Tel. 49 41 09 55): original cuisine, including seafood specialities.

Middle Range

La Treille, 10 ave de Bordeaux, 86370 Vivonne (Tel. 49 43 41 13): excellent, inventive gastronomic cuisine, 19 km from Poitiers; also has 4 simple rooms. **Auberge de la Cigogne**, 20 rue Planty, 86180 Buxerolles (Tel. 49 45 61 47): good out-of-town restaurant with garden.

Economy

Le Poitevin, 76 rue Carnot: filling regional cuisine. **Le Régal**, rue de la Régatterie: simple brasserie fare.

Entertainments

The Tourist Information office will give details of guided tours by the Caisse nationale des Monuments Historiques. In May there is a spring music festival in the town and, in July, there are festivals of dance, folklore and theatre. In October, Poitiers hosts the French Equestrian Games. Coach companies which run services and tours in the area are Les Rapides du Poitou (Tel. 49 46 27 45), S.T.A.O. (Tel. 49 01 82 67) and Voyages Bertrand (Tel. 49 01 72 62). 7 km to the north is the much publicised **Futoroscope** theme park with giant cinema screens and a special children's park.

Useful Addresses

Tourist Information is at 8 rue des Grandes-Ecoles (Tel. 49 41 21 24). The **regional tourist** office is at 2 rue Sainte-Opportune (Tel. 49 88 38 94). The **Post Office** is at 16 rue Arthur Ranc, while the **Hospital** is 15 rue Hôtel Dieu (Tel. 49 88 02 10).

Transport Options

Bicycles can be hired from **Cyclamen**, 49 rue Arsène Orillard. All buses, both town and country, stop at the train station on Boulevard du Grand Cerf.

Rest of Vienne and Deux-Sevres

Niort is the capital of the Deux-Sèvres *département* of Poitou-Charentes and is situated on the edge of the large **Marais-Poitevin**. A peaceful provincial town, Niort was once part of a fiercely contested region of France. First marauding Danes posed a threat, then English claims to the region caused it to change hands more than once. This explains the dungeon positioned on the banks of the river, which was once the inner keep of the Château of Niort built by Henry II of England and Richard the Lionheart. It now houses a museum. The pedestrianised streets near the dungeon have many old houses, particularly in the rue St-Jean which is also the location of the old Hôtel de Ville. The Vieux Ponts give an attractive view of the River **Sèvre Niortaise**, which lazily flows towards the **Marais-Poitevin**, or *Venise Verte*. **Coulon** has boat hire and a museum of the marshes, the **Musée des Marais Mouillés**. Coulon also holds a Fête des Bateliers, a boatmen's festival, in August.

Boat excursions on the rivers and marshes are also available from Arçais and many of the other villages in the area. Bicycle hire is widely available too.

Accommodation & Eating Out

Accommodation is pretty thin on the ground here, so you may be best off sticking to Poitiers and the surrounding area. Nevertheless, the following are recommended:

Middle Range

Au Marais, 46–48 quai Louis-Tardy, 79510 Coulon (Tel. 49 35 90 43): 11 rooms in rustic riverside inn; starting point for boat tours of Poitevin salt-marshes; restaurant with inventive regional cuisine.

Middle Range/Economy

Hôtel Terminus, 82 rue de la Gare, 79000 Niort (Tel. 49 24 00 38): 43 comfortable rooms in hotel near station; excellent restaurant (**Le Poêle d'Or**) serving regional cuisine.

Economy

Hôtel du Lion d'Or, 8 rue du Marché, 86300 Chauvigny (Tel. 49 46 30 28): 27 rooms in clean, friendly, family-run hotel.

13 Limousin

Since the Middle Ages Limousin has maintained its individuality despite attempts by hostile feudal lords and kings to divide its people and erode its culture. Today it is one of France's twenty-one economic regions, made up of the three *départements* of Haute-Vienne, Corrèze and Creuse, and situated west of the Massif Central.

The province is predominantly rural and agricultural, though Corrèze and Creuse have some industrial activity, and Limoges, the regional capital, has long enjoyed a reputation for high quality enamelware and porcelain.

The *départements* of Creuse and Haute-Vienne make up the northern part of the region. Creuse, with its two arrondissements of Aubusson and Guéret, is almost identical with the pre-revolutionary province of Marche. Stockbreeding is the main activity, with cereals and potatoes being grown in the south west. Chestnuts are also widely harvested, and Creuse supports mining, quarrying, spinning and food processing. The museum of Aubusson displays both classical and modern examples of the tapestries for which the town is famed. Other towns of interest are Felletin, Auzances, La Souterraine and the spa resort of Evaux-les-Bains.

Haute-Vienne, to the west of Creuse, was created from the old provinces of Berry, Limousin, Marche and Poitou. It has three arrondissements: Limoges, Bellac, and Rochechouart. Limoges, on the River Vienne, is the principal town of the *département* and a railway junction on the Paris-Toulouse line. During the Middle Ages it was divided into two separate and hostile townships and these remained apart until 1792. Both the thirteenth-century cathedral of St-Etienne and the church of St-Michel-de-Lions merit a visit, and there are museums housing collections of Limoges enamels, ceramics and porcelain. St-Julien, a centre for leather industries, is also notable for its church, begun in the twelfth century. Agriculture predominates throughout the *département*. Fodder crops, potatoes and beet are grown and there is cattle-raising here, but the chestnut, once the mainstay of the rural economy, has sadly declined.

To the south of Haute-Vienne is the *département* of Corrèze. Brive-la-Gaillarde, the principal town, has an important agricultural market. Local industries include the manufacture of mechanical and electrical appliances and food processing, and there is a firearms factory at Tulle. Lace-making, once a thriving industry, has practically disappeared. The *département* has three arrondissements: Brive, Ussel and Tulle.

Tourism in Limousin remains quite undeveloped, though, with a change in trends towards 'Tourisme Vert', Limousin has gained in popularity due to its considerable natural resources, which include lakes, forests, rivers and plateaux. (See **Level of Tourism**).

History

The name Limousin is derived from the ancient tribe of the Lemovices. These constituted a tribal association of Roman Gaul, centred on Limoges, and had their own senate and currency. There is, however, also evidence of older, prehistoric occupation from the cave dwellings near Brive-la-Gaillarde in the south-west of the region.

Limousin was controlled by the Romans until 50 BC as part of the province of Aquitaine. Later, Christianity was brought to Limoges by St Martial in the third century and his shrine became a stopping place for pilgrims on the road to Santiago de Compostella in northern Spain. Under the Merovingians who ruled the region from the sixth to the eighth century, the Pagus Lemovicinus (the district of the Lemovices) was the subject of dispute between rival kings. Then, under the Carolingians, its rulers from the eighth to the tenth century, it was incorporated into the kingdom of Aquitaine.

In the tenth century, the region was divided into a number of feudal units. The northern part was established as Marche – an endowment for the widows of the kings of France. Before the end of the eleventh century, Limousin had come under the overlordship of the Duke of Aquitaine. Its monasteries, notably St-Martial at Limoges and St-Anthony's in Brive-la-Gaillarde, were cultural centres throughout the Middle Ages. During this period Limousin was renowned for its lyric poetry and its troubadours. There was a local school of Romanesque architecture, and it was also noted for its fine art, particularly its illuminated manuscripts and decorative objects; the enamelware of Limoges and the tapestries of Aubusson are world famous. The particular culture of the Limousin has always been seen as a unifying factor in the face of repeated attempts to divide the people and fragment the region, the traditional language of which is the Spanish-sounding Langue d'Oc.

Like much of western France from the twelfth to the fifteenth century, Limousin was disputed between the English and the French. In 1152 it first came under the sovereignty of the English when Henry II married Eleanor of Aquitaine; it was finally reclaimed by Charles V (1364–80) and thereafter remained under French rule.

The next 300 years saw mixed fortunes for the area. The Wars of Religion resulted in much bloodshed. In 1771, kaolin was discovered and led to the establishment of a thriving porcelain industry. The railway arrived in the mid-nineteenth century and, with it, the necessary supplies to revitalise local agriculture and cattle breeding. Limousin's prosperity, based on the porcelain and leather industries, continued undisturbed until the Second World War, when the region was heavily bombed by the Germans and later occupied. The Pétain government, having lost Paris, set up its headquarters in nearby Vichy, and before long Limousin became a stronghold for the French Resistance. Tragically the local population paid dearly for their patriotism when thousands were massacred in cold blood as the Germans retreated from the invading Allied armies.

The return of peace saw the arrival of hydro-electric plants, and new light industries such as shoe-making. In more recent times, Limousin has woken up to its potential as a holiday region and today is capitalising on its natural assets by building up the amenities required to attract tourism.

Geography

Limousin borders the Massif Central to the north-east, east and south-east and this has a significant impact on the region's climate and weather. The high ground is subject to heavy rains and snow, but the valleys remain relatively dry. Rain falling on granite rock has meant that, over millions of years, water has collected in pools and peat bogs, and this has resulted in the formation of hundreds of small ponds and lakes of various sizes. Today these lakes have become part of an elaborate hydro-electric system and also provide opportunities for a variety of water-based activities and sports.

The *département* of Haute-Vienne has an area of some 5600 square kilometres and is crossed south-east to north-west by the River Vienne which flows through Limoges. Mountains rise to over 700 metres in the Monts de Blond range to the north-west, the Monts d'Ambazac in the east and the Monts Gargon in the south-east.

The basin of the River Creuse, which also flows south-east to north-west, through Aubusson and Guéret, forms the greater part of the *département* bearing its name, and covers some 5500 square kilometres.

Corrèze is the largest of the region's *départements*, extending to some 6000 square kilometres. In the north, the Plateau de Millevaches rises to over 900 metres and this separates the basins of the rivers Loire and Garonne. Both Tulle, the principal town of the *département* and Brive-La-Gaillarde (the largest town) stand on the River Corrèze. In the south of the *département* the River Dordogne flows westwards.

Climate

The climate in Limousin is damp and cold in the northeast (which makes for fertile pastures, particularly suitable for sheep), but generally mild and agreeable in the south and south-west. The ideal times to visit Limousin are late spring and early autumn. Spring temperatures have a maximum daily average of 21°C with an average seasonal rainfall of 61mm. This is a good time for hiking – there are fewer people on the nature trails and the forests and valleys are ablaze with spring flowers. Autumn temperatures have a maximum daily average of 22°C with an average seasonal rainfall of 70mm. For those who wish to escape the summer crowds, autumn is a sensible season to visit the region. Sports centres remain open throughout September and early October, and the autumn colours are spectacular.

Attractions

Limousin is a region of undulating green hills, wooded countryside, and peaceful shimmering lakes. Ramblers are attracted by its outstanding natural features: the Monts de Blond and the Monts d'Ambazac; the plateau known as Millevaches, and the Massif de

Monedières. They also relish the marshes, the cross-leafed heather, and the herds of grazing cattle. The numerous fast flowing rivers provide sparkling waters for trout, salmon, and grayling – and a challenge to fishermen. Lake Vassivière is situated in an area of outstanding beauty. The lake itself extends for over 2500 acres. It has beaches and natural harbours and is fed by numerous streams which form a series of small inlets; the expanse of forest and heather on its shores is punctuated with lively traditional villages.

Since the Middle Ages, Limousin has concealed its little-known, but rich, Romanesque heritage. Particularly magnificent are the abbeys of Benevent, Solignac, and Aubazine; and the collegiate churches of Dorat-Saint-Junien and Saint-Léonard.

Motor tours such as 'Following in the footsteps of Richard the Lion Heart', (see **Geographical Breakdown**), pass through beautiful, well-preserved villages such as Uzerche and Collonges-la-Rouge.

The arts of enamelwork and porcelain have spread throughout the region, and are reputed worldwide. The tapestries made at Aubusson are further witness to artistic creativity in the *département*. The cultural centres of Meymac, Vassivière, and Rochechouart and the many festivals, including the Brive book fair, all serve to maintain the region's reputation at the forefront of contemporary provincial culture.

Cuisine

Food in Limousin tends to be more refined than that in neighbouring Auvergne, whilst not as rich as that of the Dordogne. Regional cooking in Limousin is often prepared with chestnuts, onions and red cabbage, and the wild mushrooms known as *cêpes*. Mushrooms, in fact, appear in many regional dishes, and are numerous in variety. It is said that there are more varieties of mushroom in Limousin than in the whole of the British Isles. Particularly appetising are the thin *chanterelles* mushrooms, the *cêpes* and the *morels*. Local pork and beef dishes are tasty, and several cheeses are produced, such as Guéret. For dessert look out for *clafoutis*, a cherry batter pudding. No wine is produced in Limousin but the region draws in vintages from the surrounding *départements*, so wine lists tend to be comprehensive and very varied.

Level of Tourism

Tourism in Limousin is undeveloped and the region currently ranks lowest in the pecking order of French tourist regions, with only 770,000 hotel visitors a year. Out of these, only 15% come from abroad, and the average length of stay in the area is extremely short.

Until quite recently, Limousin suffered a bit of an image problem as far as tourism was concerned. People tended to have fixed ideas about the region, believing it to be old-fashioned and conservative, and unable to satisfy the increasingly sophisticated demands of modern holiday-makers. Limousin was considered a 'passing through' area, on the way to more popular regions such as the Loire or Aquitaine, not a holiday destination in itself. Its potential has therefore been largely overlooked.

The last two years have seen national and regional tourist boards making a concerted effort to put Limousin on the map. Their enthusiasm has been due in part to the 'Green Revolution' in France, which has seen an upsurge of interest in alternative holidays and a change to healthy, outdoor, nature-related vacations; in these areas, Limousin has much to offer. After fruitless attempts in the past to market Limousin's attractions in glossy brochures and promotional films, local tourist boards have revolutionised the tourist industry by specifically marketing Limousin to appeal to a particular type of visitor. Today, Limousin enjoys the reputation of being a centre for 'tourisme vert', and its once neglected natural resources are now being promoted as areas of great environmental interest.

Recent surveys have revealed that the foreigners attracted to Limousin, like their French counterparts, tend to be outdoor enthusiasts and conservation-minded too. The Dutch visit Limousin for its cycling potential; the Germans generally concentrate on watersports such as sailing and canoeing, and the British organise their holidays around the small country villages and historical monuments.

In many respects, the change in Limousin's fortunes reflects a general change in tourist trends and expectations, as people begin to move away from entertainment-based holidays to interest-based ones. Limousin has always been an ideal base for outdoor pursuits but, until recently, it has catered largely for local enthusiasts. It is ironic that it appeals now to tourists for the same reasons that it was once ignored by them: namely its simplicity, and its lack of development and sophistication. Its popularity is therefore still a relatively recent phenomenon. Time will tell whether or not regional and national tourist boards can face the challenge of maintaining sustainable tourism in the interest of conservation; but, for the present at least, it is refreshing to see that they are monitoring tourism's impact and altering their strategy accordingly.

Good Alternatives

Meeting People

An ideal way of meeting people in Limousin is to attend some of the many local festivals held throughout the year, but particularly during summer. Lists and details of these are provided by local tourist offices and the **Comité Régional du Tourisme**, Ensemble Administrative Régional, 27 bd de la Corderie, 87031 Limoges (Tel. 55 45 18 80). This regional tourist board will also supply a wealth of other information on the region.

The French Ministry for Foreign Affairs recently initiated **Opération Française 2001** to encourage exchanges between various European countries and France. Since the launch of this project, the UK has been twinned with Limousin and it is now possible for British schools to stay in residential centres in Limousin at the same time as partner French schools. For further information, contact **S.E.E. Europe**, 45 Church Street, Weybridge, Surrey KT13 8DG (Tel. 0932 840 440). This organisation can also provide information on the **Lathus Outdoor Centre**, which is situated on the Gartempe river and offers courses in a variety of outdoor pursuits.

Those interested in taking part in an archaeological dig in the region should request information from the **Direction des Antiquités**, 2 ter rue Haute de la Comédie, 87000 Limoges (Tel. 55 34 38 00).

Discovering Places

Since tourism has barely touched the surface of Limousin, coming here at all is a 'good alternative', offering the simplest recipe for discovering *la France profonde*.

History enthusiasts should consider seeing Limousin 'In the footsteps of Richard the Lion Heart'. Local tourist authorities in Haute-Vienne have gone to great lengths to revive the memory of Richard I and other English kings, by organising a historical route encompassing all the great châteaux of the area.

Another perspective is gained by following the route of medieval pilgrimage to Santiago de Compostella. In the Middle Ages Limousin became a very important religious site, due to its many abbeys and priories with their numerous religious relics. It was also a stopping place on the famous pilgrimage and the Limousin section of the ancient route offers a wealth of architectural and artistic heritage, as witnessed in such churches as the Eglise de la Souterraine and the collegiate church of St-Léonard, or the Château de Turenne and many other fortresses and monuments.

For those interested in crafts (particularly in tapestry-making), a special tour of Aubusson and Felletin is organised by the local tourist offices, enabling visitors not only to see and learn about Limousin's ancient tapestries, but also to meet some of today's tapestry makers. The Aubusson and Felletin tapestries are unique by virtue of their artistic quality, reflecting centuries of refinement.

The tourist board's suggested route for a tour of Romanesque Creuse is also highly recommended, taking you past rolling hills, streams, shady woodlands and winding lanes, as well as masterpieces of Romanesque architecture.

From June to September, the **Limousin Chestnut Association** runs tours of the Pays des Feuillardiers. The tour includes a visit to the ancient chestnus stands near Dournazac, a visit to a barrel and fencing manufacturer, and a visit to a basket-making workshop. Further information about any of the above routes or tours is available from the **Comité Régional du Tourisme** (address above).

Limousin also has **Loisirs-Acceuil** services in all three of its *départements*. As well as helping you with general information and reserving accommodation, these associations offer selections of low-impact thematic holidays in the region, all run by local people. The three addresses are: **Loisirs-Acceuil Corrèze**, Maison du Tourisme, quai Baluze, 19000 Tulle (Tel. 55 26 39 99); **Loisirs-Acceuil Creuse**, 43 Place Bonnyaud, 23000 Guéret (Tel. 55 52 87 50); and **Loisirs-Acceuil Haute-Vienne**, 4 Place Denis-Dussoubs, 87000 Limoges (Tel. 55 79 04 04).

Communications

How to Get There

Flights to Limoges airport (Tel. 55 43 30 30) are all routed via Paris. By **train**, Limoges is around 3 hours from Paris, while getting to Brive takes about 4. Eurolines do not operate a coach service to the region; their nearest stop is Poitiers (about £80 adult return from London). If you are travelling by **car**, allow at least 4½ hours to get from Paris to Limoges, either on the A 10 followed by the N 147 (via Poitiers), or on the A 71 and N 20 (via Vierzon).

When You're There

Rail – the network is not particularly comprehensive, though main lines connect La Souterraine, St-Sulpice-Laurière, Limoges and Nexon; and Limoges, Uzerche and Brive. Other lines will take you to Guéret, Felletin, Tulle, Meymac and Ussel.

Bus – long-distance coaches do not really exist in Limousin. Bus services are generally retricted to the larger towns or more popular tourist areas, and are not designed for passengers who wish to explore the more remote parts of the region.

Car – this is one region where traffic congestion should not be a problem, even in the height of summer. Though its road network is by no means dense, particularly in the area to the south and east of Limoges, even main roads are usually clear.

Cycling, Walking and Riding – Limousin is ideal cycling country; there are extensive cycle paths and bikes can be hired from local railway stations. The region offers some good walking country too, and there are a number of historical trails, as well as other paths, marked on the maps available from local bookshops. Riding stables are scattered throughout the region and can supply horses for both short outings and longer excursions. For further information regarding cycling, hiking and riding opportunities, contact the **Comité Régional du Tourisme** (see **Good Alternatives**).

Geographical Breakdown of Region

Haute-Vienne

Limoges

Limoges, situated in the centre of Haute-Vienne, on the banks of the Vienne, is the capital of Limousin. The two halves of the medieval town (St Martial on one bank and Limoges on the other), divided by the Vienne river, were on opposing sides during the Hundred Years'

War with England (1337–1553), but have now merged. However, their former boundaries can still be recognised by their narrow, winding streets which are in contrast to the spacious roads of the new town.

In younger days Limoges, built on both banks of the river, had two distinct entities. The area immediately around the cathedral was known as **La Cité**. The other half of Limoges was built around the ancient quarter of **La Ville**, situated near Place Wilson, with its narrow, picturesque streets surrounded by medieval stone walls. Unfortunately, parts of the old town fortifications have been destroyed, replaced today by characterless boulevards. La Ville is also known as **Le Village de la Boucherie** since, during the tenth century, it became home to a powerful butchers' guild. Every year on 3 October, the Butchers' festival is held to commemorate the ancient society.

The thirteenth-century cathedral of **Saint-Etienne** has an elegant, partly octagonal, bell-tower typical of the Gothic churches of the region. Notice the flamboyant portrait of St Jean and the fourteenth-century bishop's tomb.

The church of **Saint-Michel-des-Lions** (fourteenth and fifteenth century), Place du Présidial, has a tower 65 metres high with a spire surmounted by a big bronze ball; it also has some fine fifteenth-century stained-glass windows.

Below the **Place de la République** is the **Crypt of St-Martial** and the tombs of his companions, Ste-Valérie and Tève le Duc, along with other items of interest. The eighteenth-century **Palais de L'Evêché** – the old Bishop's Palace, now houses the municipal museum which has an impressive collection of old enamel, antiques and pictures. The **Musée National de Ceramique Adrien Debouché** has an outstanding collection of ceramics and porcelain, mainly Limoges but augmented with items from many parts of the world. The town is also the seat of the **Université de Limoges** founded in 1808.

The pleasant gardens of the **Jardin d'Orsay**, facing the Place Winston Churchill, contain Roman ruins.

Useful Addresses

The **Tourist Office** is on bd des Fleurus (Tel. 55 34 46 87); they run a guided tour of the town on Mondays and Thursdays in July and August. They will also give you a map of the town's bus network. A better bet for information on the surrounding area is the **Office**

Départemental de Tourisme at 4 Place Denis Dussoubs (Tel. 55 79 04 04).

Accommodation

There are no small first class hotels in the town itself. Instead try:

First Class

La Chapelle-St-Martin, N 147, 87510 Nieul (Tel. 55 75 80 17): 10 rooms and 3 suites in beautiful 19th century house in quiet surroundings 5 km from town.

Middle Range

Hôtel le Marceau, 2 ave de Turenne (Tel. 55 77 23 43): 24 rooms in family-run hotel whose restaurant has good reputation for local cuisine.

Middle Range/Economy

Hôtel au Belvédère, 264 rue de Toulouse (Tel. 55 30 57 39): 26 rooms in family-run hotel with garden; restaurant serving local specialities.

Economy

Hôtel le Musset, 2 bd de la Cité (Tel. 55 34 34 03): 29 rooms in family-run hotel with restaurant. **Auberge de l'Etape**, RN 20, ave de Brachaud (Tel. 55 37 14 33): 13 rooms in family inn with garden and restaurant. **Hôtel de France**, 23 cours Bugeaud (Tel. 55 77 78 92): spacious rooms in hotel near station.

Eating Out

First Class/Middle Range

L'Odyssée, 17 rue Charles-Michels (Tel. 55 34 58 55): cosy, family restaurant with fish specialities.

Middle Range

Domaine de Pradepont, Solignac, 87110 Limoges (Tel. 55 00 50 40): riverside restaurant in rustic manor house, serving traditional cuisine. **Cantaut**, 10 rue Rafilhoux (Tel. 55 33 34 68): regional cuisine in grand setting.

Economy

La Gratade, Le Vigen, Solignac, 87110 Limoges (Tel. 55 00 55 42): exclusively regional specialities in restaurant 9 km from town.
Café Léopold, 27 rue Haute-Vienne (Tel. 55 32 28 49): good value *plats du jour* in old town restaurant.

Rest of Haute-Vienne

Limoges is a good base for exploring the region. Green, hilly and unspoilt countryside surrounds the city, providing wonderful opportunities for ramblers, riders, cyclists and drivers. To the north-east is the **Pays d'Ambazac et des Puys et Grands Monts**, an area of low hills that descend to the gorges of the Tarion river.

Ambazac itself is a delightful twelfth-century hamlet, and well worth a visit. The church and reliquary of **St-Etienne-du-Muret** contains an exquisite eleventh-century mozarab silk dalmatic. Nearby is the **Abbey de Grandmont**, where there are the ruins of an older abbey and an interesting chapel once connected to the monastery. Due east of Ambazac, along the D5 road is **St-Laurent-les-Églises**, known for its pike fishing. Boats can be rented at the resort town of **Le Pont du Dognon** for fishing excursions onto the lake.

Nearby is **Les Billanges**, with an interesting thirteenth-century church and, just beyond, **Jonchère-St-Maurice**, whose arboretum contains many rare conifers. The best way of seeing the area is by bicycle, and these can be hired at **Laurière** nearby. From Laurière, visitors can explore the forest of **Echelles** and the grounds of the **Château de Valmath**.

Le Pays de St-Pardoux, which adjoins the Pays d'Ambazac, is an area of lakes and forest. The largest, **Le Lac de St-Pardoux**, is known for its fish, of which there are a great variety. For those interested in outdoor pursuits, this is a good place to bring your kayak, boat, windsurfer, or even just your swimming gear, for the lakes and surrounding countryside are particularly picturesque and other tourists are few and far between. **St-Pardoux** itself is an attractive village with a collection of old houses clustered together around the market square and thirteenth-century church.

Razes, between the lake and the D20 road, boasts delicious honey, a strange rocking stone, and some prehistoric dolmens of unknown origin. **Compreignac**, 4 or 5 kilometres further down the road, is the starting point of a magnificent nature trail that encompasses 120 lakes! This is the ideal place to leave the car behind, hire bikes, and really get off the beaten track to discover some of Limousin's wonderful countryside.

If you follow the course of the **Gartempe** river, you will soon come to **Bessines-sur-Gartempe**, the birthplace of the painter Suzanne Valadon. There is not much to see here except for the eleventh-century church and the ruins of the **Château des Monishes**. The Gartempe river narrows considerably here before entering a gorge and flowing through the peaceful village of **Rançon**. The bridge that crosses the river is 700 years old.

The main town in the Pays de St-Pardoux, is **Châteauponsac**. The old quarter of the town, known as **Sous-le-Moustier**, has a collection of charming old houses. Housed in the ancient Benedictine priory is the René Bauderot Museum with historical, ethnological and archaeological exhibits. A few yards away from the museum is the St Thyrse's church, built in the twelfth century, but added to in subsequent years. The decorated stone columns and wooden statues are particularly notable.

La Basse Marche, to the north of the Pays de St-Pardoux, is the meeting point of the Limoges plateau and the plains of Berry and Poitou. Unlike neighbouring regions to the south, La Basse Marche is quietly agricultural and attracts very few tourists. The principal activity in this area is stockbreeding and horse trading, and consequently there is very little in the way of accommodation, other than *gîtes* and *logis*, though there is plenty to do and see for those who enjoy the countryside.

Le Dorat is a picturesque village with several old houses and some ruined ramparts. The collegiate church of St-Pierre, once part of a monastery, is a magnificent example of medieval architecture. Its huge interior includes two small chapels, a crypt, a sacristy and a couple of innocent-looking stone lions. A religious festival is held in Dorat every seven years, in addition to the craft fair, which is an annual event.

To the south of Le Dorat, along the N147 road is **Bellac**, by far the largest town in the locality. Bellac was the birthplace of the playwright Giraudoux, and his home, La Maison Jean Giraudoux, contains a very fine library, collections of personal souvenirs, furniture, photographs and manuscripts. Other sights are the Hotel de Ville, built in the sixteenth century, and a statue of Giraudoux and six of his fictional heroines. Another landmark is the Pont de Pierre, a delightful hump-back bridge that has survived for 800 years.

Mortemart, south along the N147 road, has an attractive 200-year-old covered market place and a collection of old houses. The small hamlet grew up around the Château de Mortemart, now used for exhibitions and classical concerts. The chapel, once a part of the Augustine monastery, contains some interesting oak stalls. The countryside around Mortemart is ideal for outdoor pursuits. There is a lake at **Cieux** with good fishing opportunities, and nature trails that lead off into nearby hills.

La Vallée de La Vienne is an area of lakes and pastures near Limoges. Canoeists are recommended to stop here and dip their paddles into the River Vienne between Aixe-sur-Vienne and St-Junien. There are good overnight camping spots along the course of the river, and stretches of river to suit both the beginner and the experienced canoeist.

Rochechouart, to the west of Limoges, is a town steeped in myth. One legend has it that a beautiful viscountess was locked away in a tower with a lion by her husband, when a local courtier began spreading rumours about her reputation. When the door was unlocked, days later, the viscount found the lion obediently lying at his wife's feet. This was taken as a sign of her innocence, whereupon the rascal courtier was thrown to the lion, which then quickly recovered its appetite! In the Middle Ages, **Rochechouart Château** was renowned for its beautiful ladies in waiting. There are no ladies in waiting today, but the castle still boasts a magnificent hunting gallery lined with frescoes. There is also a splendid statue of the fabled lion! The château is home to an archaeological and ethnological museum, well worth visiting.

Thirteen kilometres away, on the opposite side of the Vienne river, stands **St Junien**, the *département*'s second largest town. It is a vibrant, busy place with prosperous leather, weaving and enamel industries. The chapel of Notre-Dame-du-Pont, overlooking the river, owes much of its elegance to Louis XI. A good way of exploring the surrounding countryside is by bicycle, which can be hired from a number of shops (ask at the Tourist Office). Visits to the **Glane Valley**, the **Brigueuil forest** and the **Château de Rochebrune** are particularly recommended. Rochebrune, once the residence of Blaise de Montluc, marshal of France and governor of Guyenne in the sixteenth century is a fine medieval fortress complete with moat and towers. The château's interior, decorated in a variety of styles, is a pleasant contrast to its austere facade. The collegiate church of St-Junien is the town's jewel; its foundations date back to the tenth century. Its statues, stonework and stained glass windows are a magnificent example of medieval masonry.

Oradour-sur-Glane, a few kilometres to the north-east, is still haunted by a tragic episode during the Second World War, when a troop of SS soldiers, retreating from the Allied invasion, massacred almost the entire population of the village in a bloody spectacle of retribution. A war memorial and museum remain.

Lying to the southwest of La Vallée de la Vienne is **Le Pays des Feuillardiers**, an area of chestnut-covered hills. The name Feuillardier is derived from the craftsmen who traditionally made barrel hoops, fencing and agricultural implements from the wood of the chestnut trees. The villages and towns in this area are generally very rustic and at most offer fairly basic accommodation. **Châlus**, historically the most interesting town in the region, owes much to Richard the Lion Heart who was fatally wounded in **Châlus Château**, a splendid twelfth-century fortress, whose dungeon, battlements and towers have survived centuries of war. For those not clued up on their medieval history, a visit to Châlus Historical Museum is highly recommended.

Set in **Le Pays Arédien**, half way between Châlus and Solignac, is the pretty village of **Nexon**, a breeding centre of Arabian horses. The fourteenth-century château was severely damaged during the Revolution, but has been fully restored. Nexon church is 400 years older, and contains some fine enamel plaques and wooden statues. **Solignac**, a few kilometres further on, has a magnificent abbey founded in 632. Its notable features are its domes and stained-glass windows. Within walking distance from Solignac are the ruins of the **Chalusset fortress** – an impressive example of medieval military architecture built in the twelfth century. The hill-top fort can only be reached on foot, but makes for a pleasant ramble.

The countryside between Solignac and Coussac-Bonneval is known for its many varities of mushroom, though a knowledge of edible fungi is advisable before eating any of the more exotic ones. **Coussac-Bonneval** itself is the site of a splendid château, home of the current Bonneval family, the descendants of Pacha Bonneval, a convert to Islam who built the castle in the Middle Ages. The tapestries and wood panelling here are outstanding. Slightly to the east of Coussac is the porcelain centre of **St-Yrieix-la-Perche**, where kaolin was discovered in the eighteenth century. The church of

Le Moustier was built on the foundations of an older abbey and boasts a bust of St-Yrieix. This makes a good base for exploring the surrounding towns and countryside. There is a railway station and good road communications, with Limoges to the north and Brive-la-Gaillarde to the south. Bicycles can be hired for excursions into the **Vallée d'Isle** and to the local lakes.

To the north-east of Le Pays Arédien is a region known as **Les Monts et Barrages**. It is an area of rivers and lakes, delightful villages, and gently rolling hills that extend to the Plateau de Millevaches. The principal town is **St-Leonard-Noblat**, an attractive centre with a remarkable **Romanesque church**. The octagonal belfry is a lovely example of the Limousin style. Inside there are some amusing carvings on the wooden choir stalls, and also some interesting capitals above the church's porch. Two local festivals are held in the town: one, known as **La Baque,** is held in July; the other, **La Quintaine** (celebrating various medieval games), in November. Also of interest is the **Gay Lussac Museum**, housing the personal effects and manuscripts of Lussac, the famous physicist born locally.

St-Leonard Noblat is an ideal spot to spend a family holiday, and there are ample opportunities for outdoor pursuits: riding, walking, tennis, swimming. For an alternative holiday, **Le Chatenet en Dognon** is a tiny hamlet a few kilometres to the north of St-Leonard, where fully equipped horse-drawn caravans can be hired. There is also a good campsite two kilometres away.

Accommodation & Eating Out

First Class

Château de Brie, Brie, Champagnac-la-Rivière, 87150 Oradour-sur-Vayres (Tel. 55 78 17 52): 5 rooms in turreted castle dating from 1500, in wooded park.

Middle Range

Moulin de la Gorce, La Roche l'Abeille, 87800 Nexon (Tel. 55 00 70 66): 9 rooms in sixteenth-century mill by lake, offering friendly welcome; renowned restaurant.

Middle Range/Economy

Hôtel les Voyageurs, Place de l'Eglise, 87390 Coussac-Bonneval (Tel. 55 75 20 24): 9 rooms in family-run hotel with garden;

restaurant known for homely regional cooking. **Domaine du Noyer**, Bersac-sur-Rivalier, 87370 St-Sulpice-Lauvière (Tel. 55 71 59 54): *4 chambres d'hôte* in sixteenth century farm complex run by charming Limousin couple; *tables d'hôte*.

Economy

Hôtel Golf du Limousin, Lac de Vassivière, Auphelle, 87470 Peyrat-le-Château (Tel. 55 69 41 34): 18 rooms in family-run hotel; restaurant finalist in 1989/90 Logis de France regional cuisine competition. **Famille le Quere**, Rouffignac, 87300 Blagnac (Tel. 55 68 03 38): *5 chambres d'hôte* on working manor house farm dating from eighteenth century; *tables d'hôte*.

Creuse

The *département* of **Creuse**, to the south-east of Haute-Vienne, is an area of rivers, lakes and forests. Like much of Limousin, Creuse is extremely rural, with only the three towns of Guéret, Aubusson and Felletin offering more than basic accommodation and other tourist-related services.

Guéret, the *département's* principal town, was once the feudal capital of the ancient French province of Marche, having grown up around a seventh-century abbey. It is a fairly large centre with a population of 13,000, though sadly many of its older buildings have been replaced by high-rise flats and offices. The Municipal Museum has a fine collection of twelfth-to fifteenth-century enamels, and the smaller Creuse Museum, near the market place, exhibits various examples of local arts and crafts. By far the finest building in the town is the Hôtel de Moneyroux (now home to the local archives), which was built in the fifteenth century.

To the north-west of Guéret, in the direction of La Souterraine, stands the **Château du Theret**, full of antique furniture, interesting paintings and other memorabilia. Nearby is the **Forêt de Charbières**, with birch, oak and pine trees, and a number of nature trails. The N145 road links Guéret with **La Souterraine**, an old Roman town. The two things to see here are the Church of the Assumption, built in the thirteenth century, and the Tour de Bridiers – all that remains of the town's medieval fortifications. La Souterraine is a lovely place to spend the day. A lake nearby offers good opportunities for swimming, windsurfing and picnicking. Not far from La Souterraine, the remains of the Cistercian Abbey of Bétête are well worth seeing.

By far the most interesting town in **La Vallée de la Petite Creuse** (which stretches from the Creuse river to the Cher in the east) is **Boussac**. The town is dominated by a magnificent château, renowned for its tapestries. The castle itself stands on the foundations of an older Roman fort, overlooking the Creuse river. During the Hundred Years' War it was besieged and virtually destroyed by the armies of Henry V, but was subsequently restored. Boussac Château, situated on what has come to be known as the **Tapestry Route**, contains a series of six tapestries called the Lady With the Unicorn. These are considered to be some of the finest medieval tapestries in Europe and attract tourists and art connoisseurs from all over the world. Tapestries apart, the château's apartments are also worth seeing.

Directly south-east of Boussac, along a pleasant country road, is **Chambon-sur-Veize**, the meeting point of two long distance footpaths that head northwest through Lepaud and Boussac. The **abbey church of Ste-Valérie** is one of the most magnificent in Limousin, and is built on the foundations of an older priory. Among the treasures to be seen here are Ribera's painting of David and Goliath, and a bust of Ste-Valérie.

Those visitors following the Tapestry Route will find that, after Boussac, their next port of call travelling south will be **Chenerailles**, with its castle and seventh-century tapestries. Chenerailles or Villemonteix Château, as it is more commonly known, was built much later in the fifteenth century. For those interested in meeting local people and experiencing traditional Limousin culture, Chenerailles is a good place to come.

There are horse fairs in the spring and autumn; and agricultural shows, and performances of medieval pageantry in the summer.

Moutier d'Ahun, 15 kilometres west of Chenerailles, is the site of a ruined abbey founded over 1000 years ago. Unfortunately, not much of what must have once been a magnificent Benedictine monastery has survived apart from some lovely wood carvings in the abbey chapel. **Aubusson** on the other hand, some 30 kilometres south, on the edge of the **Plateau de Millevaches** is the finest town in Creuse. It was the seat of a viscounty from whose rulers descended Pierre d'Aubusson, the grand master of the Order of the Hospital of St John of Jerusalem. Since the sixteenth century,

Aubusson has been famous for its carpets and tapestries. The first tapestry workshops were established in 1743 to manufacture pile carpets for the nobility. Soon after the production of carpets began at Aubusson, the pileless tapestry techniques previously in use in the district were once again adopted and, since then, the term Aubusson has come to mean a flat woven French carpet. Many of the earlier designs were of oriental inspiration, but taste soon changed to Renaissance, floral, and architectural patterns.

The Tapestry Museum is housed in the Jean Lurcat Centre where both traditional and modern examples are exhibited. For those interested in both the history and the craft of tapestry-making, a visit to the Maison du Vieux Tapissier, (rue Vieille) is strongly recommended. There are workshops and displays, as well as collections of ancient manuscripts and old furniture.

In the old quarter of the town stands the thirteenth-century **church of Ste-Croix**, which contains a magnificent tapestry depicting the Vision of Constantine.

Another interesting town on the Tapestry Route is **Felletin**, 12 kilometres away. The twelfth-century church of Ste-Valérie holds tapestry exhibitions during the summer and is well worth visiting. During the Middle Ages, the capital of Creuse was **Bourganeuf**, some 40 kilometres away from Aubusson. The town has an historical association with Prince Zizim, son of Mohamet II, who settled in comfortable exile in the Massif Central following a family feud. Bouganeuf is a delightful medieval village with several interesting things to see. Both the Hôtel de Ville, and the Tour de Zizim house some fine tapestries, and there are also the ruins of the old Château d'Auvergne. Visitors interested in long hikes, should consider the GR4, a long distance footpath that runs east/west through the *département*.

Lac Vassivière, in the south of the *département*, is situated in an area of outstanding beauty. The lake itself is surrounded by moors dotted with heather, stretches of forest and white sandy beaches. Outdoor pursuits enthusiasts, particularly those interested in watersports, will find plenty to do here. There is also a network of nature trails, riding stables, a campsite, and good fishing opportunities.

Accommodation & Eating Out

First-class accommodation is pretty rare in these parts. Try instead:

Middle Range

Hôtel du Thaurion, St-Hilaire-du-Château, 23250 Pontarion (Tel. 55 64 50 12): 11 small rooms and 1 suite in eighteenth-century hotel with excellent cooking. **Hôtel-Restaurant le Commerce**, 14 rue de Verdun, 23400 Bourganeuf (Tel. 55 64 14 55): 14 rooms in central family-run hotel whose patron, M. Jaubet, has been a chef for fifty years.

Middle Range / Economy

Hôtel Nougier, 23290 St-Etienne-de-Fursac (Tel. 55 63 60 56): 12 rooms in family-run hotel with garden; restaurant. **Hôtel de France**, rue des Déportés, 23200 Aubusson (Tel. 55 66 10 22): 21 rooms in central family-run hotel whose patron takes pride in his regional cuisine, notably the *fondu creusois*.

Economy

Le Moulin Noyé, Glénic, 23380 Ajain (Tel. 55 52 09 11): 18 rooms in family-run hotel with garden and excellent restaurant. **Hôtel de Bretagne**, Place de la Liberté, 23130 Chénérailles (Tel. 55 62 33 70): 10 rooms in family hotel with restaurant.

Corrèze

Corrèze, to the south of Creuse, is the most southerly of Limousin's *départements*, and geographically the largest and the most varied. Although it lacks both the porcelain tradition of Haute-Vienne and the tapestries of Creuse, its natural beauty more than compensates for fewer cultural attractions.

Brive-la-Gaillarde

Brive (the regional capital) lies in a fertile area where three former provinces – Limousin, Périgord and Quercy – once met. Today an agrarian/industrial economy prevails. Grain, fruit and pork are major products, and there is also some light and heavy industry. The name Brive is derived from a Latin term meaning brave or vigorous – an apt description for a town that has survived the onslaught of several foreign armies over the centuries, including the Germans in the Second World War, when the town became a stronghold for the French Resistance.

The **medieval Church of St-Martin**, on Place Charles de Gaulle, dominates the city's skyscape. The church is named after the Spanish saint who introduced christianity to the town in the fifth century and was later martyred. The carvings of mythological wildlife on the choir stalls are particularly remarkable. The **Hôtel de la Benche**, on rue Blaise Raynal houses a first-class collection of archaeological finds from all over southern France. The **Musée Edmond Michelet**, 4 rue Champanatier, commemorates the local French Resistance during the Second World War, and contains some interesting documents and wartime memorabilia.

The **Tourist Office** is in the high-rise Immeuble Château d'Eau (Tel. 55 24 08 80).

Accommodation

First Class

Château de Castel Novel, D 170, 19240 Varetz (Tel. 55 85 00 01): 33 rooms and 5 suites in park-surrounded château formerly occupied by Colette, 10 km from Brive; elegant restaurant serving gastronomic cuisine.

Middle Range

La Truffe Noire, 22 bd Anatole-France (Tel. 55 74 35 32): 32 rooms in central but quiet hotel with garden; high quality restaurant.

Middle Range / Economy

La Crémaillère, 53 ave de Paris (Tel. 55 74 32 47): 12 comfortable rooms in central hotel with garden; restaurant with welcoming atmosphere and regional specialities.

Economy

Le Champanatier, 15 rue Dumyrat (Tel. 55 74 24 14): 12 rooms in family-run hotel with restaurant. **Hôtel de l'Avenir**, 39 ave Jean-Jaurès (Tel. 55 74 11 84): 18 spacious rooms in family-run hotel handy for train station.

Eating Out

In addition to the hotel restaurants recommended above, try:

First Class / Middle Range

La Périgourdine, 15 ave Alsace-Lorraine (Tel. 55 24 26 55): traditional regional specialities in charming old restaurant.

Middle Range

Le Teinchurier, ave de Teinchurier (Tel. 55 86 90 65): good value meat dishes.

Economy

Le Quercy, 3 Place du 14 Juillet: cheap, traditional menus.

Entertainments

Brive has a huge market on Place du 14 Juillet, which is at its liveliest on Saturday mornings. Another good way of meeting local people is to attend the annual town festivals. The Twelfth Night Festival in January provides an opportunity to try pâté de foie gras and truffles, whilst July brings a summer book fair and a melon fair.

Rest of Corrèze

Tulle, the main town, famous for its lace veils, is situated on the Corrèze river. The **Cathédrale de Notre-Dame** dominates this medieval town of narrow twisting streets and high-walled buildings. From the bell tower, which is 73 metres high, there are splendid views of the surrounding countryside. Like so many of the towns in Limousin, Tulle suffered terribly during the Second World War when many of its citizens were massacred by the retreating German armies. **Le Musée de la Résistance et de la Déportation**, on quai Edmond Perrier, is both a memorial and chronicle of the towns fate during the Nazi occupation. With this and other past tragedies in mind, visitors will find the atmosphere within the cathedral fittingly sombre. The modern stained-glass windows are the only source of colour in what is otherwise a rather gloomy interior. Next to the cathedral is the fascinating **André Mazeyrie Museum**, containing various religious relics, items of porcelain and historical documents. The old quarter of Tulle is clustered around the cathedral, a series of alleyways, steps and ancient houses, built, no doubt, with the safety and defence of its citizens in mind.

For those who enjoy walking, a picnic and hike to the waterfalls at **Gimel-les-Cascades**, 12 kilometres east of Tulle, is highly recommended. The falls plunge 60 metres into a subterranean cavern – the **Gouffre de l'Inferno**. Walkers will also enjoy the climb to the ruined **Château de Ventadour**, a twelfth-century fortress perched like an eagle's nest above the village of Moustier-de-Venatadour, and the N89 road. **Ussel**, 20 kilometres north-east, has some lovely old houses lining the rue de la Liberté. Craft enthusiasts will find the collection of local work housed in the Hôtel du Juge Choriol fascinating. There are weaving exhibitions, wickerwork workshops and many other examples of local trades. In July, Ussel holds its annual sculpture and painting festival, which artists from all over the province attend. Ussel is a good base from which to explore the surrounding countryside. There is a lake nearby for fishing and swimming, and numerous nature trails. Watersports enthusiasts should head 15 kilometres south-east to the **Lac de Bort**, a magnificent reservoir 18 kilometres long. The hydro-electricity exhibition, housed in the power house is also very interesting. The village of **Bort-les-Orgues**, situated on the lakeside, is pleasant enough, though apart from the twelfth-century church of Ste-Anne, there is not much to see. Just outside the village, the **Orgues-de-Bort** rocks guard the approaches to the lake. A footpath from the car park leads up the hill to the boulders, from where there are splendid views of the *département*.

A beautiful country lane leads north-west and then south through wooded hills to **Neuvic**, a small town catering for sports enthusiasts. There is a golf course, riding stable and bicycle hire shop, and the **Lac de la Triouzoune** provides good facilities for sailors, water skiers and bathers. The Musée de la Résistance Henri Queville, in the town, commemorates the French Resistance, but particularly the local Maquis.

Just off the N89 road leading from Moustier-de-Ventadour to Ussel lies **Meymac**, a picturesque medieval town. The Marius Vazeilles Archaeological Museum, housed in the old abbey (Place du Bucher), concentrates mainly on archaeological discoveries of the Plateau de Millevaches and local history. The abbey church, the oldest building in Meymac, contains some interesting relics, among them a twelfth-century madonna.

Historians will be interested in surrounding villages such as

Mont-Besson with its ancient church and square. The whole area around Meymac offers numerous opportunities. Nearby are the Celtic and Roman sites of **Le Rat** and **Bars-les-Cars**, and several hills from which there are magnificent views. Canoeists should consider following the course of the Creuse river, which flows through some wonderful country.

Many consider the town of **Uzerche** (situated in the centre of the *département*), to be the jewel in Limousin's crown and this judgement is not without reason. It is an archetypal medieval town in every sense. Surrounded by stone walls and fortified by the Vézère river, a natural moat, its ancient buildings cluster together in a mass of grey slate, wrought-iron gates, turrets and towers. Locals say a house in Uzerche is a castle in Limousin', and this aptly describes the numerous fortified houses in the town. The interior of St-Pierre's Church is particularly magnificent and contains a series of delightful little chapels and ornate tombs. The original gateway, the Porte Bechaire, still guards the approaches to the town. Just beyond are some stone steps leading to the old fruit market on Place des Vignerons

Directly west of Uzerche is **Arnac de Pompadour**, named after Louis XV's famous mistress, Jeanne-Antoinette Poisson – Madame de Pompadour. Today, Pompadour is more famous for its stud farms and race courses than for its royal patronage. The only buildings of any historical interest in the town are the château (only the grounds are open to the public) and the Église d'Arnac, built in the twelfth century.

The countryside from Pompadour to Brive-la-Gaillarde, 60 kilometres to the south, is surprisingly bleak. Country lanes twist and wind their way through tiny hamlets, woods and hills.

The D38 road, running south of Brive, bypasses the enchanting, aptly named town of **Collonges-la-Rouge**. The buildings here are made of deep red sandstone, and are quite unlike any others in Limousin. Although, the town attracts a lot of visitors, particularly in the summer, it owes its preservation to a group of local 'friends' who formed a society for the preservation of local buildings at the turn of the century. During the Wars of Religion, Collonges-la-Rouge escaped destruction when its citizens decided to compromise by dividing the church in half; one for the Catholics and one for the Protestants. The large red Romanesque church is particularly handsome, and has an unusual belfry and beautifully carved doorway. Like Uzerche,

Collonges-la-Rouge should be savoured at leisure and not seen too hastily.

Collonges-la-Rouge is within striking distance of another delightful medieval town, **Aubazines**, situated on the main N89 road. Aubazines was the site of a twelfth-century Cistercian abbey. The abbey church, which survived the Wars of Religion, houses some remarkable stained-glass windows.

Accommodation & Eating Out

First Class

La Borderie, Le Pouret, 19270 Ussac (Tel. 55 87 74 45): 7 rooms in family-run hotel with swimming pool and gastronomic restaurant.

Middle Range

Auberge de la Marquise, 4 ave des Ecuyers, 19230 Pompadour (Tel. 55 73 33 98): 10 rooms in family-run inn with restaurant.

Middle Range / Economy

L'Espérance, Barennac Sioniac, 19120 Beaulieu-sur-Montagne (Tel. 55 91 08 54): small hotel offering vegetarian meals.

Economy

Relais St-Jacques de Compostelle, Collonges-la-Rouge, 19500 Meyssac (Tel. 55 25 41 02): 12 rooms in simple but pleasant village inn with warm welcome; restaurant. **Le Pré Fleuri**, 1090 ave Jules-Ferry, 19130 Objat (Tel. 55 25 83 92): 7 rooms in family hotel; restaurant serving regional specialities.

14 Auvergne

For the British visitor weary of the conventions of holidays in the Dordogne or the Côte d'Azur, the Auvergne may well hold the promise of being the hidden, the true France. Unfortunately however, the Auvergne has very much been discovered!

As long ago as the first century AD, the Romans had discovered the hot springs in the region and, nowadays, resorts such as Vichy in the north and Chaudes-Aigues in the south are classified spas and health resorts – indeed, there are ten of these altogether in the Auvergne. For those who prefer a different way to keep healthy, the hills of the Auvergne are criss-crossed with well-marked footpaths which, in the winter, are turned into cross-country skiing trails. There are also three downhill ski resorts, giving the region an all-year-round appeal.

For the culturally minded visitor, the Auvergne has much to offer in the way of religious architecture. A powerful Church in the twelfth century bequeathed a legacy of fine Romanesque building such as the churches of St-Nectaire and Issoire. The Auvergne can also claim a degree of gastronomic fame from the range of cheeses produced in the region, of which the most famous are bleu d'auvergne and saint-nectaire.

The people of the Auvergne, the Auvergnats, are traditionally a farming community. Fierce regional pride is said to be a characteristic of these people, although this has not prevented a large-scale exodus to the major cities, resulting in rural depopulation. The Auvergnats used to have a reputation for being reserved and unfriendly to strangers, perhaps due to their sufferings during the many wars of religion, or simply the natural characteristic of a rural community geographically isolated from the surrounding cities and thus obliged to be self-sufficient. Nowadays, you might encounter different responses to the fairly recent influx of tourists but, on the whole, sincere efforts to communicate are rewarded with a polite response and an interest in the needs of the visitor. *Cantal Sourire*

('The Cantal smile') is after all the slogan adopted by one of these regions.

History

In 800 BC, a Gallic tribe settled in this region and took for themselves the name *Arvenes*, from *Arverne* meaning land of summits. It is from this word that the Auvergne derives its name. The Arvenes settled in and around the Allier plain and, over the centuries, came to dominate the whole of the Massif Central, establishing their stronghold at Gergovie near Clermont-Ferrand. However, they couldn't resist the power of the Roman Empire which was sweeping across France and they were defeated at the battle of Alésia.

Once under Roman rule, the region experienced three centuries of peace and prosperity. Temples were erected including an important shrine dedicated to Mercury on the slopes of the Puy-de-Dome; remains can still be seen. Baths were built around the thermal springs and roads were constructed, several of which converged upon the regional capital of Augustonemetum (Clermont-Ferrand). Agriculture was developed and important ceramic industries were established at Lezoux and Les Martres-de-Veyre.

This stability was first threatened around AD 250 by raids from bands of barbarians and there then followed a time of anarchy caused by feuding war lords vying for power in the region. Amid the turmoil, Christianity, first introduced in the third century, managed to establish itself and throughout this period the Church played an increasingly important role. A monk from Aurillac became Pope in AD 999 and the announcement of the first crusade was made from Clermont-Ferrand in 1095 by Pope Urban II.

The twelfth and thirteenth centuries were a period of relative calm. The King of France supported the Church and eventually Philippe Auguste took control of the whole region. This was the time when Romanesque architecture flowered in the many beautiful churches which sprang up in the villages. It was also a time when agriculture was further developed and three-quarters of the countryside was cultivated.

The Hundred Years' War reached the Auvergne in the mid-fourteenth century. The threat of pillage from roaming bands of soldiers forced villagers to protect themselves by building fortifications. These troubles coincided with outbreaks of plague and famine. Meanwhile, the control of the region passed to the

Duc de Berry who aggravated the lives of the poor by demanding payments to subsidise the building of his palaces at Riom and Nonette.

The fifteenth and sixteenth centuries allowed the Auvergne to re-establish itself and this was the time when paper, cutlery and tanning industries were introduced to the Livradois-Forez. However, the Thirty Years' War saw another downturn in the region's fortunes. Again, pillage, famine and plague brought suffering to the people, this time coupled with a demand for the payment of higher taxes.

The French Revolution had little impact on the people of the region, although some buildings belonging to the Church and the nobility were ordered to be destroyed, but the nineteenth and early twentieth centuries saw an increasing tendency to emigrate due to overpopulation in the mountains. The situation was worsened by the destruction of the vines by disease and then by the two World Wars. The exodus threatened commerce, schools were closed, villages deserted. During the Second World War, Vichy was the home of the government of unoccupied France and the Auvergne became a stronghold for the French Resistance movement. The memorial at Mont Mouchet is a reminder of the losses they suffered.

Nowadays, the population has stabilised and the Auvergne is casting off the image of a rural backwater. Increasingly, high-tech industry is being added to the old agricultural and forestry economy; the Michelin factory in Clermont-Ferrand, established as long ago as 1832, is a major employer in the region and it is joined by chemical and textile industries (Aurillac is famous for umbrellas). Hydro-electric schemes and the growth of year-round tourism are bringing increasing prosperity to the Auvergne.

Geography

The Auvergne region forms the central part of the Massif Central, a vast granite plateau west of the Rhône Valley. Its unique feature is the range of peaks and craters, long-extinct volcanoes which have turned by the slow forces of erosion into a landscape of high green pastures and moorland, clear blue crater lakes and wooded valleys. The plateau is sliced in two, north to south, by the River Allier which first makes its appearance in a narrow gorge, then forces a wider valley, called the Limagne, before running out in the north of the region to form a flat plain on which farmers cultivate fields of maize, vines and tobacco.

West of the river, the plateau reaches the heights of the Monts Dôme, the Monts Dore and the Monts du Cantal which make up the Parc Régional des Volcans, the largest regional park in France. The Monts Dôme on the northern tip of the park are a chain of recent volcanoes, scarcely 10,000 years old, of which the most famous peak or *puy* is the Puy de Dôme itself. These *puys* may appear dark and precipitous from a distance but sharp edges have been rounded and hollows have been filled with soil and become richly wooded. The Monts Dore are older and more ravaged by glacial erosion, yet contain the highest point of the Auvergne, the Puy de Sancy (1886 metres). Before the next range of peaks rear up, the landscape levels out into the high granite tableland of the Artense and the Cezallier, a region of forests, peat-bogs and grassland. Finally, on the southern edge of the park, one single volcano, the oldest at 20 million years old, produced a series of chimneys within a lava flow 70 km in diameter. The heighest points are the Plomb du Cantal and the Puy Mary, from which radiate no fewer than twelve glacial valleys.

To the east of the Allier valley lies another regional park, the Livradois Forez. Gentler, more wooded, less dramatic than the Parc des Volcans, it comprises a series of plateaux and flattened hills, the highest of which, Pierre-sur-Haute, may on a clear day give glimpses of the Alps. South of the Livradois, the town of Le Puy-en-Velay lies in an eroded volcanic crater with three surviving plugs, needle-like outcrops, one of which sports a chapel. South-east of Le Puy, one further volcanic massif rises to Mont Mezenc (1754 metres).

The diversity of landscapes in the Auvergne gives rise to a wide range of flora and fauna. In the Parc des Volcans there are claimed to be more than two thousand types of plants; look for carpets of wild daffodil in the spring, with narcissus, violet and wild orchid, gentian and hillsides of bilberry. The woodland and forest are coniferous and deciduous, with oak and sweet chestnut in the valleys, beechwoods and silver fir on the hillsides. There are deer to be seen, wild boar, badger, mouflon (a type of wild sheep), even chamois in the more remote hills of the region. Birdlife includes owls, buzzards, the red kite, short-toed eagle and goshawk. The lakes and rivers teem with trout and carp, whilst the Allier is particularly well known for its salmon.

Climate

Thanks to its continental climate, the Auvergne caters for both summer and winter visitors. Winter can be harsh and bitterly cold.

As the clouds from the Atlantic hit the peaks of the Monts Dore and the Monts du Cantal, snow falls and the skiers arrive. In the highest regions, snow can last from December to early May. In spring, temperatures begin to pick up from April onwards although they can vary considerably. The average May temperature is 17°C.

The summer months are generally hot and dry although it can suddenly become chilly, especially in the mountains, when clouds can quickly cover the peaks and rain or thunderstorms threaten. The average July temperature is 27°C. Autumn can be a good time to visit. It is often sunny, but without the summer's oppressive heat. Even in October the average temperature is 17°C.

Attractions

Savourez l'espace – enjoy the open spaces – is the tourist board's motto for the Cantal, and it is indeed the great outdoors which forms the chief attraction of the Auvergne for tourists. They come in increasing numbers each year to walk, to climb, to explore the volcanic hills and valleys on horse-back or mountain bike, to raft or canoe down the rivers, even to experience the thrills of hang-gliding or parascending. Alternatively, the open spaces can be enjoyed in a more leisurely fashion, bird-watching, hunting for minerals or for rare orchids. Of course, in the winter it is the snow that brings visitors to enjoy the skiing. The Auvergne has three classified downhill ski resorts and 3000 km of cross-country skiing trails.

Most of these outdoor pursuits are concentrated in the two Parcs Naturels Régionaux of the Auvergne, the Parc des Volcans, the largest regional park in France, and the Parc du Livradois-Forez, although the Montagne Bourbonnaise in the Allier and the countryside surrounding the Mont Mezenc are also very attractive areas.

Traditionally, visitors came to the Auvergne to take the waters. There are ten *stations du thermalisme* of which Le Mont-Dore, Vichy and Chaudes-Aigues are the best known. Thanks to the geology of the region, Chaudes-Aigues ('hot lakes') boasts the hottest waters in Europe – 82 degrees!

For the tourist interested in architecture, the Auvergne is well known for its Romanesque churches; Notre-Dame-du-Port in Clermont-Ferrand, **Saint-Nectaire, Issoire** and **Brioude** are perhaps the best examples, whilst **Saint-Michel-l'Aiguille** in Le Puy-en-Velay is in an extraordinary position on top of a volcanic plug. Finally, **Clermont-Ferrand**, a busy university town, is a lively capital for the region.

Cuisine

Traditionally, the gastronomy of rural Auvergne is based on simple wholesome recipes using local produce. Cabbage-based soups and meat stews, supplemented with available ingredients such as mushrooms and lentils, are commonplace. Perhaps the most famous dish is *la potée auvergnat*, usually a pork, cabbage and bean stew that is gently simmered for hours, a typical method of cooking in this region.

Meat eaters can also try local specialities such as *gigot brayaude* (mutton cooked in lard with herbs and white wine) and *salade auvergnat* (green lentils mixed with ham, eggs, potatoes and mayonnaise). Not to be missed is the local *charcuterie*, Auvergne's ham being particularly renowned. Freshwater fish appear on many menus in dishes such as *saumon de l'Allier* and *les filets de truites au gratin de Cantal*, whilst game (pheasant, hare, quail) is sometimes on offer.

The region is well-known for its rye bread but above all for its cheeses. Look out for salers which is a prestigious form of cantal cheese. You might also wish to sample the blue-veined blue d'Auvergne, the cylindrically shaped fourme d'ambert and, from the Monts Dore area, saint-nectaire. If you are a fan of goats' cheese, cabécou is produced near Aurillac.

Not surprisingly, cheese is a major ingredient in several regional dishes including *la tarte au cantal* (a variation on quiche lorraine using cantal cheese with tomatoes, herbs and mustard). Vegetarians might find some suitable dishes here. Macaroni cheese, cheese soufflée and even cheese soup are popular but you will need to check that no meat has been added.

For dessert, the local specialities are fruit-based tarts or flans such as *tarte aux myrtilles* (bilberry tart) and *clafoutis aux cerises* (cherry flan). Should you wish to round off your meal with a local *digestif*, you could try the herb-based Verveine from Le Puy or Marc d'Auvergne.

Local wines include Corent, Châteaugay and Chanturgue to name but three.

Level of Tourism

Although once an example of *la France profonde*, it must be said that the Auvergne has now lost its innocence and has entered fully into the tourism rat-race. It still comes two-thirds of the way down the hit parade of French tourist regions though, hosting only 2.2% of all national visits. It has the lowest proportion of foreign visitors for any French region – only one in ten – but it does tend to attract long-stay visitors. The region has always been known as a spa resort; the *stations thermales* were well known from Roman times and have retained a regular clientèle, convinced of the beneficial effect of the waters. It is true that their products, such as Volvic mineral water, have increased their sales outside France.

It is in the mountains of the Auvergne, however, that the dramatic increase in tourism has been most felt, particularly in the Parc des Volcans. In their search for an 'unspoilt' landscape, tourists have turned from the overcrowded Alpine resorts, filling instead the roads around the Monts Dore and the Monts du Cantal. Walkers wishing to reach the peak of le Puy Mary, for example, will first have to contend with lines of parked cars and then a path heavily damaged by erosion. The summit of le Puy de Sancy can be reached by cable car as can the Plomb du Cantal – hardly an 'unspoilt' landscape. The environmental damage which is the inevitable result of developing downhill ski resorts is to be seen around Super-Lioran, the largest in central France. Of course, for the walker prepared to explore any distance from the road, glorious unspoilt countryside is there to be enjoyed. But beware – the French tourist is not averse to walking some distance before settling down for an elaborate picnic.

Inevitably, if the hillsides are under threat, then so too are the hill villages. Places which had rarely seen a tourist ten years ago have now sprouted colourful bars and restaurants. Towns such as Saint-Nectaire are now very much tourist 'resorts'.

The other regional park in the Auvergne, it should be said, does not enjoy the same degree of popularity as its neighbour. The Livradois-Forez is not as scenically dramatic, but it has a well organised tourism programme, without the crowds.

The increase in tourism has been good news for the prosperity of the Auvergne as it has gone some way towards counterbalancing the decline in the rural economy. In the Cantal, for example, 500,000 holiday-makers now visit the region annually and, with 150,000 of those coming in the winter, tourism is an all-year-round business. The visitors attract a revenue equal to 50% of that of agriculture, jobs have been created and the prosperity of the region has grown accordingly. At the same time it has to be said that the tourist authorities are aware of the dangers of tourism. The regional park status of much of the area will help protect the environment, whilst efficient publicity is attempting to direct the visitors' attention towards less well known sites such as the reservoir at Grandval where watersports are being promoted.

Good Alternatives

Meeting People

In the Auvergne much of life is geared to the outdoors and this can be the context in which to meet others with similar interests. **'Espace et Recherches'**, Château-Bas, rue du Château St-Etienne, 15000 Aurillac organises itineraries to observe bird migration, flora and fauna. **La Maison des Volcans**, Château St-Etienne, 15000 Aurillac runs courses in discovering the environment. The **Association Méandres**, Monsieur Eric Dizzaro, Le Puy Basset, 15140 Fontagnes offers donkey treks with the emphasis on discovering flora and fauna. **The Livradois-Forez Tourisme**, BP 18, 43160 La Chaise-Dieu runs a variety of 'discovery' days in its region which include Initiation à la Minéralogie, Les Fleurs du Haut Forez and A la Recherche de la Toison d'Or, which includes panning for gold! Ask for their *Monts Vallées Sejours* booklet. The **Centre Permanent d'Initiation à l'Environnement**, avenue Nicholas Rambourg, 03360 Saint Bonnet-Tronçais runs a programme of courses in such things as bird-watching, orchid and mushroom hunting.

For the less athletic, there are classes during August in making and using puppets; contact **Les Amis de la Montagne Bourbonnaise**, Place de l'Eglise, 03250 Le-Mayet-de-Montagne. The **Centre d'Animation de Trielle** organises dance, mime and theatre classes in the summer; contact M. Jacques Lours, 15450 Thiezac. Information about archaeological digs in the region can be supplied by the **Direction des Antiquités**, Hôtel de Chazerat, 4 rue Pascal, 63000 Clermont-Ferrand (Tel. 73 92 40 41).

For those interested in sampling the food of the region and meeting the people who produce it, there is a *Route des Fromages* available from the **Cantal Tourisme**, 22 rue Guy-de-Veyre, 15018 Aurillac which lists farms where you can taste and buy cheeses.

The **Tourisme du Puy-de-Dôme**, 17 Place Delille, 63038 Clermont-Ferrand has a *Circuit Gourmand* with demonstrations by bee-keepers, wine-growers and cheese-makers. The **Accueil à la Ferme** of each region has lists of farm holiday which are distributed by the tourist offices.

Festivals in the region include the May Fête de Notre Dame du Port in Clermont-Ferrand and the Easter festival of Sainte-Procule in Gannant. Gannant also hosts a world Folklore festival in July. There are various festivals to mark Assumption day (15 August), including a torchlit procession to Notre-Dame du Mont in Saint-Nectaire and to Notre-Dame du Put in Le Puy. Tourist offices will provide information of other festivals, as will the **Comité Régional du Tourisme**, 43 avenue Julien, BP 395, 63000 Clermont-Ferrand (Tel. 73 93 04 03).

Discovering Places

For those who love walking, the Auvergne is a good alternative to the busy footpaths of the Alps. The region is crossed by a dozen GR trails as well as many other marked paths. There are *Topoguides* which describe each trail. The park information centre **Parc Naturel Régional Livradois-Forez Tourisme** also produces guides to footpaths in their park as well as fully organised activity holidays. Their address is BP 17, 63880 Saint-Gervais-sous-Meymont. The administrative offices of **Le Parc Naturel des Volcans D'Auvergne** is at Montlosier près Randanne, Commune d'Aydat, 63210 Rochefort-Montagne. An organisation called **Chamina** publish a brochure of activity holidays called 'Le Colporteur' for the Massif Central. It includes pony-trekking, rafting, canoeing and mountain bike tours. Contact Chamina, 8 rue de Verdun, 15130 Arpajon/Cère for information. There are British companies who also offer walking holidays in the Auvergne including **Headwater Holidays** (Tel. 0606 48699), **Ramblers Holidays** (Tel. 0707 331133) and **Sherpa Expeditions** (Tel. 081 577 2717).

It should be noted that areas of the natural parks can get crowded in the peak season (see **Level of Tourism**); the Bourbonnais in the Allier can be a good alternative: information from the **Office Bourbonnais du Tourisme**, 35 rue de Bellecroix, BP50, 03402 Yzeure. Other activities available in the area include rock-climbing, fishing and hang-gliding.

In the winter, the outdoor enthusiasts put on their skis. Cross-country skiing is more environmentally friendly than downhill skiing as it needs no lifts or wide pistes, although some centres offering cross-country skiing also offer downhill skiing and have all the associated paraphernalia. **Auvergne Ski de Fond**, Centre Couthon-Delille, 23 Place Delille, 63000 Clermont-Ferrand will send a brochure. Two British companies who organise cross-country skiing in the Auvergne are **SVP France** (Tel. 0243 377862) and **Headwater Holidays** (Tel. 0606 48699). **Chamina** also advertise skiing holidays.

The Auvergne Tourist Board has compiled a *Route des Châteaux d'Auvergne* covering the whole region, while the Cantal tourist board has a series of *circuits touristiques* including a *circuit des églises romanes* in their 'Cantal Patrimonie' booklet. There is a *Route des Métiers* compiled by the Livradois-Forez tourist board which includes lists of crafts and local products. Brochures of locally-arranged holidays of various types are available from **Loisirs-Accueil Cantal**, 19 Place de l'Hôtel de Ville, BP 75, 15017 Aurillac (Tel. 71 48 84 84); and from **Loisirs-Accueil Haute-Loire**, 12 bd Philippe-Jourde, 43000 Le-Puy-en-Velay (Tel. 71 09 26 05).

Communications

How to Get There

There are no direct **flights** from Britain to the Auvergne and travellers have to change at Paris from where internal flights are available to Clermont-Ferrand or Aurillac.

Clermont-Ferrand is 681 km from Calais. The newly completed A71 autoroute connects the Auvergne with Paris, the A72 connects with Lyon. The journey between Paris and Clermont takes around 4 1/2 hours.

Rail tickets can be purchased from cities in Britain to Clermont-Ferrand, although passengers will need to change in Paris. There are direct trains daily from the Auvergne to Paris, but none are TGV services, so the journey takes a minimum of 4 hours 10 minutes.

When You're There

Rail – The TER network serves the main towns of the region and will also get you into the natural parks. There is a line to Riom-es-Montagne (Monts du Cantal) and Le Mont-Dore, for example, and there is a special 'panoramic' railway which follows the valley of the Dore from Courpière to Arlanc, via Ambert.

Bus – Travel by bus is not a practical alternative to the car as routes are limited and services infrequent.

Car – The new *Meridiénne*, the A71 extension will soon cut through the Auvergne in its progress towards Montpellier. It will allow speedy communications between the north and the south of the region. On the minor roads of the region, particularly around the tourist honeypots, traffic can be a problem.

Boat – The rivers of the Auvergne are used for sport rather than communications. Rafting and canoeing are popular particularly in the Gorges d'Allier, the Vallée d'Olt and the Gorge de Pradelles. Information from tourist offices or Chamina (see Good Alternatives).

Cycling – Cycling is not really a realistic form of transport except for the very fit. VTT (mountain bikes) are popular off the roads however, and are widely available for hire (see Good Alternatives). Routes include the Star of the Auvergne Summits route. Contact **La Ligue du Cyclotourisme d'Auvergne**, 68 rue Blatin, 63000 Clermont-Ferrand.

Walking – There are over a dozen G R footpaths in the Auvergne including the G R 400 which tours the volcanoes of the Cantal, the G R 412 which follows the gorge of the Allier and the G R 30 which takes the walker to some of the most beautiful lakes of the Auvergne. The regional footpath organisation, **F.F.R.P.** is at 1 rue des Tilleuls, Le Cheix-sur-Morge, 63200 Riom.

Riding – Horse . . . or donkey! Both are very popular in the region and tourist offices will have lists of places offering Equitation. (See **Good Alternatives**.) The regional association for Tourisme Equestre is at Laborie de Leynhac, 15600 Maurs.

Geographical Breakdown of Region

Allier and Puy-de-Dome

The heyday of **Moulins** was at the end of the fifteenth century when it became the capital of the Duchy of Bourbon. Nowadays, despite being the Préfecture of Allier, it is bypassed by the A71 autoroute and by most tourists who head for the mountains of the Auvergne instead. The main sightseeing attraction for the tourist is the fifteenth-century triptych in the cathedral. It was painted by the maitre de Moulins and depicts Anne of France and her husband Pierre, Duke of Bourbon either side of a Virgin and Child. The vieille ville around the cathedral makes an enjoyable area to stroll in. The **Tourist Office** is in the Place de l'Hôtel de Ville and they will supply you with a map showing points of interest. Make sure you are in the rue de l'Horloge on the hour to watch the figures of the Jacquemart family chime the time.

Known since Roman times for the supposedly beneficial effect of its carbonated waters, **Vichy** has always attracted the old and infirm. The opening of the railway at the turn of the century, filled the Parc des Sources, thermal establishments and casino.

Nowadays, the damming of the River Allier to form a large lake has diversified the appeal of the town, and young, fit people come to windsurf and enjoy the various sports facilities. Tourists can take advantage of these facilities by buying a *passeport sportif* for the Centre Omnisports. Information and bike hire are available from the Tourist Office at 19 rue du Parc.

West of Vichy are the **Gorges de Chouvigny** and the **Gorges de la Sioule** with the spectacularly situated ruins of the **Château Rocher**. A dam at the head of the Sioule has artificially enlarged the meanders at Queuille.

Heading into the regional park from **Clermont-Ferrand** the first notable town is **Le Mont Dore**. A spa in the summer ever since the Romans sampled its waters, it is now, more importantly, a ski resort in the winter, with over fifty hotels. There are guided tours of the *Etablissement Thermale* in season and walks into the surrounding hills (including the Puy de Sancy, although the 5-minute cable-car alternative makes walking rather pointless.) In the winter, there are many cross-country trails which start from the town. East of Le Mont Dore is **Saint-Nectaire**, said to have the most perfect example of a Romanesque church in the Auvergne. Of course it also gives its name to the cheese – you can visit a cheese cellar at the Maison du Saint-Nectaire (June to September). Nearby **Issoire**, a drab industrial town just off the main *Meridienne* throughroute, is the site of another, more controversial church. The Romanesque St-Austremoine was 'restored' in the last century by Anatole Dauvergne who attempted to recreate a typical medieval interior by painting the intricately carved stonework in bright colours. This does not accord with some modern taste but it makes an interesting contrast to other more sombre examples of Romanesque churches. West of Issoire, **Besse-en-Chandesse** is a good centre from which to tackle the Tour des Lacs d'Auvergne (G R 30). Besse itself is a grey–stone, fortified medieval town, typical of the Auvergne. Nearby **Super-Besse** is its modern cousin, catering for walkers and skiers.

Accommodation

First Class

Château de la Roche-Aigueperse, La Roche, Chaptuzat, 63260 Aigueperse (Tel. 73 63 65 81): 3 *chambres d'hôte*, furnished with antiques in 12th to 13th century château-fort with views of the Volcans d'Auvergne. **Château de Fragne**, Verneix, 03190 Hérisson (Tel. 70 07 80 87): 4 rooms and one suite in eighteenth-century château in large garden; open May 15th to Sept 30th; *tables d'hôte* on reservation. **Château de Boussac**, Target, 03140 Chantelle (Tel. 70 40 63 20): 3 *chambres d'hôte* and two suites in seventeenth-century turreted and moated castle in peaceful surroundings; *tables d'hôte*.

Middle Range

Château de Maulmont, Saint Priest Bramefant, 63310 Randan (Tel. 70 59 03 45): 20 comfortable rooms in imposing romantic château (a former royal hunting lodge), with impressive furnishings and excellent restaurant.

Middle Range / Economy

Hôtel le Chalet, Coulandon, 03000 Moulins (Tel. 70 44 50 08): 25 rooms in ivy-covered building with large wooded garden; good restaurant serving regional specialities.

Economy

Hôtel les Touristes, 63120 Vollore-Montagne (Tel. 73 53 77 50): 12 rooms in simple and friendly, family-run hotel; restaurant with good home cooking. **La Taverne de France**, 8 rue des Bouchers, 03000 Moulins (Tel. 70 44 04 82): friendly, central hotel above bar popular with locals.

Eating Out

In addition to the restaurants mentioned above, the following deserve special recommendation:

First Class

Le Jacquemart, 10 Place de l'Hôtel de Ville, 03000 Moulins (Tel. 70 44 32 58): inventive cuisine offered by prestigious restaurant in beautifully restored sixteenth-century house in town centre.

First Class / Middle Range

Le Moulin à Sel, 5 Place Albert 1er, 03200 Vichy (Tel. 70 97 59 72): imaginative cooking in restaurant with attractive and cosy dining room.

Clermont-Ferrand

Situated at the centre of the region, this industrial city strikes a discordant note with the surrounding rural landscapes of the Auvergne. The heart of the city, constructed largely from dark grey volcanic stone, clusters on a hillside around the cathedral. It is surrounded by modern suburbs, industrial estates and a fast ring-road. Clermont-Ferrand is really two towns; Clermont and Montferrand. However, the two have now been merged into one city with a population of 300,000.

Begin a tour of Clermont-Ferrand from the **Cathedral of Notre-Dame de l'Assomption** where the panorama from one of the towers will let you get your bearings. The cathedral itself is a light airy building thanks to the strength of the dark basalt stone which allowed the fourteenth-century architects to design slender pillars and graceful vaulting. Contrast the Gothic architecture of the cathedral with the earlier Romanesque **Notre-Dame-du-Port**, generally regarded as one of the finest examples of the style in the region. The beauty of the building, seen first from the outside with its squat octagonal lantern tower and cluster of chapels, and then on the inside with the richly decorated choir and delicately carved capitals, lies in the harmony and balance of design.

Clermont-Ferrand has a number of museums including the **Musée du Ranquet** near the cathedral, which covers the history of the city. Around the cathedral is a maze of small streets, some of which are pedestrianised. The centre of the main shopping area is the **Place de Jaude**, which has a statue of Vercingetorix, the Celtic leader said to have defeated the Romans at the battle of Gergovie. Just 2 km from the centre of Clermont-Ferrand is Montferrand which has a carefully restored old quarter with attractive half-timbered and stone houses near the tourist office.

Accommodation

Clermont-Ferrand's best small hotels tend to be located out of town:

First Class/Middle Range

Hostellerie St-Martin, Château de Bonneval, 63170 Pérignat-lès-Sarliève (Tel. 73 79 12 41): 21 rooms in quiet hotel with large gardens, 8 km from town; restaurant. **Le Radio**, 43 ave Pierre-Curie, 63400 Chamalières (Tel. 73 30 87 83): 25 rooms in Art-Deco style hotel with garden, 3 km from town; excellent restaurant using local ingredients to their full.

Middle Range/Economy

Hôtel St-André, 27 ave Union-Soviétique (Tel. 73 91 40 40): 25 rooms in hotel with restaurant. **La Belle Meunière**, 23 ave de la Vallée, 63130 Royat (Tel. 73 35 80 17): 10 rooms in peaceful turn-of-the-century hotel, 4 km from town; excellent restaurant serving traditional cuisine.

Economy

Hostellerie de la Poste, 47 ave Wilson, 63122 Ceyrat (Tel. 73 61 30 01): 6 rooms in cosy hotel, 5 km out of town; attractive restaurant serves good food. **Hôtel d'Aigueperse**, 4 rue Aigueperse (Tel. 73 91 30 62): spacious rooms in hotel handy for station. **Hôtel Foch**, 22 rue Maréchal-Foch (Tel. 73 93 48 40): welcoming, central hotel.

Eating Out

First Class

Jean-Yves Bath, Place Marché St-Pierre (Tel. 73 31 23 23): local specialities and wines in restaurant with garden. **Auberge des Touristes**, route de la Baraque, 63830 Durtol (Tel. 73 37 00 26): exceptional regional cuisine, often lightened; 5 km from town.

Middle Range

L'Aubergade, Route de la Baraque, 63830 Durtol (Tel. 73 37 84 64): elegant restaurant serving house specialities cooked from high quality ingredients, 5 km from town.

Middle Range/Economy

Vita Mine, 65 rue du Port: vegetarian restaurant.

Economy

Auberge Auvergnate, 37 rue des Vieillards: good value regional specialities. **Le Bungalow**, 30 rue Ballainvilliers: good fish and vegetarian dishes.

Entertainments

In January and February, Clermont-Ferrand hosts the **Festival du Court Métrage**, a festival of short films. The feast of **Notre-Dame-du-Port** takes place every year in May with a carnival. The **Marché St-Pierre** is open every day except for Sunday, Monday and Wednesday afternoon and is a good place to stock up on local cheeses. There are **guided tours** of Clermont-Ferrand from the tourist office in the bd Gergovie, and of Montferrand from its tourist office in the rue de Rodade. Clermont-Ferrand also boasts a full programme of **theatre, ballet and concerts**. The tourist office will have details of the current programme.

Useful Addresses

Tourist Offices are at 69 boulevard Gergovie in Clermont-Ferrand and 22 rue de Rodade in Montferrand. The office for the Puy-de-Dôme area is 26 rue St-Esprit and the regional office is 43 avenue Julien. **Chamina** (see **Good Alternatives**) is at 5 rue Pierre Le Vénérable. **The Post Office** is at 1 rue Louis Renon. The St-Jacques **Hosptial** is at 30 place Henri-Dunant (Tel. 73 62 57 00).

Transport Options

The centres of Clermont and Montferrand are both best seen on foot. There are city buses which will take you from one to the other (catch them from the Place de Jaude). The bus station is in the bd Gergovie, the train station in the ave de l'Union Soviétique. Bicycles can be hired from the train station or from **Mazeyrat**, 3 bd Gergovie.

Cantal & Haute-Loire

Further south are the **Monts du Cantal. Riom-es-Montagne**, a popular centre for walks, with an eleventh century Romanesque church, has a museum of gentians and medicinal plants. The **G R 400**, the Tour des Volcans du Cantal, can be reached from **Murat** or **Salers**. Murat is an old town of medieval houses with grey stone-tiled roofs and the home of La Maison de la Faune (a museum of birds, animals and insects); Salers is a spa town with a fine sixteenth-century church and folklore museum in the Maison des Templiers. Both towns are picturesque, both undoubtably 'touristy'. East of the Monts du Cantal is **Saint-Flour**. The old high town clusters around the fortress-like Gothic cathedral with its twin towers overlooking the Place des Armes. Nearby at **Ruynes-en-Margeride** there is an *ecomusée* with a botanical garden and an exhibition to show the relationship between man and nature. The capital of the Cantal is **Aurillac**, a large town (population over 33,000) with a well restored and pedestrianised vieille ville clustered around the 17th century church of Saint-Gérand. The Château Saint-Etienne houses the Maison des Volcans, an exhibition of volcanoes in the Auvergne and elsewhere. The Haute-Loire capital, Le Puy-en-Velay, is an excellent walking centre. It is situated on the **Sentier de Saint-Jacques de Compostella**, the **G R 65** (Le Puy was once a well known resting place on the pilgrim route), and is circled by the **Tour du Velay** footpath (G R 40). The nearby **Gorges de l'Allier** are followed by the G R 412. North of Le Puy is the **Parc Natural Régional Livradois-Forez**, a sparsely populated area of hills, rivers and forests. The main town of interest is **Ambert**, once the centre of a paper-making industry. 4km. east of the town, the **Moulin Richard-de-Bas** is the site of the Musée Historique du Papier. Ambert has an old town of narrow streets and grey stone buildings including the partly fortified fifteenth-century Gothic church.

Accommodation & Eating Out

First Class

Château de Bassignac, Bassignac, 15240 Saignes (Tel. 71 40 82 82): 2 *chambres d'hôtes* and 1 apartment in sixteenth-century former fortress in beautiful surroundings; *tables d'hôte* and *ferme-auberge* serving traditional local recipes. **Château de la Vigne**, Ally, 15700 Pleaux (Tel. 71 69 00 20): 2 *chambres d'hôte* and 2 suites in medieval château belonging to local family; open 1st June to 1st October and other times on request.

Middle Range

Hostellerie de la Maronne, Le Theil, 15140 St-Martin-Valmeroux (Tel. 71 69 20 33): 24 rooms in manor house hotel with swimming pool and peaceful surroundings; restaurant with traditional set menu. **Hôtel Mistou**, Pontempeyrat, 43500 Craponne-sur-Arzon (Tel. 77 50 62 46): 24 comfortable rooms in former mill beside river; good restaurant with fish specialities.

Middle Range/Economy

Auberge du Pré Bossu, 43150 Moudeyres (Tel. 71 05 10 70): 11 rooms in grey-stone village inn; excellent restaurant.

Economy

La Crémaillère, Les Quatre Chemins, 15000 Aurillac (Tel. 71 48 10 70): 11 rooms in cosy hotel; restaurant with generous portions of typical local cuisine. **Auberge Fleurie**, Place du Barry, 15120 Montsalvy (Tel. 71 49 20 02): 15 rooms in ivy-covered inn, run by welcoming family; restaurant popular with locals.

Le Puy-en-Velay

The most striking features of the town are the three volcanic needles which rise up from the basin in which the town sits. On one of these needles sits the **Chapelle Saint-Michel d'Aiguille**, reached by climbing more than 250 steps. The statue of **Notre-Dame-de-France** crowns the highest needle. The Cathedral of **Notre-Dame**, built in the 11th and 12th centuries from alternating stripes of dark and light stone, has an almost eastern feel with the line of domes along the nave. The old town below the cathedral is full of shops selling lace to tourists – the **Crozatier Museum** has a lace room showing the traditional lace-work for which Le Puy was famous. The **Tourist Office** is at Place du Breuil.

Accommodation

There are no first class hotels in Le Puy. Instead try:

Middle Range

Moulin de Barette, Pont de Sumène, 43540 Blavozy (Tel. 71 03 00 88): 30 rooms in pleasant hotel with gardens, 8 km from town;

good value restaurant. **Hôtel Parc**, 4 ave C-Charbonnier (Tel. 71 02 40 40): 24 rooms in hotel near park.

Economy

Hôtel des Cordeliers, 17 rue des Cordelières (Tel. 71 09 01 12): spacious rooms in friendly hotel hidden in its own courtyard and above cheap and cheerful restaurant (see below). **Grand Hôtel Lafayette**, 17 bd St-Louis (Tel. 71 09 32 85): old-fashioned atmosphere in a once-grand hotel.

Eating Out

Middle Range

Le Bateau Ivre, 5 rue Portail d'Avignon (Tel: 71 09 67 20): old town restaurant serving dishes from local ingredients. **Sarda**, 12 rue Chênebouterie (Tel. 71 09 58 94): good food in 12th century dining room with Gothic vaulting.

Economy

Café le Palais, 27 Place du Breuil: smart café with good value *plats du jour*. **Restaurant des Cordeliers** (see above).

15 The Rhône Valley

The Rhône Valley's cultural and economic heart is Lyon, which is also France's second most important city. But all around are possibilities for an unhurried kind of tourism, which allows for authentic discoveries of the area and its people. The Rhône river forms the natural axis of this crescent-shaped region and offers a note of continuity in a land of great contrasts, whose range extends from Mediterranean countryside in the south to mountains bordering Switzerland in the north.

The heavily wooded mountain ranges of the Ain *département* overlook Lake Geneva, but not far away is the quiet, flat expanse of ponds known as 'La Dombes'. This is replaced by the Beaujolais vineyards and the unusual farms of the Bresse area, with their mysterious 'Saracen' chimneys resembling miniature spires and their bunches of corn-cobs hanging beneath the balcony to dry. The landscapes of the Drôme *département* are a mixture of the Mediterranean and the Sub Alpine, while the Ardèche is famous for its spectacular gorges between which runs a river prized as a canoeist's paradise. In southern Ardèche, towards the Cévennes, you will find an area riddled with deep grottoes and weird rock formations, Around Nyons, the countryside has a distinctly Provençal flavour, while numerous *Routes du Vin* criss-cross the prestigious Côtes du Rhône vineyards which stretch south from Vienne.

Other highlights of the Rhône Valley are the châteaux of the Loire *département*; the fabulous Gallo-Roman remains at St Romain-du-Gal and Lyon; the medieval and Renaissance towns and churches scattered throughout the region; the Lyon and St Etienne museums; the unsophisticated family ski resorts of the eastern Massif Central and southern Jura; the *ecomusées* that reflect the area's industrial past; the lively pockets of traditional craftsmen, and, last but not least, the region's food.

Proudly proclaimed as the World Capital of Gastronomy, Lyon boasts many top restaurants, and the region as a whole is home to five of France's nineteen best chefs. Though the most famous creators of Lyonnaise cuisine today are all male, much is owed to the *mères* of earlier centuries, whose hearty cooking sustained many an apprentice craftsman on the Lyon stage of his 'Tour de France'. The people of Lyon and the surrounding area are still keen to stress the 'everyday' nature of their famous cuisine, and its reliance on the freshest of produce. Throughout history, the region's inhabitants have been regarded as somewhat secretive, but capable of coming up with brilliant inventions – like the hot-air balloon or the suspension bridge, Nowadays you will find a readiness among local people of many professions to share their knowledge and enthusiasm with visitors, and the vast range of locally arranged trips with 'meet-the-people' elements is impressive.

History

During the Bronze Age, the Rhône Valley was a major trade route for amber and pewter and, by 600 BC, various Celtic tribes had settled on the banks of the river. The Roman Peace, which followed the conquering of the area at the end of the second century BC, allowed trade along the Rhône Corridor to flourish further. In 43 BC, one of Caesar's lieutenants founded Lyon at the confluence of the Saône and Rhône and it was made capital of Gaul shortly afterwards. The first Christians were put to death in its amphitheatre in the second century AD, but the city began to decline when its monopoly of French wine sales was ended and Lyon soon reverted to being merely a provincial capital.

The first abbeys were founded between the fifth and ninth centuries, but churchmen constantly found themselves disputing with the Counts of Auvergne. The eighth century saw some Arab invasions of the Rhône Valley. In the ninth and tenth centuries, both the Counts of Forez and the Bishops of the Vivarais grew in power, and new abbeys such as Charay, Mazan and Les Chambons were subsequently established in the Vivarais area. It was the fourteenth century by the time the kings of France managed to persuade the region of their royal sovereignty.

Lyon first began to host trade fairs in 1419, soon becoming a large import and export centre with extensive connections. King Charles VII granted the city a monopoly on the sale of silk in 1450 and, around this time, St-Etienne started specialising in fire-arms manufacture. The University of Valence was founded in 1452. At the end of the century, King Charles VIII and his court moved to Lyon.

Preachers of the Reform gained ground with the inhabitants of the Rhône Valley in the early sixteenth century, but the Wars of Religion that subsequently took place between Protestants and Catholics had bloody consequences. Today there are still more pockets of protestantism in this part of France than in most, though the many convents here serve as a reminder of the seventeenth century counter-Reformation. Meanwhile, Lyon saw the establishment of a silk factory and the publication of various important works, both literary and scientific, including Rabelais' *Pantagruel* and *Gargantua* and Honoré d'Urfé's *Astrée*.

After the French Revolution, the Reign of Terror was particularly violent in Lyon to punish the town for its resistance. Trade and industry, notably fabric and chemical production, thrived in the nineteenth century with the advent of the railway and the Roanne-Digoin canal, though diseases affecting the silkworms of the Vivarais and the vines of Ardèche had negative consequences. Development of the River Rhône started in 1934 with the creation of the Compagnie Nationale du Rhône.

Lyon was a Resistance stronghold during the Second World War, though the Germans managed to destroy many Rhône bridges in 1944. Since the 1950s, various hydro-electric and nuclear power plants have been established in the area, which was made into the administrative region of Rhône-Alpes only in 1972. The Pilat Regional Park was created in 1974, and 1981 saw the opening of the first TGV high-speed railway line in France, linking Paris and Lyon.

The Rhône Valley has developed a reputation as a land of innovators. In 1600, Olivier de Serres, who lived in Pradel, published a treatise on farming which earned him the title 'Father of French Agriculture'. The publication of Honoré d'Urfé's *Astrée* in 1628 was a landmark in literary history, as the book is said to be the very first French novel. Annonay was the birthplace of the Montgolfier brothers, who achieved the first flight in a hot-air balloon on 4 June 1783. Marc Seguin, the inventor of the suspension bridge, the tubular boiler and one of the pioneers of the French railway, was also born in Annonay, in 1786. The physicist André-Marie Ampère and the physiologist Claude Bernard both lived and worked in the region.

Geography

The Rhône Valley forms a kind of corridor between northern Europe and the Mediterranean basin. The region is part of the larger administrative area of Rhône-Alpes and is bordered by the Hautes-Alpes, Dauphiny and Haute-Savoie to the east, Switzerland and the Jura in the north-eastern corner, Burgundy and the Auvergne to the north and west, with Languedoc-Roussillon and Provence to the south. The region makes a C-shape composed of five *départements*, starting with the Ain in the north and moving down through the Rhône and Loire to the Ardèche and Drôme in the south. The regional capital is Lyon, whose population of 420,000 rises to 1,200,000 if the suburbs are included. The second largest city is St-Etienne (207,000 inhabitants), which is the capital of Loire. The remaining departmental capitals are Bourg-en-Bresse (44,000 – Ain), Privas (11,000 – Ardèche), and Valence (68,000 – Drôme).

The River Saône north of Lyon, the Loire in the north-west, and the Rhône, France's most powerful river, which flows through the region from north to south, all pass landscapes and land use of immense variety. Unfortunately there is a worrying concentration of industry forming a chemical corridor south of Lyon; it is clearly visible from motorway and railway and spoils the views from villages like Pierrelatte.

Skiing is possible in the Monts du Forez, Pilat massif and Plateau Ardèchois of the Massif Central; in the Gex region of the southern Jura; and in the Vercors, whose plateaux are ideal for cross-country skiing. The high mountains (Crêt de la Neige – 1718 metres) and low-lying lakes of the Ain *département* are in contrast to the fertile hills of the wooded Loire while the chestnut woods and breathtaking gorges of the Ardèche, along with caves of massive proportions whose columns are like organ pipes, complement the sun-drenched slopes of the Rhône Valley as it runs along the edge of the Drôme *département*.

Among the vineyards of the region are many famous names. Beaujolais, which is really an extension of the Burgundy wine-growing area, covers 200 square kilometres of the northern Rhône *département* and occupies a privileged place in Lyonnaise gastronomy; the Côtes du Rhône are among the most ancient vineyards in France, originating with the first Greek trading centres, though they came into their own only in the mid-nineteenth century after a crisis in the silk industry. Other good wines come from the Côteaux de l'Ardèche, Bugey, Roanne, Tricastin and Die, which is known for its sparkling wine, Clairette de Die. The Rhône valley is, however, by no means exclusively devoted to the cultivation of the grape. After the vine disease of the late nineteenth century, there was considerable diversification into various types of fruit trees. Nowadays the slopes on either side of the Rhône are covered in apple, pear, cherry, peach, apricot and chestnut trees, as well as vines.

Up in the Saône valley, the ecology of the flood plains is threatened (particularly their orchids, and birds such as the corncrake), as traditional agricultural practices are abandoned in favour of more financially rewarding ones. The Conservatoire Régional is working to encourage an alternative solution which is both economically and ecologically satisfactory. Compensation is being provided for farmers who are prepared to delay their hay-making until after the chicks of the corncrakes nesting in the fields can fly. And some abandoned land is to be grazed by sheep or cows in the traditional manner to allow it to retain its marshy properties and so protect its unique fauna and flora. The Ardèche Gorges are now a protected area, and there is a nature reserve and ornithological park at Villars-les-Dombes. The bird park contains about 2000 species and is run along similar lines to the Zwin reserve in Belgium in that some birds are in aviaries, with others (around 300 species) free. The Les Dombes reserve was established in 1970 for research into aquatic plants and animals; traditional use of the lakes for fish culture is permitted and the land between the lakes is either farmed or used for commercial forestry. Rare birds include the black-necked grebe, whiskered tern and little egret. Another nature reserve, part of which is in the Rhône Valley region, is the wild strip of land known as the Hauts Plateaux du Vercors, situated in the Vercors regional park. The regional park, whose headquarters are over in Dauphiny, works closely with farmers to reconcile agriculture and tourism in this beautiful area of ridges and valleys, with its forests and mountain pastures.

One regional park belongs exclusively to the Rhône Valley and that is the Parc Naturel Régional du Pilat. It can be found to the south and east of St-Etienne and spans the whole width of the region at this, its narrowest, point. It covers 650 square kilometres of forested country whose highest peak, Mont Pilat, is 1432 metres.

It forms a kind of balcony above the river valley, made of granite from the Massif Central, and rocky outcrops known as *chirats* punctuate the hills, heaths, chestnut and oak woods, vineyards, orchards and market gardens of the park. Deer and boar can be found here as well as birds migrating back up the Rhône Valley, such as the rare Bonelli's Eagle.

Climate

The writer Claudel described the Rhône Valley's climate as the result of 'negotiation between the north and the south'. Daily sunshine levels range from two hours in November, December and January to nine in June and July. May and August are both very sunny too. The average January temperature is 3°C, rising to a 21°C average in July. Lyon has a climate all of its own and is subject to fogs in both summer and winter, whilst St-Etienne boasts 2382 hours of sunshine a year. Spring is unpredictable, with snow lying in the Forez and Pilat mountains until April. Summer tends to be dry and sunny, particularly south of Valence, but autumn brings rainy weather, which can sometimes be quite violent. In the river valleys, winter is usually cold and dry, and in the mountains there are heavy snows. Beware of the strong *mistral* wind, which can rush down the Rhône Valley with no warning.

Attractions

There is a great variety of things to see and do in the Rhône Valley region. Popular attractions include the perfectly preserved medieval village of Pérouges; the flamboyant Gothic church at Brou; Aero-City at Aubenas-Lanas, the first attraction park to focus on aerial sports; the Dombes ornithological park; the Peaugres safari park; the Modern Art Museum at St-Etienne; the various scenic railways, including the Vivarais steam train and the 15-inch-gauge Anse railway, unique in France; the relaxing spa town of Vals-les-Bains; the gorges and caves of the Ardèche, particularly the Grotte de la Madeleine and Orgnac l'Aven; the Bidon village 'Prehistorama', an exhibition on prehistory unique in Europe; and, of course, the city of Lyon.

Lyon is known for its Punch and Judy shows, as well as its Roman remains and archaeological museum, cathedral, Renaissance quarters and silk museum. Among further sights of interest are the

University of Wine, housed in a château at Suze-la-Rousse; the amazing surrealist architecture of the Palais Idéal du Facteur Cheval in Drôme; the town of Annonay, birthplace of hot-air ballooning; the unusual farms of the Bresse area; Charlieu abbey and the Bastie d'Urfé château; the *ecomusée* at Roanne; the prehistoric site at Vassieux-en-Vercors, and the shoe museum at Romans.

Less concrete sources of attraction are the gastronomy of Lyon; the winter sports facilities at the thirty-one resorts in Ain, Ardèche, Drôme and Loire; cruises on the Rhône; the craftsmen and furniture-makers of Bresse; the challenge of canoeing on the River Ardèche; the riding, orienteering, cross-country skiing and, above all, mountain biking possibilities offered by the Pilat regional park; and, believe it or not, the lively pea-shooting clubs of St-Etienne!

Cuisine

For those visitors whose main reason for coming to the area is its gastronomic prowess, it is worth mentioning the names to look out for. The acknowledged top chefs of the region are Georges Blanc (Vonnas, Ain); Paul Bocuse (Collonges-au-Mont-d'Or, nr Lyon, Rhône); Jacques Pic (Valence, Drôme); Pierre & Michel Troisgros (Roanne, Loire). A visit to one of their prestigious establishments will certainly be memorable, but, at something over £50 a head, should not be undertaken lightly. It is, however, reassuring that you are as likely to find authentic regional cuisine at the numerous simple Lyon 'bouchons' or at *ferme-auberges* throughout the region, as at one of the above restaurants.

The region is exceptionally well-placed when it comes to fresh produce, with the Charollais area for cattle; the Bresse area for poultry; the Dombes for game; the Savoy lakes for fish; the Forez and the Rhône Valley for fruit and vegetables. Out of these ingredients come such colourful creations as the *poularde demi-deuil* (pullet in half-mourning), which is truffled with cream and emerges black and white. The *quenelle de brochet* is a Lyon favourite: fish-balls made from pike. The Rhône and Loire are both famed for their charcuterie; the Forez for its crayfish and trout; the Vivarais for its simple poultry and game dishes, often cooked with the local chestnuts; and the Drôme for its pasta (*Ravioles de Royans*), game pâtés, lamb, walnuts and wild flower honeys. In Ardèche, Privas is home to the expensive *marron glacé* sweetmeat. Montélimar, in Drôme, is the capital of nougat, which was created there in 1837, and St-Etienne is renowned for its chocolates. Good cheeses include the slowly matured fourme, made from an ancient recipe in the Monts du Forez; the goats' cheeses of the Pilat and Roannais; the 'cervelle de Canut' curd cheese with garlic; the semi-pressed coucouran and creamy st-félicien.

As for wines, the variety is immense. The vineyards of Beaujolais produce internationally praised wines and the Côtes du Rhône are almost as well known. The nine top quality Beaujolais (most of which are best drunk young) are Brouilly, Côte-de-Brouilly, Chenas, Chirouble, Fleurie, Juliénas, Morgon, Moulin-à-Vent and Saint-Amour; the wines that appear under the 'Beaujolais Villages' label are worth trying too. Nowadays Beaujolais is also known for the unmatured 'Beaujolais Nouveau' which floods French wine-bars and British pubs each autumn. The finest wines of the Côtes du Rhône include Viognier (made from an ancient variety of grape now found only in this region), Condrieu and Château-Grillet (both light fresh whites), Côte-Rôtie, Hermitage, Cornas, St-Joseph and the sparkling St-Péray wine. Excellent red 'vins du pays' are produced by the twenty-one Ucova wine co-operatives south of Aubenas in the Ardèche. Othe local wines worth looking out for are those from Bugey, Montagnieu, Cerdon, and the Tricastin and Roannais vineyards. In Drôme, the Clairette de Die is a fruity sparkling wine, drunk as an aperitif, while the Ain's favourite digestif is Marc de Bugey. In the Royans area, the speciality is walnut wine, *vin de noix*.

Level of Tourism

The Rhône Valley, Dauphiny and Savoy combine to form the second most popular region in France after Paris / Ile-de-France. Together they host 13.1% of all national visits. Out of the three distinct areas, the Rhône Valley is the one with the highest proportion of foreign tourists; the first rank of these consists of the Belgians, Dutch and British, then come the Germans and, increasingly, the Italians. In 1989, the average expenditure per visitor per day was 180FF (though hotel visitors spent considerably more – 250FF), 61,693 jobs are linked directly or indirectly to tourism (i.e. 4.6% of jobs among the active population), of which nearly a third are in the Rhône *département*. Ain has the fewest jobs linked to tourism. In recent years, accommodation occupancy in June and the first half of July has been good.

Business tourism is also flourishing in Lyon, St-Etienne and Valence.

Because the Rhône and Loire *départements* have no high-altitude ski resorts, the two slack winters of 1988–89 and 1989–90 meant tourist activity at winter sports resorts here was so low that lifts were not able to function. Alpine skiing occurs mainly in the Gex region (Ain) and in the Forez hills (Loire), and most resorts are relatively small and ideal for a family clientèle. Family visits are particularly frequent at the resorts of Crozet, Lelex, Mijoux, La Faucille and Chalmazel. It is, however, worth pointing out that such resorts, because they are not particularly high up, may make excessive use of artificial means such as snow cannons to prolong the season. Avoid resorts like Chalmazel, which boasts that 'snow is assured by fifty-three cannons which work day and night to produce a twenty acre carpet of real (!) snow out of water which goes through a refrigeration system'. It may sound impressive but it is certainly not environmentally friendly. A quite different scenario occurs in the resorts of the Vercors if the snow fails to materialise; here, alternative activities, such as nature rambles by snow-shoe, are introduced. For cross-country skiers, there are no sophisticated resorts in the Rhône Valley, just small mountain villages on the Ardèche and Vercors plateaux, the Pilat massif, in the Forez hills and southern Jura, where hoteliers and farmers will accompany visitors on excursions.

The Pilat regional park used to have a rather dull reputation, and people considered it the kind of place for an old people's day out, but recently it has undergone a complete rejuvenation. Someone realised that its terrain was perfect for mountain biking ('VTT' in French). Now there are twenty-five mountain bike itineraries, for all levels, and extensive rental possibilities: the sport has become big business and the park is now one of the top places in France to practise it. Already, 4% of the 400,000 inhabitants of St-Etienne and its area have done mountain biking in the park; let's just hope the craze is not allowed to develop in an uncontrolled manner, as its effects can be potentially damaging for the environment.

The Vercors massif is particularly sensitive to tourist pressure, due to the porous nature of its rock. Litter from picnickers is more of a problem here than elsewhere, as every trace of pollution seeps straight through into the streams and rivers. The Ardèche gorges, which suffer from huge numbers of summer visitors, have recently been made into a protected site.

The large number of archaeological digs and restoration work going on in the region bears witness to the way its inhabitants value their heritage. And it is not just the older people: at Vieil Audonil, near St-Pierreville, some young people formed a team to restore the village and now there is also a wool cooperative there, whose aim is to create employment for local people.

The local government's commitment to the natural and built heritage of the region is more difficult to assess. On the one hand, it is supporting the Conservatoire Régional's efforts to rescue the Saône Valley marshlands and to preserve traditional methods of agriculture there; on the other, it proudly announced in 1990 that its ambition was to double the passenger capacity of Lyon-Satolas airport by 1993. This, combined with the 1992 opening of a new TGV station within the airport complex, is bound to add considerably to the level of tourism in this region, parts of which (notably the Lyon area and the Ardèche gorges) are already overcrowded in the high season.

Good Alternatives

Meeting People

Many of the best ways to meet local people are covered in the **Comité Régional de Tourisme**'s (CRT's) mini-guide to gastronomy and wine cellars, and its lists of regional craftsmen, technical visits and festivals. All are available from the CRT, 5 Place de la Baleine, 69005 Lyon (Tel. 78 42 50 04).

The Drome *département* boasts a Université du Vin, housed in a medieval castle with a laboratory, library and garden. It hosts guided tours for members of the public wishing to broaden their knowledge of the history of Côtes du Rhône wines, as well as 2- to 4-day courses in oenology. For further information, contact M. Avril, **Château de Suze-la-Rousse**, 26130 St-Paul-Trois-Châteaux (Tel. 75 04 86 09). Evening courses (8 p.m. to midnight), involving theory, a meal and tasting, are run by the holder of the 1978 award for best cellarwoman in France, **Mme Carré Cartal**, 6 ave de la Gare, 42700 Firminy.

Less serious wine enthusiasts will still have plenty of opportunities to meet wine-producers. The **Service Loisirs-Accueil Loire** organises visits to cellars and sampling of regional wines: contact GIE Loire-Forez, Service Loisirs-Accueil, 5 Place Jean-Jaurès, 42021 St-Etienne (Tel. 77 33 15 39). Information on the wine-tasting cellars in the Ain is available from the **Syndicat des Vins de Bugey**, bd du 133e R.I., 01300 Bellay (Tel. 79 81 30 17). For details of those in the Beaujolais area, ask the **Office de Tourisme**, 290 rte de Thizy, 69400 Villefranche-sur-Saône (Tel. 74 68 05 18). Information on the wine brotherhoods accepting applications to attend an enthronement ceremony are available from the CRT (address above). Several gastronomic brotherhoods have been set up in the Ain and details of these can be obtained from the **Maison des Pays de l'Ain**, 01370 St-Etienne-du-Bois (Tel. 74 30 50 84). One of them, the **Logis de l'Academie**, gives awards for excellence to Bresse poultry farmers and local restaurants, so look out for their seal of approval.

Not surprisingly for a region so proud of its gastronomic tradition, there are various cookery courses on offer. A 5-day course (full-board), which teaches you many Ardèche specialities, costs around 500FF. The course takes place all year round, except July, and 1-day sessions are also possible: further information from **Les Compagnons du Gerboul**, Place du Marché, 07140 Les Vans (Tel. 75 37 21 82). You could also turn your hand to 'bread-baking in wood-fire ovens and country lore': contact M. Peyrard, **Association Echanges Culturels et Artisanaux de Desaignes**, 07570 Desaignes (Tel. 75 06 60 62). Courses have also been designed which allow the visitor to 'become a privileged observer throughout a working week in one of the world-famous establishments which have made cooking and pastry-making one of the international hallmarks of the French way of life': contact **Les Etapes du Gourmets**, 47 rue Rabelais, 69003 Lyon (Tel. 78 62 09 18).

Lists of Bresse poultry breeders and 'foie gras' producers in the Ain are contained in the leaflet 'The Bresse Route – Traditions and Savoir Faire', distributed by the **Comité du Tourisme de l'Ain**, 34 rue du Général-Delestraint, BP 78, 01002 Bourg-en-Bresse (Tel. 74 21 95 00). This leaflet also contains a list of Bresse artisans, notably furniture-makers. Details of numerous craftsmen, farmers and local industries which welcome visitors are available from the CRT (address above): these range from a nougat producer and a grower of button mushrooms in a Roman quarry to an aromatic plant garden and a monastery that makes its own liqueurs. Information on some similar outings in the Drôme is available from **Mme Girard**, Tourisme en Tricastin, Mairie, 26700 Pierrelatte (Tel. 75 98 93 38). **Les Compagnons du Gerboul** (address above) operate holiday courses in local crafts in cooperation with individual artists; these include woodwork, natural dyeing, lace-making, wickerwork, spinning and pottery, as well as some more obscure crafts. Information on the craftsmen of Ain can be obtained from **M. Pillard**, Pérouges, 01800 Méximieux (Tel. 74 61 01 27). Full details of craft associations and courses on offer in the Ardèche are available from the **Comité Départemental de Tourisme**, 8 cours du Palais, BP 221, 07002 Privas (Tel. 75 64 04 66). The **Ecomusée du Roannais**, which focuses on the area's textile industry, organises economic discovery circuits of the region and visits to local enterprises: its address is Passage Général Giraud, 42300 Roanne (Tel. 77 71 31 88). Organic products from local farmers are sold by the **AVEC** cooperative, 31 rue Gervais Bussière, 69100 Villeurbanne, which is on the Lyon Metro (stop at Charpènnes or République) and open on Tuesday, Wednesday and Thursday, afternoons and Saturday mornings.

A calendar of thematic walks and excursions is contained in the Vercors regional park's leaflet, 'l'Eté de la Nature', available from the **Maison du Parc**, Chemin des Fusillés, 38250 Lans-en-Vercors (Tel. 76 45 40 33). In Ain, the centre for prehistoric research (Chenavel Castle, 01 Jujurieux, Tel. 85 57 13 27) runs beginners' courses in archaeological excavation. Information on archaeological digs in the region is available from the **Direction des Antiquités**, 23 rue Roger Radisson, 69322 Lyon Cedex 01 (Tel. 78 25 79 16 or 78 25 87 62): ask particularly about those run by Leo Lagrange Jeunes (based in Oullins); Enfants et Amis de Beauchastel (based in Beauchastel), and the Association Drômoise Chantiers, Animation et Vie Locale (based in Poet-Celard). On summer weekends, you can help restore the hamlet of Le Vieil Audon at the entrance to the Ardèche gorges; participation in outdoor recreational activities and accommodation are also possible: contact **Le Mat**, Le Vieil Audon, 07120 Balazuc (Tel. 75 37 73 80). Regional branches of the nature protection society, **FRAPNA**, run nature discovery outings and conservation days; details from the society's headquarters at Université Lyon I, 43 bd du 11 Novembre, 69622 Villeurbanne (Tel. 78 94 93 86).

Discovering Places

A list of 125 short-break ideas spread over the whole Rhône-Alpes region is contained in the 'Plaisirs à Vivre en Rhône-Alpes' brochure, available in English from **Rhône-Alpes Tourism News**, 1 Place André-Malraux, BP 297, 38016 Grenoble (Tel. 76 47 20 36). Suggestions for 2- to 8-day holidays range from gastronomy and creativity to climbing and multi-activities. Drivers or cyclists finding themselves in the Bresse area should ask the local tourist office for the leaflet 'The Bresse Route – Colours and Flavours', which describes two 100 km circuits, including detailed information on the villages passed through. Details of a 'Dombes Ponds Route' are also available from both local tourist offices and the **Comité Départemental de Tourisme (CDT) de l'Ain**, 34 rue Général Delestraint, BP 78, 10002 Bourg-en-Bresse (Tel. 74 21 95 00). Visitors to Beaujolais, in the Rhône *département*, have a choice of routes: the Route Rouge is for hedonists with limited time and a non-drinking driver, as it takes you as directly as possible from one end of the vineyards to the other, stopping only for visits to various wine-tasting 'caves'; the Route Verte, on the other hand, is more leisurely and takes you to sites of cultural and historical interest. A combination of the two might not be a bad idea.

The CDTs of the Ain, Loire, Ardèche and Drôme all organise skiing holidays, and an excellent range of detailed thematic packages (often split into Summer, Winter and Short Breaks brochures) are on offer from the CDTs of the Rhône, Ardèche and Drôme. For the Ain address, see above; the others are: **CDT Loire**, 5 Place Jean-Jaurès, 42021 St-Etienne (Tel. 77 33 15 39); **CDT Rhône**, (postal address) 146 rue Pierre Corneille, 69426 Lyon Cedex 03 (Tel. 72 61 78 90) – offices at 15 rue de Sévigné, Lyon; **CDT Ardèche**, 8 cours du Palais, BP 221, 07002 Privas (Tel. 75 64 04 66); and **CDT Drôme**, 1 ave de Romans, 26000 Valence (Tel. 75 43 27 12). Cross-country skiing on the High Ardèche plateau is organised by the **Association La Burle**, 07510 Usclades (Tel. 75 38 89 19). The **Association des Hoteliers du Vercors Drômois** also runs skiing holidays with hotel accommodation included; information from CDT Drôme. Holidays on offer from the CDT Loire range from a weekend's canoeing instruction for around 200FF to an 8-day horseriding tour of the historic and gastronomic attractions of the Forez, at around 8800FF. Other possibilities include mushroom-picking, photography and fishing, and all holidays are taken in small groups using local accommodation. The CDT Ardèche is particularly good on winter and water holidays. Its ski packages often include a variety of activities, such as mountain biking, walking and even learning a local craft, in addition to skiing itself. Information is contained in the 'Horizons de l'Hiver' brochure. Other useful leaflets are 'Ardèche Canoë-Kayak', 'Ardèche Cyclotourisme', 'Ardèche Randonnées Equestres', 'Ardèche Randonnées Pedestres' and the Loisirs-Accueil brochure, which contains an impressive range of holidays, from 420FF for two days' canoeing down the Ardèche river, to 5000FF for 9-day gastronomic circuits. The activity centre at Vallon Pont d'Arc will provide details of excursions to see the flora and fauna of the Ardèche by row-boat, flat-bottomed craft or canoe. One special trip involves groups of 4 to 6 being taken down the river by two knowledgeable boatmen and returning by taxi. Information on fishing in the Ardèche is available from the **Fédération Départementale des Associations Agréées de Pêche et de Pisciculture de l'Ardèche**, 12 bd de la République, 07100 Annonay (Tel. 75 33 26 20).

Unusual, environmentally responsible walking holidays in the Vercors Regional Park are arranged in conjunction with the National Federation of Parks, whose seal of approval has been granted. Further information from M. Patrick Rabot, **Parc Naturel Régional du Vercors**, Chemin des Fusillés, 38250 Lans-en-Vercors (Tel. 76 95 40 33). The park also produces 'Carto-Guide' walking maps, offers a 'Cheques-Loisirs' system (an economical way of paying for your leisure facilities), and a 'Ski-Adventure' package. The latter involves cross-country skiing with plenty of activities for non-skiers, such as snow-shoe walking and dog-sleigh rides; information from **ADT Royans-Vercors**, BP 3, 26420 La Chapelle-en-Vercors (Tel. 75 48 25 15). The CPIE, Maison de l'Eau, Aux Forêts, 42660 Marlhes (Tel. 77 51 82 31) offers nature discovery animations lasting an evening, half a day or a full day. Themes range from dawn chorus excursions, spring flowers and medicinal plants, to old fruit trees, rocks and houses, or mills and textiles, and must be booked at least 48 hours in advance. A guide from the CPIE is also available to come with you in your car when you are exploring the region, so that you will be able to get the most out of it. Each spring, a study camp for ornithologists is arranged at the Col de l'Escrinet in Ardèche; information from the **Association pour la Protection des Animaux Sauvages et du Patrimoine Naturel**, BP 34, 26270 Loriol (Tel. 75 62 64 86), which also runs other nature study outings.

Communications

How to Get There

The region's main international **airport** is Lyon-Satolas (Tel. 78 71 92 21), situated about 25 km east of the city, which receives daily British Airways and Air France flights from London. A daily weekday service between Lyon and Manchester is offered by Air

Littoral. If you are visiting the Ain area, you may be better off flying to Geneva international airport. The remaining national airports, which receive flights from Paris, are Valence (Tel. 75 85 28 63), St-Etienne (Tel. 77 36 54 79) and Roanne (Tel. 76 66 83 55).

Lyon-Satolas is not only an airport but a multi-purpose transport centre, 200 metres from the airport is a new TGV station, which supplements the existing one at Lyon-Perrache. The **rail** journey from Paris is only 2 hours. (It takes 2½ hours to St-Etienne.) The A6 **motorway**, known as the 'Autoroute du Soleil', also takes you from Paris to Lyon, but should be avoided like the plague in July and August.

When You're There

Rail – north-south connections within the region are excellent, with the train passing through Villefranche-sur-Saône, Lyon, Vienne, Valence, Livron and Montélimar. Lines branch off to Bourg-en-Bresse, Bellegarde, Roanne, Ambérieu, St-Etienne, Firminy, Romans and Die. Scenic steam train journeys include a 33 km trip through mountain gorges between Tournon and Lamâstre (Ardèche); a 1-hour round trip on the Commelle Vernay steam railway in Loire; and the 2 km of 15-inch gauge line, unique in France, belonging to the Anse steam railway in Rhône.

Bus – using the bus for touring makes sense only in areas like the Vercors, where there are few trains, but make sure you have a timetable (available from tourist offices), as many bus services stop running around 6 p.m. In the Ain *département*, a wide variety of coach tours is offered by **Gonnet-Bustours**, 9 bd de Verdun, BP 133, 01300 Belley (Tel. 79 81 21 09).

Car – the main motorway of the region is the A6 from Paris to the south, which passes through Villefranche-sur-Saône, Lyon, Valence and Montélimar. Bourg-en-Bresse and St-Etienne are also on the motorway network. Ardèche has been described as the greenest *département* in France, as it is completely free of motorways. All the departmental tourist boards will suggest thematic, or simply picturesque, driving circuits for visitors.

Boat – river cruises and boat-hire are popular on the Rhône and Saône rivers and the Roanne canal. Villarest lake (Loire) and Nantua lake (Ain) offer lake cruises. The Ardèche river is best explored by rowing boat, canoe or one of the flat-bottomed craft which offer excursions. Enquiries about river tourism in the region should be addressed to the **Bureau de la Plaisance**, 2 rue de la

Quarantaine, 69321 Lyon Cedex 05 (Tel. 78 42 55 83). Canoeing is particularly frequent in the Ain river and the Ardèche and Loire basins; the largest canoeing centres are Vallon-Pont-d'Arc (Ardèche) and St-Pierre-de-Boeuf (Loire). Special rules apply when canoeing between the Ardèche gorges, as they are in a nature reserve; information from the **Maison de la Réserve de Gaud** (Tel. 75 38 63 00).

Cycling – bicycles can be hired at various SNCF stations, including La Bastide/St-Laurent-les-Bains; Crest; Montbrison; Romans-sur-Isère, and Villars-les-Dombes. In the Lyon area, information on cycling is available from the **Fédération de Cyclotourisme**, 49 rue Pasteur allée A, 69300 Caluire (Tel. 78 08 26 30). Two brochures, 'A Vélo dans la Vallée du Rhône' and 'Ardèche Cyclotourisme', are full of useful suggestions for cyclists and available from the departmental tourist boards.

Riding – horseriding is particularly popular in the Ardèche, whose departmental tourist board produces a guide called 'Ardèche Randonnèes Equestres', which lists stables, farms, local riding associations and information on horse-drawn caravan and donkey excursions. The **Comité Départemental de Tourisme Equestre de l'Ardèche** is at Ferme équestre de Bressieux, St-Romain-de-Lerps, 07130 St-Peray (Tel. 75 58 52 14).

Walking – there is a total of 1760 kilometres of footpaths open to ramblers in the region. The extensive network of GR paths includes the GR 4 and 44; GR 42 and 420; GR 427; GR 59; GR 6; GR 7, 72 and 73; GR 9, 91, 93 and 95. Thematic paths cross the Pilat regional park, and the Vercors regional park has prepared 'Carto-Guide' walking guides. If you are in the Ardèche, it is worth getting hold of the 'Ardèche Randonnées Pedestres' brochure, which lists long and short walks as well as thematic and accompanied ones.

Useful Local Contacts

Addresses of the regional nature protection organisations which run excursions, such as **FRAPNA** and **ASPAS**, can be found under **Good Alternatives**. The **Conservatoire Régional du Patrimoine Naturel de Rhône-Alpes**, 54 rue St-Jean, 69005 Lyon (Tel. 78 37 98 57) is currently dealing with the rescue of the Saône Valley and the Rhône's natural alluvial forests. The headquarters of the two regional parks are: **Parc Naturel Régional du Vercors**, Chemin des Fusillés, 38250 Lans-en-Vercors (Tel. 76 95 40 33); and **Parc**

Naturel Régional du Pilat, Moulin de Virieu, 2 rue Benay, BP 17, 42410 Pélussin (Tel. 74 87 65 24).

Geographical Breakdown of Region

Ain, Rhône and Loire

Between them, the Ain with its numerous ponds and birdlife, the Rhône with its vineyards, golden stone houses and its cosmopolitan capital Lyon, and the Loire with its woods and flowery villages, offer much to the visitor.

Lyon

This famous red-roofed city enjoys a spectacular situation at the confluence of the Saône and the Rhône, as well as some impressive Roman remains and a worldwide gastronomic reputation. The city splits neatly into three sections: **Vieux Lyon** on the Saône side (west); the **Presqu'île**, which is a tongue of land between the Saône and Rhône, just before they converge; and the more **modern** quarters on the Rhône side (east). Like Paris, it is divided into *arrondissements*.

To the west of the old town is the **Fourvière** hill, where you will find the most important Gallo-Roman remains of Lyon. The hill is reached by means of steep streets or even flights of steps, known as **Montées**. Once there, you will find the Notre-Dame basilica and, off to its left up Montée de Fourvière, the **Parc Archéologique de Fourvière**. This contains an impressive **Roman amphitheatre** dating from the first century BC; a smaller **Odeon**; a **temple**; and the remains of Roman aqueducts and a cemetery. In addition, the **Museum of Gallo-Roman Civilisation** displays finds which put the monuments in context. At the bottom of the hill, Vieux Lyon, formerly the city centre, contains a protected sector of well-preserved Renaissance houses. Between and under them run little alleyways known as **Traboules**, originally used for carrying silk across the city and exploited by the Second World War Renaissance. If you start at **Eglise St-Paul** and stroll southwards, you will come across the **Nouveau Guignol de Lyon** (a Punch and Judy theatre) and the **Hôtel de Gadagne**, which houses the Lyon history museum and a fascinating museum devoted to puppets and marionettes. The main street, **rue St-Jean**, will lead you to the

Gothic **St-Jean Cathedral**, whose astronomical clock and treasury are worth visiting.

The **Croix Rousse** district, to the north of the **Presqu'île** (peninsula), is where the silk-makers and weavers of former times used to work. Their traditional methods are revived by the Cooptiss cooperative at the **Maison des Canuts** at 10–12 rue d'Ivry. Here you can see historic cloths and various old looms, including one used to teach children. At 4 rue Bodin is the long-established **Maison de l'Ecologie**, where information on the Rhône Valley's ecology can be obtained. In the **Jardin des Plantes**, the **Amphithéâtre des Trois Gaules** dates from 19 BC; good views of the Saône river can be enjoyed from **quai St-Vincent**. The **Terreaux** quarter, with its lead fountain, is pleasant, and the **Hôtel de Ville** complex is laid out in an original manner. The seventeenth- and eighteenth-century **Palais St-Pierre**, formerly a Benedictine Abbey, now houses the **Fine Art Museum**. Next-door is the **St-Pierre museum** of contemporary art. An unusual attraction is the **Museum of Printing and Banking**, both of which played a considerable role in Lyon's prosperity. Interesting glimpses of life in a hospital of the past are afforded by the **Musée des Hospices Civils**, housed in the Hôtel-Dieu. The pride of the Presqu'île is **Place Bellecour**, which contains an equestrian statue of Louis XIV. Between Place Bellecour and Lyon Perrache railway station is one of Lyon's top attractions, the **Musée Historique des Tissus**. Materials from all over the world are displayed here, as well as those particularly representative of Lyon's development in this field. Nearby is the **Museum of Decorative Arts**.

The modern part of Lyon, to the east of the Rhône, is something of a sprawl, but the **Part-Dieu** district is worth a visit, with its massive **library**, shell-shaped **Auditorium Maurice Ravel**, and 140-metre **Crédit Lyonnais** tower. To the north of here is the refreshing green space of the **Parc de la Tête d'Or**, on whose edges lie the **Natural History Museum** and the **Museum of the Resistance**.

Accommodation

Almost all the top-of-the-range hotels in Lyon are of the impersonal 100-or-more-rooms variety, but the following smaller hotels are recommended:

First Class
La Tour Rose, 22 rue Boeuf, 5e *arrondissement* (Tel. 78 37 25 90):

6 rooms and 6 apartments in elegantly decorated 17th century building; good restaurant.

Middle Range

Hôtel Créqui, 158 rue Créqui, 3e (Tel. 78 60 20 47): 28 rooms in hotel in Part-Dieu district. **Hôtel Laennec**, 36 rue Seignemartin, 8e (Tel. 78 74 55 22): 14 rooms in hotel in Montplaisir area. **Hôtel Bayard**, 23 place Bellecour, 2e (Tel. 78 37 39 64): 15 rooms in beautifully situated, central hotel.

Economy

Auberge de la Vallée, 39 ave du Chater, 69340 Francheville (Tel. 78 59 11 88): 13 rooms in charming little hotel with garden, 10 km from Lyon; good restaurant. **Les Provinces**, 10 Place St-Luc, 69110 Ste-Foy-les-Lyon (Tel. 78 25 01 55): 14 rooms in family-run hotel, 3 km from Lyon (on D75). **Hôtel Croix-Pâquet**, 11 Place Croix-Pâquet (Tel. 78 28 51 49): clean, spacious rooms. **Hôtel Alexandra**, 49 rue Victor-Hugo, 2e (Tel. 78 37 75 79): large rooms in well-located old hotel.

Eating Out

Lyon has an immense number of restaurants to suit every palate and every budget, ranging from homely little *bouchons* to the establishments of some of France's gastronomic gurus.

First Class

Paul Bocuse, Pont de Collonges (D433), 69660 Collonges-au-Mont-d'Or (Tel. 78 22 01 40): the restaurant of one of France's best and most innovative chefs; has the unusual feature of a fixed price menu for children under 12 (at around 50FF); 9 km from Lyon. **Nandron**, 26 quai Jean-Moulin, 2e (Tel. 78 42 10 26): authentic house specialities in friendly, wood-panelled-restaurant. **Léon de Lyon**, 1 rue Pléney, 1er (Tel. 78 28 11 33): lively, welcoming restaurant serving both the traditional and the modern.

Middle Range

Chez Rose, 1 rue Rabelais, 3e (Tel. 78 60 57 25): warm welcome and typical Lyonnais specialities. **La Tassée**, 20 rue de la Charité, 2e (Tel. 78 37 02 35): house specialities and selection of fine wines; reservation strongly advised.

Middle Range / Economy

Le Café Comptoir Lyonnais, 4 rue Tupin, 2e (Tel. 78 42 11 98): traditional Lyonnais cuisine in lively, bistro-style restaurant popular with locals.

Economy

L'Eau Vive, 65 rue Victor-Hugo (Tel. 78 42 32 92): wide-ranging vegetarian cafeteria. **Le Vivarais**, 1 Place Gailleton, 2e (Tel. 78 37 85 15): Lyonnais specialities in friendly atmosphere: reservation advised. **Café de Jura**, 25 rue Tupin, 2e (Tel. 78 42 20 57): one of the traditional Lyon *bouchons*. **Titi Lyonnais**, 2 rue Champonnay, 3e (Tel. 78 60 83 02): simple Lyonnais cooking in restaurant frequented by local people.

Entertainments

The tourist office offers conducted tours of the old town, the *traboules* (alternatively, a list of these allows you to make your own tour), the Trois Gaules amphitheatre or Bellecour. In addition, you could enquire at the **Service des Guides et Hôtesses**, 5 Place St-Jean, 69005 Lyon (Tel. 78 42 25 75) about their guided tours of two contemporary sites of architectural interest: the administrative centre in Part-Dieu, and the interchange complex at Perrache railway station. Addresses and details of the city's craftsmen are available from **Artisans d'Art** (M. Chaberty), 37 rue Malesherbes, 69006 Lyon (Tel. 78 89 52 05).

Every Sunday, the **Marché de la Création** takes place on the Saône quays. Theatre, concert and opera programmes are available from the tourist office (alternatively, buy a copy of the weekly *Lyon-Poche*). May brings a festival of folklore, European music and amateur theatre; in June the Villeurbanne suburb has its annual festival; September brings the marionette festival and October the Bach festival; in the weeks before Christmas you can see little candles lit in every window and there is a street procession on 8 December.

Useful Addresses

The **Tourist Office** is on Place Bellecour (Tel. 78 42 25 75) (lots of free information), with smaller branches at Perrache train station and at 3 rue Aristide-Briand in the suburb of Villeurbanne. The **Regional Tourist Board** (for whole of Rhône Valley) is based at 5

Place de la Baleine, 69005 Lyon (Tel. 78 42 50 04), and the offices of the **Departmental Tourist Board** (Rhône *département*) are at 15 rue de Sévigné. The main **Post Office** is on Place Antonin-Poncet, next to Place Bellecour. For emergency **medical assistance** phone SOS Médecins on 78 83 51 51. Otherwise the **Hospital** is the Hôtel-Dieu at 1 Place de l'Hôpital (Tel. 78 42 70 80).

Transport Options

The public transport service is called TCL and consists of the Metro and buses, supplemented by cable-cars up to Fourviére hill (from Place St-Jean, until 8 p.m.). Tickets are interchangeable and it is more economical to buy them in a *carnet* of six. On Saturdays, special *Samedi Bleu* tickets offer a good deal for those using the network a fair bit. There is a TCL information point outside the Part-Dieu train station (Tel. 78 71 80 80). Short boat trips up or down the Saône on *bateaux mouches* take place every afternoon from April to November, leaving from quai des Célestins. For cruises further afield, contact **NavigInter**, 13 bis quai Rambaud (Tel. 78 42 96 81).

The Rest of Ain, Rhône and Loire

In the north of Ain is the exclusive spa resort of **Divonne-les-Bains**, whose casino brings in more money than any other in France. In early July the town hosts an international festival of chamber music. The **Gex** area is known for its winter sports resorts, while the château at **Ferney-Voltaire** on the Swiss border will transport you back to the eighteenth century, when the writer Voltaire made it his favourite residence. You can see traditional cheese-making practices at the Fromagerie de l'Abbaye at **Chézery-Forens** (Tel. 50 56 91 97), and **Bellegarde-sur-Valserine** is a popular spot for canoeing. Further south, at **Lochieu**, is the Valromey museum of old costumes, furniture and tools, and at **Vieu-en-Valromey** there is a fair of folkore and history in early September. **Culoz** is home to the Arvière Carthusian monastery, the fourteenth-century Montverand château, and a Roman 'fairy fountain'. At **Vongnes**, a wide selection of local wines can be tasted at Le Caveau Bugiste (Tel. 79 81 05 44); it is open every afternoon in summer (weekends only the rest of the year). **Lavours** is the site of a marsh with unusual flora, as well as a fifteenth- and sixteenth-century château, a tower with a magnificent view, and a Gallo-Roman sarcophagus.

Belley is the capital of the region known as Bas-Bugey, which is a geographical anomaly, resembling neither of its neighbours in Savoy or Dauphiny. The villages of this quiet green area often grew up around a church or communal bread oven, and a medieval atmosphere still lingers in many. At Belley you can visit the Distillerie de l'Etoile, at 44 rue Ste-Marie (Tel. 79 81 02 55), where a nineteenth-century monk developed a dietetic liqueur called Kario. Bugey white brandy and other liqueurs can also be sampled – all free of charge. A cruise on **Nantua** lake is a pleasant experience, and, to the north-east, **Oyonnax** has an interesting museum devoted to the area's spinning industry. The gorges marking the course of the River Ain are impressive, as are the caves at **Cerdon**, whose series of underground tunnels contains eery rock formations. **Ambronay** is another good centre for keen canoeists.

The medieval village of **Pérouges** is very well preserved and something of a craft centre. Wisely, no cars are allowed in the village, but nonetheless it swarms with visitors during summer. At **Villars-les-Dombes** is an extensive ornithological park, where many species of birds, some in semi-liberty, may be seen. It is open from 8.30 a.m. every day of the year and it makes sense to come early in the day, before the crowds; from March to October the visit can be made by mini-train with commentary. On the outskirts of Bourg-en-Bresse, **Brou** church is a extravagant example of flamboyant Gothic art; the village specialises in various crafts and has charming old quarters. **Bourg-en-Bresse** itself is a pleasant town where you can find out about the production and maturing of milk products at the Laiterie Coopérative, 5 rue des Crêts (Tel. 74 23 18 60). The Bresse area is famous for its poultry and its enamels: a good supplier of the former is G. Pillon et Fils, Au Coq Bressan, 14 rue du 4-Septembre; enamels can be viewed and purchased at the studio of Pierre Debost, 17 rue Charles-Robin (except Sundays and Mondays). In summer, visits of the old town take place every Friday evening; they include a mini-play and are rounded off by a gastronomic buffet (information from the tourist office at Centre Albert-Camus, 6 ave Alsace-Lorraine, Tel. 74 22 49 40). In November Bourg-en-Bresse hosts a fair of gastronomy and regional produce. The town is a good base for exploring the surrounding area, with its mysterious 'Saracen' chimneys, which look like miniature spires, dominating farmhouses made with timber struts and wattle walls where corn-cobs dry beneath the eaves. In addition to poultry farmers, furniture-makers abound, producing items with distinctive Bressan 'water-leaf' designs out of the traditional woods of walnut, gnarled ash and wild cherry.

The village of **Fleurie** is in the Beaujolais wine region and hosts a wine fair at the beginning of November. You can taste local wines year-round at its Cave Coopérative des Grands Vins (Tel. 74 04 11 70), or its Caveau de Dégustation (Tel. 74 69 81 91). The name Beaujolais comes from the town of **Beaujeu**. Here you will find a museum of popular arts and traditions which focuses on wine-growing, agriculture and local crafts; the attractive medieval half-timbered 'Maison du Pays' has exhibitions and sales of local produce and craftwork, as well as information on the area. The main tourist office for the Beaujolais region is in **Villefranche-sur-Saône**; it can supply you with various leaflets including one with details of the 'Route des Pierres Dorées' in southern Beaujolais, so named because of the golden stone out of which many winegrowers' houses, often with impressive columns, are made. At **Anse** is a steam railway unique in France. The train which covers the 2 km of 15-inch gauge line can be ridden by visitors on Sundays and Bank Holidays between Easter and 30 November, and also on Saturday afternoons from June to September.

Satolas is the site of Lyon's airport and transport complex, and a tour of the hi-tech airport can be arranged for those interested. Local wines can be tasted at the Cave Coopérative des Côteaux du Lyonnais (Tel. 74 01 11 33) at **Sain-Bel**. At Easter time in **Montrottier** there is an egg hunt, during which town-dwellers come and search for eggs hidden in the countryside by young country-dwellers. At **Feurs** the Musée d'Assier presents local archaeology, history and popular arts and traditions. The lake at **Villerest** near Roanne is good for watersports, and visits by boat of the Loire gorges are possible from here. At the end of May, a medieval fête opens a festival of theatre and music. **Roanne** itself is a sensible place to start a canal charter or a cruise. The crafts of pottery, wickerwork, earthenware and leatherware can be viewed at the Maison des Remparts on Place Maréchal de Lattre de Tassigny. The Musée Joseph Déchelette is worth a visit, and the Ecomusée du Roannais (on Passage Général Giraud) should not be missed, as it offers a unique glimpse into the area's textile industry, also arranging 'economic discovery' circuits of the region and visits of local enterprises (see **Good Alternatives**). At **Charlieu** you will find a twelfth-century Benedictine abbey and a fourteenth- to fifteenth-century convent; a music festival takes place here and in **Ambierle** in July and August. Ambierle is in the Forez part of the region and has a museum, called the Musée Alice Taverne Forez, devoted to nineteenth-century Forez life. Information about the hour-long Commelle-Vernay steam train ride is available from M. Heitz, Les Berands, 42370 **Renaison** (Tel. 77 66 84 64 or 77 72 94 55). Skiing is popular in the Monts du Forez.

At **Montbrison**, the Musée d'Allard has interesting displays of local birds and minerals; the town also plays host to the annual Fourmes cheese fair on the first weekend in October. The Château des Bruneaux at **Firminy** is particularly worth visiting as it supports reconstructions of various aspects of regional life, such as an accurate model mine, whose galleries connect with the cellars of the château. The interesting architecture of Firminy owes much to Le Corbusier. The modern can also be felt in the capital of the Loire *département*, **St-Etienne**. Its Musée d'Art Moderne is an amazing structure of shiny black squares, housing the second most important public collection of modern art in France. A quite different museum is the Musée des Amis du Vieux St-Etienne, which treats the history and heritage of the town, while the recently opened Centre des Métiers d'Arts des Meilleurs Ouvriers de la France (46 rue Franklin) offers exhibition space to France's best craftspeople.

To the south-east of St-Etienne, the **Parc Naturel Régional du Pilat** straddles the region. Much information on it is available from the Maison de l'Eau at **Marlhes**, which houses the Centre Permanent d'Initiation à l'Environnement as well as a permanent exhibition on 'water', and is the starting point for a forest discovery path. For details of the CPIE's organised outings, see **Good Alternatives**. Near Marlhes, at **Allier** is the Maison de la Béate, which contains a small museum of local history, arts and traditions, open on Sundays and Bank Holidays between 1 July and 30 September. **Bourg d'Argental** is worth visiting for its architectural riches, and there is a fine belvedere above the town of **Malleval**, with its Renaissance houses, ruined castle and tree-covered slopes. The gorges on the way in to Malleval are also impressive. **St-Pierre-de-Boeuf** is a major canoeing centre, offering boat-hire and instruction. The Moulin de Virieu at 2 rue Benay, **Pélussin** is the headquarters of the regional park. Near here, at **Maclas**, home-made apple juice can be purchased from M. Juthier's farm, 'Chorée'. In late May and early June there are *Son et Lumière* evenings at **Ste-Croix-en-Jarez**, a very attractive village built inside a former Carthusian monastery. Famous wines come from **Condrieu**, a town split into the traditional and the modern by the River Rhône: the old houses and vineyards

of the right bank are in stark contrast to the motorways, railways
and chemical factories lining the left bank. Information on a wine
tasting, commentary and slide show is available from M. Desnoues,
'La Bouteillerie', 1 rue de la Croix, 69420 Condrieu (Tel. 74 59 84
96). Over on the border with Dauphiny is **St-Romain-en-Gal**, the
old Gallo-Roman part of Vienne. The Vienne tourist office run
conducted tours of its houses, market and pottery stores.

Accommodation

First Class

Château de Chervinges, Gleizé, 69400 Villefranche-sur-Saône (Tel.
74 65 29 76): 11 rooms and 6 apartments in mansion surrounded
by Beaujolais vineyards; restaurant. **Ostellerie du Vieux Pérouges**,
Place du Tilleul, Pérouges, 01800 Méximieux (Tel. 74 61 00 88): 29
rooms in half-timbered building furnished with antiques; restaurant
with regional emphasis.

First Class / Middle Range

La Huchette, 01750 Replonges (Tel. 85 31 03 55): 15 elegant
rooms and 1 apartment in quiet location; restaurant. **Mme Roux**,
Domaine de la Javernière, 69910 Villié Morgon (Tel. 74 04 22 71):
3 *chambres d'hôte* in 18th century Beaujolais manor house; *tables
d'hôte* on reservation.

Middle Range / Economy

Hôtel du Rhône, quai de Gaulle, 01420 Seyssel (Tel. 50 59 20
30): 16 rooms in unpretentious hotel on right bank of Rhône;
restaurant with regional emphasis. **Le Mail**, 46 ave du Mail,
01000 Bourg-en-Bresse (Tel. 74 21 00 26): 9 rooms in family-
run hotel.

Economy

Hôtel du Lion d'Or, 10 Place de la Liberté, 42220 Bourg-Argental
(Tel. 77 39 62 25): 7 rooms in family hotel. **Hôtel Central**, Place
du 11 Novembre, 42370 Renaison (Tel. 77 64 25 39): 8 rooms in
family-run hotel.

Eating Out

True gastronomes will probably find themselves heading for the

Ain *département*, which has the highest total of Michelin stars of any French *département*.

First Class

Georges Blanc, 01540 Vonnas (Tel. 74 50 00 10): fresh local ingredients put to imaginative use; also has 23 luxury rooms and 7 suites. **Troisgros**, Place de la Gare, 42300 Roanne (Tel. 77 71 66 97): classic gourmet cuisine; also has 24 rooms and 5 suites.

Middle Range

Castel de Valrose, 12 bd de la République, 01090 Montmerle-sur-Saône (Tel. 74 69 30 52): high quality cooking, with emphasis on fish dishes, in quiet setting; also has 10 rooms. **La Table du Pavillon**, 4 ave de la Gare, 42700 Firminy (Tel. 77 56 00 45): ideal for a meal built around a good wine. **Hôtel de l'Ancienne Gare**, 42410 Pélussin (Tel. 74 87 61 51): finalist in 1989/90 Logis de France regional cuisine competition; also has 7 rooms.

Economy

Auberge de la Plumardière, Contrevoz, 01300 Belley (Tel. 79 81 82 54): regional and fish specialities; game in winter. **Hostellerie du Valromey**, 01510 Artemare (Tel. 79 87 30 10): gastronomic cuisine and regional specialities in pleasant surroundings.

Ardèche

The Ardèche *département* has been described as France's greenest, in the sense that it has no motorways and no major railways passing through it. While most people visit the famous gorges which cut through the Mediterranean style countryside in the south, the rest of the region is often neglected.

Annonay, in the north, is where the Montgolfier brothers began their hot-air ballooning exploits 200 years ago. There is a paper-making museum here, and early December brings a festival involving a concert, a half-marathon and chestnut roasting. All around the **St-Félicien** area, the third Sunday in May is a time for celebrating local cheeses, wines, crafts and traditions. A popular steam train, known as the Vivarais train or 'Le Mastrou', takes 2 hours to wind its way along the 33 kilometres between **Tournon** and **Lamastre**. The journey, through mountain gorges and Mediterranean vegetation, is magnificent, and there is always a 20-minute stop at a charming village for the train to fill up with water and the passengers with local wine. The train runs daily in July and August, and less frequently during the rest of the year: timetable details are available from **CFTM**, 8 rue d'Algérie, 69001 Lyon (Tel. 78 28 83 34). At **St-Julien-Labrousse** is a showroom for traditional and hand-crafted items, such as sheepswool and hand-woven garments or pottery. It is run by the 'Art Artisanal Ardèchois' association and open every afternoon in July and August, weekends only in June and September. In **St-Pierreville**, 'Ardelaine' (Tel. 75 66 63 08) is a cooperative, founded to boost local employment, which shears sheep and makes the wool into finished products to sell; they have taken over an old water-powered factory to work in and their efforts are worth supporting.

Privas, home of the 'marron glacé', is the capital of Ardèche, though it has under 11,000 inhabitants. Outside town, on the Villeneuve-de-Berg road, is the Verdus Agricultural Museum which offers a historical reconstruction of rural life in Ardèche. The **Col de l'Escrinet** is a good site for bird-watching, and **Vals-les-Bains** is a popular, though somewhat sedate, spa town. There is an artists' colony at **Antraigues**, which holds an art and craft festival each August. In June there is a violet fair at **Ste-Eulalie**. South-east of **Joyeuse** is a good wine-growing area, and many of the wine-cellars lining the road can be visited. At **Aubenas-Lanas** is Aero-City, an attraction park focusing on aerial sports. Information on visiting a local cheese producer is available from Sté-Caprila, route St-Andéol-de-Berg, 07170 **Villeneuve-de-Berg** (Tel. 75 94 81 21). The restored hamlet of **Le Vieil Audon**, near **Ruoms** is worth a visit, and Ruoms itself is the site of the festival of the local wine cooperatives in mid-August. At **St-Alban-Auriolles** is the Alphonse Daudet museum of popular arts and traditions, while the Compagnons du Gerboul run a shop in **Les Vans** which sells all-original hand-crafted items by local folk using local materials. Les Vans also hosts a country art fair in August and an olive festival in July.

Vallon-Pont-d'Arc is a top canoeing centre and starting point for a visit to the Ardèche gorges. It is also possible to see the gorges by rowing boat or flat-bottomed craft and information is available from the tourist office here. The region is riddled with caves, of which one of the best known is the **Aven d'Orgnac**. Its spectacular formations include a 50-metre-high gothic arch, massive columns, and rocks resembling organ pipes and giant palm trees. It can be visited from 1 March to 15 November and also has an excellent regional prehistory museum. Wine-tasting (of the local Côtes du Vivarais wines) is possible at the Cave Coopérative here (Tel. 75 38 60 08), or at **St-Remèze** (Tel. 75 04 08 56). The gorges are protected by the **Gaud** nature reserve, whose headquarters house an exhibition on the local environment. All around are further caves: the **Aven de Marzal**; the **Grotte de la Madeleine** with its many-coloured formations; and the **Bidon** cave, whose 'Prehistorama' recreated village offers an exhibition of prehistoric life, unique in Europe. More free wine-tasting is possible at **St-Montant**'s Cave Coopérative (Tel. 75 52 61 75).

Accommodation & Eating Out

First Class

Hostellerie la Cardinale, Chomerac, 07210 Baix (Tel. 75 85 80 40): 15 rooms in luxurious hotel, close to motorway.

First Class / Middle Range

Château de Bijou, Champs la Lioure, 07210 Chomerac (Tel. 75 65 16 19): 6 comfortable *chambres d'hôte* in eighteenth-century château with park.

Middle Range

Hôtel du Château, 12 quai Marc Seguin, 07300 Tournon (Tel. 75 08 60 22): 29 rooms in riverside hotel with views of vineyards; good restaurant with local cuisine. **Mas de l'Espaïre**, Combes de Mèges, 07140 Les Vans (Tel. 75 94 95 01): 32 rooms in quiet and comfortable restored farmstead in traditional local style, surrounded by woods; swimming pool and good restaurant.

Middle Range / Economy

Hôtel du Midi, Place Seignobos, 07270 Lamastre (Tel. 75 06 41 50): 15 spacious rooms in old-fashioned hotel with highly regarded restaurant.

Economy

Manoir de Raveyron, rue Henri-Barbusse, 07150 Vallon-Pont-d'Arc (Tel. 75 88 03 59): 14 rooms in simple, atmospheric village inn with restaurant. **Le Lion d'Or**, 29 rue de la République, 07000 Privas (Tel. 75 64 11 43): 10 rooms in family-run hotel with restaurant.

Drôme

The countryside of the Drôme shows both Mediterranean and Sub-Alpine influences, and the *département* claims to have the most diverse range of local crafts in the Rhône Valley, whose southern capital is **Valence**. Built on a series of terraces above the Rhône, Valence has a large university, a variety of flourishing industries and picturesque old quarters. It has one of the most beautiful public parks in France, the **Parc Jouvet**, which has attractive floral walks. Overlooking the park is the **Champ de Mars**, whose belvedere offers a magnificent view. Down in the old town, do not miss the **Musée de Beaux-Arts**, where exhibits range from sixteenth-century Flemish to twentieth-century abstract and include many sketches and drawings by the landscape artist Hubert Robert. The Romanesque **Cathédrale St-Apollinaire** has a yellow and white tower and harmonious interior. At number 57 Grande-Rue is the Renaissance **Maison des Têtes** with its sculptured façade. The **Notre-Dame de Soyons** and **St-Jean** churches are also worth visiting, and the pedestrian zone is pleasant to stroll through.

Accommodation

Middle Range

Hôtel Seyvet, 24 ave Marc-Urtin, 26500 Bourg-lès-Valence (Tel. 75 43 26 51): 34 rooms in comfortable, family-run hotel with restaurant, 1 kilometre from town. **Hôtel de France**, 16 bd Général-de-Gaulle (Tel. 75 43 00 87): 34 rooms in central hotel.

Middle Range / Economy

Hôtel du Grand-St-Jacques, 9 faubourg St-Jacques (Tel. 75 42 44 60): 32 rooms in family-run hotel with good value restaurant.

Economy

California, 174 ave Maurice-Faure (Tel. 75 44 36 05): 30 rooms in friendly family hotel with restaurant. **Hôtel Alpes-Cévennes**, 641 ave de la République, 07500 Granges-lès-Valence (Tel. 75 44 61 34): 26 rooms in pleasant hotel, 3 km from town.

Eating Out

First Class

Pic, 285 ave Victor-Hugo (Tel. 75 44 15 32): this restaurant is run by one of France's best chefs, Jacques Pic, who marries the traditional and the innovative in an elegant setting; also has 3 comfortable, quiet rooms and 2 suites.

Middle Range

La Licorne, 13 rue Chalamet (Tel. 75 43 76 83): traditional restaurant with good-value, fixed-price menus and garden.

Economy

Le Coelacanthe, 3 Place de la Pierre (Tel. 75 42 30 68): seafood specialities in centrally located restaurant with terrace. **La Petite Auberge**, 1 rue Athènes (Tel. 75 43 20 30).

Entertainments

Valence has good cinema facilities and hosts a national 'Cinema and History' festival in April, and a 'Cinema and Literature' one in November. In July and August the Fête de l'Eté is celebrated; and July also brings the Summer Academy of Chamber Music.

Useful Addresses

The **Tourist Office** is at Maison du Tourisme, Place Leclerc (Tel. 75 43 04 88). The **Comité Départemental du Tourisme**, which gives information on the whole Drôme area, is at 1 ave de Romans, 26000 Valence (Tel. 75 43 27 12).

Transport Options

Thanks to its pedestrian precinct and park, Valence suits exploration on foot. There are also bateaux-mouches cruises, and in summer it is possible to go up the Rhône as far as Lyon, or downstream as far as Avignon.

The Rest of Drôme

At **Hauterives** is the unusual Palais Idéal du Facteur Cheval, a fascinating example of late nineteenth- and early twentieth-century Surrealist architecture. The famous wine-growing town of **Tain** l'**Hermitage** has a wine fair the last weekend in February, and, due east, at **Romans** on the River Isère, you can visit an unusual shoe-making museum or have a tour of the factory which makes the regional speciality 'ravioles' (a kind of herb-filled pasta): contact M. Bourrelier, Les Ravioles de Royans, Z.I., 26100 Romans (Tel. 75 70 16 07). From **Châtillon**, whose tourist office displays an exhibition on the environment, there is a little train through the vineyards of Die. At **St-Nazaire-en-Royans** you can visit the Thaïs cave or take a *bateaux-mouches* trip, with commentary, across its lake, which is an ornithologist's paradise. A traditional nut aperitif, called noisel, is made by M. Odeyer, Hameau de Thuire, 26190 **St-Jean-en-Royans** (Tel. 75 47 56 54), whose premises may be visited. Nearby, at **Rochechinard**, is the Maison de la Mémoire which is a museum of Royans arts and traditions. Michel Kreckelberg's Arbre du Jouet at **Oriol-en-Royans** is a source of hand-made wooden toys, while the Entreprise Bérard at **St-Laurent-en-Royans** makes a wide range of wooden articles. **St-Agnan-en-Vercors** hosts a walkers' festival in mid-July, and nearby **Luire** is the site of another cave. A permanent exhibition on the local environment is set up at the **Col du Rousset** tourist office.

There are caves at **Vassieux-en-Vercors**, as well as a museum recreating the life of the area's prehistoric flint-cutters, and one dedicated to the Resistance. At **Die**, wine-tasting is possible at the Cave Coopérative de la Clairette de Die (Tel. 75 22 02 22), where the local sparkling wine is made. Die's twelfth-century cathedral and the municipal museum, which displays local archaeological finds and items connected with local history and traditions, are also worth a visit; the latter is open every afternoon except Sunday from 15 June to 15 September and organises guided tours of medieval Die in July and August. Nearby, at **Chamaloc**, the **Maison de Parc et de la Flore** (a Vercors regional park building) is the starting point for an ecological path, as well as a bee-keeping centre, where honey-making can be watched. The famous **Lesches-en-Diois** lavender fair takes place in mid-August.

At **Saillans**, the local almond biscuit factory can be visited: information from Mme Arnaud, RN93, 26340 Saillans (Tel. 75 21 52 44 or 75 21 50 16). The Château de Blacons near **Crest** is a showroom for local paintings, jewellery, rugwork and pottery, while, at Crest itself, the Musée de la Nature has good displays of minerals and fossils, and the production of local goats' cheeses can be viewed at the Coopérative Laitière, Quartier Pied Gai, 26400

Crest (Tel. 75 25 31 41). In November there is an art and craft fair at **Etoile-sur-Rhône**. Though famous for its nougat, **Montélimar** also produces good honey; the production process can be seen on the premises of M. Claude Giraud, 4 chemin de Beausseret, 26200 Montélimar (Tel. 75 51 23 65). Traditional nougat can be purchased from Arnaud Soubeyron at Les Blaches, just off the RN7, and individuals can visit the nougat producer 'Le Sfynx' at Z.I. de Gournier, 26200 Montélimar (Tel. 75 01 50 98). Places of interest in the town include the Adhémar castle, the eleventh-century Narbonne tower, Diane de Poitier's house, and various other historic town mansions. Mme Girard of 'Tourisme en Tricastin' whose headquarters are in the Mairie at Pierrelatte (Tel. 75 98 93 38), can organise several guided tours, including one by a local stonemason at **St-Restitut** and one of the Garde Adhémar aromatic plant garden. From **St-Restitut**, you can walk to a deserted village of troglodyte caves, which are fascinating but whose atmosphere is spoiled by views of a nuclear power station in the valley.

Suze-la-Rousse is well known because its medieval château has been given a new lease of life as a 'Wine University'. This is where the famous local vintages receive approval and is open to those interested in any aspect of wine-production or tasting most afternoons (for courses, see **Good Alternatives**). In July and August the château also hosts concerts. In **Grignan**, July brings *Son et Lumière* performances to the Renaissance castle, where the writer Madame de Sévigné lived and died. Her apartments can be visited on a guided tour. If you would like to visit the **Montjoyer** monastery, where you can see a film on monastery life and purchase local liqueurs and cordials, contact Père Alexis on 75 98 51 22. **Dieulefit** is a major local craft centre, which specialises in pottery: some work is displayed at the Poterie Robin, route de Montélimar, at nearby **Le Poët Laval**; alternatively, eight local potters have showrooms at Artis, Place de l'Abbé Magnet, in Dieulefit itself. A family-run olive oil mill can be visited every day except Sunday at **Nyons**; contact Mme Autran, La Digue, 26110 Nyons (Tel. 75 26 02 52). Nyons also plays host to the 'New Olive Oil Festival' each January, and is worth a visit at any time of year for its beautiful old quarters with their covered passages, courtyards, wrought-ironwork and restored seventh-century watch-tower. In mid-July there is a lime, lavender and olive festival at **Buis-les-Baronnies**, which is complemented by the Maison des Arômes at **Montguers**, a kind of eco-museum of lavender, lime and aromatic or medicinal plants, including some distillation studios.

Accommodation

First Class

Hostellerie Manoir la Roseraie, Chemin des Grands Prés, 26230 Grignan (Tel. 75 46 58 15): 12 rooms and 1 suite in 19th century property in park, at foot of Château de Grignan; restaurant, **Domaine du Colombier**, 26780 Malataverne – Montélimar Sud (Tel. 75 51 65 86): 25 rooms in fourteenth-century castle with park and swimming pool; good restaurant. **Bastide des Hautes Tours**, 26740 Marsanne (Tel. 75 90 31 63): 4 rooms and 1 suite in medieval manor with swimming pool, beautifully situated in Provençal countryside; dinner on reservation.

Middle Range

Auberge des Quatre Saisons, Place de l'Eglise, St-Restitut, 26130 St-Paul-Trois-Châteaux (Tel. 75 04 71 88): 10 rooms in traditional stone-walled inn in perched village; good restaurant with regional dishes.

Middle Range / Economy

Hôtel Restaurant Giffon, Place de l'Eglise, Grâne, 26400 Crest (Tel. 75 62 60 64): 9 comfortable rooms in pleasant hotel with tree-shaded terrace and well-known restaurant.

Economy

Hôtel Dauphiné-Provence, 41 bd Général-de-Gaulle, 26200 Montélimar (Tel. 75 01 24 08): 19 rooms in family-run hotel with restaurant. **La Petite Auberge**, avenue Sadi-Carnot, 26150 Die (Tel. 75 22 05 91 or 75 22 13 51): 11 rooms in family-run hotel with restaurant. **M. Chaix**, quai la Mare, 26800 Etoile-sur-Rhône (Tel. 75 59 33 79): 5 *chambres d'hôte* in pleasantly situated house with kitchen facilities and living room for use of guests.

Eating Out

In addition to the above, the following restaurants deserve special mention:

First Class

Michel Chabran, N7, Autoroute Valence Nord, Pont-de-l'Isère, 26600 Tain-l'Hermitage (Tel. 75 84 60 09): restaurant run by one of the region's most famous chefs, who creates excellent dishes from predominantly local produce; also has 12 rather uninspiringly modern rooms.

Middle Range

Hôtel Restaurant le Gîte, Bellegarde-en-Diois, 26470 La Motte Chalançon (Tel. 75 21 33 58): vegetarian restaurant belonging to attractively situated country hotel.

Economy

M. Mingasson, Ferme Veyret, 26220 Dieulefit (Tel. 75 46 36 21): family-run *tables d'hôte* style restaurant on farm; also has 4 *chambres d'hôte*.

16 Dauphiny and Savoy – the Alps

In most people's minds, the Alps are connected with skiing holidays and spectacular scenery. The French Alps boast more than a hundred ski resorts, of which over forty are of international standard. The region is the only one in the world to have hosted the Winter Olympics three times, and it contains Europe's highest and most prestigious peak, Mont Blanc. But there is another side to the coin. The Alps have been described as the most threatened mountain system in the world. Forty million visitors come here each year and, though France is not the worst-affected country, environmental degradation does not respect national boundaries. What happens in one part of the range often has a knock-on effect elsewhere. Responsible behaviour on the part of tourists to France is perhaps nowhere more important than in Dauphiny and Savoy.

The area first became widely known when the 1968 Winter Olympics, based in Grenoble, were televised. But this publicity put across a rather one-sided view of the region. So impressive was its skiing potential that other attractions were all but ignored. Its well-preserved Roman remains, medieval citadels, baroque churches and numerous châteaux have usually been outshone by more recent feats of engineering, like the Mont Blanc tunnel and the cable car up to the Aiguille du Midi. The joys of year-round skiing at top-class resorts have made any regrets that small-scale farmers are losing grazing land in favour of ski runs, or that traditional local industries are disappearing, dwindle to insignificance. Fortunately, the succession of snowless winters that rounded off the 1980s has forced people to question the wisdom of putting all their economic eggs in the skiing holiday basket.

Many resorts now double as destinations for summer activity holidays. Winter alternatives are also being developed: snow-shoe walking (known as *raquettes*); nature discovery excursions; and cross-country skiing. Cross-country, or *ski de fond*, needs a far simpler infrastructure than downhill skiing and can fit in with a rural lifestyle and agricultural economy. It is a traditional means of getting around in snowy weather but can also be practised as a competitive sport. The Vercors massif is well-known for its cross-country skiing facilities, yet it is also a highly effective regional park. Summer visitors to Dauphiny and Savoy will certainly notice the large number of protected areas in the region: two national parks, one regional park (with another planned), and fifteen or more nature reserves. Away from the patches of dead hillside or artificial grass that mark the site of the previous winter's ski runs, the natural heritage of the Alps is extraordinarily rich. As well as rugged peaks and glaciers, the region offers ideal habitats for chamois, ibex and many birds of prey; several large lakes (including the French side of Lake Geneva); rivers well-stocked with fish, and others which carve out impressive gorges; caves with spectacular rock formations; a collection of spa towns; agricultural land ranging from alpine pastures to orchards in the plains, and hillside vineyards producing Savoy wines. People are independent and proud of their region, and you will find many small museums, exhibitions and festivals celebrating traditional ways of life.

It would be quite unrealistic to imagine that highly developed resorts could go back to being sleepy alpine villages, but discouraging further indiscriminate construction work by means of consumer pressure is not impossible. This does not mean that everyone should stop taking skiing holidays immediately, but just that careful thought should be given to choices of resort, accommodation and transport.

Points for Skiers to Bear in Mind

Before you automatically book this year's skiing holiday in the French Alps, consider choosing a different region that has not yet reached saturation point – the Pyrenees or the Jura, for example. Or maybe you could try your hand at cross-country skiing or some other winter sport for a change? If you do decide to go to the French Alps, you should avoid (for your own benefit as much as anyone else's) the French school holidays, which are staggered between mid-February and mid-March. Demand is so high that prices go through the roof and the slopes become grossly overcrowded.

If you have a favourite resort that you go to every winter, consider visiting it just as the snows are melting. You will probably see scarred mountainsides where the ski runs used to be, and the scarcity of the usual spring-time birds, animals and flowers will be hard to ignore. Now go to the Nature Initiation Centre at Sallanches to see what alpine vegetation and wildlife can be like without human interference. If you are shocked, maybe you should think again about your choice of resort.

When picking a resort, be realistic. Do you really need to go to a top international resort covered with black runs that you never quite pluck up the courage to use? The more people go to such resorts, the more apartments, ski runs and lifts are added, and the more environmental havoc is wreaked. Lower-altitude village resorts cause far less erosion than resorts whose facilities extend above the tree-line.

When picking accommodation, try to avoid new developments. These are often built by people from outside the area whose motives are less than altruistic. Not only do they take custom away from traditional types of accommodation such as family-run hotels and bed and breakfasts, but, if they are heavily used, developers will be encouraged to build yet more, regardless of the fact that many resorts are, environmentally speaking, unable to cope with greater numbers of visitors.

When picking your mode of transport, think very carefully before taking the car. There are already far too many private cars in the French Alps. Exhaust pollution is a major problem, as temperature inversion and lack of wind cause it to linger in the valleys where most of the roads are situated. Some resorts have come to resemble huge car parks; progress on the winding mountain roads is unbelievably slow; and each year many accidents occur because holiday-makers are not used to driving in icy conditions. In any case, if you plan to ski all week there is no need for a car. Public transport is generally quite adequate for the odd excursion, and the journey between Britain and France is usually less stressful if you take the plane, train or coach.

Once you are there, responsible behaviour is simply a matter of commonsense actions, such as keeping to the pistes, taking all litter back down the slopes, and making use of local services.

Of course, many of these considerations do not apply only when you are choosing a skiing holiday, but are relevant at all times of year and for all types of holiday in regions with as much tourist pressure on them as Dauphiny and, more especially, Savoy.

History

Relics from the Bronze Age show early habitation around the Lac du Bourget but, from the sixth century BC, a Celtic tribe known as the Allobroges settled in the area between the Rhône and Isère rivers, forcing the previous inhabitants up into the mountains. With difficulty, the Romans took charge of the region in 121 BC and developed it considerably, as can be seen from the remains at Vienne, Aimes, Aix-les-Bains and elsewhere. Despite persecution, Christianity spread in the first few centuries AD, after which the region passed to the Burgundians, followed by the Franks and the Carolingians until finally, in the early eleventh century, the Savoy area fell to Humbert aux Blanches-Mains, a vassal of the German emperor, and the Dauphiny area to Guigues I, count of Albon.

The eleventh and twelfth centuries saw the building of great abbeys and monasteries, and the founding of the Carthusian order by Saint Bruno, along with its monastery in the Chartreuse. In 1349 the ruler of Dauphiny found himself in such a political and financial mess that he had to sell his lands to the French king, bringing about the reattachment of Dauphiny to France in the form of the inheritance of the crown prince, who acquired the name Dauphin. This arrangement went on until 1628. Meanwhile, possession of Savoy was changing all the time, sometimes in favour of the French, sometimes in favour of the Empire, until the Treaty of Utrecht in 1713 when Victor Amédée, Duke of Savoy, recovered the region and was made King of Sicily. Shortly afterwards, he exchanged this post for that of King of Sardinia, so that Savoy became a Sardinian state, though it also underwent a brief period of Spanish occupation between 1742 and 1748. Towards the end of the eighteenth century, a large thermal establishment was built at the spa town of Aix-les-Bains. In 1786, the first ever ascent of Mont Blanc was completed by Balmat and Paccard, but initial excitement over this achievement was eclipsed by the French Revolution, which was the result of events set in motion by the Assembly at Vizille, in Dauphiny. Savoy was occupied by French revolutionary forces from 1792 to 1815, but was then returned to the Sardinian monarchy. In 1846, it was agreed that France would receive the lands of Savoy in exchange for helping to evict the Austrians from Italy, and April 1860 saw an overwhelming vote in favour of this move, on the part of the Savoyard people.

The railway tunnel of Mont-Cenis (also called Fréjus) was completed in 1872, linking major cities in France and Italy. Skis were introduced to the area, from Norway, only in 1889, and the first Ski Club was founded in Grenoble in 1896. The first Winter Olympics took place in 1924, at Chamonix. The Vercors came into its own in the Second World War, as a bastion of the Resistance. In 1963, the first French national park – the Vanoise – was created. The Mont Blanc road tunnel was inaugurated in 1965, in time for the Grenoble Olympics in 1968. The Vercors regional park and Ecrins national park were formed in the early 1970s, and measures to protect the mountain environment started to be taken seriously. Most recently, attention has been drawn to the region by the 1992 Winter Olympics at Albertville. 1992 also marks the 500th anniversary of the 'start of mountaineering', for which celebrations, centring on the legendary Mont Aiguille, take place in June and July.

Famous people associated with Savoy and Dauphiny include the eighteenth-century mathematician Monge and his contemporary, the chemist Berthollet; Jean-Jacques Rousseau, who chose to settle near Chambéry, where he was inspired to write much of his philosophy; the de Maistre brothers (Joseph and Xavier), eighteenth- to nineteenth-century philosophers who opposed the French Revolution and advocated an absolute monarchy; the nineteenth-century composer Hector Berlioz, born in Dauphiny; the nineteenth-century novelist, Henri Beyle, better known as Stendhal, who came from Grenoble and wrote such classics as *The Red and the Black* and *The Charterhouse of Parma*; and Aristide Bergès, who became the 'father' of hydro-electric power with his tapping of the Lancey waterfall in 1869. More recently, skiers like the Goitschel sisters and Jean-Claude Killy have 'adopted' the region.

Geography

As is clear from their historical development, Dauphiny and Savoy are in fact two separate regions, but they have been brought together, along with the Rhône Valley, in the large administrative region of Rhône-Alpes, of which they make up the 'Alpes' section. Dauphiny and Savoy are bordered by the Provençal Alps in the south, the Rhône Valley to the west, Lake Geneva and Switzerland in the north, and Italy in the east. Dauphiny (the French is Dauphiné) has only one *département*, Isère, whose capital is Grenoble (160,000 inhabitants). Savoy (whose official title is Savoie-Mont Blanc) is divided into two *départements*: Savoie in the south and Haute-Savoie in the north. The capital of both Savoie and the whole Savoy region is Chambéry (55,000 inhabitants), while that of Haute-Savoie is the pleasant lakeside town of Annecy (52,000 inhabitants). Other famous towns in the region are Aix-les-Bains and Chamonix.

The most important geographical feature is naturally the mountain range of the French Alps. The highest peaks can be found along a line drawn from the north-eastern corner of the region to roughly the centre of its southern boundary. The crystalline massifs that constitute this line are the Mont Blanc and Aiguilles Rouges; the Belledonne and Grandes-Rousses; and the Ecrins-Pelvoux. They are made of very hard rock and form rugged pinnacles, covered in snow all year round. Glaciers can still be found here, the most famous of which is the Mer de Glace, above Chamonix. The highest point of these mountains is the summit of Mont Blanc, 4807 metres above sea-level. To their west is what is known as the intra-Alpine zone. The mountains here belong to the Vanoise massif and are slightly lower, forming a minor depression between the French and Italian Alps. The landscape is one of deep valleys (notably the Tarentaise and Maurienne), steep slopes and vast pastures. Since it enjoys both heavy snow and a sunny climate, it has become the most important French skiing area, with resorts like Val d'Isère, Tignes, Courchevel, La Plagne and Les Arcs. To the east of the high crystalline peaks is a long, narrow depression that forms a fertile plain, where vines, tobacco and maize are grown. To its east are the Pre-Alps which make up a limestone mountain range, rarely above 2000 metres. There are five distinct massifs, divided from one another by river valleys. Finally, the north-western corner of the region (between Chambéry and Lake Geneva) consists of the Plateau des Bornes, with its gentle green hills and deep glacial lakes.

Though tourism has taken over from industry and agriculture as the main economic motor in many places, the rearing of cattle (usually for dairy products), forestry and hydro-electric power still play an important role. Farmers are diversifying: not only do many agriculturalists in the Vercors now grow walnuts, lime-trees and medicinal plants, in line with the re-encouragement of traditional activities by the regional park, but they also turn their hand to ski tuition or mountain guide services in winter. Fruit-growing flourished in the 1950s, but fears that many of the old varieties of fruit tree are now dying out have prompted the creation of various 'old-fashioned' orchards.

In fact, ecological protection is high on the agenda in many domains.

The Vanoise national park has fourteen kilometres of common border with the Italian Gran Paradiso park, which means that the two parks combined form the largest nature reserve in Western Europe. The Vanoise has a complex geological structure and an exceptional alpine flora of over 1000 species, including crocus, anemone and gentian. The park prides itself on its success with ibex and chamois, whose populations have increased dramatically since the park was created. Other fauna includes the marmot, fox and badger, as well as the golden eagle, buzzard, black grouse and ptarmigan. The central zone of the park is one place where roads, ski-lifts and pistes have not been allowed to penetrate, though the peripheral zone contains many winter sports resorts. The Ecrins national park, where chamois and golden eagles can also be seen, has its headquarters in the Hautes-Alpes *département* and only one third of its mountainous territory is in the Dauphiny region. The Vercors regional park, part of which is in the Drôme *département*, works closely with farmers so as to reconcile agriculture and tourism. Scattered among its series of north-south ridges and valleys are many beautiful rock formations, including caves. Pine, spruce and beech grow here, interspersed with mountain pastures, vines, walnut trees and lavender. The bear only disappeared from the wilder parts of the Vercors in 1940. There are plans for another regional park on the Chartreuse massif.

Already there are more nature reserves in Dauphiny and Savoy than in any other part of France, and the seven which belong to Haute-Savoie have their own special philosophy. There is a strong educational emphasis and, instead of blunt prohibitions, come careful explanations, always designed to show man how to fit back into nature. The idea of keeping to the marked path is shown to be to the visitor's own benefit, for animals will get used to human presence along that one trail and will not run away. Rules about not picking flowers, bringing dogs etc. are accounted for in similarly logical fashion by the Haute-Savoie reserves, which complement one another and are unique in being run by democratic associations of local people.

Climate

The great differences of altitude throughout the region, along with other factors such as relief and exposure make it impossible to generalise about the climate. As a rule, whether precipitation falls as rain or snow depends on the altitude (it is almost always snow above 3000 m); the temperature decreases by about 0.5 °C for every 100 m increase in height; and the amount of sunshine is far higher for south-facing slopes than for north-facing ones. Temperatures range from an average of −6°C in Chamonix in January to the mid-20s around Annecy in July. In the mountains, you can be fairly certain of snow cover from December through to April, though the depth of snow varies considerably from place to place and year to year. Spring is generally rainy, especially in the Pre-Alps. Summer is hot and sunny in most places (there were 1000 hours of sunshine at Annecy between June and September 1986), though evenings are chilly higher up. Autumn days are regrettably short but the skies are usually clear and blue.

Attractions

People are attracted to Dauphiny and Savoy for a number of reasons but, for many, the spectacle of its natural scenery takes second place to the comprehensive nature of its facilities. The latter are, indeed, impressive. Of its one hundred and more winter sports resorts, six offer skiing at 3000 metres from June to September; summer skiing is possible at Val Thorens, Val d'Isère, Tignes, La Plagne, l'Alpe d'Huez and Les Deux Alpes. The largest skiing area in the world is provided by the interconnected resorts of Les Trois Vallées (Val Thorens, Les Ménuires and St-Martin-de-Belleville). The French Alps also boast the largest cable-car in the world, which has room for 160 people and is situated in Courchevel. The highest cable-car in Europe takes you up 3842 metres to the Aiguille du Midi, and Europe's first urban cable-car can be found in Grenoble. Summer facilities are certainly not lacking in the French Alps either, as the increasing promotion of year-round tourism makes quite clear. At the new resort of Flaine is the highest golf course in Europe. The resorts of Valloire, La Clusaz, La Plagne and Les Arcs offer opportunities to learn or practise virtually any activity you can think of. Climbing centres exist at Chamonix and Aussois. The 'Great Lakes of the Alps' are perfect for watersports enthusiasts: Lakes Geneva, Annecy and Le Bourget (France's largest natural lake) have all-round facilities, while the smaller Lake Aiguebelette prohibits motorised sports. There are eight spa resorts in the French Alps, including France's leading spa, Aix-les-Bains.

Among other top attractions in the region are the Mer de Glace, an enormous glacier above Chamonix, which is reached by rack and pinion railway; the *Route des Grands Cols Alpins*, which offers spectacular views; various impressive hydro-electric dams; a vast Belgian-sponsored attraction park near Les Avenières; the Roman town of Vienne; the attractive lakeside town of Annecy; Grenoble, with its stunning situation and cosmopolitan atmosphere; the Mont Blanc tunnel and Mont Blanc itself. You will also find the largest cellar in the world for maturing liqueur; the liqueur in question is Chartreuse and the cellar is at Voiron, near the first ever Carthusian monastery. The Grottes de Choranche caves contain geological formations unrivalled in Europe. The chapel on the Assy Plateau is decorated with paintings by Léger, Matisse, Braque, Chagall and others, and there is a famous war memorial, designed by the architect Gilioli, on the Plateau des Glières. This was a stronghold of the Resistance, as was the Vercors plateau, and both now specialise in cross-country skiing. This sport was first registered by holiday-makers during the 1968 Grenoble Olympics, and now Haute-Savoie alone has 750 km of cross-country ski trails. Between late spring and autumn, walking in the foothills of the Alps is popular and many marked trails have been set up, especially in the regional and national parks. It is by exploring on foot that you are most likely to come across some of the more hidden attractions of the region: its Baroque churches and seventeenth-century frescoes; its châteaux and medieval citadels; its museums of local ways of life; its pastoral alpine hamlets and its nature reserves.

Cuisine

Regional cuisine varies according to where you are. In Dauphiny, you will come across the delicious *gratin dauphinois*, a dish using potatoes, cream, eggs and milk, which is occasionally varied through use of pumpkins, millet or crayfish. Walnuts are a speciality and crop up in various forms, including Grenoble walnut cake and even walnut wine. In the Vercors, you may be offered *ravioles*. These little pasta sacks are filled with a delicate mixture of soft cheese and herbs, are suitable for vegetarians, and have nothing whatever in common with tinned ravioli! Local cheeses include st-marcellin, trièves and sassenage blue cheese.

In Savoy there are many smoked hams, along with *diot* or *longeole* sausages and *attriaut* pâté. Lamb is popular, as are fish caught in the local rivers. Savoy is famous for its pastries and cakes, as well as its cheeses: tomme, beaufort, vacherin and reblochon, which is made only from the creamiest cows' milk. The true *fondue savoyarde* should be made from beaufort cheese mixed with the local white wine, Apremont.

Drinks from the region range from mineral waters through to high-proof liqueurs. The Evian and Thonon waters come from spa towns on the edge of Lake Geneva. Thonon also produces a light, refreshing white wine called Ripaille. Other highly regarded white wines from the north of the region are Seyssel, Crépy and Frangy. The Combe de Savoie, the Lac du Bourget area and the Vercors also produce agreeable wines of all types. Gentian liqueur and Marc de Savoie are popular *digestifs*, though the most famous is Chartreuse, which is made from honey combined with 130 distilled plants. The green version is 55° proof, the yellow 40°, and both are said to ensure long life!

Level of Tourism

The word *tourisme* was first introduced into the French language in 1838 by the Grenoble-born writer, Stendhal; Grenoble was also the site of the first ever French tourist board, established in 1889. The cradle of French tourism has witnessed some drastic developments during the past century. Statistics for tourism to the French Alps are rarely separated from those of the Rhône-Alpes area as a whole, which is the second most popular French region, after Paris / Ile-de-France, hosting 13.1% of all national visits. Tourism is the most important economic activity for the region and, during the skiing season, visitors to Rhône-Alpes are whisked to mountain-tops by mechanical means at a rate of 1.8 million an hour! Within Dauphiny and Savoy, the level of tourism increases steadily as you pass from Isère to Savoie to Haute-Savoie, which is the top *département* in France for winter tourism and second top for summer tourism. Haute-Savoie has also undergone an experience unique in France, in that its population has doubled in the last thirty years.

Certain facts are important to bear in mind when planning your holiday. The times of year **not** to come are between 15 February and 15 March (it's as if every schoolchild in France is on the slopes), and between 15 July and 15 August, when almost all French people and many others take their summer holidays. The tourist board is trying to persuade people to visit outside these two periods, with low-tariff *semaines blanches* for skiers, and encouragement of spring and autumn visits. In summer, the spread of the different nationalities is fairly even, with the British, Belgians and Dutch tending to prefer *gîte* accommodation, the Germans opting for hotels and the Italians renting furnished apartments. The hot summers and mild winters of the late 1980s led to certain changes in holiday trends. Summer sunshine meant that fewer people visited museums, châteaux and other indoor attractions, and fewer stayed in towns. The majority headed for the mountains, where they tended to stay longer. There were also fewer short-stay coach trips and fewer family holidays in the area. The decrease in numbers of skiers, due mainly to last minute cancellations caused by lack of snow, barely affected the large high-altitude resorts, but was catastrophic for the small-scale resorts in Dauphiny. This led such resorts (notably those in the Vercors) to rethink their policy and to develop alternative 'nature' – orientated products, which are now doing well. Unfortunately, the big resorts have not always followed this example: vast sums of money have been invested in the skiing infrastructure, for which developers have not yet seen a return; they are, therefore, doing everything in their power to coax skiers back, even if it means providing tons of artificial snow in winter and covering up the mess with artificial grass each spring.

More often than not, problems are caused by the tourism developments themselves rather than individual tourists. A development on the shore of the Petit Lac at Annecy has detracted considerably from its natural significance. Roads and tracks are often constructed above the tree-line, and ski-lifts installed, without any thought for the erosion this will cause, and the consequent loss of grazing land in some areas. Many of the sports fashionable in the Alps have negative environmental effects: a paragliding site at Le Brévent has frightened away a rare eagle, and the ski resorts in the Tarentaise wreck the habitat of the black grouse. The Chamrousse ski resort is allowed to turn into one massive car park each winter. In contrast, the new resort of Flaine has followed the example of some Swiss resorts and taken the bold step of banning cars altogether. Flaine and Avoriaz are two modern resorts that are generally regarded as successful; architecturally they are designed to compliment, even to emulate, the natural scenery.

One example of a whole area which seems to be heading in the wrong direction is the exceedingly beautiful Chamonix valley. There is a highly efficient public transport system, yet people insist on driving up and down the valley in their cars. Not only does this cause considerable pollution, but it also means the 5-minute journey from the Col des Montets down to Argentière takes 45 minutes during rush hour. And 'rush hour' lasts from 4 p.m. to 7 p.m. every day. Further up the valley, Vallorcine is a prime example of a little alpine village wrecked by the skiing industry. It used to be a thriving pastoral community; now, instead of grazing cows and flower-carpeted pastures, spring brings only bare earth where the ski runs were. Ironically, there is a project for a subsidised 'demonstration' farm here, so that children brought up in towns will have the chance to see farm animals – it's a pity it can't be the real thing! Development in the Chamonix valley goes on: another 900 beds are being created in Argentière, and complete rehabilitation of the Aiguille du Midi cable-car in 1990 increased its capacity by 40%. Unfortunately, creation of more facilities in one domain does not stop there. To take a simple example: if you build more apartments, more people will stay; the ski runs will become dangerously crowded and you will have to construct more runs, which will entail more ski-lifts; but, to make this investment worthwhile, you will have to attract even more visitors . . . and so on. It is still possible (just) to find unspoilt spots in the Chamonix valley. Instead of taking the Montenvers railway from Chamonix to the Mer de Glace glacier with its restaurants and kitschy ice-cave, go down the valley and take the chair-lift to the Glacier des Bossons, or, even better, go further up the valley to Argentière and take the cable-car to Les Grands Montets. From here it is a 1^1/2 hour walk to the Glacier d'Argentière, but you might just be the only one there.

Another area with particular difficulties due to high tourist frequentation is the peripheral zone of the Vanoise national park, but here things are looking brighter. Schemes for analysis and action have been set up, which have already been highly successful in the protection of the ibex and chamois. The Vanoise park has also been able to limit vandalism and thoughtless behaviour in and around its refuges by introducing a computerised booking system and better security (combined with an information service) in the shape of well-informed *gardiens*. Solar energy is used wherever possible in the park.

Throughout the region, problems are caused by picnickers leaving litter behind. Particularly vulnerable areas are the Col des Montets and Lac Blanc in the Aiguilles Rouges nature reserve, where people often ignore the pleas of the management to consume their lunch at the reception chalet specially designed for that purpose. Damage is also done in the Vercors regional park, as the rock here is so porous that any hint of pollution seeps straight through to one of the numerous rivers or streams. The largest nature reserve in France is to be found within the Vercors park – or, rather, it is **not** to be found, for the sites it protects are extremely fragile and people are discouraged from entering by an absolute lack of facilities.

The nature reserves and national parks are now being assisted in their efforts to protect the Alps. Alp Action is an organisation, launched in 1990 by Prince Sadruddin Aga Khan, and defining itself as 'an active partnership between the corporate sector, the scientific and conservation communities, [which] promotes practical actions for the preservation of the Alpine environment'. Leading companies are persuaded by Alp Action to sponsor certain specific projects, which at present include a prototype reserve in the Tarentaise valley, designed to combine skiing facilities with the promotion of respect for nature among tourists; a 'Code of Ethics' credit card, the adherence to whose golden rules is rewarded with discounts on transport and leisure facilities; and research into renewable energy sources and strategies to counter the effects of climate change in the Alps.

As far as local government policy is concerned, having already built many high-altitude resorts, there is now a tendency to construct more integrated ones, lower down the mountains. Of course this is a move in the right direction, but the mountains can only be saved if new construction stops altogether. The words of one local resident sum up the problem: 'Thank God for avalanches. They are the only thing which stops them developing the whole mountainside'.

Good Alternatives

Meeting People

As is usual in areas with high tourist frequentation, one of the only ways of meeting local people for whom you are not simply 'another holiday-maker passing through' is to stay in small-scale, locally owned accommodation, off the beaten track. There is any amount of this in Dauphiny and Savoy, along with many rural inns, specialising in local dishes. A list of of those in Haute-Savoie is available from the **Logis et Auberges de Haute-Savoie**, Chambre de Commerce, 2 rue du Lac, 74000 Annecy (Tel. 50 57 82 40). If you would like to learn how to prepare local dishes yourself, cookery courses are run by the **Hôtel Restaurant de la Poste**, 38850 Charavines (Tel, 76 06 60 41). You can meet up with local vintners by visiting their wine cellars or caves: information on this is available from the **Comité Interprofessionnel des Vins de Savoie**, 3 rue du Château, 73000 Chambéry (Tel. 79 33 44 16).

The regional branch of a national association allows volunteers to participate in archaeological digs and conservation work: contact **CONCORDIA – Délégation Alpes**, Les Villes Dessous, 73270 Beaufort. If you are a bird-watcher, you can meet like-minded people through **CORA** (Centre Ornithologique Rhône-Alpes), 'La Niverolle', Maison de la Nature et de l'Environnement, 5 Place Bir Hakeim, 38000 Grenoble (Tel. 76 51 78 03). As well as giving information on bird-watching in the region, the organisation arranges meetings, films etc. Adventure sports enthusiasts should get in touch with the local association specialising in their sport: a list of those in Isère can be obtained from the **Maison de l'Aventure**, 26420 La Chapelle-en-Vercors (Tel. 75 48 22 38).

If staying in one place, for example on a skiing holiday, you are obviously more likely to become involved with the local community if you choose a village resort rather than a large purpose-built one. Valmorel and Montchavin have both been successful in combining a traditional welcome with good facilities.

Discovering Places

Facilities for walkers are excellent in the region. Walkers' brochures are available from **Maison de la Randonnée**, 7 rue Voltaire, 38000 Grenoble (Tel. 76 51 76 00). The **Grande Traversée des Alpes (GTA)** organisation, based at the above address, produces a catalogue of walking trips for groups or individuals, with or without guides. Advice on walking in the Savoie *département* can be obtained from **Randonnée en Savoie**, Parc National de la Vanoise, 135 rue Docteur-Julliand, BP 705, 73007 Chambéry. A list of summer outings and films organised by the park is contained in its magazine, *L'Estive*.

Walking guides and maps (called *Carto-Guides*) are also prepared by the **Parc Naturel Régional du Vercors**, Chemin des Fusillés, BP 14, 38250 Lans-en-Vercors. A list of numerous guided excursions in July and August is contained in the Vercors park's leaflet 'L'Eté de la Nature'. The park also offers its own unique 'packages': for example, a 6-day trek across the park with mules to carry your tents and luggage, during which no habitation is seen and often no other people. This holiday designed for individuals grouped together up to a maximum of twelve people, costs around 2200FF and is just one of those offered in the Natural Parks Federation brochure '12 Voyages au Naturel'. A copy of the brochure is available from **Clés de France** (see **Introduction** p.51), and further details of this particular holiday can be supplied either by M. Patrick Rabot of the Vercors Regional Park, or by the trip's producer, **Les Muletiers du Vercors**, 38250 Villard-de-Lans (Tel. 76 95 02 21). Another walking holiday in the brochure, this time produced by **Grand Angle**, BP 10, 38880 Autrans (Tel. 76 95 23 00), costs slightly more, lasts seven days and includes hotel accommodation. One more natural park holiday is on offer in the region; this is a 6-day walking circuit in the Vanoise national park, entitled 'Magic and secret life of the glaciers', costing around 3600FF and produced by **Hexatour Savoie**, 100 quai de la Rize, 75017 Chambéry (Tel. 79 85 80 46): further information from this address, the park itself, or Clés de France.

Another way to get 'back to nature' is to stay at the **Gîte des Ecouges**, 38470 St-Gervais (Tel. 76 64 73 45). Primarily a base for children's nature discovery and activity holidays (6 years and above), this charming house also welcomes families and individuals. It is 45 minutes by foot or ski from the nearest road and 7 km from all habitation. The family who run it are well-qualified both to help you explore the rich natural surroundings and to teach you speleology and rock-climbing. The Vercors regional park operates an economical Cheques-Loisirs system, whereby you purchase a 'Cheque' consisting of units which you may spend on various sports and leisure facilities. These are on sale at all tourist offices within the park as well as the park headquarters.

A good way to get the best out of a walking trip in the mountains is to hire a qualified mountain guide (*accompagnateur en montagne*), who will usually be knowledgeable not only about the best route, but also about the flora, fauna, geology and traditions of an area. In the Maurienne, try **Philippe Lepigre**, 73480 Lanslevillard (Tel. 79 05 97 95). In the Tarentaise, the people to approach are the **Syndicat National des Accompagnateurs en Montagne**, Montcharvet, 73120 Courchevel (Tel. 79 08 15 51). A wide range of activities is on offer from the **Accompagnateurs en Montagne**, Maison de la Nature, 5 Place Bir Hakeim, 38000 Grenoble (Tel. 76 51 04 38). A lot can be learned about the environment in Haute-Savoie through attending the lectures and excursions laid on by the various nature reserves. One example is the Aiguilles Rouges reserve which offers thematic lectures every Thursday morning throughout July and August, with follow-up excursions in the afternoon. (For further details, see the **Geographical Breakdown** section on Haute-Savoie.) Students of geography or a science subject (with a reasonable knowledge of French and an interest in the natural world) can apply to spend two weeks of their summer vacation acting as a guide at the Aiguilles Rouges reserve. Training, board and lodging are provided if you apply well in advance, and this is a wonderful opportunity to discover a beautiful part of the Alps. Information is available from Jean Eyheralde, **Président de la Réserve des Aiguilles Rouges**, 101 rue de la Village, Argentière, 74400 Chamonix. True nature tourism has been developed in the village of Autrans, in the Vercors park, where François Meytras (Espace Loisirs, 38880 Autrans) will take you out (between mid-December and mid-April) for half-day, one-day, weekend or even nocturnal nature discovery expeditions, wearing snow-shoes.

Among inclusive winter holidays is 'Ski-Aventure', which covers snow-shoe walks and dog-sleigh rides as well as skiing. Information is available from **ADT 4 Montagnes**, 38250 Villard-de-Lans (Tel. 76 95 15 99). Snow-shoe, cross-country and alpine skiing holidays, in *gîtes, chambres d'hôte*, flats or hotels in Isère, are arranged by **Gîtes de France**, Maison du Tourisme, 14 rue de la République, BP 227, 38019 Grenoble (Tel. 76 44 42 28). These are also bookable through the French Government Tourist Office in London. A total of 125 short-break summer holidays (2 to 8 days) all over the Rhône-Alpes region are contained in the brochure 'Plaisirs à vivre en Rhône-Alpes' (available in English). Themes range from gastronomy, creativity and 'escape' to fishing, climbing and fitness; the brochure can be obtained from **Rhône-Alpes Tourism News**, 1 Place André Malraux, BP 297, 38016 Grenoble (Tel. 76 47 20 36). A selection of holidays (both summer and winter) of similarly wide variety, but on a smaller, friendlier scale, is offered by the **Service Loisirs-Accueil Savoie**, 24 bd de la Colonne, 73000 Chambéry (Tel. 79 85 01 09). More inclusive holidays with unusual themes such as astronomy, medicinal plants, ecology, photo-safaris and yoga, are listed by the **ADT Savoie** (same address as Service Loisirs-Accueil above) in their brochure 'Savoie Vacances Actives'. In Haute-Savoie, a booklet of all-inclusive packages is available from **Association Touristique**

Départementale Haute-Savoie Mont Blanc, 56 rue Sommeiller, BP 348, 74012 Annecy (Tel. 50 51 32 31).

Communications

How to Get There

International **airports** serving the area are Geneva-Cointrin (Tel. 22 99 31 11), which receives ten flights a day from London, five a week from Manchester, and has coach links to most resorts and towns in Savoy; and Lyon-Satolas (Tel. 72 22 72 21), which receives sixteen flights a week from London and has coach links (usually via Grenoble) to resorts and towns in Dauphiny. There is also a regular flight between the City of London airport and Chambéry-Aix-les-Bains (Tel. 79 54 46 05). If travelling via Paris, you could also choose to land at Grenoble-St-Geoirs (Tel. 76 05 71 33) or Annecy-Meythet airport (Tel. 50 22 02 41).

From Paris-Gare de Lyon, it is possible to take the high-speed TGV **train** direct to Grenoble (3 1/4 hrs) or to Annecy (3 3/4 hours). The TGV also serves Vienne, Aix-les-Bains, Chambéry, St-Gervais, Albertville and Bourg-St-Maurice. Normal express trains stop at numerous stations in the region, many of which have direct coach connections to resorts. If you are travelling up to the Alps from the Côte d'Azur in summer, be sure to use the *Alpazur* train which takes a scenic route from Nice, through Digne and Veynes, to Grenoble, Chambéry and Geneva.

Eurolines do a **coach** service from London to Grenoble, Chambéry, Annecy and Chamonix, costing around £83 adult return. If you wish to travel from Paris to Grenoble, or to 'do' the Tour du Mont Blanc circuit by coach, contact '**Europabus**', Gare St-Lazare, 17 rue d'Amsterdam, 75008 Paris (Tel. 42 70 56 00). By **car**, the journey from Paris to Grenoble or Chambéry takes just under 6 hours, if you use the A 6 motorway ('autoroute du soleil'), followed by the A 43. The former should be avoided at all costs in July and August.

When You're There

Rail – SNCF services within the Savoy and Dauphiny regions are good, though sometimes need to be supplemented with buses in steeper areas. If visiting Chamonix, train is, without doubt, the best option, as the views of the Chamonix valley beyond St-Gervais are spectacular. The train itself is also charmingly old-fashioned and, at some of the minor stations beyond Chamonix, you virtually have to flag it down like a bus! Other scenic routes include the Chemin de Fer de la Mure, 30 km of railway along gorges, overlooking rivers, round hair-pin bends, over viaducts and through mountain tunnels. The route, between St-George-de-Commiers and La Mure (near Grenoble) first opened in 1888 and trips (April–Oct) include commentary and photo-stops. Also near Grenoble is a 10 km steam-train run between La Rochette and Poncharra.

Bus – Geneva and Grenoble have regular coach connections with ski resorts and major towns. Local buses are a pleasant way to travel (most are coach quality), though allow plenty of time for journeys on winding mountain roads and bear in mind that the bus service in remoter areas will often not extend beyond about 6 p.m. Regular coach excursions in Haute-Savoie are offered by **Frossard**, 7 Place des Arts, BP 88, 74202 Thonon-les-Bains (Tel. 50 71 03 57). **Chamonix Bus**, Place de l'Eglise, 74400 Chamonix (Tel. 50 53 05 55) operates a comprehensive local bus service in the Chamonix valley, as well as summer excursions to places of interest in Haute-Savoie, Switzerland and Italy.

Car – the alpine environment is particularly sensitive to exhaust pollution so, if you can possibly avoid bringing your car, do. In summer and winter, the mountain roads get extremely crowded, so any motoring holiday to this region should be planned outside these periods. The quality of the mountain roads varies considerably, so be prepared to allow extra time even for relatively short distances.

Boat – there is no river tourism, as such, in Dauphiny and Savoy. Keen canoeists visiting Dauphiny could contact the **Comité Départemental de Canoë-Kayak**, 3 rue Moyrand, 38100 Grenoble (Tel. 76 62 80 56). There are regular cruises on Lake Geneva (known in French as Lac Léman), the Lac d'Annecy and the Lac du Bourget.

Cycling – bicycles can be hired from the SNCF stations at Aix-les-Bains, Annecy, Annemasse, Bourg-St-Maurice, Evian-les-Bains, Monestier-de-Clermont and Thonon-les-Bains. In Dauphiny, ask any tourist office for the 'Circuits Touristiques' brochure, which lists trips suitable for both cyclists and drivers. For further information, contact the **Comité Départemental du Cyclotourisme** (M. Jacques Fourna), Maison du Tourisme, 14 rue de la République, 38000 Grenoble. A challenge for really experienced cyclists is offered by the Route des Grands Cols Alpins, of 'Tour de France' fame.

Walking – facilities for both walking and cross-country skiing are excellent. The *Grande Randonnée* paths which cross the region include the GR 5, the GR 55 (through Vanoise national park), the GR 54, the GR 96, the GR 9 and the TMB or Tour du Mont Blanc, which requires 8 days and takes you through 3 different countries. Information on marked walking trails in Savoy is available from the **Association-Randonnée en Savoie**, 135 rue du Docteur-Juilliand, BP 705, 73000 Chambéry (Tel. 79 62 30 54). For information on both walking and cross-country skiing, contact **CIMES**, 7 rue Voltaire, 38000 Grenoble (Tel. 76 51 76 00). The development and promotion of cross-country skiing is the focus of **ADEPS**, ave Piétri, 38250 Villard-de-Lans (Tel. 76 95 15 89). Further details on walkers' maps, group or accompanied walks and mountain guide services can be found in the **Good Alternatives** section.

Riding – horseriding itineraries and other information are provided by the **Comité Départemental de Tourisme Equestre de l'Isère** (ARATE), Maison du Tourisme, 14 rue de la République, 38000 Grenoble (Tel. 76 54 34 36) – for Dauphiny; and the **Comité Départemental Savoie pour le Tourisme Equestre**, Maison des Sports, 6 montée Valérieux, 73000 Chambéry (Tel. 79 69 69 69) – for Savoy.

Useful Local Contacts

The number of groups with an interest in the environment is, not surprisingly, enormous. Many of them have their headquarters in the **Maison de la Nature et de l'Environnement (MNE)** in Grenoble. As over twenty organisations are based here, it is impossible to list them all, but the following deserve special mention: **FRAPNA**, MNE, 5 Place Bir Hakeim, 38000 Grenoble (Tel. 76 42 64 08) works on a wide range of environmental issues, organising campaigns and fund-raising activities, and is available to answer questions on the environment. **CORA – 'La Niverolle'** (Tel. 76 51 78 03 – address as above) is an ornithological group which offers information on bird-watching in the area and, together with FRAPNA, has produced lists of endangered animals and birds in the Isère *département* (along with the reasons **why** they are threatened). **Amis de la Terre** (Tel. 76 23 21 02 – address as above) is part of the French Friends of the Earth network. For a list of the other organisations, which include a group working on the development of environmentally responsible mountain activities, a youth education scheme and an anti-hunting lobby, write to the **MNE** itself. The address of Alp Action whose activities are described under **Level of Tourism** is **Alp Action**, Bellerive Foundation, PO Box 6, 1211 Geneva, Switzerland. Interesting ideas and projects for renewable energy production are explored by **ASDER**, 299 rue du Granier, 73230 St-Alban-Leysse (Tel. 79 85 88 50). The addresses of the region's national and regional parks are: **Parc National de la Vanoise**, 135 rue du Docteur-Julliand, BP 705, 73007 Chambéry (Tel. 79 62 30 54); **Parc National des Ecrins**, 7 rue du Colonel-Roux, 05000 Gap (Tel. 92 51 40 71); and **Parc Naturel Régional du Vercors**, Chemin des Fusillés, 38250 Lans-en-Vercors (Tel. 76 45 40 33). Detailed information on all 7 nature reserves in Haute-Savoie can be obtained from the **Division Protection de la Nature**, Direction Départementale de l'Agriculture et de la Forêt, Cité Administrative, rue Dupanloup, 74040 Annecy.

Geographical Breakdown of Region

Isère

In addition to a few famous ski resorts in the south-east of the *département*, Isère is home to the Vercors massif – stronghold of the Resistance, site of a regional park, and a cross-country skier's paradise; the Chartreuse massif – birthplace of the famous liqueur and the Carthusian order of monks; and a remarkable archaeological heritage, whose finest examples can be found in the north-west. Many unusual attractions are mentioned in the 'Promenades Insolites en Dauphiné' leaflet, available from tourist offices.

At **Beauvoir-en-Royans** in the Vercors, the Musée Delphinal presents the cultural, economic and human history of the Royans area (open late March – mid-October) At nearby **Chatte,** a pleasant hour or two could be spent at the Jardin Ferroviaire, a garden landscaped to represent scaled-down natural features, towns and villages, through which run thirty miniature trains. For home-produced cheese (including goat's cheese), try M. Girond at Le Maillet, **St-Appolinard** (Tel. 76 64 11 20). The abbey of **St-Antoine** is worth a visit; an Art and Music festival takes place there in May. M. Farconnet at Les Carrets, **St-Bonnet-de-Chavagne** (Tel. 76 38 41 15) sells mohair wool, straight from the mohair you can see grazing in the vicinity. Angora wool and jumpers are sold by M. Effantin at Les Fauries, **St-Lattier** (Tel. 76 64 59 74), and home-made honey by M. Gilet on the RN 92 into **St-Hilaire-du-Rosier** (Tel. 76 64 51 83). You can also buy St-Hilaire Kirsch from M. Revol, Les Guillots,

St-Hilaire-du-Rosier (Tel. 76 64 51 02 – meal-times only). All these people are small-scale producers whose enterprises are well worth supporting.

Pont-en-Royans is one of the highlights of the area, with its 'maisons suspendues'. The row of pastel-coloured houses hang above a rocky gorge cut by the Bourne river, supported only by wooden struts. Further along the Gorges de la Bourne are the **Grottes de Choranche**. This well-managed attraction within the regional park consists of a remarkable series of caves, discovered in 1875 and thought to extend some 20 kilometres into the mountainside. A guided tour of the first few caves reveals stalactites, stalagmites and other fascinating rock formations unequalled in Europe. There is an exhibition on the area's prehistory and plans for a museum and flint-cutting workshop. Paths starting from Choranche show the best of local natural and archaeological history and are covered in the booklet, 'Sentiers de Découverte de Choranche'. A peregrine falcon nests near the caves each year and a video-link is set up during the nesting season, so that visitors can actually watch the falcon rearing her chicks. Other videos on the natural history of the park can also be watched here, free of charge.

At **Corrençon**'s Syndicat d'Initiative there is a small exhibition and short video on the Réserve des Hauts-Plateaux du Vercors, the largest nature reserve in France, which extends southwards, covering the totally undeveloped terrain both sides of the Isère-Drôme border. In complete contrast is **Villard-de-Lans**, capital of the Vercors and the kind of place to come to if you're pining for trinket shops and such incongruities as 'Pub le Loch Ness'! What it **does** have to offer is the Maison du Patrimoine, a museum dedicated to the local area (known as 'Les 4 Montagnes') and put together from items donated by local families. **Autrans**, cross-country skiing centre and starting point of the sport's largest national competition 'La Foulée Blanche', also has a Maison des 4 Montagnes, with changing exhibitions on local traditions and natural history. The Galerie du Tramway in **Lans-en-Vercors** regularly displays work by local artists, and Mme Jacob, a wood-carver, is also based in Lans, at Le Petit Moulin. Information on the regional park can be obtained from the Maison du Parc on Chemin des Fusillés. More caves can be visited at **Sassenage**, where there is also a château. There are good views and an interesting chapel at **St-Nizier-du-Moucherotte**.

Vizille is where the events that sparked off the French Revolution started, and a museum devoted to this important phase of French history is housed in Vizille's bulky and austere Renaissance château, whose rose garden is also worth visiting. **St-Georges-de-Commiers** is the starting point for one of the most spectacular train rides in the Alps, which will take you to La Mure. If at all possible, however, make the detour to **Chichiliane**, from whose feudal castles you will see the abrupt outline of the square-topped **Mont-Aiguille**. At **La Mure** station is an exhibition commemorating the centenary of the little train from St-Georges (although the centenary year was 1988, the exhibition is still open at weekends between May and October). **Bourg d'Oisans** has a good museum of alpine minerals and fauna.

It is in this corner of the *département*, on the edge of the Ecrins national park, that you will find the well-known ski resorts of **Les Deux Alpes**, **L'Alpe d'Huez** and **Chamrousse**. The first two offer year-round skiing facilities. L'Alpe d'Huez also has, in addition to its Club Med, a Maison du Patrimoine and archaeological site. Further north, past the spa towns of **Uriage-les-Bains** and **Allevard-les-Bains**, is **Pontcharra**, starting point for a steam train ride to La Rochette, over the border in Savoie. At **Le Touvet** is a château whose park was converted into a 'water and greenery' garden in 1764. It includes an impressive water-stairs cascade but is only open on Saturday and Sunday afternoon. From Le Touvet, a 20-minute ascent by funicular railway takes you to a panoramic view-point on the Chartreuse massif. The monastery at **St-Pierre-de-Chartreuse** (built in 1084) is well worth seeing, though it is as well to arrive early if you want to miss the coach-loads. Although the monastery itself cannot be visited, you can wander round an excellent reproduction of it, which admirably recreates the atmosphere of the first ever Carthusian monastery. There is a good view-point, with museum and shop, at **La Correrie**. Do not miss the unusual church in the nearby village of **St-Hugues**, which is decorated by the artist Arcabas in a highly contemporary style. Free visits of the biggest liqueur cellar in the world are possible at **Voiron**, with a *dégustation* of Chartreuse at the end of the tour. Also at Voiron is the Mainssieux Museum of nineteenth- and early twentieth- century paintings. From **Charavines** there are boat trips on the Paladru lake; the village also has archaeology museums with displays of underwater finds.

There is a château at **Virieu** and a museum dedicated to the composer Berlioz in his home town, **La Côte-St-André**. Nearby are the Cherry-Rocher cellars and liqueur museum. **Ville-sous-Anjou** has a good natural history museum. **Vienne**, where there is a festival of sacred music in August, displays some remarkable Roman remains from 2000 years ago, including the Temple of Augustus and Livia and an impressive amphitheatre. A nursery of old varieties of fruit tree, vine and rose bush can be visited at Les Combes at **Estrablin**, beyond Pont-Evêque. Past the château at **Septème**, is the **Ville Nouvelle de l'Isle d'Abeau**. At the *ecomusée* here, you can discover all about trades and lifestyles in northern Dauphiny, past and present. You can also buy a guide to the nearby '**Domaine de la Terre**', where 65 buildings have been constructed out of raw earth, using various modern techniques. One of them, the Tour de Pisé, houses a museum. The medieval town of **Crémieu** and the Larina archaeological park at **Hières-sur-Amby** are also worth visiting.

Accommodation

First Class

Hostellerie le Marais-St-Jean, Chonas l'Amballan, 38121 Reventin-Vaugris (Tel. 74 58 83 28): 10 rooms in restored farmhouse among vineyards, just south of Vienne; restaurant.

Middle Range

Hostellerie Bouvarel, 38840 St-Hilaire-du-Rosier Gare (Tel. 76 64 50 87): 14 rooms in family hotel with swimming pool, at foot of Vercors mountains; restaurant with local specialities.

Economy

Hôtel Perazzi (formerly Familial Hôtel), 38680 Rencurel-en-Vercors (Tel. 76 38 97 68): 17 rooms in ideally situated house, built in style of region and owned by welcoming family – sauna and swimming pool; restaurant with home-made pastries and organic vegetables straight from garden. **Ma Petite Auberge**, Pajay, 38260 La Côte-St-André (Tel. 74 54 26 06): 7 rooms in charming, family-run hotel – unbeatable value; restaurant. **Mme Weber**, 38520 Ornan (Tel. 76 80 43 05): 4 *chambres d'hôte* in rustic grey-stone house on edge of Ecrins national park; *table d'hôte* – family cooking.

Eating Out

In addition to the restaurants above, try:

First Class / Middle Range

Auberge de l'Abbaye, rue Haute, 38160 St-Antoine (Tel. 76 36 42

83): gastronomic cuisine with regional emphasis, made from fresh local produce, served in characterful fourteenth-century building, overlooked by abbey.

Grenoble

Despite its spectactular situation, surrounded by mountains, Grenoble is actually one of the flattest towns in Europe. Its lively cosmopolitan atmosphere (due in part to its large university), and its wealth of interesting museums make it a good destination for a town-orientated holiday.

Grenoble is well-known in France for its excellent **Musée de Peinture et de Sculpture**, which contains works by Léger, Matisse, Picasso, Bonnard and many other household names. On the right bank of the River Isère, which is dominated by the **Fort de la Bastille**, you will find the **Eglise St-Laurent** in whose crypt is a rare Merovingian and Carolingian chapel, and the **Musée Dauphinois** which is housed in a former convent and devoted to regional arts and popular traditions. Rural poverty is sharply depicted and the well-presented exhibitions make it one of the best museums of its type. Back on the left bank, the impressive **Palais de Justice** overlooks the river. In the old quarter behind it, you will find the **Musée Stendhal,** housed in the former town hall and containing various memorabilia connected with the celebrated writer. The attractive **Eglise St-André** is thirteenth century. On the **Grande Rue**, which dates from Roman times, the **Maison Stendhal** (where the writer spent part of his childhood) can be visited; turning left down **rue J-J Rousseau**, a **Museum of the Resistance** has been installed in No. 14, actually in the apartment where Stendhal was born.

Other important sights are the spacious **Cathédrale Notre-Dame**; the seventeenth-century **Maison de Vaucanson** at 6 rue Chenoise, with its Italianate courtyard; the **Maison de la Nature et de l'Environnement** on Place Bir Hakeim, where there is always an exhibition on; and the **Natural History Museum**, behind which is the **Jardin des Plantes**, and, on the other side of Boulevard Jean Pain, the enormous **Parc Paul Mistral**. A little way outside the town centre are the **Sacré-Coeur Basilica** (opposite the railway station), and the **Centre National de l'Art Contemporain,** an impressive building called Le Magasin on Cours Berriat, created out of a disused factory, which now displays exhibitions of contemporary art.

Accommodation

First Class

Hôtel Chavant, Bresson, 38320 Eybens (Tel. 76 25 25 38 or 76 25 15 14): 8 rooms and 1 suite in beautifully decorated family-run hotel, in charming village 7 kilometres from Grenoble; restaurant with classical cuisine. **Manoir des Dauphins**, 48 cours de la Libération (Tel. 76 48 00 06): 10 rooms in gracious house, surrounded by trees; restaurant with thoughtful cooking, using fresh ingredients.

First Class / Middle Range

Hôtel Lesdiguières, 122 cours de la Libération (Tel. 76 96 55 36): 36 rooms in very comfortable hotel.

Economy

Hôtel le Globe, 38800 Pont-de-Claix (Tel. 76 98 05 25): 10 rooms in cosy, family-run hotel, a few kilometres outside Grenoble; restaurant with home cooking. **Hôtel Bellevue**, 1 rue de Belgrade (Tel. 76 46 69 34): 34 rooms in hotel with pleasant location, near river. **Hôtel Colbert**, 1 rue Colbert (Tel. 76 46 46 65): 12 spacious rooms in hotel near station.

Eating Out

First Class

Le Pommerois, 1 Place aux Herbes (Tel. 76 44 30 02): delicious, original cooking in elegant surroundings.

Middle Range

La Gambarde, 50 quai Xavier-Jouvin (Tel. 76 54 19 25): generous portions (specialities seafood and grilled meat), served in restaurant with cheerful rustic decor, near river. **Poularde Bressane**, 12 Place Paul Mistral (Tel. 76 87 08 90): highly-praised family-run restaurant (closed in August).

Middle Range / Economy

Le K'sdale, 33 ave Félix-Viallet (Tel. 76 87 14 76): fondue and raclette specialities. **La Panse**, 2 rue de la Paix (Tel. 76 54 09 54): traditional French cuisine – popular with local people.

Entertainments

The first thing to do in Grenoble is take a cable-car ride in one of the now famous bubble-like capsules, which start from the **Jardin de Ville** and take you up, across the river, to the **Fort de la Bastille**. From here, there is a splendid view of Grenoble and the surrounding mountains. There is an information point on local exhibitions and events at the **Centre National d'Art Contemporain**. The **Maison de la Culture**, just off ave M. Berthelot, is also helpful. There are various theatres in Grenoble: the Municipal Theatre, which overlooks the river, can be contacted on 76 54 03 08. On warm summer evenings, open-air theatre is performed in Place St-André. The **Maison de la Nature et de l'Environnement** (Place Bir Hakeim) is a hive of activity on Wednesday afternoons. There is an organic market in the garden and continuous projection of nature films inside, with free entry to all. Visits to Old Grenoble leave from Place St-André every Saturday at 10 a.m.

Useful Addresses

The **Tourist Office** is in the Maison du Tourisme, 14 rue de la République (Tel. 76 54 34 36). The **Post Office** is on bd Maréchal-Lyautey and the **Hospital** out in the suburb of La Tronche (Tel. 76 42 81 21). For emergency **medical assistance**, call SAMU on 76 42 42 42.

Transport Options

Grenoble boasts the largest pedestrianised street in Europe (ave Alsace-Lorraine) and a pleasantly traffic-free old town. There is a tram every 5 minutes, though the network is not as comprehensive as one might wish. Tram and bus timetables are available from the **TAG** counter in the Maison du Tourisme. The **Gare Routière** is next to the train station and has buses going to most of the surrounding towns and villages. Hiking information is available from **CIMES**, who have a branch in the Maison du Tourisme and at 7 rue Voltaire. There are trips around the old town by mini-train in summer.

Savoie

The lower, western part of the *département*, around Chambéry and the Lac du Bourget, is in sharp contrast to the mountains which dominate it, where the Vanoise national park and many of the most famous high-altitude ski resorts attempt to co-habit. Of the two great valleys which cut through the mountains, the Maurienne is less developed than the Tarentaise.

North of Aix-les-Bains, at **Albens,** the Savonnerie Artisanale de Savoie (Tel. 79 54 13 00) makes a wide variety of soaps from all-natural materials. **Aix-les-Bains** itself is best described as sedate. It has been a spa since Roman times and is now France's leading one, with 55,000 *curistes* a year. Its main attraction for those not taking the waters is the Musée Faure, a considerable collection of modern paintings, including many by top Impressionists. The archaeology museum is also worth a visit. A trip across the lake will take you to **Hautecombe Abbey** (1101), where many of the Dukes of Savoy are buried.

Chambéry, the present administrative capital of Savoie, was once capital of the Duchy of Savoy. The best view of the picturesque old quarter is from the castle, though you should also allow time for a stroll through the town. The Musée des Beaux-Arts has a fine collection of Italian paintings and the Musée Savoisien some interesting exhibits illustrating the regional trades and lifestyle. An antiques fair takes place here in May. Two kilometres outside Chambéry, you can visit the house in which Jean-Jacques Rousseau lived with Madame de Warens. Known as **Les Charmettes,** it was completely restored in 1978. To the west is **Lac Aiguebelette,** the smallest (and quietest) of the great Alpine Lakes; only non-motorised watersports are allowed here. In the Chartreuse massif, at **Entremont-le-Vieux,** a cooperative dairy can be visited and a little further on, at **St-Pierre-d'Entremont,** the Maison Intercommunale exhibits local arts and crafts. On the outskirts of Chambéry once again, the ASDER centre for renewable energy at 299 rue du Granier, **St-Alban-Leysse** is the only one in France to organise seminars for the public to instruct them how to equip their own houses with solar installations.

The town of **Montmélian** in the fertile Combe de Savoie valley is surrounded by vineyards, and the tourist office will supply information on the *Route des Vins*. In Montmélian itself, there are tours of the fort and old town. Near **St-Pierre-d'Albigny** is the Château de Miolans, a state prison from 1500 to 1792, which can now be visited; look out for the cooperative cheese dairy too. The eleventh- to fifteenth-century cathedral at **St-Jean-de-Maurienne** is worth a visit, as is the orchard created at **St-Jean-d'Arves** in order to save old varieties of fruit tree.

Valloire, a ski resort which also has good summer facilities, has an interesting gilded altarpiece in its seventeenth-century church. At **l'Orgère** (near Villarodin-Bourget), the chalet marks the edge of the Vanoise national park and the beginning of a good botanical path, as well as many other walking possibilities. The chalets at all the gateways to the park (Portes du Parc) house exhibitions and sales of local crafts. Throughout the area, authenticity of craftwork is assured by the 'Vanoise' label. The typical alpine village of **Aussois** provides an excellent alternative climbing centre for those who do not wish to add to the hordes at Chamonix. There is an alpine garden and history museum at the beautiful **Col du Mont-Cénis** (2083 m), but you will not be the only one there. **Bessans** used to be a centre of popular and religious art, some examples of which can be seen in its churches. The picturesque village of **Bonneval-sur-Arc** is a photographer's paradise, with its wooden roof-tiles, flowery balconies and surrounding meadows.

Leaving the Maurienne valley for the Tarentaise, you will come to resorts famed for their year-round skiing, such as **Tignes** and **Val d'Isère**. Not far away from the latter, at the edge of the national park, is the nature discovery path of **Le Fornet**. An exhibition of local crafts can be found at the Maison de l'Artisanat in **Séez**, with an orchard and dairy at **Bourg-St-Maurice**. The development at **Les Arcs** is extremely large-scale, with facilities for every activity, both summer and winter. The eleventh-century St-Martin Basilica at **Aime** is well worth visiting, and is in complete contrast to the 'new generation' year-round skiing resort at **La Plagne**, which is only twenty years old. There are guided visits to the cathedral and old town of **Moûtiers**, where the Académie de la Val d'Isère local history museum is interesting. A national park chalet (with craft exhibition) can be found just beyond Champagny-en-Vanoise, at **Le Bois**, where the nature discovery path is accessible to those in wheelchairs. The largest cable-car in the world, which has room for 160 people, is the one from **Courcheval** up to La Saulire. Perhaps appropriately, it is also here that the **3 Vallées** form the largest skiing area in the world. While here, decide for yourself if the new resort at **Valmorel** succeeds in integrating itself with its surroundings. It is also in this area that Alp Action's prototype reserve, **La Lauzière** (near **Celliers**), tries to combine top-class skiing facilities with conservation, and to encourage respect for nature among skiers. Near the 1992 olympic town of **Albertville** is the fortified medieval village of **Conflans**, with its fourteenth-century entrance gate and houses, and its sixteenth-century castle. At **Beaufort**, you can visit a cooperative cheese dairy where Beaufort cheese (known as the 'prince des gruyères') is produced. There is an *ecomusée* at **Hauteluce**, a charming onion-domed church at **St-Nicolas-la-Chapelle**, and, near **Ugine**, the Château de Crest-Cherel which contains a museum of ethnography.

Accommodation

First Class

L'Orée du Lac, La Croix Verte, 73370 Le Bourget-du-Lac (Tel. 79 25 24 19): 9 rooms and 3 apartments in harmoniously decorated château hotel, run by welcoming couple and overlooking Lac du Bourget; restaurant on request. **Hôtel Alba**, route du Belvédère, 73550 Méribel-les-Allues (Tel. 79 08 55 55): 25 rooms in one of the very few small-scale chalet hotels you will find in the 3 Vallées skiing area; restaurant offering genuine Savoyard cuisine.

Middle Range / Economy

Week-end Hôtel, rue du Colonel-Bachetta, 73420 Viviers-du-Lac (Tel. 79 54 40 22): 16 rooms in friendly family-run hotel in quiet surroundings by lake, 5 km from Aix-les-Bains; restaurant with simple, regional cuisine (many fish dishes).

Economy

M. Favre, Montchavin Bellentre, 73210 Aime (Tel. 79 07 83 25): 2 *chambres d'hôte* in charming stone house with wooden balconies, near Montchavin ski resort (includes cross-country skiing). **M. Bouchex**, 'Fountaine Barthoud', La Giettaz, 73590 Flumet (Tel. 79 32 92 17): 3 *chambres d'hôte* in chalet-type house, near La Giettaz ski resort; *table d'hôte* meals on request.

Eating Out

In addition to those restaurants recommended above, try the following for a special treat:

First Class

Le Bateau Ivre, 73370 Le Bourget-du-Lac (Tel. 79 25 02 66): original cuisine in 17th century salt-loft, half-way between Aix-les-Bains and Chambéry.

If buying fruit, look out for the 'Savoie' label, which means the fruit is a traditional Savoie variety grown locally.

Annecy

Annecy has all the ingredients of the perfect Alpine city. Mountains are reflected in its turquoise lake, which seems unnaturally pale but is in fact the cleanest lake in Europe. Flowers have been planted everywhere and swans swim on the river which flows past the narrow cobbled streets of the old town. Naturally, such a gem is no secret, and it pays more than ever to come off season (early October is usually still fine).

Annecy's most unusual attraction is its **Bell Museum**, situated at 3 chemin de l'Abbaye, which is the far side of avenue de France in the part of town known as **Annecy-le-Vieux** (not the same as the old town, which is called Le Vieil Annecy). The Bell Museum was founded by the Fonderie Paccard, which produced church bells for 200 years; among its creations is the bell known as 'La Savoyarde' in Montmartre's Sacré-Coeur bascilica. On avenue des Trésum, to the south of the main town, the **Conservatoire d'Art et de Histoire**, a seventeenth-century building in Sardinian style, contains a fine collection of paintings of Haute-Savoie mountain landscapes. Annecy's **château** overlooks the old town and contains a **regional museum**, somewhat eclectic in subject matter. Keen geologists should head straight for the top floor where there are interesting descriptions of the formation of the Alps. A room is also devoted to the nearby Roc de Chère and Bout du Lac d'Annecy nature reserves.

On an island in the river which passes through the old town is a twelfth century prison called the **Palais de l'Isle**. It now houses Annecy's **History Museum** and the prison cells can be visited as part of this. Other parts of the old town worth visiting are **Rue Perrière** and **Rue Ste-Claire**, with their arcaded houses; the former **Bishop's Palace** and the **Cathédrale St-Pierre**, with its Renaissance facade and Gothic interior; and the fifteenth-century **Eglise St-Maurice** and seventeenth-century **Eglise St-François**. The **Basilique de la**

Visitation is south of the château and offers a good view of Annecy. Relaxing lakeside walks can be taken in the **Jardin Public** and the **Parc du Paquier**.

Accommodation

First Class / Middle Range

Hôtel de l'Abbaye, chemin de l'Abbaye, Annecy-le-Vieux (Tel. 50 23 61 08): 11 rooms in pleasant little hotel with garden, away from town centre; excellent restaurant.

Middle Range

Palais de l'Isle, 13 rue Perrière (Tel. 50 45 86 87): 23 rooms in hotel in heart of old town, with restaurant. **Au Faisan Doré**, 34 ave d'Albigny (Tel. 50 23 02 46): 40 rooms in family run hotel; restaurant.

Middle Range / Economy

Auberge du Lyonnais, 9 rue de la République (Tel. 50 51 26 10): 9 rooms in family-run inn; excellent restaurant.

Economy

La Mascotte, 20 rue du Capitaine-Baud, Annecy-le-Vieux (Tel. 50 23 51 47): 14 rooms in family-run hotel with garden, away from town centre; restaurant. **Le Coin Fleuri**, 3 rue Filatière (Tel. 50 45 27 30): 14 rooms in family-run hotel.

Eating Out

First Class

Auberge de l'Eridan, 7 ave de Chavoires, Annecy-le-Vieux (Tel. 50 66 22 04): elegant restaurant with high-class original cuisine.

First Class / Middle Range

L'Amandier, 6 ave Mandaliaz (Tel. 50 51 74 50): excellent imaginative cuisine, including regional fixed-price menu.

Middle Range

Le Cordon Bleu, 12 rue Perrière (Tel. 50 45 51 76): small restaurant in heart of old town.

Middle Range / Economy

La Cave, 10 faubourg des Annonciades (Tel. 50 52 80 99): restaurant with Savoyard specialities.

Economy

Le Pichet, 13 rue Perrière (Tel. 50 45 32 41): *fondue savoyarde* and *raclette* specialities **Midi Pile**, 10 bis rue de la Poste (Tel. 50 45 08 10 or 50 52 82 33): restaurant with savoyard specialities; also serves snacks.

Entertainments

On Tuesday, Friday and Sunday mornings, a colourful market takes over the narrow cobbled streets of the old town (This is a perfect place for buying lunch – hot pastries and fresh fruit – to go and eat in the Jardin Publique). The **Centre Bonlieu** on Place de la Libération contains the theatre, library, shops, exhibition space and the tourist office. The latter will give information on local events (ask for the brochure 'Le Mois Annecy') and thematic visits of the old town and elsewhere. If you are in Annecy on the first Sunday in August, you will experience its annual high-point, the Lake Festival.

Useful Addresses

The **Tourist Office** is at 1 rue Jean-Jaurès (Centre Bonlieu – Tel. 50 45 00 33). The **Post Office** is on 4 rue des Glières, just off rue de la Poste. The **Hospital** is on ave des Trésums (Tel. 50 88 33 33) but for emergency **medical assistance** call SAMU on 50 51 21 21.

Transport Options

Town buses are run by **SIBRA** and a timetable is available from the tourist office or the kiosk on rue de la Préfecture. Two hour visits of the old town are organised by the tourist office; from 1 June to 30 Sept., visits in English start from the office at 2.30 p.m. on Tuesdays. The tourist office also supplies information on thematic visits and trips by horse and cart, as well as a list of beautiful walks in the surrounding area. There is a marked cycle trail round the lake and bikes can be hired from the train station or **Loca Sport**, 37 ave de Loverchy. Boat trips round the lake start from the various jetties off the Jardin Public, but the best bet is the **Compagnie des Bateaux à Vapeur**, 2 Place au Bois, whose cruises make regular photostops. Buses from the Gare Routière (next to the train station) will take you to various destinations on the shore of the lake, as well as further afield.

Haute-Savoie

The high-point of this extremely popular *département* and, in the most literal sense, of Europe itself, is Mont-Blanc. The Mont-Blanc massif, where few areas are completely free of ski-lifts, cable-cars and pistes, gives way first to rocky foothills, where the skiing facilities compete with traditional saw-mills and dairy farms, baroque churches and medieval castles, and then to the lowlands around Annecy and Lake Geneva.

A current Alp Action project centres around a valuable marsh belonging to the village of **St-Martin-Bellevue**, north-east of Annecy. An ancient pond is being revitalised in order to re-encourage aquatic plants and animals which used to thrive here; an overpass for visitors is planned. On rue Blanche in **Thônes** there is a museum of the local area and its history, and on the route d'Annecy out of Thônes, at **Les Aravis**, you can visit the local cheese cellars. The château at **Menthon-St-Bernard** has been inhabited by the same family ever since the eleventh century and its rich interior and library make it worth a visit (open every afternoon between 1 May and 30 September; Thursday Saturday and Sunday only the rest of the year). Archaeological digs and a museum can be visited on July and August afternoons at **Faverges**. One of Haute-Savoie's nature reserves is the Bout du Lac d'Annecy, near **Doussard**. A family of beavers now lives here and Alp Action has plans to restore the fourteenth-century Beauvivier watch-tower in order to create a public observatory. A museum of local history is housed in a seventeenth-century former school on rue Hauteville, **Rumilly** (open summer holidays only), and at **Marcellaz-Albanais** is the Musée de l'Enfance, which is one of the handful of European museums devoted wholly to the childhood environment, especially toys and books (open Sunday, Monday, Wednesday and Thursday afternoons, 1 April to 31 October). At **Sévrier**, a Bell Museum can be visited (all year except December; every day except Monday), and you can also see a foundry at work on weekends between June and September. In July and August, the Musée du Bois is open in **Seyssel**, where scale models by a master cabinetmaker are on display. Among the vineyards of **Frangy** is the Château de Clermont, a magnificent Renaissance building which contains collections of local pottery, sculpture, paintings and agricultural equipment. Popular arts and traditions are also the subject of the Musée Paysan at **Viuz-en-Sallaz**, near **St-Geoire**. Reconstructions of an alpine chalet and farm are among exhibits in the Fessy museum of regional art and folklore, south-east of **Douvaine**. The Musée du Lac at **Nernier**, right on Lake Geneva (*Lac Léman*), is also worth visiting.

On a headland in Lake Geneva is the medieval craft village of **Yvoire**. The garden of the château here is called the Labyrinthe aux Oiseaux, and part of it (the former kitchen garden) has been made into a Jardin des 5 sens (Garden of the five senses), which can be visited from May to October. At **Thonon-les-Bains**, the Château de Sonnaz houses a museum of the Chablais area, and there is also a fishing museum. The sixteenth-century castle at **Ripaille** has formal gardens, an arboretum and an old oak forest surrounding it. Inside is an exhibition about the Delta de la Dranse nature reserve, near **Publier**, where there are guided visits between May and September. At **Evian-les-Bains**, the Notre-Dame de Grâce church is impressive and there are trips round the water-bottling plant in summer. It is also a major starting point for boat trips on Lake Geneva (including one to Lausanne, on the Swiss side).

Away from the lake, on the Italian border, is the much-praised new ski resort of **Avoriaz**, whose architecture aims to reflect the surrounding landscape. At the Musée des Musiques Mécaniques in **Les Gets**, you will find one of the best European collections of music-boxes, gramophones and other music machines. Once a week, it is possible to visit the workshop where they are restored (contact M. Bouchet, Tel. 50 79 72 84). At **Samoëns**, the Jardin Alpin de la Jaysinia is a conservatory of rare alpine plants. The reception chalet for the Sixt-Fer à Cheval nature reserve is at **Fer à Cheval**. It is open from mid-June to mid-September and gives advice on exploring the reserve, which is on steep terrain and aims to present the fascinating relationship between man and the mountain. The chalet also hosts exhibitions, organises visits of the reserve (every Friday in July and August) and other thematic outings, runs a lecture series (Tuesday evenings in July and August), and maintains a discovery path at the Fond de la Combe. An *ecomusée* at **Sixt** also focuses on the reserve. The modern ski resort of **Flaine** is a car-free zone and boasts the highest golf course in Europe.

In the restored Château des Rubins, at **Sallanches** in the Chamonix valley, is the coordination centre for all the Haute-Savoie nature reserves. Open all year round, audio-visual effects make the visit like a mountain walk, where you can see Alpine forests, wetlands, rivers, pastures and geology. Alp Action is at present transferring the centre's 20,000 slides onto a videodisk, so that they may eventually be made available to the public in video form. Already 25,000 visitors a year come to the centre, which is computer-linked to all seven of the Haute-Savoie nature reserves and can answer almost any question you have concerning nature in the Alps. On the **Assy Plateau**, look out for the chapel which is decorated with paintings by modern artists including Léger, Matisse, Braque and Chagall. At **Mégève** is the local Musée du Val d'Arly, and **Passy** is home to the Plaine Joux nature reserve museum. The reserve itself is an area of cliffs and gorges, and the chalet at Plaine Joux will inform you of its thematic excursions and Thursday lectures.

The best way to travel between **St-Gervais** and Chamonix is by train; you will see some breathtaking scenery, marred only by the occasional corrugated iron building and the wide, but often congested, road beneath you. At **Les Contamines-Montjoie** is another nature reserve, which runs botanical excursions, lectures and exhibitions in summer, and slide shows in winter. There is a museum of the mountainside on Place de l'Eglise in **Les Houches**, and **Les Bossons** is the place to stop if you want to see an impressive glacier, within easy access of the village, yet remarkably uncrowded.

Chamonix itself is beautifully situated beneath Mont Blanc, but sadly spoilt by all the trappings of fame and fortune, including a restaurant complex built smack on top of the Mer de Glace glacier. Many people climb a little way up one of the Mont Blanc range, just for the sake of it; yet they are inevitably disappointed by the views. If you care more about the scenery than the prestige value of climbing Mont Blanc, it makes more sense to climb the Aiguilles Rouges, which are right opposite the more famous range and therefore offer spectacular views. Chamonix is the starting point for the Aiguille du Midi cable-car. It is also home to the Maison de la Montagne and the Musée Alpin, both on Place de l'Eglise. Information on the myriad sports which can be practised here is available from the tourist office. Further up the valley in **Argentière**, you can gain access to a virtually unvisited glacier, the Glacier d'Argentière. For exact details, ask at the chalet of the Aiguilles Rouges nature reserve, which is situated on the **Col des Montets**. The chalet, open from 1 June to mid-September, contains exhibitions including replicas of natural milieux, a library and a laboratory, where you can use the microscopes and other equipment under the guidance of the assistants. As well as recommending itineraries, the reserve runs guided visits on its discovery path, lectures and other excursions. Local ways of life are reflected in the Musée Vallorcin at **Vallorcine**.

Accommodation

First Class

Les Prés Fleuris sur Evian, route Départementale 24, 74500 Evian-les-Bains (Tel. 50 75 29 14): 12 rooms in calm hotel (with restaurant), surrounded by meadows and overlooking Lake Geneva; friendly welcome, but closed October to late May.

Hôtel de l'Abbaye, route du Port, 74290 Talloires (Tel. 50 60 77 33): 31 rooms and 2 apartments in former seventeenth-century abbey (with restaurant), which hosts exhibitions of regional paintings and classical music concerts in its cloisters, and overlooks Lake Annecy.

Middle Range

Hostellerie les Près du Rosay, 285 route du Rosay, 74700 Sallanches (Tel. 50 58 06 15): 15 rooms in Savoyard building, next to health centre; excellent gourmet restaurant.

Middle Range / Economy

Hôtel Restaurant le Jorat, Bogève, 74250 Viuz-en-Sallaz (Tel. 50 36 61 15): 12 rooms in tranquil green valley near Crépy vineyard; restaurant with seasonal specialities.

Economy

Mme Olianti, Chalet 'les Mazets', 210 Croix des Moussoux, 74400 Chamonix (Tel. 50 55 83 08): 4 *chambres d'hôte* in mountain chalet.
Mme Brissand, Résidence Bellevue, Argentière, 74400 Chamonix (Tel. 50 54 10 63): 6 *chambres d'hôte* in quiet village.

Eating Out

First Class

Auberge du Père Bise, route du Port, 74290 Talloires (Tel. 50 60 72 01): traditional family-run inn with lakeside garden, famed throughout the region for its excellent cuisine; also has 25 rooms and 9 suites.

Middle Range

Auberge Gourmande, 74140 Massongy Douvaine (Tel. 50 94 16 97): interesting cuisine served in elegantly decorated restaurant with open fire in winter and terrace in summer, situated near Crépy vineyards.

Economy

Auberge Rurale du Pralet, Chaumont, 74270 Frangy (Tel. 50 44 71 27): old-fashioned Savoyard cooking in rural inn near vineyards.

17 Provence – Alpes

Provence is often thought of as the idyllic summer holiday destination, conjuring up, as it does, visions of cloudless skies, ripe vegetables and smiling sun-brown people. The Alps, on the other hand, are considered the perfect place for a winter holiday, with their crisp snow, soaring peaks and international reputation. It is rarely made clear that the two areas are not only contiguous, but actually part of the same region.

Yet the 'Provence-Alpes' of this chapter are not necessarily those of popular myth. The term Provence is often used loosely as a synonym for the south of France, but its heart is, without doubt, in the small *département* of Vaucluse. Situated inland, to the east of the Rhône, the trappings of the Côte d'Azur are gone but the essence of Provence remains. The next-door *département*, the Alpes-de-Haute-Provence, has elements of both the Provençal and the Alpine; and finally, in the Hautes-Alpes, the Alpine emerges triumphant. But although these southern Alps offer what is arguably the most spectacular high mountain scenery in Europe, it is not here that you will find the famous international ski resorts – those are mainly in the northern Alps of the Savoy region. Instead, the countryside is relatively unspoilt and, though resorts exist, they are on nothing like the same scale. Much of the land even has national or regional park status.

Provence-Alpes offers more than its fair share of superlatives: the most important collection of Gallo-Roman remains in France, including the best-preserved archway; the most spectacular lime-stone gorge in Europe; a village whose pottery was good enough for Louis XIV at Versailles; the highest town in Europe (Briançon); the highest village in Europe (St-Véran); the highest garden in Europe (Jardin Alpin du Lautaret); and a mountain (the Barre des Ecrins) only 700 metres lower than Mont Blanc. The backdrop to all this magnificence is pleasantly low-key and rural, with no large cities at all. Instead you will find Provençal farmsteads, vineyards along the banks of the Rhône, and fertile plains used for market gardening. Lavender fields abound, and the scent mingles with that of numerous herbs to produce the classic smell of Provence. Festivals and country markets still flourish, and the region possesses a wealth of Christian art and architecture: from wrought-iron bell-towers and ancient statues of Christ to little roadside shrines. Fortified castles overlook villages which cling to the hillside. In the mountains, each community has its own architectural style according to the requirements of its geographical situation. Carving wooden furniture and toys is the speciality here: it used to be a hobby of shepherds on the long evenings when the sheep had come down from the pastures for winter, and now it is a welcome source of supplementary income. You will find particular hospitality among the mountain dwellers, especially once you have shown that you are prepared to respect their environment and adapt to their ways.

Tourism is important to the regional economy and this is reflected in the incredible range of locally arranged, low-impact excursions and holidays. The wide selection makes it virtually impossible to pick out one theme or activity. The answer to the dilemma may be to come in spring . . . The region's climate is so exceptional that, in April or May, you can enjoy a 'winter' break in the Hautes-Alpes, then transfer to the Vaucluse for your 'summer' holiday!

History

It was in the fifth century BC that the Celts began to settle in the foothills of the Alps; Hannibal crossed Provence and the Alps in 218 BC. By 14 BC the whole area belonged to the Roman Empire. The fourth and fifth centuries AD saw the spread of Christianity and the creation of bishoprics such as Digne, Riez and Sisteron, followed by the fall of the Roman Empire in AD 451. After this, the Franks annexed the area, only to lay waste to much of it in the eighth century. Finally, in 843, the Treaty of Verdun left Provence to King Lothaire, though the tenth and eleventh centuries saw it become first part of Burgundy, then part of the Holy Roman Empire. The Comté of Forcalquier was formed towards the end of the eleventh century, but had merged into the Comté of Provence by the middle of the thirteenth. Meanwhile many monastic communities had been founded in the Alps and upper Provence.

Charles of Anjou's government brought a certain stability to the region, but in 1274 the Comtat Venaissin (the area around Avignon) was ceded to the papacy. From 1316 to 1403, both popes and anti-popes took up residence at Avignon, which was bought by Clement VI from Queen Jeanne of Provence in 1348, and the town enjoyed considerable expansion. A crusade against Vaudois heretics in the alpine valleys took place at the end of the fifteenth century. In 1538, Charles Quint invaded Provence and, in 1539, French was decreed the region's administrative language. Conflicts between Catholics and Protestants worsened, until the Protestants finally obtained freedom of worship at the end of the sixteenth century. A century later, the Duke of Savoy invaded the southern Alps and, in 1707, Prince Eugène of Savoy penetrated Provence. The 1713 Treaty of Utrecht meant that France lost part of the Briançon area, but gained the Ubaye and the principality of Orange. The eighteenth century was a time of agricultural and commercial expansion. By 1791 the Comtat Venaissin was also annexed to France.

The nineteenth century brought attempts to re-establish the Provençal regional identity in all fields, but rural living standards declined. In the plains, the vines suffered disease, and mountain villages became virtually deserted as their inhabitants left for the rapidly industrialising towns. In 1933 the National Rhône Company was established, in order to harness the river. Battles took place in the Ubaye in the Second World War. The tapping of natural resources continued after the war, with the creation of the dam and reservoir at Serre-Ponçon, and of hydro-electric power stations on the Durance river in the 1950s and 1960s. The 1970s saw the foundation of several national and regional parks, and the development of agriculture and tourism.

Famous people from this region include various medieval troubadours; Pierre Gassendi, a seventeenth-century philosopher and priest from Champtercier; Jean Giono, a major novelist, famous for his Provençal settings, who died in 1970; and the distinguished Avignon archaeologist, Fernand Benoit.

Geography

The three *départements* described here as Provence-Alpes are situated in the south-east of France, just above the Côte d'Azur. They belong to the region known as Provence-Alpes-Côte d'Azur (sometimes abbreviated to PACA), but, from a tourist's point of view, they form a different type of destination to that of their coastal neighbours. The regional capital of PACA is down in Marseille. The smallest *département* of Provence-Alpes is the Vaucluse, whose capital is

Avignon (92,000 inhabitants); the Alpes-de-Haute-Provence has Digne-les-Bains as its capital (only 16,500); and the capital of the Hautes-Alpes is Gap (32,000).

Where it passes through the Vaucluse, the Rhône river has formed plains, known as the Combat Venaissin, which have been made extremely fertile by means of irrigation, and now constitute one of France's most important market-gardening areas. The Vaucluse is the top French producer of tomato conserves, melons, apples, grapes and cherries, and is also a prime source of fresh tomatoes, garlic, courgettes, onions, asparagus and pears. The market-garden plots are sheltered from the wind by cypress trees. It is along the Rhône above Avignon that the vineyards which produce the famous Côtes du Rhône wines grow. Further east, the Luberon and Ventoux mountains also offer the right soils and sites for vine growing. The limestone massif of Mont Ventoux rises out of the Comtat plain to a height of 1909 metres. Its summit is covered in fields of little white stones, but the rest is a good example of reforestation: in the early nineteenth century it was known as 'the peeled mountain' because man had cut down all its natural forests, but now it has considerable forest cover once again, which provides shelter for much wildlife. To the south, beneath the lavender fields and sheep pastures of the Vaucluse plateau, underground waters have formed interesting chasms, coming to the surface – dramatically – at Fontaine-de-Vaucluse. Further south still are the rugged Luberon hills, which belong to a regional park.

Three rivers (the Aigues, the Ouvèze and the Durance) flow down from the Alps, through Provence and into the Rhône. All three look mild enough in summer, but turn into torrents when there is heavy rain or melting snow: according to an eighteenth-century Provençal saying, 'the three curses of Provence are the Durance, the Mistral and Parliament'. Today, however, the Durance has been tamed and its force put to use in providing electricity. Its tributary, the Coulon, flows through the valley of Apt, where many fruit trees grow. Fruit is also a major crop of the plains on either side of the Durance, as it crosses the Alpes-de-Haute-Provence *département*. The southern border is marked by the River Verdon, with its spectacular limestone gorges. It is towards the north-east of the *département*, around Digne, that the Pre-Alps start. These mountains are rugged and vegetation is sparse. On the border with the Hautes-Alpes, parts of the Durance and Ubaye rivers have been made into the vast Serre-Ponçon reservoir, one of the largest in Europe. North and east of here, the mountains are higher, culminating in the northern tip of the Mercantour massif, which reaches over 3000 metres, and the Ecrins massif, whose highest peak is 4102 metres. Valleys cut through the mountains, and glaciers have left behind them turquoise lakes.

One traditional industry of the region is ochre quarrying near Apt. In the area around Moustiers-Ste-Marie, traditional lavender growing is threatened by the development of artificially synthesised lavender. A speciality of the Vaucluse is truffles, the much sought-after underground fungus which can fetch up to £300 a kilo!

The flora and the fauna of the region are extremely varied, ranging from the typically Mediterranean to the typically Alpine: lavender gives way to gentian, rosemary to edelweiss, thyme to cornflower, and olive trees to larches; the butterflies and lizards of Provence are replaced by the golden eagles, marmots and chamois of the Alps. There are two national parks with areas in the region: most of the Ecrins is in the Hautes-Alpes, and the northern part of the Mercantour is in the Alpes-de-Haute-Provence. The Ecrins national park is the largest in France, but is little known abroad, 10% of its area is occupied by glaciers, and the flora found there includes the 'Queen of the Alps', Alpine Mugwort and the Lady's Slipper Orchid. There is a long-term policy of trying to restore the park's fauna to the levels of primitive times, wherever appropriate, and the ibex was reintroduced in 1977. Tourism has brought greater prosperity to the region, stemming the exodus to towns. The same is true in the Queyras regional park (also in the Hautes-Alpes), which contains some of Europe's highest villages. The other regional park in the area is the Luberon, most of which is in the Vaucluse, though it overflows into the Alpes-de-Haute-Provence. Here, there are many remote walks, where you may come across rare fritillary butterflies or the largest European lizard, despite the fact that much of their *garrigue* (limestone moorland) habitat has been lost through coniferous afforestation. Projects of the park include the rescuing of old species of fruit tree and the protection of the beaver and birds of prey. One of the last refuges of the original European population of beavers is the River Durance. The Luberon also contains 28 sites of geological interest from the tertiary era, which show the remarkable flora and fauna of 35 million years ago. Near Digne, in the Alpes-de-Haute-Provence, a geological reserve has been created, where you can see, among other things, the skeleton of an Ichthyosaurus. Other protected sites include the Verdon gorges and Mont Ventoux.

Climate

The region's climate is predominantly Mediterranean, with hot, dry summers. There are usually about 90 days in the year designated 'hot' (average temperature above 25°C). In the Vaucluse, for example, the average temperature in July is 22°C, and in October it is 18°C. Autumn is a period of violent storms followed by days of brilliant sunshine. Spring tends to be somewhat cooler, with occasional heavy rain. It also brings with it the strong Mistral; this wind from the north-west only lasts a few days, but rushes down the Rhône Valley, reaching speeds of up to 250 kph at the summit of Mont Ventoux. Generally speaking, precipitation in the Vaucluse is around 65 cm a year, spread over about 87 days. The Alpes-de-Haute-Provence claims to have over 300 sunny days a year, and its spa town, Pra-Loup, has been officially designated a 'zone climatique', which means that it enjoys exceptionally fine weather. In the mountains, winter brings the ideal combination of deep snow, bright sunshine and blue sky.

Attractions

The principal attractions of Provence-Alpes are its scenery and climate, and the opportunities for enjoying these which range from gentle walks to climbing frozen waterfalls; along with its historical sites and well-preserved regional culture. The most famous sites are the Palace of the Popes in Avignon and the Roman monuments in the Vaucluse, particularly the theatre and triumphal arch of Orange, which have been designated a UNESCO World Heritage site. Between Avignon and Digne are numerous impressive churches, many of which have graceful arches, rose windows and worn stone carvings. To balance the high-profile attractions of Roman, Romanesque and Gothic architecture, are numerous simple rural buildings: squat Provençal farmsteads, known as *mas*; sheepfolds and pigeon houses; wells and fountains; bell-towers and wayside oratories. These are part of 'La France profonde', and offer a special insight into the region's past. Some traditional industries are still practised – lavender growing, bee-keeping, olive oil production – along with crafts like wood-carving and the making of *santons*, which are figures of clay and cloth, placed in Christmas cribs. People often visit Provence at Christmas time to experience the traditional celebrations, but there are local festivals and fairs throughout the year. Active appreciation of the area's natural beauty is often carried out on foot; there are many accompanied nature (or geology) walks, as well as cross-country and alpine skiing possibilities. The variety of sports which can be practised here seems limitless and includes ones which take you on the water, into the air or beneath the ground.

Cuisine

Many elements of the regional cuisine coincide with that of the Côte d'Azur – *pistou* vegetable soup, *aïoli* garlic mayonnaise, and ratatouille, for example – but others are more typical of inland or mountain cooking. Fish is used less, but there is more game, more lamb and a noticeable predeliction for truffles and other wild mushrooms in various forms. Anchovies and black olives are also used liberally. Typical *entrées* might include sausage from Sault, Ventoux truffles, asparagus from Lauris, and cured ham. Thrush pâté is also common, especially round Mont Ventoux. Among other game dishes are pheasant, hare and even chamois. Many main courses revolve around lamb (perhaps from Valréas or Sisteron) or mutton. Vegetables are often served imaginatively here, and mushroom-based dishes include scrambled egg and truffles, and truffles in a pastry shell. Artichokes, aubergines, courgettes, tomatoes and fennel are also common. In the mountains, most areas have their own special variety of home-made pasta. Cheeses include the tomme of Ubaye and many goat's milk cheeses, such as valréas, picodon and banon. There are plenty of sweet specialities, ranging from fruit tarts in the mountains, and fresh fruits (figs, melons, grapes, peaches, pears, apples, cherries, apricots and strawberries), to *papalines* from Avignon, and sweets made from honey, almonds or marzipan. The Apt region is the world capital for candied fruit.

The most famous regional wines are the Côtes du Rhône (especially Châteauneuf-du-Pape), but there are also good wines from the Ventoux and the Luberon, the Gigondas and the Vacqueyras. The Durance valley is the source of other red and rosé wines, and a pleasant sparkling wine comes from Pierrevert. For dessert wines, try the Muscat de Beaumes-de-Venise or the Grenache de Rasteau. Walnut and orange wine are also produced in the Alpes-de-Haute-Provence. Liqueurs are made from gentian, thyme and yarrow.

Level of Tourism

Statistics for the Provence-Alpes-Côte d'Azur region rarely distinguish between coastal and inland destinations. It is, however, safe to assume that, although PACA as a whole is the third most visited region in France, the three inland *départements* of Provence-Alpes receive far fewer visitors than those of the Côte d'Azur. Though there has been an explosion of short-stay holidays recently, most people still tend to come here for their main holiday, and around 34% of visitors are from abroad. Those from Britain tend to be in the 16 to 44 age range and come mainly for activity or sporting holidays, but they also show an interest in the environment, culture and heritage of the region. Gordes and villages in the Luberon hills are considered trendy sites for second homes and, although the influx of outsiders can lead to tensions, it has also served to revitalise areas which were rapidly becoming depressed.

Tourism-related problems are usually to do with the sheer volume of cars and/or people in individual places. One example is the Col du Lautaret. This narrow pass, in the Ecrins national park, is the site of the highest garden in Europe, where mountain plants from all round the world can be seen and where research is carried out. In summer it receives up to 3500 vehicles a day. By the late 1980s, this had taken its toll on the site, which was unable to cope with the volume of visitors and became thoroughly degraded. A recent project has, however, brought new facilities including better buildings, clearer signposting, discovery paths and audio-visual animations, and things are looking up. The Luberon regional park, in the Vaucluse, suffers regularly from forest fires, sometimes started through the carelessness of tourists. In order to lessen the risk of fire, and in the interests of nature protection and traditional activities such as truffle-hunting, much of the mountainous central sector is closed to cars in summer. This has the added advantage that ramblers can enjoy unusually peaceful walks. The Luberon park also favours the creation of special paths, so as to 'canalise' its visitors. The Queyras regional park has a central zone forbidden to motor vehicles too. It has considerable problems with the erosion of footpaths, but these are being tackled.

The area's parks do their best to protect not only the environmental heritage of the region, but also its architectural features. Numerous restoration projects are underway, for the most part concentrating on small-scale rural edifices, such as oil mills, pigeon houses, bread ovens, fountains, wells, washing places, belfries, shrines and chapels. One reason for this is to attract tourists. Many rural parts of the region are still suffering badly from the exodus of young people to towns, which inevitably deals a crushing blow to the local economy. In the Ecrins national park, tourism has, without doubt, brought greater prosperity to the inhabitants, but the real success story is the Queyras regional park. In 1957, floods destroyed many houses and the Queyras was in grave danger of dying. But the whole population pulled together so as to integrate tourism and agriculture, focusing on the 'pilot' village of Ceillac. In 1977, regional park status was granted and certain rules and priorities were established: dilapidated buildings were restored and the area underwent a general clean-up; no new building was allowed to be over nine metres high, or built outside existing villages; and tourism initiatives concentrated on nature discovery in summer and cross-country skiing in winter. The efforts paid off, and the population, which had been decreasing rapidly, actually grew by 21% between 1975 and 1982. The inhabitants are proud of their achievement and convinced that 'Le tourisme vert' has saved their valley from 'désertification'; visitors come to the area for its well-preserved countryside and for contact with the local population. And as the economy was becoming too reliant on tourism, the people are again concentrating on agriculture.

Good Alternatives

Meeting People

An unusual place to stay, where you can meet people and participate in working parties and courses, is the **Centre du Haut-St-Jean**, route de Pelleautier, 05000 Gap (Tel. 92 51 31 21). There are both rooms and camping facilities at this old farmhouse, which has an organic garden and bakes its own bread. Working parties tackling areas in need of conservation are organised by the **Conservatoire Régional du Patrimoine Naturel de Provence**, and the person to contact about them is Marte Busse, Ecomusée de St-Martin-de-Crau, 13310 St-Martin-de-Crau (Tel. 90 47 02 01). If you are interested in learning a typical Provençal sport or game, you could get in touch with M. Vial, 6 rue Pasteur, 05000 Gap (Tel. 92 51 03 46), who is in charge of the **Ligue de Provence de Pétanque et Jeu Provençal**. Exhibitions and courses about the everyday life of local people, which take place in an old priory, are arranged by the **Conservatoire du Patrimoine Ethnologique de la Haute-Provence**, Mane, 04300 Forcalquier (Tel. 92 75 19 93). In the Alpes-de-Haute-Provence, courses of crafts, including pottery, *santon* making, weaving, sculpture, stained-glass making and wooden-toy making, are offered by some local craftsmen. For information, contact either the **Chambre des Métiers des Alpes-de-Haute-Provence**, 23 allée des Fontainiers, 04000 Digne (Tel. 92 31 23 77), or the **Artisans des Alpes du Sud**, 135 rue Saunerie, 04200 Sisteron. The following organisations also offer courses: **Association Petit Pas**, Chaloux, Simiane-la-Rotonde, 04150 Banon (Tel. 92 76 29 13) – yoga, dance, climbing, horse-trekking, walking; **Le Château en Verdon**, St-Laurent-du-Verdon, 04480 Quinson (Tel. 92 74 50 14) – crafts and sport; and **Ecologie et Artisanat**, Ferme de la Thomassine, 04100 Manosque (Tel. 92 74 40 24) – organic agriculture. Other associations whose activities combine meeting local people with discovery of the region are treated below.

Discovering Places

If you are visiting the Vaucluse by car, a brochure for drivers, called 'A few selected excursions' can be obtained from the **Chambre de Tourisme du Vaucluse**, La Balance, Place Campana, BP 147, 84008 Avignon (Tel. 90 86 43 42). You could also ask for information on the 'wine roads', available from the **Comité Interprofessionel des Vins des Côtes du Rhône**, 41 cours Jean-Jaurès, 84000 Avignon (Tel. 90 86 47 09). The opportunities for those wishing to see the countryside in an active manner are almost limitless. Accompanied walks and thematic excursions are organised by the **Maison du Parc Naturel Régional du Luberon**, 1 Place Jean-Jaurès, 84400 Apt (Tel. 90 74 08 55).* For information on cross-country skiing in the lesser-known massifs of Ubaye, Haut-Verdon, Mercantour and the Digne Pre-Alps, contact the **Association Départementale des Relais et Itinéraires (ADRI)**, 19 rue de la Mairie, 04000 Digne (Tel. 92 31 07 01). ADRI also gives advice on hiking and publishes free brochures about guided walks and activity holidays: send an international reply coupon to **ADRI-CIMES**,

---

* A holiday entitled 'The forgotten paths of Luberon' is run by the park under the auspices of the Natural Parks Federation, and marketed by **Clés de France** (see **Introduction** p. 51). The 6-day walking circuit, during which your luggage is transported by mules, takes place in April, May and September and cost around 2800FF, including comfortable B&B accommodation.

Centre d'Information Montagne et Sentiers, 42 bd Victor-Hugo, 04000 Digne, and state whether you require the summer/autumn brochure or the spring/winter one. In July and August, geology courses of 1 to 5 days' duration are run by the **Centre de Géologie**, Quartier St-Benoit, 04000 Digne (Tel. 92 31 51 31), which also arranges trips combining either geology and hiking or geology and (advanced) riding.

The **Parc Naturel Régional du Queyras**, avenue de la Gare, BP 3, 05600 Guillestre (Tel. 92 45 06 23) organises ecological, wildlife and sporting excursions in many parts of the park, as well as guided botanical walks in the Réserve du Val d'Escreins. There is also a 6-day exploration of the park on foot and by mountain bike, called 'Around the highest village in Europe', approved by the Natural Parks Federation and marketed by **Clés de France** in Paris (see **Introduction** p. 51). The holiday is designed for individuals grouped together up to a maximum of twelve people, and the price of around 3300 FF includes full-board in charming 2-star hotels, transfer of luggage, mountain-bike-hire and the services of qualified local guides. For more information, contact either Clés de France or M. Kovacic, **Office de Promotion du Tourisme en Queyras**, 05170 Aiguilles (Tel. 92 46 76 18).

Information on adventure and activity holidays, which include climbing frozen waterfalls and excursions by dog-sleigh, is available from the **Comité Départemental de Tourisme des Hautes-Alpes**, 5ter rue Capitaine-de-Bresson, 05002 Gap (Tel. 92 53 62 00). Half and one-day rafting and hydrospeed excursions are organised by the **Association Verdon Animation Nature** (R. Verdegen), Le Couvert, 04360 Moustiers-Ste-Marie (Tel. 92 74 60 03). The **Centre d'Activités Pleine Nature**, La Colle-St-Michel, 04170 Thorame-Haute (Tel. 92 83 47 84), runs cross-country skiing, ski-trekking and dog-sleigh excursions in winter, and riding, archery and nature courses in the Mercantour national park in summer.

An excellent and comprehensive tour operator is '**Plein-Air-Nature**' (Brigitte Eckert), BP 129, 04000 Digne (Tel. 92 31 51 09), a non-profitmaking association, run by local people, which aims to 'develop the practice of activities in the heart of nature in the Alpes-de-Haute-Provence, through discovery and training courses'. Accommodation is either in tents or with local people in small farmhouses, where you can enjoy traditional food. The courses/holidays vary from 2 to 8 days in length, the number of participants is between 5 and 12, and the themes range from canoeing, potholing and walks focusing on literature, architecture, botany or gastronomy, to nature photography, astronomy, and the opportunity to meet local shepherds. Special holidays are arranged for youngsters between 8 and 17. **François and Sarah Couplan**, 5 rue Albert-de-Lapparent, 75007 Paris (Tel. (1) 47 83 38 01), do two unusual 5-day walking trips: the first, entitled 'Surviving out of Nature', involves taking the absolute minimum with you and searching for food; the second, 'Edible and Medicinal Weeds', provides the kind of practical information not available in books. The **Centre de Découverte de l'Espace Pastoral**, Les Deux Moulins, Gontard, 04300 Dauphin (Tel. 92 79 58 33), offers a trip which allows you to get to know the pastoral environment and alpine way of life. For more conventional tours, usually by coach, contact the regional operator **Alpes Azur Tourisme**, 7 ave Général-Leclerc, 04000 Digne (Tel. 92 32 18 36). A selection of short breaks throughout the PACA region, ranging from the sporting, healthy and ecological to the cultural and gastronomic, is contained in the '52 Activity Weekends' brochure, available from the **Comité Régional du Tourisme – PACA**, Immeuble CMCI, 2 rue Henri-Barbusse, 13241 Marseille (Tel. 91 39 38 00).

Communications

How to Get There

There is no international **airport** in the region itself, but Marseille (Tel. 42 89 09 74) and Nice (Tel. 93 72 30 30) airports are convenient for the southern part of Provence-Alpes. There are also coach connections from both of them to all ski resorts in the Alpes-de-Haute-Provence. Distance-wise, visitors to the Hautes-Alpes are better off using the smaller airport of Grenoble-St-Geoirs, though they will probably have to travel via Paris.

It is possible to take the high-speed TGV **train** as far as Grenoble, from where there are connections to Veyne, Gap, Embrun, L'Argentière-la-Bessée and Briançon. Orange and Avignon are both on the main line which runs from Mâcon and Lyon to the south.

By **car**, the journey time from Paris to Orange (via the A 6 and A 7) is something over 6½ hours; if you are travelling to Gap, it will take more than 7 hours (via the A 6, A 43, A 48 and N 85). Eurolines run a **coach** service from London to Serres, Sisteron and Digne, costing around £90 adult return.

When You're There

Rail – the main stations are those mentioned under **How to Get There**. Unfortunately, the east-west connections leave a lot to be desired: Manosque, for example, has to be approached either via Veynes (to the north), or Aix-en-Provence (to the south), despite the fact that it is due east of, and not far from, Avignon. This lack is, however, made up for by an efficient bus network. The Chemins de Fer de Provence run a steam-train service between Nice and Digne, and some trains which take you right up to Geneva. In summer, a steam train known as the Pine Cone express runs the scenic route between St-André-les-Alpes and Puget-Théniers.

Bus – good coach services criss-cross the region, with the main starting points at Grenoble, Avignon, Marseille and Nice. Other towns served regularly include Briançon, Orange, Vaison-la-Romaine, Châteauneuf-du-Pape, Fontaine-de-Vaucluse, Manosque, Digne, Castellane, Sisteron, Barcelonnette, Gréoux-les-Bains and Riez. In main towns like Avignon, coach services are often timetabled to suit train arrivals and departures. For coach tours in the area, try **Agence Alpazur**, 7 ave Général-Leclerc, 04000 Digne (Tel. 92 32 18 36).

Car – there is very little motorway in the region, the exceptions being the A 51 between Manosque and Sisteron, and a very short stretch of the busy A 7 ('autoroute du soleil') between Orange and Cavaillon. There is by no means a dense road network, partly due to the mountains, but some minor roads do allow for off-the-beaten track exploration.

Boat – for information on Rhône cruises, which can be joined at Avignon, contact **Naviginter**, 3 rue de l'Arbre Sec, 69001 Lyon (Tel. 78 27 78 02). Other cruises on the Rhône – some on barges – are organised by **Grands Bateaux de Provence**, Allée de l'Oulle, 84000 Avignon (Tel. 90 85 62 25). Boats can be rented from **Les Péniches du Pont d'Avignon**, Relais Nautique, 84000 Avignon (Tel. 90 32 49 58 or 90 70 07 37). Many lakes in the region have sailing and canoeing facilities. Information on canoeing in the Hautes-Alpes is available from the **Comité Départemental de Canoë-Kayak**, BP 21, 05200 Embrun.

Cycling – bicycles may be hired from the SNCF stations at Digne, Manosque, Sisteron, Embrun, Gap, Avignon, L'Isel-sur-la-Sorgue and Fontaine-de-Vaucluse. Cycle itineraries along country lanes between Cavaillon and Apt and tracks from Apt to St-Martin-de-Castillon are suggested by the Luberon regional park (address below). Other information about cycling in the Vaucluse is available from the **Comité Départemental de Cyclotourisme** (M. Gouttebaron), 2 rue Lavoisier, 84000 Avignon (Tel. 90 88 30 74). For details of 10 cycle rides in the Forcalquier district, contact **Hôtellerie Rurale de Haute-Provence** (M. Laurens), Président Hôtel St-Clair, 04230 St-Etienne-les-Orgues (Tel. 92 76 07 09). Other infomation can be obtained from the **Comité Départemental des Alpes-de-Haute-Provence** (M. Exubis), 'La Cassette', 22 ave St-Véran, 04000 Digne (Tel. 92 31 28 23). Cycling and mountain biking are both popular in the Queyras.

Walking – numerous GR paths cross the region, including the GR 4, GR 5, GR 6 and GR 9. General information on the area's hiking possibilities is available from the **Comité Régional de la Randonnée Pédestre**, 123 allée des Temps Perdus, 84300 Cavaillon (Tel. 90 71 26 05). Details on both hiking and cross-country skiing in the Alpes-de-Haute-Provence is supplied by **ADRI**, 9 rue de la Mairie, 04000 Digne (Tel. 92 31 07 01). A cross-country skiing interpretation path has recently been set up at Larche, in the Mercantour National Park.

Riding – the Vaucluse is a good horseriding area, with many farms offering rides. A leaflet called 'A Cheval dans le Vaucluse' is available from the **Comité Départemental du Tourisme**, Place Campana, BP 147, 84008 Avignon. Horse-drawn caravans can be hired from M. Moyne, 'Saint-Sauveur', 84320 Entraigues-sur-Sorgues (Tel. 90 83 16 26). In the Alpes-de-Haute-Provence, contact the **Comité Départemental d'Equitation** (M. Robert), Jausiers, 04400 Barcelonnette.

Useful Local Contacts

Various sites of ecological interest are managed by the **Conservatoire Régional du Patrimoine Naturel de Provence**, Ville-Vieille, Caussols, 06460 St-Vallier-de-Thiey (Tel. 93 09 29 95). Information on all the parks and protected areas in the region is available from the **Agence Régionale pour l'Environnement**, BP 17, 13320 Bouc Bel Air, or from the **DRAE**, 17 rue Thiers, 13100 Aix-en-Provence. The headquarters of the parks with areas in the Provence-Alpes region are: **Parc National des Ecrins** (administration), 7 rue Colonel Roux, BP 142, 05004 Gap (Tel. 92 51 40 71), or **Parc National des Ecrins** (information/documentation), Maison du Parc, 05290 Vallouise (Tel. 92 23 32 31); **Parc National du Mercantour**, 23 rue d'Italie, 06000 Nice (Tel. 93 87 86 10); **Parc Naturel Régional**

du Queyras, avenue de la Gare, BP 3, 05600 Guillestre (Tel. 92 45 06 23); and **Parc Naturel Régional du Luberon**, Maison du Parc, 1 Place Jean-Jaurès, 84400 Apt (Tel. 90 74 08 55).

Geographical Breakdown of Region

Avignon

This rampart-surrounded city on the bank of the Rhône was the seat of the Popes throughout the fourteenth century, but is probably more famous for its nursery-rhyme 'pont' and summertime Drama Festival.

The central attraction of Avignon is the sprawling white Gothic **Palais des Papes**. The papal palace looks almost like a military fortress, with buttressed towers rising straight out of the rock on which it is built. The part known as the **Old Palace** contains the consistory hall and chapel, both of which display fine frescoes; the banqueting hall, with spectacular eighteenth-century tapestries; St-Martial's Chapel (more frescoes); and the Pope's robing room and bedchamber. In the **New Palace** are the enormous Clementine Chapel and two audience chambers. Completely separate is the **Petit Palais**, which is situated at the other end of **Place du Palais**. This building was the seat of the bishopric in the fourteenth century, and now contains a labyrinth of art galleries, whose offerings range from Romanesque sculpture to Botticelli, but the sheer volume of work can make it slightly undigestible. Also on the Place du Palais is the **Cathédrale Notre-Dame-des-Doms**. This is a large Romanesque building with a rich Baroque interior, whose most interesting feature is its dome. Beyond the cathedral is the elegant **Rocher des Doms** Garden, which offers magnificent views over the Vaucluse. If you follow the Rhône downstream, you will come to the **Pont St-Bénézet**, which is the original 'Pont d'Avignon' – or **was** . . . Now only four of its twenty-two arches remain, the rest having been swept away by the swollen river back in the seventeenth century. There are good views across the Rhône from the town's ramparts. Wandering through the streets of Avignon, you will come across various town mansions (*hôtels*) of note, though there is no 'old town' as such. The most picturesque streets are probably **rue des Teinturiers, Rue des Lices** and **rue du Roi René**. At the end of the latter, the **St-Didier Church** is typical of the Provençal style of the fourteenth century. The **Eglise St-Pierre**, with its impressive Renaissance panels, is also worth a look.

Among museums to be visited is the **Calvet Museum**, which contains a collection of paintings, furniture and local prehistory. Next door, the **Requien Museum** is a good source of information on local natural history. The **Musée Lapidaire** contains some fascinating sculptures, and the **Palais du Roure** is now a museum of Provençal ethnology and archaeology. On the Place de l'Horloge, a spacious leafy square dominated by the town hall, exhibitions on the local area are displayed in the **Maison d'Exposition des Pays de Vaucluse**.

Accommodation

Most of the best hotels are situated outside the main town.

First Class

Les Frênes, avenue des Vertes-Rives, 84140 Avignon-Montfavet (Tel. 90 31 17 93): 14 rooms and 4 suites in nineteenth-century country mansion, 5 km from Avignon; restaurant with fresh produce and regional wines.

First Class/Middle Range

Hôtel les Agassins, Le Pigeonnier, route d'Avignon (RN 7), 84130 Avignon-Le Pontet (Tel. 90 32 42 91): 25 comfortable rooms in contemporary Latin-style décor, 1 km from town; restaurant with high-quality cuisine. **Auberge de Cassagne**, 450 allées de Cassagne, 84130 Avignon-Le Pontet (Tel. 90 31 04 18): 14 rooms and 2 suites in charming old Provençal house, 1 km from town; excellent restaurant.

Middle Range/Economy

Auberge de Bonpas, route de Cavaillon, 84140 Avignon-Montfavet (Tel. 90 23 07 64): 10 rooms in family-run hotel; restaurant.

Economy

Hôtel le Parc, 18 bis rue A-Perdiguier (Tel. 90 82 71 55).

During the festival, it is unwise not to book accommodation in advance. If you have not booked, try the **CEMEA** service, 8 rue Frédéric Mistral (Tel. 90 86 50 00).

Eating Out

First Class

Brunel, 46 rue de la Balance (Tel. 90 85 24 83): excellent regional cuisine, near Palais des Papes. **Hiély-Lucullus**, 5 rue de la République (Tel. 90 86 17 07): highly regarded cuisine in beautiful setting.

Middle Range

Le Petit Bedon, 70 rue Joseph-Vernet (Tel. 90 82 33 98): Provençal dishes using produce from local farmers; wines from small producers. **Le Muller's**, 81 ave d'Avignon, 84130 Avignon-Le Pontet (Tel. 90 31 02 75): imaginative cooking in friendly restaurant.

Economy

La Ferme St-Pierre, 1551 ave d'Avignon, 84140 Avignon-Montfavet (Tel. 90 87 12 86): regional, country dishes in old farmhouse, 5 km from town. **Le Pain Bis**, 6 rue Armand-de-Pontmartin (Tel. 90 86 46 77): mostly vegetarian dishes using all-organic ingredients.

Entertainments

Saturday is market day, with an antiques market on Place Crillon, a flower market on Place des Carmes and an organic market round Porte Magnanen. Sunday brings a flea market to Place des Carmes. There seems to be some kind of festival going on in Avignon throughout the year, but the famous Theatre and Dance Festival takes place in July and August, attracting over 250,000 visitors. Plays, dance, mime and music take over the streets, and cinemas show five or six different films each day. Programmes and information are available from **Maison Jean Vilar**, Hôtel de Crochans, 8 rue de Mons (Tel. 90 86 59 64). Avignon is a good destination for theatre-lovers the rest of the year as well – the town theatre is on Place de l'Horloge. **La Tache d'Encre**, 22 rue des Teinturiers, is a lively *café-théâtre*. At Christmas time, there is a living crèche at midnight mass.

Useful Addresses

The **Tourist Office** is at 41 cours Jean-Jaurès (Tel. 90 82 65 11), with a branch at the train station. The Vaucluse **Chamber of Tourism** is at La Balance, Place Campana (Tel. 90 86 43 42). The **Post Office** is on ave du Président-Kennedy. The two **Hospitals** are

Ste-Marthe, Porte St-Lazare, Tel 90 82 99 28 and Durance, 305 rue Raoul-Follereau (Tel. 90 89 91 31). For emergency **medical assistance**, dial 90 82 65 00.

Transport Options

In December, walking tours of the ramparts take place. Bicycles can be rented at the train station and from Cycles Peugeot, 19 rue Florence. Town buses are good, and services to surrounding areas excellent. Ask at the tourist office about the horse-drawn caravan and steam-train tours which leave from Avignon. Avignon pleasure harbour is often a stopping place for those heading south to the Mediterranean. The **Grands Bateaux de Provence** (Allée de l'Oulle) run cruises, and small boats can be hired from the **Locations Nautiques du Pont d'Avignon**.

Vaucluse

The *département* of the Vaucluse, described as the vegetable garden of France, represents the heart of Provence. The countryside's dominant colours are deep purples, oranges and greens. Its name comes from the Latin for 'closed valley', and the Vaucluse is bordered by the valleys of the Rhône, with accompanying vineyards, and the Durance; it is overlooked by Mont Ventoux.

The historic town of **Carpentras** has a cathedral typical of the southern Gothic style, the oldest synagogue in France (fifteenth century), and several museums of regional interest, including the Musée Comtadin. Towards the end of every November, a fair of crafts and agriculture takes place, as it has for over 460 years, and January, February and March bring the Truffle Market. The famous wine town of **Châteauneuf-du-Pape**, on the bank of the Rhône, also holds a festival, the Fête de la Veraison, on the first weekend in August. The changing of the grape colour from green to red is celebrated with an antiques fair and medieval craft market. Winegrowers' tools are displayed at the Musée du Père Anselme. Nearby **Orange** is certainly worth visiting. Its Roman Triumphal Arch, founded around 35 BC, is the best-preserved in France, with some interesting bas-reliefs, and its first century theatre is also in remarkable condition, hosting various concerts and operas each summer. Near **Bollène**, where a Provençal festival is held in September, you will find the remains of the ancient town of Aeria and a village which was still inhabited by cave-dwellers at the beginning of this century. **Valréas** is extremely picturesque, with covered passages in the old town and the eighteenth-century Château de Simiane, now the town hall, where there is an art exhibition in summer.

The Roman ruins of **Vaison-la-Romaine** are very impressive, and understanding is enhanced by a visit to the archaeology museum. If you are in the area at Christmas, try to go to the Nativity Pageant at **Séguret**, and look out for the church's wrought-iron bell-tower if passing through **Gigondas**. The other side of the attractive Dentelles de Montmirail mountains ('dentelles' means lace), at **Caromb**, there is a museum of old tools and a wine festival in August. Make sure you explore **Mont Ventoux** (**not** when the Mistral is blowing though). It offers spectacular views over the region, numerous walks, and a couple of small ski resorts with cross-country skiing facilities.

Down at **Apt** are the headquarters of the Luberon regional park. The Maison du Parc, at 1 Place Jean-Jaurès, is a reception centre with exhibitions, slide shows, tasting and sales of local wines and produce, and a Fossil Museum. The area is geologically fascinating and Apt is a good starting point for walks. Every Saturday, a colourful market takes over the town: look out for Jean-Luc's organic vegetable stall and Marianne and Didier's home-produced goat's cheese. The Salon des Santonniers, where the clay crib-figures known as *santons* are made and sold, is worth a visit in December. The regional industry is ochre-mining, and you can see amazing red ochre cliffs at **Rustrel**. Near **Viens** are the Sentiers des Bories; two signposted trails lead visitors to these ancient dry stone dwelling places of unknown origin. Local archaeological finds, fossils and traditional tools can be seen at the Musée Marc Deydier at **Cucuron**, the other side of the Grand Luberon mountain. The Sunday morning country market at **St-Martin-de-la-Brasque** is worth a visit. Another park reception centre is at **La Tour d'Aigues**, where museums of local history and earthenware are housed in the interesting Renaissance château. There is a museum of basket-making at **Cadenet**, and a Provençal villa-style château at the attractive village of **Lourmarin**. If you take the **Combe de Lourmarin** through the surrounding holm oak scrub, you will come to **Buoux** fort and rock dwellings.

At nearby **Bonnieux**, the history of breadmaking is told in an interesting manner at the Musée de la Boulangerie. This is also the starting point for the cedar forest botanical path, where huge Atlas cedars dating from 1860 can be seen. Another discovery path, this time focusing on local agriculture, starts from **Goult**. At the craft village of **Roussillon** begins the Ochre Trail; this

45-minute walk points out the geology and ecology associated with the orange ochre cliffs of the area. The up-market village of **Gordes**, where many town-dwellers have second homes, has an interesting stained-glass museum and an olive oil mill, where the history of the industry is explained. There are a large number of stone huts (*bories*) in the vicinity and many have been restored to create a rural habitat museum, called the Village des Bories. The nearby Cistercian Abbey at **Sénanque** is a popular attraction. At **Fontaine-de-Vaucluse** there is a Museum of Santons and Provençal Traditions. Various underground streams come to the surface here, making for interesting geological effects. The Thouzon caves, near **Le Thor**, can be visited every day from Easter to late October (and Sunday afternoons the rest of the year).

Accommodation

First Class

Mas de Garrigon, rue de Saint-Saturnin d'Apt, Roussillon, 84220 Gordes (Tel. 90 05 63 22): 8 rooms in modern building of traditional style; friendly atmosphere, but young children not accepted; restaurant.

First Class / Middle Range

La Table du Comtat, Séguret-Village, 84110 Vaison-la-Romaine (Tel. 90 46 91 49): 8 rooms in welcoming hotel in medieval village; restaurant with imaginative use of local produce and wonderful view.

Middle Range

Mas des Capelans, RN 100, 84580 Oppède (Tel. 90 76 99 04): 9 rooms in old Provençal farmhouse surrounded by vineyards; restaurant with family cooking – reservation essential, **Hostellerie les Florets**, route des Dentelles, 84190 Gigondas (Tel. 90 65 85 01): 15 rooms in calm location; restaurant with local cuisine and wines from family's own vineyard.

Economy

Relais de Roquefure, Près le Chêne, 84400 Apt (Tel. 90 74 22 80): 16 rooms in family-run hotel; restaurant. **Hôtel du Parc**, Les Bourgades, Fontaine-de-Vaucluse, 84800 L'Isle-sur-Sorgue (Tel. 90 20 31 57): 12 rooms in family-run hotel with restaurant.

Eating Out

In addition to the restaurants mentioned above, the following are recommended:

Middle Range

Restaurant le Relais, route d'Orange, 84290 Ste-Cécile-les-Vignes (Tel. 90 30 84 39): quality cuisine – reservation advised. **Hôtel-Restaurant le Mirvy**, route de Manosque, 84240 La Bastide-des-Jourdans (Tel. 90 77 83 23): local produce including game and truffles; 10 rooms available. **Hôtel des Voyageurs**, 84490 St-Saturnin-d'Apt (Tel. 90 75 42 08): finalist in Logis de France regional cuisine competition 1989/90; also has 14 rooms.

Alpes-de-Haute-Provence

In many ways, this *département* offers the best of all worlds. It has a remarkable climate and an unspoilt range of mountains, rising to a height of 3412 metres; in its villages, you will find traditional architecture, crafts and hospitality; and the herbal scents of Provence seem to linger everywhere.

On the border of the Luberon regional park, near **Céreste**, is the attractive Carluc Priory. The village of **Simiane-le-Rotonde** is known for the unusual circular keep of its medieval castle, and for its classical concerts. Those with more contemporary interests will want to visit **St-Michel-l'Observatoire**, where the observatory belonging to the national centre for scientific research is open to the public. It is worth passing through the pretty village of **Dauphin** and, perhaps, visiting its Centre de Découverte de l'Espace Pastoral on your way to **Mane** and **Forcalquier**. Mane was fortified by Vauban and, at the nearby Salagon Priory, there is an 'Ethnological Conservatory' which holds exhibitions and courses on the local everyday life. Forcalquier itself has an impressive cathedral and convent, and hosts a Festival of Haute-Provence in the first half of August. If you are in **Oraison** in December or January, make an appointment to visit the family-run olive oil mill: Moulin à l'huile Paschetta, 6 ave Charles-Richaud (Tel. 92 78 61 02). **Volx** specialises in making *santon* figurines, modelled and hand-painted to represent the inhabitants and tradesmen of a typical Provençal village at worship.

The fortified town of **Manosque** also makes *santons*, and its narrow alleys are steeped in history, overlooked by Renaissance houses, twelfth-century gates and wrought-iron bell-towers. The little spa town of **Gréoux-les-Bains** has a château founded by the Knights Templar and, in a Templar tower, at nearby **St-Martin-de-Brômes**, there is an interesting Gallo-Roman museum. The **Valensole** plateau is the site of many lavender plantations and distilleries, which can usually be visited if you ask the person in charge. The lavender fields are at their best in July. On the Route de Manosque, coming in to Valensole, is a Bee Museum and shop, run by bee-keeper André Nevière. Look out for the church's elaborate bell-tower, and make sure you attend one of the *santon* fairs if you are there in late July or early August. The pretty village of **Riez** has several interesting museums: the Musée Lapidaire, which contains Gallo-Roman remains; the 'Nature en Provence' museum; and a Bee Museum at Miellerie de la Ferrage. **Moustiers-la-Marie** has a strong pottery-making tradition and it was from the craftsmen here that Louis XIV ordered the dinner service for Versailles. The history of Moustiers pottery is explained in the Musée de la Faïence. Sailing and other watersports can be practised in a spectacular setting, just below the most beautiful limestone gorge in Europe, on the lakes of the **Verdon**. It is worth looking out for the Notre-Dame de Roc church and the seven-sided tower at **Castellane**, and the Vauban citadel at **Entrevaux**. Beyond the attractive village of **Annot** are **Senez** Cathedral and a fossil museum at **Barrême**.

The administrative capital of the *département* is the spa town of **Digne-les-Bains** (usually referred to simply as Digne). The town is quite touristy in a sleepy sort of way, with tree-lined boulevards and street cafés. The Notre-Dame du Bourg church is worth a visit, along with the Second World War museum and the Geological Reserve at St-Benoit, with its exhibitions and 'Ichthyosaurus Path'. In mid-December there is a *santon* fair at **Champtercier**. The **Rochers des Mées** rock formations, on the bank of the River Durance, are impressive, and at **Peyruis**, you can visit a family-run olive oil mill in December and January (call the Moulin à l'huile Dumardaric on 92 68 04 12 first). Some say that the fortified town of **Sisteron** is the northernmost point of the true Provence. In July and August, concerts are performed at its citadel, which offers spectacular views over the Durance.

Seyne-les-Alpes was also fortified by Vauban and is a village ski resort in an area reminiscent of Switzerland. The winding road south from **Pra-Loup** (a town famous for its excellent climate) will take you to **Allos**. Here, there is a visitor centre belonging to the Mercantour national park, a pleasant, bright blue lake, and a path which allows you to explore the mountainside, offering possibilities of seeing marmots and curiously twisted larch trees. It is worth continuing down the road to see the Fort-de-France at **Colmars**. Back at **Barcelonnette** is another visitor centre for the Mercantour Park, as well as opportunities for skiing and discovery of the local flora. The town has associations with Mexico, as many of its inhabitants emigrated there as pioneers. A 'Museum of the Valley' is situated on ave de la Libération, and a Craft Centre on rue Traversière. There are village cross-country ski centres at **Jausiers**, **Ste-Anne-à-Condamine**, **Larche**, where there is an interesting interpretation path, and **St-Paul-sur-Ubaye**, which has a museum of agricultural techniques.

Accommodation

For a list of rural hotels, contact the **Association de l'Hôtellerie Rurale de Haute-Provence**, Chambre de Commerce et d'Industrie, 60 bd Gassendi, 04000 Digne (Tel. 92 31 03 14).

First Class

Hostellerie de la Fuste, La Fuste, 04210 Valensole (Tel. 92 72 05 95): 10 rooms and 2 suites in old Provençal villa in park; fabulous restaurant using local ingredients.

First Class / Middle Range

La Bonne Etape, Chemin du Lac, 04160 Château-Arnoux (Tel. 92 64 00 09): 12 rooms and 6 suites in traditional coaching inn; excellent restaurant with imaginative use of freshest produce.

Middle Range

Hôtel Mistre, 65 bd Gassendi, 04000 Digne (Tel. 92 31 00 16): 19 attractive rooms in central family-run hotel; restaurant with local specialities.

Economy

Hôtel Central, 26 bd Gassendi, 04000 Digne (Tel. 93 31 31 91): 22 rooms in nineteenth-century town house. **Hôtel la Chaumière**, 04140 Seyne-les-Alpes (Tel. 92 35 00 48): 10 rooms in family-run hotel; restaurant.

Eating Out

The hotel-restaurants mentioned above are recommended. A list of restaurants serving local dishes is available from the **UDOTSI**, Rond-Point du 11 Novembre, 04000 Digne (Tel. 92 31 29 26). Particularly good is the *Middle Range* restaurant, **Auberge de Reillane**, Le Pigeonnier, route de Céreste (D 214), 04110 Reillane (Tel. 92 76 45 95), which serves regional dishes using local ingredients.

Briançon

The small town of Briançon (12,000 inhabitants), in the Hautes-Alpes, is the highest one in Europe, situated in a strategic position, at the crossroads of four valleys. Fortifications make parts of it rather austere, but the views are breathtaking.

The old town, which is situated above the newer quarters, dates mainly from the early eighteenth century when Vauban was commissioned to fortify it. There is an excellent view from the **Champ de Mars**. Access to the Ville Haute is through four gates. At one of them, the **Porte Pignerol**, there is an exhibition on Vauban; it also houses the tourist office. The simple fortified church of **Notre-Dame**, whose interior is more richly decorated, is another reminder of Vauban's influence. The upper town is divided by the steeply sloping streets known as the **Grand Gargouille** and **Petite Gargouille**, down the middle of which run streams, originally used for dousing fires. Picturesque houses line both streets, which are linked by the colourful **Place d'Armes**. The **Asfeld Bridge** over the Durance is impressive. Ask at the tourist office about the organised visits of Vauban's **Citadel**. Archeological finds are on display in the **Musée des Cordeliers**, along with fifteenth- and sixteenth-century frescoes.

Accommodation & Eating Out

Despite the popularity of Briançon with tourists, especially in July and August, there are no small-scale first class hotels.

Middle Range

Hôtel Cristol, 6 route d'Italie (Tel. 92 20 20 11): 18 rooms in family-run hotel; restaurant. **Le Vauban**, 13 ave Général-de-Gaulle

(Tel. 92 21 12 11): 44 comfortable rooms in hotel with restaurant and garden, near Durance river.

Middle Range / Economy

Auberge le Mont-Prorel, 5 rue René-Froger (Tel. 92 20 22 88): 18 rooms in family-run chalet hotel; good restaurant. **Le Lièvre Blanc**, rte de Grenoble, 05240 Villeneuve-la-Salle (Tel. 92 24 74 05): 26 rooms in family hotel with mountain guide proprietor, in pretty village 6 km from Briançon; good restaurant with generous portions.

Economy

Hôtel de la Chaussée, 4 rue Centrale (Tel. 92 21 10 37): 21 rooms in family-run hotel; restaurant. **Hôtel Paris**, 41 ave Général-de-Gaulle (Tel. 92 20 15 30): 22 rooms in hotel convenient for station; restaurant.

Entertainments

Information on current events is available from the tourist office and from the Cultural Centre on ave de la République. A music festival on the theme of 'Art and Mountains' takes place in the first fortnight of July, and, from mid-July to mid-August, theatrical *Son et Lumière* performances occur. Other entertainment is of the fresh-air variety, with skiing and walking coming top of the list, followed by numerous other sporting possibilities.

Useful Addresses

The **Tourist Office** is at Porte de Pignerol, BP 48, 05100 Briançon (Tel. 92 21 08 50). The **Post Office** is on route d'Italie. An information centre dealing with the Briançonnais sector of the **Ecrins National Park** is at Villa Belledonne, 35 bd du Lautaret, 05100 Briançon (Tel. 92 21 08 49).

Transport Options

The town itself can easily be explored on foot, but shuttle buses between the railway station and skiing areas are regular. There are 200 km of ski runs and a range of cross-country skiing possibilities. Snow-shoe excursions are also organised. All year round, Briançon makes a good base for numerous short but spectacular walks: to the Fort des Salettes, Croix de Toulouse and Puy St-André, for example.

Haute-Alpes

In this *département*, you can discover the natural riches and incredible scenery of various protected areas, and experience some of the smaller ski centres of the Alps. Cross-country skiing is possible from December to May and resorts are divided into the following categories by the tourist board: Nordic Spaces, Natural Valleys, Village Resorts and Mixed Ski Resorts. Generally speaking, resorts in the first three categories, situated on the Queyras and Champsaur massifs are likely to be less developed and more authentic – and staying at one of these outside the winter sports season will help the economy of villages desperate to attract a year-round clientèle.

In the **Champsaur** area, you can visit the little cheese museum known as the Laiterie du Col Bayard at **Laye**; the Rural Museum of the Haut-Champsaur at St-Jean-St-Nicolas, **Chabottes**; and the 'La Casse' Rural Museum at Prapic, **Orcières**. Nearby **Gap** is the capital of the Hautes-Alpes. It has some pretty medieval streets, most of which are pedestrianised; a cathedral built with different coloured stones from the surrounding region; an eighteenth-century town hall; and a departmental museum, whose main collections are local archaeology and pottery. In July, festivals of music and drama take place. Gap is a good base for walks and excursions. Further south, at **Tallard**, there is a fourteenth-century castle, which hosts a festival of old music in July and August, and where a museum on the Maltese Knights is planned. The enormous artificial lake of **Serre-Ponçon** offers comprehensive watersports facilities. At **Embrun** there is a cathedral reminiscent of that in Gap; the town is also a centre for regular guided walks.

Montdauphin is a village fortified by Vauban, with an impressive citadel and arsenal. Concerts are held here in summer. At **Guillestre**, on avenue de la Gare, are the headquarters of the Queyras regional park, where information on the surrounding area can be obtained. The road which follows the course of the River Guil is spectacular, especially in autumn. **Ceillac** is a village ski resort and the 'pilot' village of the park. It has a lot of character, and several farmhouses with inner courtyards. At Château-Queyras, there is a medieval fortress, and a crypt dedicated to the geology of the area, where audio-visual techniques are used to show how the Alps were created. At nearby **Château-Ville-Vieille**, you will find a craft and local produce centre. The village resort of **St-Véran** (1990 to 2040 metres) is the highest village in Europe. Most houses are eighteenth-century chalets made of larch trunks and have attractive balconies. A craft centre is situated in the village resort of **Aiguilles, Vallouise** is where you will find the information centre for the Ecrins national park; it also holds a large pottery market in August. If you walk to **Tête Noire**, you will see flora and fauna dating from the Ice Age. The highest European garden is near **Le Monêtier-les-Bains**, at **Col du Lautaret**. Here, at 2100 metres, many high natural milieux have been recreated and over 2000 mountain species can be seen in 60 rock gardens, criss-crossed by streams, ponds and waterfalls. The garden is open only between late June and early September. Mid-August brings the festival of bread and mountains to nearby **Villars-d'Arène**.

Accommodation

Middle Range

Hôtel les Châlets du Villard, Le Villard, 05350 St-Véran (Tel. 92 45 82 08): 26 rooms in ideally situated chalets; restaurant. **Auberge du Choucas**, 17 rue de la Fruitière, 05220 Monêtier-les-Bains (Tel. 92 24 42 73): 13 rooms in old Alpine farmhouse; half-board preferred; restaurant.

Economy

Hôtel Fons-Regina, Quartier de Fontreyne, 05000 Gap (Tel. 92 53 98 99): 21 rooms in family-run hotel; restaurant.

Eating Out

In addition to the restaurants above, the following are recommended:

Middle Range

Manoir de Malcombe, route de Veynes, 05000 Gap (Tel. 92 53 78 76): inventive cuisine in eighteenth-century manor house. **Relais de la Poste**, 35 rue Berthelot, 05400 Veynes (Tel. 92 57 22 25): prize for the promotion of regional cuisine in 1988/89 Logis de France competition; 12 rooms available.

18 Côte d'Azur

Mention the Côte d'Azur and you are almost bound to provoke some response. This can vary from appreciative murmurings about the perfect climate, palm-fringed beaches, blue sea and beautiful people, to sceptical remarks concerning concrete monstrosities, pollution of the Mediterranean, inflated prices and unbearable crowds. Of course, neither attitude is wholly justified. The Côte d'Azur exhibits elements of both, but to see it **only** in terms of the above criteria is to miss around 90% of what it has to offer.

In the 1970s and early 1980s, one's hotel had to be as close to the beach as possible, so as not to lose a moment of that precious sun-bathing time. The inevitable consequences were some overdeveloped stretches of coast. Nowadays, however, as people demand more of their holiday than to roast on the sand and risk skin cancer, visitors are looking further afield. There is a growing awareness that the coastline is just the southernmost edge of the three *départements* situated between the Rhône delta and the Italian border, and that there are still some remarkably wild areas, both here and inland. The *départements* of the Côte d'Azur boast two national parks: Mercantour, situated at the geographic and climatic crossroads of the Mediterranean south and the Alpine north; and Port-Cros, the only island park in Europe. In addition there is the Camargue regional park, one of the three most important coastal wetlands in Europe; two marine parks, where fishing and leisure activities are limited; and various protected sites.

The tourist board is beginning to encourage people to look beyond the 'sun and sea' image hitherto projected. If you do so, you will find lavender fields and flower-filled meadows, walled hill villages and ancient castles, traditional crafts and ways of life, and a rocky landscape dotted with sturdy pine trees and orange-roofed houses. The frenetic pace of Monte Carlo's casino is a world away from the lazy Latin atmosphere of towns where old men play *boules* and sip *pastis* on tree-shaded squares. Local crafts include the carving of olive wood, hand-weaving, and wrought-ironwork, sometimes in evidence on church bell-towers. At lively markets, people haggle in Provençal dialect over the fresh vegetables so important in regional cooking. During the Christmas period, you will see elaborate cribs containing clay figures in costume, known as *santons*.

If this side of the Côte d'Azur is often obscured by its glossy image, so too are the area's cultural assets. The number of high-quality museums and art galleries is remarkable, and old towns like Grasse and Arles should not be overlooked simply because they are located inland. Festivals, large and small, take place throughout the year. Active visitors will find they can practise almost any kind of sport: in spring, you can swim from Nice beach in the morning and be on the ski slopes by lunchtime! The foothills of the Alpes-Maritimes also offer walks through pleasant fields and along spectacular gorges. Perhaps the greatest advantage of a holiday on the Côte d'Azur, over and above its sheer beauty, is the diversity of possible activities within such a relatively small area.

History

The habitation of the Côte d'Azur goes back a long time; near Menton, skeletons have been found which date from 30,000 BC. More recent signs of human presence are visible in the Mercantour national park's Vallée des Merveilles, where there are countless rock carvings, some produced by Bronze-Age shepherds between 1800 and 1500 BC. From 1000 BC, the area came under Ligurian occupation, though, around 600 BC, Phoenician sailors founded the Greek colony Massalia, which would later be called Marseille. They introduced the olive and the vine to the area and set up trading posts along the coast. By this time there were also Celts in the region, but Ligurians, Greeks and Celts were all defeated when the Romans invaded in the second century BC. Roman civilisation spread during the first few centuries AD, taking in towns like Fréjus, Antibes, Nice, Aix-en-Provence and Arles. The latter became Rome's granary as both agriculture and trade flourished. The fourth, fifth and sixth centuries saw the advent of Christianity and repeated invasions until, finally, the region fell to the Franks in 536. During the ninth and tenth centuries, the Saracens continually attacked the Côte d'Azur, from both sea and land, until their defeat in 972.

In 1032, the whole of Provence became part of the Holy Roman Empire, though the Counts of Provence continued to enjoy considerable independence. After changing hands several times and serving as the starting place for the great thirteenth-century crusades, Provence (minus Nice, which belonged to Savoy, and Monaco) was reunited with France in 1486. This caused a certain resentment among local people, for whom it signified a loss of their Latin roots. In 1501, the Parliament at Aix-en-Provence became a supreme court of justice. The following decades saw the invasion of the region by soldiers of the Holy Roman Empire; the declaration that French, not Latin, was to be the administrative language; and an attack on Nice by French and Turkish troops. The Wars of Religion raged in the late sixteenth century, with the Protestant minority coming off worst. In 1691, Nice was captured by the French but was returned to Savoy five years later, only to become part of the kingdom of Sardinia in 1718. In 1720, a boat arriving at Marseille brought a terrible plague, which caused the deaths of 90,000 people in the course of two years. The eighteenth century saw the first British families coming to live in Nice. The publication of Tobias Smollett's *Travels* marked the start of a strong British association with the Côte d'Azur. Between 1793 and 1814, Nice was ruled by France, after which time it returned to the King of Sardinia. In the nineteenth century, the poet Frédéric Mistral led the regional cultural movement known as the Provençal Renaissance. It was not until 1860 that Nice belonged definitively to France. The Monte Carlo casino opened in 1878 and the Riviera's reputation for winter tourism spread.

The region was affected by the First World War only through the loss of young men, which exacerbated the general rural depopulation and left the area poverty-stricken. In 1940, the Italians occupied Menton and some of the coast and, in 1942, the Germans invaded the whole of Provence, which was liberated in 1944. Since the war, the summer tourist trade has continued to expand, rapidly alleviating the problem of poverty. Hydro-electric power stations were built on the River Durance in the 1960s, major motorways were constructed in the 1970s and 1980s, and the high-speed TGV train line between Paris and Marseille was completed in 1981. Meanwhile, the Algerian war of 1958 brought many ex-patriate refugees. Along with Algerians, Spaniards and Italians, who came to the area as labourers, they have become an integral part of the cosmopolitan community on the Côte d'Azur.

The numerous celebrities who have settled on the Côte d'Azur include various Impressionist painters, Scott Fïtzgerald, Coco Chanel and countless film stars. Among native Provençaux are the sixteenth-century astrologer Nostradamus; the eighteenth-century moralist, the Marquis de Vauvenargues; Fragonard, an artist best known for his exquisite erotic paintings; the Neo-Impressionist Paul Cézanne and the novelist Emile Zola, who was his boyhood companion; the chef, Auguste Escoffier, creator of *Pêche Melba*; the dramatist and poet Edmond Rostand, who wrote *Cyrano de Bergerac*; and the comic screen actor Fernandel.

Geography

The exact limits of the Côte d'Azur are often left rather vague. Two regions include it in their name: the large (five *département*) region of Provence-Alpes-Côte d'Azur (abbreviated to PACA); and the small (one *département*) region of Riviera-Côte d'Azur. The three coastal *départements* treated in this chapter are Bouches-du-Rhône, Var (both PACA), and Alpes-Maritimes (Riviera). The terms Riviera and Côte d'Azur are often used interchangeably. Strictly speaking, however, the Riviera is just the stretch of Mediterranean coast between Nice and Menton, near the Italian border; whereas the Côte d'Azur extends from Les Lecques (between Marseille and Toulon) to Menton. This chapter follows the coast even further west, through the part of the area known as Provence, to the natural boundary of the Rhône delta. The capital of PACA and of the Bouches-du-Rhône *département* is Marseille (879,000 inhabitants); Toulon (182,000) is capital of the Var; and Nice (339,000) is capital of the Alpes-Maritimes and, consequently, the Riviera. Other sizeable towns are Aix-en-Provence (125,000) and Arles (51,000), both in Bouches-du-Rhône.

In the west of the region, the Rhône river splits, just above Arles, into the Petit Rhône and the Grand Rhône. The Petit Rhône marks the edge of the Bouches-du-Rhône *département*, and the area between the two rivers forms the Camargue regional park. Here, the Rhône's alluvial deposits have created huge lagoons, separated from the sea by strips of sand. The largest of these is the Vaccarès Lagoon, which is a nature reserve. The surrounding land consists of wild expanses of salt-marsh. There is also a 100 km-long beach and areas of salt steppe-land, where semi-wild white horses and Camargue bulls are reared. Further east, the Berre Lagoon is divided from the sea by the limestone coastal hill chain known as the Estaque. From Marseille to Le Ciotat, the outstanding coastal feature is the series of deep inlets called *calanques*: fingers of red-brown rock thrust into the sea, with rugged cliffs and little islands. Inland, the Provençal landscape is equally varied, with a collection of plains, hills and massifs. East of the Grand Rhône and behind the coastal industrial zone of Fos-sur-Mer is the Plaine de la Crau. This appears to be a desert of large pebbles, with sparse vegetation, but was traditionally used as winter pastureland for sheep. It is unique in France but has been disappearing at an alarming rate thanks to industrial expansion, irrigation schemes, a new motorway and intensive forestry. At long last, an area of it was purchased by the Conservatoire Régional in 1989, so that its remarkable flora and fauna are not lost altogether. To the north are the attractive white limestone Alpilles hills and, further along the Durance river, which forms the border with the Vaucluse *département*, is the Montagne Ste-Victoire, a limestone massif with astonishing caves and caverns, situated close to Aix-en-Provence.

The coastline of the Var *département*, from Les Lecques to shortly before Cannes, starts off in the west with sharp indentations and steep cliffs, broken by occasional beaches. The Giens peninsular, near Hyères, points to a series of islands. The first, Porquerolles, is predominantly forest and is a botanical reserve. Some of the forest is treated as an annex to the national park situated on the next island, Port-Cros. This is Europe's only island national park and more than half the total area of the park is underwater. The island has rocky shores and abrupt cliffs, with fossilised dunes forming natural sculptures at Le Tuf. Some of the island's flora and fauna are of a type not found on the coast of the mainland, but they are essentially typically Mediterranean: the sad truth is that this is one of the few places where they are found intact. The underwater flora and fauna are exceptionally rich and include almost all the interesting species to be found in the Mediterranean. Opposite Port-Cros' main town is a small islet called Bagaud, which is a strict nature reserve and closed to the public. On the coast of the mainland at this point, the Maures massif, densely wooded further inland, meets the sea, forming promontories like the still largely unspoilt St-Tropez peninsula, as well as broad bays. Beyond St-Raphaël, the Esterel massif causes a change in the coastline, with breathtaking views of rugged rocks and narrow inlets. Not far inland there are mountains of considerable height, notably in the Ste-Baume massif. Between the various short mountain chains are valleys planted with vines, cereals and olives. In the northern Var, along its border with the Alpes-de-Haute-Provence *département*, are the spectacular gorges and Grand Canyon of the River Verdon.

The last stretch of the Côte d'Azur belongs to the Alpes-Maritimes *département* and includes the Riviera proper. Between Cannes and Nice, there is only one promontory, the Cap d'Antibes; otherwise the shore is a succession of wide bays, some sandy, some stony. Beyond Nice, however, the Pre-Alps come right up to the sea-shore, rising away from it in terraces which, eventually, reach a height of over 3000 metres on the Italian border. The beautiful mountains along the border, with their gorges, Bronze-Age engravings, mountain lakes and alpine flora and fauna, are protected by the Mercantour national park.

Traditional industries along the Côte d'Azur include salt-works at Hyères, bauxite mining near Brignoles, cork production in the Maures forest, market-gardening in the Rhône Valley, and rice-growing in the Camargue. There are also vineyards, olive groves, almond trees, cereal crops and lavender fields. Some old industries have, of course, died out, to be replaced by new ones like tourism and high-technology research.

The immense variety of natural habitat on the Côte d'Azur means that a large proportion of France's animal and plant species can be found here. In addition there are several unusual species, some endemic to the region. Typical Mediterranean forest, which can be found on Port-Cros island, consists of evergreen oak, cork oak, aleppo pine, palm trees and imported eucalyptus. In the Pre-Alps, you will find holm oak, larch, olive, laburnum and rhododendron, as well as colourful alpine meadows. Thirty rare species of plant, found nowhere else in the world, exist in this part of the region; they include the pink-spiked *Saxifraga Florulenta*. Migrating birds stopping at Port-Cros include the golden oriole, little egret and gannet; shearwaters breed there. In the Camargue, over 300 migrant species have been recorded, and pink flamingoes inhabit the park year-round. Grouse, ptarmigan, buzzards and the short-toed and golden eagle can be found in the Pre-Alps. Port-Cros is the last remaining French site where the Tyrrhenian painted frog lives. Likewise, the mainland's Maures massif offers the final refuge for France's most endangered reptile, Hermann's Tortoise, though even this habitat is under threat. The Rhône cricket is now found only in the Crau plain. Mammals living in the Mercantour park include stoat, hare, marmot, deer, wild boar, chamois, ibex and mouflon. The Mediterranean itself is ideal for rockfish, flatfish, eels, octopuses, crabs and lobsters.

Climate

For centuries, people have been drawn to the Côte d'Azur by its climate. As a rule, summers are long, hot and extremely dry, winters cool and fairly wet. Temperatures range from about 10°C in February to 30°C or so in August, and the average for the year is around 16°C. In 1988, Nice had 74 days with a temperature of over 25°C; 79 days when it rained; 30 windy days; and not a single day of frost, snow, hail or fog. In general there are approaching 300 sunny days a year and the sea temperature is above 20°C from June to September, averaging a blissful 25°C in August. When the Côte d'Azur gets windy, it does it in style; the famous north-west wind known as the *mistral* is very strong and often blows up suddenly. In the Pre-Alps, inland from Nice, summer temperatures are more moderate, though the sun shines as much as ever. In winter, though the nights are cold, you can often explore the snow-covered landscape in just a T-shirt during the day. Visitors to the Camargue should avoid July and August; quite apart from being crowded with people, it is also humming with vicious mosquitoes.

Attractions

In 1887, the poet Stephen Liégard decided the French Riviera deserved to be distinguished from the Italian one, and christened France's most beautiful stretch of coast the Côte d'Azur. The name first conjures up visions of sparkling blue sea (the Mediterranean is, indeed, Europe's bluest sea), but time has added countless other associations, which all serve to attract people to the area. The myth status which the region has attained is the basis of its success – and the tourist authorities are convinced that its image of exclusivity and luxury must not be allowed to slip one iota, if this success is to continue.

Naturally, a large part of the Côte d'Azur's appeal comes from its beaches, whose beauty is enhanced by a translucent light, peculiar to the region and a source of inspiration to so many artists. Of the sandy beaches, the best are at Cannes and La Napoule. In 1989, Nice was declared one of the eight towns in the world most diligent in keeping its beach and water clean. People are often surprised, however, to find that Nice has a pebble beach, not a sandy one. After Nice, the most famous resorts are Cannes, with its film festival; Monaco, with its harbour, palace and casino; Menton, with its Italianate buildings and nearby mountains; and Antibes, home to the national Picasso museum. Further west, Marseille is an immensely atmospheric city and provides a good base for exploration of the rocky inlets known as *calanques*, where climbing can be practised. Boat trips from Cannes and Antibes to the Iles des Lérins are popular too. A lush green backdrop to the beaches is supplied by semi-tropical vegetation, including palms and fruit trees. An effort to 'green' the area has led to the opening of many exotic gardens, of which the ones in Monaco and Eze are the most famous. The number of golf clubs is also growing fast. Many tourists come to the region for the party atmosphere of the Nice carnival just before Lent, or else in May, hoping to catch a glimpse of their favourite film-star at Cannes. Further attractions of the Côte d'Azur are its ostentatious shops and its casinos. It boasts four of the top ten casinos in France, and the one in Monaco brought in a staggering £87 million in 1989!

The Côte d'Azur is also known for its museums and, more particularly, its galleries of twentieth century art. Although few tourists cite them as their main reason for coming, most people do go to at least one museum or gallery in the course of their visit. There are three national museums on the Côte d'Azur: the Picasso museum in Vallauris, near Antibes; the Chagall museum in Nice; and the Fernand Léger museum in Biot. The first two receive more than 120,000 visitors a year, along with the Matisse museum in Nice (recently revamped), the Maeght Foundation of modern art in St-Paul-de-Vence, and the newly created Parc des Miniatures in Nice. The real star is, however, the Oceanography museum in Monaco; in 1988, this welcomed nearly 910,000 visitors, making it the eighth most popular museum in France. A less well-known museum of high quality is the museum of the Camargue, which was declared European museum of the year, back in 1979.

The Romans left behind traces in many towns. Roman monuments in Arles, together with their Romanesque counterparts, have been made into a UNESCO World Heritage site. The Côte d'Azur has a small spa town, Berthemont-les-Bains, and various leisure parks with names like Aquasplash and Marineland. One attraction which people do not automatically associate with the Côte d'Azur is skiing. In fact, the Maritime Alps (or the 'Alpes d'Azur', as the tourist board has christened them) offer 600 km of alpine skiing at three big resorts (Auron, Isola 2000, Valberg) and twelve smaller ones. Another reason for coming in winter is the wealth of Christmas traditions which still go on here. Other attractions which are often missed are the national and regional parks; the markets taking place in old town centres; the possibilities of wild walks along Europe's highest cliffs, 122 metres above the sea, or pleasant strolls through alpine pastures; traditional festivals and pageants; the fine frescoes, altar-screens and wrought-iron bell-towers of many churches; and, generally, exploration of the region's fascinating *arrière-pays* or 'hinterland'.

Cuisine

The staple ingredients of the cuisine are garlic (known as the 'truffle of Provence'), onions, olive oil and herbs, along with many fresh vegetables such as tomatoes, peppers, courgettes and aubergine and, quite often, fish. This is one place in France where vegetarians will be spoilt for choice. Do not leave without trying the delicious *soupe au pistou*, a vegetable soup with red beans and tomatoes. Fish soups are also popular. You will certainly encounter *aïoli*, which is a garlic mayonnaise (usually served with boiled vegetables or fish). White fish with *aïoli* is known as *bourride*; other fish dishes are *anchoïade* (made with anchovies), *brandade* (made with cod), and the famous *bouillabaisse* fish stew. Thrush used to be a popular dish, but is less so now (mainly because hunting has scared them all away); you may still, however, come across a reminder of the hunting tradition in the form of expensive song-bird pâtés. Specialities vary around the region, though leg of lamb (*gigot*) is served almost everywhere. Camargue specialises in a beef dish called *estouffade de bœuf* and is also known for its asparagus. Arles is famed for its sausages. *Poutargue* is a purée of fish eggs from Martigues. Marseille offers *pieds et pacquets*, a dish involving sheep's tripe, salt pork and white wine. The mountains above Nice specialise in *bresaou*, smoked salted mutton, as well as goat's and sheep's cheeses. Nice itself has its own special ratatouille, and *gnocchi* (ravioli stuffed with beet). This is also the best area for olives, which crop up in many dishes including the onion pizza known as *pissaladière*. Other local specialities include *pissare*, a marrow or courgette dish, and socca, an oven-baked pancake made with chick-peas. Melons and apricots are grown in the region and you will often find them in preserved form. Other sweet specialities include nougat, honey sweets, orange creams, *navettes* (small, boat-shaped cakes) from Marseille, and lavender or rosemary honey.

Though not particularly famed for its wines, you will find plenty of variety among local ones. The best known are Bandol, Cassis, Palette, Coteaux d'Aix-en-Provence, Coteaux des Baux and Côtes de Provence. The Côtes de Provence alone has 44,000 acres of vineyard. Though the region is best known for its rosé wines, 30% of Côtes de Provence are white and 5% red. The region's other staple drink is the strong aniseed-flavoured *pastis*.

Level of Tourism

Tourism is the most important economic activity of the Côte d'Azur. 1985 was a record year, receiving 8.5 million tourists, and since then the total has hovered slightly below that level. Not only do 10% of tourists to France end up on the Côte d'Azur, an unbelievable 1% of all world tourists make this strip of Mediterranean coastline their destination. Unfortunately, the authorities regard this high share of the market as something which must not be relinquished, even though maintaining it means a minimum expansion of 5 or 6% per annum. Such growth is bound to be particularly damaging for the Côte d'Azur because, unlike most other destinations, it already has a century's worth of tourism development behind it and space has become scarce.

One reason the tourist industry is so valuable is that the clientèle here spends a lot. Over half of those who arrive by plane in August choose a 4-star or luxury hotel. Although the short-stay phenomenon has increased recently, the majority of visitors are here for their main holiday, and even the less well-heeled allow themselves the odd splurge, following the reasoning that, once you're in such an extravagant place, you might as well live it up! Around 40% of tourists come from abroad, mostly from Italy, Germany, Britain, the USA and Spain, though there has been a marked increase in Japanese visitors too. The year-round influx usually involves the Italians coming in winter; the 'culture-vultures' (predominantly the over-45s) at Easter; congress visitors in spring; the Germans in May; the sun-lovers in summer, with the Spanish choosing

July and the French August; the British and another round of Germans in September; and huge numbers of congress visitors in October. European coach excursions often include Nice in their itinerary, but over half the tourists come in their own car and the vast majority organise their holiday independently. In the Alpes-Maritimes *département*, 38% stay in hotels and 20% in second homes, of which there are already 150,000, with more being purchased every year. The main *département* for camping is the Var.

Most people cite 'rest and relaxation' as their motive for coming to the Côte d'Azur, but an increasing number of visitors are there for either sport, culture or business. The clientèle is extremely loyal: 80% of visitors have been before and 90% intend to return. Over 90% are happy with their holiday, though, interestingly enough, the people most likely to express dissatisfaction are those who have been coming every summer for years. The most common causes for complaint are the prices and the snootiness of shop-keepers. This latter phenomenon is surely part of the automatic human tendency to lash out at people on whom you know you are over-dependent. Although it is undeniable that tourism brings a good deal of income to the region, the negative consequences are considerable.

Tourists often double the population of coastal areas in season, and 41% of active inhabitants in the Alpes-Maritimes feel they owe their job, at least in part, to tourism. This 'single-crop' type of economy is sometimes considered unhealthy, especially when many of the jobs it creates are seasonal. Resentment is, however, rarely explicit and you are unlikely to encounter it unless you are insensitive enough to acquire an ostentatious second home in an area where local people feel the water in your swimming pool could be put to far better use on their dried-up crops! Intensive agriculture, along with tourism and high-tech industry, has already led to the virtual extinction of traditional farming methods. Space is at such a premium that the economic alternatives boil down to either exploiting land to its maximum or selling it to the developers. The space factor also means that many new hotel projects, though perhaps more tasteful than those of the 1970s, still fall into the large-scale, several-storey category – despite the 1979 United Nations Priority Actions Programme, among whose aims was the harmonisation of tourism development with the environment. Recent investments have concentrated on new motorways, luxury Cannes hotels, the

Monaco casino and a 1000-bed Club Med village at Opio. Plans for the future are in the same vein: large, top-of-the-range hotels, golf courses, holiday villages, casinos and sports facilities. The tourist board is, however, attempting to alleviate stress on the infrastructure not only by building more hotels, but by encouraging visitors to come off-season and to base themselves in less well-known resorts. Subsidies are being offered to local people wishing to set up *gîte* accommodation inland. The concretisation of the coast is also being counteracted by the creation of numerous parks and gardens. Underground car-parks are camouflaged under green space; an entire district of Nice is being turned into a botanical garden; and a new village called Antibes-les-Pins is based on famous gardens of the past. All this serves to enhance the exotic image of the Côte d'Azur and, though it is an artificial development, it is, nonetheless, a positive one.

Most of the environmental damage inflicted in the Côte d'Azur must be laid at the door of the tourist industry rather than individual tourists. There are, however, exceptions. Every year forest fires are started by people having barbecues or dropping cigarettes. In 1990, 37,000 acres of forest were burnt in the Maures plain. In addition to all the other fauna and flora destroyed, it is estimated that 10,000 rare tortoises died. Various other problems have been countered with drastic measures. In the Mercantour park's Vallée des Merveilles, the valuable Bronze-Age engravings were being vandalised and stolen. Many people wished to close the area to the public altogether, but the park favoured a less absolute line. Now, tourists are restricted to three marked paths and are only allowed off the paths when accompanied by a trained guide. Rangers are on site to enforce these rules and, so far, they seem to be working. There are strict rules on Port-Cros Island Park too. The island has already had one lucky escape: back in 1909, it only just avoided being sold to an American consortium with plans for sky-scrapers and a race course. Today there are still only twenty or thirty permanent inhabitants and the environment and wildlife are considered so precious that no risks are taken. Smoking and dogs are not allowed outside the only town; no motor traffic except administrative vehicles is permitted; the speed of boats is restricted; camping and picking flowers are forbidden. People are obviously not dissuaded from visiting though, as the island, like the Camargue, suffers from high numbers in summer.

Good Alternatives

Meeting People

On the Côte d'Azur, meeting local people is only really possible if you make an effort to leave tourist trails behind. In order both to escape the crowds and to appreciate the charm of the *arrière-pays* and its inhabitants, it is worth choosing to stay in locally-owned accommodation inland. There are some *chambres d'hôte* and numerous *gîtes*, whose situation allows for day-trips to the beach, but also for other excursions and, above all, independence. And, who knows, a shift to this type of accommodation might even persuade developers it is no longer worth their while to build large hotels on the coast.

The best places to soak up the local atmosphere are markets, fairs and festivals. A calendar of festivals and a list of fairs, markets and museums of popular arts and traditions in the Bouches-du-Rhône is available from the **Comité Départemental du Tourisme**, 6 rue du Jeune Anacharsis, 13001 Marseille. Information on festivals in the 'Alpes d'Azur' is contained in the brochure 'Vacances en Fêtes' from **L'Union Départementale des Offices du Tourisme des Alpes-Maritimes**, 2 rue Deloye, 06000 Nice. Typical markets, where shepherds and sheep arrive early in the morning at the village square, take place in Guillaumes and St-Etienne-de-Tinée. Antique fairs are frequent in the area above Grasse. In the Bouches-du-Rhône, it is possible to buy local produce, such as wine, snails, plants, fruit juice, olives, confectionery, cheese, fruit and vegetables, and honey, directly from the producer; a list of addresses can be obtained from the **Comité de Promotion des Produits Agricoles des Bouches-du-Rhône**, 22 ave Henri-Pontier, 13626 Aix-en-Provence (Tel. 42 23 06 11). If you wish to be shown round the premises, you should make an arrangement with the proprietor in advance. One way to combine a holiday with learning something useful is to attend a cookery course. The **Comité Régional du Tourisme**, 55 Promenade des Anglais, 06000 Nice organises courses at classy establishments, with top chefs, in Nice and Mougins; but infinitely more appealing is a course in country cooking, which takes place every summer in an attractive mountain village, where the villagers demonstrate local dishes. For further information, write to the **Bureau de Tourisme**, Place Felix-Faure, BP 12, 06450 St-Martin-Vésubie (Tel. 93 03 21 28). Conservation volunteers could offer their services at one of the *chantiers* run by the **Conservatoire Régional**. Information about these is available from Marte Busse, **Ecomusée de St-Martin-de-Crau**, 13310 St-Martin-de-Crau. Details about joining archaeological excavations in the Bouches-du-Rhône and the Var can be obtained from the **Direction des Antiquités Préhistoriques et Historiques**, 21–3 bd du Roy René, 13617 Aix-en-Provence (Tel. 42 27 98 40). Those with good French could go along to one of the seminars (on topics such as local architecture, forestry or crafts), run by the **Ecomusée de la Roudoule**, Place des Tilleuls, 06260 Puget-Rostang (Tel. 93 05 02 81).

Discovering Places

If you know where to look, there are plenty of lesser-known corners to explore in the Côte d'Azur. A list of all the protected areas in Provence, along with individual maps and leaflets, is available by writing either to the **Agence Régionale pour l'Environnement**, BP 17, 13320 Bouc-Bel-Air; or to the **DRAE**, 17 rue Thiers, 13100 Aix-en-Provence. Information on the 'hinterland' of the Alpes-Maritimes is contained in the brochure *Moyen et Haut Pays*, available from **UDOTSI**, 2 rue Deloye, 06000 Nice (Tel. 93 80 84 84). There are numerous local companies which organise excursions. SNCF offer regular bus excursions through the company Beltrame et Fils, which leave from St-Raphaël and various other towns in that area, and have a different destination every day of the week. Details are available from **Agence SVA Beltrame et Fils**, Gare Routière, 83700 St-Raphaël (Tel. 94 95 95 16). **SAMUR** is an operator offering both coach and boat excursions – info: **SAMUR**, Bastide St-Claude, Chemin de St-Claude, 06600 Antibes (Tel. 93 33 25 22). Another good coach operator, some of whose itineraries include steam-train rides, is **Santa Azur**, 11 ave Jean-Médecin, 06000 Nice (Tel. 93 85 46 81). Activity holidays of 1 to 3 days are organised from May to November by the **Service Commercial**, Chemins de Fer de Provence, 40 rue Clement Roassal, BP 387, 06007 Nice (Tel. 93 88 34 72). Activities to choose from are mountain biking; rafting and canyoning (a combination of climbing, diving and caving); or plain old walking. You can even combine all three on a 7-day holiday. Wine tours are possible in the Var: ask the **Comité Départemental du Tourisme du Var**, 1 bd Foch, 83300 Draguignan (Tel. 94 68 58 33). A range of holidays is offered by **Loisirs-Accueil Bouches-du-Rhône**, Domaine du Vergon, 13770

Mallemort (Tel. 90 59 18 05). The **Comité Régional de Tourisme – PACA**, Immeuble CMCI, 2 rue Henri-Barbusse, 13241 Marseille (Tel. 91 39 38 00), produces a booklet (called '52 Activity Weekends') of numerous two, three and four-day breaks in the Bouches-du-Rhône and Var (as well as the other PACA *départements*), all organised by local tour operators and ranging from the healthy, active or ecological to the cultural or gastronomic.

Walking is certainly the best way to see the countryside, and there are many guided and thematic walks organised, particularly in the Mercantour national park. Reaching the Bronze-Age engravings of the Vallée des Merveilles requires a 3-hour walk, so allow a full day to get there and back. Tende is the nearest town and information on guided visits is available from the tourist office there. Alternatively, contact the **Bureau des Guides du Val des Merveilles**, BP 12, 06430 Tende (Tel. 93 04 62 64), which does 1, 2 and 3-day expeditions. Information on nature rambles in the park is available from the **Parc National du Mercantour**, 23 rue d'Italie, 06000 Nice (Tel. 93 87 86 10). Nature discovery weekends are organised by the **Bureau des Guides du Val d'Entraunes**, Hôtel de la Vallière, 06470 St-Martin-d'Entraunes (Tel. 93 05 51 07). Perhaps the widest range of thematic excursions is offered by **Michel Bosquet**, 89 bd Las Planas B4, 06100 Nice (Tel. 93 52 88 51), with whom you can study flora, fauna, birdlife and geology; practise photography in the mountains; and, from January to Easter, go walking in snow-shoes. Husband-and-wife team Gérard and Christine Kieffer have formed a company called **Itinerrances**, (Villeplane, 06470 Guillaumes, Tel. 93 05 56 01), which offers family walks with pack-mules, botanical walks, longer treks and snow-shoe walks, all enhanced by a home-made meal on their farm.

A 7-day walking tour called the 'Alpes d'Azur and the Valley of Marvels' is run in the park for individuals grouped together up to a maximum of twelve people. The price of around 4200FF includes full-board, transport in a Land-Rover, bivouac material and the daily presence of a trained local guide. The holiday enjoys the seal of approval of the Natural Parks Federation and can be booked either through **Clés de France** (see p. 51), or directly with the **Bureau des Guides du Val des Merveilles** (address as above). If you wish to visit the astronomy centre at Caussols, contact **PARSEC**, 2 passage du Petit Parc, 06000 Nice (Tel. 93 42 66 16). Information on the mountainous area known as 'la Suisse Niçoise', including organised holidays and courses, is available from **Interval**, Mairie de St-Martin-de-Vésubie 06450 (Tel. 93 03 20 08).

Communications

How to Get There

There are direct **flights** from the UK to both Marseille (Tel. 42 89 09 74) and Nice (on both British Airways and Air France). Air UK now runs a service between London and Nice too, while Air Littoral has recently introduced a Manchester-Nice route and has plans for a Manchester-Marseille service. Nice Côte d'Azur International Airport (Tel. 93 21 30 30) is one of the busiest in France. The Paris-Nice flight used to be extremely expensive, but competition means that fares are decreasing and passenger numbers growing, so that it is now the second most frequented route in Europe, after Paris-London. There is another international airport at Cannes-Mandelieu (Tel. 93 90 40 40).

There are frequent daily SNCF **train** services between Paris and major stations on the Côte d'Azur. The high-speed TGV train puts Nice at $7^{1}/2$ hours from Paris, and Marseille at under 5 hours.

Eurolines offers a direct **coach** service from London to Marseille, with connections to Grasse, Cannes, Antibes, Juan-les-Pins and Nice, costing around £100 return for an adult. Driving down south in your own car can be a long and expensive business. The motorway journey from Paris to Marseille takes around 8 hours non-stop and will set you back about £30 in tolls.

When You're There

Rail – within the region, train services along the coast are frequent and offer fabulous views (remember to sit on the coastal side). The route (west to east) is Arles, Marseille, La Ciotat, Bandol, Toulon, Les Arcs, Fréjus, St-Raphaël, Cannes, Juan-les-Pins, Antibes, Cagnes-sur-Mer, Nice, Monaco, Menton and on into Italy. Minor lines fork off to Port-de-Bouc and Hyères (both on the coast), but trying to reach anywhere inland (with the exception of Aix-en-Provence, which is on a main line) proves extremely problematic. From Nice there is a train which runs north-east through the Roya valley (Breil-sur-Roya) to Tende (and, eventually, on to Turin). In order to go anywhere north-west of Nice, you should take the scenic steam railway run by the **Chemins de Fer de Provence**, known as the 'Train des Pignes', which takes you along the Var valley up to Digne (in the Alpes-de-Haute-Provence). Information is available from Gare du Sud, 33 ave Malaussena, 06000 Nice (Tel. 93 88 28 56); if you are there between June and September, try to take the 'Alpazur' service, as this offers a free commentary on the journey.

Bus – there are regular bus services within the region and the network is particularly comprehensive in the Alpes-Maritimes. In addition to linking all the coastal destinations between Nice and Menton, buses run inland to Vence, St-Paul, Grasse, St-Martin-Vésubie, Valberg, Auron and Isola 2000. Information is available from the **Gare Routière Nice-Côte d'Azur**, Promenade du Paillon, 06300 Nice (Tel. 93 85 61 81). For coach excursions, see **Good Alternatives** section.

Car – unless you are planning a touring holiday inland, it is probably not worth bringing or hiring a car, as the bus and train service along the coast is perfectly adequate. If you are driving, the journey between Marseille and Nice takes around 2 hours. The A 50 runs part of the way along the coast (as far as Toulon), with the A 8 following a route further inland. Many interesting places to explore can be found on the minor inland roads.

Boat – almost every coastal town offers the possibility of boat trips. Les-Saintes-Maries-de-la-Mer is the starting point for visits of the Camargue. The most popular trip goes to the Isles des Lérins from Antibes and Cannes. A ferry from Hyères, Le Lavandou or Toulon will take you to Port-Cros national park and the other Iles d'Hyères. From St-Raphaël, you can use the **Bateaux Bleus** service to visit the blood-red *calanques* of the Esterel massif; the Maures massif and the Sardinaux isles; the Ile Ste-Marguérite; and St-Tropez, along the coast. From Nice, you can even take a day-trip to Corsica, if you don't mind having only 2 hours on shore once you're there. Arles is a starting point for cruises on the Rhône, organised by **Naviginter**. Information on canoeing in the 'Alpes d'Azur' is available from the **Comité Départemental des Alpes-Maritimes**, c/o Antoine Calvo, 6 rue Diderot, 06100 Nice.

Cycling – cycling is a good way to see many parts of the Côte d'Azur, notably the Camargue and the Grasse and St-Auban hills. The following SNCF stations have bikes for hire: Aix-en-Provence, Antibes, Arles, Bandol, Cagnes-sur-Mer, Cannes, Hyères, Juan-les-Pins and St-Raphaël. Tourist offices will give you details of other outlets. A list of cycle clubs in the Alpes-Maritimes is available from the **Fédération Française du Cyclotourisme**,

Comité Départemental 06, c/o Rémy Bernage, 22 bus rue Trachel, 06000 Nice. A brochure on cycling holidays in the Var can be obtained from the **Association Varoise de Développement du Tourisme de Randonnée**, Conseil Général du Var, 1 bd Foch, 83005 Draguignan (Tel. 94 68 97 66). Mountain bike rental and excursions are possible at **Domaine du Grenouillet**, 83 Agay/rte de Valescure (Tel. 94 82 81 89).

Walking – numerous GR paths criss-cross the region, though those in the mountains north of Nice (GR 5, GR 52 and GR 52A) are open only between late June and early October and should be tackled only by experienced mountain walkers. There are, however, many other paths suitable for everybody – the GR 51 (excellent views of the Riviera); the GR 4; the GR 9; the GR 99; and shorter coastal paths. The route used by Napoleon in 1815 can be followed inland from Golfe-Juan. Details of walks from 1½ hours to 12 days are contained in the leaflet 'Alpes-Maritimes Randonnée', available from the **Comité Départemental de la Randonnée Pédestre**, 2 rue Deloye, 06000 Nice and from the Mercantour Park headquarters (address below). The **Club Alpin Français**, 14 ave Mirabeau, 06000 Nice (Tel. 93 62 59 99), does excursions on Wednesdays and Sundays. For further information on thematic walks, see **Good Alternatives** section. Cross-country skiing is a good way to see the Alpes-Maritimes in winter, and skiing information is available from local tourist offices.

Riding – information can be obtained from the offices of the **Association Régionale de Tourisme Equestre Provence Côte d'Azur** (ARTEPROCA) at Mas de la Jumenterie, route de St-Cézaire, 06460 St-Vallier-de-Thiey (Tel. 93 42 62 98). For the Var *département*, contact the **Association Varoise de Développement du Tourisme de Randonnée** (address under **Bicycle**). Horseriding in the Camargue is particularly popular.

Useful Local Contacts

The **Conservatoire Régional du Patrimoine Naturel de Provence**, Ville Vieille, Caussols, 06460 St-Vallier-de-Thiey (Tel. 93 09 29 95) does some essential work, looking after ecologically fragile sites and, where appropriate, creating discovery paths for the public. Information on sites of ecological and architectural interest can be obtained from the **DRAE**, 17 rue Thiers, 13100 Aix-en-Provence. The addresses of park headquarters are as follows: **Parc National de Port-Cros**, Castel Ste-Claire, rue Ste-Claire, 83400 Hyères (Tel. 94 65 32 98); **Parc National du Mercantour**, 23 rue d'Italie, 06000

Nice (Tel. 93 87 86 10); and **Parc Naturel Régional de Camargue**, Mas du Pont de Rousty, 13200 Arles (Tel. 90 97 10 40).

Geographical Breakdown of Region

Bouches-du-Rhône

This is a *département* with many highlights, including the impressive Roman monuments inland and the unique coastline, starting with the Camargue marshes and changing into high cliffs and rugged inlets.

At **Graveson**, in the north-western corner, there is an abbey and a perfume museum. The Château du Roi René, which overlooks the Rhône at **Tarascon** is worth a visit, especially the last weekend in June, when the town celebrates its folklore festival, the Fête de la Tarasque. At **St-Rémy-de-Provence**, a museum is devoted to the Alpilles, a chain of white limestone hills rich in flowers and insects, situated just to the south. The town hosts a market of local wines and produce on the last weekend in July. There is also an archaeological museum that houses many of the finds made at the nearby Roman ruins of **Glanum**. **Les Baux-de-Provence** is a bit of a tourist trap, but has various interesting museums, including a Musée des Santons, where the clay figures used in Christmas cribs are displayed. If you happen to be here at Christmas time, the Midnight Mass includes a nativity pageant. Part of the extremely fragile **Crau Plain** has recently been made into a nature reserve and may be visited as part of a 2-hour guided tour, arranged by the *ecomusée* at **St-Martin-de-Crau** (Tel. 90 47 02 01). This museum was created from a former sheep-pen and houses a collection of old tools associated with traditional agricultural techniques and sheep-rearing as well as fauna and geology displays. From 1 April to 30 September, it is open 9–12 and 3–7; and from 10 October to 31 March it is open 10–12 and 2–5 (except Monday).

Just outside Arles is the beautiful **Montmajour** Abbey. The Roman town of **Arles** should certainly be seen, though the bullfights now staged at its impressive amphitheatre may not be to everyone's taste. The Museon Arlaten, a sixteenth-century Gothic mansion at 29 rue de la République, is a folk museum that offers insights into Provençal culture. There are also museums of Christian and Pagan art. Boat trips on the Rhône start from Arles, and this is a good way to see the area that was Van Gogh's hunting ground. South-west, at

Le Mas du Pont-de-Rousty, is the Musée Camarguais, an essential starting point for those who wish to understand the Camargue. The museum is combined with a discovery path that allows you to see irrigation and cultivation techniques, reed-picking, pastures for the horses and bulls, and bird refuges. At the **Pont-de-Gau** is an information centre and ornithological park, where birds can be observed both in aviaries and in the wild; Camargue bulls can also be seen. This is open from February to November. To the north of the **Etang des Launes** is an unusual landscape, which incorporates contemporary architecture into a natural setting. A 1¹/2 hour circuit allows you to explore the area, on which information is available from the tourist office at **Les-Saintes-Maries-de-la-Mer**. This village, right on the coast, is considered the capital of the Camargue. A gipsy pilgrimage takes place here at the end of May. Tours of the Petit Rhône leave from the Capitainerie at the port; there is also a marked circuit for walkers, as well as bike-hire possibilities. A 20 km path along a dyke or the beach takes you through the Réserve Nationale de Camargue: La Capellière. Near **Salins-de-Giraud**, in the **Domaine de la Palissade**, is a Nature Initiation Centre, with exhibitions and an aquarium. From here you can go on a guided visit of one of three discovery paths (ranging from 1¹/2 to 4 hours), all of which introduce you to the flora and fauna of the surrounding lagoons.

The other side of the industrial area around the **Port de Fos** is the town of **Martigues**, which has been described as the Venice of Provence. Further round the enormous **Etang de Berre** is **Marignane**, which (in addition to being next to Marseille Airport) has a Museum of Popular Arts and Traditions, and a *Son et Lumière* in early September. **Salon-de-Provence** is a charming town, situated among olive-groves, with a Musée de Salon et de la Crau. Nearby, at **Pelissane**, is the sixteenth, seventeenth and nineteenth-century Château de la Barben, which has magnificent gardens. Near **La Roque-d'Anthéron**, where the Canal de Marseille and the River Durance run parallel, is the Cistercian Silvacane Abbey, which hosts classical concerts in summer. **Aix-en-Provence**, in a wine-growing area, is another 'must', though those on a limited budget may wish to make it a day-trip, as it is expensive. This sophisticated town, which was the birthplace of Cézanne, has a circuit of monuments associated with the artist. The Saint-Sauveur cathedral and cloisters should be visited, as should the Tapestry and Old Furniture Museum, and the Musée du Vieil Aix. The **Ste-Victoire** mountain, to the east, was a favourite source of inspiration for Cézanne. Further south, **Aubagne** has a fair of ceramics and *santons*, which lasts for the whole of August. In July, **La Ciotat**, on the coast, holds big markets of local produce, known as Les Provinciades. Neighbouring **Cassis** has a wine festival in early September, and a Museum of Popular Arts and Traditions. From Cassis, you can take a boat to the **Calanque d'En Vau**. This finger of land, whose cliffs are some of Europe's highest, is attached to a deserted wasteland of limestone scree, across which the hardy can walk all the way to Marseille.

Accommodation

First Class

Château de Vergières, Domaine de Vergières, 13310 St-Martin-de-Crau (Tel. 90 47 17 16): 7 rooms in mansion in middle of farming country; open 1 March to 15 November; *tables d'hôte* available if reserved. **Mas de la Fouque**, rte du Petit Rhône, 13460 Les Saintes-Maries-de-la-Mer (Tel. 90 47 81 02): 12 rooms in luxurious family hotel; Camargue horses for hire; pleasant restaurant.

Middle Range

Domaine de Roquerousse, rte d'Avignon, 13300 Salon-de-Provence (Tel. 90 59 50 11): 17 rooms in calm hotel with park; restaurant specialising in local produce and game. **Mas des Carassins**, 1 chemin Gaulois, 13210 St-Rémy-de-Provence (Tel. 90 92 15 48): 19 rooms in nineteenth-century farmhouse with views of Alpilles hills.

Economy

Hôtel des Arts, 30 bd Victor-Hugo, 13210 St-Rémy-de-Provence (Tel. 90 92 08 50): 17 rooms in friendly rustic-style hotel; restaurant serves simple, local dishes. **Hôtel le Commerce**, 2 rue St-Clair, 13260 Cassis (Tel. 42 01 09 10): 16 rooms in family hotel; restaurant.

Eating Out

In addition to the hotel restaurants mentioned above, the following are recommended:

First Class

Moulin de Lambesc de Tante Yvonne, rue Benjamin-Raspail, 13410 Lambesc (Tel. 42 28 02 46): old Provençal recipes served in 15th century mill; reservations essential.

First Class / Middle Range

Restaurant l'Olivier, 1 bis rue Reattu, 13200 Arles (Tel. 90 49 64 88): modern Provençal cuisine in old Arles town-house.

Marseille

Marseille, though one of the oldest cities in France, is now the most important commercial port on the French Mediterranean. Yet it has plenty to charm the visitor, not least its fascinating old harbour and the unique atmosphere generated by the ethnic mixture of its population.

The best place to start is the **old port**, which is worth walking all the way round. There is something appealing about the way old boats and new are moored side-by-side – a phenomenon which is less common as you travel east and the ports become more exclusive. The mouth of the port is guarded by **Fort-St-Jean** and **Fort-St-Nicolas**, both of which offer excellent views. Near the latter are the pleasant **Parc du Pharo** and **St Victor's Basilica**. This fortified church, parts of which date from the eleventh and twelfth centuries, is famous for its catacombs. At the end of boulevard Tellène you will find a steep ramp leading to the **Basilique Notre-Dame-de-la-Garde**, from where there is a stunning panorama of the city and surrounding area. If you have time, go on to **Parc Borély** on the outskirts of the city. This vast park, next to the **Botanical Gardens**, belongs to an eighteenth-century castle, which houses an interesting **Museum of Mediterranean Archaeology**. If you head back towards the centre, just off rue St-Férréol is the **Cantini Museum**, which concentrates on contemporary art, but also has a section of seventeenth- and eighteenth-century ceramics.

Straight down rue St-Férréol is **La Canebière**, the most famous street in Marseille, now a bustling shopping area (though not particularly safe at night). The other side of the Canebière is the **Jardin des Vestiges**, an archaeological garden containing some ruins of Greek fortifications dating from the second century BC. Through the garden is the **History Museum**, which is particularly good on the early history of Marseille. More recent times are treated in the **Musée du Vieux Marseille**, which is a kind of folk museum of the nineteenth and early twentieth centuries and includes Provençal furniture and a collection of *santons*. The nearby **Musée des Docks Romains** reveals first century docks and warehouses, discovered by chance thanks to a Second World War bomb. Beside the ruined eleventh-century **Old La Major Cathedral** is its nineteenth-century counterpart (of the same name), which is an impressive building in Romano-Byzantine style. The beautiful old hospice known as the **Vieille Charité** is now a cultural centre which houses exhibitions.

Other places to visit are the **Palais Longchamp**, an imposing nineteenth-century palace that houses the **Musée des Beaux-Arts** and the **Natural History Museum**; the **Grobet-Labadié Museum**, a town-house decorated with antiques and paintings, situated at the end of boulevard Longchamp; and **Château-Gombert**, where there is a very good **Museum of Popular Arts and Traditions**, open Monday, Wednesday, Saturday and Sunday afternoons only. Nearby are some caves with stalactite and stalagmite formations, known as the **Grottes Loubière**. Ask the tourist office about walks along the coast, past Le Corbusier's **Cité Radieuse**, to see the *calanques*; and boat excursions to the legendary **Château d'If**, a former state prison, built in the sixteenth century and made famous by Dumas' novel *The Count of Monte Cristo*.

Accommodation

First Class

Le Petit Nice, Anse de Maldormé, 160 Corniche J-F-Kennedy, 7e *arrondissement* (Tel. 91 52 14 39): 17 luxurious rooms in calm location.

Middle Range

St-Ferréol's, 19 rue Pisançon, 1er (Tel. 91 33 12 21): 19 rooms in hotel quite close to port. **Hôtel Petit Louvre**, 19 Canebière, 1er (Tel. 91 90 13 78): 31 rooms in hotel right in the heart of Marseille; good value restaurant.

Middle Range / Economy

Hôtel Mistral, 31 ave de la Pointe Rouge, 8e (Tel. 91 73 44 69 or 91 73 52 45): 23 rooms in family-run hotel with restaurant.

Economy

Hôtel Edmond Rostand, 31 rue Dragon (Tel. 91 37 74 95): cosy hotel in town centre.

Eating Out

First Class

Le Passedat, Le Petit Nice, Anse de Maldormé, 160 Corniche J-F-Kennedy, 7e *arrondissement* (Tel. 91 52 14 39): fabulous restaurant where father-and-son team add fresh ideas to traditional Provençal recipes.

First Class / Middle Range

Restaurant le Palatain, 49 rue Sainte, 1er (Tel. 91 55 02 78): traditionally-based but imaginative cuisine: closed mid-July to early Sept. **Restaurant Miramar,** 12 quai du Port, 2e (Tel. 91 91 10 40): seafood specialities in old port restaurant.

Middle Range

Cousin-Cousine, 102 Cours Julien, 6e (Tel. 91 48 14 50): light, imaginative cooking. **Au Jambon de Parme,** 67 rue de la Palud, 6e (Tel. 91 54 37 98): Provençal and Italian cuisine in a Louis XVI dining room.

Economy

Chez Madie, 138 quai du Port, 2e (Tel. 91 90 40 87): family restaurant with Provençal emphasis. **Chez Soi,** 5 rue Papère (Tel. 91 54 25 41): family cooking with local specialities. **La Dent Creuse,** 14 rue Sénac (Tel. 91 42 05 67): country-style restaurant with cheap menus.

Entertainments

Some of the best entertainment is provided if you get up early and go along to the fish market on quai des Belges, which is bursting with local colour. From late November to 6 January, Marseille holds a Foire aux Santons, where traditional clay and cloth crib figures are on sale. For information on nightlife here, ask the tourist office for Marseille Poche, but remember it is unwise to go alone to the North African quarter (rue Ste-Barbe and bd d'Athènes) at night. In summer, open-air theatre, opera and concerts take place in the courtyard of the Vieille Charité, at Château-Gombert and at the Borély Château. There are some twenty theatres in Marseille, perhaps the best known of which is the **Théâtre de la Criée**. There is also a lively *café-théâtre* called **L'Avant-Scène** on Cours Julien.

Useful Addresses

The main **Tourist Office** is at 4 la Canebière (Tel. 91 54 91 11) and there is a branch at the train station in summer. The **Comité Départemental du Tourisme des Bouches-du-Rhône**, which will give you information on the whole *département* is at 6 rue du Jeune Anacharsis, 1er (Tel. 91 54 92 66), and the **Comité Régional de Tourisme Provence-Alpes-Côte d'Azur**, which can give information on the entire PACA region is in Immeuble CMCI, 2 rue Henri-Barbusse (Tel. 91 39 38 00). The **Post Office** is 1 Place Hôtel des Postes. For **medical assistance**, phone 91 52 84 85.

Transport Options

Most attractions in Marseille are situated within walking distance of the old port but, for some, you will be glad of the efficient and comprehensive bus network. Tickets for the Metro, tramway and buses are interchangeable and can be purchased more economically in *carnets* of six. There are only two Metro lines and one tramway line, which are easy to get used to. For the buses, you will need a copy of the free 'Plan du Réseau RTM'. It is possible to travel by bus to destinations as far out as St-Antoine, Château-Gombert, Allauch, Aubagne and La-Madrague-de-Montredon. For spectacular coastal views, take bus number 83 from the old port to Parc Borély. Rather expensive bus tours leave the tourist office at 10 a.m. every day in summer. Alternatively, take the Petit Train de la Bonne Mère, which offers a 50-minute tour (with commentary) of Old Marseille, including the port and the two basilicas. The ferryboat *le César* plies the route between Place aux Huiles and quai Marie every half-hour; the main Gare Maritime is on quai des Belges and boats leave here regularly for the Château d'If, the Ile de Frioul and the *calanques*.

Var

The Var is a green *département*, whose interior is well worth exploring, criss-crossed with rivers but susceptible to forest fires.

Six-Fours-les-Plages is a typical resort town on a peninsula, and a good base for coach and boat excursions; it has an interesting Heritage Museum in the town hall. The Fort Balaguier at nearby **La Seyne-sur-Mer** houses a Naval Museum. **Toulon** is a major port; its sixteenth-century Royal Tower is worth a visit, as is the Musée du Vieux Toulon. If you leave the coast here and head inland across the quite considerable Ste-Baume massif, you will come to **St-Maximin-la-Ste-Baume**. Here can be found the greatest Gothic monument in Provence, the St-Maximin Basilica and Convent, which holds many concerts. Further inland, the town of **Barjols** boasts 33 fountains, which come into their own when it celebrates the Fête de St-Marcel. The northernmost edge of the Var is marked by the Verdon river, which widens into the **Lac de Ste-Croix** before forming the **Grand Canyon du Verdon**, a deep gorge beside which runs a road known as the Corniche Sublime, which provides spectacular views. To the south-east, beyond a large military zone and the town of Fayence, is the **Lac de St-Cassien**. This is the only freshwater lake in the Var and is a reserve for waterfowl. An educational path has recently been put in place by the Conservatoire Régional at the **Marais de Fondurane**.

At **Draguignan** there is an impressive church tower, topped with wrought-ironwork, and a Museum of Popular Arts and Traditions of Middle Provence. The classical collegiate church of St-Martin at **Lorgues** is worth visiting on your way to **Entrecasteaux**, where there is a castle with a garden, which houses a bizarre collection of paintings and artefacts. Near **Le Thoronet** is a Cistercian abbey. At **Vidauban** Mairie, one room is set aside as a Rustic Museum and **Le-Luc-en-Provence** has an archaeological museum concentrating on the central Var. **Brignoles'** Palace of the Counts of Provence houses a museum of the Pays Brignolais, which includes early Christian altarpieces and a typical local kitchen. Brignoles is also the place to come if you wish to cram a visit of all France's major sights into a few hours! A five-acre park called France in Miniature is landscaped just like France, with geographical features and famous monuments in the appropriate places. There is a garden of contemporary sculptures at **Châteauvert**.

Back on the coast, **Hyères**, which has a Museum of Popular Arts and Traditions, is the best starting point for trips to the **Hyères Islands**. For details, contact the Office de Tourisme, Park Hôtel, avenue de Belgique (Tel. 94 65 18 55). **Porquerolles Island** is densely forested and a botanical reserve; at Fort-Ste-Agathe there is a museum dedicated to the history of the islands, and at Le Hameau

Agricole a botanical exhibition; you can also hire bikes on the island. **Port-Cros Island** is a national park. The information centre is in the port, which is the island's only village; Etissac fortress houses a museum of marine life, and one of the various thematic walks actually goes below sea-level. It is possible to take a boat back to **Le Lavandou**, from where you can head inland to **Collobrières** in the Massif des Maures. Here you will find the lovely old Carthusian monastery of La Verne. Further on, at **Gonfaron**, is the Village des Tortues, which really deserves support. This tortoise re-population centre, founded in 1985, aims to increase the number of Hermann's tortoises on the Maures massif. No tortoise is taken from the wild (they are all donated by their owners or born at the centre), and each one is released into the wild after five or six years. A visit to the centre is fascinating, particularly in June, when the eggs are laid, and September, when they hatch. Opening times are 9 a.m. to 7 p.m. every day (except in Jan. and Feb.) and it is possible to help the cause by 'sponsoring' a tortoise. At **Grimaud** is a ruined castle, dating from the 13th century, and a museum of local arts and traditions.

The St-Tropez peninsula is surprisingly unspoilt, and **St-Tropez** itself has a citadel worth visiting. At **Fréjus** is an episcopal city, with a thirteenth-century cathedral and cloisters, which house an archaeological museum and where concerts are performed in summer. The remains of a Roman arena may also be visited. Nearby **St-Raphaël** is an excellent base for coach trips inland and boat trips to various islands; it also has an archaeological museum. Just along the coast, at **Anthéor**, you can see the blood-red *calanques*, typical of the area.

Accommodation

If you are staying a week or more, St-Raphaël tourist office can provide you with a list of furnished apartments. The following accommodation is recommended:

First Class

Château d'Entrecasteaux, 83570 Entrecasteaux (Tel. 94 04 43 95): 3 rooms in seventeenth- and eighteenth-century château with Le Nôtre gardens. **Château de Ferlande**, route de St-Côme, 83270 St-Cyr-sur-Mer (Tel. 94 26 29 17): 1 *chambre d'hôte* and 2 apartments in old Provençal manor house amid vineyards. **La Ferme d'Augustin**, Plage de Tahiti – St-Tropez, 83350 Ramatuelle

(Tel. 94 97 23 83): 34 rooms in luxury hotel with rustic furnishings, very near beach.

Middle Range

Château d'Artigues, 83560 Artigues-Rians (Tel. 94 80 39 27): 23 rooms in newly renovated sixteenth-century château; excursions possible; restaurant using only fresh produce, notably fish. **Château de Trigance**, 83840 Trigance (Tel. 94 76 91 18): 8 rooms in converted eleventh-century hill-top castle, furnished in medieval style: restaurant. **Castel Lumière**, Le Portail, 83330 Le Castellet Village (Tel. 94 32 62 20): 6 rooms in hotel in medieval village with view of vineyards and sea; restaurant offering traditional cuisine and local wines.

Economy

Le Logis du Guetteur, Place du Château, 83460 Les Arcs (Tel. 94 73 30 82): 11 rooms in converted eleventh-century fort; good restaurant. **Hôtel Notre-Dame**, 15 ave de la Libération, 83610 Collobrières (Tel. 94 48 07 13): 16 rooms in family hotel; restaurant.

Eating Out

In addition to the restaurants mentioned above, try:

First Class

Les Chênes Verts, rte de Villecroze, 83690 Tourtour (Tel. 94 70 55 06): light Provençal cuisine.

First Class / Middle Range

Restaurant le Bistro des Princes, 449 ave Franklin Roosevelt, 83000 Toulon (Tel. 94 42 45 31): brasserie-style dishes with local wines.

Middle Range

Auberge St-Vincent, Carrefour du Pont du Brusc – RN 559, 83140 Six-Fours-les-Plages (Tel. 94 25 70 50): seafood specialities.

Nice

As capital of the Riviera-Côte d'Azur region, Nice likes to play on its reputation for the sophisticated and the exclusive but it is actually one of the more approachable Riviera resorts and has a beautiful Old Town, where *trompe l'œil* façades reflect a strong Italian influence.

On arrival in Nice, heading for the **Promenade des Anglais** and the sea is virtually instinctive. The famous Promenade runs along the sea-front and would be an idyllic place for a stroll . . . without the traffic. Even so, it offers a wonderful choice of views: on one side, the sea stretches to the horizon, peppered with colourful windsurfers; on the other, imposing hotels with legendary names line the road. If you walk along the Promenade des Anglais from its western end, you will soon come across the **Masséna Museum** on your left. This is built in the style of a First Empire Italian villa and contains paintings and altarpieces by artists of the early Nice school, as well as exhibitions on the theme of local customs and history. Further on is the **Jardin Albert 1er**, which leads into the **Place Masséna**, a smart Italian-style square, out of which extends the main shopping street, **ave Jean-Médecin**. There are more gardens on the other side of the square and, between these and the 'château' hill, is the triangular area of narrow winding lanes and flights of steps which makes up Nice's **Old Town**. The main sights here are the seventeenth-century **Cathédrale Ste-Réparata**, the ornate **Eglise St-Jacques**, and the Genoese-style **Palais Lascaris**, whose elaborate rooms may be visited. If you head back to the sea-front, look out for the **Chapelle des Pénitents Noirs**, a Baroque chapel which boasts the oldest known altar screen of the early Nice school. The attractive **Cours Saleya** used to be the Old Town's promenade. If you continue along rue des Ponchettes, you will come to the steps (or lift) that lead to the '**château**'. In fact, there is no castle, but the hill that was once the site of Nice's fortress is known by that name. It offers a 360° panorama, some excavations of Roman and Greek ruins and a pleasant walk past an artificial waterfall. Beyond the 'château' is Nice's port, and beyond that the **Terra Amata Museum**, which has prehistoric exhibits, including a replica of a 400,000 year-old camp, made by hunters near the town.

Near Place Garibaldi are the **Natural History Museum** and the modern, boat-shaped complex known as the **Acropolis**, where contemporary works of art are exhibited, both outside and in. If you follow the Boulevard Carabacel, you will come to the **Musée Marc Chagall**. This is the most impressive collection of Chagall's works and includes the seventeen paintings of his 'Biblical Message', as well as a tapestry, a mosaic, and numerous engravings and sketches.

Beyond here, along and around the boulevard de Cimiez, is the most exclusive residential part of Nice. At the end of the boulevard, past the statue of Queen Victoria (who used to stay here), are the **Roman Ruins**. There is a comprehensive bath complex and an arena, where summer spectacles are now held. A seventeenth-century Italian villa, called the **Arena Villa**, houses two museums: the **Archaeological Museum** exhibits finds from the excavations while the **Matisse Museum** displays paintings, drawings, sculptures and a tapestry, which give a rounded picture of the artist's development. Nearby is a **Fransiscan monastery**, with a beautiful abbey and a Fransiscan museum, situated in terraced gardens.

It is also worth visiting the six-domed **Russian Orthodox Cathedral**, just off boulevard du Tzarewitch; the **Fine Arts Museum**, on ave des Baumettes; and the **Gallery of Naive Painting**, on ave du Val Marie, at the western end of Promenade des Anglais. Children will particularly enjoy two attractions on the outskirts of town: the **Parc Phœnix**, described as 'animated gardens', which boasts the largest greenhouse in the world; and the **Parc des Miniatures**, which uses scale models to tell the 400,000 year history of the Riviera.

Accommodation

The First Class hotels are all quite large, but two of them deserve a mention, as they would make a stay in Nice into the holiday of a lifetime.

First Class

Hôtel Négresco, 37 Promenade des Anglais (Tel. 93 88 39 51): 150 rooms in 1912 building, listed as historic monument – unadulterated luxury. **Hôtel Westminster**, 27 Promenade des Anglais (Tel. 93 88 29 44): 110 rooms in charming turn-of-the-century building, with art collection.

Middle Range

Le Petit Palais, 10 ave Emil-Bicckert (Tel. 93 62 19 11): 25 rooms in stylish hotel in quiet residential area. **Hôtel Excelsior**, 19 ave Durante (Tel. 93 88 18 05): 45 rooms in quiet district near centre. **Mme Olivier**, 61 rte de St-Pierre-de-Féric (Tel. 93 97 02 08): 4 *chambres d'hôte* in pleasant house, 4 km north-west of town centre: *tables d'hôte* available.

Middle Range / Economy

Le Relais de Rimiez, 128 ave de Rimiez (Tel. 93 81 18 65): 24 rooms in family-run hotel.

Economy

Hôtel les Gémeaux, Grande Corniche, 149 bd de l'Observatoire (Tel. 93 89 03 60 or 93 26 90 38): 12 rooms in family-run hotel to north-east of town. **Hôtel Clemenceau**, 3 ave G-Clemenceau (Tel. 93 88 61 19): central hotel with bright, comfortable rooms. **M. Papasseudi**, La Plaine des Fleurs, 65 Vieux Chemin de Crémat (Tel. 93 37 80 92): 4 *chambres d'hôte*, 7 km north-west of town centre. **Hôtel Montreuil**, 18 bis rue Biscarra (Tel. 93 85 95 90): small, centrally-located hotel.

Eating Out

First Class

Le Florian, 22 rue Alphonse-Karr (Tel. 93 88 86 60): wide range of excellent dishes with Provençal emphasis: closes from 10 July to 20 August. **Coco Beach**, 2 ave Jean-Lorrain, Cap de Nice (Tel. 93 89 39 26): impressive seafood restaurant with sea views.

Middle Range

Le Chapon Fin, 1 rue du Moulin (Tel. 93 80 56 92): very good Niçois specialities. **Au Rendez-Vous des Sportifs**, 120 bd de la Madeleine (Tel. 93 86 21 39): authentic Niçois restaurant, off the beaten track.

Economy

Lou Pistou, 4 rue de la Terrasse (Tel. 93 62 21 82): excellent value local fare. **Le Démodé**, 18 rue Benoit-Bunico (Tel. 93 85 70 86): traditional Nice cuisine, using utterly fresh produce. **La Fontaine**, 22 rue Benoit-Bunico (Tel. 93 80 58 99): local recipes in cosy, old town restaurant. **Le Saëtone**, 8 rue d'Alsace-Lorraine (Tel. 93 87 17 95): traditional dishes in central location.

Entertainments

The best entertainment in Nice is free: walking along the sea-front and through the flower market that takes place in Cours Saleya, or window shopping in the new and exclusive Carré d'As complex.

There is a theatre or, alternatively, the '**Expobouffe**' *café-théâtre*, at 24 rue Benoit-Bunico (Tel. 93 80 75 40). It is possible to take a guided tour (in English, if required, and including a tasting) of a traditional confectionery workshop: **Confiserie du Vieux Nice**, quai papacino (Tel. 93 55 43 50). You can also visit an olive oil mill, the **Moulin Alziari**, 318 bd de la Madeleine (Tel. 93 44 45 12). At most times of year, there is some festival or other going on in Nice. The most famous are: the Clairvoyance and Astrology Festival in March; the Nice Carnival, just before Lent; the May Fête; the Sacred Music Festival in June; and the International Folk Festival in July.

Useful Addresses

The main **Tourist Office** is on ave Thiers, right beside the railway station (Tel. 93 87 07 07), but be prepared for queues here. Another branch is at 5 ave Gustave V (Tel. 93 87 60 60). The two major **Post Offices** are at 23 ave Thiers and Place Wilson. For emergency **medical assistance** phone 93 53 03 03. There is a 24-hour chemist at 7 rue Masséna.

Transport Options

Most of Nice can be covered on foot, and the tourist office does a guided tour of the Old Town; ask also about their mini-train tours. From the train station, bus 12 goes to the beach; for further information on town buses, ask at the TN headquarters at 10 ave Félix-Fauré. Bicycles, scooters and motorbikes can be hired from **Nicea Location Rent**, 9 ave Thiers (Tel. 93 82 42 71). Ferries leave from quai du Commerce for Corsica (buy tickets at SNCM office, 3 ave Gustave V). There are also cruises along the Riviera in summer.

Alpes-Maritimes

Most visitors to the Alpes-Maritimes come to the resorts along its 70 km of coastline, yet an astounding 90% of the region is mountainous. Inland, villages of pink and ochre houses, with curved local tiles, perch on hillsides where alpine flowers grow . . . and the sparkling wealth of the Riviera seems miles away.

At **Mandelieu la Napoule** there is a botanical path, where you can see typical Mediterranean plants, either on your own or with a guide. Try to visit the photography museum in the pleasant village of **Mougins**. The hills behind are good walking country.

It is possible to visit an apiary (afternoons only) at the Château de l'Aubarede, **Le Cannet-Rocheville**, and, in Le Cannet itself, do not miss the St-Sauveur-Tobiasse Chapel. The famous resort town of **Cannes** has a lovely sandy beach, a flower market and many art galleries. You can also go on boat trips to the beautiful **Iles des Lérins**; go to chamber music concerts at the Chapelle Ste-Anne; and visit the traditional confectioner's shops, Blachère and Maiffret, on rue Pasteur and rue d'Antibes, respectively. At **Vallauris** are the National Picasso Museum and several potteries, and at **Antibes** the garden of the Villa Thuret is worth visiting (weekdays only). Between Antibes and **Biot** is 'Marineland', where children will enjoy the Petite Ferme Provençale with its baby animals. Biot is home to the National Fernand Léger Museum, whose architecture is inflenced by the painter's work. Nearby is a Museum of Local History, which displays, among other things, local pottery. At **Villeneuve-Loubet** is the Museum of Culinary Art, situated in the house where the famous chef Auguste Escoffier was born. At **Cagnes-sur-Mer**, you can visit Renoir's house and studio, which have also been turned into a museum, and the Château de Cagnes.

If you head inland from here, taking the **Corniche du Var**, you will encounter more ancient castles, as well as walled villages and spectacular views from the western bank of the Var river. At **St-Paul-de-Vence** is the Maeght Foundation, a magnificent twentieth-century art gallery. There are numerous other art galleries and artists' studios to visit, as well as a local history museum. Between **Vence**, where you can visit a nougat factory at 28 ave Colonel-Meyer, and **Tourrette-sur-Loup** is the Notre-Dame-des-Fleurs Château, a former Benedictine abbey, which now houses a Museum of Perfume and Liquor, Tourrette-sur-Loup is another place where you can browse in numerous artists' and craftsmen's (particularly weavers') studios. They line the Grand Rue of this charming medieval village. At **Pont-sur-Loup**, a confectioner's (the Confiserie des Gorges du Loup) offers tours, and at **Gourdon** there is a fortified castle, which houses a Museum of History and Naive Painting and has magnificent gardens. Along the Loup river there are beautiful gorges and marked paths for walkers. Look out for the fifteenth and sixteenth-century altar paintings in the **Bar-sur-Loup** church, and try to visit the fifteenth-century olive oil mill at **Opio**. The next stop should certainly be France's perfume capital, **Grasse**. The town is surrounded by flower-covered slopes and filled with public gardens. Three perfumeries can be visited:

Galimard, Molinard and Fragonard, which dates from 1783. There is also a Perfumery Museum, a Villa-Museum displaying works by members of the Fragonard family, and a Museum of Provençal Art and History.

Further north, at **Roquesteron** and **Gilette**, there are botanical paths, and at **St-Martin-du-Var** you can visit the Duranus Pottery. It is worth taking the road or footpath along the Gorges de Vésubie to **Utelle**, where the church has interesting fifteenth- and sixteenth-century altar paintings. Another good walking area is around **Puget-Théniers**; information on a geological trail here is available from the Ecomusée de la Roudoule at **Puget-Rostang**, which has exhibitions, publications and seminars on local arts, crafts, ways of life, environment and history. **Valberg** is a major ski resort and the site of a Mercantour national park visitor centre. At **Châteauneuf d'Entraunes**, the Moulin de la Barlatte has recently been made into a small *ecomusée*. Further visitor centres are at **Entraunes** and **St-Etienne-de-Tinée**, where there is a challenging hiking trail. **Auron**'s Chapelle St-Erige displays the oldest frescoes in the region. Further south, the Ste-Croix church at **St-Dalmas-Valdeblore** is an example of early Norman architecture, unique in France. Some of the guided tours to the **Vallée des Merveilles**, with its important collection of over 100,000 open-air stone engravings from the Bronze Age, start from **Fontanalbe** and others from the **CAF des Merveilles**. There are parking facilities at the Lac des Mesches and a visitor centre at **Tende**. A historic church organ and extremely fine frescoes are to be seen in **La Brigue** church. There are many more religious buildings of great interest in the attractive village of **Saorge**, perched on the side of the upper Roya Valley. You will also find the studio of Pierre Franca (ave Dr-Davéo), a traditional olive-wood carver. Another specialist of this local craft is M. Rech whose studio is in the Veil quarter of **Breil-sur-Roya**, where there is also an Ecomusée du Haut-Pays, with displays on the natural environment, history and economic life of the Roya and Bévéra valleys, and a Baroque church with a noteworthy organ. Many marked trails and a botanical path start from **Sospel Lucéram** church has a beautiful old altar screen. It is also worth visiting the pretty hill villages of **Peillon** and **Peille**, where there is an *ecomusée* in the Mairie. Spectacular views over the sea can be had from **Castellar** and **Ste-Agnes**, which, at 750 metres, is the highest coastal village in Europe.

Its Italianate buildings, Grecian villas, old harbour and semi-tropical fruit trees (oranges and lemons) make **Menton** one of the Riviera's most famous resorts. It has a Museum of Local Prehistory and several parks and gardens worth visiting, notably those of Les Colombières, with their magnificent view, and the exotic Val Rameh gardens. You can also have a tour of a local jam maker's, the Confiture Herbin (rue du Vieux Collège). The area around **Roquebrune Cap Martin** is one of pines and olive trees, including one olive tree a thousand years old, probably the oldest in the world. A museum devoted to the Middle Ages is housed in the town's castle. The principality of **Monaco**, a sovereign state of under 1 square mile, is the most popular excursion destination on the Riviera, with its palace, hanging gardens, waxworks, oceanography museum, prehistorical anthropology museum, observatory caves, exotic garden of cacti and, of course, the world-famous Monte Carlo Casino. At **La Turbie** there is a 50-metre high Roman monument, called the Trophée des Alpes. The **Cap d'Ail** offers wonderful views of Monaco and stages outdoor plays and concerts in the pine-surrounded Cocteau Amphitheatre. At **Eze-Village** there are Galimard and Fragonard Perfumeries, which can be visited, as well as an exotic garden with some remarkable cacti. At **Beaulieu-sur-Mer**, the Villa Kerylos is a faithful reconstruction of an ancient Greek private residence; the Ile de France villa in **St-Jean-Cap-Ferrat** houses a fine art collection and has spectacular gardens. **Villefranche-sur-Mer** has a medieval old town and a museum of works by the sculptor Volti in a sixteenth-century citadel, whose gardens contain numerous exotic fruit trees.

Accommodation

First Class

Hôtel-Restaurant le Saint-Paul, 86 rue Grande, 06570 St-Paul-de-Vence (Tel. 93 32 65 25): 18 luxurious rooms in sixteenth-century house, decorated in Provençal style and situated in heart of village; highly recommended restaurant. **Château de Cipières**, 06620 Cipières (Tel. 93 59 98 00): 1 *chambre d'hôte* and 6 suites in luxurious mansion: *tables d'hôte* available. **La Colombe d'Or**, Place de Gaulle, 06570 St-Paul-de-Vence (Tel. 93 32 80 02): 27 rooms in exclusive family hotel.

Middle Range

Auberge de la Madone, 06440 Peillon-Village (Tel. 93 79 91 17): 21 rooms in charming hotel in medieval hill-top village; restaurant.

Hostellerie de l'Ancienne Gendarmerie, D 2565, Le Rivet, 06450 Lantosque (Tel. 93 03 00 65): 6 rooms and 3 suites in riverside setting: restaurant.

Economy

Auberge des Seigneurs, Place du Frêne, 06140 Vence (Tel. 93 58 04 24): 7 rooms in medieval house with period furniture; restaurant with Provençal specialities. **Mme Barrois**, Le Bosquet, 06620 Pont-du-Loup, Bar-du-Loup (Tel. 93 42 56 69): 3 *chambres d'hôte* in owner's house. **M. German**, Domaine Ste-Madeleine, 06380 Sospel (Tel. 93 04 10 48): 4 *chambres d'hôte*; farm produce for sale and private swimming pool.

Eating Out

Look out for restaurants displaying the *Charte de la Restauration* sticker – they are members of the Fédération Départementale des Restaurateurs. In addition to those mentioned above, the following **First Class** restaurants are recommended: **Le Moulin de Mougins**, 424 Chemin du Moulin, Notre-Dame-de-Vie, 06250 Mougins (Tel. 93 75 78 24): exquisite cuisine in old mill. **Château Eza**, 06360 Eze-Village (Tel. 93 41 12 24): luxurious cliff-top hotel-restaurant.

19 Languedoc-Roussillon

Visitors who reach this region after travelling through the rest of France often have the impression of arriving in another country. The bright sunshine, in evidence most of the year round, gives the Languedoc-Roussillon its vivid colours, and creates the relaxed pace of life for which the region is famous. Much of Languedoc-Roussillon seems more Spanish than French, with its bullfights and suntanned Mediterranean people, speaking with a strong local dialect that would appear to be more intelligible in Barcelona than in Paris. Day-to-day life is led very much out-of-doors, in pavement cafés, on promenades, with festivals and dances held in village squares. The sense of a world apart is reinforced by the locals' keen sense of their own historical identity, separate from that of the rest of France. The two ancient languages of the region, Occitan and Catalan, are still much in evidence – most obviously in the bilingual street names in some towns and the gold-and-red striped flag of the ancient region of Languedoc flying over some town halls or appearing as bumper stickers on cars. After centuries of what is perceived as the region's colonisation and suppression by the north, anti-Paris feelings are still strong, but mainly among the older generation. The region's main cultural contribution came between eleventh and thirteenth centuries, in the form of the long lyrical Occitan verses of the troubadours, which were recited in courtly circles all over Europe. Both parts of the region are currently in the throes of a local cultural revival, making great efforts to keep their ancient languages alive. In Roussillon, Catalan is still in everyday use, with French a second language for many. Languedoc's Occitan language survives as a patois in some rural corners, but there have been attempts to revive this. It is now taught in schools and in the region's universities, and poetry and novels are written in it. Although there is no great movement for independence – decentralisation has satisfied most people's desire for autonomy – there are still occasional outbursts of regional passion, such as during the 1970s when vine-growers protested violently at wine imports from other EC countries.

Tourism has taken over from vine-growing as the region's main industry, as the demand for cheap, low-quality wine has fallen. Those from other parts of France regard the wines of Languedoc-Roussillon somewhat disdainfully, erroneously believing them *all* to be the poorer quality 'vins ordinaires' that the region used to pour so abundantly into Europe's wine lake. In fact, during the past thirty years, most of the poor quality vines have been uprooted, and many of the region's vineyards have been replanted to produce AC ('appellation contrôlée') wines and have been officially upgraded. Languedoc-Roussillon was put firmly on the tourist map during the 1960s and 1970s, as a result of the French government's ambitious project, designed to breathe life into the region's stagnant economy, to attract tourists away from the neighbouring Côte d'Azur and Costa Brava. The large-scale development of the coastline by the state in partnership with the private sector led to seven modern resorts being built on sites previously the domain only of mosquitoes: Port Camargue, La Grande Motte, Carnon, Cap d'Agde, Gruisson, Port-Leucate and Port-Barcarès. The project has been the subject of ongoing debate since its launch in 1963. On the positive side, the resorts are well spaced-out along the coast, leaving wide areas in between, protected mainly by the Conservatoire de l'Espace Littoral. Ecologists, however, claim that the chemical blitz that was used to rid the coastline of its mosquito population was environmentally harmful, and that the new concrete resorts have had considerable impacts on wildlife habitats through pollution, land drainage and general disturbance. In any case, there is no doubt that these resorts are what attract the majority of Languedoc-Roussillon's summer visitors, who have increased in number from half a million in 1964 to today's figure of 5 million.

History

The hybrid region of Languedoc-Roussillon was formed in 1964, combining part of the ancient region of Languedoc with French Catalonia, or Roussillon, whose history and development were completely different.

The original inhabitants of Languedoc were Iberian tribes, but they readily absorbed the customs of the other civilisations who made this territory their own. The Greeks who settled in towns such as Agde and Marseillan around 500 BC, and brought the vine to the region, were followed by the Romans, 400 years later. The main legacy left by the Romans was the construction of many aqueducts, temples and roads, which remain among the region's greatest attractions. With the disintegration of the Roman empire. Languedoc was invaded by successive waves of Visigoths then, more briefly, Moors. The latter were driven out in the eighth century and feudal rule by the Counts of Toulouse gradually took their place. The long history of the region's detachment from the rest of France began with the Counts of Toulouse, whose complete independence from the French monarchy eventually led to their cruel annihilation by the crown. The excuse for this was the counts' support for the region's Cathars, whose doctrine was held by the Catholic Church to be heretical. The Counts of Toulouse were overwhelmed in the Albigensian Crusade (1208–1244), launched by Philippe Auguste of France and Pope Innocent III. The knights of the Ile-de-France, led by Simon de Montfort, rooted out and destroyed the Cathars and with them Languedoc's own troubadour culture.

The proximity of the frontier with Spain and the constant risk of war had caused the inhabitants of the region to construct many castles and fortified towns, such as Carcassonne and Aigues-Mortes. During the Albigensian Crusade, the Cathars took refuge in the many hill-top castles which still bear their name. It was after the region fell into the possession of the French crown that it began to be called 'Languedoc' – because its inhabitants did not speak French, but the 'langued'oc', in which 'oc' was the word for 'yes', not 'oui' as in the north. The popularity of Protestantism in the region was the next marked difference between it and the rest of France. After the religious wars of the sixteenth century, the Edict of Nantes allowed many Languedoc towns to practice their Protestantism. But the revoking of this edict by Louis XIV led to an uprising by the Huguenot Camisards based in the Cévennes Hills, in the north of the region. The Camisard War (1702–4) resulted in the ruthless crushing of the rebels by the crown. But, despite this, the Cévennes are still a stronghold of the Protestant faith in France.

Roussillon, the other part of this modern region, has a common history with the rest of the region of Catalonia, south of the Pyrenees, except for a brief period during the thirteenth and fifteenth centuries, when Roussillon was part of the Kingdom of Majorca. The Palace of the Kings of Majorca in Perpignan is a legacy of that era. After that, it alternated between French and Spanish rule. It was part of Spain for the 150 years leading up to 1659, with the signing of the Treaty of the Pyrenees, which established the present Franco-Spanish frontier, granting everything north of the Pyrenees to Louis XIII of France. Culturally, the people of Roussillon remain Catalans, with their own Catalan language still very much alive, and strong links with the people of Spanish Catalonia across the border.

The rebellious spirit of the people of Languedoc-Roussillon had its fullest expression in the recent century, when the region was the centre of Resistance activity during the Occupation of the Second World War. The members of the Resistance movement took their name, 'maquisards', from the local scrubland ('maquis') in which they hid from the occupying forces.

Geography

The Languedoc-Roussillon region stretches along the Mediterranean coast from the border with Spain to the mouth of the Rhône, a distance of 240 km. The lie of the land resembles a vast amphitheatre facing the sea, whose successive layers demonstrate the variety of the landscape: hills and mountains, then limestone plateaux or *causses*, then the flat coastal plain. The Pyrenees and the Cévennes Hills have firs and pines on the higher slopes, with forests of cork oak and beech further down, broken in parts by areas of 'maquis' or scrubland. These slopes are famed for the variety and abundance of their wild herbs, mushrooms and the wild flowers that attract vast numbers of butterflies in spring and summer. The wild boar, chamois and wild cat are still common in the Pyrenees, while the brown bear has been reduced to near-extinction by human inroads into its habitat.

In front of the mountains lie the *causses*, limestone plateaux inside of which lie grottoes, huge underground cathedrals with bizarre stalactites and stalagmites. The *causses* themselves, used mainly for sheep-grazing, are intersected by narrow but deep canyons or gorges, cut by rivers such as the Tarn and the Hérault. The low hills leading down to the plain are characterised by the distinctive *garrigue*, a low, impenetrable scrub of broom and dwarf oak, scented by the presence of thyme, lavender, mint, and other aromatic herbs. The fertile coastal plain is dominated by the vineyards which produce 40% of France's wine, including most of its cheap table wine. Between these, lie large *étangs*, or coastal lagoons of salt water, separated from the sea itself by sand-dunes. The *étangs* are rich in wildlife that includes leeches, larvae, molluscs and alevins and, in summer, are home to flocks of bright pink flamingoes, creating a breathtaking sight as they take off or land. The coast itself alternates between areas of intensive tourism development and large areas of genuine wilderness.

Languedoc-Roussillon is well-endowed with national and regional parks and nature reserves. A full 25% of all France's protected sites are to be found in this region, including most of its coastal strip. Its seven natural reserves amount to a total of nearly 20,000 acres. The Haut-Languedoc Regional Park's position makes it of great botanical interest, as its flora gradually changes from that of the Mediterranean to that of the Atlantic zones. Mammals inhabiting the forests and hills of the park include the mouflon (a form of wild sheep) and the wild boar. The *causses*, mountain forests and gorges of the Cévennes National Park, France's largest park, attract a wide range of inhabitants including several raptors, such as the reintroduced griffon vulture, the short-toed eagle and golden eagle, as well as wild boar and deer.

The region is made up of five *départements*. Pyrénées-Orientales, Aude, Hérault and Gard lie along the coast, while Lozère lies inland. The university town of Montpellier, with 200,000 inhabitants, is the regional capital.

Climate

Apart from in its mountain regions, the Languedoc-Roussillon benefits from weather which is predictable and typically Mediterranean. Summers are long, hot and dry, with temperatures consistently around 30°C. Winters are cooler, but short. Rain, when it falls, tends to come in spring and autumn. The Pyrenees and the Cévennes are cooler in winter, with snow on their peaks sometimes as early as October through to May. The region is occasionally disturbed by violent winds: the Mistral, which blows down the Rhône Valley, and cools the sea; the Tramontane, so-called because it comes across the mountains; and the Marin which blows off the sea, bringing wet weather.

Attractions

There is no doubt that the sunshine and clear blue skies that this region enjoys for most of the year are among its main attractions. The outdoor life is what most tourists come for, whether this is sitting on the beach, or indulging in more active pursuits such as canoeing, hill-walking, or horseriding in the region's hinterland and mountains. The landscape itself provides many attractions, from wildlife study in the extensive wetlands of the **Camargue** to hill-walking amid the strange alien beauty of the *causses*, with their underground grottoes such as the **Grotte des Demoiselles**. The **Pyrenees** conceal a multitude of unspoilt villages waiting to be explored. The **Cévennes Hills** have a quiet beauty of their own and, even in summer, provide a dignified contrast to the frantic commercialism of the crowded urban resorts on the coast. The attractions of the Cévennes include the **Musée du Désert**, telling of 200 years of Huguenot history, the **Cirque de Navacelles**, and the **Ecomusée du Mont-Lozère**. Sightseeing also focuses on the human imprint on the natural environment: the lofty **Cathar castles**, the three-tier Roman aqueduct at **Pont du Gard**, the **Maison Carré** temple in Nîmes, two of Europe's best-preserved medieval walled towns, **Carcassonne** and **Aigues-Mortes**, and Perpignan's stately **Palace of the Kings of Majorca**. Many of the region's cities have attractive historic centres, such as those of **Montpellier, Nîmes, Perpignan**, and **Béziers**. But the small towns and villages of Languedoc-Roussillon's coast and countryside are popular too: **Collioure, Sète, Grau du Roi, Auduze, Pézenas**, and **St Guilhem-le-Désert** are among the most attractive. Water is the focus for many tourist attractions and activities, not only the long coastline, on which quiet **beaches** can still be found, but also the **gorges** of the Rivers Hérault, Tarn and Vis, for canoeing and swimming, and the beautiful seventeenth-century **Canal du Midi**, for holiday cruising.

Cuisine

Languedoc-Roussillon is best known for its fish, seafood and charcuterie as well as the abundance of peaches, apricots, lemons, strawberries and cherries, which ripen much earlier here than in other parts of France. Bass (*loup*) and angler fish (*baudroie*) are always fresh and appetising, as are the mussels and oysters from the *étang* at Leucate. Anchovies are a regional delicacy, from the mouthwatering *anchoide* (anchovy paste) of Nîmes to the anchovy *salade composée* of Collioure. A well-known dish of the region is the very rich *cassoulet*, a combination of lamb, pork, or bacon, with sausages, onions, garlic, white beans and tomatoes. *Pelardon* is a favourite goats' milk cheese, sold in small discs, and often appearing toasted as *chèvre chaud*, with lettuce and walnuts, as a starter. This is one of the few dishes of the region suitable for vegetarians. Another is *aligot*, a potato-and-cheese dish of Lozère.

Regarding the region's wines, the best are the rich and fruity reds: Corbières, Faugères, Fitou, and Saint Saturnin. The white Côtes de Roussillon is a light dry wine which goes well with the local seafood and shellfish. Also worth trying as an aperitif or with the dessert are the sweet wines produced in the region: Muscat de Frontignan, Muscat de Lunel, Rivesaltes and Banyuls.

Level of Tourism

With almost 5 million tourists a year, Languedoc-Roussillon is third in the roll-call of France's tourist regions. The region is highly dependent on its income from tourism, earning almost 12% of its gross domestic product from this industry, the second highest proportion in France after Corsica. Its 50,000 British visitors a year form the fourth largest foreign-visitor group (14%), coming well behind the Germans, Dutch and Belgians. But the region's most numerous visitors by far are the French themselves. In summer, 88% of tourists come from other parts of France – mainly the Ile-de-France: about one in five of all French summer visitors is a Parisian. This is typically a long summer holiday destination for the French, the average length of stay being around 20 days. Among the French, there is great loyalty towards the region as a destination. About three-quarters of all its French visitors have already spent a holiday in Languedoc-Roussillon. This preponderance of French visitors gives the region's tourism its characteristics: the main season is very short – three-quarters of all visits to Languedoc-Roussillon are crammed into the period between 15 June and 15 September; 92% of all tourists use their own cars to get there, and secondary residences constitute by far the most popular type of accommodation – 63% of the region's accommodation stock is composed of second-ary residences, the vast majority of which belong to the French themselves. Most tourism in the region is highly concentrated into a small fraction of the land area. It ranges from the intense concentration of the modern coastal resorts and towns just in from the coast, which account for 69% of all tourist nights, to the much lower impact tourism of the countryside inland, where only 10% of all tourist nights are spent, and the mountains, with 21%.

Languedoc-Roussillon is largely an independent tourist's destination. Most tour operators' products in the region are confined to the coastal strip – camping and caravanning holidays, rented holiday flats, and cruising on the Canal du Midi. Away from the coast, tourism retains the character of a cottage industry, with a multitude of small-scale and highly personal enterprises offering accommodation such as the *gîte rural* or the family hotel, and activity and interest holidays for small groups. Nevertheless, many of these small businesses are well-organised: each of the *départements* of Aude, Lozère, and Pyrénées-Orientales has its own Loisirs-Accueil reservation service, bringing together a wide range of rural tourism products. (See **Good Alternatives**).

The A9 autoroute can be extremely busy during July and August as it is the main route to Spain. During the last weekend in July or the first in August, traffic levels are at their highest, and cars go along this section of the A9 at a snail's pace. For a more leisurely and much more scenic route through the region, use the Route du Piémont – see **Good Alternatives**. July and August are also the months to avoid if you want to see the Pont de Gard or the small historic towns of Carcassonne, Pézenas, or Aigues-Mortes – all well worth seeing, but overrun by tourists in summer. Likewise, the new coastal resorts of La Grande Motte, Carnon, Cap d'Agde, Gruissan, Port-Leucate, and Port-Barcarès are full to bursting during July and August, in strong contrast to the almost desolate calm found there at other times of the year. Fortunately, away from these resorts, it is easy to find quiet beaches. Try l'Espiguette, Marseillan-Plage, Fleury d'Aude, or any of the beaches between Canet and St Cyprien-Plage.

Surprisingly, perhaps, for a region with a strong anti-Paris tradition, there is very little (expressed) resistance to the annual influx of tourists. In the past, farmers resented the arrival of so many, and grumbled about the volume of traffic on country roads and the sometimes inconsiderate behaviour of hikers. But since the decline of the region's cheap winegrowing industry, this previous pocket of resistance has now joined those who see tourism as a great hope for Languedoc-Roussillon. Many of them have taken up the EC grants which are available to the region's farmers to help them purchase the amenities they need to receive tourists – such as equipment for camping sites on their land. There remains some underlying resentment towards the Dutch, who have the reputation of spending very little in the region, arriving in cars loaded up with enough Gouda cheese and other Dutch produce to last the entire holiday (a reputation supported in fact by official tourism figures showing that the Dutch spend least per head, of all foreign visitors). The British, on the other hand, are regarded locally as a quiet and unobtrusive race, quite happy to spend two weeks relaxing peacefully in the remoter parts of the region.

The Regional Council's plans for the expansion of Languedoc-Roussillon's tourism centre around efforts to increase the quality of the accommodation and facilities, and lengthening the season. The region's sparsely-populated *arrière pays*, the countryside inland, is regarded as virgin territory for tourism, with great potential for small-scale, low-impact development in the future. Elsewhere, the construction of golf courses, such as that at St Cyprien, is seen as a way of attracting the up-market visitor, despite the enormous problems involved in keeping golf courses green under the summer sun. Business tourism, in the form of conferences and trade fairs, is being encouraged, and Montpellier's Corum conference centre is the region's latest showpiece in this respect. Foreign markets are being targeted for publicity campaigns, as these are more likely than the less flexible French to be persuaded to visit the region in the low-season.

Good Alternatives

Meeting People

Languedoc-Roussillon provides many opportunities for meeting French people in their own workplaces, and gaining an insight into how well-known brand name products are made, or how artisan work is still carried out. The Comité Régional de Tourisme's free leaflet, 'Découverte Economique', gives details of visits – most of them free – from Noilly Prat to IBM. It includes: **Perrier's** guided tours around its source and bottling plant – contact: Source Perrier, Les Bouillens, 30310 Vergèze (Tel. 66 87 62 00); tours of the factory belonging to **Cantalou**, France's biggest chocolate exporter – contact: Chocolaterie Cantalou, route de Thuir, 66011 Perpignan Cédex (Tel. 68 85 11 22); visits to a reconstruction of a typical farm of the *causses* region – contact: **Ferme Caussenarde de Hyelzas**, 48150 Hures la Parade (Tel. 66 45 65 25); and visits to a salt-marsh, with a commentary on how sea salt is extracted – contact: **Compagnie des Salins du Midi et des Salines de l'Est**, Exploitation salinière, D 979, 30220 Aigues-Mortes (Tel. 66 53 82 88).

Alternatively, you could put yourself to work by joining a group doing voluntary work on a *chantier* in the Cévennes national park. Projects range from restoring an abandoned farmhouse to clearing a GR route. You need to arrange your own transport and accommodation, but tools are provided and accompanied tours of the park are given in reward for your labour. Ask (well in advance) for the leaflet 'Chantiers bénévoles' from the Parc National des Cévennes, Château de Florac, 48400 Florac (Tel. 66 45 01 75). Conservation *chantiers* in the Gard *département* are also run by **Les Compagnons du Cap**, Pratcustals, Arply, 30120 Le Vigan (Tel. 67 81 82 22). Information on joining an archaeological dig in the region is available from the **Direction des Antiquités**, 5 bis rue de la Salle L'Evêque, BP 2051, 34026 Montpellier (Tel. 67 66 03 77).

Discovering Places

The **Conservatoire Régional de la Faune, de la Flore et des Espaces Naturels du Languedoc-Roussillon** organises guided visits to a variety of natural sites in the region, including the *étangs* of Palavas, the gorges of the River Gardon, and the Camargue. For information, contact CORFFEN, Maison de l'Environnement, 16 rue Ferdinand Fabre, 34000 Montpellier (Tel. 67 79 77 50). Three of the region's **Centres Permanents d'Initiation à l'Environnement** (Environmental Discovery Centres) run a programme of tours of the local fauna and flora: for the wildlife of the Narbonne *étangs* and barge-trips, contact the CPIE, Ecluse de Mandirac, 11100 Narbonne (Tel. 68 48 35 48). For a look at the eagles and vultures of the Causses de Larzac, and tours of its dolmens and menhirs, contact the CPIE du Larzac Méridional, Presbytère Laclastre, 34520 St Maurice Navacelles (Tel. 67 44 63 81). For the birds and elusive mouflons of the Haut-Languedoc, contact the CPIE du Haut-Languedoc at the regional park address below.

The **Parc Naturel Régional du Haut-Languedoc** and the **Cévénnes National Park** also offer very reasonably-priced activity holidays, from horseriding and accompanied walks to cycling and nature study tours. Details from the parks themselves: Haut-Languedoc, 13 rue du Cloître, 34220 St-Pons-de-Thomières (Tel.

67 97 02 10). Cévennes – address above. **Tailhos Découvertes** in the Haut-Languedoc is a small-scale tourism enterprise typical of those operating in the parks. It provides *ferme-auberge* accommodation, with catering based on their own farm produce, plus a range of activities, including mountain biking, potholing and canoeing. Half-board is from 150FF per person per day. Contact: Mr and Mrs Hinsinger, 34220 St-Pons-de-Thomières (Tel. 67 97 27 62).

Well worth considering, also, are the activity holidays offered by the inhabitants of two Pyrenean villages far away from the parts of the region colonised by mass tourism. **Mantet** at an altitude of 2000metres in a national nature reserve rich in wildlife and wild flowers, was abandoned in the 1960s. Its 27 residents now earn their living through a combination of farming and tourism. Mountain biking, horseriding, climbing and gorge walking are among the activities on offer. Full-board in the activity holiday centre, guides, and use of equipment costs about 250FF per person per day. General contact for the village: Odile Guinel, La Bouf'tic, 66360 Mantet (Tel. 68 05 51 76). The tiny Pyrenean village of **Olette** also serves as an excellent base for activity holidays. **Exodus Expeditions** – 9 Weir Road, London SW12 0LT (Tel. 081 675 5550) offer 15-day packages based in Olette, with accompanied hikes every day to other mountain villages, at around £770 per person, all-inclusive. Otherwise, shorter, more flexible hiking holidays, with *gîte* accommodation, can be tailor-made for those passing through the Pyrenees, or with less time to spare. Contact: Elizabeth Prevot, CCI antenne de Prades, 10 Place de le République, 66500 Prades (Tel. 68 05 21 41).

Languedoc-Roussillon's three **Loisirs-Accueil** reservation services bring together a rich offering of reasonably-priced products on a small-scale and run by local people. A 3-day tour of the Cathar Castles of the Aude, with half-board in a 2-star hotel costs around 800FF. One-week breaks learning yoga techniques in the Lozère, with *gîte* accommodation are available at around 2000FF per person, full-board. A 6-day study tour of Pyrenean fauna and flora on horseback, with *gîte d'étape* accommodation, costs about 2000FF. Contact the Loisirs-Accueil services direct, for details of these and the many other holidays: **Loisirs-Accueil Aude**, 39 boulevard Barbès, 11000 Carcassonne (Tel. 68 47 09 06); **Loisirs-Accueil Lozère**, Place Urbain V, B P 4, 48002 Mende Cedex (Tel. 66 49 24 25); **Loisirs-Accueil Pyrénées-Orientales**, quai de Lattre-de-Tassigny, 66000 Perpignan (Tel. 68 34 55 06).

France Naturellement offers specialist-led holiday/study tours, for groups of six or twelve people, concentrating on the region's national parks and nature reserves. The director is English, and a qualified environmental scientist, specialising in the conservation and management of rural areas. The typical cost of a 1-week study tour for twelve people travelling together works out at around 8800 FF per person, for tour transport, specialist leader's and local lecturer's fees, meals, and comfortable accommodation. Alternatively, dormitory-style accommodation in field-study centres is available at lower prices. Contact Marianne Carr, 66730 Pezilla-de-Conflent (Tel. 68 97 71 41). **Knights of Languedoc** run tailor-made tours of the region, with accommodation in family-run hotels and châteaux. Four or five night gourmet itineraries cover the Cévennes, gorges and *causses*, or Lower Languedoc and the Haut Languedoc National Park, or Carcassonne and Catalonia, from around £195 per person in the low season to £300 in the high season, for half-board accommodation. A range of special interest holidays is also available, including regional cookery courses and tours of the Camargue. For details contact: Ben and Alissa Knight, La Liniere, 34600 Bedarieux or their London office (Tel. 071 704 0589).

Finally, one of the best choices for those driving through the Languedoc-Roussillon is the inland alternative to the busy autoroute 9. Avoid the wear and tear on your nerves, and explore some of the region's best countryside at the same time, by taking the parallel route through the region, about 60 km in from the coast. Called the Route du Piémont by the Regional Council, who are making efforts to promote it, this is a series of national and departmental roads through some of the region's most interesting parts, skirting the Cévennes and the Haut Languedoc Regional Park. Details from the **Comité Regional de Tourisme**, 20 rue de la République, 34000 Montpellier (Tel. 67 92 67 92), who will also supply general information on the whole region.

Communications

How to Get There

Get to Languedoc-Roussillon by **air** from Britain by taking a Dan Air flight from Gatwick to Montpellier or Perpignan, or an Air France flight from Heathrow to Montpellier (twice weekly). There are domestic flights from Paris to Montpellier, Nîmes, Béziers, and Perpignan. Montpellier is also served by flights from Bordeaux, Nice, and Lyon.

Direct TGV **trains** from Paris, Gare de Lyon, run to this region and connect its major cities, beginning with Nîmes (4¼ hours from Paris), then Montpellier and Béziers. Slower trains run along the same route, also serving Sète, Agde, Narbonne and Perpignan.

A direct **coach** service from London to Nîmes Montpellier and Perpignan, is operated by Eurolines, costing around £95 adult return. The car journey from Paris to Perpignan takes nearly 9 hours and can be extremely costly in tolls if you use the motorway.

When You're There

Rail – branches from the busy main line mentioned above stretch inland to the region's other pricipal cities: from Narbonne to Carcassonne, and from Nîmes to Alès and Mende. Picturesque 'tourist' trains operate on certain routes, such as the 'petit train jaune' in the Pyrenees, or the Cévennes steam train connecting Anduze and St Jean du Gard.

Bus – in the region itself, a fairly dense network of coach services serves destinations in the mountains and hills back from the coast. Efficient and punctual coaches operate from the coach stations or 'gares routières' in the following towns: Nîmes – rue Sainte-Félicité (Tel. 66 29 52 00); Montpellier – rue Jules Ferry (Tel. 67 92 01 43); Narbonne – quai Victor Hugo (Tel. 68 32 07 60); Perpignan – avenue Général Leclerc (Tel. 68 35 29 02).

Car – the only two motorways in the region are the A9 all along the coast, and the A61 connecting Narbonne and Carcassonne to Toulouse. For alternatives to the A9, see **Good Alternatives** section. Inland there are plenty of minor roads which make exploring the region a pleasure.

Boat – the Canal du Midi and the Canal du Rhône à Sète run the entire length of Languedoc-Roussillon. Between Easter and November, no special permit is needed to hire a houseboat for a relaxing cruise through the region. The leaflet 'Tourisme Fluvial', produced by the Comité Régionale de Tourisme lists the many local companies which hire out craft on the canals.

Walking – There are some 4000km of *Grande-Randonnée* footpaths in Languedoc-Roussillon, from the Pyrenean GR36 to the GR4 across the 'causses' of Lozère. Tourist offices will supply details and the topo-guide references, as well as suggestions for the region's many shorter, local hikes. An excellent way of meeting French people, and seeing some of the region's best countryside at the same time, is to join in some of the walking tours organised by

Languedoc-Roussillon's rambling associations. All welcome foreign visitors, and can be contacted through each *département's* **Comité Départemental de Randonnées** (Ramblers' Committees): Aude: 13 rue de la République, 11000 Carcassonne (Tel. 68 72 60 61); Gard: Centre Raymond Gourdon 5 rue Raymond Marc, 30000 Nîmes; Hérault: Chambre d'Agriculture Place Chaptal, 34076 Montpellier Cedex (Tel. 67 92 88 00); Lozère: Place Urbain V BP 4, 48000 Mende (Tel. 66 65 34 55); Pyrénées-Orientales: 1 rue des Roses, 66500 Ria (Tel. 68 96 46 41).

The Comité Régional de Tourisme's free guide, 'Randonnées', gives details of the region's footpaths, professional guides, cycling tours, riding tours, and opportunities for cross-country skiing.

Useful Local Contacts

For the address of the **Conservatoire Régional** and the national and regional parks, see **Good Alternatives** section. It might also be of interest to contact **L'Association Languedoc-Roussillon pour la diffusion de l'Ecologie scientifique**, 34270 St Jean de Cuculles (Tel. 67 55 28 86), or the **Société de Protection de la Nature du Languedoc-Roussillon**, Place Eugène Bataillon, 34000 Montpellier (Tel.67 63 47 62).

Geographical Breakdown of Region

Pyrénées-Orientales & Aude

Perpignan

A truly Mediterranean city, Perpignan is a colourful collection of charming squares and shared avenues of plane trees, mimosa and palms. Ask for the the tourist office's leaflet 'Flaneries à Perpignan', for a list of all the main attractions. The **Palace of the Kings of Majorca** in rue des Archers is an outstanding example of medieval military architecture, with some fine Gothic buildings and two chapels in the thirteenth-century citadel. The pink dome of the fourteenth-century château of **Le Castillet** in Place de la Victoire gives it an almost oriental appearance. Inside is housed the Casa Païral – the **Musée d'Arts et Traditions Populaires du Roussillon**. From its terrace, there is a spectacular view of the city, the Roussillon plain, the sea, and the Pyrenees. Nearby, the **Cathédrale Saint-Jean** in the Place Gambetta dates from 1324, and stands as an excellent example of southern Gothic.

Built in the typical small red bricks of the region, its richly ornate interior features a Romanesque chapel dating from 1025, and some beautiful stained-glass windows. To continue your sightseeing *and* have a rest at the same time, walk the short distance to the **Place de la Loge**, for a seat in one of the outdoor cafés. From there, you can admire the fine medieval buildings, including the **Hôtel de Ville** and **La Loge de Mer**, the former Bourse de Commerce of the region, but now housing a fast-food outlet! The **Musée d'Histoire Naturelle** in the Place Fontaine-Neuve has a rich collection dedicated to the fauna and flora of the South of France.

Accommodation

There are no small first class hotels in Perpignan. Instead try:

Middle Range

Hôtel de la Loge, Place de la Loge (Tel. 68 34 54 84): 29 antique-furnished rooms in central hotel with welcoming owners. **Hôtel de France**, 16 quai Sadi-Carnot (Tel. 68 34 92 81): 31 comfortable rooms and 4 apartments in waterfront hotel; excellent restaurant.

Middle Range / Economy

Hôtel Kennedy, 9 ave P-Cambres (Tel. 68 50 60 02): 25 rooms in hotel on edge of town behind citadel.

Economy

Hôtel le Bristol, 5 rue Grande des Fabriques (Tel. 68 34 32 68): large rooms in good, though quiet, location. **Hôtel de la Poste**, 6 rue Fabriques-Nabot (Tel. 68 34 42 53): 32 spacious rooms in friendly, central hotel; restaurant.

Eating Out

First Class

Le Chapon Fin, 18 bd Jean-Bourrat (Tel. 68 35 14 14): light cuisine using local ingredients, in typical Catalan dining room.

First Class / Middle Range

Le Relais St-Jean, Place de la Cathédrale (Tel. 68 51 22 25): changing selections of high quality food served in pleasantly situated restaurant popular with local people.

Middle Range

François Villon, 1 rue du Four St-Jean (Tel. 68 51 18 43): excellent regional restaurant in room with vaulted ceiling.

Economy

Le Perroquet, 1 ave Général de Gaulle: good Catalan-style menus. **Le Palmarium**, Place Argo: good value restaurant with canal-side terrace. **Restaurant des Iles**, 14 rue Grande la Monnaie (Tel. 68 34 40 14): good for vegetarian dishes.

Entertainments

Even in summer, Perpignan's streets are quiet after 10 p.m. but the action continues in its restaurants and bars, which are lively until well after midnight. During Holy Week, at the end of March, the town throbs with music and festivities celebrating the Catalan peoples' religious traditions. Try to be there for the breathtaking Sanch procession and the 'sardanes' – Catalan folk dances in front of the Castillet.

Useful Addresses

The **Tourist Office** is in the Palais de Congrès, Place Armand Lanoux (Tel.68 34 13 13 or 68 66 30 00). The **Comité Départemental de Tourisme** at quai de Lattre-de-Tassigny (Tel.68 34 29 94), has information on the whole Pyrénées-Orientales *département*. The **Post Office** is on quai de Barcelone, and the **Hospital** on ave du Maréchal Joffre (Tel. 68 61 66 30).

Transport Options

Perpignan's network of narrow streets is best explored on foot. Bicycles are available for hire from the SNCF station (Tel. 68 51 10 44), or Cycles Mercier, 1 rue du Président Doumer (Tel.68 85 02 71). There is a good town bus service, but buses are scarce after 9 p.m.

Rest of Pyrénées-Orientales and Aude

Begin your exploration of the most southerly and mountainous region of Languedoc-Roussillon with its charming Catalan villages, in **Prades**, in the verdant Têt valley – also known as **Le Conflent**. Each July and August, in the abbey of Saint-Michel-de-Cuxa, this town hosts the Pablo Casals Festival, in honour of the great cellist who lived there from 1939 to 1960. Continue along the road after the abbey to the Col de Millères, from where you can climb to the 2785m-high peak of the **Canigou** – an hour's hike, but well worth the view! The nearby village of **Villefranche-de-Conflent** is the starting point for the Petit Train Jaune de Cerdagne, which runs the 63km between here and **Latour-de-Carol**. With open carriages in summer, this is one of the most spectacular ways of seeing the Pyrenees, passing through **Bolquère/Eyne**, the highest station in Europe open to commercial traffic. Get off at **Montlouis** for a well worthwhile detour north into the **Capcir** region. **Formiguères**, the largest town, which was chosen by the Kings of Majorca as their summer resort in the thirteenth century, is a good centre for mountain hikes. But make a point of seeing some of the smaller mountain villages such as **Espousouille, Réal, or Fontabiouse**, which all provide excellent examples of Capcir's rural architecture. Back to Montlouis, continue west into the **Cerdagne** region, whose climate makes it a natural centre for research into solar energy. You can visit the huge solar furnace in **Odeillo** and the thermodynamic solar plant of Thémis, in **Targassonne**. North of Odeillo, **Les Bouillouses** is a classified natural site of 4450 acres, at over 2000m altitude, with several lakes of dazzling beauty.

Visit **Carcassonne** out of season only, to have the tranquillity to enjoy the perfection of this hill-top medieval town. Although the walled 'cité' is the main attraction, the rest of the town, the 'vine basse' contains a good example of southern Gothic architecture in the fourteenth-century Cathédrale Saint-Michel, as well as the Eglise Saint-Vincent, with its flamboyant steeple. Spend some time looking into the fine courtyards of the lower town's many 'hôtels particuliers', before climbing up to the cité. The famous **cité** is surrounded by a double wall and 52 towers. The Basilique Saint-Nazaire, known as the jewel of the cité, has its original Romanesque nave, but a Gothic choir, as well as a tombstone said to be that of Simon de Montfort. The twelfth-century Château Comtal, stronghold of the cité, can be visited on a guided tour only. But much of the cité's charm can be appreciated simply by strolling around its narrow streets, or the *lices*, the space between the two walls. While doing so, look to the left of the Porte Narbonnaise, the cité's largest entrance, to see the various materials used in the construction of the ramparts by the various occupants of the cité.

Carcassonne is at its liveliest during its festivals. The August

Médiévales festival sees the inhabitants, in medieval dress, reconstruct the daily life of those times. There is jousting, a medieval market, and a *Son et Lumière* show lights up the cité at night. Go in June for the Troubadours festival of medieval music, or in July for the Festival of the Walled Town, with theatre, music and dance. The tourist office is at 15 boulevard Camille-Pelletan (Tel.68 25 07 04), with a summer annexe in the Porte Narbonnaise, the cité (Tel. 68 25 68 81). Information on the whole Aude *département* is available from the **Comité Régional de Tourisme**, 39 boulevard Barbès (Tel. 68 71 30 09). Everywhere in Carcassonne is within easy walking distance, but for an effortless 20-minute tour of the ramparts, take the 'petit train' from the Porte Narbonnaise, which goes around the outside of the cité.

Not to be missed are the Cathar castles and the Roman and Gothic abbeys of the Aude, which are essential elements of the religious heritage of Languedoc-Roussillon. Excellent tours of these, lasting several days, are offered by the Loisirs-Accueil Aude (see **Good Alternatives**). If your time is limited, head north from Carcassonne towards the **Montagne Noire** and the sublime **4 Châteaux de Lastours** which put up a brave resistance during the Albigensian Crusade. While in the area, make a trip to the Abbaye de Caunes-Minervois, which dates from the eighth century, and the nearby Grottes de Limousis, with its strange rock and crystal formations. If heading towards Perpignan on the D118 and D117, your journey takes you to the Benedictine abbey of **Saint Polycarpe** and that of **Alet**, and the Cathar strongholds of **Peyrepertuse**, **Quéribus**, and **Aguilar**, perching on their lofty promontories. Nearby is the village of **Tautavel**, which gives its name to the 450,000 year old 'Homme de Tautavel', whose remains were discovered here in the 1970s. A museum in the town is devoted to this man, the oldest in Europe, and the other findings from the archaeological dig.

Accommodation

First Class

Domaine d'Auriac, route Ste-Hilaire, 11000 Carcassonne (Tel. 68 25 72 22): 23 luxurious rooms in nineteenth-century residence with park, 3 km south of Carcassonne; restaurant, **Hôtel le Cité**, Place de l'Eglise, 11000 Carcassonne (Tel. 68 25 03 34): 23 rooms and 3 apartments in Gothic house with garden, situated on the ramparts of the walled city itself.

First Class / Middle Range

Relais des Chartreuses, 66160 Le Boulou (Tel. 68 83 15 88): 10 rooms (no singles) in hotel in sheltered country setting, with swimming pool; restaurant serving French and Moroccan cuisine (half-board obligatory in July and August). **Château des Tilleuls**, Liaison rapide Perpignan-Thuir, 66680 Canohes (Tel. 68 55 05 67): 30 rooms in eighteenth century manor house and farm in wooded park, 10 minutes from Perpignan; restaurants serving good regional cuisine.

Middle Range

Hôtel Montségur, 27 allées d'Iena, 11000 Carcassonne (Tel. 68 25 31 41): 21 rooms in late nineteenth-century house with period furniture; excellent restaurant (**Le Languedoc**) nearby.

Middle Range / Economy

Hôtel Corrieu, La Llagonne, 66210 Montlouis (Tel. 68 04 22 04): 28 rooms in hotel with good value restaurant. **Le Cottage**, 21 rue Arthur-Rimbaud, 66700 Argèles-sur-Mer (Tel. 68 81 07 33): 30 rooms in quiet family hotel near sea, with good Mediterranean cooking.

Economy

Hôtel les Thermes Romains, 11190 Rennes-les-Bains (Tel. 68 69 87 04): spa town inn. **Villa Amphitryon**, 286 ave Général-Leclerc, 11000 Carcassonne (Tel. 68 71 67 47): pleasant, friendly hotel.

Eating Out

In addition to the restaurants mentioned above, try the *First Class* **Auberge du Pont-Levis**, Porte Narbonnaise, La Cité, 11000 Carcassonne (Tel. 68 25 55 23), for excellent cuisine in pleasant surroundings.

Herault

Around the gorges of the River Hérault lie a multitude of fascinating natural sites and places rich in historical significance. The High Valley of the Hérault offers opportunities for activities ranging from canoeing and cycling to geological outings and creative arts courses. Get details of these from: the Pays d'Accueil Pic St Loup - Haute Vallée de l'Hérault, BP 18, 34270 St-Mathieu-de-Treviers (Tel. 67

55 34 34), and the Pays d'Accueil Gorges et Vallée de l'Hérault (Tel. 67 57 58 83).

St Martin-de-Londres is a superbly-restored medieval village which boasts an elegant eleventh-century of Romanesque church and, a few kilometres away, the fourteenth-century chateau of Notre-Dame-de-Londres, with several rooms open to the public. La Grotte des Demoiselles in **St-Bauzille-de-Putois**, known locally as the Fairies' Grotto, is a natural underground cavity of cathedral-like dimensions, with vast stalagmites and stalactites. Wear a sweater, even in summer, as the sunshine never penetrates this bizarre creation of nature. Move from the depths of the earth to the heights, travelling a few kilometres to **Pic St Loup**, 658 metres high, for an excellent view of the surrounding region, and perhaps a *dégustation* of one of the full-bodied 'Crus du Pic St Loup'. Take the road to **Viols-en-Laval** to visit the prehistoric village of Cambous, a remarkable reconstruction of the settlement that existed on this site 4000 years ago, painstakingly recreated according to the archaeological discoveries made here.

The ancient town of **Clermont l'Hérault** offers many fine examples of medieval architecture, including the 'Chateau féodal des Guilhem', which dominates the main square. Use the town as a base for exploring the surrounding attractions: 8km away lies the Cirque de Mourèze, with its weird rock formations created by the erosion of the limestone. **Saint-Guilhem-le-Désert's** imposing Romanesque abbey and magnificent cloisters make it a real honeypot in summer: go out-of-season - and climb the ruin-topped hill behind the village for the panoramic view. Worth a stop also is the nearby Pont du Diable, with its pebble beach and canoes for hire, for exploring the deep river gorges. At **Béziers**, visit the Centre International de Documentation Occitane, for exhibitions, books, and videos on the Occitan language: 7 rue Rouget-de-Lisle (Tel. 67 28 71 62). Three nearby towns well worth a visit are **Pézenas**, **Mèze** and **Agde**. Pézenas is known as the Versailles of the south, because of its superb sixteenth and seventeenth-century architecture, all perfectly preserved. Its annual Molière festival pays homage to the playwright, who visited the town several times with his troupe. Allow time to visit the fascinating Lagunage de Mèze, an environmental research centre concerned with aquaculture and the breeding of tropical fish. Agde, founded by the Phoenicians 2500 years ago, has a beautiful old town and a cathedral built of black volcanic bricks.

Accommodation & Eating Out

First Class

Château de Grézan, 34480 Laurens (Tel. 67 90 28 03): a former Commandery of the Templars, famous for its wines, this incredible fortress-style château offers 2 apartments, for weekly rental only; restaurant.

Middle Range

Château de Ponderach, route de Narbonne, 34220 St-Pons-de-Thomières (Tel. 67 97 02 57): 9 rooms in country house (family home) with grounds and welcoming hostess; restaurant with classical and regional cuisine.

Middle Range / Economy

Le Mas de Coulet, 34190 Brissac (Tel. 67 73 74 18). **Hôtel-Restaurant Capion**, bd de l'Esplanade, 34150 Gignac (Tel. 67 57 50 83): 8 rooms in traditional hotel in heart of vineyard; good restaurant and wines.

Economy

Grand Hôtel, 2 rue Courtellerie, 34800 Clermont-l'Hérault (Tel. 67 96 00 04).

Montpellier

The region's administrative capital, Montpellier is a beautifully constructed city of harmonious architecture, with one of the largest and most intact historic centres in Europe. Its attractive squares and colourful pedestrian streets are animated by the presence of the city's young and lively population.

The Tourist Office's leaflet 'Montpellier in the Heart of History' points out the main attractions to be taken in while strolling around the city. The city's seventeenth- and eighteenth-century **hôtels particuliers** (townhouses) are famed for their elegance. The **Hôtel des Trésoriers de France** and the **Hôtel des Trésoriers de la Bourse**, a quiet oasis in the heart of the city, are typical examples. Montpellier's famous **Medical Faculty** dates from the fourteenth century. In the building are portraits of doctors who have practised there, including Rabelais and Rondelet, as well as an **Anatomy**

Museum - not for the squeamish! Nearby, on the boulevard Henri IV, is the Faculty's **Botanical Garden**, France's first, containing a wide variety of medicinal plants. **St Peter's Cathedral**, built in 1364, is Montpellier's only religious building to survive the Wars of Religion. For a complete contrast, cross the historic centre to arrive at the city's modern district of **Antigone**. Designed by the Catalonian architect, Ricardo Bofill, this neo-classical city-within-a-city attracts the admiration of planners and architects from all over the world. It is best seen at night, when the dramatic lighting makes it look like an opera set. Back in the historic centre, the **Musée Fabre** on boulevard Sarrail, established in 1825, has paintings, by Delacroix, Courbet, Ingres and Bazille, as well as sculpture and pottery.

Accommodation

First Class

Chevalier d'Assas, 18 rue d'Assas (Tel. 67 52 02 02): 14 rooms in charming hotel with garden on edge of main town.

First Class / Middle Range

Demeure des Brousses, route de Vauguières (Tel. 67 65 77 66 and 67 64 03 58): 17 rooms in 18th century Languedoc country residence with park, 4 km east of town; good restaurant (**L'Orangerie**) – half-board obligatory in high season.

Middle Range

La Maison Blanche, 1796 ave Pompignane (Tel. 67 79 60 25): 38 rooms in hotel with park; restaurant. **Hôtel Noailles**, 2 rue Ecoles-Centrales (Tel. 67 60 49 80): 30 rooms in seventeenth-century house in central location.

Middle Range / Economy

Hôtel la Peyronie, 4 rue des Petetes (Tel. 67 52 52 20): 20 rooms in family-run hotel with restaurant.

Economy

Hôtel Fauvettes, 8 rue Bonnard (Tel. 67 63 17 60): hotel with garden and near Jardin des Plantes, **Hôtel Majestic**, 4 rue du Cheval Blanc (Tel. 67 66 26 85): well-situated good value hotel.

Eating Out

First Class

Le Chandelier, 3 rue Leenhardt (Tel. 67 92 61 62): generous, seasonally changing menu in Italian setting. **Le Mas**, route de Vauguières, (Tel. 67 65 52 27): charming restaurant with extensive local wine list, in converted eighteenth-century farmhouse with garden, 4 km east of town.

First Class / Middle Range

La Réserve Rimbaud, Quartier des Aubes, 820 ave St-Maur (Tel. 67 72 52 53): classical cuisine in beautiful house with riverside terrace, popular with local people.

Middle Range

Isadora, 6 rue du Petit Scel (Tel. 67 66 25 23): seafood specialities served in cellar in old town. **Le Ménestral**, 2 impass Perrier, Place de la Préfecture (Tel. 67 60 62 51): excellent restaurant housed in thirteenth-century former grain-house.

Economy

Le Vieil Ecu, 1 rue des Ecoles Laïques: converted 16th century chapel with terrace serving good selection of food. **Yakanooga**, 10 rue du College Duvergner: fish specialities in pleasant restaurant with terrace. **Le Tripti-Kulaï**, 20 rue Jacques-Coeur (Tel. 67 66 30 51): vegetarian cuisine.

Entertainments

Walking tours of the city, daily in summer and on Wednesdays and Fridays at other times of the year, set off from the Tourist Office at 3 p.m. The attractive main square, **Place de la Comédie**, is pedestrianised and contains several outdoor cafés, whose customers are endlessly entertained by mime artists and street musicians, all summer. The **Languedoc Cultural Centre**, 20 rue Lakanal (Tel. 67 79 65 51), has a programme of cultural events. On Saturday and Tuesday mornings, there is a **market** selling organic produce on the boulevard des Arceaux.

Useful Addresses

The main **Tourist Office** is in Le Triangle, just off Place de la

Comédie (Tel. 67 58 67 58 or 67 79 15 15). Information on the whole Hérault *département* from the **Comité Départemental du Tourisme**, 1 Place Marcel-Godechot (Tel. 67 54 20 66). The offices of the **Comité Regional de Tourisme** have information on the whole region: 20 rue de la République (Tel. 67 92 67 92). The **Post Office** is on Place Rondelet, and the Saint-Eloi **Hospital** at 2 ave Bertin-Sans (Tel. 67 33 90 50). For emergency **medical assistance** call SAMU on 67 63 00 00.

Transport Options

Montpellier's centre is best seen on foot, and there are many pedestrianised streets. For a touch of class, take a ride around the city on a horse-driven **open carriage**. Tours depart from the Esplanade Charles de Gaulle. **Bicycles** are available for hire from Accueil SNCF in the railway station (Tel. 67 34 20 00). There is a good local **bus** service, although after 8 p.m. they are infrequent.

Nimes Gard and Lozère

The claim of this city to be the Rome of France is justly based on its extensive Roman remains. Nîmes' centrepiece is its well-preserved **Arena**, a Roman amphitheatre built between the first century BC and the first AD, and still used for bullfights and a prestigious jazz festival every July. To continue the Roman theme, walk to the Place de la Comédie for the fifth-century **Maison Carré**, a neat little Gallo-Roman temple, which houses a **Musée des Antiques**, displaying sculptures dating from the time of the temple's construction. Just outside the network of narrow streets of the Old Town is the eighteenth-century **Jardin de La Fontaine**, containing two monuments of note: the **Temple of Diana**, a Gallo-Roman sanctuary, and the **Tour Magne**, a pre-Roman watchtower, from which there is a spectacular view over the city. Back in the Place aux Herbes, is the **Cathedral Notre-Dame et Saint-Castor**, dating from the 11th century, but damaged to such an extent in the Wars of Religion that it had to be practically rebuilt in the nineteenth century.

Accommodation

First Class / Middle Range

L'Orangerie, 755 rue Tour de l'Evêque (Tel. 66 84 50 57): 31 rooms in hotel with garden; restaurant. **Hostellerie Relais du Moulin**, route d'Arles (Tel. 66 84 30 20): 21 rooms in hotel with garden, 4 km from town; restaurant.

Middle Range

Hôtel les Tuileries, 22 rue Roussy (Tel. 66 21 31 15): 10 rooms in fairly central hotel.

Economy

Nouvel Hôtel, 6 bd Amiral Courbet (Tel. 66 67 62 48): friendly, attractive hotel. **Le Lisita**, 2 bd des Arènes (Tel. 66 67 62 48): comfortable rooms in excellent location; restaurant. **Hôtel de France**, 4 bd des Arènes (Tel. 66 67 47 72): equally excellent location

Eating Out

First Class

Alexandre, 4 rue de l'Aéroport, 30128 Garons (Tel. 66 70 08 99): seasonal and regional specialities in hotel with garden, 9 km from town. **L'Enclos de la Fontaine**, quai de la Fontaine (Tel. 66 21 90 30): gastronomic cuisine.

Middle Range

Mas des Abeilles, route de St-Gilles (Tel. 66 38 28 57): seafood specialities in restaurant with garden, 2¹/2 km from town. **Le Magister**, 5 rue Nationale (Tel. 66 76 11 00): imaginative regional cuisine in elegant surroundings

Economy

L'Oeuf à la Côte, 29 rue de la Madeleine: old town restaurant with terrace, concentrating on poultry and egg dishes. **Les Hirondelles**, 13 rue Bigot: restaurant with traditional fixed price menu and popular with local people.

Entertainments

On Fridays, there is an organic food and local produce market in the boulevard Jean Jaurès. Pentecost is when Nîmes' streets throng with visitors who come for the bullfights, flamenco dancing and pavement artists. The last week in September sees the annual Grape Harvest Fair, with exhibitions of folk art and bullfighting.

Useful Addresses

Tourist Office: 6 rue Auguste (Tel. 66 67 29 11). Information on the whole Gard *département* from the **Comité Départemental du Tourisme**, 3 Place des Arènes (Tel. 66 21 02 51). The **Post Office** is on bd de Bruxelles, and the **Hospital** is the Gaston Doumergue, 5 rue Hoche (Tel. 66 27 41 11). In a **medical emergency** phone SAMU on 15.

Transport Options

There is an inexpensive and efficient local bus service. For bus trips further afield, including into the Camargue, ask at the 'gare routière'. Bicycle hire from the SNCF station (Tel. 66 23 50 50).

Rest of Gard and Lozère

On its route east from the Cévennes to the River Rhône, the Gard flows through exquisitely-scented garrigue country. **Le Vigan** is an attractively verdant little town dominated by the Cévennes Hills, which are the theme of its Cevenol Museum of Art and Popular Traditions. Nearby lies the geological oddity of the Cirque de Navacelles, a gigantic depression dug out of the *causses* by the River Vis, enclosing an entire village 300 m down in a steep valley. **Valleraugue**, 10 km away, is a typical Cévennes village, and the starting point for the 4000 Steps, a one-day hike to the top of Mount Aigoual. Maps of the route are available from the tourist office. **St-Hippolyte du Fort** is the setting for an *ecomusée* dedicated to the region's silk-making industry, and the 13th century Château de Ribaute les Tavernes.

Barely 2 km from **Anduze** is the Bambouseraie de Prafrance, an exotic forest of bamboo trees growing in the area's special microclimate. Travel there on the steam train which runs between Anduze and **St Jean du Gard** – home to the Museum of the Cévennes Valleys, dedicated to the life and traditions of the Cévennes. Nearby in **Mialet** is the very moving Musée du Désert, describing two centuries of Huguenot history.

The beautifully-preserved Renaissance town of **Uzès** is worth a visit, if only for the Municipal Museum in the former Bishop's Palace, with its André Gide Room and fine display of regional ceramics. Only 3 km away is the Museum of Agriculture and Loco-motion in **Arpaillargues**, with working farm machinery through the ages. Rejoining the Gard on its journey east, be sure not to miss the majestic Pont du Gard, a legacy of the Roman period, and the highest aqueduct-bridge ever built by them. Walk across it if you have a head for heights. If not, swim underneath it!

Languedoc-Roussillon's national and regional parks in the north of the region include some of its most scenic attractions. Still further north in Lozère, France's most sparsely-populated *département*, is the weird lunar landscape of the *causses*. **The Parc Naturel Regional de Haut-Languedoc** offers a multitude of opportunities for nature study outings and visits to places of interest. Try to get to the exotic Mediterranean Gardens of **Roquebrun** for the 300 species of plants there. **St-Pons-de-Thomières** is also worth a trip, not only to visit the headquarters of the park, but the Museum of Prehistory and the town's unlikely-looking cathedral, as well as the nearby Grotte de la Devèze. For information on the **Parc National des Cévennes**, make for the town of **Florac**, where you will find the park's Information Centre (open June to October only) housed in the beautifully-restored Château de Florac. East of Florac, on Mount Lozère, the highest of the Cévennes, is a fascinating *ecomusée*, describing the hard life of those who lived, and still live and work, on this harsh granite peak, with its poor soils and inclement weather. Start your visit at **Pont de Montvert**, where the main *ecomusée* building is located. In the other direction from Florac lies Aven Armand, a wonder of nature well worth the trip. Descend 200 m in the funicular train, to find yourself in the underground grotto's 'Virgin Forest' – entirely composed of giant, tree-shaped stalagmites. Travelling north, **Mende** is worth a stop, for its fine fourteenth-century cathedral. The Comité Départemental de Tourisme on Place Urbain V (Tel. 66 65 34 55) has information on the whole Lozère *département*. Continue on through **Marvejols**, 5 km north of which is situated the Zoological Park of Gévaudan, with bears, bison, chamois, and the wolves which have made it famous. Finally, on this deserted plateau, the most northerly part of the Languedoc-Roussillon, lies the surprisingly elegant **Château de la Baume**, open for visits during the afternoon.

Accommodation

First Class

Château de la Caze, La Malène, 48210 Ste-Enimie (Tel. 66 48 51 01): 19 rooms in medieval fairy-tale château with moat; traditional cuisine served in restaurant in converted chapel. **Les Etapes du**

Ranquet, route de St-Hippolyte, 30140 Tornac-Anduze (Tel. 66 77 51 63): 10 rooms in welcoming house surrounded by oak trees; swimming pool and excellent cuisine using local produce.

First Class/Middle Range

Château d'Ayres, 48150 Meyrueis (Tel. 66 45 60 10): 24 rooms in historic house with good restaurant.

Middle Range

La Renaissance et St-Sauveur, rue de la Ville, 48150 Meyrueis (Tel. 66 45 60 19): 20 rooms in two converted town mansions; cuisine from fresh local produce. **Hôtel de l'Atelier,** 5 rue de la Foire, 30400 Villeneuve-lès-Avignon (Tel. 90 25 01 84): 19 rooms in carefully restored and centrally situated old townhouse with courtyard.

Economy

Hostellerie du Seigneur, Place du Seigneur, 30126 Tavel (Tel. 66 50 04 26): 7 simple rooms in cosy central hotel in vineyard country; restaurant with good family cooking. **Hôtel du Gevaudan,** rue des Aigues Passes, 48000 Mende (Tel. 66 65 14 74): 11 rooms in family-run hotel with restaurant.

Eating Out

In addition to the restaurants mentioned above, try the following for a special treat:

First Class/Middle Range

Le Manoir, Mas de Cazalet, 30250 Sommières (Tel. 66 77 74 01): gastronomic restaurant serving regional specialities in medieval setting (including an art gallery in the vaulted cellars), surrounded by park, woods and vineyards.

20 Midi-Pyrénées

Midi-Pyrénées is the largest administrative region in France, being about the size of Belgium. Stretching from the Spanish border in the south right up to the Auvergne, the region has naturally been subjected to a wide variety of influences over the centuries, making it a land of startling contrasts. Predominantly rural, its extensive red-brown plains of cereals are broken up by dramatic gorges, carved out by the various rivers which criss-cross the region. Almost without warning, the Pyrenees mountain range rises dramatically above the southern plains, with its snowy peaks and plunging valleys, some of which are protected by the Western Pyrenees national park.

A wide range of outdoor activities can be practised in the challenging terrain of the Pyrenees, which are thankfully nowhere near as developed as the Alps. It is nonetheless to the mountains that the majority of visitors head. The least well-known *départements* are those of Tarn, Tarn-et-Garonne and Aveyron, situated further to the north and east. Here you will find tranquil countryside where high plateaux called *causses* are riddled with caves and habitation seems limited to occasional farms or fortified hill-top villages, often situated on river bends and known as *bastides*. These can also be found in the region's gastronomic capital, the Gers *département*, where Armagnac is produced. Pleasant, hearty wines are widely available, the most famous of which is probably Gaillac. Local cuisine is heavily based on the fruits of the land, with every menu including at least one duck or goose dish.

The agricultural riches of Midi-Pyrénées are largely a result of its mild and sheltered climate, but also of the dedication of its farming folk. Despite a considerable exodus earlier this century from the countryside to towns like Toulouse and even Bordeaux (over in Aquitaine), a great many people are still involved in farming, both on a commercial and a subsistence level. Many families have farmed the same land for generations, with very few real changes in their way of life in spite of new agricultural techniques.

The region's major city is Toulouse – *la ville rose* – which is the capital of the French aviation industry. It also has the largest student population in France, after Paris, but manages to combine the progressive with the traditional: from the tenth to the thirteenth centuries, most of southern France was ruled by the Counts of Toulouse and this has not been forgotten. Many parts of Midi-Pyrénées quite obviously have their roots deep in the Middle Ages; colourful festivals and a simple lifestyle in country areas contribute to this impression.

After the rural localities and historic red-tiled towns, the region's main tourist attraction, Lourdes, is bound to come as a disappointment if the purpose of your visit is not religious. Even if you are prompted by faith, this major centre of Roman Catholic pilgrimage, famed for its alleged powers of healing, may seem more like a shrine to those who make money from the sale of kitschy mementos. The sophistication of the tourist infrastructure here is unique in the region. It is sad that it is the only glimpse of Midi-Pyrénées some people get. Many make a bee-line for Lourdes, or else simply pass through the region on their way to Spain or the Mediterranean. The tourist board is currently trying to persuade people to stop and savour the lesser-known corners of this – in many ways – old-fashioned land. Following their advice would not be such a bad idea.

History

The earliest evidence of the region's inhabitants are the cave paintings at Niaux and Bédeilhac in the Ariège-Pyrénées. It is estimated that prehistoric cave dwellers produced these around 10,000 BC. It was in 56 BC that the Romans conquered the south of France, subduing the Celts and Gauls and leaving straight roads, spas and vineyards as their legacy to the region. The city of Toulouse was also founded in Roman times, originating as a crossing point on the River Garonne for Romans travelling to Iberia.

The fifth century AD brought a hundred years of rule by the Visigoths. By the eighth century, the land of Gasconia (today's Gascony, much of which is in the Gers *département*) was well-established with its own Latin-based Occidental language known as the Langue d'Oc, which bore more resemblance to Spanish than to French. In the lands further south, meanwhile, the Basque language held sway. Pilgrims making for Santiago de Compostella in northern Spain began to cross the region in considerable numbers from around AD 950. By the end of the first millennium, the south of France had developed its own distinct identity, very different from that of the north. Its people looked to the Counts of Toulouse to rule them, rather than to the French king in distant Paris. And Toulouse in turn looked to the king of Aragon in Spain.

During the eleventh century, Toulouse became a centre of sophisticated civilisation, where Arab and Jewish influences blended to produce brilliant poetry and sculpture. The quiet, refined life of the region was, however, shattered with the repercussions of Catharism. The name Cathar is derived from the Greek word meaning purity, and the beliefs of the Cathar Christians differed markedly from those of Orthodox Rome, according a greater role to the devil and seeing reincarnation as the only way to resolve good and evil. Most Cathars were merchants and nobles with a strong ethic of hard work and pure living. Their priests were known as *parfaits* and the religion quickly took hold in the region, with bishops presiding at Albi, Toulouse, Agen and Carcassonne. The Church, however, considered their beliefs heresy and Rome sought to destroy them. The persecution of the Cathars was prolonged and they were forced to retreat to strategic defensive strongholds on mountain-tops like Montségur, their capital. But the Inquisition crusades, led by Simon de Montfort, were relentless and, by 1250, nearly 1 million Cathars had been massacred. This upheaval offered a chance for the French monarchy to step in and take control of the south-west of France.

The religious conflicts and Anglo-French wars of the Middle Ages resulted in the construction of fortified towns called *bastides*. The Pyrenees also has a legacy of churches, built on the pilgrimage routes to Santiago de Compostella and in defence settlements against the Moors; many are fine examples of Romanesque architecture. From the mid-15th century, Toulouse began to benefit from its production of a blue dye called *pastel* (woad). Following a fire in 1464, much of the city was rebuilt, and the timber-framed buildings which had been destroyed were replaced by elegant new constructions of the characteristic small red bricks which gave the town the name Ville Rose. It was the introduction of indigo from India which put the brakes on Toulouse's prosperity, causing it to go into decline.

In 1539 the Edict of Villers-Cotterets imposed French as the official language and the Langue d'Oc grew rarer, until its cultural revival in the nineteenth century, which continues today. The 1659

Treaty of the Pyrenees finally brought this geographically isolated region, which had (and, to some extent, still has) clear social structures of its own, under the rule of France. A major means of communication for the region, the Canal du Midi, linking Toulouse and the Mediterranean, was completed in 1681 after fourteen years of impressive work by an army of 12,000 workers. In the nineteenth century, Alexandre Dumas chose to model the character of d'Artagnan, hero of *The Three Musketeers*, on a real country gentleman from Gascony. It was not until the First World War that the fortunes of Toulouse began to change; Monsieur Latécère decided to move his aircraft factory there from Lille and this was the start of the city's development as the centre of the French aviation industry. During the Second World War, the Pyrenees offered a good source of escape routes. Recent events of regional importance include the influx of North African immigrants after the Algerian war and the creation of the Western Pyrenees national park in 1967.

Geography

The Midi-Pyrénées region is situated in south-west France, bordered by the Massif Central to the north, Aquitaine to the west, Languedoc-Roussillon to the east and, to the south, the Pyrenees mountain range, which forms a natural frontier between France and Spain. There are eight *départements* which make up this region: Lot and Aveyron in the north, whose regional capitals are Cahors and Rodez respectively; a middle band comprising Gers (capital Auch), Tarn-et-Garonne (capital Montauban), and Tarn (capital Albi); and finally the southern *départements* of Haute-Pyrénées, whose capital is Tarbes but which also contains Lourdes, Ariège (capital Foix), and Haute-Garonne. It is the last-mentioned *département* in which Toulouse, the regional capital, is to be found. The city has a population of around 350,000 (or 600,000 if you include the suburbs) and is far-and-away the largest town in the region.

Of the eight *départements*, two – Hautes-Pyrénées and Ariège – are predominantly mountainous, with the former containing (as the name suggests) some of the highest and most dramatic peaks of the range. This mountainous area occupies roughly a quarter of the region, giving way to foothills and then to plains, the Toulousain basin, and the limestone Plateaux des Causses. The other *départements* are all named after the rivers which flow through them and have had such an influence on their landscape. Through the plains, these rivers cut undulating valleys and steep gorges, and their meanders have provided the perfect sites for hill-top villages and fortresses. All the rivers add their strength to the mighty Garonne, which flows through Toulouse and on to Bordeaux and the Atlantic. Another important waterway is the Canal du Midi, linking Toulouse to the Mediterranean.

The Parc National des Pyrénées Occidentales stretches for 100 kilometres along the Franco-Spanish border and encompasses over 100,000 acres, comprising lakes, valleys and many peaks of more than 1000 metres. The park was established in 1967, after fierce opposition from the local communities who previously owned the land. Nowadays, together with the Spanish Parque Nacional de Ordesa y Perdido, it aims to protect the natural wildlife and vegetation of the remote mountains. The park is accessible for hiking, climbing and licensed fishing, but hunting and collecting of natural species are forbidden; the only shelter in the park is provided by mountain refuges.

One of the park's most important sites is the Cirque de Gavarnie, a huge glacier in the form of an amphitheatre, where a 423-metre waterfall (one of France's biggest) crashes downwards. Apart from the glaciers and naked rock, the park contains mountain-pine forest up to a height of 2400 metres, and a varied flora of 400 or so indigenous species, including the Pyrenean pheasant's eye and Pyrenean gentian. The main flowering months are June, July and August. Bird species include eight pairs of Europe's rarest bird of prey, the bearded vulture; other types of vulture inhabit the park as well as the golden eagle and capercaillie. The park has successfully increased the number of Pyrenean chamois (known as the *isard*) to over 3000, and marmots are abundant. In the 12% of the land which is afforested, you will find wild boar, genet, badger and marten. Grazing land occupies 50% and provides for 37,000 sheep, 5000 cattle and 800 horses. The rarest animals are the lynx and brown bear, which live in the park's peripheral areas; the population of the latter has declined drastically as a result of human destruction and disturbance of its forest habitat. Its protection was declared a special project by President Mitterand soon after taking office, but there have been no encouraging results as yet, although current initiatives include the introduction of bears from Russia. Among species already declared extinct by the World Wide Fund for Nature is the Pyrenean ibex.

A number of nature reserves, including Néouville and Ossau, extend the area of the park's protection, and the Conservatoire de Sites Naturels de Midi-Pyrénées takes responsibility for planting fruit trees to help maintain the brown bears' food supply. Among the Conservatoire's other projects are the protection of some Ger's lakes inhabited by turtles; the preservation of peat-bogs in northern Aveyron; and the promotion of traditional cereal crop cultivation. In areas of the Tarn *département*, Occitan and Cathar traditions are kept alive by the Haut-Languedoc regional park, founded in 1973.

Climate

Most of the region enjoys a mild climate with plenty of sunshine, especially in the lower lands, which are sheltered by the mountains and well away from the temperamental coasts. Summers here in the plains are long and hot, with temperatures often reaching 25°C in June and September, while those in July and August are even higher. In winter, frosts are rare and leaves generally remain unshed for many months in the still, clear air. In spring and autumn there can, however, be unsettling winds and erratic weather as a result of the easterly 'vent d'autan'.

In the mountains, afternoon thunderstorms are not uncommon in July and August and the weather can be oppressive if you are walking long distances. Snow usually falls after Christmas here, and the western end of the range is generally damper than the east, with lowest temperatures averaging about −2°C in the centre around Andorra. Allow a temperature drop of approximately 1/2 to 1°C for every 100 metres in altitude.

In both the mountains and the lowlands, September is usually the most pleasant time of year to visit, though this is not a region where any great restrictions on holiday dates are imposed by the climate.

Attractions

The most important attractions in Midi-Pyrénées, certainly in terms of visitor numbers, are both pilgrimage sites: the cliff-top village of Rocamadour and the town of Lourdes. The latter is where, in 1858, the Virgin Mary appeared to the fourteen-year-old Bernadette Soubirous in a grotto, a total of eighteen times. Pilgrims began to visit the site and it developed a reputation for helping, sometimes even curing, the ill and handicapped, and today it is still one of the most important places of pilgrimage in the Christian world.

Elsewhere, the attractions of the Midi-Pyrénées region tend to be its relaxing expanses of countryside, combined with its pockets of interesting historical sights. Toulouse has many attractive and distinctive features. Its characteristic red-brick ecclesiastical and secular buildings, its squares, fountains, arcades and bridges, are all being appreciated by increasing numbers of visitors. Other towns of architectural and historical significance include Cahors, Rocamadour and Moissac, while *bastide* villages like Cordes, and monuments like Monségur fortress or Albi's astoundingly red fortified cathedral, are also major attractions. Albi has the additional interest of the Toulouse-Lautrec museum, Castres has a Goya museum, and Montauban a museum devoted to Ingres.

The Pyrenees offer a wealth of outdoor activities: hiking the GR 10 footpath, climbing, fishing, downhill and crosscountry skiing, hang-gliding and nature observation. Cycling, the national sport, draws many French groups and individuals to tackle the mountains and, in summer, the Tour de France attracts large crowds of spectators as it passes through the region. Elsewhere, water-sports enthusiasts are lured by fast-flowing rivers; the Gorges d'Aveyron is a popular centre. Traditional pageantry events like the Fêtes-de-Foix and the summer music festivals which take place in Toulouse and throughout the region add to its appeal, while its seventeen spa towns with their numerous hydrotherapy centres are still popular with French *curistes*.

Cuisine

The Midi-Pyrénées is famous for its cuisine, which is predominantly duck and goose-orientated. The birds are fattened and most commonly served as *foie gras* (liver), *confit* preserved in fat or *magret* (breast). Potatoes and salad are the main accompaniments and these dishes are on almost every restaurant menu. Market stalls display selections of *confits*, as well as quail, rabbit, hare and *marcassin* (young wild boar), which usually form the main ingredients for stews known as *civets*. Throughout the region housewives as well as farmers keep hens, ducks and geese, and roadside stalls selling *foie gras* are common. Regional home-cooking involves converting lesser parts of birds or game into tasty fare including *cassoulet* (a Toulouse speciality of goose, kidney beans and other vegetables and meats), *garbure* (a soup of vegetables and wing-tips), *gésier* (gizzard), as well as the famous *pâté de foie gras*. Even the poultry enthusiast can suffer from a surfeit, and vegetarians will be wringing their hands! On larger menus, relief is provided in the shape of the region's freshwater fish. Trout, salmon and pike-perch (*sandre*) are frequent, while sea fish and oysters from neighbouring Aquitaine are often available.

The village of Roquefort produces its famous blue cheese, made from ewe's milk and matured in caves. Other cheeses are produced in the Pyrenees: those from cow's milk tend to have a black rind, those from ewe's milk an orange rind. Many farmers also make *chèvre* – goat's cheese. Walnuts are widely grown, as are soft fruits such as plums. Honey is particularly thick and delicious in the mountains. The region's pâtisseries offer a variety of fruit, nut and honey tarts, along with *croustades* – appetising Armagnac-flavoured apple or plum pastries.

Wines are produced extensively throughout the region and, although less famous than those of neighbouring Bordeaux, are very acceptable. Among the best red wines are Cahors, from the Lot valley, Madiran from Gers, Fronton from Haute-Garonne and Gaillac from Tarn. Some wine producers offer tours followed by *dégustation*. Gers is the centre for the production of the famous Armagnac, a brandy made from grapes grown on sandy soil and distilled only once (Cognac comes from chalky areas and is distilled twice). Floc-de-Gascoyne is an aperitif made from inferior Armagnac and grape juice. Violets (the emblem of Toulouse) are made into the town's own special liqueur, known, appropriately enough, as Violet. This can also be found as a sugar coating on the local chocolates.

Level of Tourism

Historically, the Midi-Pyrénées region has always had a close connection with tourists or travellers of one sort or another. Since the Middle Ages, people have made pilgrimages through south-west France to Santiago de Compostella in Spain, and Bernadette's visions at Lourdes in the latter part of the last century provided the spark for another, still continuing, wave of pilgrimages. In the past, people visiting these places necessarily lingered in towns along their route. Nowadays, with the advent of the autoroute and the airport, latter-day pilgrims drive down to Spain or the Med, barely noticing Midi-Pyrénées. Even those heading for Lourdes tend to fly in and out without ever exploring the surrounding area.

Despite this, Midi-Pyrénées still ranks highly in the league of French touristic regions, hosting around 5.7% of all national hotel visits. Of its visitors, about 23% come from abroad, with the British and the Germans constituting some 50% of the region's foreign tourists. The rise in popularity of skiing attracted the wealthy, outdoor visitor and, until recently, these and the pilgrims were pretty much the only tourists to visit the region. Changing trends in tourism, combined with regional government initiatives, mean that people are now taking their summer holidays here too, and Midi-Pyrénées is now firmly on the tourist map. At present, most tourists visit the region in July and August, though the British also come in May and June, whilst September is popular with the Germans. Most Europeans bring their own cars, though there are a fair number of German coach trips and the Americans usually opt for car-hire. Toulouse is a popular short-break destination, while many longer holidays are spent in self-catering accommodation in the countryside.

Toulouse has its tourism-related problems, mainly involving the sheer volume of traffic, but some relief should be afforded by the new Metro, currently under construction. This project is being approached in a sensible manner, with the facades of the old buildings in Place Esquirol being carefully maintained, while their interiors are being converted into Metro stations.

Skiing in the Pyrenees is on a much smaller scale than in the Alps, and keen downhill skiers should give the Pyrenees a thought; firstly, because the welcome you receive will be that much more personal and authentic, and secondly, because, unlike the Alps, the Pyrenees have not yet reached saturation point. At present, most skiers here come from the south and west of France, whilst nearby Andorra draws the mass-market European charter flights. Most of the skiing takes place in the Hautes-Pyrénées, on the fringes of the national park, which, thankfully, places restrictions on the expansion of ski tourism. Despite this, there are plans afoot, which threaten to construct roads and tunnels and to allow ski-lifts in the park. Most French tourists come to ski in February, during the school holidays, so avoid this month if you prefer lower prices and empty slopes (though, even in February, the Pyrenees are nowhere near as crowded as the Alps).

Lourdes is still the region's main honeypot and, during its

high season (Easter to late September), the town is thronged with coachloads of visitors. The Basilica of Saint Pius X was built in 1958 with direct access for up to 20,000 pilgrims, both handicapped and able-bodied. This underground arena indicates the scale of Lourdes' development. The regional government has an ambivalent attitude towards the fact that the airport is built so close to Lourdes that the majority of visitors do not spill out into the area surrounding the town. On the one hand, it means that tourism is controlled and that the ecologically fragile mountains on Lourdes' doorstep, with their narrow roads and passes, are not subjected to the expansion of infrastructure which increased visitor numbers would necessarily entail. On the other hand, tourists are receiving a one-sided view of the region and the only local people to benefit from the business are the hotel owners and trinket sellers of Lourdes itself. In the face of this dilemma, the regional tourist board has decided to concentrate its efforts on encouraging motorists visiting Lourdes, or heading south to Spain or the Mediterranean, to spend more time in the rest of the region as they pass through. Country people and farmers are offered incentives and training schemes to enable them to provide a high-quality network of *chambres d'hôte* and *ferme-auberge* accommodation throughout the countryside, so that they too will benefit. The tourist board is gearing up to an expected increase in visitors with their slogan 'A region that is taking off'. Fortunately, in Midi-Pyrénées the land mass is sufficiently large to accommodate greater numbers of visitors without problems – provided this is managed appropriately.

Good Alternatives

Meeting People

A list of the region's festivals, of which there are many extremely colourful examples throughout the year, can be provided by the **Comité Régional du Tourisme**, 12 rue Salambo, BP 2166, 31022 Toulouse (Tel. 61 47 11 12). A good selection of general information, which will whet your appetite for the region, is contained in their brochure 'Holidays in Midi-Pyrénées'. The region, especially the Pyrenees, is being promoted as an 'activity playground', so you can be sure that, whether your interest is climbing, fishing, cycling, white-water rafting or high-altitude flower photography, you will find like-minded people pursuing the same activities.

If you wish to help promote conservation in the Pyrenees, you might be interested in **Vacances Militantes**. These bring together people of mixed backgrounds and ages to work on conservation projects, such as the building of bird sanctuaries or maintenance of footpaths. For further information, contact **Uminate** (José Cambou), 47 rue Arago, 31500 Toulouse (Tel. 61 58 14 31).

Those interested in joining an archaeological dig could make enquiries at the **Direction des Antiquités Historiques**, 2 rue des Paradoux, 31000 Toulouse (Tel. 61 55 15 77); if your field of interest lies even deeper in the past, try the **Direction des Antiquités Préhistoriques**, 37 bis rue Roquelaine, 31000 Toulouse (Tel. 61 62 01 45).

Jeanne Gosselin has a large country house where she runs 5-day courses in pottery, sculpture, weaving, painting or interior design, with rooms in the house and camping in the grounds. For further details, contact her at 'Certe', 09700 Gaudies (Tel. 61 67 01 56).

Two to 5-day canal cruises, during which study courses are held about the region through which your barge passes, are organised by the **Peniche d'Initiation à l'Environnement Atlantique-Mediterranée**, 14 rue de Tivoli, 31068 Toulouse (Tel. 61 33 50 81).

Discovering Places

An alternative manner of discovering the Pyrenees is offered by Jean-Sébastian Gion, born and bred in the Haute-Pyrénées, who arranges summer and winter discovery excursions, slide shows, courses and much else, both for already established groups and for individuals grouped together. He acts as a guide on the excursions, which are designed for those who want to explore and learn about the Pyrenean environment, and provides a completely new perspective. Further information is available from him at the **Maison de la Découverte Pyrénéenne**, 3 route de Tarbes, 65200 Bagnères-de-Bigorre (Tel. 62 95 45 20).

A visit to the **Pyrenees National Park** is highly recommended. Maisons du Parc, located at strategic points throughout the range, offer a variety of services to the public, providing permanent and temporary exhibitions on the unique ecosystem of the Pyrenees, as well as organising conferences and debates on conservation issues. Park wardens are also happy to arrange a variety of mountain-related activities, such as hiking trips and photographic excursions. Day-long walking, hiking and climbing excursions are run by the **Association des Amis du Parc**, 20 rue Samonzet, 64000 Pau (Tel. 59 27 15 30). If you wish to participate in a mountain excursion lasting several days, including an introduction to flora and fauna observation, geology, country ways, fishing or high-altitude speleology, contact **CIMES – Pyrénées**, BP 88, 09200 St-Girons (Tel. 61 66 40 10). For further information on the park's facilities and activities, contact the **Parc National des Pyrénées Occidentales**, 59 route de Pau, 65000 Tarbes (Tel. 62 93 30 60). For those interested in flora and fauna, **Tambao Randonnées Pedestres**, Gigors, 26000 Crest (Tel. 75 76 42 32) organise hiking excursions into the Pyrenees to observe indigenous species of animal and plant life.

In Ariège, Mme Bertolino has a large, renovated country manor house with 10 comfortable rooms and 1 suite, whose facilities can be used by groups for business seminars and receptions. Individuals are more likely to be interested in the language courses which take place here; these are for all ages and abilities and there is the possibility of one-to-one tuition. Mme Bertolino also keeps horses so horseriding trips (2 to 3 days) can be arranged, as well as 3-day circuits exploring the Cathar castles of the area. The atmosphere of the house is a family one; cooking involves traditional regional specialities, and, in addition to riding, a number of activities including skiing and cycling can be practised. For details contact Mme Bertolino at **Montagnac**, St-Félix-de-Tournegat, 09500 Mirepoix (Tel. 61 68 72 75).

A 24-room hotel which offers weekend to 6-day activity or discovery holidays in the Lot is the **Auberge du Vieux Quercy**, Le Bourg, 46110 Carennac (Tel. 65 38 69 00). Activities range from mountain-biking and pony-trekking to fishing, canoeing or swimming in the Dordogne river, while visits include local markets, traditional festivals, underground caves and nearby museums and sites. For coach trips (1 to 5 days), some including accommodation, starting from Toulouse or Lourdes, see **Bus** section of **Communications**.

A small British holiday company based in the Pyrenean village of Barèges is **Borderline**; they offer a variety of outdoor holidays in Barèges and a walking tour which crosses over into the Ordesa national park in Spain. They have extensive local knowledge and use exclusively local guides and experts for their various activities which include bird-watching and discovery of the alpine flora. You can contact Borderline at Les Sorbiers, rue Ramond, 65120 Barèges (Tel. 62 92 68 95).

All eight of the Midi-Pyrénées *départements* have a **Loisirs-Accueil** service, offering advice in many areas, reservation of accommodation, and a selection of locally arranged low-impact trips in the *département*. Their respective addresses are as follows:

Ariège: BP 143, 09003 Foix (Tel. 61 02 09 69). **Aveyron:** APATAR, Carrefour de l'Agriculture, 12006 Rodez (Tel. 65 73 77 33). **Haute-Garonne:** 70 bd Koenigs, 31300 Toulouse (Tel. 61 31 95 15). **Gers:** Maison de l'Agriculture, route de Tarbes, 32003 Auch (Tel. 62 63 16 55). **Lot:** 53 rue Bourseul, BP 162, 46003 Cahors (Tel. 65 22 19 20). **Hautes-Pyrénées:** 6 rue Eugène-Tenot, 65000 Tarbes (Tel. 62 93 03 30). **Tarn:** Hôtel du Département, 81014 Albi (Tel. 63 60 33 83). **Tarn-et-Garonne**, Hôtel des Intendants, Place du Maréchal-Foch, 82000 Montauban (Tel. 63 63 31 40).

Communications

How to Get There

Toulouse-Blagnac and Lourdes-Ossun are the region's two international **airports**, to which Air France, British Airways and Dan Air fly from various British airports. Air Littoral now flies from Manchester to Toulouse. Air Inter operates domestic scheduled services to both Lourdes and Toulouse, while TAT flies from Paris to Albi and from Nantes to Toulouse.

By **train**, the fastest journey time from Paris to Cahors is 5 hours, while going as far as Toulouse takes 6. In summer, Eurolines operate a **coach** service from London to Tarbes and Lourdes, which works out at just over £100 adult return. By **car**, the journey down from Paris to Toulouse takes over 8 hours as there is no direct autoroute.

When You're There

SNCF bring out a **TER** (Transport Express Régional) leaflet, which is extremely useful if you are planning a holiday using public transport, as it includes all regional services including those on SNCF coaches. The leaflet is available from all Midi-Pyrénées travel agents and stations.

Rail – the region's main rail line passes through Cahors, Montauban and Toulouse, before splitting off to Boussens, St-Gaudens, Montréjeau (connection to Luchon), Tarbes and Lourdes in the west; and

Castelnaudry and Carcassonne in the east. A minor line also continues down to Foix, Ax-les-Thermes and La Tour-de-Carol in the south. Other lines from Toulouse will take you to Auch, St-Sulpice-Tarn (connections to Castres and Mazamet), Tessonnières, Albi and Rodez. Millau and Castelsarrasin are also on the network, which is fairly comprehensive, though you should allow time for some rather circuitous routes.

Bus – the region's bus services are not particularly regular, tending to run short journeys to get villagers to town on market day rather than daily services. Even longer distance services are less than convenient, as they rarely allow a return on the same day. Coach operators based in Toulouse and Lourdes do, however, run some good trips to the surrounding area, ranging from 1 to 5 days and often including accommodation. Their addresses are **CTT Voyages / Occitanie Tours**, 21 Place du Salin, 31000 Toulouse (Tel. 61 52 47 85); and **L'Accueil Pyrénéen**, 26 ave Maransin, BP 67, 65102 Lourdes (Tel. 62 94 15 62).

Car – the only motorways in the region are the A 62 from Bordeaux and the Atlantic to Toulouse, and the A 61 on from Toulouse to Narbonne and the Mediterranean. Otherwise there is a network of good N roads between the main towns, and attractive D roads for more leisurely exploration. If you are planning to drive in the mountains during winter, remember to take snow chains.

Boat – the Canal du Midi and the Canal Latéral à la Garonne are popular waterways for narrow boat and cruising holidays. Boats can be hired locally for one-way journeys as well as round trips.

Cycling – bicycles can be hired at rail stations in the main towns and can be transported by coach as well as train. Only attempt cycling in the Pyrenees if you are fit and have a good bicycle, but remember that mountain biking is prohibited in the national park.

Walking – the Pyrénées are ideal for walking, rambling and hiking. The GR 10 traverses over 500 km of the Hautes-Pyrénées and is suitable for all good walkers. The 'Haute Randonnée Pyrénées' (HRP), however, requires mountain trekking experience. These footpaths are clearly signposted and marked on maps available from the national park information centres. More challenging hikes and climbs are led by park guides (see **Good Alternatives**). For lower level walking, try the GR 653 which crosses the Gers *département*.

Useful Local Contacts

The **Conservatoire des Sites Midi-Pyrénées**, which supervises all sorts of conservation activities, is based at 31 rue de Cugnaux, 31300 Toulouse (Tel. 61 59 21 38). Another conservation group, specialising in the protection of larger animals is **Groupe Grande Faune**, 16 ave des Charmettes, 31500 Toulouse. Information on environmental protection in the Lot *département* can be obtained from **Lot Nature** (M. Heaulme), St-Cirice, 46090 Cahors. In the Pyrenees, information concerning all sorts of ecological issues and occupations in the mountains is provided by the **Centre d'Information Montagne et Sentiers** (CIMES), BP 88, 09200 St-Girons (Tel. 61 66 40 10). Try also the **Centre Permanent d'Initiation à l'Environnement**, rue de la Hount Blanque, 65200 Bagnères-de-Bigorre (Tel. 62 95 49 67); or the **Association des Amis du Parc**, 20 rue Samonzet, 64000 Pau (Tel. 59 27 15 30). The address of the headquarters of the Western Pyrenees national park is **Parc National des Pyrénées Occidentales**, 59 route de Pau, 65000 Tarbes (Tel. 62 93 30 60). The **Parc Naturel Régional du Haut-Languedoc** can be reached over the border in the Hérault *département*, at BP 9, 13 rue du Cloître, 34220 St-Pons.

Geographical Breakdown of Region

Haute-Pyrénées, Haute-Garonne and Ariège

The Haute-Pyrénées is at the heart of the mountain range, with the highest peaks on the French side and the most dramatic remnants of glaciation. Haute-Garonne has its share of physical and historical interest, concentrated around the young River Garonne, but all too often eclipsed by the attractions of its capital, Toulouse. Whilst Ariège (whose full name is Ariège-Pyrénées) holds greater appeal in its foothills, with their mementos of earlier civilisations.

The highlight of the town of **Tarbes** is the Jardin Massey, a pretty landscaped park, dating from 1850 and containing a fifteenth-century cloister. Apart from being a major place of Christian pilgrimage, nearby **Lourdes** is also the gateway to the Haute-Pyrénées. Unless you have come as a pilgrim, it is advisable to see it and move on, so as to avoid the pricey and crowded accommodation found in all such commercialised resorts. The main places of interest are the Massabielle Grotto, where the fourteen-year-old miller's daughter, Bernadette, had her various visions of the Virgin, including one during which a new spring trickled forth as she scratched the earth. It is the waters of this spring which, ever since, have been believed to have healing powers, and it is to this spot that sick people from all round the world have come to be cured. Above and beside the grotto are two basilicas, the Rosaire and the vast underground arena of St-Pius X; also nearby are the Musée Bernadette and the Musée d'Art Sacré du Gemmail. Across the **Gave de Pau** is Bernadette's birthplace, the Moulin des Boly, and the Cachot, her home. The most imposing building, however, is Lourdes castle. This medieval hill-top fortification can be reached on foot or by escalator and it houses the Musée Pyrénéen, which exhibits aspects of the lifestyle and crafts of the whole Pyrenean region. This, like most of the amenities of Lourdes, is open between Easter and mid-October, as is the cable-car on the town's outskirts, which takes you up to the **Pic Béout** for a splendid view of the whole area. A relatively peaceful picnic and recreation spot is the Lac de Lourdes. At Easter, a festival of sacred art and music takes place in the town.

Some of the most impressive sights of the surrounding area are its caves, notably the **Grottes de Bétharram** and **Médous**, the former of which is more interesting, though, of course, more commercialised. The latter are near the town of **Bagnères-de-Bigorre**, where a traditional local festival with mountain singers takes place in August. The road south from Lourdes will bring you the French Pyrenees at their most magnificent – the **Bigorre** area, with its peaks, misty valleys, historic villages and cheerful spa towns, such as **Argelès-Gazost**. The left fork of the road follows the Gave de Pau towards its source and takes you to the **Cirque de Gavarnie**. **Gavarnie** itself is simply a collection of souvenir shops, which hosts the Pyrenees Festival each July, but the Cirque is one of the most impressive sights of the national park: an amphitheatre of rock, cupped beneath a glacial rim, from which the Grand Cascade falls about 440 metres. The track running round the top naturally gives spectacular views. Part of the same formation are the less-trodden **Cirques de Troumouse** and **d'Estaubé**, also on the route of the HRP footpath. Another beauty spot is around **Pont d'Espagne**, a few kilometres south of **Cauterets** along a road flanked by several gushing waterfalls. Around Pont d'Espagne is marvellous walking country and, in addition to the GR 10, many local footpaths take you along the Marcadau valley to **Pont du Cayan** and **Pont d'Estalaunque**.

Further down the valley, **Barèges** makes a good base for

walks to **Montagne Fleurie** and is near the 2720-metre **Pic du Midi de Bigorre**. Another good location for mountain proximity and splendid views is the charming village of **St-Savin**. The fourteenth-century Romanesque abbey church dates back to times when religious orders ruled the area. The village was also once inhabited by the unfortunate 'Cagots'. Originally lepers, these were social outcasts who became accomplished craftsmen. The church doorway of St-Savin reveals how they used to observe mass from outside. The **Baronnies** is an interesting area of foothills, north of **Arreau** and the picturesque **Vallée de Campan**. Made up of four parishes, it is off the beaten tourist track but rich in woodland and wildlife, with a network of caves such as those at **Labastide**.

To the east is **St-Bertrand-de-Comminges** in Haute-Garonne. Some remains of the original Roman settlement here are still in evidence, though much was destroyed when an eleventh-century Gascon nobleman, Bertrand de l'Isle Jourdan, decided to have a cathedral built here. This Romanesque cathedral of the, later canonised, St-Bertrand dominates the present town. The cathedral's choir is an amazing piece of work, comprising sixty carved stalls vividly depicting religious and secular images of sins and virtues. The ramparts and adjoining medieval houses are features of the walled village, where there is a Classical Music season in July (including concerts in the cathedral). Another charming, though much simpler, Romanesque church is that of **St-Just**, sitting below at **Valcabrière**.

Nearby, the **Grottes de Gargas** display engravings of mammoths, deer, bison and horses, as well as hand paintings, some of which have curiously short fingers. **Bagnères-de-Luchon**, where the Romans first built thermal baths, has enjoyed popularity as a lively and elegant spa since the eighteenth-century. **Luchon**, where there is a folk song festival in July and a flower festival in August, is a good base for walks to **Maladeta** or **Port de Venasque** (2445 metres). Views of spectacular lakes and waterfalls reward those who complete the challenging walks from the **Vallée du Lys**.

Like its neighbouring *départements*, Ariège has some high altitude ski resorts, spas and walking bases, notably at **Axles-Thermes** near the Andorra border. Previously known as **Pays de Foix**, it is however, more notable for its limetone foothills, broken up by hill-top forts, hidden valleys, river plains and cave systems. **Foix** is the area's capital, where you can take a boat trip on the underground River **Labouche**, past unusual rock formations and waterfalls, emerging with a view of the medieval castle and its three towers. At **Tarascon-sur-Ariège** you can visit the magnificent **Grottes de Niaux**. These labyrinths of prehistoric cave paintings compare in importance with those of the more colourful Lascaux caves in Dordogne. The caves are open all year round and the Salon Noir contains paintings of bison, deer, ibex and horses. The connecting caves of **Lombrives**, with their intricate stalagmite and stalactite formations can also be visited.

The Ariège foothills were the last Cathar strongholds and the castles at **Montségur, Roquefixade, Usson** and **Puivert** are all well worth seeing. The citadel at Montségur is perched on a hilltop, 1000 metres up. It is not surprising that, in 1243, it took a 9-month siege finally to overthrow the Cathars. Nowadays it takes a half-hour steep climb to get to the top. Nearby **Mirepoix** is a good example of a *bastide* town, and medieval pageants take place both here and in Foix each summer, while the area's commercial centre is the medieval town of **Pamiers** with its canals and markets.

Accommodation & Eating Out

Accommodation in this area tends to be surprisingly cheap, with a good selection of *chambres d'hôte* and small family-run hotels, as well as the odd château:

First Class

Château de Camon, Dominique du Pont, 09500 Mirepoix (Tel. 61 68 14 05): 5 rooms in sixteenth-century château in beautiful village; restaurant and tea rooms in former abbey and its gardens.

Middle Range

L'Oustal, Unac, 09250 Luzenac (Tel. 61 64 48 44): 5 attractive rooms in simple village inn; restaurant serving generous portions of regional specialities and popular with locals. **Jean-Marie Kühn**, Ferme St-Genès, Le Carlaret, 09100 Pamiers (Tel. 61 67 16 31): 5 *chambres d'hôte* (for non-smokers) in a beautifully restored farmhouse; vegetarian cooking, swimming pool and horseriding on American Appaloosa horses.

Economy

Auberge du Poids Public, 31540 St-Félix-Lauragais (Tel. 61 83 00 20): 13 rooms in friendly village inn with good views; excellent regional cuisine. **Famille Ventelon**, Hameau de Rousseau, Cos, 09000 Foix (Tel. 61 02 95 90); *chambres d'hôte* in country home furnished from family antique shop; *tables d'hôte* shared with family, offering an abundance of typical regional home cooking. **Hôtel le Viscos**, 65400 Saint-Savin (Tel. 62 97 02 28): 16 rooms in family-run hotel with restaurant.

Toulouse

The pink bricks and medieval grandeur of this famous southern city combine with a forward-looking confidence in technology, providing the setting for unashamed enjoyment of food and entertainment as well as a love of art and culture, in full evidence to the visitor.

Today's city has a large old quarter of narrow medieval streets, encircled no longer by a wall but by busy boulevards. In the centre, the Garonne is spanned by two bridges, **Pont Neuf** and **Pont St-Pierre**, which stand either side of the original Roman fording point, Chaussée de Bazacle. Of the 230 listed buildings, many are extremely impressive. **Le Capitole**, which occupies one side of the **Place du Capitole**, was completed in the eighteenth-century. It houses the Hôtel de Ville, the Opera and the Salle Henri-Martin, which displays his works. Many other paintings hang in the Salle des Illustres and beside the Grand Escalier. The **Donjon du Capitole** at the rear is the sixteenth-century keep, which houses the Tourist Office.

The **Basilica of St-Sernin** is arguably the finest example of Romanesque architecture, dating back to the eleventh century when it was built to accommodate pilgrims *en route* to Santiago de Compostella. Its octagonal, five-tiered tower is the city's main landmark. The interior contains a wealth of Romanesque sculptures, including one of St Sernin and his killer, the bull, and there is a crypt full of various saintly relics. From the basilica, **rue du Taur** leads to **Notre-Dame du Taur**, a fourteenth-century church, also dedicated to the martydom of St Sernin by the Romans in AD 257. The **Couvent des Jacobins** is a Gothic masterpiece of monastic design, completed in 1340 for the Dominican order. It incorporates a church whose main feature is a palm tree-like central column; there is also a bell-tower, a refectory used for art exhibitions and cloisters used for summer music festival performances. The **Cathédrale St-Etienne** was built, demolished and added to between the thirteenth and seventeenth centuries. Its rose window and seventeen chapels are its most interesting attractions.

Some of the grandest buildings in Toulouse were constructed by two successful pastel merchants. These are the **Hôtel de Bernuy** and **Hôtel d'Assézat** mansions. The **Musée des Augustins**, which occupies the Augustinian monastery and cloisters, has collections of Romanesque, Renaissance and Gothic sculpture, as well as religious art. Other good museums include the **Natural History Museum** and the archaeological **Musée St-Raymond**. The **Parc du Château de la Reynerie** on Impasse de l'Abbé Salvat is an exotic eighteenth-century garden, ideal for a quiet stroll.

Accommodation

First Class

Grand Hôtel de L'Opéra, 1 Place Capitole (Tel. 61 21 82 66): 54 luxurious rooms in ideally situated, central hotel with garden; highly regarded restaurant.

First Class / Middle Range

La Flânerie, route Lacroix-Falgarde, 31320 Vieille-Toulouse (Tel. 61 73 39 12): 12 rooms in hotel with views over valley and park, 9 km from town.

Middle Range

Hôtel de Diane, 3 route de St-Simon (Tel. 61 07 59 52): 35 comfortable and attractively furnished rooms in family-run, turn-of-the-century hotel with garden, 8 km to south-west of town centre; restaurant with good regional dishes next-door. **Hôtel Royal**, 6 rue Labéda (Tel. 61 23 38 70): 31 rooms in quiet, though central, hotel with Spanish-style courtyard.

Economy

Hôtel du Grand Balcon, 8 rue Romiguières (Tel. 61 21 48 08): good value rooms in central hotel where St-Exupéry once stayed. **Hôtel St-Antoine**, 21 rue St-Antoine (Tel. 61 21 40 66): elegant rooms in quiet, well-located hotel.

Eating Out

First Class

Restaurant Vanel, 22 rue Maurice-Fontvieille (Tel. 61 21 51 82): extremely inventive regional cuisine. **La Belle Epoque**, 3 rue

Pargaminières (Tel. 61 23 22 12): high-quality light cuisine served in atmospheric surroundings.

Middle Range

La Bascule, 14 ave Maurice-Haurion (Tel. 61 52 09 51): traditional local dishes with a modern touch. **Au Chat Dingue**, 40 bis rue Peyrolières (Tel. 61 21 23 11): good quality at a reasonable price.

Economy

Chez Carmen, 97 allées Charles-de-Fitte (Tel. 61 42 04 95): home cooking in bistro-style restaurant, popular with locals. **Les Caves de la Maréchale**, 3 rue Jules-Chalande: elegant restaurant in former wine cellar on pedestrian street. **Auberge Louis XIII**, 1 bis rue Tripière: restaurant with garden, popular with students.

Entertainments

From July through to September there is a summer music festival, with concerts both classical and contemporary. September also brings an intenational piano festival. On Sunday mornings the area around the Basilique St-Sernin is the site of a large flea market. News-stands will supply you free of charge with a copy of 'Regard', which lists concerts and plays. For atmosphere in the evenings try the Café Florida on Place du Capitole, or the Père Bacchus or Van Gogh, side by side on Place St-Georges.

Useful Addresses

The **Tourist Office** is at the Donjon du Capitole (Tel. 61 23 32 00) The Comité Régional du Tourisme, which will supply information on the whole of Midi-Pyrénées, is at 12 rue Salambo (Tel. 61 47 11 12). The Post Office is at 9 rue Lafayette (opposite the tourist office), and the **Centre Hôpitalier** is on Chemin de Vallon (Tel. 61 53 11 33). In a **medical emergency**, call 61 49 33 33.

Transport Options

A good way of seeing the main sights is to join one of the daily walking tours run by the tourist office. They also do bus excursions to nearby sights. Town buses leave from Place du Capitole, and the new Metro system can also come in handy. A pleasant cycle ride is through the Grand Rond to Allée Paul Sabatier.

Gers, Tarn-et-Garonne and Tarn

These *départements* contain expanses of sparsely populated agricultural land, made interesting by steep, winding river gorges, underground caves, hill-top towns and the remains of medieval fortifications.

Gers, the *département* to the west of Toulouse, is renowned for its agricultural abundance, while its inhabitants are accredited with gastronomic excellence, a considerable talent for good living and unusual boastfulness! A 'Festival du Bon Vivre' is held annually at **Condom**, where the gastronomic sequences of *Babette's Feast* were filmed. It is around here, in the northern Gers, that the famous Armagnac brandy is produced. Châteaux can be visited for tasting and buying and the **Château de Cassaigne** has an exhibition about Armagnac production. This former residence of the bishops of Condom is open all year. The town has various other interesting buildings, notably the Cathédrale St-Pierre, in Gascon Gothic style, and its adjacent sixteenth-century cloisters. Condom is a pleasant base for visiting the many nearby castles and towns such as **Fourcès, Montréal, Larressingle** and **La Romieu**. Many of these are the fortified medieval villages known as *bastides*, built in strategic hill-top locations by the Counts of Toulouse after the thirteenth-century crusades against the Cathars. One of the most interesting examples is Fourcès.

Auch, the capital of Gers, is worth visiting if only for the Cathédrale Ste-Marie, whose 113-stall choir has oak carvings of grotesque figures from Biblical and mythical stories. The Gascon, Arnaud de Moles, painted the stained-glass windows in the early sixteenth century, and there is also a statue of d'Artagnan from 1931. The Musée des Jacobins, housed in the Jacobean convent, exhibits archaeological finds and traditional Gascon artefacts.

Over the departmental border, in Tarn-et-Garonne, **Moissac** is a good place to see one of the region's finest abbey churchs, the St-Pierre, and its adjoining cloisters, which were rebuilt in the eleventh century. The church doorway and the extensive carvings on the cloister's arches and walls are the main features to look out for. In summer the traditional Chasselas festival is held at Moissac. The Bishop's Palace at nearby **Montauban**, which is the departmental capital, is used as an art gallery for works of the town's famous citizen, Jean-Auguste Dominique Ingres. Born in 1780, he was the last great French Classical painter, in oppositior to Delacroix, France's foremost Romantic painter. Montauban also has an interesting market square in Place Nationale, and hosts a music festival in summer.

The Tarn *département*, to the east, is one which is still relatively 'undiscovered'. Most people make a flying visit to its capital, Albi, and ignore the rest. However, nearby **Cordes** is a fine example of a hill-top *bastide*. Built in the thirteenth century, it prospered as a centre for leatherwork, weaving and lacework. It is now an artists' colony once again, with its steep cobbled main street lined with studios selling regional crafts and produce. A falconry festival is held here in July. Another attractive hill village is **Castelnau-de-Montmirail**, whilst **Gaillac**, as well as being an important wine-producing centre, boasts the magnificent seventeenth-century classical Parc de Foucaud. South-east, at **Castres**, is the Musée Goya, housed in episcopal buildings designed by Mansart with gardens by Le Nôtre, and exhibiting collections of Spanish painting including some works by Goya. Here you are on the edge of the Haut-Languedoc regional park, where cultural animation plays a considerable role in keeping Occitan and Cathar traditions alive. The Maison Fuzier in **Malzamet** presents the strong local traditions linked to death and, throughout the park, traditional music and farm crafts are promoted. The Montagne Noir *ecomusée* at **Labastide** offers a window on the culture and economy of this fragile region, whose mountains are virtually deserted and whose valley villages, formerly producers of textiles, are now in recession. The museum plays a considerable role in working to save the regional heritage.

Accommodation

First Class

Château de Garrevaques, Garrevaques, 81700 Puylaurens (Tel. 63 75 04 54 and 61 52 01 47): 8 *chambres d'hôte*, 2 suites and 1 large apartment (sleeps 7 to 11) in château with park, swimming pool and tennis court; possibility of the services of a chauffeur-cum-guide; *tables d'hôte*. **Hôtel Restaurant Château Saint-Roch**, 'Le Pin', 82340 Auvillard (Tel. 63 95 95 22): 10 rooms in beautiful, imposing château with park; restaurant.

Middle Range

Le Logis des Cordeliers, rue des Cordeliers, 32100 Condom (Tel. 62 28 03 68): though a new building, this peaceful hotel blends well with the surrounding medieval stone-walled quarter of Condom and has a restaurant in an adjacent Gothic chapel. **Hostellerie du Vieux Cordes**, rue St-Michel, 81170 Cordes (Tel. 63 56 00 12): 21 rooms in medieval inn with views of old town; good cuisine.

Economy

Mme Malbreil, 'Naussens', 81150 Castanet (Tel. 63 55 22 56): welcoming *chambres d'hôte* on a farm. **Mme Galea**, 'Les Dantous Sud', 82100 Castelsarrasin (Tel. 63 32 26 95): *chambres d'hôte* in comfortable house with swimming pool; *tables d'hôte* with traditional home cooking.

Eating Out

In addition to the above, the following are recommended:

First Class

Hôtel de France, Place de la Libération, 32000 Auch (Tel. 62 05 00 44): the regional cuisine of Gascony at its best; also has 30 comfortable rooms.

Economy

Ferme-Auberge du Château de la Hitte, 32330 Gondrin (Tel. 62 28 28 23): excellent regional dishes served on reservation; also offers simple *ferme-auberge* accommodation.

Albi

This lovely red-brick town, with its amazing fortified cathedral, looks equally picturesque on both sides of the River Tarn. Albi's main attraction is the thirteenth-century **Cathédrale Ste-Cécile**, which looks more like a castle to defend the town, recalling the days when priests also had to be soldiers. Built in the deep red brick found throughout the town and which gave Albi the nickname 'le Rouge', the cathedral cannot fail to impress. Its interior is interesting too, filled with colourful sixteenth-century frescoes, including one of the seven deadly sins, and fabulous *trompe l'oeil* marble. Albi's other claim to fame is that it was the birthplace of the painter Henri de Toulouse-Lautrec. The Palais de la Berbie houses a museum of his work which includes all his famous posters of Paris nightclubs. The house where he was born (the Maison Natale de Toulouse-Lautrec) is in **Vieil Albi**; it is still owned by his family but can be visited from

July to mid-September. The sleepy dark streets of this part of town are a favourite haunt of artists and craftspeople keen to sell you their creations. The peaceful **Eglise St-Salvy** is also worth a visit.

Accommodation

First Class

La Réserve, route de Cordes, 'Fonvialane' (Tel. 63 60 79 79): 20 rooms in quiet riverside inn (with swimming pool), just outside town; excellent restaurant.

Middle Range

Le Modern'Pujol, 22 ave Colonel-Teyssier (Tel. 63 54 02 92): 19 rooms in family-run hotel with restaurant.

Middle Range / Economy

Le Vieil Alby, 25 rue Toulouse-Lautrec (Tel. 63 54 14 69): 10 rooms in family-run hotel in old town; excellent restaurant. **Relais Gascon et Auberge Landaise**, 1 et 3 rue Balzac (Tel. 63 54 26 51): 17 rooms in charming family establishment with restaurant.

Economy

Laperouse, 21 Place Laperouse (Tel. 63 54 69 22): 22 rooms in family-run hotel with restaurant. **Hôtel du Parc**, 3 ave du Parc (Tel. 63 54 12 80): 18 rooms in quiet situation near park.

Eating Out

In addition to the restaurants above, try:

First Class

Francis Cardaillac, Tilbury, 81150 Marssac (Tel. 63 55 41 90): historic regional recipes with a modern touch, served in restaurant with garden, 10 km from town.

Economy

Auberge St-Loup, 26 rue de Castelviel: medieval inn offering menus of local specialities.

Entertainments

In June and July, Albi seems awash with celebrations: from the Feu de la St-Jean bonfire to theatre, film and music festivals. Details are available from the tourist office. In the mornings there is a vast indoor market on Place du Marché, while Saturday morning brings an open air market to Place Ste-Cécile. Watching the artisans at work in the old town is also interesting.

Useful Addresses

The **Tourist Office** is on Place Ste-Cécile (Tel. 63 54 22 30). The **Post Office** is on Place du Vigan, and the **Centre Hospitalier** is on rue de la Berchère (Tel. 63 47 47 47).

Transport Options

The best way to explore Albi is certainly on foot, though bicycles can be rented at the train station. Ask at the tourist office about bus excursions to neighbouring towns and villages.

Aveyron & Lot

The rocky gorges and limestone *causses* of Aveyron and the woods and historic towns of Lot make these interesting parts to explore.

North of Albi, in the south-west of Aveyron, **Najac** is a picturesque fortified village perched 150 metres above one of the gorges gouged out by the River Aveyron. It is in this area that the gorges are at their most impressive. Further east, you will find the small town of **St-Affrique** with its ornate Notre-Dame church. Prehistoric dolmens can be visited around here, as well as the caves where the famous Roquefort cheese undergoes its 2 to 3-month maturation process. The departmental capital, **Rodez** is also worth a visit, with its pink sandstone Gothic cathedral – unusual in these southern parts.

To the north is the craft town of **Espalion**, where a honeycomb of medieval buildings flank the river in the old town. Nearby **Estaing** is very picturesque, with a castle topping the hill behind. In winter there are skiing possibilities in this area, around **Laguiole**, though the business remains comfortably small-scale. The village of **Ste-Geneviève** on the River Argance has an attractive church. By following the river, you will come to the **Barrage de Sarrans** which has created an artificial lake crossed by a suspension bridge; good views can be enjoyed from the platforms which jut out from the cliff here, and from **Laussac**, a pretty hamlet on a promontory. **Entraygues** is a pleasant, tree-shaded town with a riverside quay and the D 42 road heading south-east from here hugs the gorges of the Lot river, which, though not high, are steeply wooded. Perhaps the highlight of the area is the town of **Conques**, where a music festival is held in summer. Its attractive cobbled streets, uneven flights of steps, three-towered Romanesque church and houses of pink-brown stone are a photographer's paradise, and in summer you will not be the only one appreciating them. An out-of-season visit is, however, a quite different experience – and thoroughly recommended.

Over the border in the Lot *départment* is the spectacularly situated village of **Rocamadour**; it has long been a pilgrimage destination and is now a tourist attraction as well – allegedly the second most visited site in France, attracting around 1½ million visitors a year. The Pilgrims' Steps (216 of them) will take you to its Cité Religieuse (there is also an elevator!), and, even higher up, its château. The illuminated spectacle, 'les Lumières du Temps à Rocamadour' takes place here during the first two weeks in August. Another festival, this time jazz, takes place at nearby **Souillac** in July. **Gourdon-en-Quercy** is a historic town and there are interesting prehistoric cave paintings near it in the **Grottes de Cougnac**.

The Lot river carves its way across the region to the south of here. It is the centre for the production of the heavy red Cahors wines, whose vineyards line the banks. The river valley is one of the most attractive stretches of scenery in the whole region; it is also an ideal place to stay, with its off-the-beaten-track villages, such as **Puy-l'Evêque**, perched above its north bank; its traditional old towns like **St-Cirq-Lapopie**; its prehistoric cave paintings at the **Grotte du Pech-Merle**; and, not least, its capital Cahors.

Accommodation & Eating Out

First Class

La Pescalerie, 46330 Cabrerets (Tel. 65 31 22 55): 10 rooms in eighteenth-century manor house in beautiful countryside; exceptionally warm welcome and restaurant offering home-cooked meals from the freshest local ingredients.

Middle Range

La Pélissaria, St-Cirq-Lapopie, 46330 Cabrerets (Tel. 65 31 25 14): 8 rooms in grey-stone hotel with garden and views over valley; restaurant. **La Source Bleue**, Moulin de Leygues, Touzac,

46700 Puy-l'Evêque (Tel. 65 36 52 01): 12 rooms in 11th century paper mill with friendly owners; restaurant with fish specialities. **Hôtel Belle Rive**, Au Roc du Pont, 12270 Najac (Tel. 65 29 73 90): 31 rooms in family-run hotel; restaurant was winner in the 1989/90 Logis de France competition for the promotion of regional cuisine.

Middle Range / Economy

Relais les Vieilles Tours, Lafage, 46500 Rocamadour (Tel. 65 33 68 01): 10 rooms in restored manor house in secluded setting; meals from fresh local produce.

Economy

Auberge du Pont Romain, 12320 Conques (Tel. 65 69 84 07): 7 rooms in family-owned inn with restaurant. **Hôtel Bellevue**, Place de la Truffière, 46700 Puy-l'Evêque (Tel. 65 21 30 70): 15 rooms in family-run hotel with wonderful views and restaurant.

Cahors

The historical capital of the Quercy province, Cahors grew up in one of the most pronounced meanders of the River Lot and flourished during the thirteenth century. A signposted walk guides you through the medieval streets of Cahors' **Badernes** quarter. Some of the main sights there are the **Cathédrale St-Etienne**, with its impressive twelfth-century tympanum over the doorway and the fourteenth-century paintings on the two domes above the nave; the **Maison Roaldes**, where King Henry IV stayed, and the remains of the castle ramparts. The **Pont Valentré** bridge is reputed to be the world's finest example of a medieval bridge. It was built in 1360 and has 3 towers, each nearly 50 metres high, and 6 pointed Gothic arches. One of the best viewing points is on the far bank beside the **Fontaine des Chartreux**, the original Roman spring which supplies drinking water to the city. In Cahors, even the modern boulevards of the city centre offer fine views of the river.

Accommodation & Eating Out

In Cahors there are numerous small, family-run establishments with restaurants serving regional cuisine.

First Class

Château de Mercuès, Mercues (Tel. 65 20 00 01): 19 rooms and 4 suites in 13th century riverside château with park, 7 km from town; good traditional restaurant.

Middle Range

Hôtel Beau Rivage, Laroque-les-Arcs (Tel. 65 35 30 58): 15 rooms in tranquil spot on outskirts of town; good regional restaurant. **Hôtel Terminus**, 5 ave Charles-de-Freycinet (Tel. 65 35 24 50): 31 comfortable rooms in turn-of-the-century family-run hotel; excellent restaurant (**Le Balandre**), serving good house specialities.

Economy

Hôtel de la Paix, 30 place St-Maurice (Tel. 65 35 03 40): 22 rooms in family-run hotel with restaurant. **L'Escargot**, 5 bd Gambetta (Tel. 65 35 07 66): 10 rooms in centrally situated family hotel; restaurant, **L'Orangerie**, rue St-James: this restaurant offers a mixture of vegetarian dishes and regional speicalities.

Entertainments

There is not usually much on in Cahors itself: its strong point is as a base for touring (plenty of wine-tasting *caves* in the vicinity). The tourist office will supply a free guide to regional wines. There are Wednesday and Saturday markets in front of the cathedral and a Blues Festival comes to town in mid-July.

Useful Addresses

The **Tourist Office** is on Place Aristide-Briand (Tel. 65 35 09 56). The **Post Office** is on rue Wilson, and the **Centre Hospitalier** is on the same street (Tel. 65 35 47 97).

Transport Options

The tourist office runs tours of the old town and mini-bus tours of the area in summer. Bike rental is available from the railway station or from **Combes**, 117 bd Gambetta. Buses to neighbouring towns and villages leave from the train station.

21 Aquitaine

Modern Aquitaine is an area of great variety. The name, originally Roman, was revived in 1964 for one of France's twenty-one economic regions. It comprises five *départements*: Dordogne, Gironde, Landes, Lot-et-Garonne and Pyrénées-Atlantiques, each with a distinctive character. For the most part it is a rural region and, other than Bordeaux, contains no big cities. It is therefore an ideal choice for visitors who enjoy touring by car and for lovers of the countryside.

Dordogne, which is almost identical with the ancient Périgord, is in turn divided into the four *arrondissements* of Périgueux, Bergerac, Nontron and Sarlat, and is the most northerly of the *départements*. Its rivers and forests, caves and grottos, medieval towns and châteaux, along with a distinctive cuisine, have made it a popular area with tourists

Southeast of Dordogne is the *département* of Lot-et-Garonne, an agricultural area of crops, cattle-raising and dairy farming. Fruit-growing is particularly important and the *département* is noted for its plums, from which Prunes d'Agen is made. Vineyards produce some good wine (notably Dual and Marmande) and this is one of France's main tobacco growing areas. The towns of Agen, Marmande, Nerac and Villeneuve-sur-Lot give their names to the *département*'s four *arrondissements*.

Gironde, to the west of Dordogne, containing the *arrondissements* of Bordeaux, Blaye, Langon, Lesparre, Médoc and Lesbourne is celebrated for the vineyards, (Médoc, St-Emilion, Pomerol) which are concentrated mainly in the north of the *département*. The principal city, Bordeaux, is in the heart of one of France's major industrial and commercial areas.

The western part of the *département* is mainly flat and covered in pine forest with a coastline that is fringed with sand-dunes, lagoons and marshes, broken to the south by the Arcachon Basin and its ring of seaside resorts.

During the Middle Ages Gironde was traversed by three different routes to the shrine of Santiago de Compostella in northern Spain.

Sandy beaches continue south for almost 130 kilometres into Landes whose two *arrondissements*, Mont de Marsan and Dax, contain several small modern resorts. Pyrénées-Atlantiques is situated south of Landes, on the border with Spain, which lies behind the mountain barrier of the Pyrenees. This is the land of the Basques and their language still survives here. The area is rich in regional culture, crafts and legend. Basque architecture too is distinct: low farmhouses with painted wooden timbers and shutters are a particular feature of this area. The Basque region also has strong sporting traditions. Pelote is the local game, though rugby is very popular, the region providing the backbone of the French national team. A local form of bullfighting takes place here in which, as in Provence, the bull is not killed.

Pau, the principal city, together with Bayonne and Oloron, lend their names to the *département*'s *arrondissements*. St-Jean de-Pied-de-Port, formerly the capital of Navarre, guards the Pass of Roncevaux that once linked the two halves of the important medieval kingdom of Navarre.

The tourist industry is an important source of income for the area (see **Level of Tourism**), and there are several spa towns as well as the seaside resorts of Biarritz and St-Jean-de-Luz. The Aquitaine region is now known throughout the world for the wines of the Bordeaux vineyards, and the ancient caves of the Dordogne where, in 1940, two schoolboys discovered the remarkable Lascaux cave paintings.

History

Dordogne has been inhabited since prehistoric times, and the valley of the Vézère in the southeast of the *département* provides extensive evidence of early man's presence through the cave drawings and paintings at Les-Eyzies-de-Tayac and Lascaux.

In Julius Caesar's account of Gaul, Aquitaine is described as the area between the Pyrenees and the River Garonne. Later, under the Emperor Augustus, it was made a Roman administrative district and its borders were extended to the River Loire and the Massif Central. Further administrative changes were made under the Emperor Diocletian, when Aquitaine was divided into three provinces. The region is celebrated in the works of Ausonius, a fourth century poet and native of Bordeaux. In the fifth century it came under the rule of the Visisgoths but, by AD 507, it was controlled by the Franks.

The following century the Normans began to invade the region from the north, leaving their customary trail of destruction behind them, until they finally settled in Normandy. However, it was not until the end of the millennium that Aquitaine settled into a more peaceful rhythm. In the Pyrenees, particularly, the history of this time remains deeply rooted in legend. Roland, Charlemagne's illustrious nephew, is believed to have fought against the Moors in the Western Pyrenees, aided by a miraculous sword, Durandal, which is said to have been presented to him by an angel. Roland died on the Pass of Roncevaux, ambushed by Arab marauders, but his name lives on in epic poetry, in local place names and in legend.

It was Charlemagne who first established Aquitaine as a kingdom, though it was reduced to a duchy under the Counts of Poitiers in the tenth and eleventh centuries. The last duke, William X, married his daughter, Eleanor of Aquitaine, to King Henry II of England. After his death, the dukedom was disputed for centuries between England and France, but it never again existed as a single unit, finally being divided up into the provinces of Poitou, Guyenne and Gascony.

The Black Prince's army, largely composed of French soldiers, regained the region in 1356, in what is known locally as the second Battle of Poitiers. This was a short-lived victory however, for it ended thirteen years later when the French retained Aquitaine and it was placed under the rule of Jean Duke of Berry, brother of Charles V.

By this time the struggles between the Frankish kings and the Dukes of Aquitaine (who were also kings of England) were acquiring a more nationalistic fervour, and, with the crowning of Charles the VIII in 1423, Aquitaine was becoming French in character. What today is the western part of the *département* of Pyrénées-Atlantiques, formed part of kingdom of Navarre until 1589, when Navarre's king became Henry V of France. Thereafter it was united with France, and French kings bore the title 'King of France and Navarre'.

Throughout the Middle Ages, pilgrims from all over Europe traversed the region on their way to the shrine of Santiago de Compostella. In the sixteenth century, religious battles replaced baronial and nationalistic ones when, in the wake of the Protestant Reformation, many were converted to the Protestant faith. In the following century, the Girondist Party of the French Revolution was formed in Bordeaux. A few years later, however, the city became the scene of dreadful counter-revolutionary wars, when Royalist peasants rose against Republican forces. The citizens of Bordeaux, and the region generally, were to suffer again in 1814, when the English fleet blockaded Aquitaine's harbours during the Napoleonic Wars. Following Napoleon's defeat, Bordeaux and Gironde declared their allegiance to the Bourbons.

During both the First and Second World Wars, Bordeaux became a refuge for the fleeing French governments of the day, and came to symbolise the centre of French Resistance. In fact, during the Second World War, despite heavy bombing of the region, the Germans were never able to flush out the French Resistance which eventually, in 1944, liberated Bordeaux and much of Aquitaine almost unaided by Allied forces.

The reputation of the region's wines has, ever since Roman times, been zealously maintained. However, in 1974, there was a scandal of unprecedented proportions. Eight wine shippers and merchants from Bordeaux were convicted of fraudulently adulterating 40,000 hecto-litres of wine.

Geography

Dordogne lies on the western slope of the Massif Central. As it drops to the west its barren plateaux become gradually more afforested. Towards the north, upland meadows rise to 400 metres.

Seven major rivers cross the *département*, one of which, the Dordogne, gives it its name. These rivers flow through scenic valleys which support wheat, maize, potato, and tobacco crops as well as fruit. There are large expanses of sweet chestnut forest, and walnuts are grown for their oil.

Lot-et-Garonne, the smallest of the region's *départements*, lies in the middle of the Aquitaine basin. It is crossed south-west to south-east by the River Garonne, on which stands Agen, the *département*'s principal town. Agriculture, especially fruit and tobacco, are the dominant industries. Gironde is the largest *département* in France. It bears the name of the river and estuary formed by the confluence of the Rivers Garonne and Dordogne.

The coastline is straight, sandy and flat; much of the land in the north-east was reclaimed in the nineteenth century and is now pine forest. Coastal lagoons provide facilities for a variety of watersports though there are no natural harbours, with the exception of the Arcachon Basin.

Over three-quarters of Landes consists of the forest of Les Landes, the most extensive in France. This also includes the Landes de Gascogne regional park. Formerly a windswept land of sand, moor and marsh, dotted with lakes and ponds, the sand-dunes were stabilized in the nineteenth century, and much of the area drained by canals and finally afforested with pines to provide a source of timber and turpentine. Fire has been a constant hazard, but the area now supports a thriving forestry industry supplying paper and saw mills with raw material. There is an exhibition and interpretation of the local rural economy in the regional park (see **Geographical Breakdown**). Also part of the park is the Banc d'Arguin Nature Reserve, a low, sandy island in the Arcachon Basin, which has interesting flora and bird fauna, notably the Sandwich tern which nests there.

Pyrénées-Atlantiques borders the regions of Midi-Pyrénées to the east, the Landes to the north, the Bay of Biscay to the west, and the Pyrenees mountains to the south. The highest peak in the *département* is Pic d'Anie at 1830 metres. Several easily accessible passes at 915 metres link the area with Spain, the most famous of which is Roncevaux. Green, upland meadows are grazed by sheep and cattle whilst, in the valleys, grain and potatoes are grown and poultry raised. In 1951, huge deposits of natural gas were discovered at Lacq near Pau, much of which is used locally to generate the electric power required for the aluminium and plastics industries and for the manufacture of fertilisers.

It cannot be denied that the scenery of the majority of Aquitaine is flat and, in conventional terms anyway, uninteresting. The Pyrenees mountain range is in stark contrast to this. The mountains form a natural frontier between France and Spain, stretching from the Atlantic, where green hills rise gently from the ocean, to the Mediterranean where dramatic cliffs fall steeply to the sea.

Historically and geographically, the two principal regions of Pyrénées-Atlantiques – the Basque country in the south west, and Béarn in the central Pyrenees, have remained fiercely independent and somewhat divorced from national politics and affairs. This sense of regionalism has often given outsiders the impression that the Pyrenees are remote and inhospitable. Remote they can seem, particularly in winter, but inhospitable they are not. The Basques and the Béarnaises, though proud of their distinct culture and traditions, are friendly and colourful people.

The mountains of the western Pyrenees are incorporated into the Pyrenees national park, formed in 1967. The park is a protected strip of land running for over a hundred kilometres along the French/ Spanish border. There are numerous species of indigenous flora and fauna in the Pyrenees, though, tragically, the brown bear was hunted almost to extinction during the last century and today only a dozen or so survive. As for flora, gentian, saxifrage and edelweiss are plentiful and grow on the highest passes, whilst in the valleys white buttercups, columbines, bellflowers and lilies flourish. Apart from the few surviving bears, other large mammals which roam the hills include wild boar and goat, the Pyrenean chamois or 'isard', and the extremely rare lynx. There are also foxes, badgers, martens, otters and marmots. Ornithologists should look out for the golden eagle, Bonnelli's eagle, and the vultures sometimes seen gliding over the high mountain plateaux in search of carrion. The lower slopes are home to eagle owls, snow finches, woodpeckers and jays.

One of the means that French ornithologists have adopted to protect birds has been to buy tracts of land through which migrants travel. In 1979, a group of naturalists subscribing to the organisation **FIR** (Fund for Intervention on Behalf of Raptors, BP 27, 92250 La Garenne Colombes, Tel. (1) 47 71 02 87) leased the pass of Orgambideska in the western Pyrenees. This initiative enabled them to ban hunting hides in the area. Among the birds to be seen here are black kites, Montagu's harriers, swallows, yellow wagtails, honey buzzards and black storks.

Climate

Aquitaine's diverse landscape of mountains, coastline and plains means that the climate varies considerably from *département* to *département*. In Dordogne, the climate is mild and damp in the valleys, but more continental to the east. Lot-et-Garonne has a largely maritime climate whereas, in Gironde, the autumns and winters are mild and the summers hot and dry. In the capital, Bordeaux, the highest rainfall and the lowest temperatures occur in November, December and January. In August the average daily maximum temperature hits 26°C, though the temperature usually remains above 20°C from May through to September. The combination of mountains and sea in Pyrénées-Atlantiques dictates that *département*'s climate: during the summer there are frequent rainy spells and plenty of mist, but sea breezes often clear the skies in the afternoons leaving clear sunny days. In the valleys, the combination of heat and damp makes for a humid atmosphere, whereas the mountain tops tend to be warm and fresh. There is no permanent snow in Pyrénées-Atlantiques. The best times to visit Aquitaine are during spring and autumn. Autumn is the ideal season for hiking in the Pyrenees; it is cooler, prices are generally lower and there are fewer tourists. It is not advisable, however, to walk in the Pyrenees after October, as snow falls early and most mountain refuges close.

Attractions

Regional tourist board brochures on Aquitaine boast of its wonderful scenery, famous wines and its great historical heritage. In spite of the fact that one comes to expect this kind of description from tourist board handouts, anyone who has visited Aquitaine would agree that the region has great variety and much to offer. Its scenery differs greatly in contour from *département* to *département*. There are rolling green hills in Dordogne; flat windswept beaches in Gironde; marshes and forest in Landes; and high mountains in Pyrénées-Atlantiques.

Wherever one chooses to travel in Aquitaine, the past is a constant companion: prehistory in Dordogne; military history in the numerous *bastides*; and legend in the valleys of the Pyrenees. A visit to the caves of the Vézère Valley, which has been designated a World Heritage site by UNESCO, is highly recommended. Nowhere else in Europe are so many ancient sites concentrated within such a small area. To recommend a tour of the Bordeaux châteaux to wine buffs is, surely, superfluous. Even those who are not particularly interested in the wine trade will find many of the wine châteaux architecturally pleasing. A visit to the historic town of Bordeaux itself is also a 'must'.

The forests and beaches of the Landes and the mountains of Pyrénées-Atlantiques are areas of great natural beauty, and should be included on any tour of the region. Unlike the Riviera or the Alps, where it is sometimes difficult to get away from the hordes of people, there is ample space here. It could be said, in fact, that space is Aquitaine's most precious resource and, fortunately, much has been done to preserve it. (See **Level of Tourism**)

Cuisine

One of Aquitaine's charms is its regional cuisine. The Dordogne, famous for its truffles and *pâté de foie gras*, attracts gourmets from all over the world. Other dishes to look out for in Dordogne include: *confit* (potted preserved meat, usually goose or duck) and *pommes sarladaises* (potatoes served with truffles and goose fat). The Bordeaux palate differs considerably. Here the specialities are salt-marsh lamb from Pauillac, lamprey eels, wood pigeon, oysters from Arcachon, and cured ham in Bordelais sauce. Basque cuisine is distinctly 'homey': the fare of shepherds, fishermen, climbers and hill farmers. Fresh mountain trout, tuna (from St-Jean-de-Luz), fresh squid and sardines are particularly recommended.

Pyrenean food is both tasty and simple. It is also ideal after a day spent out in the mountains. Dishes such as ham, mixed meat stew (potted duck or goose), haricot bean stew and Basque fish stew are popular locally.

It is also worth mentioning that Aquitaine, particularly the Dordogne, is one of the few places in France where vegetarian restaurants are positively numerous.

France's greatest wine producing area is Bordeaux. The four principal vineyards in the area are Medoc (red wine); Graves (white dessert wine); St-Emilion and Pomerol (red wine); and Sauternes (sweet white wine). It must be said, however, that wine from Bordeaux is expensive and one is more likely to pick up a bargain back home than here. Popular wines appearing on menus all over the south-west include the following: Bergerac, an excellent red wine; Château Mont Bazillac, a good sweet white wine; Cahors, a fruity red wine; Béarn, light red, white and rosé wines; and Jurançon, unusual white wines, both dry and sweet.

Level of Tourism

Tourism in Aquitaine is well developed and it currently ranks fourth in the pecking order of French tourist regions. It is predominantly a long-stay region and 77% of the 3.7 million hotel visitors who come to Aquitaine every year are French. Other than the French, Aquitaine is popular with the Belgians, Dutch and Germans, and to a lesser extent, the British (who predominantly visit the Dordogne and the vineyards of Gironde).

Though tourism has brought some changes to the region (notably in the form of facilities catering for visitors, accommodation and new service industries), it has not dramatically affected the lives of the local people. Parts of Aquitaine have, in fact, been popular tourist sites for over a century. In the nineteenth century, Biarritz enjoyed the patronage of European royalty, as did the beaches of the Arcachon Basin. Pau has been popular with the British since Peninsular War campaigners settled there, and the waters of the spa town of Dax have attracted French visitors ever since the Middle Ages, when pilgrims frequented the thermal baths for their healing qualities.

The main tourist centres of Aquitaine are the *départements* of Dordogne, Gironde and Pyrénées-Atlantiques. The tourist industry in Lot-et-Garonne and Landes is little developed, the one exception being the beaches of the Arcachon Basin, which attract thousands of people during the summer months.

Lacking in large towns (excepting Arcachon) and without a tourism tradition, the Landes was ripe for development when France's population of holiday-makers spilled over from the custom-built resorts of the Riviera. The local government proved equal to the challenge, however, and today the coast of the Landes amply accommodates visitors, not only from other parts of France, but also from Holland, Germany and Britain. Due to local government policy, the modest resorts of the Arcachon Basin have been spared the construction of the unsightly tower-block condominiums so apparent on the Riviera. Instead, a more sympathetic form of accommodation was advocated by the **Conservatoire de L'Espace Littoral** (the French equivalent of the National Trust, but specifically for coastal areas), in the form of caravan sites. Though caravan sites too can be an eyesore, and prejudicial to the local ecosystem, they only remain in place for three months of the year, whereas apartment blocks become permanent fixtures of the coastline.

Tourism on the Aquitaine coast depends overwhelmingly on family-run enterprises, which is part of its attraction. Visitors to the Arcachon Basin often return to stay in the same establishments year after year. Seasonal unemployment, caused by the short summer season, has put pressure on local business to expand in order to encourage out-of-season tourism, though it is debatable whether the demand exists for a longer season.

Fortunately the beaches and dunes here are so vast that the volume of bathers seems insignificant when compared with the endless miles of sand. At the expense of a little energy, visitors prepared to abandon the comfort of the large, well-equipped camp sites and to walk a few kilometres, will be richly rewarded with plenty of space, peace and tranquillity.

Despite the fact that Dordogne today is a popular tourist centre, it is refreshing to see that the detrimental effects of tourism have been kept to a minimum. This has been partly due to the quality of visitors that Dordogne has historically attracted. They have never been of the sun-and-sand type – all too eager to soak up rays, compete for available space and invest nothing. Dordogne has traditionally appealed to families and the retired, many of whom, until the recent recession, bought second homes in the area. The impact of this has been considerable. The property market has brought great wealth to the area, and the desire to conserve and preserve the beauties of the region is obvious to the visitor. The fact that so many Dordogne enthusiasts have bought holiday or retirement property in the *département*, emphasises the degree of investment and commitment that visitors have been prepared to make to the area, though this very devotion can naturally bring with it its own problems, notably in areas where British immigrants outnumber the local population. Since the tourist industry is so well developed here, prices are considerably higher than those in the other *départements* of Aquitaine.

The local government and tourist board in Dordogne have been faced with a number of problems. On the one hand, the prosperity that the tourist industry has generated has been welcomed by local people. On the other hand, the detrimental effects of mass tourism have also been felt. The most obvious example of the negative impact can be seen at the Lascaux caves, where, in 1940, some remarkable prehistoric paintings were discovered. So numerous were the visitors to Lascaux when the caves were opened to the public that, within twenty years, the paintings began to deteriorate and, in the 1960s, it was decided that the site should be closed. What had not been appreciated was that a great number of visitors crammed into the small grotto would affect the level of humidity in the atmosphere surrounding the paintings. The carbon dioxide generated by the volume of people visiting the cave encouraged a green algae to grow on the interior walls. Today, visitors are denied the genuine article and instead view a replica of the original paintings, which, though it can never live up to the ancient masterpiece, offers an example of sensible tourism practice which could be applied, with positive consequences, elsewhere. Fortunately a lesson was learned from the experience, and now the number of visitors to the caves of the Vézère Valley as well as to many other monuments in Dordogne is strictly monitored, thus ensuring that the mistakes of the past will not be repeated.

Gironde's attractions have had their attendant problems too, in the shape of traffic. Due partly to the pressures of tourism, a controversial proposal to build a motorway from Clermont-Ferrand to Bordeaux has met with considerable opposition from local conservationists, who have formed a pressure group called 'Non à l'Autoroute'. The plan, if implemented, would involve the destruction of acres of fields and forest, not to mention the pollution created by the volume of traffic passing through the area.

The Pyrenees remain a relatively unexplored and undeveloped range, eclipsed somewhat by the popularity of the Alps (with their superior skiing opportunities and higher peaks). In fact the Pyrenees, the western hills particularly, are not ideal for downhill skiing. This is partly due to the parallel steep-sided valleys running north/south from the peaks to the plains, making communication from east to west difficult. Relatively few mountain passes are accessible by car. Another notable feature of the range is the lack of major high-altitude resorts and of sophistication of any kind. Visitors tend to be outdoor enthusiasts – interested in fishing, climbing or hiking, not the jet-setters of some Alpine resorts. This difference is reflected in the limited range of accommodation offered and the relatively low cost of food and a bed. Hotels and other related services tend to be family-run. Those looking for luxury hotels, varied nightlife and entertainment will be disappointed. However, for those who are satisfied with good country fare at the end of a tiring day in the mountains, genuine hospitality and a cheap clean room for the night, the towns and villages of the Pyrenees will live up to expectations; and their overall charm is only enhanced by the fact that, in contrast to much of the Alps, the high mountain areas remain unscarred by cable-car pylons.

The formation, in 1967, of the Western Pyrenees national park ended the indiscriminate hunting of mountain fauna, and its administration has provided other regions in France with a model example. Conservation in the park is impressive and, since its foundation, animals such as the brown bear and Pyrenean chamois (known as the 'isard'), previously under threat of extinction, have found sanctuary, and numbers are slowly recovering.

Another protected area of Aquitaine is the regional park of the Landes and Gascony where, at Marquèze in the middle of the forest, a traditional Landais farm has been built as part of a project to promote traditional farming techniques.

It is advisable to visit Aquitaine, particularly Pyrénées Atlantiques and Landes, out of season. The Pyrenees in autumn and spring are beautiful, as are the Atlantic coast and the forests of the Landes. During the summer, walking in the mountains can be uncomfortably warm, and Dordogne and Gironde are particularly crowded during July and August. Even the most enchanting château can lose its appeal under such conditions.

Good Alternatives

Meeting People

An ideal way of meeting people in Aquitaine is to attend the many local festivals and celebrations that are held in the region throughout the year, but particularly during the summer. Lists and details of these events are provided by local tourist offices and the regional tourist board (**Comité Régional du Tourisme**, or CRT), which can be contacted at 21–23 rue de Grassi, 33000 Bordeaux (Tel. 56 44 48 02).

If you wish to help promote conservation in the Pyrenees, you might be interested in **Vacances Militantes**. These bring together people of mixed backgrounds and ages to work on conservation projects, such as the building of bird sanctuaries or maintenance of footpaths. For further information, contact **Uminate** (José Cambou), 47 rue Arago, 31500 Toulouse (Tel. 61 58 14 31). Details of how you can join a group of paying guests involved in conservation activities, such as reafforestation in the Dordogne, are available from **Le Jardin Sauvage**, St-Aulaye, 24410 Echourgnac. **Chantiers de Travail**, 34 rue Leytaine, 33000 Bordeaux, also organise projects to work on the restoration of local historical monuments. Those interested in joining an archaeological dig in the region should contact the **Direction des Antiquités**, 6 bis cours de Courgue, 33074 Bordeaux (Tel. 56 51 39 06).

In Gironde, the **Centre d'Etudes et de Diffusion de Techniques**, Mombrier, 33710 Bourg (Tel. 57 64 30 13) organises holiday courses in local crafts. Two holidays, each lasting two weeks, are run in July and August, and you can join courses in lacquer-work, woodwork and porcelain-making. The centre not only promotes local crafts, but it also enables participants to meet local practioners of the various crafts and to see a dimension of traditional Gironde life usually denied to the conventional tourist. For those interested in alternative medecine, opportunities to learn about the medicinal qualities of plants is offered by **AUBE: Centre de Développement Personnel**, Sablou, 24900 Montignac Lascaux (Tel. 53 51 97 70).

An association known as **Découverte et Vie Super-Détente**, based at 48 bis rue des Haies, 75020 Paris (Tel. (1) 43 48 00 01) organises sporting holidays for young people and has a centre in Arcachon (Gironde), which offers a variety of sports courses as well as walking holidays. Pelota tournaments take place regularly in the Basque region and you can be sure of meeting local people if you attend one of these; a calendar is available from the **Agence de Tourisme du Pays Basque**, BP 247, 64108 Bayonne (Tel. 59 59 28 77).

Discovering Places

Good ways of exploring the region are offered by the **Landes de Gascogne** regional park and the **Pyrénées Occidentales** national park. Much can be learnt about the former at its *ecomusée*; branches of this are situated in forest clearings and they aim to encourage traditional husbandry skills once widely practised in the area. There is also an ornithological park and a bee farm (see **Geographical Breakdown**). One excellent way to get to know the Landes region is to take a 7-night discovery holiday called 'In the intimacy of the tree of gold'. This is organised by the park, marketed by **Clés de France** (see **Introduction**, p.51) and approved by the Natural Parks Federation. The holiday, which is designed for individuals grouped together up to a maximum of 14 people, is available from April through to October, and the price of around 4700FF includes full-board in a charming, traditional 2-star hotel, three gastronomic meals, exploration by canoe, boat and bicycle, entrance fees for visits, local entertainment evenings and the daily presence of a park guide. Further information can be had either from Clés de France or direct from Mme Renaud, **Parc Naturel Régional des Landes de Gascogne**, Place de l'Eglise, 33830 Belin-Beliet (Tel. 56 88 06 06). The park headquarters can also provide information on canoeing, accompanied or unaccompanied walks, cycling and' mountain biking, whether you require tips on the best spot for an afternoon excursion, or arrangements made for a 6-day holiday including equipment hire.

A visit to the **Pyrenees National Park** is equally highly recommended. Park houses, located at strategic points throughout the range, offer a variety of services to the public. They provide permanent and temporary exhibitions on the unique ecosystem of the Pyrenees, as well as organising conferences and debates on park administration and conservation. Park wardens are also happy to arrange a variety of mountain-related activities, such as hiking trips and photographic excursions. Day-long walking, hiking and climbing excursions are also run by the **Association des Amis du Parc**, 20 rue Samonzet, 64000 Pau (Tel. 59 27 15 30). If you wish to participate in a mountain excursion lasting several days, including an introduction to flora and fauna observation, geology, country ways, fishing or high-altitude speleology, contact **CIMES – Pyrénées**, BP 88, 09200 St-Girons (Tel. 61 66 40 10). For further information on the park's facilities and activities, contact the **Parc National des Pyrénées Occidentales**, 59 route de Pau, 65000 Tarbes (Tel. 62 93 30 60).

Guided visits and slide shows are put on in July and August by the Landes division of the National Forests Office; contact the Service Départemental, **Office National des Forêts**, 40012 Mont-de-Marsan (Tel. 58 75 30 59). For those interested in flora and fauna, **Tambao Randonnées Pedestres**, Gigors, 26000 Crest (Tel. 75 76 42 32) organise hiking excursions into the Pyrenees to observe indigenous species of animal and plant life.

If you are interested in alternative energy and technology, you could visit the **Biolands** centre at Le Sen, 40420 Labrit (Tel. 48 51 46 34). The organisation which runs it collects four tons of pine needles daily, grinds them up and then distils them to make oil. The waste material from the distillation process is then transformed into humus and, after drying, into fuel. Heat for the distillation is produced by burning wood chips from local sawmills.

Cycling is increasingly being seen as a positive alternative to other forms of transport in Aquitaine, as elsewhere, and an ideal way of discovering the countryside. Three of the organisations running cycling holidays in the region are **Vélocité**, 3 rue Tauzia, 33000 Bordeaux; **Aquitaine Alternative**, 4 impasse des Minimettes, 33000 Bordeaux; and **Sépanso**, Béarn MJC Lau, ave du Loup, 64000 Pau.

Three of Aquitaine's *départements* have **Loisirs-Accueil** services.

These offer a variety of activity and discovery holidays, run by local tour operators and following a low-impact philosophy. Their addresses are: **Loisirs-Accueil Dordogne-Périgord**, 16 rue Wilson, 24009 Périgueux (Tel. 53 53 44 35); **Loisirs-Accueil Gironde**, 24 rue Esprit des Lois, 33000 Bordeaux (Tel. 56 52 61 40); and **Loisirs-Accueil Lot-et-Garonne**, 4 rue André Chénier, 47000 Agen (Tel. 53 66 14 14).

Communications

How to Get There

If you wish to travel by **air**, both British Airways (Tel. 081 897 4000) and Air France (Tel. 071 499 9511) operate services from Heathrow and Stansted to Bordeaux-Mérignac airport (Tel. 56 34 84 84). Air Littoral run a Manchester-Bordeaux service.

Fifteen daily **trains** put Bordeaux at less than 5 hours from Paris, to be reduced to 3 hours with the opening of the new TGV Atlantique line.

Bordeaux is at the crossroads of various major European routes if you are travelling by road. The drive from Paris can take under 6 hours on the A 10 motorway, while Eurolines run a direct **coach** service from London to Bordeaux, Bayonne and Biarritz, with connections to Dax and Pau in summer. The return fare for an adult hovers around £100.

When You're There

Rail – in general the connections are good in the north of the region and down the west coast, but less so elsewhere. The main coastal line runs through Bordeaux, Facture (connection to Arcachon), Morcenx, Dax, Bayonne, Biarritz and Hendaye on the Spanish border. From Bayonne there are connections to St-Jean-de-Pied-de-Port and St-Jean-de-Luz, as well as Puyoô, Pau and Oloron-Ste-Marie. The only major station in the region's centre is Mont-de-Marsan, accessible from Morcenx, though both Bordeaux and Périgueux have connections with Agen, Bergerac and Sarlat, as well as with each other.

Scenic train rides are possible on the Train de la Rhune, Col de St-Ignace, Sare, 64310 Ascain; the Train Touristique d'Artouste, Artouste Fabrèges, 64440 Laruns; and at the Ecomusée de la Grande Lande, Marquèze, 40360 Sabres.

Bus – from Hendaye on the Spanish border, regional services operate to Bayonne and Biarritz. From Bordeaux there are services to Pauillac, St-Emilion and Labrede, as well as a network of many smaller local lines.

Car – only two autoroutes cross the region for any distance: the A 62 follows the course of the River Garonne between Bordeaux and Toulouse, passing through Longon and Agen; and the A 64 links Bayonne and Pau. The N 10 road across the Landes and along the coast is also good, though it is more rewarding to explore using some of the numerous D roads you will find inland. Some are signposted as tourist routes (there are eleven of these in Gironde alone), which means that they are particularly attractive (and, consequently, rather more crowded than the unmarked D roads).

Boat – those keen on river touring, either by hiring their own boat or joining an organised cruise should contact **Aquitaine Tourisme Fluvial**, 12 Place de la Bourse, 33076 Bordeaux (Tel. 56 79 50 00). Canoeists are particularly well catered for in the Gironde, where they can paddle away on the Leyre, the Médoc rivers, the Isle, the Ciron, the Dronne and the Dropt. Further information from the **Comité Départementale de Canoë-Kayak**, 38 quai des Chartrons, 33000 Bordeaux (Tel. 56 44 97 75).

Cycling – bicycle hire is available from the stations at Agen, Arcachon, Bagnères-de-Bigorre, Bayonne, Bordeaux-St-Jean, Dax, St-Jean-de-Luz, Soulac-sur-Mer and Vic-en-Bigorre. If you are interested in a cycling holiday in the Pyrenees, the **Comité Départemental de Cyclotourisme** (Alexandre Bibes), 16 rue de l'Operne, 64200 Biarritz will recommend suitable maps and bike-hire shops. Gironde has the largest network of cycle paths in France, along the coast or through the Landes forest: information from the **Comité Départemental** at 22 résidence 'la Bredinière', 33650 Labrede (Tel. 56 20 34 96). For details of organisations running cycling holidays, see **Good Alternatives**.

Walking – numerous footpaths, including the GR 8 which links the Pointe de Grave and the Lac de Cazaux, and the forest trails, former tow-paths and vineyard tracks of the Gironde, can be found all over Aquitaine and are covered by 'topo-guide' maps, available from most stationers. For the more intrepid there are the Pyrenees, which are a walker's paradise. Until quite recently they remained relatively unknown to British hikers. At present there are two trails which traverse the complete Pyrenean range: the GR 10, a lower level route, remains entirely within France, while the HLR is a higher ridge route, which avoids roads and at times crosses the frontier into Spain. Those with limited hiking experience should stick to the lower route, since the HLR traverses some steep and often snow-covered slopes, where an ice axe and crampons would be required. Details of locally–run guided walks can be found under **Good Alternatives**.

Riding – Dordogne, Pyrénées-Atlantiques and the Landes are all ideal for pony-trekking, and riding provides a good means of exploring the countryside, whether you prefer forests, plains or mountains. Custom-made trips are offered by two riding centres in Pyrénées-Atlantiques: the **Auberge Cavalière**, Accous, 64490 Bedous (Tel. 59 34 72 30); and the **Baso Béarnaise**, Zaldi Xuri, 64120 St-Palais (Tel. 59 65 70 78). In the Dordogne, riding trips can be arranged by the **Saint-Sauveur** riding school, St-Sauveur, 24520 Mouleydier. For further information on riding in Aquitaine, contact the **Centre Hippique du Lycée Agricole et Forestier**, 33430 Bazas (Tel. 56 25 03 21).

Useful local contacts

The **Conservatoire des Sites d'Aquitaine**, created only in 1990, groups together the regional associations for the study and protection of nature and plans to undertake actions for the promotion of conservation. Its address is Maison de la Nature, 3 rue de Tauzia, 33800 Bordeaux (Tel. 59 91 33 81). In the Pyrenees, information concerning all sorts of ecological issues and occupations in the mountains is provided by the **Centre d'Information Montagne et Sentiers** (CIMES), BP 88, 09200 St-Girons (Tel. 61 66 40 10). Try also the **Centre Permanent d'Initiation à l'Environnement**, rue de la Hount Blanque, 65200 Bagnères-de-Bigorre (Tel. 62 95 49 67); or the **Association des Amis du Parc**, 20 rue Samonzet, 64000 Pau (Tel. 59 27 15 30). The address of the headquarters of the western Pyrenees national park is **Parc National des Pyrénées Occidentales,** 59 route de Pau, 65000 Tarbes (Tel. 62 93 30 60), while that of the **Parc Naturel Régional des Landes de Gascogne** is Place de l'Eglise, 33830 Belin-Beliet (Tel. 56 88 06 06).

Geographical Breakdown of Region

Dordogne & Lot-et-Garonne

Dordogne, the most northerly of Aquitaine's départements, lies between the coastal plains of the Atlantic and the slopes of the

Massif Central. It is crossed by numerous rivers, including the Dordogne itself.

Dordogne has always been popular with the British, who have traditionally travelled south in search of pleasant countryside, peace and tranquillity. Perhaps the reason for this is that, in many ways, it is appreciated as a home from home: a French Wye Valley, or the Cotswolds with a difference. Nature in Dordogne does not impose itself grandly as in the Alps or the Pyrenees. Rather, an unusual harmony between man and the environment has existed in the area for hundreds of years, with the result that Dordogne's considerable natural beauty has been enhanced by human creation. The most ancient and obvious example of this are the cave paintings of the Vézère Valley, depicting the many species of prehistoric animal which once roamed the plateaux. In more recent centuries châteaux were built on the banks of the Dordogne, and the fertile land was used to grow fruit, vines, and chestnut forests.

Brantôme, situated 40 kilometres north of Périgueux, is a quiet peaceful town. It is an ideal centre for those seeking a cottage holiday, though it is not recommended as a base for exploring the wider Dordogne Valley. The River **Dronne** which flows through the town has great charm. In Brantôme itself there is an eighteenth-century abbey, behind which stands a splendid Romanesque belfry.

Nearby is the **Château de Hautefort**. This is one of the most magnificent Renaissance castles in the area, and dominates the surrounding countryside. In 1968, a fire tragically destroyed much of the building, and not all the chambers have been restored to their former glory. The château is surrounded by classical gardens. In the twelfth century the castle was the residence of Bertrand de Born, the famous troubadour, to whom Dante refers in his epic poem *The Inferno*.

The monastic ruins of **Chancelade** are also easily accessible from Brantôme. They include a museum of religious art, and the abbey nearby, at **Merlande**, contains some fascinating carvings around its arcades. From Brantôme, a visit to the beautiful village of **St-Jean-de-Cole** is well worth the effort. The picturesque hamlet and market village has a delightful eleventh-century church. The Brantôme tourist office is on ave de Pierre-de-Bourdeilles (Tel. 53 05 80 52), near the abbey. They can provide circuit maps of the town.

Unless you have your own transport, Brantôme is not easy to get to. There is only one bus a day serving the surrounding country, though, in the summer months, the tourist office organises a bus visit to the Dronne Valley and Bourdeilles castle (bus schedules are provided by the office).

Seven kilometres south-west of Brantôme is the **Château de Bourdeilles**. Pierre de Bourdeilles, better known as 'Brantôme', and author of *The Lives of Famous Men and Great Captains*, lived here before setting off around the world in search of adventure. The castle is situated on a fortified terrace above the Dronne river. If you do not have transport and do not fancy the hike, canoes can be rented in Brantôme (Porte de Reformes, Tel. 53 05 80 46) enabling you to paddle your way to the castle and back.

The town of **Périgueux**, south of Brantôme is almost two thousand years old. Despite its antiquity, however, it is not a particularly interesting place as a holiday base, though the cathedral is worth a visit. Seen from afar, the Cathedral of St-Front looks distinctly oriental, with its dome and eastern style belfry. St-Front, built in the style of a Greek cross is reminiscent of St Mark's in Venice and reminds one of the crusades that inspired its construction. The remains of a Gallo-Roman tower – the Tour de Vesone is located in a medieval quarter of the town, the modern town having been built around a series of ancient boulevards and alleyways. The Périgord museum, nearby, contains prehistoric exhibits, among them the tusk of a mammoth and the skeleton of the Chancelade man.

If you wish to give someone a genuine souvenir from Périgueux, you might want to visit the Périgueux distillery, which has been producing fruit liqueurs for hundreds of years. An interesting display shop adjoins the factory.

There are two carnivals in Périgueux. Summer celebrations last throughout July and August and include an international festival of mime, featuring performances from all over the world. This theatrical event is considered to be one of the most prestigious of its kind in France. There is also a summer festival of French song, which attracts artists from all over France, who gather to compete for the coveted 'Trophée Platine'. The traditional Mardi Gras celebrations attract about 30,000 people every year and provide a good opportunity to see some traditional Occitan costumes.

South-west of Périgueux, along the *route nationale*, lies **Bergerac** on the western fringe of the Dordogne river. It is famous throughout France for its tobacco. Unfortunately not much of the old town remains. The Place du Feu contains a statue of the immortal Cyrano and, near the river, some sixteenth- and seventeenth-century buildings have been restored. There is a fascinating tobacco museum (tobacco was first introduced to France in 1560 – apparently it was suggested that a dose of it might cure Catherine de Medici's migraines), which recounts the history of the industry and contains a fine collection of pipes and snuff boxes. There is also a Maison du Vin nearby which can provide visitors with details of local wine-producing châteaux.

The **Château Feudal De Beynac**, perched like an eagle's nest 140 metres above the surrounding Périgord Valley, is situated between the Vézère Valley and the town of Souillac. It is one of the most impressive fortresses of the central Dordogne, and much of the original castle (besieged in the thirteenth century by Simon de Montfort) remains intact. Of particular interest are the double surrounding wall with two moats, and the barbican outworks. The large state room with a fine chimney breast, decorated with frescoes and wood-panelled walls, is a splendid, example of Renaissance work.

Sarlat, situated on a beautiful stretch of the Dordogne river, is arguably one of the finest medieval market towns in Europe. It is also a very good base from which to explore the surrounding area. Unfortunately it gets extremely crowded during the summer season. There are a number of beautifully restored houses in the area east of the main street, particularly around the Place du Peyrou. One of the oldest buildings is the monastery, founded by Clovis in the twelfth century.

Sarlat is Dordogne's liveliest town, with a street festival of drama in July every year attracting thousands of tourists. There is also a film festival in November. Sarlat receives about 600,000 visitors each year, so the tourist industry is well developed. To avoid the crowds, and the inevitable congestion they cause (not to mention the inflated summer season prices), visiting out of season is highly recommended.

About 14 kilometres from Sarlat is the fortified town of **Domme**, 150 metres above the Dordogne river. Here are some wonderful caves, all of which are easily accessible from the town's market place. They are particularly well known for their magnificent columns and their unusual colour. The town's prison, built by the Knights Templar is also worth visiting.

More caves can be seen 25 kilometres from Sarlat at the **Gouffre de Proumeyssac**. The huge amphora-shaped cavern, through which a subterranean river flows, contains a variety of organ-pipe stalactites.

Les Eyzies is not a particularly memorable town. It is, however, an ideal centre from which to visit the many caves for which the Périgord region is famous. Beneath the Périgord plateau runs a huge network of subterranean caverns, rivers, lakes and caves, formed millions of years ago by water draining through the porous limestone rock. Today many of these caves are accessible, enabling visitors to see an extraordinary array of stalactites, stalagmites, columns of petrified water and mineral deposits. For sheer grandeur, the caves of the Massif Central cannot be beaten. The caverns of the Dordogne are sometimes overcrowded and claustrophobic and long queues at their entrances are the norm. However, what cannot be seen anywhere else in Europe (within such a concentrated area) is the variety of cave paintings to be found in the Dordogne, and especially around the Vézère Valley. These are believed to have been painted during the Magdalenian period (15,000 – 8,000 BC). This period of prehistory marks the end of the Ice Age, when plateaux were covered in tundra and beasts such as bison and mammoth flourished. The caves mentioned below have been particularly recommended by the Périgord tourist office.

One and a half kilometres northwest of Les Eyzies, along the D47 road, is the **Grotte du Grand Roc**. Though containing no cave paintings, its rare colouring and coral-like stalactites are remarkable. Set in a cliff face, the cave commands a panoramic view over the Vézère Valley.

Two kilometres down the road from Les Eyzies, is the **Grotte du Font Gaume**. This cave was discovered in 1901 and found to contain some of the finest Magdalenian paintings in the region. Among the paintings is a magnificent frieze of bison and reindeer. The caves are very popular so it is advisable to arrive early in the morning. Two kilometres further down the road is **Combarelles**. The drawings here were discovered in 1902. Along with the paintings at Font Gaume, these pictures of bison, monkey, reindeer and mammoth are considered to be among the finest in Europe. The caves are situated on the Breune river, 5 kilometres from Les Eyzies.

Twenty kilometres north-east of Les Eyzies, at Montignac, is the replica of the **Lascaux** cave (the original is now closed to the public). The caves were found in 1940 when two schoolboys, looking for their dog, stumbled into them. The remarkable clarity of the paintings discovered at Lascaux cannot be seen in many other caves in the region. All forms of prehistoric bestiary are represented, along with many other signs and symbols which have led archaeologists to believe that the cave was used, not as a dwelling, (no other artefacts have been found), but as a shrine or temple. The facsimile here is well worth a visit.

At **Le Regourdou**, 460 metres above Lascaux, the remains of a Neanderthal man were discovered. The cave, once a sepulchre for both humans and animals, is believed to have been used by an ancient tribe belonging to the cult of the bear. The museum of prehistory here is well worth visiting.

South-east of the Périgord plateau, and separated from Dordogne by the **Lot river**, is the *département* of **Lot-et-Garonne**. Although the countryside becomes fertile as it approaches the Garonne river, Lot-et-Garonne is neither a particularly interesting, nor beautiful, area. **Agen**, the largest town in the *département*, is busy and industrial, but it is famous throughout France for its fruit. The specialities here are prune and plum confectionery, and fruit liqueurs. There is, however, little of interest to see in Agen except its museum, which houses a collection of Spanish masters, among them Goya.

Accommodation

First Class

Le Moulin de l'Abbaye, 1 rte de Bourdeilles, 24310 Brantôme-en-Périgord (Tel. 53 05 80 22): 16 sumptuous rooms and 5 apartments in thirteenth-century abbot's house, mill and miller's house, with beautiful views; excellent restaurant serving lighter versions of regional favourites, cooked with local ingredients. **Manoir de Hautegente**, 24120 Coly (Tel. 53 51 68 03): 6 *chambres d'hôte* in beautiful ivy-covered manor house with grounds, near the Dordogne Valley; restaurant in evenings. **Château de Barry**, 47320 Clairac (Tel. 53 84 35 49): 8 comfortable *chambres d'hôtes* in quiet eighteenth-century château in heart of vine-growing area; *tables d'hôte* on reservation.

Middle Range

La Sauvagère, RN 21, Galinas, 47340 La Croix Blanche (Tel. 53 68 81 21): 12 charming rooms in vine-clad hotel offering friendly welcome, 10 kilometres north of Agen; good restaurant. **La Combe**, 24620 Les Eyzies-de-Tayac (Tel. 53 06 94 68): comfortable accommodation on small farm; meals using home-grown vegetables and home-made bread.

Economy

L'Auberge du Soir, 24310 Brantôme (Tel. 53 05 82 93): 8 rooms in family-run hotel; restaurant with local specialities. **Hôtel du Midi**, 18 rue Denis-Papin, 24000 Périgueux (Tel. 53 53 41 06): 25 rooms in family-run hotel with restaurant.

Eating Out

Vegetarians will be pleasantly surprised to find that, in this rare corner of France, they are catered for outside the crêperies and pizza parlours to which they will doubtless have grown accustomed!

First Class

L'Aubergade, 52 rue Royale, 47270 Puymirol (Tel. 53 95 31 46): lightened regional cuisine, making the most of seasonal ingredients and natural flavours.

Middle Range

La Couleuvrine, 1 Place de la Bouquerie, 24200 Sarlet-la-Canéda (Tel. 53 59 27 80): subtle cuisine in thirteenth-century former guard-room, part of 18-room hotel. **Hôtel la Forge**, Place Victor-Hugo, 24150 Lalinde (Tel. 53 24 92 24): good restaurant with vegetarian options; part of family-run hotel with 21 rooms.

Economy

Le Farou, Orliac, 24170 Belvès (Tel. 53 29 13 14): vegetarian evening meals using organic produce, served in beautiful surroundings; also offers rooms in old country house.

Gironde & Landes

To the west of Dordogne is the *département* of Gironde, the largest in France. Much of the land to the north-west was reclaimed in the nineteenth century in order to prevent land erosion. The windswept dunes were first planted with gorse, which rapidly took root. This greatly improved the quality of the soil and later enabled foresters to plant pine trees.

Bordeaux

The main tourist attraction in Gironde is Bordeaux, along with its surrounding vineyards. Bordeaux is by no means idyllic: it is busy, noisy and polluted and many of its once grand buildings are now shabby and grimy; however, it remains an exciting and vibrant place. It is also an excellent base from which to explore the surrounding region. There are major rail links with other towns and plenty of places to stay.

The centre of the city is a splendid mixture of architectural styles and owes much of its physical attraction to the Marquis of Tourny, who was responsible for erecting many elegant buildings and squares. The River Garonne curves around the **port**, with its ancient quays, warehouses, factories and mansions, many of them built in the eighteenth-century 'grand monumental' style. Situated on the right bank of the river, across a nineteenth-century bridge, is **La Bastide** and the ruins of a Roman amphitheatre.

The **Grand Theatre**, built in 1780, is one of the finest in France. Its double staircase and statue-crowned colonnade inspired Garnier's plan for the Paris Opera House. The **Esplandes de Quinconces**, nearby, is one of the largest squares in Europe, containing statues of Montaigne and Montesquieu.

Another of Bordeaux's showpieces is the Gothic cathedral of **St-André**, built between the eleventh and fifteenth centuries. Notice the magnificent set of carvings above the exterior doorway, and its grimacing gargoyles!

Bordeaux is also home to some wonderful museums and galleries. The **Musée d'Aquitaine**, housed in the faculty of letters, contains some interesting ethnographical and historical collections but concentrates mainly on the vocations and trades that have made Bordeaux famous – notably the wine trade. The **Museum of Fine Arts**, in cours d'Albert near the cathedral, was founded in 1801 and contains one of the finest collections in France, housing works by Titian, Perugin, Giordano, Pierre de Cortone, Rubens and Breughel. The **Museum of Decorative Arts**, set in a beautiful mansion surrounded by gardens, exhibits collections of furniture, ceramics, metalwork and pottery.

Accommodation

First Class

Le Saint-James, 3 Place Camille-Holstein, 33270 Bouliac (Tel. 56 20 52 19): 18 rooms in interestingly renovated old house in vineyards, 9 km from town; top-class restaurant with inventive cuisine.

First Class / Middle Range

Le Grand Hôtel Français, 12 rue du Temple (Tel. 56 48 10 35): 35 comfortable rooms in fairly central hotel.

Middle Range

Hôtel Sèze, 23 allées de Tourny (Tel. 56 52 65 54): 24 rooms in hotel in green part of town, near parks. **Hôtel Etche Ona**, 11 rue Mautrec (Tel. 56 44 36 49): clean, friendly hotel, ideally situated in centre of town near Grand Theatre.

Economy

Hôtel la Boétie, 4 rue de la Boétie (Tel. 56 81 76 68): comfortable rooms in friendly hotel, situated in quiet street near Fine Arts museum. **Hôtel d'Amboise**, 22 rue de la Vieille Tour (Tel. 56 81 62 67): pleasant hotel in pedestrian area.

Eating Out

First Class

Jean Ramet, 7–8 Place Jean-Jaurès (Tel. 56 44 12 51): subtle, imaginative cuisine and friendly welcome. **Le Vieux Bordeaux**, 27 rue de Buhant (Tel. 56 08 04 21): traditional regional cuisine with modern touch, in elegant surroundings.

First Class / Middle Range

Le Récif de Cancale, 22 cours du Chapeau-Rouge (Tel. 56 44 37 95): seafood specialities, using the freshest fish, in beautiful 18th century house next to Grand Theatre.

Middle Range

La Tupina, 6 rue Porte de la Monnaie (Tel. 56 91 56 37): the best place to come for typical regional cuisine and some Bordeaux wines at reasonable prices.

Middle Range / Economy

Dominique, 2 cours de l'Intendance (Tel. 56 52 59 79): excellent value fixed price menu with wide choices, in elegant dining rooms.

Economy

La Flambée, 26 rue de Mirail (Tel. 56 92 71 02): good seafood, among other house specialities. **L'Athenée**, 44 rue des Trois Conils (Tel. 56 92 71 02): cosy restaurant with reasonable prices.

Entertainments

If you're looking for studenty cafés, try the area around Place de la Victoire (term-time only). Those with more sophisticated tastes might take their enquiries about wine along to the **Maison du Vin**, 1 cours du 30 Juillet (Tel. 56 52 82 82), which gives free tastings and will provide a comprehensive list of all the wine producing châteaux in the area.

Useful Addresses

The **Tourist Office** is at 12 cours du 30 Juillet (Tel. 56 44 28 41), and there are also information kiosks at the airport and bus station. The **Post Office** is 52 rue Georges-Bonnac, and the **Hospital** is Hôpital St-André, 1 rue Jean-Burguet (Tel. 56 79 56 79). For emergency **medical assistance** ring SAMU on 56 96 70 70.

Transport Options

The train station is half an hour's walk from the town centre; alternatively take bus 7 or 8. The tourist office and train station can both supply you with the economical 1 or 3-day *Carte Bordeaux Découverte* bus ticket, which is worthwhile if you plan to do a lot of sightseeing. Between mid-May and mid-October the tourist office also offer a day's wine tour by bus of many wine-producing châteaux in the area. The bus station is at 14 rue Fondaudege, serving various local destinations. Bicycles can be hired from the train station.

Rest of Gironde & Landes

A tour of Bordeaux's many vineyards is highly recommended for those who enjoy their wine. There are numerous vineyards to visit, but these are just some of the ones particularly recommended by the Bordeaux tourist board.

Château Margaux: you do not need to make an appointment prior to visiting the château. There is a guided tour of the vineyards and also a visit to the cooper's yard, where visitors can see the cooper at work.

Château Malle: this château at **Preignac** is famous for its dessert wine. The castle itself is a magnificent Baroque building and is worth visiting even if you are not interested in wine. The tour of the vineyards also includes a wine tasting.

Château La Rivière: a 'fairy-tale castle' perhaps best describes its considerable charm. It is a relatively unknown château, but the owners offer a genuine welcome to visitors who make an appointment prior to visiting.

Château Mouton Rothschild: this is one of the most elegant châteaux in the region. The grounds also contain a fascinating museum on wine and the wine trade, as well as a wine shop.

In general the vineyards of the Bordeaux area lack the charm of those of the Loire. The countryside is by no means spectacular and there is a lack of accommodation and good eating places. The one notable exception is **St-Emilion**, 40 kilometres east of Bordeaux. It commands a magnificent position on a hill, surrounded by ramparts. Of particular interest is the church which was hewn out of the rock face. The houses in St-Emilion are built of an unusual golden red stone and the town also boasts a magnificent medieval fortress. On the banks of the Gironde river stands the fortified port of **Blaye**. Its castle, and the Vauban-built **Fort Médoc** opposite, once defended the coast of Gironde.

The national N10 road, running south-west, links Bordeaux with the *département* of **Landes** and, further south, Biarritz in Pyrénées-Atlantiques. Up until the nineteenth century, the Landes coastline was an immense, inhospitable wasteland of scrub and sand. The latter, deposited by the sea and wind, formed extensive dunes which were blown up to 50 kilometres inland; it choked all existing vegetation and made human habitation impossible. In 1788, however, an engineer by the name of Bremontier set in motion a plan to stabilise the dunes. He constructed an elaborate system of dykes and embankments backed by rows of stakes, which caused the sand to pile up along them. Gradually the palisade was moved inland and the dunes were sown with coarse grass whose fast growing roots matted the loose sand together. Further inland gorse, furze and broom were grown, providing shelter for the slower growing pines. But the land was still subject to erosion since, below the shallow soil, lay a thick layer of rock which prevented drainage. In the nineteenth century, under the guidance of another enlightened engineer named Chambrebort, a project was initiated to shatter the rock. It was successful and, as a result, thousands of acres were planted with pine and cork oak, and the country became rapidly fertile. Within thirty years Landes had a thriving timber industry from which railway sleepers, pit-props and housing material were made. For the first time in the chronicled history of the region the dunes of the Landes were used as grazing pasture for sheep.

With the growth of the pine forests came the hazard of forest fires. 1949 saw the worst of many infernos, when 370,000 acres were razed. Although great progress has been made in the way of fire prevention (the regulation governing camping and picnicking, for example is extremely strict), fire remains a constant menace.

Today, the reformation of the Landes is complete, and the *département* possesses an immeasurably rich source of 2¼ million acres of pine forest. Unfortunately, in some areas the replacement of sand pine is not much of an improvement: views of the Pyrenees have been obscured, and acres of pine become rather monotonous. Occasionally, however, there are clearings amongst the trees which reveal farms and small hamlets. A good way to find out about the traditional life of the Landes is to visit the *ecomusée* at **Marquèze**, in the heart of the **Regional Park Of The Landes**. The buildings, most of them replicas of nineteenth-century wooden farmhouses, include a small station with a direct line to **Sabres**. Here there is a bird sanctuary and a collection of workshops. At **Luxey**, a branch of the *ecomusée*, pine resin is distilled for the production of alternative fuel. The centre is open on Saturdays and Sundays. For further information write to **Parc Naturel Régional des Landes de Gascogne**, Préfecture, 40011 Mont-Marsan; or telephone 58 06 24 25.

The oil wells around Parentis-en-Born somewhat mar the scenery, and the noise of the military firing range nearby is apt to impinge on holiday tranquillity. Another unsightly area is the military base at Biscarossa which sprawls for some 20 kilometres. As for traditional Landes culture, **Mont-de-Marsan** holds Spanish-style 'Corridas' during the summer months. Those not in favour of blood sports will be pleased to know that the bull is not killed but honoured in a Landais bullfight.

To the north of the regional park is the town of **Bazas**, with an attractive town centre and old arcaded houses. The Gothic cathedral of **St-Jean Baptiste**, restored this century, overlooks an expanse of cobbled streets. Just south of Bazas is the Gallo-Roman spa town of **Dax**, known principally for its therapeutic waters. The resort of **Arcachon**, along the Landes coast, is an attractive town. Particularly elegant is its shaded promenade which juts out to sea. Arcachon is a good place for cheap oysters but bathing off the coast is poor. Better beaches can be found at nearby **Pyla-Sur-Mer** and **Pilat Plage**

Situated at the outflow of the River Eyre is the **Parc Ornithologique du Teich**, occupying 300 acres of marshy delta. The **Reservoir du Poisson** was built to encourage migratory species of bird to frequent the sanctuary, and now herons, storks, wild geese, ducks and swans are among the regular visitors to the area. Keen bird-watchers should make a special point of visiting the site, where exceptionally good facilities have been provided for observing the various species. The sanctuary also includes an environmental centre, an aquarium and a museum containing exhibits of local marine life. To the north there are a number of small resorts which cater for campers and sailors. The area is good for watersports such as wind-surfing and sailing.

Accommodation

First Class

Château de Brugnac, Bossugan, 33350 Castillon-la-Bataille (Tel. 57 40 58 56): 3 rooms and 2 suites (the latter situated in a keep built by Edward I of England), in 13th to 14th century castle with wonderful views; *tables d'hôte* on request, **Château de Monbet**, St-Lon-les-Mines, 40300 Peyrehorade (Tel. 58 57 80 68): 3 rooms in quiet seventeenth-century château with large park.

Middle Range

Château Layauga, Gaillan-Médoc, 33340 Lesparre (Tel. 56 41 26 83): 7 rooms in elegant house close to both the Atlantic and the major vineyards; gourmet restaurant with finest wines. **Le Royal Brion**, 10 rue du Pin Vert, 33600 Pessac (Tel. 56 45 07 72): 26 rooms in atmospheric hotel with gardens, not far from Bordeaux.

Economy

Auberge de la Commanderie, rue des Cordeliers, 33330 St-Emilion (Tel. 57 24 70 19): 15 rooms in friendly old hotel, located near attractive town square. **Le Gascoigne**, 79 cours Hericart de Thury, 33120 Arcachon (Tel. 56 83 42 52): good simple B&B.

Eating Out

First Class / Middle Range

Les Ardillières, route de Lacanau, 33160 Salaunes (Tel. 56 58 58 08): rustic-style restaurant with wooden beams and open fire, serving regional specialities; also has 40 rooms.

Middle Range

Les Huitières du Lac, 1187 ave du Touring Club, 40150 Hossegor (Tel. 58 43 51 48): excellent seafood restaurant, with views over lake; also has 9 rooms.

Economy

Coquille, 63 bd du Général-Leclerc, 33120 Arcachon: good value for oysters, mussels and a bottle of Graves.

Pyrénées-Atlantiques

To the south-west of Landes is the *département* of **Pyrénées-Atlantiques**, one of the most varied and interesting parts of Aquitaine. Occupying the small south-western corner of the *département*, where the mountains meet the Altantic Ocean, is the **Basque** region of France. Fiercely regional, and proud of their culture, language and traditions, the Basques (in both France and Spain) are a colourful and friendly people. This part of the Pyrenees is characterised by low, lush, and densely forested hills. The small hill villages with whitewashed buildings, rust-coloured timbers, shutters and roof tiles are particularly charming. The traditional sports of the Basques are Pelota (played against a fronton wall) and rugby.

Bayonne, on the coast, was once a port which exported wine to Britain and the rest of Europe during the Middle Ages. The fine fourteenth- and fifteenth-century **cathedral** has some interesting stained-glass windows. The older cloisters were built in the thirteenth century. Not far from the cathedral are the ruins of some fortifications and ramparts built by Vauban – the renowned military engineer from the reign of Louis XIV. There are two museums in the town; the **Musée Basque,** is considered to be one of the finest regional museums in France, and the **Musée Bonnat** houses a distinguished collection of paintings and drawings. The Tourist Office is in the Hotel de Ville (Tel. 59 55 50 70), Place de la Liberté. It organises tours of Bayonne and the Basque country.

Directly west of Bayonne is the seaside resort of **Biarritz,** beautifully sited on the Basque coast. It was once a favoured summer resort of Napoleon III, Bismarck and Queen Victoria. Today, however, you are more likely to see surfers than royalty. The seafaring inhabitants used to be whalers when whales abounded in the Bay of Biscay. Unfortunately, Biarritz has kept little of its former style – with the exception of the sumptuous Hotel Palais, which once belonged to the Empress Eugénie. The old villas and the Russian Orthodox church are sadly in need of repair. It is still, however, a very pleasant town, though apart from the **Museum of Oceanography**, and the beaches, there is not much to occupy visitors.

Nearby **St-Jean de Luz** is still an important tunny port. Fishing boats bound for the Newfoundland fisheries once set sail from here. The thirteenth-century church of St-Jean-de-Baptiste, where Louis XIV married his Spanish Infanta, is a splendid example of Baroque style. There are safe and sandy beaches here, good for sailing and surfing. The St-Jean festival takes place on 21 June. There are stalls selling fresh tuna, street musicians, dancing and fireworks. Another festival, the Nuit de la Sardine, in mid-July, features an orchestra Basque singers and more tuna.

St-Jean-de-Pied-de-Port, east of St-Jean-de-Luz, at the foot of the Pyrenees, is a picturesque town on the River Nive. It is a lively and attractive place to stay, and a good base for walkers and cyclists as the Pyrenees are easily accessible from here. There is a strong Basque spirit to the town, and the wooden buildings with their shutters and whitewashed walls are typical of the region. In the Middle Ages, St-Jean-de-Pied-de-Port, was a stop off for pilgrims on their way to Santiago de Compostella in Spain, and churches in the area still bear the shell motif, which was the saint's emblem. It was then the ancient capital of Navarre, and controlled the approaches to the **Roncevaux Pass**.

The cobbled rue de la Citadelle, leads to the fifteenth-century fortress. From this point, Spain is some 8 kilometres away. From the Église Notre-Dame-du-Pont (which once doubled as part of the town's fortifications), there are some magnificent views. The **Iraty forest**, 22 kilometres south, near the bird sanctuary of **Orgambideska**, is good hiking country (maps can be obtained from the Tourist Office). Particularly delightful is the 9-kilometre **Larreluch trail** running from Iraty to the **Chalet Pedro**, where, at the end of a hard day's walk hikers can enjoy fresh mountain trout.

Accommodation

First Class

Château d'Urtubie, 64122 Urrugne (Tel. 59 54 31 15)): 6 rooms in fortified fourteenth-century castle, extended in eighteenth century, and steeped in history.

First Class / Middle Range

Château d'Ilbarritz, 64210 Bidart-Biarritz (Tel. 59 23 00 27): 11 rooms in imposing late nineteenth-century château with magnificent ocean views, 3 km from Biarritz; good restaurant.

Middle Range

La Forestière, route de Laruns, 64260 Louvie-Juzon (Tel. 59 05 62 28): 15 spacious rooms in small hotel with garden and views of the Pyrenees; restaurant serves standard traditional fare. **Hôtel Arraya**, 64310 Sare (Tel. 59 54 20 46): 21 rooms in traditional sixteenth-century Basque house, once a stopping place for pilgrims, in typical Basque village; very good restaurant.

Economy

Hôtel Ohantzea, Aînhoa, 64250 Cambo-les-Bains (Tel. 59 29 90 50): 10 rooms in old timber-framed house near Spanish border, owned by same family for generations; friendly welcome, garden and restaurant. **Les Flots Bleus**, 41 perspective Côte des Basques, 64200 Biarritz (Tel. 59 24 10 03 or 59 01 29 54): 9 rooms in family-run hotel with sea views and restaurant.

Eating Out

First Class

Léonie, 6 rue Garat, 64500 St-Jean-de-Luz (Tel. 59 26 37 10): local specialities with modern touch, served in cosy restaurant.

Middle Range

Arrantzaleak, Chemin de Halage, 64500 Ciboure (Tel. 59 47 10 75): fresh fish specialities and warm welcome, 5 km from St-Jean-de-Luz.

Middle Range / Economy

Le Vieux Logis, route des Grottes, 64800 Lestelle-Bétharram (Tel. 59 71 94 87): traditional regional cuisine in busy auberge; also has 14 rooms.

Economy

La Négresse, 10 bd de l'Aérodrome, 64200 Biarritz (Tel. 59 23 15 83): lively restaurant serving different dishes according to season.

Pau

Pau, in neighbouring **Béarn**, once the capital of Navarre and currently the departmental capital, has been popular with the British since 1820, when Peninsular War campaigners settled there. However, the social upheaval caused by the First World War dispersed much of the rich clientèle who used to frequent it. Today, Pau is once more a prosperous town. It owes much of its industrial reconstruction to the evolution of seed corn, which attracted research into alternative agricultural methods. The discovery of natural gas at Lacq, moreover, brought great wealth to the area and led to the development of a research centre. More recently, the relocation to Pau of industries from other parts of France (particularly in the field of aeronautics and metallurgy) has been welcomed locally.

It is a colourful, friendly city, with plenty to do and see. It is also a good base for exploring the Pyrenees.

The fourteenth- and fifteenth-century **castle** was the birthplace of Henri IV (1589–1610) one of France's most distinguished kings. In nearby **Lescar**, there is a **Romanesque church** with twelfth-century mosaics and Renaissance stalls. Panoramas of the Pyrenees are particularly fine from here in winter. Pau contains two first-class museums. **Le Musée National du Château de Pau** houses a magnificent collection of tapestries. It was the birthplace of **Marshal Bernadotte**, Napoleon's general, who later became Charles XIV of Sweden. The **Pau Fine Arts Museum** is also well worth a visit.

Accommodation

First Class / Middle Range

Hôtel de Paris, 80 rue E-Garet (Tel. 59 27 34 39): 41 comfortable rooms in conveniently located hotel. **Castel du Pont d'Oly**, 2 ave Rauski, 64110 Jurançon (Tel. 59 06 13 40): 7 rooms in hotel with garden and excellent restaurant, 2 km out of town.

Middle Range

Hôtel de Gramont, 3 Place Gramont (Tel. 59 27 84 04): 31 comfortable rooms in pleasant, family-run hotel near château.

Economy

Hôtel Ossau, 3 rue Alfred de Lassence (Tel. 59 27 07 88): friendly hotel with comfortable rooms, views of the Pyrenees and good home cooking. **Hôtel de la Pomme d'Or**, 11 rue Maréchal-Foch (Tel. 59 27 78 48): welcoming, good-value hotel.

Eating Out

First Class

Pierre, 16 rue L-Barthou (Tel. 59 27 76 86): gastronomic restaurant with seasonal house specialities and good regional wines.

Middle Range

Le Saint-Jacques, 9 rue du Parlement (Tel. 59 27 58 97): excellent regional cooking in popular restaurant; reservation recommended. **Ruffet**, 3 ave C-Touzet, 64110 Jurançon (Tel. 59 06 25 13): good-value rustic-style restaurant with garden, 2 km from Pau.

Economy

Le Panache, 8 rue Adoue: generous portions in elegant surroundings. **Chez Olive**, 9 rue du Château (Tel. 59 27 81 19): simple, tasty food in homely restaurant.

Entertainments

The Pau festival, which involves plays, firework displays and ballet performances, is held every year in the last week of June. This is also the time for the Pyrenees stage of the Tour de France, which local people follow avidly; a detailed schedule is available from the